Economic Commission for Europe

ECONOMIC SURVEY OF EUROPE IN 1991-1992

Prepared by the
SECRETARIAT OF THE
ECONOMIC COMMISSION FOR EUROPE
GENEVA

NEW YORK, 1992

NOTE

The designations employed and the presentation of the material in this publication do not imply the expression of any opinion whatsoever on the part of the Secretariat of the United Nations concerning the legal status of any country or territory or of its authorities, or concerning the delimitation of its frontiers.

UNITED NATIONS PUBLICATION

Sales No. E.92.II.E.1

ISBN 92-1-116540-7
ISSN 0070-8712

PREFACE

The present *Survey* is the forty-fifth in a series of reports prepared by the secretariat of the Economic Commission for Europe to serve the needs of the Commission and to help in reporting on world economic conditions.

The *Survey* is published on the responsibility of the secretariat, and the views expressed in it should not be attributed to the Commission or to its participating Governments.

The pre-publication text of this *Survey* was completed in early March 1992 as a document for the 47th session of the Economic Commission for Europe. The final text, incorporating minor changes, was completed on 10 April 1992.

EXPLANATORY NOTES

The term "eastern Europe" as employed in the text and tables of this publication is used exclusively for presentational convenience and comprises Albania, Bulgaria, the Czech and Slovak Federal Republic, Hungary, Poland, Romania and, in most cases, Yugoslavia, all of which, despite the considerable differences between them, currently find themselves in transition to the market system.

Similarly, the terms "the eastern countries" and "the east" are used for reasons of brevity, to refer to the European transition countries jointly.

Accordingly, the terms "east-west trade" and "east-west economic relations", which formerly reflected the relations between the two groups of countries with different economic systems, are now used in this publication solely for presentational convenience, to denote the relations between the economies of eastern Europe and the former Soviet Union now in transition to the market system on the one hand and the market economies on the other.

The following symbols have been used throughout this *Survey*:

A dash (-) indicates nil or negligible;

Two dots (..) indicate not available or not pertinent;

An asterisk (*) indicates an estimate by the secretariat of the Economic Commission for Europe;

A slash (/) indicates a crop year or financial year (e.g., 1990/91);

Use of a hyphen (-) between dates representing years, for example, 1989-1991, signifies the full period involved, including the beginning and end years.

Unless the contrary is stated, the standard unit of weight used throughout is the metric ton.

The term "billion" signifies a thousand million.

References to dollars ($) are to United States dollars unless otherwise stated.

The following abbreviations have been used:

CIS	Commonwealth of Independent States
CMEA	Council for Mutual Economic Assistance
ECE	Economic Commission for Europe
EEC	European Economic Community
FAO	Food and Agriculture Organization of the United Nations
GDP	Gross domestic product
GNP	Gross national product
GSP	Gross social product
IMF	International Monetary Fund
NMP	Net material product
OECD	Organization for Economic Co-operation and Development
OPEC	Organization of the Petroleum Exporting Countries
SDR	Special drawing rights

CONTENTS

CHAPTER 1

The transition economies in 1991: an overview

CHAPTER 2

Western Europe and North America

2.1 OUTPUT AND THE COMPONENTS OF DEMAND IN 1991	11
2.2 INFLATION AND LABOUR MARKETS	20
(i) Costs and prices	20
(ii) Labour markets	23
2.3 TRADE AND CURRENT ACCOUNT DEVELOPMENTS	28
2.4 COUNTRY NOTES	31
2.5 THE SHORT-TERM OUTLOOK	37

CHAPTER 3

Eastern Europe

3.1 THE TRANSFORMATION PROCESS IN 1991 AND OUTLOOK FOR 1992	39
(i) Introduction	39
(ii) Reform programmes: too much stabilization?	39
(iii) Reform results to date: more pain than gain?	45
(iv) Economic lessons	47
(v) Political economy of transition	51
(vi) The illusion of a painless transformation disappears	53
(vii) Political lessons	55
(viii) Short-term prospects: the need for political stabilization	56
3.2 OUTPUT AND DEMAND	57
(i) Output	57
(ii) Domestic absorption	62
(iii) Sectoral developments	63
(iv) Labour market developments	67
3.3 FOREIGN TRADE AND EXTERNAL BALANCE	74
(i) An overview	74
(ii) Trade and payment relations with the west	77
(iii) Eastern trade	83
(iv) Short-term prospects	89
3.4 MACROECONOMIC STABILIZATION: EFFORTS AND RESULTS	91
(i) Price liberalization and the fight against inflation	91
(ii) Fiscal and monetary performance in 1991	93
(iii) The social burden of inflation	95
(iv) Spending and saving behaviour of households	97
(v) A note on comparability of budgetary and monetary statistics	99

CHAPTER 4

The economies of the former Soviet Union

4.1	THE SOVIET ECONOMY IN 1991	103
	(i) Introduction	103
	(ii) Output and demand	104
	(iii) Sectoral developments	106
	(iv) Internal balance	107
	(v) Labour market	109
	(vi) Trade and payments	111
4.2	POLITICAL DISINTEGRATION AND ECONOMIC FRAGMENTATION	114
	(i) Legislation and current developments before August 1991	114
	(ii) The abortive Union Treaty of August 1991	114
	(iii) Last attempts to save the Union	116
	(iv) The birth of the Commonwealth of Independent States	117
	(v) Trade between independent states	118
4.3	THE TRANSFORMATION PROCESS AFTER THE AUGUST COUP	120
	(i) Introduction	120
	(ii) Monetary stabilization	120
	(iii) The decontrol of prices	122
	(iv) The privatization process	123
	(v) Internationalization	128
	(vi) Economic relations among successor states: issues and options	128
	(vii) Some possible ways forward	131
4.4	THE SUCCESSOR STATES OF THE SOVIET UNION	136
	(i) Introduction	136
	(ii) Russia	138
	(iii) Ukraine	146
	(iv) Belarus	153
4.5.	THE BALTIC STATES	159
	(i) Introduction	159
	(ii) Developments during 1991	159
	(iii) Institutional changes	161
	(iv) Relations with Moscow and the CIS	163
	(v) Relations with the outside world	166
	(vi) Prospects	167
4.6	PROSPECTS FOR 1992 AND BEYOND	170

CHAPTER 5

International support for eastern transformation

5.1	APPROACHES TO ASSISTANCE AND COORDINATION	173
	(i) Support for eastern Europe	173
	(ii) Support for the ex-Soviet Union	177
5.2	FINANCIAL ASSISTANCE	180
	(i) Eastern Europe	180
	(ii) Commonwealth of Independent States	184
5.3	WESTERN TRADE POLICIES AND IMPROVEMENT OF MARKET ACCESS	187
	(i) Measures implemented in 1990-1991	187
	(ii) Measures to be implemented in 1992	187
	(iii) The Uruguay Round and eastern Europe	189

CHAPTER 6

On property rights and privatization in the transition economies

6.1 PROPERTY RIGHTS CONCEPTS 191
    (i) Introduction 191
    (ii) Key concepts and the thrust of the chapter 192
    (iii) Property rights and privatization on the transition agenda 193
    (iv) Privatization in market economies — lessons for the east? 194

6.2 ON ESTABLISHING PROPERTY RIGHTS 198
    (i) The role of property rights in resource allocation 198
    (ii) Denied property rights and restitution 200
    (iii) Implicit, vested, and accrued property rights: phenomena of late communism 201

6.3 PRIVATIZATION AS AN ITEM OF TRANSITION POLICY 204
    (i) Basic definitions 204
    (ii) The dispute about the meaning of privatization 206
    (iii) The private sector and its role in the transition 208

6.4 THE MOTIVES FOR AND OBJECTIVES OF PRIVATIZATION 211
    (i) Economic motives 211
    (ii) Political motives 213
    (iii) Social framework 213
    (iv) Reducing the role of labour intransigence 214
    (v) Wealth distribution 214
    (vi) On prioritizing the aims of privatization 214

6.5 OBSTACLES TO PRIVATIZATION 217
    (i) Salient problems 217
    (ii) Technical obstacles 219
    (iii) Economic obstacles to privatization 223
    (iv) Managerial problems of privatization 225
    (v) Attitudinal problems associated with privatization 227

6.6 MECHANISM OF PRIVATIZATION 230
    (i) Spontaneous privatization 231
    (ii) Free distribution of state assets 232
    (iii) Distribution of user rights 241
    (iv) Sale of state-owned assets 241
    (v) The privatization of financial institutions 244
    (vi) The question of land 244

6.7 EXPERIENCE AND AGENDA 247
    (i) Lessons from the experience with privatization to date 247
    (ii) The agenda for the near term 251

CHAPTER 7

Migration from East to West: a framework for analysis

7.1 INTRODUCTION AND HISTORICAL BACKGROUND 257
    (i) Introduction 257
    (ii) East-west migration: the cold war and recent developments 258

7.2 EUROPEAN EXPERIENCE OF INTERNATIONAL LABOUR MIGRATION IN THE 1960s 261
    (i) The extent and nature of labour migration from southern Europe in the 1960s 261
    (ii) The expected benefits and unexpected disadvantages of labour migration in the 1960s 262

7.3 IMPACT OF ECONOMIC CONDITIONS IN TRANSITION COUNTRIES ON MIGRATION 267
    (i) Projections of labour force growth for eastern Europe and the former Soviet Union 267
    (ii) General economic pressures for migration arising from the transition 267
    (iii) Possible sectoral and occupational effects on the potential for migration 269
    (iv) Prospects for emigration in individual countries 272
    (v) Influences from western Europe 273

7.4 EAST-WEST MIGRATION: PROSPECTS AND POLICY CHOICES 274

Statistical appendices

Statistical appendices ... 277

Appendix A. Western Europe and North America ... 279

Appendix B. Eastern Europe and the Soviet Union ... 292

Appendix C. International trade and payments ... 311

LIST OF TABLES AND CHARTS

Page

Chapter 2

Table

2.1.1	Quarterly changes in real GDP, 1990-1991	13
2.1.2	Annual changes in real GDP in western Europe and North America, 1989-1992	13
2.1.3	Changes in manufacturing production in western Europe and North America, 1989-1991	14
2.1.4	Capacity utilization rates in manufacturing industry, 1979-1991	15
2.1.5	Contribution of demand components to real GDP growth in western Europe and the United States, 1989-1991	15
2.1.6	Real private consumption expenditures in western Europe and North America, 1989-1991	16
2.1.7	Household net savings and net lending ratios, 1985-1991	17
2.1.8	Real gross fixed capital formation in western Europe and North America, 1989-1991	17
2.1.9	Real public consumption in western Europe and North America, 1989-1991	18
2.1.10	Volume of trade in goods and services in western Europe and North America, 1989-1991	19
2.2.1	Contribution to the change in the GDP deflator, 1990-1991	24
2.2.2	Contribution to the change in the domestic demand deflator, 1990-1991	25
2.2.3	Changes in employment by sector, 1979-1991	26
2.3.1	Changes in the volume of exports and imports, 1990-1991	28
2.3.2	Germany: Value of merchandise imports, 1990-1991	29
2.3.3	Terms of trade, 1990-1991	30
2.3.4	Current account balances, 1989-1991	30

Chart

2.1.1	Annual growth rates of real GDP, 1980-1991	12
2.1.2	Consumer confidence in the European Community and the United States, October 1989-February 1992	12
2.1.3	Quarterly index numbers of industrial output, 1985-1991	14
2.1.4	Consumer credit and personal saving in the United States, 1960-1991	18
2.1.5	The slowing down of the west German engine of growth, 1989-1991	18
2.2.1	Monthly changes in consumer prices, 1990-1991	21
2.2.2	Intermediate and final output prices in manufacturing industry, 1990-1991	22
2.2.3	World market prices of raw materials, in US dollars and ECUs, 1991	23
2.2.4	Unemployment rates in western Europe and the United States, 1970-1991	27

Chapter 3

Table

3.1.1	Eastern Europe: Characteristics of stabilization-cum-reform programmes	40
3.1.2	Eastern Europe: Stabilization results in 1991	45
3.1.3	Reform-cum-stabilization programmes in Poland, Bulgaria and Czechoslovakia: Planned targets and actual results	46
3.1.4	Czechoslovakia, Hungary and Poland: Changes in real incomes of population, 1990-1991	53
3.1.5	Czechoslovakia, Hungary and Poland: Changes in the structure of personal incomes, 1989-1991	54
3.2.1	Eastern Europe: Basic economic indicators, 1986-1991	59
3.2.2	Eastern Europe: National product, 1988-1992	59
3.2.3	Eastern Europe: Domestic production and absorption, 1989-1991	60
3.2.4	Eastern Europe: Gross fixed investment, 1986-1991	61
3.2.5	Eastern Europe: Volumne of foreign trade, 1988-1991	61
3.2.6	Eastern Europe: Industrial output, 1986-1991	64
3.2.7	Gross agricultural production, 1986-1991	65
3.2.8	Changes in employment and unemployment, 1989-1990	68
3.2.9	Eastern Europe: Unemployment, 1990-1991	68
3.2.10	Registered vacancies	69
3.2.11	Unemployment rates by sex	70
3.2.12	Regional dispersion of unemployment rates in September 1991	70
3.2.13	Employment change by industrial branch between 1990-QI and 1991-QIII	71
3.3.1	Eastern Europe: Foreign trade, by direction, 1989-1991	74
3.3.2	Eastern Europe: Trade balances, 1989-1991	74
3.3.3	Eastern Europe: Changes in foreign trade value and trade balances by partner region, 1989-1991	76
3.3.4	Eastern Europe: Foreign trade with the west, 1989-1991	77
3.3.5	Exports of Czechoslovakia, Hungary and Poland to the west by commodity, 1990	81

		Page
3.3.6	Eastern Europe and the Soviet Union: Convertible currency current account balances in 1990-1991	81
3.3.7	Eastern Europe and the Soviet Union: Balance of payments in convertible currencies, 1990-1991	82
3.3.8	Eastern Europe and the Soviet Union: Medium- and long-term funds raised on the international financial markets, 1988-1991	83
3.3.9	Eastern Euorpe and the Soviet Union: Gross debt vis-a-vis BIS and OECD reporting institutions, by type of debt, 1989-1991	84
3.3.10	Undisbursed credits commitments of BIS Reporting Banks vis-a-vis eastern Europe and the Soviet Union	85
3.3.11	Eastern Europe and the Soviet Union: Joint ventures and foreign direct investment: 1990-1991	85
3.3.12	Eastern Europe and the Soviet Union: Foreign currency reserves, 1988-1991	86
3.3.13	Eastern Europe: External debt in convertible currencies, 1989-1991	86
3.3.14	Eastern Europe: Preliminary balance of payments outlook and financing needs in 1992	90
3.4.1	Rapid price liberalization: forecasts and reality	92
3.4.2	Price liberaliztion and the fight against inflation: The radical approach	92
3.4.3	Rate of inflation, 1990-1991, month over preceding month	93
3.4.4	Rate of inflation, 1990-1991, period-over-preceding year	93
3.4.5	Fiscal revenues and expenditures in 1991	94
3.4.6	Changes in standard of living, 1988-1991	94
3.4.7	Minimum wages, average wages and consumer prices	95
3.4.8	Average pensions in 1990	96
3.4.9	Share of food expenditures in total outlays of workers' and employee households and in total retail sales	98
3.4.10	Households' savings on convertible currency accounts	99
3.4.11	Inter-enterprise credits, as a non-registered component of the money supply in 1991	100
3.4.12	Domestic state debt, as of end-1991	100

Chart

3.1.1	Two depressions in eastern Europe	42
3.2.1	Net material product produced	58
3.3.1	Effective western market demand facing eastern Europe and the Soviet Union, 1990-1992	78
3.3.2	Exports of Czechoslovakia, Hungary and Poland to the developed market economies, by destination, 1988-1991	79
3.3.3	Exports of Czechoslovakia, Hungary and Poland to the developed market economies, by commodity, 1988-1991	80

Chapter 4

Table

4.1.1	USSR/CIS: Output, employment, costs and prices, 1987-1991	105
4.1.2	USSR/CIS: Incomes, prices and expenditure, 1987-1991	106
4.1.3	USSR/Successor states: Money supply, 1987-1991	107
4.1.4	USSR/Successor states: Incomes and credits, 1987-1991	108
4.1.5	USSR/CIS: Foreign trade, by direction, 1989-1991	109
4.1.6	USSR/CIS: Trade balances, 1988-1991	109
4.1.7	USSR/Successor states: Balance of payments, 1990-1991	110
4.1.8	Soviet Union: Foreign trade with the west 1989-1991	111
4.3.1	USSR: Employment by form of organization of the workplace, January-September 1991	124
4.3.2	Russian Federation: Non-state entities outside agriculture	125
4.3.3	Russian Federation: Development of family farms, 1991	126
4.4.1	Soviet successor states: Selected economies data, 1990	137
4.4.2	Soviet successor states: Selected population indicators	138
4.4.3	Soviet successor states: Share in Soviet output by products, 1990	139
4.4.4	Soviet successor states: Economic performance in 1990 and 1991	140
4.4.5	Soviet successor states: Foreign trade, 1991	140
4.4.6	Russian Federation: Basic economic indicators, 1987-1991	141
4.4.7	Russian Federation: Balance of payments in 1990-1991	142
4.4.8	Ukraine: Basic economic indicators, 1987-1991	147
4.4.9	Belarus: Basic economic indicators, 1987-1991	154
4.5.1	Estonia: Basic economic data, 1990	160
4.5.2	Estonia: Year-on-year changes in the economy, 1985-1991	161
4.5.3	Latvia: Basic economic data, 1990	162
4.5.4	Latvia: Selected economic indicators, 1985-1991	163
4.5.5	Lithuania: Basic economic data, 1990	164
4.5.6	Lithuania: Selected economic indicators, 1985-1991	165
4.5.7	Baltic states' merchandise trade values, 1989 or 1990	166
4.5.8	The Baltic states: Net export values of consumer items, 1989	167

Chapter 5

Table

5.2.1	Asistance committed by the G-24 to eastern Europe	181
5.2.2	Global assistance committed to eastern Europe	181
5.2.3	G-24 disbursements and other financial flows to eastern Europe in 1990	183
5.2.4	Eastern Europe: Gross financial resource flows, 1990, and outlook for 1991 and 1992	183
5.2.5	Eastern Europe and the Soviet Union: Net transfers of financial resources: 1990-1991	185
5.2.6	International assistance to the CIS states	186

Chapter 6

Table		Page
6.1	Distribution of firms by type, as of end-1991	195
6.2	Privatization of agricultural land	196
6.3	Restitution measures approved or planned in main sectors of the economy	200
6.4	Share of the socialized sector in 1987	208
6.5	Gemany: Size distribution of firms in mining and manufacturing in 1989	209
6.6	The main motivations for and goals of privatization	212
6.7	The main obstacles to privatization	218
6.8	The role of the stock exchange in privatization	228
6.9	The main mechanisms of privatization	231
6.10	Privatization of public utilities and housing	232
6.11	Distribution schemes for industrial assets	235
6.12	Privatization in the financial sector	243
6.13	Privatization of retail trade and catering	244
6.14	The privatization process in east Germany	247
6.15	The petty privatization process in Hungary	247
6.16	Macroeconomic indicators by ownership structure in Poland	248
6.17	Number of transformation of economically active firms in Poland	249
6.18	Legislative acts relevant to privatization	250
6.19	Tentative proportion of assets to be sold and auctioned off in the Russian Federation during 1992-1994	251
6.20	Normative revenues and asset shares to be privatized in the Russian Federation during 1992	251

Chart		
6.1	Transformation of property rights	203

Chapter 7

Table		
7.1	Net emigration from eastern Europe, 1987-1989, and the former Soviet Union to western Germany, 1987-1991	259
7.2	Asylum seekers from eastern Europe in Germany, 1987-1991	260
7.3	Annual population change due to net migration from southern Europe, 1960-1989	262
7.4	Stocks of southern European workers in other European countries in 1974 and 1989	263
7.5	Structure of civilian employment in southern Europe in 1960 and 1970	264
7.6	Population and labour force growth between 1960 and 1974 in southern Europe: Actual figures and estimates assuming no labour migration	265
7.7	Eastern Europe and the former Soviet Union: Projected population and labour force growth between 1990 and 2000	268
7.8	Estimates of GDP per capita in southern Europe adjusted for purchasing power differences, 1960-1989	269
7.9	Typical estimates of GDP per capita in eastern Europe and the former Soviet Union in 1987, adjusted for purchasing power differences	270
7.10	Sectoral structure of employment in eastern Europe and the former Soviet Union in 1989	271

Statistical Appendices

Appendix A. Western Europe and North America

Appendix table		
A.1	Gross domestic product	280
A.2	Private consumption	281
A.3	Public consumption	282
A.4	Gross domestic fixed capital formation	283
A.5	Volume of exports of goods and services	284
A.6	Volume of imports of goods and services	285

		Page
A.7	Current account balances	286
A.8	Industrial production	287
A.9	Consumer prices	288
A.10	Average hourly earnings in manufacturing	289
A.11	Total employment	290
A.12	Annual unemployment rates	291

Appendix B. Eastern Europe and the Soviet Union

B.1	Net material product	293
B.2	Net material product used for domestic consumption and accumulation	294
B.3	Monthly nominal wages	295
B.4	Money incomes of population and volume of retail trade	296
B.5	Real wages and per capita real incomes	297
B.6	Consumer prices	298
B.7	Dwellings constructed	298
B.8	Total gross investment	299
B.9	Total gross fixed assets	300
B.10	Employment	301
B.11	Gross industrial production	302
B.12	Industry: Gross investments, gross fixed assets and employment	303
B.13	Gross agricultural output	304
B.14	Agriculture: Gross investments, gross fixed assets and employment	305
B.15	Export and import volumes	306
B.16	Energy production: Electricity, coal and crude oil	307
B.17	Steel production	308
B.18	Grain production	309
B.19	Saving deposits of the population	310

Appendix C. International trade and payments

C.1	World trade: Value, by region	312
C.2	World trade: Volume change, by region	313
C.3	Western Europe and North America: Trade volume change	314
C.4	Eastern Europe and the Soviet Union: Exports by main directions, 1970-1990	315
C.5	Eastern Europe and the Soviet Union: Imports by main directions, 1970-1990	316
C.6	East-west trade: Value of western exports, by country of origin	317
C.7	East-west trade: Value of western imports, by country of destination	318
C.8	East-west trade: Western trade balances by western country	319
C.9	East-west trade: Western exports, imports and balances by eastern country	320
C.10	Eastern Europe and the Soviet Union: Balance of payments in convertible currencies	321
C.11	Eastern Europe and the Soviet Union: Gross debt, foreign currency reserves and net debt in convertible currencies	322

Chapter 1

THE TRANSITION ECONOMIES IN 1991: AN OVERVIEW

Introduction

For the world economy, 1991 was one of the worst years of the entire post-war period. Global output fell for the first time since 1945 and the growth of world trade fell for the third year in succession. In the market economies of western Europe and North America, output growth was virtually zero with a small increase in Europe offset by a fall in North America. An expected recovery in North America and the United Kingdom was forecast for the second half of 1991, but this failed to appear and compensate for the sharp slow-down in Germany and Japan. Current forecasts point to a feeble recovery in 1992.

In eastern Europe the depression associated with the break-up of centrally planned economies deepened further with domestic output levels falling by some 14 per cent. One of the most momentous events of the post-war period occurred with the dissolution of the Soviet Union in December: the year was marked by fruitless efforts to negotiate a new union treaty against a background of growing economic dislocation and large falls in the level of activity.

Despite the great hopes and opportunities created by the revolutions of 1989 in eastern Europe, the general mood is now quite pessimistic. This is no doubt exaggerated and reflects in part the breaking of previous illusions about the ease and speed with which the transformation of the former "planned" economies could be brought about. Nevertheless, the problems are considerable. It has proved fairly easy to break up the old structures but extremely difficult to build the new. Fixed investment is still falling rapidly in the transition economies: that has to be reversed if the reform process is to succeed and burgeoning unemployment levels to be checked. A growing fear is that the increasing economic strains will lead to disillusion and impatience, with both the idea of the market economy and with the democratic process.

If the western governments wish to reduce these growing risks, a much greater commitment to the success of the reform process will be needed on their part.

The Soviet Union and the CIS

In 1991 the *Soviet Union* effectively broke up when the Presidents of Russia, Ukraine and Belarus declared their republics to be independent and signed the Minsk Agreement of 8 December creating the Commonwealth of Independent States (CIS). By 21 December another eight republics had joined the CIS whose aims now included the building of "democratically law-governed states". On 25 December Mr. Gorbachev resigned the presidency of the USSR and on 26 December the Soviet Union ceased to exist.

Much of 1991 had been dominated by attempts to negotiate a new relationship between the republics and the Union and these appeared to have succeeded when a draft agreement was initialed in the summer. Although this draft treaty is likely to have proven unviable, especially in the economic sphere, the reduction in the authority of the Union was such that it was a principal cause of the August coup. From that point, the republics rapidly asserted their full independence. However, economically, the successor states of the Soviet Union are still highly interdependent and one of the most urgent tasks now facing them is to create institutions and working arrangements for managing their mutual relations in a constructive manner.

The accelerating economic decline of the Soviet Union in 1991 was due essentially to massive disruptions in the supply-side of the economy as a highly specialized division of labour began to break down. With the collapse of central "planning" control and the acceleration of inflation, barter transactions among enterprises have replaced centrally determined enterprise flows settled in roubles. The breakdown of central authority and the emergence of elected local leaders, sensitive to the needs of their constituents, led to restrictions on the outflow of goods, especially consumer products, to other regions. Since the division of labour in the Soviet Union was highly differentiated in terms of geographical distribution as well as function, these developments were particularly damaging and strengthened the tendency toward republican mercantilism. Against this background of increasing barter, curbs on inter-republican transactions and the general dislocation of traditional economic arrangements, there was a large decline in output.

For 1991 as a whole, net material product in the Soviet Union/CIS fell by 15 per cent and GDP by 17 per cent. This follows reductions of 4 and 2 per cent respectively in 1990. The downturn was gathering pace throughout the year and accelerated sharply in the last quarter. Short-term forecasts are virtually impossible in the current state of turmoil, but another large fall in output seems probable in 1992. An aggregate decline of 25-30 per cent between 1989 and 1992 would not be implausible in the light of what has happened in eastern Europe (see below). Although the fall in output last year affected all the individual republics, there were large variations among them.[1]

Consumers have suffered and possibly by more than is indicated by the estimate of a 15 per cent fall in the volume of private consumption, since it is generally believed that the official consumer price index understates the true rise in prices. The compression of already relatively low living standards is continuing in the independent republics in the early months of 1992 and is raising fears that the fragile political and social consensus for market reforms will be increasingly difficult to maintain without substantial help from abroad. These fears are reinforced by the prospect of rapidly rising unemployment in the course of 1992. Statistics on unemployment in the former Soviet Union and in its successor states do not provide a reliable picture of its current extent. At the end of 1991, one million people were registered as unemployed in the labour offices of the CIS members. At the end of 1990 Goskomstat estimated the total, according to ILO definitions, at 2 million. Current unofficial estimates, which vary widely, start at around 4 million, but it is extremely difficult to judge the accuracy of such numbers. What does seem clear is that unemployment is now a serious problem and, in the light of experience in eastern Europe, is likely to grow rapidly as soon as any real restructuring of the economy gets under way.

Although a great deal of legislation to support the transition to a market economy was passed in 1990 and especially in the first half of 1991, the principal failures concerned the fundamentals of privatization, price liberalization, monetary and fiscal policies and the pursuit of currency convertibility. In the presence of such lacunae, progress in other areas will have little effect and, in a "second best" world, may be counterproductive. This can be seen clearly in the case of inflation. Open inflation in the Soviet Union first appeared in 1985 as a result of policy errors and the side-effects of partial decentralization. After 1989, and particularly in 1991, there was a marked increase in the fiscal autonomy of the republics. Given the maintenance of a single currency and a passive, accommodating monetary policy at the centre, the republics were able to run up fiscal deficits knowing that the inflationary consequences would be diffused across the entire Union. In such circumstances there was little incentive for the republics to embark on a serious attempt at macroeconomic stabilization and, given the deteriorating relationship between the union and the republics, there was little chance of monetary control being established at the centre.

A solution to this conflict, between the fiscal autonomy of the republics and the continued existence of a single currency and ineffective monetary control, is now the most urgent task facing the successor states of the ex-Soviet Union. Without a solution, macroeconomic stabilization will be impossible; and without stabilization the collapse of supply links between enterprises and republics will continue to the point of destruction.

Given the lack of mutual confidence among the successor states and their fears of a re-assertion of control from Moscow, and not to mention the strength of national pride in newly-won independence, one possible solution would be to move towards an open trading area with separate currencies. This would require an effective currency reform and a coherent macroeconomic stabilization programme in each republic. The prime institutional requirement is to find ways of establishing monetary control (the absence of effective bank regulations and credit control in the Baltic States is the main reason for their delay in introducing their own currencies). A problem here is that central banks in many of the republics, including Russia, are responsible to parliaments, which tend to be relatively tolerant of inflation. An alternative method of control might be to set up *currency boards*, which would effectively tie the money supply to changes in the balance of payments. The disadvantage is that the currency boards would probably require much more western assistance than the amounts required for stabilization funds to support the internal convertibility of the rouble and any new republican currencies; the advantage is that, assuming there is effective regulation of the commercial banks, the currency board is likely to be a more effective means of financial stabilization.

A final ingredient of a programme to establish stable economic relations among the successor states is the need for effective payments arrangements among the different currencies. The issues involved here are much the same as those discussed in the proposal for a payments union among the former CMEA members.[2] The essential objective of a payments union is to avoid an excessive contraction of trade during the period of transition towards current-account convertibility of the republican currencies. Two years ago the warnings of a severe collapse in intra-CMEA trade were ignored and suggestions that a payment union might be useful as a transition measure were brushed aside. There are signs that the lessons of that collapse have been noted by some CIS members and that they are keen to avoid a repetition.

The above measures, if put into effect quickly, would establish a framework for macroeconomic stabilization and for stopping − and perhaps reversing − the rush toward autarky in the successor states of the former Soviet Union. However, if the measures are to be successful, substantial assistance will have to be provided by western countries and the international institutions. This will have to include large-scale technical assistance in setting up banking and payments institutions as well as significant financial help.

The "republicanization" of monetary control will have to be supported by measures to control budget deficits, which means controlling public spending and/or maintaining or increasing tax revenue. Cuts in spending are extremely difficult when all the political pressures are for increases to soften the growing hardships arising from falling real consumption levels, rising unemployment, and dislocation in the supply of goods. Western grant aid in the form of food, medicine and

---

1 For details on the different republics, see chapter 4.4.

2 See United Nations Economic Commission for Europe, *Economic Survey of Europe in 1989-1990*, United Nations, New York, 1991, chapter 3.4.

medical equipment can assist here in a wider role than a purely emergency one. On the side of revenue, technical assistance is urgently required to set up and operate effective tax collection systems.

The stabilization problem is now very urgent. Without significant help from the west in 1992, it is doubtful that domestic efforts alone can be successful. And without effective stabilization it is unlikely that the longer-run programmes for privatization, market liberalization and industrial restructuring can make any progress. Nevertheless, in the absence of adequate help from abroad, the CIS members will probably try to do something on their own and in doing so they are likely to focus on the two sectors where, despite the degradations of the former economic system, their products are still internationally competitive. The first is *natural resources*, although their development is hampered by supply-side problems which could eventually be overcome with the help of foreign capital and technology; the second is the *armaments* industry, which could probably resume export growth fairly quickly. An export drive in military weapons, however, would not perhaps be the most welcome form of self-reliance from the point of view of the "new world order".

Eastern Europe

In eastern Europe the difficulties of transforming former Soviet-type systems into decentralized market economies became ever more apparent in 1991. Levels of output continued to fall sharply, even in the few countries where an upturn had been expected, and most people have had to bear large cuts in their standards of living. The popular enthusiasm for a new order that characterized the political revolutions of 1989 has given way to widespread feelings of anxiety and disappointment — and even bitterness that the pace of economic change has been unable to match the speed of political development. The fact that the earlier hopes of rapid economic transformation — encouraged by western advisers and politicians no less than those in the east — were unrealistic is now irrelevant. Political leaders, not only in eastern Europe, but also in the west, now have the task of preserving and reinforcing support for economic transformation in the face of increasing current hardships and the disappointment of initial expectations. In particular, they will have to counter the populist and reactionary charge that the hardships of the transition are in fact the "inevitable" properties of a market economy. In this task they will need the practical support of the international organizations and institutions.

It is generally accepted that the revolutions of 1989 were not foreseen. This was a major failure of political appreciation and of social science in both the western countries and in the east. Yet despite this demonstration of a general lack of understanding of the dynamics of economic and social change, the revolutions were quickly followed by western advisers explaining why there was "no alternative" to doing this or that if the transition to a market economy were to be successful, and by politicians declaring that the transition would be swift and painless. Given the failure to anticipate the upheavals of 1989, a greater amount of pragmatism might have been more appropriate, especially since one implication was that knowledge of the "initial states" from which the transition countries were departing was, at best, rudimentary. This began to be acknowledged at the beginning of 1991. In Germany, officials admitted that they had seriously underestimated the effects of "shock-therapy" on the *Länder* which had been subject to forty years of communist rule.[3] In his New Year's address, President Vaclav Havel referred to the "unpleasant surprises" of the previous year and announced that "the reconstruction we had planned for and looked forward to will take longer and cost far more that we first thought. What a year ago appeared to be a rundown house is in fact a ruin."[4]

These errors of analysis are having serious consequences. In Germany, the unexpected escalation in the budgetary costs of supporting reconstruction in the former GDR has led to a sharp increase in inflationary pressures and, via the impact of higher German interest rates working through the exchange rate mechanism of the EMS, is having a depressing effect on the prospects for the recovery of activity throughout western Europe. The electorates in the west (including North America) are unprepared for the scale of international assistance that will probably be required to ensure that the transition processes become self-sustaining; and those in the east are also unprepared for the likely duration of their hardships. As suggested above, the political task of keeping the transition processes on course is now much more difficult than it was two years ago.

Another complication in creating realistic expectations and sustaining popular support for the transition process in eastern Europe is that the destination is usually described in terms of a unique western model which bears little relation to western realities. One of the most powerful attractions of market economies and democratic systems is that they greatly enlarge the scope for choosing different arrangements for the conduct of economic and social affairs. There is no single western model of democracy or of a market economy: around a core set of institutions and values there is considerable variation between, for example, western Europe and the United States and Japan and even within western Europe alone. It is also highly misleading to represent western market economies as being ruled solely by market forces. The great achievement of the western democracies, especially since the depression of the 1930s, has been to combine market driven efficiency and resource allocation with a concern for equity and social justice. Moreover, the fairly widespread existence of market failure, in the form of externalities or non-competitive behaviour, has led to a variety of forms of government intervention ranging from nationalization to various forms of regulation. The workings of western market economies have therefore been greatly modified by government intervention, the specific forms of which vary considerably

---

[3] See the interview with Mr. Otto Schlecht, State Secretary at the Economics Ministry, Bonn, in the *Financial Times*, 29 April 1991.

[4] President Havel's address was published in English in *The New York Review of Books*, 7 March 1991, pp.19-20.

among countries and have changed markedly over time. The policy debates and innovations of the 1980s have not really altered this picture: the state has handed over (or back) certain activities to the private sector in some countries and there have been important changes in the institutions and forms of regulation of competitive behaviour. These changes have met with varying degrees of success, but one of the major criticisms made of them — in both the United States and the United Kingdom, for example — is that they have led to greater inequality.[5] This alone is likely to lead to a reappraisal of the policies of the 1980s and to a renewed search for ways of improving the trade-off between equity and efficiency in the 1990s. To ascribe the relative success of the western market economies *solely* to the uninhibited workings of free market forces both simplifies and underestimates their achievement: it has been the interactive evolution of a whole range of democratic, social and economic institutions and practices which have ensured the survival of western "capitalism" and repeatedly falsified the Marxist prediction of its imminent collapse. This is a richer — and more inspiring — picture of "the market economy" than the "stripped-down" market efficiency model that is commonly presented to the electorates of eastern Europe and of the successor states to the Soviet Union.

Many of the people in these countries must now be wondering whether the invisible hand of the market is really an iron fist. In eastern Europe the depression deepened further in 1991 with domestic output levels falling on average by about 14 per cent. This follows an average fall of 10 per cent in 1990 and 2 per cent in 1989. Since 1988 the aggregate fall in output is nearly 25 per cent.

No country escaped the collapse of output in 1991, but the differences were considerable: in Bulgaria the fall was some 23 per cent; in Romania, Yugoslavia and Czechoslovakia, it ranged between 13 and 16 per cent; while in Hungary and Poland it was about 8 per cent.

All sectors have been hit by the recession. The fall in industrial output was particularly large in 1991: it averaged about 19 per cent with declines ranging from 12 per cent in Poland, the third successive year of falling output, to a reported 60 per cent in Albania, the poorest and least industrialized country in Europe.

Agricultural output also continued to fall, for the third year in succession, although the drop of 1 per cent was less than in 1990. In Yugoslavia output is actually reported to have risen, in both the social and private sectors, and there was also a small increase in Romania.

Although the development of the services sector is expected to provide an important boost to economic growth in the medium run, so far this has failed to materialize. However, the decline in the output of services has been less than for output as a whole, so there has been some shift in its share of national output. There is also probably a greater diversity of trends within services than in other sectors of the economies of eastern Europe: transport and trade have been badly affected by the falls in agricultural and industrial output, while health, education and other public services are being hit by the tightening of fiscal policies. However, business and financial services appear to be growing in Hungary and there has been some expansion in the communications sector in Poland.

In surveying this general picture of collapsing output in eastern Europe, a decline which appears to be on the scale of the depression of the 1930s, a number of considerations have to be borne in mind. The first concerns the quality of the statistics on which the picture is based. Although many problems in this respect have been around for a long time, there has probably been a deterioration in the last few years as national statistical offices begin to switch to new methods of collection of, in many cases, completely new sets of statistics.[6] One consequence of this reorganization is that the private sector, particularly small enterprises, and new activities are still not being accurately reflected in the statistics. There is also a shift in reporting bias. Under the former "administered" regimes, enterprises tended to overstate their output levels in various ways in order to satisfy centrally determined targets and to boost their claims for bonuses and an increased allocation of investment funds. Now, the incentive is to understate production in order to avoid paying taxes, an incentive which is strengthened by the embryonic state of tax collection and enforcement systems. These factors probably lead to some exaggeration in the measured decline of production, but until better official figures are produced and published no-one really knows the extent of the overstatement. Anecdotal evidence and a general consideration of the various factors influencing activity suggest that it is unlikely to be so large as to alter radically the general picture of a severe decline in production. In Poland and Hungary, the private sector is relatively more important than elsewhere and it does appear to have been quite dynamic in 1991 in industry, construction and in some service sectors. This is a most encouraging development and one which is probably not fully reflected in the output figures — nevertheless, it is unlikely to have more than partially offset the collapse of the still very much larger state sectors.

The extent of the downturn in eastern Europe is much greater than originally expected, although the disparity probably reflects the unrealism of the initial expectations as much as surprise developments. The proximate causes of the downturn were the introduction of large changes in relative price structures, which are central to price liberalization measures, and the restrictive macroeconomic policies introduced to curb accelerating inflation and government budget deficits. The simultaneous introduction of such policies in several countries generated negative multiplier effects throughout the region, which in turn were greatly amplified by the collapse of trade among the members of the former CMEA. The collapse of trade with the Soviet Union had a major impact on eastern Europe, especially in the countries of south-eastern Europe where the disruption caused by shortages of energy and

---

[5] See Dieter Helm, Colin Mayer and Ken Mayhew, "Microeconomic Policy in the 1980s", *Oxford Review of Economic Policy*, Vol.7, No.3, Autumn 1991.

[6] See United Nations Economic Commission for Europe, *Economic Bulletin for Europe*, vol.43, New York, 1991, pp.4-5.

other supplies was exacerbated by severe foreign exchange constraints. These various domestic and exogeneous factors have interacted and intensified their ultimate impact on levels of activity.

Nevertheless, in spite of all these factors it is important to emphasize that a recession in output was unavoidable. The transition from a Soviet-type economy to a market economy must involve a large relative price shock as the system moves from an administered price structure to one based essentially on competitive world market prices. This shift in relative prices will benefit some activities in the transition economy, but it will weaken the competitiveness of others and of some to the point of extinction. Thus a proportion of the capital stock is rendered economically unprofitable, virtually overnight. How large a proportion will be "knocked out" in this way will depend on a number of factors including the initial disparity between domestic and world prices and on whether there are any arrangements in place to extend the adjustment period. It seems reasonable to assume that a very large proportion of the east European capital stocks have been rendered economically obsolete in the manner described, especially in the industrial sector.[7] So far, little progress has been made in reducing pollution and other environmental costs in the transition economies: but when action does get under way it will almost certainly lead to further reductions in the viable capital stocks, either through direct regulation or through the internalization of external costs.

Rebuilding the productive capacity of the former centrally planned economies requires a strong recovery in fixed investment, but the pre-conditions for this are not yet in place. Gross fixed investment fell on average by 23 per cent in 1991,[8] following declines of 2 and 14 per cent in 1989 and 1990 respectively. In other words, fixed investment has fallen by more than one third since 1988. The fall in fixed investment is general and in some countries (Bulgaria, Poland and Romania) has been under way since 1989. Over the last few years (see below, table 3.2.4) investment has fallen by about 19 per cent in Poland and Hungary and by nearly 50 and 60 per cent in Romania and Bulgaria.

The question of fixed investment is at the heart of the transformation process and the conditions for its recovery are largely co-terminous with those required for the transition itself. Private investment — foreign and domestic — is at present held back by a multitude of uncertainties concerning not only the medium-term economic outlook but also the putting into place of the entire structure of laws and institutions which are necessary conditions for a market economy to function. The one country which appears to have made significant progress in this regard is Hungary which attracted nearly $2 billion of foreign direct investment last year: nevertheless, even there, total investment is still falling and there are still few signs of any restructuring in industry.

Privatization is generally proving much more difficult than expected. In the leading tier of reformers (Czechoslovakia, Hungary and Poland) it is moving slowly and elsewhere it has hardly begun. It therefore seems likely that for some time to come there will still be a relatively large state-run sector in the east European economies. This will create problems for incentives in general and for the propensity to invest in particular. Private enterprises will be faced with continued uncertainty over the structure of their domestic markets and the managers of state enterprises, in the absence of clear pre-privatization programmes (such as break-up (see below) and commercialization (see chapter 6)), will have little or no incentive to invest.

It is widely assumed that once effective stabilization policies have corrected internal and external imbalances, and with a price reform carried through and a realistic exchange rate in place, private investment will take off to complete the transformation process. However, as the above observations imply and the current situation in Poland suggests, the timing of the two processes may not be synchronized. How can this "timing" gap be overcome? There seems to be little point in urging governments to "speed up" the creation of new legal structures and market institutions. These are complicated matters and governments are already going as fast as they can. A more effective approach might be to consider more active and explicit industrial policies on the part of governments: these would include a whole range of "supply-side" measures to raise capacity and competitiveness, increase public infrastructure investment, introduce effective training programmes (including for management), and establish a monitoring system to reveal bottlenecks and market failures and encourage a quick response to remove them. The suggestion of a more active role for governments may produce ideological reactions on the part of some advisers, but this is a nettle that may have to be grasped if the stabilization-structural transformation sequence does not proceed as it is assumed to do. If east European governments were to decide on such a course, it would be advisable to do so with the help and advice of one of the international organizations (such as OECD) familiar with such policies in the western market economies.

Controlling *inflation* is a difficult task for the transition economies. They need to introduce programmes of price liberalization and secure significant changes in the structure of relative prices, while at the same time the legacy of institutions and practices from the previous regime continues to undermine the effectiveness of the traditional tools of macroeconomic policy. Thus, credit policy is frequently being attenuated by the large-scale resort to inter-enterprise credits; and rising unemployment may be accompanied, perversely, by rising wages.[9] The jump in the price level following price reforms was generally much larger than expected and although inflation rates subsequently subsided they

---

[7] Detailed studies are still in short supply, but the existence of negative value added, when measured at world prices, has been shown to exist in several manufacturing industries. See G. Hughes and P. Hare, "Competitiveness and Industrial Restructuring in Czechoslovakia, Hungary and Poland", *European Economy*, Commission of the European Communities, Brussels, Special Edition, No.2, pp.57-110.

[8] This figure excludes Yugoslavia.

[9] On this, see chapter 3.2 below.

remain high. In Poland, inflation fell sharply in the first seven months of 1991, but it then accelerated again in the second half of the year, to 44 per cent a year in December. So far, policy makers in Czechoslovakia have been rather more successful in this respect: after the price reform of 1 January 1991, prices rose sharply in the first quarter but decelerated rapidly thereafter, a performance which partly reflects the more favourable conditions in which the Czechoslovak reform was launched but also the very tight control of budgetary policy. However, there was a some acceleration again at the end of the year. In south eastern Europe, the control of inflation is proving even more difficult: there has been a sharp acceleration in Romania and Yugoslavia since last summer, to annual rates of 367 per cent and 644 per cent respectively in December. In Bulgaria the initial acceleration in the rate of inflation following the price reform last February was sharply reduced by the spring, but thereafter it rose again and by December was running at an annual rate of 78 per cent.

The persistence of high inflation rates in the transition economies is in many ways a consequence of their "transitional" state: the "command" economy has been abandoned but many of its microeconomic features remain, weakening or undermining the effectiveness of fiscal and monetary policy. Some improvement can probably be made to the effectiveness of anti-inflationary macroeconomic policies — improvements in tax systems, perhaps a more determined use of incomes policies — but a significant and sustained reduction of inflation will also need more positive supply-side responses to the new relative price structures.

In 1990 one sign that the "soft budget constraint" was still operating in the transition economies was the relatively low levels of *unemployment* that were prevailing despite the large and widespread falls in output. This has changed considerably in the last year: the number of persons registered as unemployed in eastern Europe more than doubled in the year to December 1991 when it stood at just under 6 million (excluding the former German Democratic Republic). Unemployment rates in Bulgaria and Poland were some 10-11 per cent in December and some 7-8 per cent in Czechoslovakia and Hungary. In Yugoslavia the rate at the end of the year was nearly 20 per cent. Although there are many uncertainties surrounding the precision of these figures, there seems to be little doubt that there has been a dramatic rise in joblessness in eastern Europe.

As in the western market economies, the burden of unemployment has tended to fall more heavily on women than on men, on the young, and on manual workers rather than the more educated. The number of long-term unemployed (those without a job for more than a year) also appears to be rising although, given that open unemployment is a recent phenomenon in eastern Europe, it is still relatively small compared with the numbers prevailing in western Europe. Since, as noted above, the restructuring of the transition economies is still in its early stages, both the levels and duration of unemployment can be expected to continue rising even beyond the time at which output begins to recover.

Democratic institutions and the process of economic transformation

Many of those arguing for the so-called "shock therapy" approach to the transformation of eastern Europe do so, at least partly, because they fear that the forces of reaction are still strong and that incompetence and/or corruption in the bureaucracies may be holding back the transition process.[10] This may exaggerate (or misinterpret) the situation insofar as many officials and bureaucrats can adapt quickly to changed conditions: as Edward Gibbon noted, also writing about a collapse of regime, "officers of the police or revenue easily adapt themselves to any form of government".[11] Not all government officials will possess the same degree of flexibility, but the key issues obviously include, just as in other sectors of the transition economy, the questions of skills and retraining, and the structure of incentives. Also, the administrative systems themselves will require radical alteration since they were designed to serve a very different political system from the one now being established. Moreover, it is not always a simple matter to distinguish between the faults of individuals and the much larger failings of the system in which they are required to operate. However, from the perspective of building support for the transition process, let alone from that of common justice, the distinction needs to be made.[12]

Clearly if the economic reforms were to fail — or to look as if they might fail — then these same officials would be looking for the next best alternative rather than fighting for the current objectives. So the expectations of economic success are certainly crucial for gathering and maintaining both popular and bureaucratic support for the transition process. But, having said that, it might be questioned whether it is sensible to burden economic instruments with political and administrative considerations. Instead of, for example, trying to speed up the privatization process so as to remove the influence of incompetent or unqualified officials, it might be wiser to target the deficiencies in administration directly rather than risk a dangerous backlash from a flawed economic reform.

It is important to acknowledge the close interdependence between the objectives of economic reform and reconstruction, democratic institution building and security issues in the transition economies, but it is also wise to remember the macroeconomic policy advice to match targets and instruments. In broad terms, administrative instruments should be used to support institutional objectives, and economic instruments should not be overloaded with political targets. The question

---

10 See Anders Åslund, letter to the *Financial Times*, London, 6 March 1992.

11 Edward Gibbon, *The Decline and Fall of the Roman Empire*, Oxford University Press, World's Classics Edition, 1903, Vol.1, p.75.

12 One qualified observer has argued that the majority of personnel running the courts in the Soviet Union were honest and decent people. "But the system as a whole, the entire mechanism of law enforcement ... led to a perversion of the law and the erosion of human rights for all — the accused, the investigators and the judges themselves." Anatoly Sobchak, *For a New Russia*, London, 1992.

of privatization can be used to illustrate this point. In *western* Europe, the privatization policies of the last decade or so have been essentially concerned with improving economic efficiency, although some proponents have stressed the adjustment of the border between the democratic state and civil society as a matter of principle. In eastern Europe the matter of economic efficiency is of course very important, but privatization is also regarded as the most prominent sign of the overthrow of the entire conception of the organic state.[13] In other words, privatization in the former communist countries is intimately connected to the creation of democratic states and the re-assertion of the claims of civil society. It is not surprising therefore that there are considerable pressures for privatization to be carried out as quickly as possible. However, the speed of privatization which might satisfy democratic and political objectives could be too fast for avoiding deleterious economic outcomes. It has been persuasively argued[14] that the state monopolies of the former centrally planned economies should be broken up *before* they are privatized — otherwise, the highly concentrated production structures, characteristic of Soviet-type economies, would be maintained with a high probability of continued economic stagnation and weak incentives for improving economic efficiency. Such an outcome would not only increase the tensions noted above but would also make it easier to reverse the process at a later date — a possibility which is precisely what the proponents of rapid privatization claim to be avoiding. There are, in addition, many other technical and quasi-technical problems which must be overcome if privatization is to be economically successful.[15] Skating over such problems in order to speed up the process could lead not only to sub-optimal outcomes but also to a backlash against the private sector as a whole.[16] There is, however, already an extensive framework[17] for providing technical expertise and assistance in the building and strengthening of democratic and administrative structures in the transition economies — and no doubt this could be strengthened further. Moreover, a number of conditions concerning respect for democracy, the rule of law and human rights, have already been set as requirements for receiving economic assistance from the G-24 countries and from the European Bank for Reconstruction and Development.[18] There is, thus, both a framework for western assistance for strengthening democratic institutions in eastern Europe and the implicit threat of sanctions against a country which violates the pre-conditions for assistance. If the framework is used to the full and the threat remains credible, the fears of democrats in eastern Europe will be reduced and the political overload removed from policies for economic restructuring.[19]

Western economic assistance

It is the view of most observers, in all parts of Europe, that the nascent democracies of eastern Europe would be gravely threatened by a failure of the process of economic transformation. In order to avoid such an outcome, the governments of the western market economy countries have launched a number of initiatives to assist the countries of eastern Europe and the CIS in their attempts to restructure their economies according to market principles. In the past year there has been an increase in the flow of official financial resources to the transition economies, an expansion of technical assistance, and an improvement in access to western markets for eastern products. The established international financial institutions, the World Bank and the IMF, have increased their assistance to eastern Europe and they have now been joined by the European Bank for Reconstruction and Development which was inaugurated in April 1991.

One of the most important developments has been the improvement of *market access* to the European Community, which is the largest single western market for eastern goods. Quantitative restrictions on most manufactures had been abolished or suspended by the beginning of 1991 and all the east European countries received General System of Preferences treatment. Agricultural, steel and textile products are subject to separate arrangements, but for the latter two there has been some loosening of restrictions. Important gains in access were obtained by Czechoslovakia, Hungary and Poland as a result of their bilateral Association Agreements with the European Communities, which were signed in December 1991. These provide for the phasing in of free trade in non-agricultural goods between the parties to the Agreements over a ten-year period.[20] Again, separate provisions apply to sensitive products such as textiles and steel, although there are improvements in both areas. There was, however, little improvement for agricultural products. Nevertheless, the

---

[13] The term is used as in T.D. Weldon, *States and Morals*, London, John Murray, 1962 edition.

[14] David M. Newberry, "Sequencing the Transition", London: *CEPR Discussion Paper Series*, No.575, August 1991.

[15] For an extensive discussion, see chapter 6 below.

[16] There is, for example, a lack of expertise in many areas in government and state enterprises which needs to be remedied. There are widespread hopes that privatization and restructuring can be speeded up with the help of western private capital, but many government officials lack experience in dealing with western companies and are unfamiliar with international management contracts and competitive bidding methods. Mr. Anthony Pellegrini, Head of the World Bank's infrastructure division, has recently expressed concern in this regard with respect to the water industry in eastern Europe, where some western firms have offered local government authorities contracts containing "dubious terms". See *Financial Times*, 12 March 1992.

[17] For example, contacts between parliamentarians are maintained through the Western European Union, the Council of Europe, the Inter-Parliamentary Union, and so on. Also, within the CSCE, the Office for Democratic Institutions and Human Rights will serve as an information exchange for technical assistance available for institution building in the new democracies.

[18] These pre-conditions for economic assistance are also among the five conditions, laid down by the Foreign Affairs Council of the European Community on 16 December 1991, which would have to be met before the independence of any of the Yugoslav Republics would be recognized.

[19] Uncertainty and the threat of instability in eastern Europe has also been greatly increased by the disintegration of the Soviet Union. This has not only created severe economic disruption through the sudden collapse of trading links, but has also added to the fears of the east European countries for their security. A framework for cooperation on security issues *per se* is also developing and includes the CSCE and the new North Atlantic Cooperation Council which met for the first time on 20 December 1991.

[20] For details of the Agreements see chapter 5.3 below.

Agreements offer important market opportunities for the east European partners and constitute a significant step towards their full integration into the European economy. One disappointment for the three transition economies was that a date was not fixed for their eventual accession to full membership of the European Community. The setting of a date, however far away, could have had a positive effect in encouraging foreign direct investment in the three countries. Also, some policy makers would have welcomed such a date as a source of pressure in maintaining their progress towards a market economy: a succession of intermediate targets would have had to have been met according to the pre-determined timetable.

Trade liberalization is also under way to varying degrees in the other market economies. The EFTA has concluded a free trade agreement with Czechoslovakia and negotiations are continuing with Hungary and Poland; and the United States has improved access under the Trade Enhancement Initiative. It is important that this general movement to liberalize access continues and that it be extended as quickly as possible to all the economies in transition.

At the present moment, the outcome of the Uruguay Round is still in the balance, but a successful conclusion could provide important benefits to the eastern countries. Apart from the gains from a general lowering of trade restrictions, an agreement to lower protection of agriculture in the developed market economies could especially benefit the export earnings of countries such as Bulgaria, Hungary, Poland and Ukraine.

Despite the considerable publicity given to the growing number of financial commitments to the transition economies, the amount of genuine aid (grants and concessional finance) from the west has been small. Between January 1990 and June 1991 the total of *commitments of assistance* by the G-24 countries to eastern Europe amounted to $32 billion. Commitments extended to the CIS between September 1990 and January 1992 amounted to nearly $79 billion. Of the pledges to eastern Europe, however, only about one fifth consists of grant aid, although there is in addition a certain grant element in some bilateral loans. The bulk of the assistance to eastern Europe and the Soviet Union consists of non-concessional finance and is, therefore, debt-creating. Virtually all loans have been made at market conditions, although there is some implicit subsidy since the eastern countries either have little access to the international capital markets or have to pay a large premium over base interest rates.

The figures for commitments do not of course indicate the actual flows of funds into the transition economies. In the case of the CIS (ex-Soviet Union) *gross disbursements* in 1990-1991 were about $25 billion, less than one third of commitments. Disbursements lag behind commitments for a variety of reasons and may not occur at all if certain conditions or targets are not met by the potential recipient.

For 1990 it is estimated that total *gross financial flows* — private and official capital plus debt restructuring — to eastern Europe were $9.7 billion, of which $1.7 billion (less than one fifth) was official aid. Only rough estimates are possible for 1991, but these suggest a doubling of the total gross flow to some $19.8 billion. However, this improvement is not expected to continue: because of an anticipated fall in IMF and G-24 lending, the total in 1992 is expected to be around $14.5 billion. In all three years debt restructuring accounts for a large proportion of the gross flow.

In terms of the *net transfer of resources* the situation is even less promising. In 1990 there was a net outflow of financial resources from eastern Europe as the withdrawal of funds by commercial banks and large payments for debt servicing by Poland and Hungary more than offset the inflow of new funds. In 1991 there was a net *inflow* of $4.4 billion, with only Poland continuing to have a net outflow, but it is difficult to be confident that this improvement will continue in 1992. For the Soviet Union, an official net inflow of medium- and long-term assistance of some $6.5 billion in 1990-1991 was more than offset by the withdrawal of a net $15 billion of private short-term credit.

Western official financial aid for the countries of eastern Europe, and for the successor states of the Soviet Union, is, so far, considerably smaller than the sums implied either in a "Marshall Plan equivalent" ($16.7 billion a year) or in the suggestion of the President of the Commission of the European Communities to provide the equivalent level of support as the Community gives to its own depressed regions ($23 billion a year, excluding the former Soviet Union).[21]

Inflows of private capital into the eastern countries have generally been disappointing. Foreign direct investment in Hungary and Czechoslovakia has been encouraging but elsewhere it is negligible. Private banks abroad have reduced their lending, including to these two countries, and in general, as noted above, private capital has tended to flow out of the region. This suggests that one of the main elements in the western approach to helping the transition — promoting structural change with large amounts of foreign private capital — has not yet started to work.

As regards the mobilization of funds for *balance of payments* support for the east European countries, the record has been mixed. When it appeared in 1990 that most east European countries would face a financing gap in 1991, partly as a result of the Gulf crisis and higher oil prices, the G-24 and the international financial institutions moved quickly to arrange the necessary credits. These operations proved successful for Czechoslovakia and Hungary, but the necessary financing could not be raised for Bulgaria and Romania. In several cases donor countries did not contribute as much as had been expected. However, the flexibility of the current arrangements also proved inadequate. Creditors tend to adhere to their established practices and timetables for disbursing funds, and there is no arrangement to take up the slack if a major G-24 con-

---

21 United Nations Economic Commission for Europe, *Economic Survey of Europe in 1989-1990*, New York, 1990, p.13.

tributor falls behind schedule in meeting its commitments or fails to contribute as agreed.

While some transition countries built up their reserves during 1991, and are perhaps less dependent on the quick disbursal of G-24 funds, the avoidance of further economic and social dislocations in Albania, Bulgaria and Romania is likely to continue to depend on timely access to funds.

There continues to be a problem with the overall framework for coordinating assistance to the transition economies. At the last ministerial meeting of the G-24, in November 1991, ministers noted the need for more effective support for the transition process and in particular for a more rapid disbursement of resources, increased information sharing among donors to avoid duplication, and closer cooperation between the international financial institutions and the G-24.[22] This may be difficult to achieve given the desire of some G-24 governments and international institutions to guard their independence in such matters and the lack of clear institutional arrangements for overall coordination.

The question of coordination[23] is not just a question of keeping registers of projects and avoiding duplication among donors, important though that may be. Arrangements also need to be made for assessing assistance in relation to the requirements of the transition countries — *and* for assessing those requirements.

Aid and technical assistance are essentially forms of government intervention designed to overcome bottlenecks to economic growth which, for one reason or another, are not being removed by market forces. In countries where the price mechanism is weak, economic rigidities are likely to persist. By definition, this is true, to widely varying degrees, of the transition economies. For private capital to take over the driving role in the transition process, it is necessary to identify first the constraints on private sector growth and the ways in which they might be overcome with official assistance. It is also necessary to identify which of the constraints is binding at any given time in any given country. Thus, in some of the development models of the 1960s, it was customary to identify constraints arising from inadequate levels of domestic saving or from shortages of foreign exchange: either could restrain the rate of fixed investment, but for effective policy formulation it was necessary to know which one should be targeted. Other constraints may arise from a shortage of skilled labour or, as is likely to be the case in the transition economies, from the absence of crucial elements in the institutional structure required for the existence of (reasonably) efficient markets. To formulate consistent sets of economic policies and focus assistance where it will be most effective thus requires a macroeconomic framework in which government objectives (concerning the growth of output, the unemployment rate, etc.) are related to the effective limits to growth.

So far, none of the transition economies or aid-providing countries appear to have adopted such a broad approach to coordination. The background papers occasionally and voluntarily prepared for meetings of the G-24 by the transition countries typically report on recent progress with reform, on recent economic developments and the short-term outlook. Only Poland has produced a fairly comprehensive account of the reforms and projects the government hopes to implement, but even this only refers to the coming year and does not address the issues in a framework such as that suggested. In this respect a great many useful lessons can be learned from the way in which Marshall Aid for western Europe was organized in the Organization for European Economic Cooperation.

Another advantage of a clearer and more coherent framework for organizing western assistance for the transition process is that it could play an important role in building confidence in the various reform and restructuring programmes. In some countries, especially some of the members of the CIS, there is a problem of confidence on the part of populations who have seen a series of "plans" come to nothing (or very little) and remain very sceptical towards new sets of proposals. In such circumstances, the credibility of a new reform programme could probably be enhanced with the support of a major international group such as the IMF or the G-7. However, to have a significant effect on expectations, the programme should be seen to have been thoroughly analysed and discussed and the support of the international community must be publicly known.

More broadly, a clearly defined framework could provide a more "general safety net" for the transition process in which the inevitable mistakes could occur without damaging confidence. It is in such a context that the ECE secretariat has proposed[24] the creation of a Second European Recovery Programme in which the commitment of western governments to the ultimate success of the transition process would be made more explicit. Many historians point to the important role of the confidence effects of Marshall Aid and the United States' commitment to its success in the reconstruction of western Europe after the war. Today, only the new east German *Länder* have a similar degree of commitment to the success of their transformation programme.

However, this does raise the question of the strength of western governments' practical commitment to the reconstruction of eastern Europe and the former Soviet Union. As noted above, the amounts of genuine aid being given to them are very small and there seems little prospect of a significant increase in the immediate future. Many western governments feel constrained by their own budgetary problems and by the deteriorating short-term prospects for their own economic growth. With rising unemployment at home, it is difficult for foreign assistance to qualify as a high priority. Some

---

[22] The coordination of emergency aid and other assistance to members of the CIS was discussed at the Washington Conference on 22-23 January 1992 and will be followed up at another conference in Lisbon in the Spring.

[23] For a more detailed discussion of the coordination issue, and one which places it in the context of proposals for a Second European Recovery Programme, see United Nations Economic Commission for Europe, *Economic Survey of Europe in 1989-1990*, New York, 1990, pp.25-26, *Economic Survey of Europe in 1990-1991*, New York, 1991, p.7, and *Economic Bulletin for Europe*, vol.43, New York, 1991, pp.8-9.

[24] See United Nations Economic Commission for Europe, *Economic Bulletin for Europe*, vol.43, New York, 1991, pp.7-9.

governments clearly hope that the problems of the transition economies can be left in large measure to the IMF and the World Bank. However, the IMF is still denied the 50 per cent increase in its quota which is necessary to meet the growing demands on its resources, especially from the eastern countries, and a $1.3 billion increase in the capital of the IFC (an affiliate of the World Bank) is still not approved although it is being asked to increase its support for private sector projects. The danger is that the growing introspection of some of the leading western countries will only be broken by the onset of a major crisis in one of the transition economies and that this could lead subsequently to hasty measures which would probably be less than optimal.

Chapter 2

WESTERN EUROPE AND NORTH AMERICA

Against earlier expectations, there was a general weakening of economic growth in 1991 and several countries remained or moved into recession. Against this background, inflationary pressures tended to ease and conditions in the labour markets deteriorated. An upturn in output growth is now expected for the second half of 1992 but forecasts are surrounded by more than the usual margin of uncertainty and the downside risks may be considerable. Economic growth in western Europe and North America is unlikely to average more than 1.7 per cent in 1992.

2.1 OUTPUT AND THE COMPONENTS OF DEMAND IN 1991

Economic growth slows further ...

There was a further slow-down in economic growth in the western market economies of the ECE region in 1991 (chart 2.1.1). A strengthening of growth rates, projected by many forecasters for the second half of 1991, did not materialize: instead, the dominating pattern was one of sluggish or falling activity levels against a background of declining business and consumer confidence.

In fact, consumer confidence had started to weaken perceptibly already in 1990, reflecting a variety of factors, which differed in importance among the various countries. However, the decline accelerated sharply in the second half of 1990 as a result of the crisis in the Persian Gulf. The speedy conclusion of the Gulf war, at the end of February, boosted consumer confidence in March, but this turned out to be only a temporary rebound: in the second half of 1991, consumer confidence fell sharply, both in western Europe and the United States, and at the end of 1991 was close to the levels recorded during the recession of 1981/1982 (chart 2.1.2). As was argued in this *Survey* last year,[25] it was by no means obvious, despite widespread assumptions to the contrary, that the end of the Gulf war would lead to a rapid recovery of confidence, thereby ensuring that the recession would be brief and shallow. It is clear (chart 2.1.2) that the Gulf crisis created a large negative deviation from an established downward trend — a mini-cycle attached to a longer downturn.

... and the cycle is more synchronized

A feature of recent conjunctural developments is a reduction in the degree of cyclical desynchronization that had emerged among the major economies in 1990, and which had seemed set to continue had the earlier forecasts for 1991 been realized.[26] The closer synchronization in 1991 largely reflects the failure of the recovery to appear in the United States and the United Kingdom, where earlier declines in quarterly real GDP were followed by virtual stagnation in the second half of 1991 (table 2.1.1). At the same time growth slowed down significantly in Germany and Japan. GDP in west Germany started to fall in the third quarter of 1991, compared with the preceding quarter, and stagnated in the final quarter. On the basis of the usual definition,[27] the German economy therefore was on the edge of recession in 1991, although, admittedly, overall activity levels have remained quite high. In France, there was steady but moderate economic growth in the first three quarters of 1991, but with the overall slow-down in foreign demand, notably from Germany, activity levels weakened considerably in the final months of the year. In Italy economic growth resumed in the first quarter of 1991 following a decline in real GDP in the final quarter of 1990, but the pace of economic activity slackened in the following quarters. There was also a sharp deceleration in economic growth in Japan in the second half of the year.

Among the smaller economies of western Europe, for many of which quarterly GDP data are not available, recessionary forces prevailed in the course of 1991 in Finland, Sweden and Switzerland; in a number of the

---

[25] United Nations Economic Commission for Europe, *Economic Survey of Europe in 1990-1991*, New York, 1991, pp.37-38.

[26] See United Nations Economic Commission for Europe, *Economic Survey of Europe in 1990-1991*, New York, 1991, pp.9-10.

[27] That is, two successive quarterly declines in real GDP.

CHART 2.1.1

Annual growth rates of real GDP, 1980-1991

(Percentage)

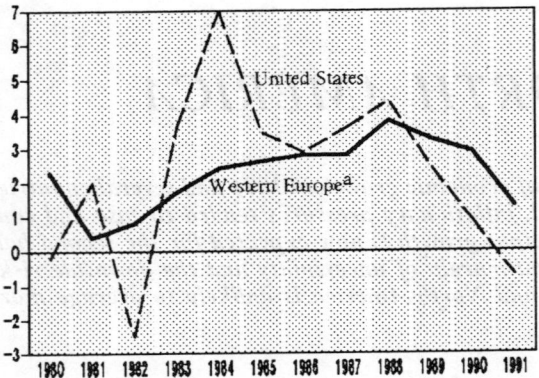

Source: ECE/DEAP.

a 17 countries, see table 2.1.2.

CHART 2.1.2

Consumer confidence in the European Community and the United States, October 1989-February 1992

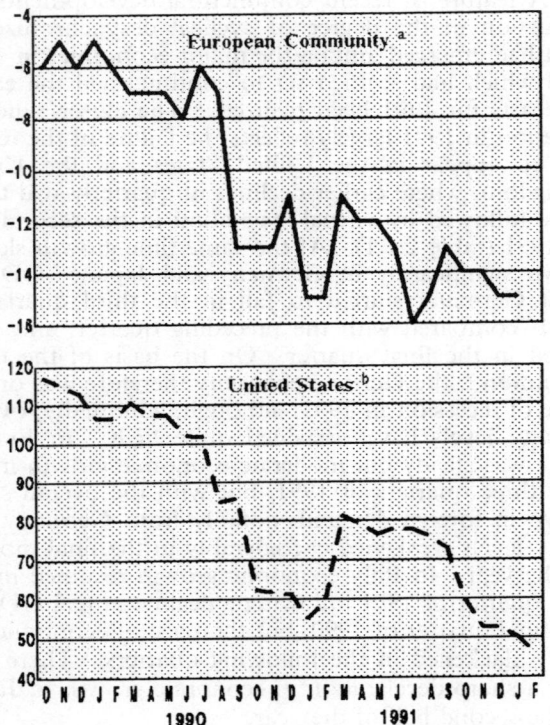

Source: Commission of the European Communities, *European Economy*, Supplement B, monthly; United States Department of Commerce News, *Survey of Current Business* and Consumer Research Center, New York.

a Net balances between respondents giving positive and negative answers to several specific questions. For details see any edition of the source.

b Conference Board Index of consumer confidence, 1985 = 100.

other countries, output growth faltered and approached a standstill in the second half of the year.

... but there are large differences in policy stances

The marked cyclical desynchronization of the major economies in 1990 led to striking differences in the stance of policy.

Thus, in the United States, monetary policy was considerably relaxed in the course of 1991 in order to stimulate domestic demand. In contrast, in Germany and (for most of 1991) in Japan, monetary policy was tightened in an attempt to choke off inflationary pressures. Higher interest rates in Germany, in turn, have reduced the room for manoeuvre of monetary policy in most other west European countries which are either members of the European Monetary system (EMS) or are adhering to exchange rate targets *vis-à-vis* the Deutschmark or the ECU. The level of German interest rates is not appropriate for most of these countries given the deterioration of their domestic activity levels. However, any attempt to boost activity is likely to conflict with the aim of maintaining fixed exchange rates within or without the EMS. Thus, in the United Kingdom nominal short-term interest rates were only lowered in the course of 1991 in tandem with the falling inflation rate, meaning that real interest rates remained very high. In France, which had not followed the increase in German official interest rates in August 1991, a lowering in the central bank's intervention rate in October by one quarter of a percentage point was more than reversed in November, when the French franc came under pressure in the EMS. Subsequently, the French monetary authorities raised interest rates still further, in the wake of the Bundesbank's decision in December to lift the discount rate to its highest level in the post-war period.

An important factor constraining domestic demand in several countries, notably the United States and the United Kingdom, has been the need to correct structural financial imbalances in the private sector. The arduous and lengthy adjustment process involved has reinforced prevailing pessimistic expectations: reduced borrowing and higher savings have offset the stimulative effect of lower interest rates in these two countries.

An important factor in the slow-down of growth in western Europe in 1991 was the weakening of the demand stimulus emanating from German unification. In the second half of 1990 and the first half of 1991 the surge in German import demand had still provided some offset to the recessionary forces prevailing in North America and the United Kingdom. However, the stimulus was sharply reduced with the tightening of German monetary and fiscal policy in the second half of 1991.

In the United States, the progressive and considerable easing of monetary policy in the course of 1991 has so far failed to stimulate domestic demand growth. This lack of response is not only a reflection of the normal lags with which economic agents respond to changes in interest rates, but is also due, in large measure, to the high levels of private sector debt and asset price deflation which have been depressing the propensity to spend. High private sector indebtedness has also had a weakening effect on domestic demand in the United Kingdom and the three Nordic countries. In

TABLE 2.1.1

Quarterly changes in real GDP, [a] **1990-1991**
(Percentage change over previous period)

	1990				1991			
	Q-I	Q-II	Q-III	Q-IV	Q-I	Q-II	Q-III	Q-IV
France	1.4	-	0.7	-0.3	0.3	0.7	0.7	..
Germany	2.0	0.5	2.0	0.5	1.5	0.5	-0.5	..
Italy	0.7	0.1	0.4	-0.1	0.6	0.4	0.1	..
United Kingdom	0.6	0.9	-1.3	-1.0	-0.7	-0.5	0.1	-0.4
United States	0.4	0.4	0.1	-1.0	-0.6	0.3	0.4	0.2
Canada	0.6	-0.2	-0.3	-1.2	-1.2	1.4	0.2	-0.2
Japan [b]	0.9	2.0	0.7	1.0	2.0	0.7	0.4	-0.1
7 major economies	0.7	0.6	0.3	-0.4	0.1	0.4	0.3	..

Source: ECE secretariat estimates, based on national statistics.

a Data are seasonally adjusted.
b GNP.

TABLE 2.1.2

Annual changes in real GDP in western Europe and North America, 1989-1992
(Percentage change over previous year)

	1989	1990	1991	1992 [a]
Western Europe	*3.3*	*2.9*	*1.0*	*1.5*
4 major economies	3.1	2.7	1.0	1.4
France	3.9	2.8	1.0	1.5
Germany	3.2	4.7	3.4	1.5
Italy	3.0	2.0	1.0	1.4
United Kingdom [b]	2.2	0.9	-2.4	1.3
13 smaller economies	3.5	3.2	1.0	1.6
Austria	3.7	4.9	2.7	2.3
Belgium	3.8	3.7	1.5	2.0
Denmark	0.8	1.7	2.2	2.3
Finland	5.4	0.4	-6.2	-1.0
Greece	3.5	-0.1	1.0	1.3
Ireland	5.9	6.0	2.0	2.3
Netherlands	4.0	3.9	2.0	1.3
Norway	0.4	1.8	1.5	2.3
Portugal	5.4	4.2	2.7	2.2
Spain	4.8	3.7	2.5	2.5
Sweden	2.4	0.6	-0.7	-
Switzerland	3.9	2.2	-0.5	0.9
Turkey	1.9	9.2	1.5	2.8
North America	*2.5*	*0.9*	*-0.8*	*1.8*
United States	2.5	1.0	-0.7	1.8
Canada	2.5	0.5	-1.5	2.3
Total above	*2.8*	*1.7*	*-*	*1.7*
Memorandum item:				
Japan	4.6	5.6	4.5	2.4
Total above including Japan	*3.1*	*2.4*	*0.7*	*1.8*

Source: National statistics.

a Forecast.
b UK output measure of GDP at factor cost.

addition, the banks have tightened their lending standards, which had been considerably relaxed in the 1980s.

In the United States the value of commercial and industrial loans by banks fell in 1991. Changes in total bank lending reflects, of course, the interaction of both demand and supply factors, whose relative importance is difficult to isolate. Thus, the overall deterioration in the economic environment will tend to dampen demand for credit by the private sector. Also, as their financial situation deteriorates in the recession, many loan applicants will no longer meet the normal standards of credit worthiness, entailing a corresponding reduction in loans extended. However, in addition to these factors, the steep rise in provisions for bad debts, notably in the real estate sector, has weakened the balance sheets of many banks and reduced their willingness or capacity to increase lending. A further constraint on lending has been the need to meet the agreed Bank for International Settlement (BIS) capital adequacy ratios. All these factors together have led to more restrictive bank policies, which appear to have played an important role in the reduction of commercial and industrial loans in the United States in 1990-1991.[28]

Lower growth in western Europe, contraction in the US

Against the background described above, *real GDP*, the broadest measure of total economy output, rose in western Europe by barely 1 per cent in 1991 compared with 2.9 per cent in 1990 (table 2.1.2).

As usual, there are significant inter-country differences, but the main feature is a general deceleration in economic growth (Appendix table A.1). Most striking are the very large fall of real GDP in Finland (a decline of 6.2 per cent in 1991) and the long and deep recession prevailing in the United Kingdom. Among the other countries, Sweden and Switzerland also experienced an absolute fall in total economy output for the year as a whole, although the declines were rather small. Only Denmark and Greece escaped the general deceleration of economic growth, although it was still fairly weak in the latter.

In the United States, the relatively modest rise in output in the second and third quarters of 1991 was not sustained: real GDP growth was virtually flat in the final quarter, and for the year as a whole, total output was 0.7 per cent less than in 1990. The weak US performance was a major factor behind the decline in real GDP in Canada in 1991.

Total *industrial production* remained very sluggish in 1991. In western Europe there was hardly any

---

[28] See Ronald Johnson, "The Bank Credit 'Crumble'", *Quarterly Review*, Federal Reserve Bank of New York, 1991, Vol.16, Number 2, pp.40-51.

TABLE 2.1.3

Changes in manufacturing production in western Europe and North America, 1989-1991

(Percentage change over previous year)

	1989	1990	1991 [a]
Western Europe	4.2	2.3	-1.0 *
4 major countries	4.4	2.1	-0.5
France	4.5	1.4	-0.5
Germany	5.2	5.5	3.0
Italy	3.3	-0.3	-2.5
United Kingdom	4.2	-0.4	-5.0
12 smaller countries	3.9	2.8	-1.5 *
Austria	6.6	8.6	1.5
Belgium	4.2	4.9	-4.5
Denmark	..	..	..
Finland	2.8	-0.1	-11
Greece	2.3	-2.8	..
Ireland	11.7	4.7	3.5
Netherlands	4.1	4.0	1.0
Norway	1.5	1.0	-2.0
Portugal	2.7	5.0	..
Spain	4.3	-	-1.0
Sweden	3.8	-2.7	-8.5
Switzerland	2.8	2.6	-0.5
Turkey	2.2	9.5	1
North America	2.7	0.5	-2.5
United States	2.9	0.9	-2.0
Canada	0.3	-5.4	-6.5
Total above	3.5	1.4	-1.5 *

Sources: National statistics; ECE secretariat estimates.

[a] Estimates rounded to nearest 0.5 percentage point.

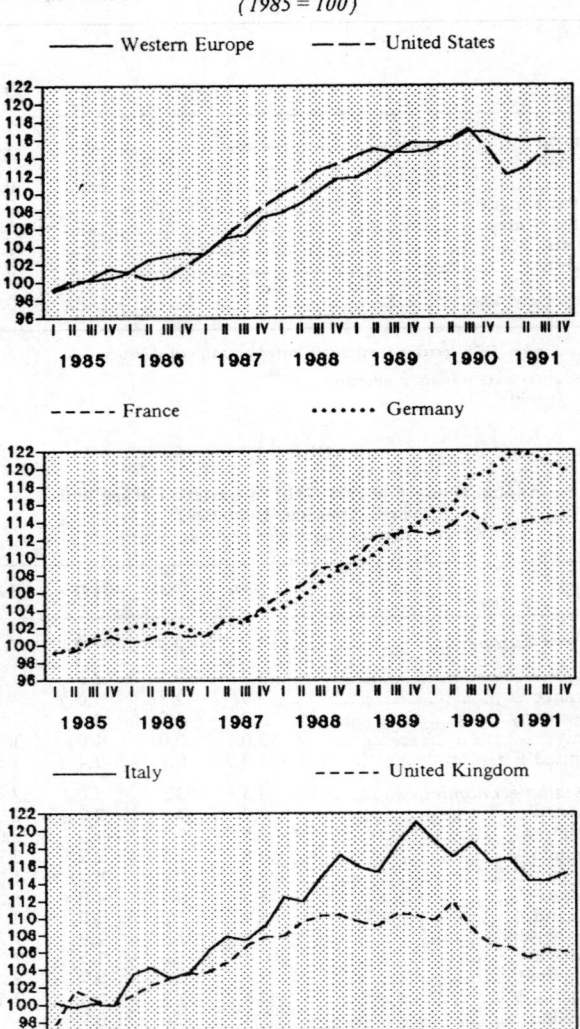

CHART 2.1.3

Quarterly index numbers of industrial output, 1985-1991

(1985 = 100)

Source: ECE DEAP.

Note: Data are seasonally adjusted.

change from the average level in 1990 (Appendix table A.8). In the United States, industrial output increased slightly during the first three quarters but faltered thereafter. On average, the level of output in US industry in 1991 was still 2 per cent lower than in 1990. The overall weakening of industrial activity in the last year or so in western Europe and the United States is shown in chart 2.1.3, which also reveals the different cyclical growth patterns in the four major economies of western Europe.

On average, total industrial output held up better than manufacturing production in 1991, a reflection of the better performance in mining and energy, which boosted aggregate output levels in the Netherlands, Norway and the United Kingdom. For the west European countries combined, manufacturing output started to fall in the final quarter of 1990 and continued to do so throughout 1991. On average, manufacturing output in western Europe fell by about 1 per cent in 1991, but in several countries the reductions were much larger (table 2.1.3). In North America, manufacturing output fell by 3 per cent in 1991 (compared with 1990), a figure which masks a very much larger fall in Canada, where production has declined by some 12.5 per cent since 1989. As was the case for real GDP, a slight recovery of output in the second and third quarters of 1991 was not sustained in the final quarter.

Against the overall background of weakening demand for goods both at home and abroad, industrial *capacity utilization rates* were falling in the course of 1991. This development has been a major influence in reducing cost-push pressures. However, it is noteworthy that in several countries utilization rates in the final quarter of 1991 were still above or close to those recorded at the previous cyclical peak in 1979/80. This is especially the case in Germany (table 2.1.4). Nevertheless, business surveys suggest that, on balance, there has been an increase throughout western Europe in the number of firms expecting available capacity to be more than sufficient to meet demand in the months ahead. Given the sharpness of the recession, considerable slack capacity existed at the end of 1991 in Finland and the United Kingdom.

In the United States, the rate of capacity utilization in manufacturing also fell markedly in 1991. Towards the end of the year, average utilization rates were some 8 percentage points lower than at the previous cyclical peak. It appears therefore that the upturn, when it occurs, should be sustainable for quite some time without

TABLE 2.1.4

Capacity utilization rates in manufacturing industry, 1979-1991
(Per cent)

	Previous peak [a] 1979 1980	Quarterly rates [b] 1989 Q-IV	1990 Q-I	1990 Q-II	1990 Q-III	1990 Q-IV	1991 Q-I	1991 Q-II	1991 Q-III	1991 Q-IV *
France	85.3	88.3	88.0	88.4	87.2	86.5	85.4	84.1	83.8	84.0
Germany	86.0	88.6	88.8	89.4	89.0	89.5	89.5	88.6	88.2	86.6
Italy	77.3	80.8	80.2	80.2	80.0	79.1	78.2	77.4	76.5	77.1
United Kingdom	87.6	88.3	88.1	87.1	86.2	84.0	81.3	78.7	76.8	77.7
Austria [c]	86.0	86.0	..	..	..	86	..	..	..	85
Belgium	78.8	82.2	81.1	81.0	80.6	81.5	80.4	79.4	79.1	78.5
Finland [d]	90.0	87.0	89.0	89.0	87.0	87.0	82.0	82.0	77.0	77.0
Greece	..	77.2	77.3	76.2	77.9	76.7	78.6	76.7	76.5	76.9
Ireland	68.1	76.4	78.7	75.5	75.2	77.4	76.2	74.2	74.3	77.2
Netherlands	83.0	86.1	86.0	86.1	86.0	85.9	84.8	85.1	84.7	83.7
Portugal	..	86.1	86.0	86.1	86.0	85.9	84.8	85.1	84.7	83.7
Spain	..	81.1	80.1	79.3	79.9	80.2	78.2	77.6	76.7	77.7
Sweden	83.7 [e]	88.4	88.0	88.0	87.1	86.6	85.5	84.0	83.4	..
Switzerland	87.0	89.4	89.6	89.5	88.7	88.5	85.0	83.6	83.4	..
United States	86.5	82.9	82.7	82.8	82.9	80.8	78.0	77.9	78.7	78.6*
Canada [f]	87.3	82.0	80.3	79.1	77.9	74.0	71.2	72.5	73.5	..

Sources: Belgium, France, Germany, Greece, Ireland, Italy, the Netherlands, Portugal, Spain, United Kingdom: Commission of the European Communities, *European Economy*, supplement B, November 1991; table 1 (data refer to January, April, July and October); Sweden: *Statistiska Meddelanden* (Industrins Kapacitetsutnyttjande − Series I, 13 SM 9104); Canada and the United States: OECD, *Main Economic Indicators*, Paris; Austria: Oesterrichisches Institut für Wirtschaftsforschung, *Monatsberichte No.1*, 1992, and previous issues; Switzerland: Bundesamt für Statistik, *La vie économique*, No.1, 1992, and previous issues; Finland: *Bank of Finland Monthly Bulletin No.1*, 1992 (direct communication).

[a] Quarterly high; for the United States monthly high.
[c] Data refer to November of each year.
[e] No data are available for 1979.
[b] Quarterly rates are seasonally adjusted.
[d] Only semi-annual data are available.
[f] Revised series after 1988.

TABLE 2.1.5

Contribution of demand components to real GDP growth in western Europe and the United States, 1989-1991
(Percentage points)

	Domestic demand					Foreign balance			
	Private consumption	Public consumption	Fixed investment	Stocks	Total	Exports	Imports	Net	GDP
Western Europe									
1989	1.8	0.1	1.4	0.2	3.6	2.5	-2.8	-0.3	3.3
1990	1.8	0.4	0.7	-0.1	2.9	2.1	-2.1	-	2.9
1991	0.9	0.3	-0.2	-0.4	0.6	1.7	-1.3	0.4	1.0
United States									
1989	1.3	0.3	0.1	0.3	1.9	1.0	-0.4	0.6	2.5
1990	0.8	0.6	-0.3	-0.7	0.5	0.8	-0.3	0.5	1.0
1991	-0.1	0.2	-1.2	-0.3	-1.4	0.7	-	0.7	-0.7

Source: ECE secretariat calculations based on national and international sources.

Note: Differences between totals and sum of components are due to rounding.

creating cost pressures which might risk the progress made in lowering the rate of inflation. Wage cost pressures may also be reduced compared with earlier upturns because of the labour shake-out in many service sectors.

Pervasive weakening of domestic demand

Looking at changes in real GDP from the demand side, it is clear that the major factor behind the slowdown in overall output growth since 1989 has been the significant weakening of domestic demand, which in turn partly reflects the lagged effects of tighter economic policies. The contribution of the major demand components to real GDP growth during 1989-1991 is presented in table 2.1.5. The data show the sizeable weakening of private consumption and fixed investment, and the relatively strong role played by the downturn of the stock cycle in western Europe. Some offset to the weakness of domestic demand was provided by changes in the net foreign balance in 1991.

In the United States, domestic demand had a negative impact on total economy growth in 1991, but half of that was offset by the positive contribution of increased net exports.

TABLE 2.1.6

Real private consumption expenditures in western Europe and North America, 1989-1991
(Percentage change over previous year)

	1989	1990	1991
Western Europe [a]	3.0	3.0	1.4
France	3.2	3.1	1.5
Germany	1.7	4.7	2.4
Italy	3.6	2.7	2.4
United Kingdom	3.5	1.0	-1.7
13 smaller countries	3.0	3.1	1.7
North America	2.0	1.2	-0.2
United States	1.9	1.2	-0.1
Canada	3.2	1.3	-1.1

Source: National statistics.

[a] 17 countries, see Appendix table A.2.

Deteriorating economic environment dampens household spending ...

Real private consumption in western Europe rose by about 1.5 per cent in 1991, about half the rate recorded in the two preceding years (table 2.1.6). The deceleration in consumer demand mirrors the overall deterioration in the economic environment. Increasing slack in labour markets and the associated rise in unemployment has dampened growth of personal incomes and depressed consumer confidence. In such an environment precautionary savings are generally stepped up and changes in *household savings ratios* were in fact a drag on higher consumption growth in 1991. High real interest rates have made borrowing less attractive and have increased the debt servicing burden on indebted households. In a number of countries, the household sector is also under pressure to correct financial imbalances (a strong rise in household indebtedness) which had been built-up in the 1980s (see below) and this has also constrained spending in favour of higher savings. On occasion, special factors, such as the tax increases in Germany in July 1991, have also played an important role in slowing down the growth of private consumption.

In the United States, real private consumption actually fell by 0.1 per cent in 1991: real disposable income growth was virtually flat, and there was a slight rise in the household savings ratio. Recent revisions of US national accounts data have led to a general, albeit relatively small, upward revision of the savings ratios for the 1980s.[29] These changes do not affect, however, the overall downward trend of the savings ratio in this period. Despite the recent increase in the saving ratio, its level remains rather low compared with the 1970s and with many other developed market economies.

A brief digression: saving and net lending of households

There have been considerable swings in *household saving ratios* in a number of west European countries (Finland, Norway, Sweden and the United Kingdom) since the mid-1980s, with large declines, being reversed in the last two years or so (table 2.1.7).

Household saving is the difference between current period disposable incomes and consumption expenditures. Not all expenditure, however, is financed from current period income. Consumer borrowing allows for the possibility of consumption expenditures exceeding disposable incomes and this is reflected in a negative savings ratio.

The fall in savings relative to disposable incomes in the four countries mentioned above was partly associated with the deregulation of their financial markets, which has facilitated borrowing and correspondingly reduced the dependence on own funds. Deregulation also led to greater innovation and competition among financial institutions and effectively increased the liquidity of non-financial assets, mainly housing. Weaker lending standards and the associated possibility of higher gearing also contributed to a boom in property markets, which in turn enhanced the scope for borrowing, given the link between the value of property (used as collateral) and loans by banks.[30]

With the overall deterioration in the economic environment, notably the rise in nominal and real interest rates, the slow-down in the growth of real incomes and the collapse of the housing boom with, in some cases, large falls in asset values, the debt burden associated with higher debt levels has been difficult for many households to sustain. It is therefore not surprising to see a strong upturn in the saving ratio (table 2.1.7) and a slow-down or fall in borrowing since 1989.

It should be recalled, moreover, that households purchase not only consumer goods and services but also capital goods. Broadly speaking, if aggregate household savings exceed the corresponding expenditures on investment goods (mainly housing) then the household sector is effectively a net lender of funds to economic agents in other sectors, with financial institutions acting as intermediaries. Conversely, negative net lending means that the household sector is effectively borrowing funds from other sectors. It is striking that, in the four countries for which data are given in table 2.1.7, household net lending was negative for a number of years in the latter half of 1980s: in other words, savings were insufficient to meet expenditure on the household capital account. In the three Nordic countries, incomes were insufficient to cover even consumption expenditure, a shortfall which was accentuated by borrowing to purchase capital goods, viz. housing. This phenomenon was especially pronounced in Norway between 1985 and 1988. The rapid fall in the savings and net lending ratios implied a considerable stimulus to domestic demand originating in the household sector. The recent large increase in the two ratios

---

[29] See US Department of Commerce, *Survey of Current Business*, vol.71, No.11, November 1991. For the period 1977-1990, there was a modest downward revision in the annual saving rates only for 1977 and 1989.

[30] Within the life-cycle and permanent income hypothesis of consumption, increases in property values should lead to a reduction in the savings of owners since they allow for higher consumption at given income levels.

TABLE 2.1.7

Household net savings and net lending ratios, 1985-1991
(Percentage of disposable income)

	1985	1986	1987	1988	1989	1990	1991
Finland							
Savings	5.8	3.6	3.5	0.5	2.0	3.6	9.1
Net lending	3.3	1.4	2.1	-0.9	-2.3	0.2	8.0
Norway							
Savings	-2.7	-6.1	-6.2	-2.4	1.0	2.0	5.0
Net lending	-9.1	-13.2	-13.1	-7.4	-1.5	-	6.8
Sweden							
Savings	1.9	0.4	-3.4	-5.1	-4.5	-1.1	1.0 *
Net lending	1.6	0.6	-4.6	-5.7	-4.0	-1.5	2.5 *
United Kingdom							
Savings [a]	9.8	8.5	6.9	5.4	7.1	9.2	10.2
Net lending	3.3	1.3	-1.1	-4.3	-1.2	2.1	..
Memorandum item:							
United States							
Savings	6.4	6.0	4.3	4.4	4.4	5.1	5.3
France							
Savings [a]	14.0	12.9	10.8	11.4	11.9	12.0	12.5 *
Germany							
Savings	11.4	12.3	12.6	12.8	12.5	13.9	13.8

Source: National statistics.

a Gross savings.

reflects, in turn, the sizeable contractionary effect of overall household demand on the level of economic activity.

TABLE 2.1.8

Real gross fixed capital formation in western Europe and North America, 1989-1991
(Percentage change over previous year)

	1989	1990	1991
Western Europe [a]	6.9	3.2	-0.7
France	7.5	3.9	-1.5
Germany	7.0	8.8	6.9
Italy	4.6	3.0	-1.0
United Kingdom	6.8	-2.4	-10.3
13 smaller countries	7.7	2.0	-0.9
North America	1.0	-1.8	-7.4
United States	0.4	-1.6	-7.6
Canada	5.6	-3.3	-5.7

Source: National statistics.

a 17 countries, see Appendix table A.4.

In the United States during the 1980s, there was a marked fall in the savings ratio and a considerable increase in consumer debt relative to disposable incomes (chart 2.1.4). There is, of course, no direct proportional relationship between changes in the savings ratio and the consumer debt-income ratio. Nevertheless, the long-term changes in these two variables, shown in chart 2.1.4, suggest that financial deregulation, and the associated easing of borrowing facilities, may have been one factor behind the steep fall of the saving ratio during the 1980s. More recently, the US household savings ratio has started to rise again, and there has been a marked fall in the consumer debt-income ratio, to a level recorded around 1985-1986. Compared with the changes noted above for the four west European countries, however, the overall sluggishness of the US saving ratio in recent years stands out (table 2.1.7 and chart 2.1.4). This may point to a slower rate of adjustment in unwinding the high levels of personal debt in the United States, which, in turn, is likely to maintain upward pressure on the US saving rate and, consequently, to dampen the growth of consumption expenditure.

... and fixed investment declined

Fixed investment fell slightly in *western Europe* in 1991 compared with 1990, although total expenditure remained quite high on average when viewed against the large increases recorded between 1986 and 1990. To some degree therefore, the weakening of investment reflects a "natural" growth pause after a period when capital formation was driven not only by strong output growth and rising profits but also by the need to make up for the relatively weak performance of the 1970s, when a backlog of potential innovations had built up, and to prepare for the impact of the completion of the EC's internal market, scheduled for the beginning of 1993.

TABLE 2.1.9

Real public consumption in western Europe and North America, 1989-1991

(Percentage change over previous year)

	1989	1990	1991
Western Europe [a]	0.7	2.4	1.5
France	0.1	3.1	0.8
Germany	-1.7	2.1	1.2
Italy	0.9	1.0	1.5
United Kingdom	0.9	3.1	2.4
13 smaller countries	2.5	2.5	1.7
North America	1.6	3.2	1.0
United States	1.5	3.2	0.2
Canada	2.9	3.1	2.7

Source: National statistics.

[a] 17 countries, see Appendix table A.3.

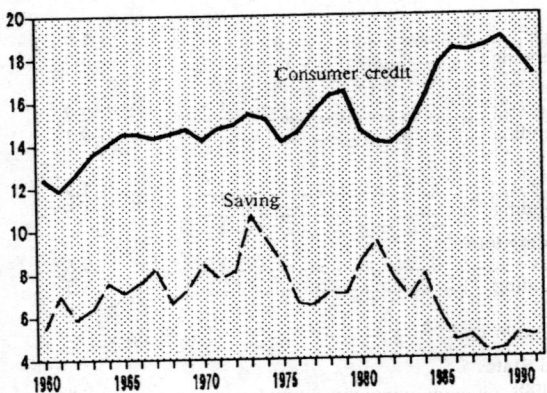

CHART 2.1.4

Consumer credit and personal saving in the United States, 1960-1991

(As percentage of personal disposable income)

Source: ECE/DEAP based on national statistics and OECD, *Main Economic Indicators*, Paris.

Notes: Consumer instalment credit outstanding at the end of each year. Personal disposable income and saving data pertain to the final quarter of the corresponding year; the data are seasonally adjusted and expressed at annual rates. Data for credit, saving and incomes for 1991 are for the third quarter.

The proximate cause behind the sluggish performance in 1991, however, was the dampening impact of tight policies on domestic demand, reinforced by the faltering of growth abroad. High interest rates curbed notably the demand for housing investment in many countries, but business investment also weakened considerably. With the outlook for growth remaining weak, capacity utilization rates declining and profit margins shrinking, investment plans were reduced and the emphasis has been shifting again to investment designed to rationalize production rather than to augment capacity.

Nevertheless, among the four major west European economies there are striking contrasts in investment performance in 1991, ranging from a slump in the United Kingdom through stagnation in France and Italy to still robust growth in Germany (table 2.1.8). The drastic cuts in fixed investment in the United Kingdom, apart from the recession, also reflect the adjustments in the company sector designed to consolidate exceptionally large financial imbalances. The strong year-on-year growth for Germany masks a virtual stagnation of fixed investment as from the second quarter of 1991. Among the smaller economies, there was a general tendency for investment spending to fall in 1991 (Appendix table A.4). Fixed investment plummeted by 13.5 per cent in Finland; and there were smaller, but also considerable, declines in Sweden and Switzerland.

Weak domestic demand and persistent problems of oversupply in the market for housing and office space were important factors behind the large fall in total fixed investment in the *United States* in 1991 (table 2.1.9). With the pace of activity slackening and capacity utilization rates falling, there was a large fall in purchases of industrial equipment. Residential investment fell strongly in 1991, for the fifth consecutive year, but there was a strengthening of investment in single family housing in the course of 1991. Nevertheless, the latter was still significantly below its level in 1990.

Overall output receives modest support from public consumption ...

The support for total output growth from *public consumption* (table 2.1.9) has been relatively modest in

CHART 2.1.5

The slowing down of the west German engine of growth, 1989-1991

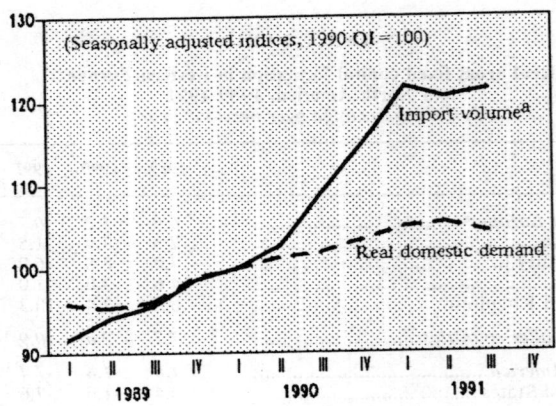

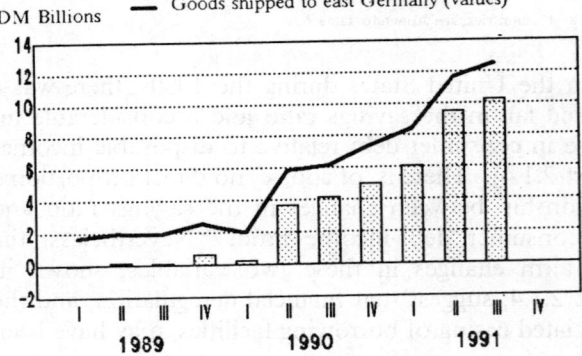

Source: ECE secretariat Common Data Base.

a Imports of merchandise.

TABLE 2.1.10

Volume of trade in goods and services in western Europe and North America, 1989-1991
(Percentage change over previous year)

	Exports 1989	Exports 1990	Exports 1991	Imports 1989	Imports 1990	Imports 1991
Western Europe [a]	7.8	6.5	4.7	8.4	6.1	3.5
France	10.3	5.2	4.0	8.2	6.4	3.2
Germany	10.1	10.3	12.1	8.4	10.2	11.0
Italy	10.0	7.5	1.2	9.0	6.7	3.5
United Kingdom	4.2	5.0	0.7	7.4	1.0	-2.9
13 smaller countries	6.5	5.2	3.3	8.7	5.9	2.2
North America	8.9	7.0	5.1	3.9	1.9	0.2
United States	11.3	7.8	6.6	3.7	2.2	0.3
Canada	0.6	3.8	-0.6	5.2	0.6	-0.3

Source: National statistics.

[a] 17 countries, see Appendix tables A.5 and A.6.

1991 in both western Europe and North America, reflecting the general tightness of fiscal policies, still dominated by the overriding objectives of deficit reduction and fiscal consolidation. In western Europe this process should become even more pronounced over the next years given the recent Maastricht agreement on convergence criteria pertaining to budget deficits and public sector debt which member countries of the EMS have to meet as a precondition for full membership of the European Monetary Union.[31]

The pronounced weakening of economic activity in 1991, however, has led to a widespread increase in budget deficits, reflecting the combined impact of lower than expected tax revenues and higher than projected transfer payments.

... but stronger help from the foreign balance

The slow-down in economic growth has led to a general deceleration in both export and import growth in *western Europe*, largely a reflection of the close economic links that exist between the countries in the region (table 2.1.10). Demand from overseas has also remained rather weak, notably as a result of falling output in North America and a marked deceleration of domestic demand in Japan.

The relatively strong annual growth rates of exports for many countries in 1991 conceal a general and significant deceleration in the second half of the year, notably as a result of the weakening of domestic demand in Germany. German import demand, in 1991 as a whole, was still an important support for higher domestic activity in many countries of western Europe. Chart 2.1.5 illustrates the impact of unification on the growth of German domestic demand and the considerable boost it provided to demand for foreign goods. The lower panel of the chart shows that a sizeable proportion of the increase in German imports was shipped to east Germany to satisfy the pent-up demand for western goods. This demand could not be met by west German producers alone since, *inter alia*, capacity utilization rates were already very high.

The very strong export growth for west Germany in 1991 (an increase of about 12 per cent) is entirely accounted for by economic transactions with east Germany, which are recorded in the foreign balance. Exports to foreign countries actually fell by 1.6 per cent compared to 1990.

The annual export performance for goods and services was quite favourable in a number of smaller economies in 1991, notably Austria, Greece, Ireland and Spain (Appendix table A.5). In contrast, exports fell considerably in Finland, largely on account of the collapse of demand from the former Soviet Union and the phasing out of the bilateral trading arrangement. Exports declined also in Sweden and Switzerland.

On the import side (Appendix table A.6), countries in recession obviously reduced their demand for foreign goods. This was particularly pronounced in Finland (a fall of 13 per cent) and Sweden (a decline of 6.5 per cent). In contrast, imports continued to grow strongly in 1991, as compared with 1990, in Austria, Portugal and Spain, largely a reflection of the continued strength of domestic demand.

On balance, changes in the real net foreign balance made a positive, and occasionally a substantial, contribution to economic growth in most countries in 1991. Changes in real net exports were a drag on overall growth only in Austria, Italy, Portugal and Spain.

Weak domestic demand largely accounts for the fact that imports into the *United States* hardly changed in 1991 compared with 1990. Export growth slowed down as a result of the increasing sluggishness of foreign demand, a tendency which was reinforced by the appreciation of the US dollar *vis-à-vis* the Deutschmark during the first eight months of 1991. In sum, the change in real net exports added some 0.7 percentage points to overall economic growth in 1991, slightly more than in 1990, but still insufficient to offset the 1.4 per cent fall in domestic demand.

---

[31] The agreement stipulates that a country's budget deficit shall not exceed (or not be significantly higher than) 3 per cent of GDP; in a similar vein the ceiling for public debt was put at 60 per cent of GDP.

2.2 INFLATION AND LABOUR MARKETS

(i) Costs and prices

In 1991 inflation moderated in the western countries of the ECE region. Measured by the consumer price index, the rate of inflation in 18 western economies of the ECE region[32] fell from 5.5 per cent in 1990 to 4.9 per cent in 1991 (Appendix table A.9). The downtrend was generally stronger in the high inflation countries and hence, the convergence toward lower inflation rates in the region increased significantly during 1991. The rate of inflation during the year accelerated only in Germany, the Netherlands, Ireland, Switzerland (during the first half) and Turkey. Disinflation was greatest in the Nordic countries, in the South European countries (except Turkey) and, particularly, in the United Kingdom and the United States. Year-on-year rates of inflation in the fourth quarter of 1991 were the lowest since the first quarter of 1987 in the United States (3 per cent) and the fourth quarter of 1988 in the 13 industrialized west European countries taken together (4.2 per cent).

"Underlying" inflation rates, which refer to consumer prices excluding seasonal and volatile food and energy prices, continued their downtrend which started in the last quarter of 1990, although with much less momentum than the total index (chart 2.2.1). In western Europe the "underlying" rate fell strongly during the first half of the year but then stabilized at nearly 4 per cent, largely because of increases in indirect taxes, duties and prices of public utilities in various countries (most notably in Germany, the Netherlands and the United Kingdom). It is also probable that there was an acceleration in the growth of unit labour costs in most countries as a result of lower productivity growth. While the rates of change in both the total consumer price index and the "underlying" rate were relatively similar in western Europe, in North America the "underlying" rate of inflation increased faster than the total index during the second half of the year, reflecting to a large extent the dampening effect of the fall in the dollar prices of food and energy on the total consumer price index. This favourable development in commodity prices was partially offset for the west European economies by the appreciation of the dollar, particularly during the second and the third quarters.

Within the consumer price index, changes in the prices of manufactured goods decelerated strongly throughout 1991, both in western Europe and particularly in North America, reflecting to a large extent the impact of falling raw material and energy prices on the production costs of manufactures. Over the 12 months to December 1991, the rate of change fell from 3.5 per cent to 1.5 per cent in western Europe[33] and from 7 per cent to 1 per cent in North America. In contrast, the rate of increase in the prices of services strengthened in western Europe and decelerated much more slowly than the prices of manufactures in North America. Over the same 12 months, the rate of increase in service prices increased from just below 4 per cent to 4.5 per cent in western Europe and fell from 6 per cent to 4.5 per cent in North America. The persistently higher rate of increase of prices in the service sector than in manufacturing reflects a number of factors including the relatively higher labour intensity of services and their relative insulation from changes in world commodity prices. Moreover, despite increasing internationalization in the last decade, services are still not subject to the degree of international competition that exists in the markets for manufactures and primary commodities.

Input and output prices and average hourly earnings in manufacturing industry

In the western market economies of the ECE region, manufacturing industry's output prices in 1991 rose less than in 1990 and its raw material and intermediate goods prices actually fell (chart 2.2.2). In *western Europe* input prices continued the downtrend, which started in 1990. There was a brief recovery in the second quarter reflecting the rise in world oil prices during April-July, the effect of which on the domestic prices was amplified by the strong appreciation of the dollar against the European currencies. During the second half of the year input prices resumed their fall at a faster rate. For the year as a whole, west European manufacturing industry's input prices fell by 0.8 per cent, nearly twice as much as in 1990. On the other hand, the year-on-year rise in output prices fluctuated at around 3 per cent during the first half of 1991 but then moderated significantly during the rest of the year as a result of weaker domestic and foreign demand and falling input prices. The annual rate of increase was less than 2 per cent in the last quarter compared with 3.0 per cent during the first half of the year.

In the *United States*, the year-on-year rise in manufacturing industry's input prices, after accelerating significantly during the second half of 1990, weakened considerably in the first quarter of 1991. Thereafter, they began to fall and in the last quarter were 2.3 per cent lower than a year earlier. The increase in output prices, after climbing to 7 per cent in late 1990, moderated significantly during 1991 and much faster than in western Europe. Output prices actually fell in November and December for the first time in five years.

---

[32] Excluding Turkey where inflation was 65.5 per cent in 1991.

[33] Weighted average of France, Germany, Belgium, Denmark, Norway, Switzerland.

CHART 2.2.1

Monthly changes in consumer prices, 1990-1991
(Percentage change over corresponding month of the preceding year)

—— Total   ---- Excluding food and energy

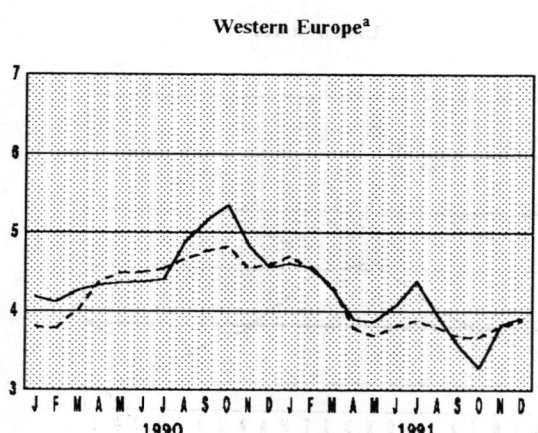
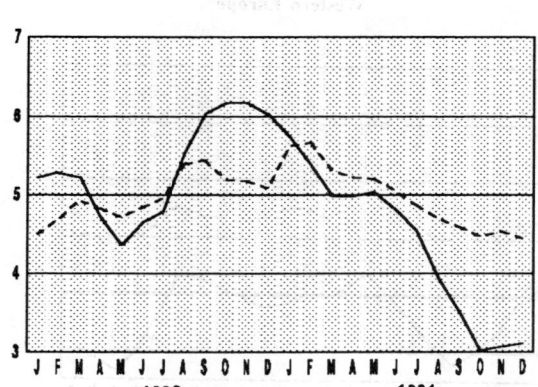

Source: National sources.

^a Weighted average of 10 countries, excluding Italy, Finland and Sweden.

The difference between the changes in output and input prices in manufacturing remained more or less stable in western Europe, except in the last quarter when it increased because of falling input prices. In the United States, the margin fluctuated during the first half of 1991 and then narrowed throughout the rest of the year due to the significant moderation in output prices. For 1991 as a whole, the differential growth between output and input prices in western Europe was 3 percentage points, the same as in 1990, but in the United States it fell from 4.5 percentage points to nearly 2.6 points. These different trends in the differential might be explained by the stickier and higher rates of growth in unit profits and, in particular, unit labour costs in western Europe than in the United States, which prevented a large part of the favourable material cost development from being passed on to consumers.

Although there was some deceleration as compared to 1990, average hourly earnings in west European manufacturing industry still increased by some 6.7 per cent in 1991 compared with 3.3 per cent in the United States (Appendix table A.10). Thus, despite some moderation in nominal earnings, real hourly earnings (deflated by the consumer price indices) continued to improve in most west European countries (except in Greece and Sweden) by some 1.5 per cent in 1991, much the same as in the previous two years. In North America, and particularly in the United States, however, real hourly earnings deteriorated further in 1991 (by nearly 1.5 per cent) for the fifth consecutive year.

World commodity prices

Commodity prices reached a cyclical peak in September 1990, since when the prices of most commodities have fallen. Oil prices, which had risen during the Gulf crisis to nearly $40 per barrel by the end of September 1990, had declined already to below $25 by the beginning of 1991 and fell to $19 by the end of February. Between April and July the dollar price of oil and, hence, total energy prices, recovered somewhat. But thereafter the downtrend in oil prices resumed and at the end of 1991 energy prices were nearly 30 per cent lower than at the end of 1990 (chart 2.2.3). The underlying weakness in the oil price is due to the weak demand for oil in the main industrial countries and to large production increases by some producers, notably Saudi Arabia.

The dollar prices of non-oil commodities also fell, by 11 per cent during the 12 months to December 1991. Prices for industrial raw materials had already been falling since the beginning of 1989 because of weaker demand, but the decline accelerated during 1991 for a number of commodities, particularly metals,[34] by the expansion of supply and sharply reduced world demand. The markets for food and beverages were marked again by good harvests and at the end of 1991 their prices were only 2.2 per cent higher than a year earlier.

The appreciation of the US dollar (by just under 6 per cent against the ECU over the 12 months to December) during most of 1991 dampened some of the positive effects of these lower commodity prices on European inflation rates. Nevertheless, in ECU terms

---

[34] Production and consumption of most traded metals would have been roughly in balance in 1991 if it had not been for the unexpectedly fast collapse of domestic demand in the USSR. The former Soviet Union's exports to the west of aluminium, copper and nickel grew sharply. In addition, east European imports of lead, tin and zinc collapsed.

CHART 2.2.2

Intermediate and final output prices in manufacturing industry,[a] 1990-1991
(Percentage change over corresponding month of the preceding year)

——— Intermediate product prices   - - - - - - Final output prices

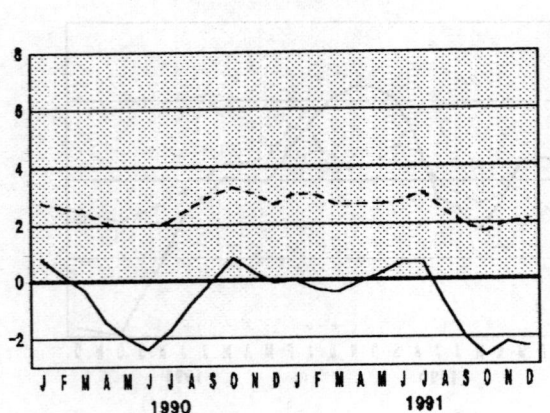
Western Europe[b]

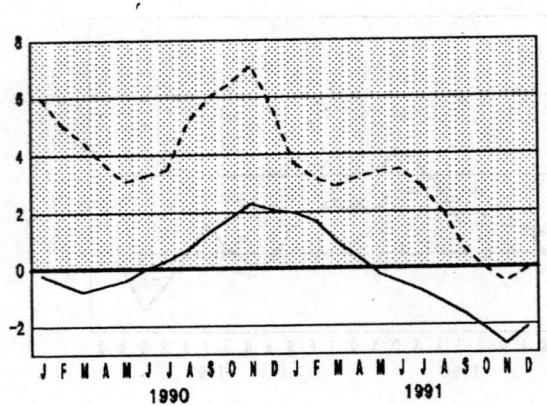
United States

Source: ECE secretariat Common Data Base, based on national sources.

[a] For definitions of indices, see United Nations Economic Commission for Europe, *Economic Survey of Europe in 1982*, New York, 1983, pp. 32-33.
[b] Weighted average of 12 countries, excluding Italy.

the fall in energy prices during the 12 months to December 1991 was still 23 per cent and that in non-energy prices was 5 per cent.

Wage and non-wage labour costs

Reflecting the increased slack in most labour markets and the maintenance of tight monetary policies in most of western Europe, inflationary pressures arising from wage and non-wage labour costs did moderate in 1991, but not by enough to offset the weakening of productivity growth. Weak, and even falling, productivity in some industries, particularly during the first half of the year, mainly reflected the lagged response of employment to the downtrend in output growth and was the major cause of the continued high growth in unit labour costs during 1991 in most west European countries (5.7 per cent on average, slightly higher than in 1990). On the other hand, the growth of wage and non-wage labour costs per person employed in western Europe moderated somewhat but was still rising much more than the overall inflation rate in most countries (on average, 6.4 per cent in 1991 compared with 6.9 per cent in 1990). In some countries labour costs per head in 1991 even accelerated (Germany, Austria, Denmark, Ireland, the Netherlands and Switzerland) or increased as fast as in 1990 (France and Canada). In the United States, despite virtually zero productivity growth for 1991 as a whole, unit labour costs increased by 4.1 per cent, a much slower rate than in western Europe and Canada and also slightly less than in 1990 thanks to a relatively lower increase in wages. The growth of unit labour costs also decelerated in some of the west European countries: Italy, the United Kingdom and the Scandinavian countries. However, in the former two and Sweden the rates of change were still very high (7.8, 8.3 and 7.2 per cent respectively) and in Denmark and Norway the moderation was mostly due to better productivity growth in 1991 rather than to increased flexibility of wages.

GDP and domestic demand deflators

In 1991, the *rate of change in the GDP deflator*, the broadest measure of inflation and which reflects domestic cost pressures on prices, accelerated slightly in western Europe and Canada and moderated for the second consecutive year in the United States (table 2.2.1). However, the rate of change also slowed down in some west European countries: Italy, Finland, Ireland, Norway, Sweden and the south European countries excluding Turkey.

The acceleration and/or the stickiness in inflation rates measured by the GDP deflator in 1991 was mainly due to the continued strong growth in *unit labour costs* and to large increases in indirect taxes in many countries. As in 1990, three fifths of the average west European increase in the GDP deflator in 1991 was due to unit labour costs, while the contribution of indirect taxes was nearly 17 per cent. The contribution of indirect taxes was particularly large in Germany (more than a quarter of the increase in the GDP deflator), Italy, the United Kingdom and Sweden: indirect taxes net of subsidies increased by some 15 per cent in the former two and nearly 10 per cent in the latter two. The contribution of indirect taxes to the change in the GDP deflator in North America was nearly one third.

Significantly weaker demand and intensified competition put pressure on profit margins in 1991 and so the downtrend in the rate of change in *unit profits* for the total economy, which started in 1990, continued. In western Europe, unit profits increased by 2.7 per

CHART 2.2.3

World market prices of raw materials, in US dollars and ECUs, 1991
(December 1990 = 100, semi-logarithmic scale)

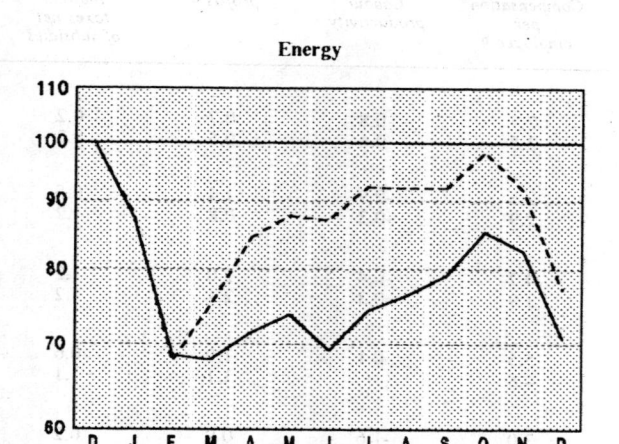

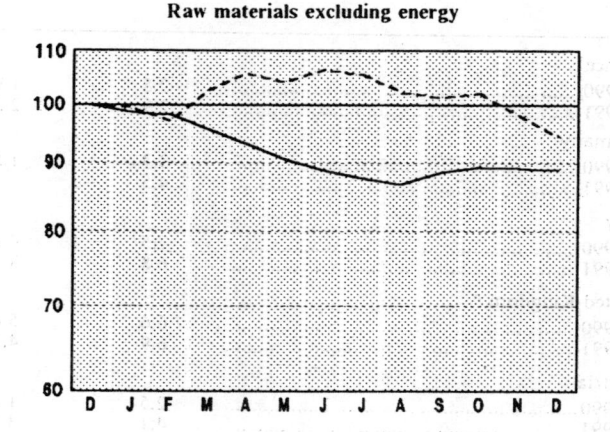

Source: The dollar index is published in Hamburg Institute for Economic Research (HWWA), *Intereconomics*, Hamburg (bi-monthly). The conversion to ECUs was made by the ECE secretariat on the basis of the US dollar-ECU exchange rate published in IMF, *International Financial Statistics*, Washington, D.C., (monthly).

cent (compared with 3.7 per cent in 1990); in the United States there was virtually no increase at all, while in Canada they fell for the second consecutive year. Consequently, the contribution of the change in unit profits to the increase in the GDP deflator during 1991 fell to one fifth in western Europe, was zero in the United States and actually pulled down the inflation rate in Canada (as it also did in Finland and Ireland).

The change in the domestic demand deflator, which measures the overall rate of domestic inflation by taking into account the terms of trade, continued to accelerate slightly during 1991 in western Europe; it stabilized in Canada and moderated significantly in the United States (table 2.2.2). Among the west European countries domestic inflation slowed down only in Italy, Belgium, Finland, Norway and Sweden, while it remained stable in the United Kingdom. Nevertheless, except for Belgium and Norway, the domestic inflation rates of these countries were still the highest in the western industrialized world.

As in 1990, import prices in 1991 did not put pressure on domestic inflation rates except in a few smaller west European countries (Ireland and to a much lesser extent in Austria, and the Nordic countries). For western Europe as a whole, the implicit price deflator of imports increased by 0.5 per cent in 1991 compared with 0.2 per cent in 1990. This slight acceleration was due to the weaker effective exchange rates of the European economies (except the United Kingdom) since the suppliers' prices fell for all the countries concerned except for Ireland and Sweden. Thus, as in 1990, the main factor behind the rise in domestic prices in 1991,

both in western Europe and North America, was the rise in domestic factor costs, particularly labour costs and indirect taxes.

(ii) Labour markets

In 1991, despite the easing of participation rates in most of the western ECE countries,[35] due to the higher rate of growth in the working-age population, the labour force continued to grow strongly (0.6 per cent). However, because of weaker economic activity, the average level of employment fell slightly (-0.2 per cent) for the first time in nine years and thus there was significant increase in unemployment. The average rate of unemployment has risen in every month since mid-1990, reaching 8.3 per cent at the end of 1991 compared with 6.9 per cent 18 months ago. However, this overall picture of the labour market situation conceals large differences among individual countries, partly a reflection of the increased desynchronization of national growth cycles which characterized most of 1990 and the first part of 1991. In other words, given the usual lagged response of employment to changes in output, labour markets in individual countries in 1991 generally reflected the sharp differences in output growth in 1990. Among the six major economies those in severe recession (Canada, the United States and the United Kingdom in particular) experienced significant job losses; in two (France and, especially, Italy) there were gains in employment albeit smaller than in 1990; while in Germany, in marked contrast, employment growth,

---

[35] See Appendix table A.1 for the list of countries.

TABLE 2.2.1

Contribution to the change in the GDP deflator, 1990-1991

(Percentages)

	Change in the GDP deflator [a]	Unit labour costs Total	Compensation per employee [b]	Labour productivity	Unit profits [c]	Unit indirect taxes net of subsidies
France						
1990	2.8	1.9	2.7	-0.8	0.7	0.2
1991	2.9	2.2	2.8	-0.6	0.5	0.2
Germany						
1990	3.4	1.5	2.5	-0.9	1.4	0.5
1991	4.5		2.9	-0.3	0.8	1.2
Italy						
1990	7.5	4.2	4.7	-0.4	2.0	1.2
1991	6.8	3.5	3.9	-0.3	2.1	1.2
United Kingdom [d]						
1990	6.6	5.4	5.5	-0.1	1.9	-0.6
1991	6.9	4.7	4.8	-	1.1	1.1
Austria						
1990	2.5	1.4	3.0	-1.6	0.9	0.2
1991	4.1	3.1	3.5	-0.4	0.4	0.6
Belgium						
1990	3.0	1.8	3.2	-1.4	1.0	0.2
1991	3.2	1.9	2.6	-0.7	1.1	0.2
Denmark						
1990	2.1	0.7	2.0	-1.2	1.7	-0.3
1991	2.1	0.3	2.1	-1.7	1.6	0.2
Finland						
1990	5.2	5.0	6.0	-0.9	-	0.3
1991	3.9	5.4	4.7	0.7	-2.0	0.5
Ireland						
1990	1.3	-	1.3	-1.3	3.5	-2.2
1991	1.1	1.7	3.2	-1.4	-1.1	0.5
Netherlands						
1990	2.9	1.1	2.0	-0.9	1.1	0.7
1991	3.0	1.9	2.4	-0.5	0.8	0.3
Norway						
1990	4.5	1.7	3.0	-1.2	2.8	0.1
1991	2.6	1.5	2.8	-1.4	1.1	-
Sweden						
1990	9.4	7.1	6.9	0.2	0.3	1.9
1991	-7.4	3.8	4.4	-0.6	2.4	1.3
Switzerland						
1990	5.3	3.9	4.5	-0.5	1.3	-
1991	5.7	5.0	4.7	0.3	0.4	0.3
Western Europe [e]						
1990	4.6	2.9	3.6	-0.7	1.3	0.4
1991	4.8	3.0	3.4	-0.4	1.0	0.8
United States						
1990	4.1	2.5	2.8	-0.3	1.1	0.4
1991	3.6	2.4	2.4	-	0.1	1.1
Canada [d]						
1990	3.0	3.4	3.2	0.1	-0.4	-
1991	3.2	3.2	3.3	-0.1	-1.1	1.0

Source: National accounts. Small discrepancies are due to rounding.

[a] GDP at market prices.
[b] Wage and non-wage labour costs per person employed.
[c] Includes capital consumption.
[d] Based on data for three quarters.
[e] Weighted average of 13 countries.

TABLE 2.2.2

Contribution to the change in the domestic demand deflator, 1990-1991
(Percentages)

	Change in domestic demand deflator	Changes in GDP deflator excluding exports [a]	of which due to: Import prices Total	Exchange rates [b]	Export prices of suppliers [c]
France					
1990	2.6	3.0	-0.3	-1.7	1.3
1991	3.0	2.7	0.3	0.6	-0.3
Germany					
1990	3.0	3.2	-0.2	-1.8	1.6
1991	4.2	3.9	0.4	0.5	-0.1
Italy					
1990	7.4	6.8	0.6	-0.9	1.5
1991	6.2	6.0	0.2	0.5	-0.3
United Kingdom [d]					
1990	6.3	5.6	0.7	-0.1	0.8
1991	6.2	6.9	-0.7	-	-0.8
Austria					
1990	1.7	1.6	0.1	-3.0	3.1
1991	5.0	4.2	0.8	0.8	-
Belgium					
1990	3.6	4.2	-0.7	-4.2	3.5
1991	3.2	3.2	-	0.3	-0.3
Denmark					
1990	2.8	3.4	-0.6	-2.8	2.3
1991	3.0	2.6	0.5	0.7	-0.3
Finland					
1990	5.5	5.2	0.3	-1.3	1.7
1991	5.2	4.6	0.6	1.3	-0.7
Ireland					
1990	3.3	6.1	-2.8	-4.6	1.8
1991	4.2	3.1	1.1	1.0	0.1
Netherlands					
1990	2.3	3.4	-1.1	-3.1	2.0
1991	2.8	2.8	-	0.6	-0.6
Norway [d]					
1989	4.9	4.4	0.4	-1.2	1.6
1990	4.1	3.7	0.4	1.1	-0.7
Sweden					
1990	9.8	8.9	0.9	-0.3	1.2
1991	8.0	7.3	0.7	0.3	0.4
Switzerland					
1990	4.5	4.8	-0.3	-3.4	3.2
1991	5.1	4.9	0.2	1.0	-0.8
Western Europe [e]					
1990	4.4	4.4	-	-1.6	1.6
1991	4.6	4.5	0.1	0.5	-0.4
United States					
1989	4.4	4.0	0.4	0.8	-0.3
1990	3.5	3.5	-0.1	-	-0.1
Canada [d]					
1990	3.6	3.2	0.4	0.4	-
1991	3.6	3.6	-0.1	-0.5	0.4

Source: National accounts and IMF, *International Financial Statistics*, Washington, D.C. Small discrepancies are due to rounding.

[a] Calculated as the residual of the change in the domestic demand deflator minus the contribution of the change in import prices.
[b] Effective exchange rates (reciprocal of IMF MERM rates).
[c] These are the prices of imports in terms of the national currency of the country of origin.
[d] Based on data for three quarters.
[e] Weighted average of 13 countries.

TABLE 2.2.3

Changes in employment by sector, 1979-1991 [a]
(Average annual changes)

	1979-1989	1989	1990	1991 [b]	1979-1989	1989	1990	1991 [b]
	(Thousands)				*(Percentages)*			
Western Europe [c]								
Total	710.7	221.0	220.3	34.4	0.5	1.6	1.6	0.2
Industry	-531.7	40.4	58.7	-56.7	-1.1	0.9	1.3	-1.3
Services	1 569.2	198.5	189.0	123.1	2.1	2.4	2.2	1.4
North America								
Total	2 059.4	260.0	67.6	-127.9	1.7	2.0	0.5	-1.0
Industry	173.2	38.5	-49.5	-163.3	0.5	1.1	-1.4	-4.8
Services	2 021.0	218.2	119.6	29.6	2.5	2.4	1.3	0.3

Source: National statistics; OECD, *Quarterly labour force statistics*, No. 4, 1991, Paris; OECD, *Labour force statistics 1969-1989*, Paris; ECE secretariat estimates.

[a] Civilian employment; labour force survey data which differs from the national accounts data used in the text in discussing changes in total employment and productivity.
[b] Based on data of first three quarters.
[c] Excluding Greece, Portugal and Turkey.

for the year as a whole, continued with the same vigour as in 1990 (Appendix table A.11).

A similar divergence of cyclical labour market situations is also apparent among the smaller economies where a strong growth of employment in Austria and Portugal contrasts with significant job losses in the Nordic countries, Ireland, Switzerland and Greece.

Declining or lower rates of increase in employment in the majority of the countries of the region and the continued relatively strong expansion in the labour force, especially in western Europe,[36] naturally led to an increase of labour market slack in 1991. In western Europe the number of people unemployed increased by nearly 1.5 million, to an average of 16 million in 1991, which corresponds to 8.7 per cent of the labour force compared with 8.1 per cent in 1990 (Appendix table A.12).

In North America, where both economies were in recession and employment had already started to decline in the second half of 1990, unemployment increased much faster in 1991: a rise of nearly 1.8 million jobless people took total unemployment to nearly 10 million at the end of 1991. Nevertheless, in North America the unemployment rate (6.9 per cent) was significantly lower than in Western Europe. In the United States, the December unemployment rate was 7 per cent, the highest level for five years. In the same month the average west European rate was 9.1 per cent, its highest level for three years. In most of the west European countries the average unemployment rate has risen from cycle to cycle. After seven years of expansion, in 1989-1990 the rate of unemployment in the majority of west European countries (except Finland, Sweden, Portugal and Italy), and also in Canada, was still higher than in the trough of the previous cycle (1979-1980). In the United States, however, the rate of unemployment at the end of the last business cycle fell below its previous trough (1978-1979), chart 2.2.4.

The 1980s were not only a decade of high unemployment, by historical standards, but also of significant changes in the structure of unemployment. Youth and female unemployment rates have reached record levels and long-term unemployment rose significantly, both in number and as a proportion of total unemployment during the 1980s. These structural changes, and in particular the increase in the share of the long-term unemployed, go a long way to explaining the persistence of higher unemployment rates in western Europe. In the United States, the rate of flow both into and out of unemployment is higher and hence the average duration of joblessness is shorter.[37]

The recent rise in unemployment has a particular aspect which, in addition to the increase in the total, has affected consumer confidence and employment expectations. For decades services have been the engine of employment growth. During the 1980s, the service sector in the United States created 20 million new jobs and its share of total employment reached 70 per cent at the end of the decade. In western Europe, both the growth rate of services and their share of total employment was smaller than in the United States. Nevertheless, in the majority of countries it was the most dynamic sector for employment creation during the 1980s (table 2.2.3).

In previous downturns unemployment hit mostly blue collar workers in the manufacturing sector. In the current recession white collar joblessness has risen in line with the increase in total unemployment. Most services, from banking to retailing, with the principal exception of health care, are going through a restructuring process similar to that in manufacturing a decade ago. The drive to control costs and improve profits has resulted in recruitment freezes,[38] early retirements, layoffs, consolidations and takeovers. This more widespread diffusion of unemployment throughout a greater number of sectors and occupations, in addition to other

---

[36] Western Europe includes four south European countries.

[37] "The 1988 'steady state' average duration for the US unemployment was 3 months compared with 10 months for UK, 16 months for Germany and 50 months for Belgium". G.D.N. Worswick, "The scope for macroeconomic policy to alleviate unemployment in western Europe", UN/ECE Discussion Papers Series, Vol.2, No.4, New York, 1992 (forthcoming).

[38] For example, in the United Kingdom, there was a rise in job vacancies during the fourth quarter. However this seems to have been associated with a reduction

CHART 2.2.4

Unemployment rates in western Europe[a] and the United States, 1970-1991
(Percentage of total labour force)

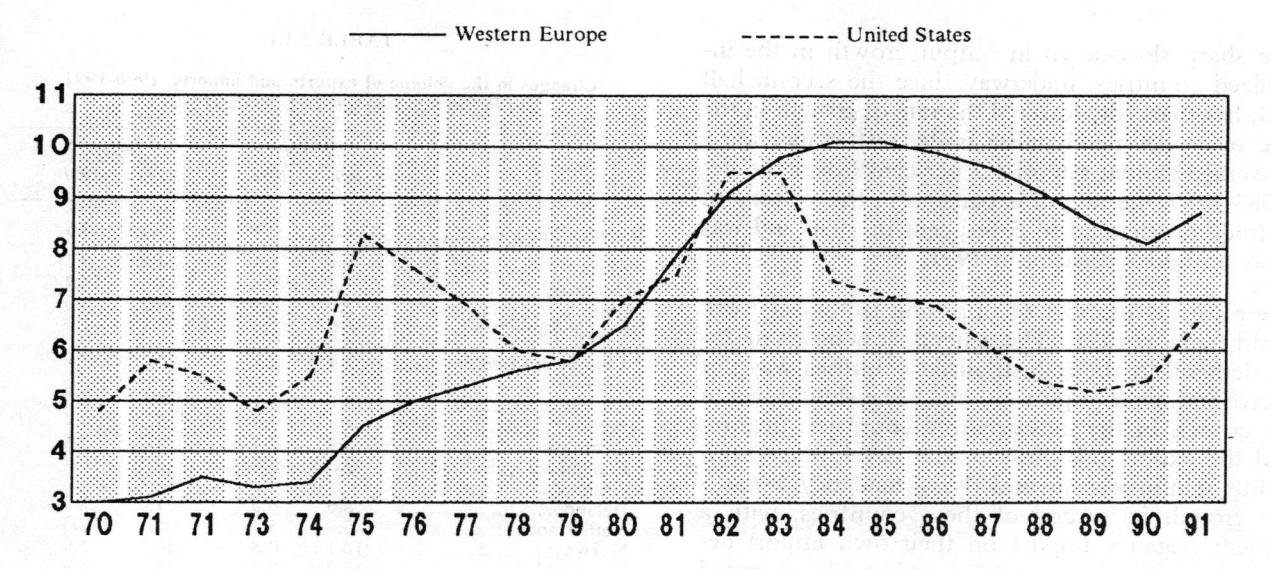

Source: See Appendix table A.12.

[a] Total of 17 west European countries.

factors such as high levels of household indebtedness in some countries, has increased uncertainty among a wider range of employees than in the past and may help to explain why consumer confidence and retail sales data are so far out of line with the actual development of economic activity. The slow-down or falls in output are generally modest (except in the United Kingdom and a few smaller west European countries) and gains in real wages have been significant almost everywhere except in the United States.

Given the present levels of consumer confidence, the expected upturn is likely to be much more gradual than previous recoveries and thus cyclical unemployment rates will continue to rise for longer than in the past. In most countries, this implies a further deterioration in long-term unemployment.[39]

Rising unemployment, with a rising proportion of long-term unemployed, will increase considerably the levels of government expenditure, which in some cases are already swollen by higher interest rates. On average, OECD governments are already devoting the equivalent of 2 per cent of GDP to labour market measures.[40] These expenditures are expected to grow considerably in the near future.[41]

---

in recruitment as the number of new vacancies notified to job centres and the (seasonally adjusted) number of people placed in jobs by the employment service both fell. Department of Employment, *Employment Gazette*, London: HMSO, January 1992.

[39] In the United Kingdom the proportion of persons unemployed for more than 6 months has been forecast to rise from 44 per cent of total unemployment at the start of 1991 to around 60 per cent by 1993. This may limit the extent to which rising unemployment helps to moderate earnings growth. National Institute of Economic and Social Research, *National Institute Economic Review*, No.138, London: November 1991, p.17.

[40] OECD, *Economic Outlook*, Paris, December 1991, p.38.

[41] On the question of possible migration into western Europe from the eastern countries, see chapter 7 below.

2.3 TRADE AND CURRENT ACCOUNT DEVELOPMENTS

The sharp slow-down in output growth in the industrialized countries, underway since the second half of 1989, has markedly lowered the rate of growth in the volume of world merchandise trade. After increasing at an average annual rate of 6.2 per cent[42] over the period 1983-1989, the rate of expansion in the volume of world trade decelerated to 5 per cent in 1990 and was probably around 3 per cent in 1991.

There were a number of opposing factors at work on world trade in 1991. The general slow-down in domestic demand in the industrialized countries was not conducive to higher import growth. The slow-down in output growth in the industrialized countries, in turn, affected the export prospects of the developing countries, thus reinforcing an underlying tendency towards weaker growth in several of these countries, with a subsequent negative impact on their own import demand. No significant support for world trade emanated from the reforming countries of eastern Europe and the successor states of the former Soviet Union, all of which are going through a very deep stabilization-cum-structural adjustment recession. Accordingly their import demand, which is mainly directed to the industrialized countries, remained depressed. The same applies to their mutual trade in the aftermath of the dismantling of the CMEA trading arrangements.

The factors making for an overall deceleration in the rate of expansion of world trade were partly offset by the direct and indirect demand effects associated with German unification, although the overall stimulus tapered off abruptly in the second half of 1991 largely on account of the tightening of German policies. World trade was, moreover, also supported by a surge in import demand associated with reconstruction programmes of countries in the Middle East affected by the Gulf war and by the continuing buoyancy of domestic demand in several of the newly industrializing countries in south-east Asia.

A major feature of international economic transactions in 1991 was the remarkable shift in current account positions among the three major economies: there was a dramatic decline in the US current account deficit, while the German current account swung from huge surplus into deficit. At the same time the pronounced decline in the Japanese surplus in 1990, compared with previous year, was more than reversed in 1991.

TABLE 2.3.1

Changes in the volume of exports and imports, 1990-1991
(Percentage change over previous year)

	Exports 1990	Exports 1991	Imports 1990	Imports 1991
Western Europe	4.3	2.4	5.8	3.8
France	5.1	4.5	4.8	2.5
Germany [a]	1.4	1.4	11.5	13.4
Italy	2.8	0.7	4.2	3.0
United Kingdom	6.6	1.4	1.3	-2.9
4 major economies	3.4	1.9	6.0	4.9
Austria	8.5	3.1	8.6	6.0
Belgium	3.3	4.8	5.2	4.4
Denmark	5.9	7.4	3.7	3.8
Finland	3.3	-8.8	-4.2	-16.7
Greece	..	..	..	..
Ireland	8.6	6.5	7.0	2.9
Netherlands	5.7	5.4	5.7	2.3
Norway	10.1	-0.8	10.5	1.9
Portugal	12.0	-0.2	15.6	6.9
Spain	12.2	10.6	9.2	10.8
Sweden	-	-2.0	1.0	-6.3
Switzerland	4.5	-1.3	2.7	-1.4
Turkey	..	..	..	..
11 smaller economies	5.7	3.1	5.6	2.2
North America	6.7	5.9	1.4	0.7
United States	7.4	7.6	1.8	0.4
Canada	4.5	0.6	-0.4	1.7
Japan	5.5	2.4	5.8	3.1
Total above	5.0	3.2	4.6	2.9

Source: National statistics and ECE secretariat estimates.

Note: Regional aggregates have been calculated by the ECE secretariat using 1989 trade weights. Data for Norway exclude ships, oil platforms, crude oil and natural gas.

[a] Excluding the five new *Länder*.

Trade volumes

The annual growth in the volume of *merchandise exports* in western Europe slowed to approximately 1 per cent in 1991, down from 4 per cent in the previous year (table 2.3.1). Among the four major economies, the relatively strong export performance of France stands out, a reflection of improved competitiveness but also of favourable special factors. A major factor dampening German export growth — already in 1990 — was the weakening of international growth, and notably the pronounced slow-down in the demand for investment goods: capital goods are a major specialization of German industry. In addition, in 1991 there were the trade diversion effects associated with unification, as west German firms focused on meeting the steep rise in domestic demand, mainly from the eastern,

---

[42] Calculated as the arithmetic average of volume changes for exports and imports, respectively. For data up to 1990 see United Nations, *Monthly Bulletin of Statistics*, vol.XLVI, No.1, January 1992, Special Table: B, pp.240.

TABLE 2.3.2

Germany: [a] **Value of merchandise imports, 1990-1991**
(Indices: 1990 Q-III = 100) [b]

Origin	1990 Q-III	1990 Q-V	1991 Q-I	1991 Q-II	1991 Q-III	1991 Q-IV
European Community	110.1	120.1	126.1	124.4	124.7	123.8
United States	36.9	96.9	101.0	117.7	124.0	107.3
Eastern Europe [c]	98.2	109.1	114.5	120.0	123.6	127.3

Source: Deutsche Bundesbank.

[a] Excluding the five new *Länder*.
[b] Data are seasonally adjusted.
[c] Including the former Soviet Union.

but also from the western part of the country, which drove capacity utilization rates to very high levels. It is estimated that the value of merchandise exports by east German firms declined by 53 per cent in 1991 compared with the previous year. These shipments accounted, however, for only 3 per cent of total German exports in 1991.

Among the smaller economies, there was notably a sharp fall in exports volumes in Finland in 1991, reflecting mainly the breakdown of markets in the eastern countries. Exports also fell in Sweden and Switzerland.

A general factor supporting export growth in western Europe was the strong import demand originating in Germany after unification. Against a background of already high capacity utilization rates in west German manufacturing industry in the first half of 1990, the surge in demand in the new *Länder* for western goods in the second half of that year spilled over to foreign suppliers. Also, the stimulus which unification provided to west German activity strengthened the demand for foreign goods.

Although German import demand levelled off in the second half of 1991, year-on-year import growth rates were considerable. It appears that member countries of the European Community benefited much more than EFTA countries from the strengthening of import demand in Germany in 1990-1991 (table 2.3.2). This was notably the case for France and, among the smaller economies, for Belgium, Denmark, Portugal and Spain. Among the EFTA countries, export growth to Germany was particularly buoyant for Austria, Finland and Norway.

Exports remained a major source of economic growth in the United States in 1991. In volume terms they rose by nearly 7 per cent reflecting *inter alia* improved price competitiveness and strong demand from western Europe, notably Germany. The strong year-on-year export growth rate masks, however, a considerable slow-down in the final months of 1991, in line with the further weakening of economic growth in western Europe, which offset the potential stimulus deriving from the depreciation of the dollar *vis-à-vis* the Deutschmark and the Yen in the second half of the year.

Changes in *import volumes* in the industrialized countries in 1991 reflect largely the overall deceleration in growth of domestic demand. In western Europe the volume of imports rose by about 3.5 per cent, compared with nearly 6 per cent in the preceding year. As can be seen from table 2.3.1, however, there was considerable variation in relative import changes among the various countries in 1991, reflecting the different levels of activity. Among these various changes, the plunge in imports by 17 per cent for Finland in 1991 is particularly noteworthy. Slackening domestic demand was also the major factor behind the sizeable slow-down in US import demand and the slight decline in Canada. For the United States, the fall in import value in 1991 was more than offset by the decline in unit values, partly reflecting the appreciation of the US dollar during the first half of 1991. The volume of merchandise imports rose by about 2.5 per cent in 1991.

Terms of trade

The aggregate terms of trade of the industrialized countries with the rest of the world improved in 1991, broadly offsetting the deterioration in the preceding year. This mainly reflects the fall in oil prices after the Gulf crisis and the overall weakness of primary commodity prices.

Changes in the terms of trade of individual industrialized countries, however, do not exhibit a uniform pattern. They reflect, in addition to relative price changes in trade with developing countries, changes in trade prices with other industrialized countries. Among the larger economies, only Germany had a deterioration in its terms of trade, a combination of rising unit values for imports and a slight fall for exports (table 2.3.3). Among the smaller countries, there was a general deterioration in the terms of trade in 1991, the major exceptions being Spain and Switzerland.

Current account balances

There were striking changes in the relative current account positions of the major economies in 1991 (table 2.3.4). These were mainly related to the Gulf war and to the differential strength of domestic demand.

In the United States, the current account deficit plunged to some $8.6 billion for 1991 as a whole, down from $92.1 billion in the preceding year. This reflects, in broadly equal measure, a significantly reduced deficit in merchandise trade and a swing in net unilateral transfers from negative to positive for 1991 as a whole, the first ever in the post-war period. The improvement in the trade account was brought about by a combination of favourable terms of trade changes, robust export

TABLE 2.3.3
Terms of trade, [a] **1990-1991**
(Percentage change over previous year)

	1990	1991
Western Europe	**0.9**	**0.1**
France	0.2	0.4
Germany [b]	1.5	-2.4
Italy	2.9	1.3
United Kingdom	1.0	3.4
4 major economies	*1.1*	*0.2*
Austria	0.8	-1.8
Belgium	-1.6	-0.2
Denmark	1.5	-1.0
Finland	-2.9	-2.0
Greece	..	..
Ireland	-3.7	-0.8
Netherlands	2.1	-
Norway	2.8	-1.4
Portugal	0.1	-0.6
Spain	0.7	1.9
Sweden	1.9	-0.4
Switzerland	1.6	2.1
Turkey	..	..
11 smaller economies	*0.5*	*-0.1*
North America	**-1.8**	**3.6**
United States	-1.8	3.6
Canada	-2.2	-
Japan	**-5.9**	**7.0**
Total above	**-0.4**	**1.5**

Source: National statistics and OECD, *Economic Outlook*, No.50, 1991, Paris.

Note: Regional aggregates of unit value indices were calculated by the ECE secretariat using 1989 trade weights.

[a] Ratio of unit volume index of exports to that of imports.
[b] Excluding the five new *Länder*.

TABLE 2.3.4
Current account balances, 1989-1991
(Billion US dollars)

	1989	1990	1991
Western Europe	**7.3**	**-7.3**	**-50.7**
France	-4.6	-8.4	-5.1
Germany [a]	57.2	47.9	-20.6
Italy	-10.6	-14.5	-18.9
United Kingdom	-33.4	-26.9	-10.5
4 major countries	*8.6*	*-1.9*	*-55.1*
Austria	0.1	1.0	-0.1
Belgium	3.6	3.6	4.1
Denmark	-0.9	1.5	2.2
Finland	-5.8	-6.7	-5.8
Greece	-2.6	-3.5	-1.7
Ireland	0.5	1.4	2.0
Netherlands	9.6	10.3	10.5
Norway	0.2	3.8	5.4
Portugal	0.2	-0.2	-0.6
Spain	-10.9	-16.8	-16.7
Sweden	-3.3	-5.8	-4.3
Switzerland	7.0	8.6	8.9
Turkey	1.0	-2.6	0.5
13 smaller countries	*-1.3*	*-5.4*	*4.4*
North America	**-123.9**	**-111.0**	**-31.8**
United States	-106.4	-92.1	-8.6
Canada	-17.5	-18.8	-23.4
Japan	**57.0**	**35.9**	**72.6**
Total above	**-59.6**	**-82.4**	**-9.9**

Sources: National statistics; IMF, *International Financial Statistics*, February 1992; OECD, *Economic Outlook*, No.50, December 1991.

[a] Including the five new *Länder*.

growth and a slight fall in imports. The swing in unilateral transfers was due to payments made by Saudi Arabia, Kuwait, Germany and Japan to meet the costs of the Gulf war. Given the one-time nature of the latter and the relatively weak growth prospects in western Europe and elsewhere in 1992, the US current account deficit is expected to rise strongly again in 1992.

The German current account deficit shifted from a surplus of DM 77.4 billion in 1990 to a deficit of DM 33.4 billion in 1991, a swing of some DM 110 billion. In 1991 the deficit corresponded to 1.2 per cent of German GDP. The bulk of these changes is accounted for by the steep fall in the trade surplus. In addition, there was a considerable rise in the traditional deficit on the unilateral transfer account: this was caused by special payments to the Soviet Union related to the repatriation of Soviet troops and by the already mentioned payments to the United States in connection with the Gulf war. The result of these changes was that Germany became a net capital importer in 1991. The aggregate changes in the capital account, however, conceal the fact that the country was still a net exporter of long-term capital in 1991, although the surplus was much smaller than in 1990.

After declining markedly in 1989 and 1990, the surplus on the current account in Japan surged to $72.6 billion in 1991, more than double the figure for 1990. This was largely due to changes in the trade account, where rising exports and falling imports led to a rise in the trade surplus to some $103 billion, a gain of about $40 billion compared with 1990. A striking feature is that Japan became a net importer of long-term capital in 1991, totalling about $36 billion, compared with a net outflow of more than $40 billion in 1990.

2.4 COUNTRY NOTES

Germany

The overall economic situation in Germany continues to be marked by the huge contrast between the western and the eastern parts of the country. Fiscal policy is mainly concerned with the immense transfer payments, largely debt-financed, to support the east German economy. Monetary policy, in turn, is aiming to check the inflationary consequences of a large fiscal deficit and mounting labour cost pressures. There has therefore evolved a sharp divergence in the stances of fiscal and monetary policy since the second half of 1990, with the former clearly expansionary and the latter gradually shifting from a broadly neutral to an increasingly restrictive stance.

Overall output growth faltered in west Germany in the second half of 1991, reflecting the combined impact of the longer than expected downturn of the international business cycle, the tightening of economic policies and the stabilization — at a high level — of east German demand for western goods. The steep fall in activity levels in the former GDR since the second half of 1990 appears to have come to end in spring of 1991, but since then the economy has been bumping along the bottom. The timing of a broad and self-sustained upturn remains, however, a major uncertainty. Positive signs have been emerging from the construction sector which, supported by massive public sector projects, has started to expand strongly in the course of 1991, as can be judged from order statistics. In manufacturing the long and arduous process of establishing international competitiveness is gradually getting under way; but considerable increases in labour productivity (largely on account of labour shedding) have so far been offset by equally steep rises in labour costs, designed to quickly close the gap between east and west German wage levels. Progress in privatization has been considerable; at the end of 1991 more than 5,000 companies or company units had been sold by the *Treuhandanstalt*, but broadly the same number of firms is still owned by the privatization agency.

The strains exerted by unification on public sector budgets is reflected in net transfer payments to east Germany amounting to about DM 115-125 billion to east Germany in 1991, or about 4.5 per cent of west German GNP.[43] These payments have been the major factor behind the overall public sector deficit of DM 110 billion or some 4 per cent of total German GNP in 1991.[44] Nevertheless, it is noteworthy that this is much less than projected earlier, a reflection of stronger than expected growth in income taxes and the fact that funds already allocated are blocked because of the limited absorptive capacity of the east German economy.[45]

In the face of mounting inflationary pressures, the Bundesbank raised official interest rates in several stages from February 1991: the Lombard rate at the end of the year was 9.75 per cent, compared with 8.5 per cent a year earlier, and the discount rate was 8 per cent, its highest level in the post-war period. At the beginning of December, the new target range for the growth of M3 between the fourth quarters of 1991 and 1992 was fixed at 3.5 to 5.5 per cent, which incorporates the Bundesbank's desired annual inflation rate of 2 per cent — a signal of its determination to reduce inflation to well below its current level.

Economic forecasts prepared for west Germany in autumn 1991 pointed to a growth rate of total output of 2 per cent in 1992. These forecasts were based on favourable assumptions about a recovery in the United States and in western Europe, which would have brightened export prospects. It was assumed, moreover, that pay claims by trade unions would be moderate, thus facilitating the stabilization task of the Bundesbank and raising the probability of lower interest rates sometime in the first half of 1992. However, with the delay of the recovery in the United States and western Europe, forecasts for export growth have been lowered. And claims for large wage increases have led to a major clash between monetary policy and wage policy. Monetary policy, moreover, is receiving only little support from fiscal policy. Although the federal budget deficit is projected to fall in 1992 compared with 1991, the overall public sector deficit is set to increase further on account of higher transfer payments to east Germany. The lowering of inflationary pressures therefore depends to a large extent on the current wage round, but given the deterioration in the general economic environment and the tightening of monetary policy in late 1991, forecasts for GDP growth in the western *Länder* in 1992 have already been reduced to 1.5 per cent. For east Germany an increase in real GDP by some 10 per cent is projected.

---

[43] These transfers are designed *inter alia* to bolster the incomes of private households, provide generous incentive schemes for business investment and to push ahead with badly required improvements of infrastructure. The figure pertains to net transfers, i.e., after taking into account, *inter alia*, taxes accruing to the federal budget and the overall effect of unification on west German growth and corresponding tax revenues. Gross transfer payments amounted to some DM 170 billion in 1991, nearly 90 per cent of east German GNP and 6.5 per cent of west German GNP. The data pertaining to transfer payments were taken from "Jahresgutachten 1991/1992 des Sachverständigenrates zur Begutachtung der gesamtwirtschaftlichen Entwicklung", *Deutscher Bundestag*, Drucksache 12/1618, 18 November 1991, table 36, p.136.

[44] This is the deficit according to the financial statistics concept which, as compared with the national accounts concept, is a more appropriate measure of the claims made by the public sector on capital market resources. The deficit according to the national accounts definition corresponded to some 3 per cent of GNP in 1991. Note that all these figures exclude borrowing by the *Treuhandanstalt*, which is recorded in the accounts of the enterprise sector.

[45] Administrative bottlenecks appear to be a major constraint.

Pay increases agreed in the steel sector early in 1992 are seen, however, to conflict with the stabilization goal. Also, money supply growth at the beginning of 1992 was far above the Bundesbank's target range, largely reflecting a strong expansion of loans to finance private sector investment projects in east Germany. Generous interest rate subsidies and other incentives have had a strong immunizing effect against higher market rates. Against this overall background it is unlikely that German interest rates will be lowered in the first half of 1992 and even a decline in the second half of the year cannot be taken for granted.

France

The overall pace of economic activity remained quite moderate in France in the course of 1991. Growth resumed in the second and third quarters; however, in the final quarter, faltering exports and a pronounced weakening of domestic demand led to stagnation in GDP. The large increase in unemployment was a factor behind the weakening of consumer confidence and a rise in the saving ratio. Investment plans have been progressively reduced since autumn 1990 against a background of weakening demand, shrinking profit margins and high interest rates. Exports were a major support to overall activity levels in 1991, a result of favourable demand from Germany and the depreciation of the franc against the US dollar in the first half of the year.

Tight policies have lowered the French inflation rate below that of Germany in 1991 as a whole, but this success has been bought at the cost of high and rising unemployment, which became a major preoccupation of policy makers in the course of 1991.

Attempts to find some extra room for manoeuvre by allowing French short-term interest rates to fall below those of Germany were short-lived, despite the reversal of the inflation rate differential in favour of France. Concerns about the position of the franc in the ERM led to a sharp increase in interest rates in November — and, in December, French rates quickly followed the rise in German rates.

The Government's budget plans for 1991 were affected by the unexpectedly strong slow-down in economic growth. As a result, the fiscal deficit was much larger than projected. However, the working of automatic stabilizers should not be mistaken for a change in the underlying stance of fiscal policy, which has been tight since 1983. The 1992 budget, adopted in autumn 1991, projects a further increase in the budget deficit but the overall economic impact of the budget is estimated to be slightly restrictive.

The Government's forecast for 1992, made last October, points to an acceleration in GDP growth to 2.2 per cent, with exports and private consumption being the major driving force. However, the slow-down in Germany and the persistent uncertainty about the timing of the cyclical upturn in the United States and the United Kingdom, together with the constraints which high German interest rates impose on French monetary policy, all suggest that the actual outcome is likely to be much less.

Italy

The marked slow-down of economic growth in Italy in 1991 masks a striking robustness of private consumption supported by continuing increases in employment and strong earnings growth. Fixed investment fell, a reflection of lower profit margins and weakening demand prospects. Deteriorating competitiveness was an important factor in the recent sluggishness of exports, which also depressed industrial output.

Monetary policy is constrained by the high public sector debt, which exerts upward pressure on interest rates, and by the exchange rate limits imposed by the ERM. Although inflationary pressures abated somewhat in 1991, the inflation rate is still markedly higher than in the majority of other EMS countries. The convergence criteria established for the EMU should therefore act as a further constraint on monetary policy in the years ahead. Some limited room for manoeuvre was used to reduce the discount rate by half a percentage point from 12 to 11.5 per cent in May 1991, partly reflecting measures adopted previously to limit the growth of public debt. Any further relaxation of monetary policy was impeded *inter alia* by the need to attract capital inflows to finance the rising current account deficit. As in the case of France, the authorities had no option but to follow quickly the tightening of German monetary policy in December 1991.

Fiscal policy is marked by the need to come to grips with the huge budget deficit, which in 1991 amounted to some 10.5 per cent of GDP, slightly less than in 1990 but higher than targeted. The government budget for 1992, adopted at the end of December 1991, is projecting a broadly unchanged fiscal deficit relative to GDP for 1992. Moreover, this embodies assumptions about proceeds from privatization and the growth of the economy which may now be too optimistic. Public sector debt continues to run at more than 100 per cent of GDP which, as is also the case with the budget deficit, is far above the EMU convergence criteria.

Economic forecasts for 1992 point to a growth rate of real GDP of around 1.5 to 2 per cent; as for the other countries of western Europe, the actual outcome will be very sensitive to the timing and pace of an upturn in foreign demand.

United Kingdom

The recession in the United Kingdom was the most severe among all the major economies in 1991. The fall in output was the largest in any single year in the post-war period. Although the recession appeared to have bottomed out in mid-year, it was followed by stagnation rather than recovery and by a renewed fall in GDP in the last quarter of the year. It was the unexpected downturn in consumer spending in the second half of 1990 which tipped a slowing economy into recession and it was the failure of consumer spending to recover in 1991 which confounded forecasts of general recovery in the second half of the year. Despite a sharp fall in the rate of inflation and in interest rates, the household savings ratio continued to rise and, for the year as a whole, private consumption fell.

Like the United States, the economy of the United Kingdom is bedevilled by the high levels of indebtedness of both the households and business sectors. This is a legacy of the unsustainable boom of the late 1980s which was fuelled by a sharp reduction in interest rates and income tax rates in 1988 and by a massive expansion of cheap credit. This last factor was a consequence of financial deregulation which led to a wave of financial innovations and to easier lending standards as financial institutions struggled to maintain market share in an intensely competitive environment. The credit boom led to a sharp rise in asset price-inflation, particularly in private housing where the owner-occupier retained considerable tax advantages, and financial liberalization enabled house-owners to extract a large part of their equity, boosted by capital gains, to support consumption. Thus, it appears that one of the unexpected results of financial deregulation was to amplify the effect of changes in wealth on private consumption.

The depth of the present recession is basically due to the tightening of monetary policy between mid-1988 and October 1990 which led to large increases in the costs of debt servicing and, subsequently, to reduced borrowing and a sharp cutback in spending. The monetary squeeze also triggered a prolonged slump in the housing market and a sharp fall in house prices which has created considerable uncertainty and a sharp fall in confidence in the personal sector. These domestic sources of recession were augmented during the last 18 months or so by the Gulf crisis, the effects of higher interest rates in Germany, operating through the commitment to the ERM, and by the more pessimistic outlook for the world economy.

The prospects for the United Kingdom economy in 1992 have deteriorated sharply since last autumn. In his Autumn Statement,[46] the Chancellor presented the government's spending plans on the assumption of a 2.2 per cent growth in GDP in 1992, but this is expected to be considerably reduced when he presents his Budget on 10 March 1992. The principal independent forecasters are now expecting GDP growth of about 1.2 per cent this year.[47]

The policy options for strengthening the economy are limited. Although nominal interest rates have fallen significantly since the autumn of 1990, real rates remain high and have actually increased over the past year. But an easier monetary stance − in the sense of lowering real interest rates to a level more appropriate to the state of the economy − is constrained by the level of German rates. The discussion of possible measures to support recovery in the United Kingdom have therefore focused in fiscal policy. An increase in government spending of 3.5 per cent in real terms was announced last November and will come into effect in the 1992/93 financial year. But it is also widely assumed that further measures will be announced with the Budget on 10 March. In both the independent forecasts quoted above, it is assumed that tax cuts and/or other adjustments will produce a fiscal stimulus of some $2 billion.

United States

When the United States economy resumed growth in the second quarter of 1991, this seemed to confirm expectations that the recession, which began in summer 1990, would be only short and shallow. Monetary policy had been eased progressively in February, April and September with the aim to choke off contractionary forces. However, in the final quarter, the pace of activity slackened in an environment characterized by deteriorating employment prospects and plunging consumer confidence. The monetary authorities reacted to the erosion of confidence and fears of a renewed recession by cutting the discount rate to 3.5 per cent, its lowest level since 1964. At the same time, the federal funds rate was allowed to go down to 4 per cent, so that real short-term interest rates are close to zero.

It has become evident that the forces which could make for a cyclical recovery are being tied down by the structural imbalances accumulated over the past decade. These include the large increases in the indebtedness of the corporate and household sectors, the overbuilding in the commercial real estate sector and the enduring federal budget deficit. Some progress has been made over the past year or so in unwinding the private sector debt problem (see above), but financial imbalances still appear to be a major constraint on spending behaviour.

Concerns about the weak performance of the economy led to a considerable relaxation in monetary policy in the course of 1991. Between the beginning and the end of the year the discount rate was reduced progressively from 6.5 per cent to 3.5 per cent, and the federal funds rate was lowered by 3 percentage points to 4 per cent. Rapid growth of M1 suggests that there is abundant liquidity in the banking sector; at the same time the fall in the prime rate from 9.5 per cent to 6.5 per cent between January and December of 1991 suggests that credit growth is now largely demand constrained.

Fiscal policy has been relatively tight since 1986; but in 1991 the budget deficit rose considerably on account of the economic slow-down and built-in stabilizers. The margin for discretionary changes in fiscal policy designed to stimulate the economy is effectively very limited given the already very high budget deficit. Also the budget agreement reached in 1990 stipulates that any discretionary change in fiscal policy must be deficit-neutral.

At the beginning of 1992, short-term prospects for the US economy are very difficult to judge. Most forecasts point to a recovery in the second half of 1992 but, overall, only moderate growth is projected for the year as whole. It is not too difficult to identify the sources of a possible upturn: lower inflation and interest rates have a favourable effect on real income growth and this should support private consumption. Also, as progress is made in reducing debt levels, spending can

---

[46] HM Treasury, *Autumn Statement 1991*, London: HMSO (Cm 1729), November 1991.

[47] Latest (February 1992) forecasts of the London Business School and the National Institute of Economic and Social Research, for GDP growth in 1992, are 1.2 per cent and 1.3 per cent respectively.

be expected to rise again. Low interest rates and advantageous prices should also help to stimulate the demand for housing; some progress in this direction was already made in 1991. It is also likely that there will be an upturn of the inventory cycle; and export growth will be supported by the recent depreciation of the dollar against the Deutschmark and the yen.

A further easing of monetary policy cannot be excluded but is unlikely to have much of an effect, given that real interest rates are already very low and that they can do little to accelerate the unwinding of the private sector debt problem. Amidst widespread fears of a renewed weakening of the economy, the administration has launched at the end of January 1992 a fiscal policy package, parts of which still have to be approved by Congress, designed to stimulate domestic demand. However, the net stimulus of the proposed measures is likely to be fairly modest.

The smaller economies

There has been increasing cyclical desynchronization among the 13 smaller countries of western Europe over the last two years or so. Some economies moved into recession (Finland, Sweden, Switzerland) while in many others, despite a cyclical downturn setting in, growth still remained quite robust. In Portugal, the economy was still in a phase of overheating, and in Denmark and Greece, which had been out of phase with the other countries in the mid-1980s, there was a slight acceleration in the growth of real GDP in 1991.

In *Austria* a relatively high momentum of economic activity was maintained in 1991. Robust domestic demand growth dampened the impact of the marked slow-down in export growth on overall economic activity levels. Large income gains in conjunction with higher employment (in construction, trade and services) supported private consumption, while construction, in spite of high interest rates, was boosted by strong demand for industrial buildings, office space and housing. Export performance, which in the earlier part of 1991 was still benefiting from strong demand emanating from Germany, deteriorated in the second half of the year to the extent of losing market shares captured in 1990, notably in Germany. The consequence of a reduced growth in net exports in the presence of strong domestic demand was a record deficit in merchandise trade and a swing in the current account from a sizeable surplus in 1990 to a small deficit in 1991. Fiscal policy continued to aim at budget consolidation and the public sector deficit was further reduced in 1991, although the federal budget deficit was broadly unchanged. Monetary policy continued to be directed at maintaining an unchanged exchange rate of the schilling *vis-à-vis* the Deutschmark. Austria's favourable inflation performance enabled it to raise its discount rate by less (0.5 percentage points) than the increase introduced by the Bundesbank in mid-August.

For 1991 as a whole, real GDP growth decelerated to about 3 per cent, compared with 4.6 per cent in 1990. Given the overall deterioration in the international economic environment, growth forecasts for 1992 were lowered in December to 2.5 per cent, down from the 3 per cent forecast in late summer. However, the revised forecast was completed before the further tightening of German monetary policy on 20 December 1991.

In *Belgium*, private consumption was the mainstay of overall growth in 1991, while fixed investment slowed down considerably. Relatively strong growth of enterprise investment was partly offset by a decline in housing investment. Inflationary pressures have eased marginally, and the current account surplus rose slightly relative to GDP. The high level of public sector indebtedness, some 115 per cent of GDP in 1991, remains a major policy preoccupation. Interest payments on debt outstanding accounted for more than 20 per cent of total government expenditure last year.

In *Denmark*, economic performance has been steadily improving since 1989, following the cyclical trough of 1987-1988, which was the result of restrictive fiscal policies designed to redress the large current account imbalance. Private consumption was the main source of growth in 1991. Business investment remained very sluggish, while housing investments continued to fall and were some 40 per cent lower than in 1986. Exports, boosted by demand from Germany, continued to be a major support to output growth in 1991; import growth remained moderate, but picked up with the mild recovery of private household expenditures. The current account, which moved into surplus in 1990 after being in deficit for the preceding 25 years, improved further and for 1991 the surplus amounted to some 1.5 per cent of GNP, a considerable swing from a deficit of 5.4 per cent of GDP in 1986. Inflation has fallen to a very low level and, for 1991 as a whole, was the lowest in the industrialized countries. However, employment has continued to fall and the unemployment rate has risen above 10 per cent. The government budget deficit increased to some 1.8 per cent of GDP in 1991, compared with only 0.5 per cent in 1989. In 1992 fiscal policy is set to stabilize government expenditure in real terms and to reduce the budget deficit.

Finland is in its worst recession of the post-war period. Exports slumped as a result of the collapse of the Soviet market, depressed demand in its major western trading partners, and an overvalued exchange rate. The Finnish markka was linked to the ECU in June 1991 but in November the authorities floated the currency against a background of strong capital outflows. A de facto devaluation of the Finnish markka was quickly followed by a formal devaluation by 12.3 per cent. Highly indebted households have reduced their consumption in the face of high interest rates and falls in both nominal and real house prices. The considerable increase in the general government budget deficit, associated with the sharp downturn in economic activity, will require fiscal restraint for years to come.

There was a sharp slow-down in economic growth in *Ireland*, which mainly reflects the sluggishness of fixed investment, notably buildings, after two years of very strong expansion, and the dampening effect of weak international demand on exports. Public consumption remained sluggish, given the overriding objective of fiscal policy to reduce the public debt/GNP ratio towards 100 per cent by 1993.

Restrictive fiscal and monetary policies, designed to reduce serious macroeconomic imbalances, entailed the virtual stagnation of domestic demand in *Greece* in 1991. But the associated dampening of import demand and a considerably improved export performance led to a GDP growth of 1 per cent. In contrast, sluggish exports and an import boom in 1990 had completely offset the rise in domestic demand. Some progress has been made in curbing the current account deficit, but the resilience of high inflation and a public sector borrowing requirement close to 16 per cent of GDP remain major policy problems.

In the *Netherlands* economic activity weakened in 1991 as the stimuli from domestic tax reductions at the beginning of 1990 and from German unification began to weaken. As a result, both domestic demand and export growth weakened in 1991. The still relatively robust growth in private consumption was partly due to a fall in the savings ratio, given only little growth of real disposable incomes. Business investment faltered as a result of the slower pace of demand, lower capacity utilization, a squeeze in profit margins and higher interest rates. The budget deficit in 1991 reached 3.5 per cent of GDP, so that fiscal policy has hardly any scope left for stimulating demand.

Norway has been out of phase with the west European business cycle since the collapse of the oil price in 1986/87 which led to a decline in real GDP in 1988. Since then the economy has been steadily recovering. Real GDP growth in 1991 was only slightly lower than in 1990 because of the strong growth in exports of oil and natural gas. Data for the first three quarters of 1991 show that private consumption fell slightly, reflecting a sharp rise in the savings ratio by about 4 percentage points, thus absorbing, as in Sweden, all the growth in real disposable income. These developments are explained by the need to rebuild financial positions which deteriorated sharply as a result of the rise of indebtedness in the 1980s. The net financial wealth of the household sector is recovering only slowly and in 1991 was still lower than in 1984. The sluggishness of total fixed investment masks strong growth in manufacturing and mining and a continuing fall in construction. Inflationary pressures have abated compared with 1990 and the strong growth of oil and gas exports led to a considerable increase in the current account surplus for 1991. Forecasts for 1992 envisage an acceleration in output growth on the mainland from 0.8 per cent in 1991 to 2.6 per cent in 1992. Fiscal policy will be broadly expansionary and is designed to stimulate demand and employment growth.

In *Portugal*, the pace of economic expansion slowed down in 1991, reflecting a lower growth of domestic demand at a high level: overall the economy was still overheating in 1991. The real foreign balance continued to be a drag on overall output growth. There was a further deceleration in the rate of fixed capital formation in 1991. Nevertheless, real fixed investment was about 75 per cent higher than in 1985, largely a reflection, as in Spain, of the integration effects of full EC membership in 1986. The large budget deficit (6.1 per cent of GDP in 1991) and a high inflation rate are major concerns for economic policy. The budget for 1992 aims to reduce the deficit to 5.2 per cent of GDP.

In *Spain*, the slow-down in economic growth gathered pace in the course of 1991. There was a further deceleration in the growth of private consumption in 1991 and investment rose only slightly. But it is noteworthy that the investment boom since 1986 has driven real expenditure to about 75 per cent above its level in 1985. Investment is set for a moderate expansion as from 1992, especially since the stimulus associated with the world exhibition and the Olympic games will have tailed off in 1992. Some offset to the weakening of domestic demand was provided by an increase in real net exports of goods and services.

The recession has deepened in *Sweden*. After sluggish growth in 1990, real GDP fell by nearly one per cent in 1991. Industrial output fell further and was on average 10 per cent lower than in 1989, a reflection of weak domestic demand and a marked deterioration in international price competitiveness. Both domestic and foreign demand declined in 1991. Private consumption stagnated, as strong growth in real disposable incomes all went into savings. A similar pattern was observed in 1990. The savings rate has been on a marked upward trend since 1989. There was a large fall in fixed investment, reflecting in the main the deteriorating prospects for industry. A high rate of consumer price inflation remains a major problem for economic policy. The current account deficit shrank somewhat in 1991 mainly because of lower imports. Monetary policy is focused on stabilizing the exchange rate of the krona against the ECU. Interest rates were raised to contain exchange rate pressures and in May 1991 the krona was linked to the ECU to forestall expectations of an imminent devaluation. To stem considerable capital outflows, the monetary authorities raised the official interest rate on December 5 from 11.5 per cent to 17.5 per cent. However, before Christmas the rate had already been lowered again to 14 per cent.

Given the effects of automatic stabilizers, the recession has led to a sizeable increase in the budget deficit, which the government hopes to contain by cutting its expenditure. In autumn 1991 a tax package was adopted, designed to lower taxes on business capital and incomes and generally improve supply-side responses. The government forecasts a growth rate of 1.3 per cent for GDP in 1992, but private forecasters are more pessimistic and point to the possibility of a further decline.

Real GDP fell in *Switzerland* in 1991 as a whole, but the decline, which began in autumn 1990, appears to have come to a halt in the third quarter of 1991. The immediate cause behind this weak performance is the depressing effect of high interest rates on fixed investment, notably construction investment.[48] With the large fall in industrial capacity utilization rates in the course of 1991, expenditures on machinery and equipment also declined. Household consumption weakened on account of a slow-down in real disposable income growth (reflecting declining employment) and a rise in

---

[48] It is noteworthy that the construction sector in Switzerland is relatively large (7.6 per cent of GDP) compared with the west European average of 5-6 per cent. These figures refer to 1985, the latest year for which sectoral national accounts data are available for Switzerland.

the savings ratio. Output levels were supported for some time by strong demand from Germany but this was not sufficient to offset the sluggishness of demand in other markets. A major policy concern remains the high inflation rate, which subsided somewhat in autumn but year on year has hardly changed. Nevertheless, the maintenance of the restrictive stance of monetary policy has contributed to an easing of inflationary pressures, which should become more visible in the course of 1992.

Growth forecasts for 1992 prepared by private and official institutions reveal strikingly large differences. Inflationary pressures are expected to subside only gradually, and the scope for a more relaxed stance of monetary policy is limited given the focus on stabilizing the exchange rate against the Deutschmark. Consumer confidence is weak and real disposable income is unlikely to increase significantly. Exports are likely to be subdued given the country's high dependence on the German market and its specialization on investment goods, for which international demand is likely to pick up only in the later stages of a recovery. On the whole, therefore, only a moderate recovery is likely in 1992.

In *Turkey*, the rapid acceleration in the pace of economic growth in 1990 could not be maintained: real GNP growth slowed to 1.5 per cent in 1991 compared with 9.2 per cent in the previous year. Domestic demand fell as a result of weaker private sector fixed investment and, especially, a significant run-down of stocks. In contrast, a considerable slow-down in import growth in conjunction with an improved export performance made for a significant positive contribution of net exports to overall GNP growth in 1991, following a strong offset in 1990. The budget deficit rose to 11 per cent of GNP in 1991 and has been a major source of increasing inflationary pressures. After being in considerable deficit in 1990, the current account swung into a small surplus in 1991, partly the result of favourable changes in net unilateral transfers. The new government's short- and medium-term economic programme, presented in January 1992, aims at further privatization, a reduction of subsidies to state companies, and a tax reform. These measures are designed not only to improve the overall performance of the economy but also to reduce the budget deficit, which in turn should help to bring down the inflation rate. Official forecasts are for real GNP growth of 5.5 per cent in 1992.

Economic growth remained very sluggish in *Canada* in the course of 1991, in spite of the progressive lowering of interest rates since the second half of 1990. After a strengthening in the second quarter, real GDP growth faltered again in the third, and is estimated to have fallen in the final quarter. For the year as a whole, real GDP was about 1.5 per cent below its level in 1990. The decline in domestic demand accelerated in 1991 and at the same time the positive growth contribution from real net exports was much reduced. Private consumption fell as sluggish employment and low earnings growth depressed real disposable incomes. Households were also striving to reduce their debts. In general, consumer confidence remained therefore weak, a tendency which was supported by bleak employment prospects. Total fixed investment also declined for the year as a whole, although residential construction picked up after the first quarter of 1991 under the stimulus of lower mortgage rates. The stock decumulation that started in the first quarter of 1990 was only temporarily interrupted in the first quarter of 1991 and the declining trend resumed thereafter.

At the beginning of 1992 the government has lowered its GDP growth forecast for 1992 to 2.7 per cent, which compares to a forecast of 3.1 per cent by OECD in autumn 1991.

2.5 THE SHORT-TERM OUTLOOK

The western market economies are now passing through a period of weak economic activity and great uncertainty. In 1992, there is likely to be greater convergence around a low growth rate of output but also lower rates of inflation. The failure of the expected recovery to appear in the second half of last year and, in particular, the marked weakening of activity in a number of economies in the last quarter, has led to a significant lowering of growth forecasts for 1992. It now looks increasingly possible that average GDP growth in western Europe this year is unlikely to be much more than 1.5 per cent, with most of any pick-up occurring in the second half. Even this forecast is surrounded by considerable downside risks.

In the United States there are hopes that the one-point cut in the discount rate last December will provide a boost to the economy and there are a few tentative signs of recovery in interest-sensitive expenditures such as car sales and housing starts. Nevertheless, consumer confidence is at a record low level and domestic demand is likely to remain fairly weak in the first half of 1992. But exports should improve in response to the weaker dollar in the last quarter of 1991. At best, a moderate, sustained upturn could be under way in the second half, giving an annual increase in real GNP of some 1.8 per cent. This would imply an average growth rate in the ECE market economies (western Europe and North America) of about 1.7 per cent in 1992.

Although the prospect is for a fairly anaemic recovery after, perhaps, several more months of recession or flat activity, most governments see little scope for policy initiatives to strengthen the upturn. In Europe attention is especially focused on monetary policy in Germany. It was hoped that the December increase in German interest rates would lead quickly to a moderation in wage demands. However, the steelworkers' settlement was higher than what the Bundesbank thought desirable and until it is clear that it will not have a knock-on effect on subsequent settlements (in engineering and in the public sector, for example), there is unlikely to be any easing of monetary policy. Also, money supply growth is currently above the Bundesbank's target range of 3.5-5.5 per cent, which is another reason why interest rates are unlikely to fall in the near future. At the end of 1991 it was widely expected that German interest rates might begin to fall in the spring, but this now seems unlikely to occur before the second half of the year.

This creates difficulties for the other members of the ERM, who are unable to lower their own rates to levels more appropriate to their weaker levels of activity. In real terms, interest rates are high and have actually risen over the last year and are likely to rise still further in the first half of 1992. Given the marked convergence in west European inflation rates, and in particular the narrowing or the elimination of the differential over the German rate, there is little scope for further cuts in nominal interest rates in most countries. Some small improvements might be possible if signs of a sustained recovery in the United States led to an appreciation of the dollar against the Deutschmark and a weakening of the Deutschmark within the ERM. (If expectations of a recovery in the United States fail to materialize, the pressures would work in the opposite direction.) But, essentially, a significant easing of interest rates in western Europe must await a reduction in German rates.

Although monetary policies in western Europe are constrained by commitments to maintaining exchange rate parities within the ERM and by inflationary pressures in Germany, there is little prospect of any offsetting relaxation of fiscal policy. Although budget deficits have tended to increase with the operation of the automatic stabilizers, most governments are continuing their efforts to stabilize discretionary spending and reduce borrowing requirements in relation to GDP. A few governments do intend to allow some discretionary widening of their budget deficits — notably Finland, Norway and the United Kingdom — but the majority are intending to reduce them. In this respect the most notable change is in Germany where large cuts in the Federal budget deficit are planned for 1992 and 1993. An additional constraint on fiscal policy in some countries is the requirement to meet the convergence criteria prior to European Monetary Union. General government borrowing requirements should not be greater than 3 per cent of GDP and the government debt to GDP ratio should be 60 per cent or less, or at least on trend towards the reference value. Countries such as Belgium and Italy may have to pursue very tight policies in order to meet such targets by 1996.

In contrast to western Europe, the United States has become a "low interest rate zone" as the authorities have tried to boost a stagnant economy with a significant easing of monetary policy and large cuts in interest rates. The failure of the highly indebted economy to respond to this stimulus last year led to a large cut (of one percentage point) in the discount rate in late December, to a number of measures designed to improve the margins of commercial banks, and, at the end of January, to the President's proposal for a number of tax changes intended to boost activity without enlarging the still widening budget deficit. However, the latter are necessarily relatively modest since any further significant addition to the deficit could weaken financial confidence.

The extended slow-down of growth in the market economies partly reflects the normal cyclical forces at work after the long boom of the 1980s. These forces did not appear to be very strong 18 months ago, a fact which was reflected in most forecasts of a mild and relatively brief "growth" recession. That scenario has only been significantly revised in the last six months or so.

There has thus been a considerable failure in economic forecasting and appreciation. In a number of countries, the effects of financial deregulation in the 1980s were not fully appreciated and it has taken a long time for it to be widely accepted that the ensuing high levels of corporate and personal debt — and the subsequent attempts to reduce them — are powerful breaks on economic recovery. In western Europe the current monetary policy constraint is in large measure a consequence of a serious underestimation of the difficulties of transforming the former GDR into a market economy. It is the presence of these major structural problems which suggest that any assumption of a normal recovery — which is embedded in the standard short-term forecasting models — should be treated with great caution. The so-called "credit crunch" is a simple and somewhat misleading label to describe a complicated process of reversing the debt build-up and correcting for its consequences. On the demand side, borrowers have increased savings, reduced expenditure and lowered their outstanding debt. On the supply side, financial institutions are repairing their balance sheets from the damage caused by the bad credits which they advanced during the boom and are reluctant to lend to any but the most creditworthy borrowers who, in turn, are reluctant to borrow. How long this process of adjustment will take, and whether it will have longer term effects on consumer confidence, is unknown. Similarly, the timing of a recovery in the former GDR and the rate of reduction of inflationary pressures in Germany are also uncertain. Thus, the existence of high real interest rates in a period of recession is likely to be prolonged. In a situation where the "coefficient of ignorance" has risen sharply there is probably some bias towards pessimism. However, it is possible that consumer demand could recover more quickly than expected: consumers have already surprised policy makers and forecasters on several occasions. Nevertheless, the emerging consensus is for a slow and uncertain recovery in 1992 with consumer confidence remaining fragile and subject to a high risk of setbacks.

Chapter 3

EASTERN EUROPE

This chapter provides an account of the principal macroeconomic developments in eastern Europe in 1991 and discusses the prospects for 1992. The first section, 3.1, reviews the transformation process in the first years after the 1989 revolutions. Section 3.2 highlights recent changes in output and demand, and section 3.3 those in foreign trade and the external balance of the east European countries. Section 3.4 focuses on macroeconomic stabilization efforts and results.

3.1 THE TRANSFORMATION PROCESS IN 1991 AND OUTLOOK FOR 1992

(i) Introduction

The process of transforming the centrally planned economies of eastern Europe into market economies based on the principles of political democracy, which was started in 1989 in a climate of popular enthusiasm and optimism, has lost much of its momentum and vigour in the last two years. Once filled with hope, the countries in transition have increasingly become an area of disillusion, anxiety and socio-political tensions. Ambitious economic reform programmes have not been able to fulfil many of their promises and have failed to bring about a quick and tangible improvement in the living standards of the population. The prolonged economic downturn, persistent inflation and declining consumption have all led to general disappointment and frustration, which has been exacerbated by the dismantling of the job security and welfare programmes inherited from the communist era.

The deep economic recession is central to the rapidly changing socio-political climate in eastern Europe. In 1991 the economic performance of all east European countries deteriorated substantially: in most countries national product has been falling steadily since 1989 and in the combined GDP/NMP of six countries of the region[49] declined further by some 14 per cent in 1991. The cumulative drop of output registered over the last two to three years in some countries has attained proportions that are unmatched even by the Great Depression of 1929-1933 (chart 3.1.1). Unemployment has been rising steadily, reaching levels which are potentially explosive in societies which have been accustomed for decades to almost complete job security. In some countries national and ethnic conflicts are adding to political instability, making future prospects even more gloomy and uncertain.

While they display marked differences in their initial socio-economic conditions, the scope and pace of their institutional reforms and their political landscapes, all east European countries have followed a broadly similar path of transformation. In 1991 three basic phenomena could be identified which were common to all of those countries: (a) they were all engaged in the process of implementing comprehensive reform-cum-stabilization programmes (although the designs of the programmes and the degree of implementation differed considerably); (b) they have all been in deep recession (with falls in national product varying from some 8 per cent in Hungary to 23 per cent in Bulgaria); and (c) the early results of reforms in all countries have generally been much worse than was initially anticipated.

The growing gap between expectations and reality in east European countries is a source of serious concern among policy-makers and observers in both east and west. Heavier than expected costs of transformation not only erode popular support for reforms, but they also undermine the position of reform-minded governments and contribute to political instability. This could lead to a succession of short-lived democratic governments with an eventual shift of power to populist and even extremist political groups. The consequences could be daunting: not only could the reform process be brought to a halt, but instability and unrest could eventually spill over to the rest of Europe. Unless confronted in a swift and decisive manner, these challenges may prove to be too difficult to handle for the fragile democracies in the post-communist countries.

---

[49] Bulgaria, Czech and Slovak Federal Republic, Hungary, Poland, Romania and Yugoslavia.

TABLE 3.1.1
Eastern Europe: Characteristics of stabilization-cum-reform programmes

Feature	Bulgaria	CSFR	Hungary [a]	Poland	Romania	Yugoslavia
Programme start	1.Feb.1991	1.Jan.1991	continuous	1.Jan.1990	1.Nov.1990	19.Dec.1989
Price liberalization (coverage in %)	Instant 70%	Instant 85% (increased to 90% in July and 95% in Nov. 91)	Gradual	Instant 90% (6-month freeze on energy prices after initial 400% increase)	Gradual (80% in four stages from 1.11.1990 to 15.11.1991)	Instant 80% (6-month freeze on energy and public sector prices, after initial rises)
Monetary policy	Moderately restrictive (refinancing rate: 54% per month)	Restrictive	Moderately restrictive	Restrictive (controls of net domestic assets of the banking system; initial refinancing rate: 36% p.m. positive real)	Accomodative (credit ceilings, refinancing rate of 12.5%; negotiated bank interest rates)	Temporary restrictive; (controls of net domestic assets of central bank; initial discount rate: 23% p.a. negative real)
Fiscal policy	Moderately restrictive	Restrictive (fiscal adjustment of 1% GDP)	Moderately restrictive	Restrictive; (planned fiscal adjustment of 7% of GDP: increased tax discipline)	Moderate (gradual reduction of subsidies)	Temporary restrictive; (planned fiscal adjustment of 5% of GDP)
Wage policy	Liberal (with limits on minimum wage growth)	Restrictive (excess wage taxes)	Moderately restrictive (excess wage taxes)	Restrictive (partial backward indexation with punitive taxes)	Unrestricted (periodical indexation)	Initially restrictive; (6-months freeze on nominal wages, aborted)
Exchange rate policy	Sharp initial devaluation (900%; float rate)	Devaluation (fixed rate for "basket")	Gradual devaluations (crawling peg)	Sharp initial devaluation (46% against US dollar; fixed rate)	Devaluation and unification of rate	Initial devaluation (20% against D mark; fixed rate, aborted)
Nominal anchors	Yes (money supply, incomes)	Yes (exchange rate, wages)	No	Yes (exchange rate, wages)	No	Yes (discount rate, wages, exchange rate)
Real anchors	No	Yes (money supply, interest rate)	Yes (money supply)	Yes (interest rate)	No	No
Internal convertibility for firms	Yes	Yes	Yes	Yes	No (Planned for end 1991)	Yes (aborted)
Internal convertibility for households	Limited	Limited	No	Yes	No	Yes (aborted)
Capital account convertibility	No	No	No	No	No	Restricted
Foreign trade liberalization	Limited	Extensive	Gradual	Extensive (no import quotas, few export quotas)	Limited	Extensive (few import and export quotas)
Foreign investment regulations	Liberal	Liberal	Liberal	Partly liberal (profit transfer restricted)	Restricted	Liberal
Small-scale privatization	Yes, limited	Yes	Gradual	Extensive	Yes, limited	Limited
Large-scale privatization	No	Yes, delayed	Limited	Slow	Planned (July, 1991)	Slow
Property restitution	Under review	Yes	No	Selective	No	No
Banking reform	Initialized	Initialized	Advanced	Initialized	Initialized	Initialized
Stock exchange	No	No	Yes (1989)	Planned (April 1991)	No	No
External assistance	Yes (IMF stand-by credit)	Yes (IMF stand-by credit; stabilization fund)	Yes (IMF extended 3-years facility in 1991)	Yes (IMF stand-by credit; stabilization fund)	Yes	Yes (IMF stand-by credit)

Sources: Compiled from: F. Coricelli, R.R. Rocha, op.cit., p.197; D.M. Nuti, "Economic Inertia in the Transitional Economies of Eastern Europe", European University Institute, Florence, 24-25 January, 1992, mimeo; D.Popescu, "Interrelation between Convertibility and Trade in Romania", European University Institute, Florence, 24-25 January, 1992, mimeo; M. Hrncir, J. Klacek, "Stabilization Policies and currency convertibility in Czechoslovakia", *European Economy*, Special Issue, No.2, 1991; D. Rosati, "The Polish road to capitalism: A critical appraisal of the Balcerowicz Plan", *Thames Polytechnic Papers on Political Economy*, New Series No.2, Spring, 1991; *Bulgarian Economic Outlook*, BTA, No.3, 20 January 1992.

Note: Unless otherwise stated, the data reflect stipulations of the initial stabilization-cum-reform programmes adopted in particular countries.

[a] Hungary was the only country which did not introduce a standard stabilization plan similar to other eastern countries, and this column has been inserted in the table for the sake of completeness. The data presented refer to economic policies followed in Hungary in 1991.

(ii) Reform programmes: too much stabilization?

The unprecedented wave of political changes which swept through European countries in 1989, cleared the way for the abandonment of the discredited system of central planning and the adoption in its stead of the market mechanism. One after another, the ex-communist countries adopted comprehensive programmes of reforms, aimed at a single, albeit all-important, strategic objective: the establishment of a modern market economy of a western type with a strong private sector and based on democratic principles. This strategy received strong support from the international community, with the IMF and the European Economic Community being particularly active in providing financial assistance and technical advice to the transition countries of eastern Europe.

Emerging from the communist era, the east European economies were in a very precarious state, with falling output, soaring inflation, widespread shortages and unsustainable levels of external debt. Large economic imbalances called for urgent stabilization plans to prevent economic collapse and to prepare the ground for broad institutional reforms. The economic programmes adopted in all countries embraced both institutional reform as well as stabilization, although the proportions between the two strands and the detailed provisions of economic policy varied from country to country.

The stabilization packages applied in the east European economies and sponsored by the IMF were based on the liberal-monetarist philosophy which dominated mainstream economic thinking in the 1980s. The standard approach to economic adjustment was to limit drastically government involvement in the economy through cutting subsidies, liberalizing prices and deregulating economic activities and then letting the market do the job. The programmes typically included strong deflationary measures in the form of monetary and fiscal restrictions, coupled with partial or full price liberalization, aimed at reducing domestic demand; the devaluation of domestic currencies and some form of incomes policy. Institutional changes focused on foreign trade liberalization, the introduction of some degree of convertibility, the privatization of state-owned enterprises and reform of the financial sector.

While sharing the common strategic and medium-term goals of market reforms and macroeconomic stabilization, east European countries followed varying transition policies. Large differences in initial macroeconomic conditions and varying experiences of market reforms in the past influenced the initial design and time schedule of reforms in individual countries. As a result, each country was at a different stage of transformation in 1991.

While *Hungary*, by virtue of its early start with the 1968 New Economic Mechanism, was commonly considered as a front runner of market reforms in eastern Europe, it nevertheless followed a strategy of gradual and carefully prepared changes, and was in some respects overtaken by other countries which opted for bolder and faster reforms. Hungary is the only country in the group which managed to escape going through a painful stabilization operation, mainly because its macroeconomic situation was assessed as relatively balanced. On the other hand, Hungary was able to introduce successfully a vast range of institutional reforms, including a two-tier, competitive banking system, a modern taxation system, liberal foreign investment regulations, and key elements of financial markets.

Yugoslavia and *Poland* were the first countries to introduce drastic stabilization programmes under the aegis of the IMF on 19 December 1989 and 1 January 1990 respectively. The Yugoslav case is somewhat different from the Polish one, both with respect to initial conditions as well as to the programme results. Yugoslavia had virtually no inflationary overhang (free prices), enjoyed a considerable degree of economic decentralization and a nearly convertible currency.[50] However, the Yugoslav programme was aborted in the second half of 1990, as the federal government was unable to keep incomes under control and to continue with monetary restrictions. Later in 1991, political and national disputes pushed the country into a civil war and the programme of economic stabilization collapsed with the disintegration of central government controls over the economy.

The first comprehensive reform-cum-stabilization programme, designed to meet the specific needs of post-communist economies, was the Polish plan associated with the name of Deputy Prime Minister Leszek Balcerowicz. It served as a prototype for other transitional countries: largely similar plans were introduced in the *Czech and Slovak Federal Republic* on 1 January 1991 and in *Bulgaria* on 1 February 1991.

Table 3.1.1 provides a comparative summary of the main features of stabilization-cum-reform programmes in east European countries.

The common characteristics of all programmes included attempts to curb inflation through various combinations of monetary, fiscal and wage restrictions, sweeping price liberalization, the laying down of foundations for market institutions, the privatization of state-owned assets, and the opening of domestic economies to international markets. Macroeconomic policy packages applied in turn in Yugoslavia, Poland, Czechoslovakia and Bulgaria can be described as "heterodox" stabilization programmes, combining macroeconomic restrictions with so-called nominal anchors, and supported by external financial assistance (IMF stand-by credits, stabilization funds).[51] They have been commonly referred to as *shock*, or *"big-bang"* programmes, as their most conspicuous feature was a drastic and massive change in the key economic parameters (prices, exchange rates, interest rates, removal of subsidies, elimination of administrative controls),

---

[50] See: F. Coricelli, R.R. Rocha "A Comparative Analysis of the Polish and Yugoslav Programmes in 1990", in P. Marer, S. Zecchini, (eds.), *The Transition to a Market Economy*, OECD, Paris, 1991, vol.I, pp.189-243.

[51] Typical "heterodox" programmes applied in Latin America or Israel included also some form of price controls over a limited period of time.

CHART 3.1.1

Two depressions in eastern Europe
(GDP at constant prices)

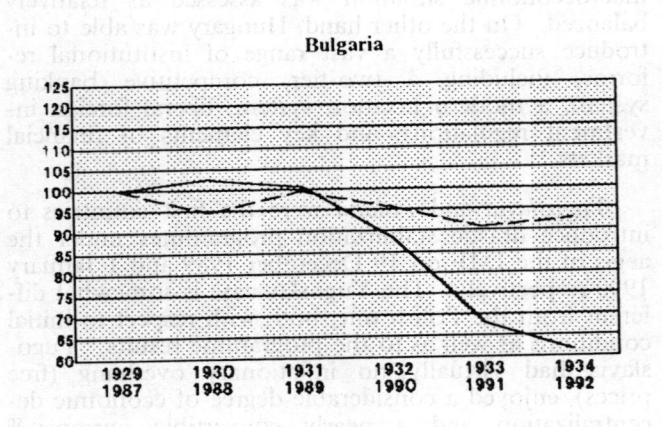

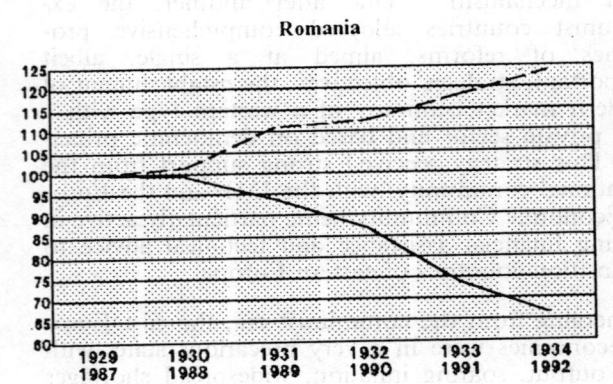

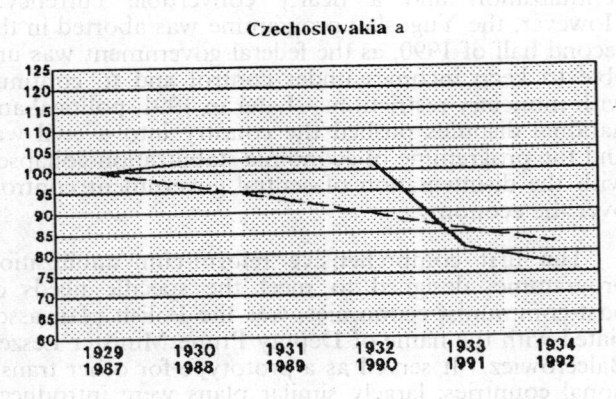

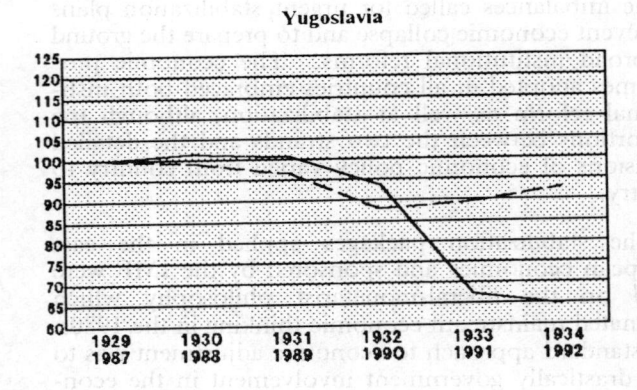

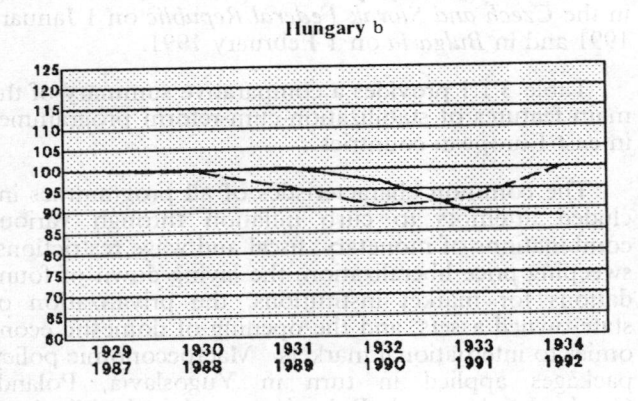

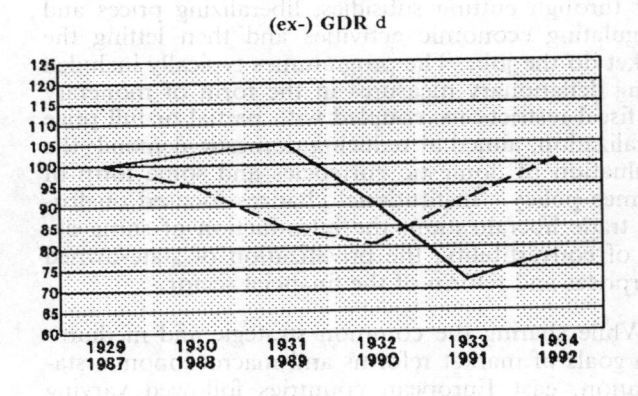

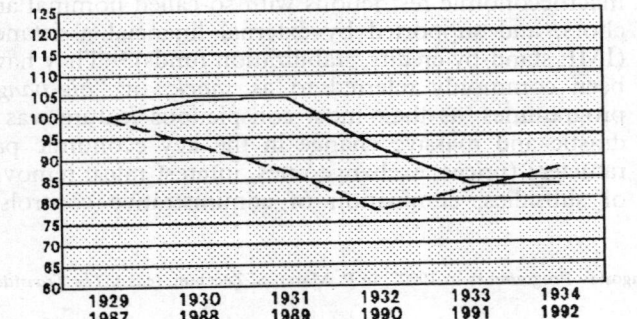

– – – – (1929-1934) ——— (1987-1992)

Bulgaria

Romania

Czechoslovakia a

Yugoslavia

Hungary b

(ex-) GDR d

Poland c

Source: M.C. Kaser, E.A. Radice, (eds). *The Economic History of Eastern Europe 1919-1975*, Vol.I. and B.R. Mitchell, *European Historical Statistics 1750-1975* for historical data; ECE secretariat Common Data Base for 1987-1991; project LINK forecast for 1992, (New York meeting March 1992).

a NMP for 1987-1990.
b Net Domestic Product, 1929/1930 financial year = 100; NMP for 1992.
c GNP for pre-war years; NMP for 1992.
d Pre-war Germany for 1929-1934; NMP for 1988, 1989.

typically introduced up front in one comprehensive package.

In contrast, *Romania*, and most importantly *Hungary*, have decided to follow a more gradual adjustment strategy. The latter country was able to capitalize on its earlier efforts to introduce elements of market mechanism over the last two decades, and to benefit from generally better macroeconomic conditions. Romania's choice for a gradual strategy has probably been prompted by the not-so-encouraging earlier Polish experience and by the lack of strong political support for the government.

The distinction between *shock treatment* and *gradualism* gave rise to extensive discussions among economists and policy-makers on the advantages and shortcomings of the two approaches. The issue has become highly controversial in the context of the early results of different stabilization policies pursued in Hungary and Poland, the two most advanced reforming countries.

Both approaches have their merits and demerits. The gradual evolution "into" a market system has the advantage of being more easily accepted by the population and is less likely to raise social protests — at least in the initial stage — as the inevitable costs of transition can be extended over a longer period. It also allows, at least in theory, for a more elaborate preparation of particular reform components, thus diminishing the risk of making policy mistakes. Thus, the "Schumpeterian" evolution gives time for a step-by-step, "creative" absorption of new elements by the economic system, which changes only gradually.

However, disadvantages connected with the gradual approach may easily outweigh the benefits. Resistance on the part of various social groups with vested interests may build up over time, effectively slowing down the reform process, and eventually bringing it to a halt. Examples may be found in the half-hearted, "stop-and-go" reform attempts in Yugoslavia after 1952, Hungary after 1972 and Poland in the 1970s and 1980s. Also, where there are large initial imbalances (such as high inflation and massive shortages), the failure to produce a noticeable improvement of living conditions and material standards may undermine the political position of the government, thereby reducing its willingness and ability to continue with the reform process, and sometimes even providing an excuse for a return to centralist methods.[52]

On the other hand, the "shock" therapy typically produces a sudden fall of real incomes and savings, at least for large groups of the population (mostly wage-earners), and may indeed provoke social unrest. This political risk can be offset to some extent by the improved market situation, the elimination of queuing and the higher quality of goods and services but, in general, the readiness of the population to sacrifice present consumption for highly uncertain future gains is rather limited, except under very special circumstances (such as in the aftermath of a political breakthrough or under dictatorial rule). However, the stabilization results of the "shock" therapy normally come rather quickly and the resulting efficiency gains can be substantial. In short, the choice between the two approaches involves weighing greater economic benefits against increased social costs. No clear-cut rules can be formulated in this respect without referring to specific country local conditions.

The debate on the speed of transition is sometimes flawed in that it fails to recognize the need to differentiate between stabilization and institutional change and it sometimes ignores the necessary time lags between policy measures and policy results (targets). While stabilization policies are expected to produce results in the short-term, institutional measures, even if implemented immediately, may be expected to yield the desired results only after some time; the same applies to industrial policies and other structural measures.

Systemic reforms during the transformation from plan to market consist of revamping the whole legal system in the economy and changing the pattern of social behaviour accordingly, while necessary structural adjustment essentially results from new investment. In both cases time is required, and even if the process can be advanced at varying speed, no "shock-type" change is possible. The only institutional "big-bang" implemented so far was the wholesale adoption of western German laws and regulations by the former GDR; but for obvious reasons this is a very specific case, which neither can nor should be emulated in other east European countries. True, some *liberalization* measures, such as price liberalization, currency convertibility or the removal of foreign trade restrictions, can be introduced at one stroke, even though they are of an institutional character. However, it should be noted that these changes cover only a small fraction of the institutional reforms needed to put the market mechanism in place and, besides, in most cases their primary and most immediate functions were essentially to help to stop inflation and to contribute to macro-stabilization. Otherwise, the scope for an *instantaneous* institutional (or structural) transformation is rather limited. Thus, the "shock-versus-gradualism" dilemma may be applicable only to a subset of transformation policies: while the choice certainly exists in the area of macroeconomic stabilization, it is far more limited in the areas of institutional reform and of structural change.

In the last issue of the *Economic Bulletin for Europe*, the ECE secretariat argued in favour of a more gradualist strategy of transformation.[53] The argument is based on the complexities involved in such a revolutionary change in economic structure and social behaviour and on the need to create a new institutional framework before the incentives of a market economy can begin to work effectively. It may have also been influenced by the unexpectedly high social costs incurred during the early stages of the transition in some east European countries (most notably Poland).

The problem is that *in practice* it may be difficult to adhere to this logic. It is obvious that the transition

---

[52] H. Gabrisch, K. Laski, et al., "Transition from the Command to a Market Economy", *WIIW Forschungsberichte*, No.163, Vienna, 1990.

[53] See United Nations Economic Commission for Europe, *Economic Bulletin for Europe*, vol.43, New York, 1991, pp.6-7.

to a market economy cannot be accomplished through "mounting a cavalry attack", but should be perceived as a process extending over longer periods. In this sense, the gradualism concept refers clearly to the *results* of the process, which can materialize only in a longer perspective. But does it mean that the necessary *policy decisions* should also be prepared and taken gradually, or rather should they be taken up front? Attempts to establish a market mechanism overnight are certainly unrealistic but, on the other hand, the required core reform decisions should not be unnecessarily delayed. In particular, extending the stabilization operation over a lengthy period may be a very dangerous mistake. Finally, it should also be noted that a choice between "shock" and gradualism is not always feasible in practice. The option for gradual transformation was quite realistic (if not the only one) for Hungary in the late 1960s, but it was no longer open to some other countries in the end of 1980s, because of unsustainable domestic and external imbalances and unexpected external shocks.

Hungary and Poland represent the two opposite policy patterns in this respect and while both programmes have been analysed extensively, no clear and unambiguous conclusion can be drawn as to the superiority of one approach over the other. In both cases the results so far are at best mixed, given the different initial conditions in each country.[54]

In addition to the speed of reforms, other fundamental policy dilemmas to be solved at the outset of the transition include the sequencing of reforms, the degree of openness and the extent of the social safety net.

While the *sequencing* issue received some attention in the context of stabilization programmes in developing countries, it has gained a new dimension in the recent discussions on east European transformation. Perhaps the most challenging problem was the need to reconcile the accepted economic principle that "everything depends on everything else" with the sheer impossibility of introducing all the required changes at the same time. In conditions of high inflation, macroeconomic stabilization emerged as the first priority; however, it was not at all clear how the predominantly state-owned economy would react to financial stabilization measures in the absence of market institutions. Therefore some authors suggested that institutional reforms should come first, and financial stabilization only later on.[55] This is certainly a valid point, yet a lot depends on the extent of domestic imbalances. Under rampant inflation with massive shortages and a collapsing social order, instantaneous stabilization through drastic financial measures may be the only option available. Its social costs are likely to be higher in the absence of a developed market structure but decisive and resolute action may be more easily accepted by a tormented population. On the other hand, postponing the stabilization when the economy is collapsing would probably lead to a loss of control over the reform process, as evidenced by the disastrous results of policies of procrastination in the former Soviet Union.

Among the specific policy measures, the timing of introducing *price liberalization* and *convertibility of the domestic currency* have probably been most controversial. Early decisions on both issues have been regarded as crucial for establishing a minimum package of economic incentives and competition. Opponents point out the limited efficiency of early price liberalization under monopolistic structures and a weak financial system; they also consider premature convertibility as recessionary in the short run and unsustainable in the long run.

In the case of the economic liberalization of the western European countries in the post-war period, convertibility came only at the end of the process; but, according to some observers, this experience is largely irrelevant in the current situation of post-socialist economies.[56] Correct relative prices and the spur of foreign competition are key elements for any market-oriented reform, and therefore early convertibility (for current-account transactions) appears as a necessary step.

No prior experience existed as to the desirable level of *domestic protection* for the transition period. Poland started its programme at the beginning of 1990, with a very high overall protection level, consisting essentially of a deeply undervalued domestic currency, which was further reinforced by an average tariff protection of 12 per cent. Persistent inflation under the fixed nominal exchange rate, and extensive liberalization of import tariffs in mid-1990, dramatically reduced the level of protection and by the second quarter of 1991 the Polish economy had moved to the other extreme, with one of the most liberal foreign trade regimes in the world (no import quotas, 3-5 per cent average tariff incidence, and an undervalued dollar exchange rate). In Bulgaria, the initial level of protection also turned out to be rather high, due to the sharp devaluation of the lev and restricted convertibility. In contrast, in Czechoslovakia the initial devaluation was moderate[57] and customs tariffs were very low, so that the government imposed

---

[54] It should be noted that the "shock-versus-gradualism" dilemma in the Polish context is not always interpreted correctly. The Polish "shock" referred essentially to the stabilization part of the programme, while the institutional part has in fact been implemented only gradually, and is still far from being completed. The zloty devaluation, the four- to sixfold increase in energy prices, the sudden elimination of subsidies, the general liberalization of prices and increases in interest rates were all done simultaneously and on a large scale, producing a tremendous change in the economic environment. On the other hand, however, many institutional reforms, though initialized at the beginning of the programme, were expected to yield results only after some time (for example, privatization, the reform of the banking system, and the establishment of capital markets), and some others have not been started yet (such as fiscal reform). Therefore what one has witnessed in the Polish context was something like a "handicapped shock" therapy, which applied only to the stabilization operation, so that its effectiveness should be evaluated only in the narrower context of the stabilization goals. This is a distinctively different strategy of transformation from that adopted in the case of German unification, where both the stabilization and institutional change were brought about simultaneously within several months in 1990.

[55] See e.g., R. Dornbusch, "Strategies and Priorities for Reform", in P. Marer, S. Zecchini (eds.), *The Transition to a Market Economy*, OECD, Paris, 1991, p.169-183.

[56] See e.g., R. Portes, "The Transition to Convertibility for Eastern Europe and the Soviet Union", *CEPR Discussion Paper*, No.500, London, 1990.

[57] Between September and end-December 1990 Czechoslovakia devalued the koruna twice from 15 Kcs/$ to 28 Kcs/$, i.e., by nearly 90 per cent. In Poland the series of devaluations preceding the programme implementation brought the dollar rate from the average 3,077 zl/$ in November up to 9,500 zl/$ in end-December 1989, i.e., by more than 300 per cent.

a 20 per cent import surcharge to prevent excessive imports of consumer goods (reduced to 15 per cent in July 1991). However, both the high and low protection levels at the beginning of stabilization programmes did not seem to have been results of a deliberate trade policy but were rather more or less unexpected "side" effects of efforts to restore and maintain internal balance.

All the reform programmes included provisions for the protection of social groups which were likely to suffer the most drastic falls in living standards. *Social safety nets* included such components as unemployment compensation, indexation schemes for pensions and transfer payments, minimum wage legislation and controlled prices for certain basic goods and services. The share of budgetary expenditures earmarked for social protection has been relatively high, mostly because of numerous social programmes inherited from communist times, and the level of compensation payments was considered as rather generous.[58]

(iii) Reform results to date: more pain than gain?

In all east European countries, the stabilization-cum-reform programmes failed to meet the macroeconomic targets set by governments or specified in agreements with the IMF. In some cases the shortfalls are substantial. Were these forecasts too optimistic, or were some obstacles encountered which could not have been foreseen? Or were mistakes made in the design and implementation of the programmes? Table 3.1.2 illustrates the scale of recession in six central and east European countries, while table 3.1.3 gives a summary of planned and actual results of reform programmes in Poland, Bulgaria and Czechoslovakia.

It can be observed that the actual contraction of output was much stronger than anticipated in all countries, with the industrial sector being hardest hit by the recession. The increase in unemployment, although high by east European historical standards, did not, however, match the fall of output, due to structural rigidities in labour markets. Real wages sharply declined in all countries, as a result of various wage control schemes and higher than anticipated inflation. On the positive side, one should note the reactions of the government accounts and of the trade balance, which were generally favourable in most countries (except for Romania and Yugoslavia). The discrepancies between specified goals and actual results differed among countries, apparently reflecting different combinations of policy measures and circumstances.

Judging from the evidence provided by macro-economic statistics, the first phase of stabilization was moderately successful on the financial side, and rather disappointing on the real side. All "strong" programmes proved to be relatively effective in bringing down inflation within a few months of the initial price jump, although the sustainability of these results is questionable. In Yugoslavia, inflation was reduced from the monthly rate of 59 per cent in December 1989 to zero levels in May to June 1990; but inefficient control over money supply led to an increase of the inflation rate in the second half of the year and the subsequent abandonment of the programme in 1991. In Poland, underlying inflation rooted in various cost and inertial factors turned out to be much more persistent and after the initial deceleration from almost 80 per cent in January 1990, inflation has continued at a rate of 3-5 per cent per month since April 1990. In Czechoslovakia, the initial adjustment was weaker, and prices practically stabilized five months after they were liberalized. In general, the "shock" therapy seems to be more effective in curbing high inflation than "gradual" programmes, as evidenced by comparisons with the Romanian data.

TABLE 3.1.2

Eastern Europe: Stabilization results in 1991
(Percentage change over preceding year)

Country	GDP	Inflation (CPI)	Unemployment [a]	Industrial output
Bulgaria	-26 [b]	250	10.7	-27
Czechoslovakia	-16	58	6.6	-23
Hungary	-(7-9)	35	8.3	-19
Poland	-9	70	11.5	-12
Romania	-13	344 [c]	3.1	-19
Yugoslavia	-15 *	164	19.6	-21

Source: National statistics and ECE estimates.

[a] End-1991.
[b] NMP.
[c] December 1991 relative to October 1990.

Price liberalization under monetary and fiscal restraint proved to be very effective in restoring market balance in countries suffering from endemic shortages. Rapid improvement in the market situation was most visible in Poland; but a similar effect can already be observed in Bulgaria. Similarly, policies worked very well in stabilizing the foreign exchange market: in both countries black market premiums were brought down to negligible levels almost instantaneously and demand for foreign exchange stabilized, responding to the fall in real incomes and to changed expectations.

The "shock" programmes also appear to have had stronger positive impacts on fiscal and external balances than the more gradual policies. The budget position in Poland and Czechoslovakia improved strongly during the first semester of programme implementation in reaction to the temporary increase in the profitability of enterprises following price liberalization. However, once these short-term effects disappear, the fiscal balance may be expected to deteriorate because of the continued recession, as was the case of Poland in 1991. The improvement of the external position may last longer, depending on the extent of the initial undervaluation of the domestic currency. In Poland, a substantial trade surplus was built up during the first year of stabilization, resulting from the initial devaluation and the sharp contraction of domestic demand, but it is likely to dissipate gradually because of the continuous real appreciation of the domestic currency which is in-

---

[58] Unemployment benefits in Czechoslovakia and Poland were set at relatively high levels (e.g., 70 per cent of average wage in Czechoslovakia), opening room for abuse. Anecdotal evidence suggests that many unemployed workers undertake unregistered commercial activities, while still receiving unemployment benefits (see e.g., I. Dryll "Bezrobocie — fikcja czy dramat?", *Zycie gospodarcze*, No.5, 1991).

TABLE 3.1.3

Reform-cum-stabilization programmes in Poland, Bulgaria and Czechoslovakia: Planned targets and actual results
(Percentage changes over previous period, percentage shares, levels in thousands, billion dollars or roubles)

Macroeconomic variable	Poland 1990 Targets	Poland 1990 Results	Poland 1991 Targets	Poland 1991 Results [a]	Bulgaria 1991 Targets	Bulgaria 1991 Results [a]	Czechoslovakia 1991 Targets	Czechoslovakia 1991 Results [a]
GDP	-3.1	-11.6	+3.5	-9.0	-11	-23	-(5-10)	-16.0
Inflation:								
CPI, first quarter	75	132	23	26	..	..	25	35
CPI, whole year [b]	95	249	36	60	< 200	474	35	58
Unemployment:								
as per cent	2.0	6.3	..	11.4	5.0	10.7	7-12 [c]	6.6
in thousands	400	1,123	..	2,155	..	419	..	524
Industrial output	-5.0	-23.4	..	-14.2	..	-27	..	-23
Budget balance:								
in money terms	-5.5 [d]	-31.0 [d]	..	..	..	..	..	..
as per cent of GDP	-0.5	+0.5	-0.5	-3.4	-3	-5.8	+1.0	-2*
Trade balance:								
in billion dollars	-0.8	+3.8	..	-0.1	-2.0	2	-2.5	+0.9
in billion TR	+0.5	+4.4	..	+0.4	..	..	..	..
Change in international reserves, in billion dollars	..	+2.4	+0.7	-1.3	..	..	..	+2.2

Sources: Compiled from: G.W. Kolodko, "Transition from Socialism and Stabilization Policies: The Polish Experience", *Rivista di Economica Politica*, June 1991, pp.289-330; D.K. Rosati, "The Stabilization Program and Institutional Reform in Poland," Kiel Institute of World Economics, 1991; *Rzeczpospolita*, 23 April 1991; M. Hrncir, J. Klacek, "Stabilization policies and currency convertibility in Czechoslovakia", *European Economy*, Special Issue, No.2, 1991; J. Charap, K. Dyba, M. Kupka, "The reform process in Czechoslovakia: An assessment of recent developments and prospects for the future", *Communist Economies*, Fall 1991; *Bulgarian Economic Outlook*, BTA, No.3, 20 January 1992, and national statistics.

a Preliminary.
b December-December.
c Target planned for three years.
d Trillion zloty.

evitable in all countries where nominal exchange rate anchoring is pursued for too long. In Czechoslovakia, the response of the export sector in 1991 was less spectacular, partly because of the larger share of sales directed to former CMEA markets, partly because of the recession in the west and partly because the initial adjustment of the exchange rate was lower. A similar reaction of the foreign sector was observed in Bulgaria, where the trade balance turned from deficit to a modest surplus by the end of 1991.

The *external environment* worked against countries which started their programmes later. When Poland launched its all-embracing reform programme in late 1989, not only did it receive strong support from the international community as the first country from the former Soviet bloc to carry out market reforms (this support culminated in the debt reduction agreement of March 1991), but also it benefited from a relatively favourable situation on international markets. High levels of economic activity in western countries allowed Polish firms to increase significantly their convertible currency exports, thus cushioning the sharp fall in domestic demand. At this time, the majority of CMEA imports were still paid for in transferable roubles, and the Gulf war was not imminent. In contrast, for Czechoslovakia and, especially, Bulgaria the launching of reform programmes in the beginning of 1991 coincided with the dismantling of the CMEA trade and payments system and the recession in the west reduced their possibilities for shifting sales from domestic to foreign markets.

Economists largely agree that the biggest problem with the stabilization programmes is that they tend to be strongly contractionary, although the scale of their recessionary impact is a controversial issue. The depth of economic recession in eastern Europe is sometimes disputed on the grounds that official statistics in these countries exaggerate the actual fall in output. Three main arguments are typically raised in this context. First, *macroeconomic statistics* are considered to be rather unreliable, both as regards the quality of data as well as in the methodologies used. Some of these problems have existed for years, but many are a direct consequence of the transition process itself. For instance, national accounts statistics are based on incomplete data, quarterly data for GNP or NMP series are not computed, the activities of the service sector are monitored only partially and trade statistics are plagued by a host of conversion and classification problems. Perhaps the most significant deficiency is that official statistics fail to take full account of the rapidly growing private sector — including the "shadow" economy (concerning, in particular, imports of consumer goods, retail trade and non-material services). For this reason it may be assumed that officially reported data on most important macroeconomic variables (like GDP, output, employment, individual consumption) should be revised upwards, although the scale of the revision is unclear.[59]

The second argument underlines the process of *industrial restructuring* which is taking place in east

---

59 Despite its other merits, the "statistical" recession argument is sometimes overdone, when applied to the reporting practices of state-owned enterprises. While enterprises had indeed incentives to cheat on the degree of fulfilment of planned targets under central planning, these incentives largely disappeared with the abolition of central command planning, which in some countries had taken place years earlier (Yugoslavia 1954, Hungary 1968, Poland 1982).

European economies. Some observers point out that in fact the recession is not as deep as it appears, the reason being that many activities have been discontinued because under the newly-established set of market prices and more realistic exchange rates these activities turned out to yield negative (or very low) value added.[60] While the existence of value-added "subtractors" in formerly centrally planned economies can hardly be disputed (especially in energy consuming sectors, because of the excessively low energy prices under central planning), the actual scale of the distortion remains problematic (it also varies among countries),[61] and it is unclear how the problem should be addressed by economic policy (whether and which of these activities should benefit from some temporary protection). But the most important caveat to this argument is that if negative value-added activities are indeed shed, the overall level of welfare should increase rather than decrease. It is quite difficult to demonstrate that this is in fact taking place.

In a similar vein, it is sometimes argued that the observed recession simply reflects the *elimination of uncompetitive production* which cannot find outlets under new conditions. That is certainly true, but the reasons for this low competitiveness may vary from structural or microeconomic inefficiency to macroeconomic restrictions imposed on domestic demand and/or market imperfections. And if the latter is true, then some activities, which could possibly become competitive after restructuring, will disappear because the macroeconomic policy is excessively restrictive and capital markets are underdeveloped. Moreover, the market-oriented transformation was expected not only to eliminate the inefficient activities, but also to stimulate the expansion of those which are more efficient so that a dramatic fall in overall production was not seen as a real possibility.

Altogether, while there is certainly a grain of truth in the assertion that the actual recession is not as acute as it may appear from official statistics, it seems that the difference is probably not as large as some observers claim.[62] Moreover, the positive supply response is not as vigorous and forthcoming as initially expected. In any case, it would be definitely misleading and even dangerous to consider the present recession as something like a statistical "mirage". The deep contraction of output and employment is a matter of fact, which may or may not be disputed by academics, but should not be ignored or belittled by policy-makers. Even if real levels of living standards are indeed less affected than the statistics may suggest, an expectation gap has none the less emerged between the reality and what was initially expected, no matter how naive or overly optimistic were these expectations.

One of the consequences of this gap is the rapidly deteriorating political situation in east European countries. The unexpected outcome of parliamentary elections in Poland, the strikes by Romanian miners and the gradual erosion of social support for market reforms in Hungary and Czechoslovakia all demonstrate that the costs of transition are becoming unbearable for large groups of the population.

(iv) Economic lessons

Possible explanations of the excessive recession in eastern Europe cover a large range of exogenous and endogenous factors. Some of them are of a strictly economic character, while others result from bitter political disputes and internal conflicts.

The question which should perhaps be asked in the first place is whether the transition from central planning to a market economy must inevitably be associated with a deep recession? After all, it was a common belief that the traditional communist system was so terribly inefficient that simply changing the government and removing the repressive communist powers would make a substantial difference in terms of economic efficiency and, consequently, in living standards. As some observers put it, if the initial situation had been as bad as it had appeared — that is if the distortions had been so great and these economies so mismanaged — there must have been some programmes that would clearly have made everyone better off.[63]

Two years of experience with the transition demonstrate that this view was probably overly optimistic and that some recession is indeed unavoidable. But this recognition should not divert attention from possible mistakes in the process of planning and implementing the transformation. Ample evidence exists to support the view that the inevitable costs of transition have been amplified in many cases by a combination of unfounded assumptions, wrong estimates, inconsistent policies, and simple lack of action.

To be sure, *some recession* is probably inevitable. For one thing, the shift from central planning to a market mechanism requires the laying off of labour to open the way for restructuring and to establish a pool of unemployed workers commensurate with the natural unemployment rate.[64] For another, destruction is easier and faster than creation: it takes less time to discontinue

---

[60] See e.g., R. McKinnon, *The Order of Economic Liberalization: Financial Control in the Transition to a Market Economy*, Baltimore, Johns Hopkins University Press, 1991.

[61] Attempts to estimate the share of negative value added industries in east European countries were undertaken by some authors, but important caveats remain as to the quality of data used and some methodological assumptions (V. Konovalov "Poland: Competitiveness of Industrial Activities, 1961-1986", The World Bank, Washington, D.C., 1989 (mimeo); P. Hare and G.Hughes, *Competitiveness and Industrial Restructuring in Czechoslovakia, Hungary and Poland*, CEPR Discussion Paper Series, No.543, London, 1991).

[62] Some analysts believe that if black and grey markets are counted in, production may have held level in Poland, where the officially reported fall in GDP was 8-9 per cent in 1991 (see *Time*, 17 February 1992, p.9). For a similar argument in the context of the Hungarian economy, see *Figyelö*, 27 February, 1992, p.13.

[63] R. Portes "The Path of Reform in Central and Eastern Europe: Introduction", *European Economy*, Special edition No.2, Commission of the European Communities, Brussels, 1991.

[64] K. Laski "Transition from Command to Market Economies in Central and Eastern Europe: First Experience and Questions", Vienna Institute for Comparative Economic Studies, 1991, mimeo.

inefficient activities than to move resources to efficient uses, because in the latter case typically some investment is needed and new technology cannot be put in place overnight. This loss of output and employment is however only temporary and should disappear after the initial reallocation of resources is completed; moreover, these losses should be partly contained by the efficiency gains which are likely to appear after the communist system has been dismantled. On the other hand, the losses will probably be higher under the "big-bang", because the asymmetry between destruction and creation effects will be larger. Finally, some losses appear to be unavoidable because of the exhaustion of some resources which were overexploited under central planning. For example, natural resources were run down without considering their protection and replenishment, and health standards were reduced.

But it is doubtful whether these factors can fully account for the massive and protracted downturn in economic activity which has been observed in eastern Europe. Other explanations have therefore to be sought. Among those which derive from economic considerations, three groups of factors seem to be of major importance: (a) errors in the initial design of stabilization-cum-reform programmes, (b) policy mistakes during the implementation of the programme and (c) external shocks, and especially the demise of the CMEA and the collapse of the Soviet market.

(a) Initial programme structure

Part of the blame for the lack of expected successes has been frequently put on the *initial design* of reform programmes implemented in eastern Europe. Here the critique falls into several categories. Some commentators indicate that stabilization packages were as a rule *too restrictive*, and led to an excessive fall of domestic absorption through a tight monetary and fiscal squeeze. In this view, the ensuing recession was caused by a combination of demand-side (reduced real incomes and wealth) and supply-side (credit squeeze, monopolistic behaviour) factors.[65]

It is sometimes argued that the main reason behind the excessive restrictiveness of stabilization policies was a significant overestimation of the size of the inflationary overhang in post-communist economies. The notorious shortage syndrome, so characteristic of centrally planned systems, had led the authors of the stabilization programmes (both national policy-makers and international experts) to believe that only very drastic deflationary measures could effectively eliminate the excess liquidity *and* restore flow equilibrium. The result was that probably too many instruments aimed at demand reduction were put in place and that they not only washed out the inflationary overhang but also sharply reduced the "normal" demand level by reducing real incomes and wealth.[66]

A variant of this argument refers to technological factors. Faced by the sudden change of relative prices and liquidity squeeze, firms in the transition economies reduced their *inventory stocks* and other liquid assets (e.g., foreign exchange holdings), accumulated in the past. While the resulting fall of demand for production inputs may have indeed been contractionary, its impact is temporary and cannot be responsible for a prolonged contraction (in Poland, the fall in stock levels in the first half of 1990 was followed by a rise in inventories in the second half of the year and in 1991).

Another line of reasoning points to a *lack of balance* of the stabilization-cum-reform programmes, which focused primarily on stabilization goals, presumably not paying enough attention to the supply side and, especially, to institution building. The theoretical framework applied to design the transformation was perhaps excessively influenced by IMF experience with stabilization and structural adjustment programmes in developing countries, with too little attention given to the specific conditions of post-socialist economies (lack of behavioural patterns resulting from central planning).

The conventional approach may need to be revised in the light of east European experience in 1990-1991. Perhaps the most important observation is that the *pattern of reaction of economic agents* in the predominantly state-owned and monopolized economies to standard monetary and fiscal restrictions is different from that seen in market economies. When they are affected by a financial squeeze, firms in eastern Europe tend first to reduce output and raise prices, then they suspend payments to their suppliers, negotiate various reliefs with banks and the government, then send workers on unpaid leave and only after having exhausted other possibilities do they start to reduce employment. Restructuring programmes such as mergers and joint ventures, even if contemplated, rarely materialize in the form of concrete projects in the absence of an immediate threat of bankruptcy.

The (implicit) assumption that the behavioural patterns of economic agents are similar to those observed in the west ignores the fact that enterprises in the east have been faced by a different structure of incentives. The lack of genuine owners of capital, an unclear allocation of property rights, the absence of any threat of takeover or acquisition, the excessive powers of Workers' Councils and/or labour unions and meagre competitive pressure from outside all make state firms' behaviour very inertial and conservative. Critics of the standard stabilization programmes argue that these programmes neglected the need for an immediate and radical overhaul of existing incentive structures, and

---

[65] See e.g., O. Blanchard, R. Dornbusch, P. Krugman, R. Layard and L. Summers, "Reform in Eastern Europe" (The WIDER Report), World Institute for Development Economics Research (WIDER), Helsinki, 1990; G. Calvo, F. Coricelli, "Stabilizing a Previously-Centrally-Planned Economy: Poland 1990", paper presented to "Economic Policy: A European Forum" hosted by CERGE, Prague, 17-19 October, 1991, mimeo; D.M. Nuti, "Economic Inertia in the Transitional Economies of Eastern Europe", European University Institute, Florence, January 1991, mimeo; G.W. Kolodko, "Transition from Socialism and Stabilization Policies", loc.cit.; D.K. Rosati, "Sequencing the Reforms in Poland", in P. Marer and S. Zecchini, (eds.) *The Transition to a Market Economy*, Paris, OECD, 1991, vol.I, pp.208-225.

[66] For example, contrary to common beliefs, the real money stock in Poland did not decline during stabilization. The level of M2 in real terms diminished only by 3 per cent between October 1989 and July 1990, while output declined by almost 20 per cent and at the same time the market equilibrium was restored. This may suggest that in fact there was no inflationary overhang prior to stabilization programme, and that the expectations-induced increase of real cash balances (declining velocity) of households may have significantly reduced domestic demand in the first half of 1990.

thus failed to produce a positive supply response from enterprises.

Finally, the stabilization packages were criticized for their internal structure and choice of policy tools. The most controversial was probably the concept of *nominal anchoring*, constituting a key element in all "shock" programmes. Experience from stabilization episodes in developing countries has indicated that nominal anchors can serve as effective brakes on domestic inflation, provided they are accompanied by monetary and fiscal restraint. But when applied in the economies in transition, this concept becomes more problematic. The policy of the fixed exchange rate in Poland, which was aimed at reducing the inflation rate, proved to be rather costly in terms of output and employment. The initial devaluation, intended to anticipate the corrective inflation following the price liberalization, turned out to be excessive as excess liquidity in the hands of households was significantly overestimated. The "overshooting" of the exchange rate had both a strong inflationary impact through a sharp increase of input prices and was also contractionary in the initial period, because of reduced real incomes, especially in the non-tradable sector. The steep initial devaluation of the lev in Bulgaria from 3 lev per dollar in 1990 to 28 lev per dollar on 1 February 1991 had similar and much stronger effects.[67] If maintained for too long in a situation of high domestic inflation, the fixed exchange rate policy leads to a substantial real appreciation, a heavy loss of competitiveness in the tradable sector, and a gradual depletion of international reserves.

Alternatively, when wages are used as a nominal anchor, the side effects are equally deleterious. The main theoretical argument for a tax-based incomes policy is that it alleviates inflation and reduces the unemployment costs of stabilization.[68] Moreover, a restrictive wage policy seemed even more appropriate in the economies in transition, where state firms are labour-managed, and thus tend to pay higher wages at the cost of profits.

But the specific wage policies actually applied in eastern Europe, which led to a substantial fall in real wages, proved economically counterproductive, socially unfair and politically dangerous. Falling real wages reduced the incentives for labour reallocation, allowed inefficient sectors to maintain overemployment and inhibited productivity growth. The flattened wage structure inherited from the past was not changed, the labour market mechanism remained distorted and migration abroad was encouraged. The redistributive effects of wage controls in favour of lower paid workers may also be pro-inflationary (as overall savings ratios would be expected to decline following the redistribution).

The recent experience of some east European countries suggests that nominal anchors can be useful instruments of anti-inflationary policies only within a specific policy package and only for a short period of time. If used simultaneously with sweeping price liberalization, they can produce severe distortions and "overshooting". If extended beyond the period of rapid disinflation (varying between three and six months), they are bound to delay necessary restructuring, and eventually they may "anchor" the economic recovery rather than inflation. Real anchors (like the real money supply) may therefore be more suitable once the initial phase of disinflation has been completed.[69]

The stronger than expected recession also calls for a revision of the design of the social safety net. These social programmes were based on overly optimistic scenarios of economic recovery. The generous unemployment benefits and high pension payments, in combination with both low retirement ages and the various indexation schemes adopted in many countries, proved unsustainable under recessionary conditions and in view of falling government revenues. They also give rise to numerous abuses and significantly increase problems of "moral hazard".

(b) Current economic policies

Another reason for the excessive recession may be rooted in misguided *economic policies* following the initial stage of transition. The Polish experiment may be particularly instructive in this respect, because it started earliest so that the impact of economic policy can be examined over a longer period of time. When the Polish economy showed signs of a modest recovery in the second half of 1990, inflation also accelerated and the government decided to tighten monetary policies in an attempt to bring inflation under control. Financial restrictions were further strengthened in 1991 and continued throughout the year. That policy can hardly be considered appropriate. While the monthly inflation rate diminished from some 5 per cent in the last quarter of 1990 to 3 per cent in the last quarter of 1991, industrial output dropped over the same period by 12 per cent, and unemployment almost doubled to 11 per cent. Clearly, the macroeconomic cost of reducing the inflation rate by two percentage points proved to be very high.

One reason for this may have been the erroneous interpretation of the *source* of inflationary pressures in the second half of 1990. While the government linked inflation to growing demand fuelled by increases in wages and expanding credit, a cost-push explanation may have been more plausible. Sharp increases in energy prices in the wake of the Gulf war in the summer of 1990 and the gradual shift to dollar prices for CMEA imports exacerbated the earlier corrective increases of some domestic prices (coal, transport tariffs, turnover taxes), and temporarily boosted inflationary expectations. Moreover, the seasonal increase of food prices in the autumn was mistakenly viewed as a symptom of inflation going out of control. Hence, macroeconomic

---

[67] Bulgaria, however, decided to float its currency against the dollar, and the rate dropped to 14 lev per dollar after several months, before rising again to 24 lev per dollar at end-1991.

[68] See, e.g., R. Dornbusch, "From Stabilization to Growth", op.cit.

[69] See e.g., D.M. Nuti, "Progress in trade reforms, missing links, convertibility: A discussion", in United Nations Economic Commission for Europe, *Reforms in Foreign Economic Relations of Eastern Europe and the Soviet Union*, New York, 1991, pp.49-53.

demand reducing measures were used to attack the cost-push inflation, with the inevitable result being that the economy slid further into a deep recession.

The lesson which should be drawn is that after the first phase, when inflation goes up following price liberalization and then comes down due to restrictive stabilization measures, inflation may continue at an underlying rate determined mainly by cost and supply factors. This type of inflation requires different anti-inflation policies from those adopted to combat the initial, demand push inflation. Furthermore, anti-inflation policy targets should not be overly ambitious and should be weighed against the costs of lost output and employment: the rewards from reducing the monthly inflation rate from, say, 50 per cent to 5 per cent are much bigger than those from reducing it further from 5 to 1 per cent. In this context, the target of a 1 per cent monthly inflation rate, aimed at in Poland or Bulgaria only a few months after the launching of the programme, is very costly to attain if it is feasible at all.

Another reason for the excessive recession was probably the adopted policy of the *fixed exchange rate*. The level of the nominal exchange rate in Poland remained unchanged for more than 16 months, despite rapidly growing domestic prices (prices rose by more than 340 per cent per cent between January 1990 and May 1991). This reflected the policy priorities of the Polish government, which was more concerned about the inflationary repercussions of a devaluation and about the credibility of its exchange rate policy than about the deepening recession. But this may have not been the best economics. Imports increased sharply in 1991, while exports stagnated, international reserves declined and interest rates continued to be high, all contributing to the continuation of the recession. Under conditions of fiscal and monetary restraint, a recovery would require an offsetting mechanism for "crowding-in". A competitive real exchange rate would provide such a mechanism, at least in the medium run.[70] This experience demonstrates that, after the initial large devaluation, the currency should not be allowed to appreciate too much in real terms, and that the inflation target should not dominate exchange rate policy after the initial period of price stabilization. Instead, it should gradually be supplemented by other targets, most notably that of maintaining the competitiveness of the tradeable sector.

The third lesson is that *monetary policy* should not be too restrictive for too long. While correctly considered to be the most powerful tool for dampening demand-pulled inflation, the monetary policies adopted during stabilization proved to be both more contractionary and less efficient than expected. The policy of setting a positive real interest rate under conditions of high inflation and keeping a fixed exchange rate leads to sharp fluctuations in nominal interest rates and high levels of real interest rates. This policy should be modified as soon as inflationary expectations have been reduced. While adhering to the long-run target of non-negative real interest rates, the monetary authorities should make credit policy generally more flexible and in line with real growth targets. When inflation is falling, long-term interest rates should be lower than short-term rates and investment credits in preferred areas should be encouraged. Otherwise, the recession is likely to continue beyond the initial period of extinguishing high inflation.

In the specific circumstances of eastern Europe, monetary and credit policy instruments transplanted from industrialized economies may not work properly. The tight credit policy of the commercial banks, imposed in the form of high interest rates and bank-specific credit ceilings, led enterprises to resort to other sources of financing, most notably to borrowing from each other. The sharp increase of inter-enterprise credits, which typically assume the chain form, is a notorious phenomenon in east European economies in the first phase of transition, as firms try to escape the financial squeeze imposed by restrictive stabilization policies. In Czechoslovakia, the amount of inter-enterprise credits increased from Kcs 7.1 billion in January 1990 to 53.9 billion in December 1990, and to more than 130 billion in October 1991 (an equivalent of some 15 per cent of GDP and an increase by ten times in real terms).[71] In Poland the level of inter-enterprise indebtedness was very high already in 1989, but after a temporary decline in the summer of 1990, it started to grow again in the fourth quarter of 1990, probably responding to a tightening of credit policy. The proportion of inter-enterprise credit to the total short-term credit extended by commercial banks increased from 68 per cent at the end of 1989 to 170 per cent at the end of 1991; this is an emphatic illustration of the limited scope for imposing financial discipline on enterprises in eastern Europe through the "official" banking system. Similar problems are observed in Hungary, Romania and Bulgaria.[72]

The economic consequences of excessive inter-enterprise credits are very harmful. First, they effectively neutralize the impact of monetary policy at the macroeconomic level by allowing firms to circumvent credit restrictions. Second, they distort microeconomic adjustment, because the allocation of inter-enterprise credit is typically across-the-board and not based on any economic considerations. As a result, there is no distinction between good and bad firms. Third, financial discipline weakens, as no interest is charged on inter-enterprise credits.[73]

---

[70] See R. Dornbusch, "Policies to Move from Stabilization to Growth", *CEPR Discussion Paper Series*, No.456, London, 1991.

[71] See J. Charap, K. Dyba, M. Kupka, "Reform Process in Czechoslovakia", op.cit., p.20-21.

[72] See e.g., Bulgarian National Bank, *News Bulletin*, Semi-Annual Report, January-June 1991, No.5, 1 September 1991, p.3.

[73] Some authors tend to disregard these costs, arguing that interenterprise credit is an illiquid monetary asset and is, therefore, of limited danger to the overall effectiveness of monetary policy (S. Gomulka, "Poland", in P. Marer, S. Zecchini (eds.), *The Transition to a Market Economy*, op.cit., vol.I, p.67), but this view is not sustainable. Even if the total money supply does not change, its structure shifts towards more liquid assets. If firms are not restricted in spending categories, they can increase or continue to pay wages through an increase in interenterprise "borrowing", even though banks refuse to provide financing. Additional liquidity is injected in the economy, corresponding to the increase of interenterprise credit. Furthermore, if many firms behave in a similar manner, a chain of liabilities is established, slowing down the restructuring process and contributing to the overall overindebtedness of the enterprise sector.

Two general conclusions can be drawn. First, the mistake which is likely to have been made during the first phase of transition is the failure to recognize in time the impact of the fundamental change of macroeconomic conditions in eastern Europe. Emerging unemployment, the elimination of shortages and restoration of basic monetary equilibrium are all symptoms of transforming the Kornai-type, supply-constrained economies into Keynesian-type, demand-constrained ones. A gradual shift in macroeconomic targets from anti-inflation to anti-recession, and in policies from demand reduction to supply support measures, is therefore required to open the way for a transition from stabilization to recovery and growth.

On the other hand, the focus on macro-stabilization, dominating the first phase of transition, should be quickly balanced with more emphasis on extensive institutional reforms, especially in the banking sector and financial regulation, as well as on structural policies. The frustrating inertia observed in eastern Europe should not probably be taken as proof of the inability of *all* state firms to adjust; it rather demonstrates that the correct incentives have not yet been put in place or are not strong enough. Privatization is probably the most important instrument of structural change; but it is necessarily slow and costly. Other possibilities should not be neglected, especially in dealing with large firms in the state sector. Corporatization, "commercialization" and other institutional measures can be carried out relatively fast and at low cost, and yet they can substantially increase the flexibility of state enterprises in responding to market signals. If not accompanied by the required institutional changes, macroeconomic restrictions are destructive and the real costs imposed by the stabilization effort could be largely wasted.

(c) *External shocks*

There is no doubt that 1990-1991 was a period of unprecedented external shocks for east European economies. The recessionary impact of domestic reforms was further exacerbated by a series of unfavourable *external developments*, including the Persian Gulf war, the dismantling of the CMEA and the political and economic disintegration of the Soviet Union. The increase in energy prices, followed by the shift to convertible currency payments and world market prices in mutual trade adversely affected the *terms of trade* of east European countries: while forced to pay higher prices for imported fuels and raw materials, they faced at the same time a sharp decline of demand for their traditional exports of manufactured goods. The most important export market in the region – the Soviet Union – collapsed in 1991, partly because of a shortage of convertible currency, partly because of increasingly inefficient and chaotic foreign trade and foreign exchange controls, and partly because of sheer political disintegration. As a result, exports from eastern Europe to the ex-Soviet market declined in 1991 by 35-40 per cent in volume terms. Moreover, a considerable part of the deliveries have not been paid for by Soviet importers, adding to the financial difficulties of east European enterprises.

While the adverse impact of the eastern trade collapse on domestic recession in the east European economies is undisputed, its scale and magnitude remain a controversial issue. In official statements of many east European countries, the fall of Soviet import demand is frequently cited as the main cause of their recession; but this impact is almost certainly overestimated, especially in "northern-tier" countries. Preliminary calculations for Czechoslovakia and Poland suggest that domestic, policy-induced factors have exerted a much stronger contractionary impact.[74]

But the "Soviet trade" factor has been probably of much greater significance in the case of Bulgaria, where the share of the Soviet Union in exports was extremely high, and where, unlike in Hungary or Poland, the reorientation of trade to other markets only started in 1991. Moreover, the Bulgarian economy was also adversely affected by its almost total isolation from international financial markets following the unilateral suspension of foreign debt servicing at the beginning of 1990.

(v) Political economy of transition

The core of the economic and political transformation in eastern Europe lies in replacing the inefficient system of totalitarian central planning by a market democracy. But the long-term benefits require some sacrifices in the short run. Who gains and who loses in the transformation? What is the political economy of this process? It is interesting to examine to what extent those social groups which have supported the transformation in the hope of gaining better living standards may actually count on receiving benefits from the transition. As can be seen from the experience of eastern Europe, the distribution of transition costs follows a specific pattern, which may become an important source of frustration and instability in the young democracies.

In "The Road to a Free Economy", Janos Kornai addresses his free-market manifesto to various social groups. He not only maintains that capitalists will benefit from the market-oriented transformation but seeks to reassure the reader that many other groups will also be better off: liberals will be happy to see their ideas implemented, young people will be offered new exciting opportunities, consumers will enjoy the elimination of shortages, and pensioners will welcome stopping inflation.[75] This seems to be an overly optimistic view. The most likely outcome is that in the short period only two categories are likely to gain: entrepreneurs (actual and would-be) and owners of property. With the latter category practically extinct under communist rule, and with the so-called middle class confined to the rudimentary private sector, this leaves rather a narrow

---

[74] United Nations Economic Commission for Europe, *Economic Bulletin for Europe*, vol.43, New York, 1991, p.68-69, and J. Klacek et al, "Ekonomicka reforma v CSFR (prubezne hodnoceni)", *Politicka ekonomie*, No.9-10, 1991, p.727.

[75] J. Kornai, *The Road to a Free Economy*, Norton, New York, 1990, pp.179-191.

social base to support the transformation process. The contrast between the large majority coalition *before* the transformation and the small minority reaping immediate benefits *after* the transformation is indeed baffling.

A closer look into the distribution of costs and benefits among various social groups reveals that economic burdens are mostly borne by wage-earners and farmers. The Polish and Czechoslovak cases are particularly illustrative of this tendency. In table 3.1.4 changes in the real incomes of the population are shown, while table 3.1.5 illustrates changes in income distribution among particular groups.

While the figures presented also reflect changes in sectoral manpower allocation (with large shifts from the public to the private sectors), the pattern of income distribution during the first year of stabilization in Poland (1990) and Czechoslovakia (1991) displays striking similarities. Total real incomes plummeted in both countries by 26 per cent and 29 per cent, respectively, with incomes of wage-earners (by more than one third) and especially private farmers (by more than half) falling the most. The two pivotal social groups were thus hit hardest in the first period of transformation. These groups were also net losers in Hungary, although the changes in real incomes in that country were more moderate. The private non-agricultural sector, which in 1990 was the main gainer in Hungary and Poland, has seen its position stagnating in 1991. By contrast, recipients of transfer payments seem to be best protected: in all three countries their share in total incomes increased substantially. But the unusually high proportion of pensions and other social transfers to wages in Poland, reaching almost 70 per cent in 1991, is something of a curiosity for a country in deep crisis.[76]

In sum, in view of very large layers of losers in the initial stage of transformation, and in particular the unexpected distribution of its burden, it is hardly surprising that reforming governments in east European countries are struggling for political survival only a few months after being brought to power by an overwhelming majority of the population. Such a policy of income distribution would probably be assessed as politically dangerous for any government in a western country.

It should be noted however, that the analysis of changes in real incomes and savings in the economies in transition from one system to another is obstructed by statistical and measurement problems. The key issue is how to measure the real wage (savings level) in a shortage economy. It is well known that the statistical real wage (defined as a nominal wage deflated by the price index) does not reflect the real purchasing power. On this premise, some authors claim that even though statistical real wage has fallen, the people may actually be better off because of the elimination of shortages.[77]

This is, however, a debatable view. That the elimination of shortage is a good thing is uncontroversial. But how this relates to the real wage is more complex. First of all one does not have a clear picture of the size of shortages in a centrally planned economy; experts' opinions differ in this respect.[78] It may be that shortages were largely induced by the excess demand for goods, caused by the high velocity of money in an inflationary situation and would disappear in a stable-price, no-shortage environment.[79]

But more importantly, this view ignores the income distribution aspect. Shortages imply rationing by queuing, and this clearly benefits low income groups as higher income groups can afford to pay black-market premiums over official prices. After the liberalization, when prices reach market-clearing levels, no rationing is required, and queuing is no longer necessary. While high income groups can afford to pay higher prices, low income groups are no longer able to trade leisure time for goods and may be forced to reduce their consumption because some categories of goods have become simply too expensive and thus unaffordable. Whether society as a whole is better off (in the short run) cannot be now determined for sure, as the social utility function is in principle unknown.

One (crude) indicator may be the change in real consumption levels, but, again, it does not contain any information about the pattern of distribution. In Poland, real consumption declined by 15 per cent in 1990 and increased only by 2 per cent in 1991, while in Czechoslovakia the drop of consumption during the first year of stabilization programme (1991) is estimated at some 25 per cent. The decline of consumption in Bulgaria in 1991 was at least of the same magnitude, if one takes into account the fall of real (statistical) incomes of population by more than 60 per cent. Taking into account the rapidly increasing income and wealth differentiation (stemming from the rapid expansion of the private sector), this suggests that there must have been a significant deterioration of living standards for large groups of population in all three countries.

An important cost of transformation is connected with the unemployment. As mentioned earlier, the shift to a market system must lead to "some" unemployment, not only because the market economy operates with a "natural" level of unemployment, but

---

[76] This is not only connected with the very low retirement age limit in Poland, but also may be a symptom of excessive social safety programmes, including overly generous unemployment compensation schemes (on this issue, see R. Holzmann, "Safety Nets in Transition: Concepts, Recent Developments, Recommendations", in P. Marer, S. Zecchini, *The Transition to a Market Economy*, op.cit., Vol.II, pp.155-180).

[77] D. Lipton, J. Sachs, "Creating a Market Economy in Eastern Europe", *Brookings Papers on Economic Activity*, No.1, 1990. Some authors pushed this argument to the extreme, pointing to the *increase* of nominal wages when converted to dollars and asserting on that basis that an average worker was in fact better off (J. Sachs, "A Tremor, Not Necessarily a Quake, for Poland", *International Herald Tribune*, 30 November, 1990). But this is a false argument. One cannot speak about improvement if statistical wage increased from $108 to $131, because the purchasing power of the dollar declined over the same period by more than half.

[78] See e.g., R. Portes, D. Winter, "Disequilibrium estimates for consumption goods markets in centrally planned economies", *Review of Economic Studies*, 1980, vol.47, and W. Charemza, "Alternative paths to macroeconomic stability in Czechoslovakia", *European Economy*, Special Edition No.2, 1991, p.41-56, for disparate estimates.

[79] The real money stock (M2) in Poland declined only by 3 per cent between November 1989 and June 1990; but the economy moved over this period from endemic shortages to general financial equilibrium.

TABLE 3.1.4

Czechoslovakia, Hungary and Poland: Changes in real incomes of population, 1990-1991
(Percentage change from prior year) [a]

Item	Czechoslovakia 1990	Czechoslovakia 1991 [b]	Hungary 1990	Hungary 1991 [b]	Poland 1990	Poland 1991
Total incomes	-2.4	-29.7	0.8	-9.4	-26.6	3.0
of this:						
Wages	-7.3	-34.9	-1.5	-7.5	-37.2	-8.4
Social transfers	-5.2	-24.0	0.9	-7.3	-18.2	26.2
Incomes in agriculture	-8.5	-53.3	-13.4	-35.3	-62.4	-39.3
Private sector	-	-	32.9	-1.8	33.5	1.0
Other incomes	24.9	-9.7	..	..	-6.0	5.2

Source: Compiled from national statistics.

[a] Nominal incomes deflated by consumer price index (Czechoslovakia: 1990 = 110.0, 1991 = 157.9; Hungary 1990 = 128.9, 1991 = 135.2; Poland: 1990 = 717.8, 1991 = 170.3).
[b] January-November 1991 over January-November 1990.

also because the supply side asymmetry between the destruction and creation of new jobs during the transformation leads initially to frictional lay-offs. Unemployment has indeed risen in east European countries, but again its levels have gone far beyond the limits which were originally envisaged. Moreover, unemployment levels seem to be rather inelastic with respect to the labour policies applied. Poland and the former GDR provide two extreme examples of income-employment policy. Although quite different policies were adopted, unemployment levels are high in both countries.[80] Eventually, in either case the cost of unemployment and reduced job security is to be borne primarily by wage earners.

(vi) The illusion of a painless transformation disappears

The transformation from a centrally planned to a market economy, like every revolution, is aimed at revamping the institutional structures of east European economies and societies. But, unlike some other revolutions, which were animated by the idea of improving social justice and equity, the current transformation in the east in the economic area was based on the explicit idea of improving efficiency. While quite sound in the longer perspective, in the more immediate future this increase in efficiency is unlikely to occur without a radical departure from previously widely accepted understanding of social justice and equality. So, paradoxically, the transformation, being an escape from the utopia of extreme egalitarianism, may have been based on some important illusions, at least at the level of popular consciousness.

The abandonment of central planning and the switch to a market economy was generally supported by major groups of the population: workers, farmers, intellectuals. But this broad coalition, which brought about the revolutionary change, contains the seeds of its own destruction. The platform of national unity has essentially been built not on common future goals but rather on common past experience: all coalition groups were dissatisfied and frustrated with their lives under the socialist regime, especially against the backdrop of western consumption standards. Their desire to replace the traditional centrally planned system with the market economy and political democracy stemmed from a firm belief that they would *all* be quickly better off under the market system. But this proved to be *the big illusion*: because the transformation into a market economy includes, *inter alia*, a temporary decline in average standards of living due to a fall of production, and a radical departure from traditional egalitarianism and paternalistic interventionism, some important social groups, like wage-earners and farmers, are bound to lose, not win, at least in the short run.

The socio-political platform of the first post-communist coalitions was surprisingly narrow. In fact, the only point which is commonly shared without reservations is that the communist regime must be discarded, and a "democratic" system established (typically, with no specifics given). This "negative" programme is perhaps attractive enough for establishing a broad majority coalition to win the first free elections and to form the first non-communist government. But it is insufficient to carry on with the transformation process beyond the initial shift of power. Bitter conflicts emerge on the day following the takeover, and the anti-communist coalition falls apart within few months, as the big illusion disappears when confronted with the reality of rapidly rising prices, falling wages and emerging unemployment. Romania provides perhaps the most dramatic example of this process, but the decomposition of the Solidarity movement and the subse-

---

[80] Poland avoided massive unemployment in the beginning of the stabilization programme because of the strong position of the Workers' Councils and restrictive incomes policies in the form of punitive taxes imposed on wage increases exceeding pre-determined rates (the limits were set at 0.2-0.6 of monthly inflation rates). Low wages and their *upward rigidity, inter alia*, allowed enterprises to survive the first period of financial restrictions without any significant adjustment, and to hoard labour even though output fell drastically already in January 1990 and recession continued throughout 1990 and 1991. Thus, employment levels were protected at cost of real wages. But the price Poland probably paid for this policy was a significant slow-down in industrial restructuring: the long and severe contraction in 1990-1991 was not accompanied by a more pronounced reallocation of resources, labour in particular. As a result, after two years of continuous stabilization, unemployment is still rising (it reached 2.2 million people, or 11.4 per cent of the active labour force in end-1991), as firms have to shed labour, faced with continuous financial squeeze. In *East Germany* a different strategy was applied. The 1:1 conversion rate adopted for West and East German marks together with generously revised wage contracts both led to a substantial increase of east German wage levels. Being confronted by high wages and their *downward* inflexibility, enterprises had no choice but to lay off labour massively. Thus, real wages were protected at cost of employment levels. The unemployment rate in GDR jumped to some 10-15 per cent already after several months in 1990, but then stabilized (excluding part-time workers). But the industrial restructuring, stimulated by massive inflows of capital from the former Federal Republic of Germany, is taking place at much faster pace than in Poland.

TABLE 3.1.5

Czechoslovakia, Hungary, Poland: Changes in the structure of personal incomes, 1989-1991
(Shares in total personal incomes, in percent)

Item	Czechoslovakia 1989	1990	1991 [a]	Hungary 1989	1990	1991 [a]	Poland 1989	1990	1991
Wages	59.7	56.8	53.5	45.1	45.3	45.9	45.7	39.1	32.4
Social transfers	19.7	19.1	21.1	21.5	21.8	22.8	15.9	17.7	21.7
Agriculture	6.4	6.0	4.1	12.9	11.3	8.2	13.5	6.9	4.8
Private sector	-	-	-	7.3	9.6	10.3	8.2	14.9	14.8
Other incomes [b]	14.2	18.1	21.4	13.2	12.0	12.8	16.7	21.4	26.3

Source: As for table 3.1.4.

[a] January-November 1991.
[b] Including consumer credits and foreign transfers; in Czechoslovakia including compensation for price increases paid since July 1990 (140 Kcs per month per employee).

quent political fragmentation in Poland is also very illustrative. Impressive mass popular movements held together only when the enemy was still in power; after the breakthrough the national unity coalition tended to break apart and be replaced within a very short time by a mosaic of various political parties and groups, fighting each other with surprising hostility.

Can it be avoided? Can economic conflicts on a large scale be prevented in the post-communist era? The experience gained so far is not encouraging. First of all, the multitude of political orientations is a natural reaction after many decades of totalitarian rule. But more important is the underlying logic of the transformation into a market system: higher efficiency in the economy can in principle be achieved only at the cost of much wider wage and income differentiation and, hence, deeper inequalities than in the past.[81]

A major part of the big illusion may be explained by the combination of the demonstration effect from western Europe with the euphoric expectations prevailing when the regime was finally removed. People in eastern Europe expect an immediate improvement in their standard of living, because they see how their western neighbours live. In addition, it has been a common habit to blame the "system" for any unhappiness. Now the system is being changed and for the common man things have in many respects got worse. Thus, in a sense, the new democratic governments of eastern Europe are becoming victims of their own statements from before the transformation: they are simply unable to make their expectations come true.

Another part of the big illusion comes from ignoring the time factor. The time lags between policy actions and expected outcomes were largely unknown when the reforms were started but generally they seem to be much longer than was expected. When it launched its economic programme in January 1990, the Polish government promised that the economic recovery would begin in the second half of 1990; but the recession has continued throughout 1990 and 1991, and recent estimates predict that GDP may decline by a further 3-4 per cent in 1992 before a recovery comes. This means that pre-transformation levels of per capita GDP in Poland may not be reached before the year 2000. Not surprisingly, the people feel bewildered or even deceived. This frustration is likely to result in calls for social and economic protectionism during the transition and, if not addressed properly, may give rise to frequent changes of governments.

The distribution of the burden of the costs of the transition, which can be observed in the east European countries (as discussed in the preceding section), works clearly against the short-term economic interests of workers and other wage earners, and also affects low income groups more severely. Indeed, the core social groups supporting the transformation are bound to be its primary victims.[82]

The result is that shortly after the transformation process begins, an enormous *expectation gap* emerges. With illusions disappearing, the popular support for necessary reforms weakens, and the socio-political base of new governments quickly disintegrates. This is the most dangerous challenge facing the new democracies in eastern Europe. The resulting political turmoil ap-

---

[81] It is sometimes argued that countries can achieve growth and at the same time guarantee everyone a floor level of income and employment security, i.e. the trade-off between equity and efficiency does not exist, at least in the short run. While this may be true for relatively minor policy changes which can be welfare-improving, the equity vs. efficiency trade-off certainly exists in case of fundamental systemic revolutions, when changes affect both the incentive structure and the institutional framework of the economy (for a discussion of conceptual issues, see e.g., K.J. Arrow, "The Trade-Off Between Growth and Equity", in H.I. Greenfield, A.M. Levenson, W. Hamowitch, E. Rotwein (eds.), *"Theory of Economic Efficiency: Essays in Honor of Abba P. Lerner"*, The MIT Press, Cambridge, Mass., 1979, pp.1-12; for empirical evidence, see E.K. Browning, W.R. Johnson, "The Trade-Off between Equality and Efficiency", *Journal of Political Economy*, 1984, vol.92, No.2).

[82] This explains the astonishing eclipse of the Solidarity labour union in Poland. As the symbol of anti-totalitarian resistance, Solidarity won national elections by a landslide in 1989; but immediately after the political breakthrough, the union was manoeuvred into an awkward and politically unsustainable situation: on the one hand it was politically committed to support the new, democratic government and thus its very restrictive economic policy (this government was after all installed by Solidarity itself), while on the other hand it was coming under strong pressure from rank-and-file workers organizations to protect their economic interests against the hardships of stabilization policies. As it quickly turned out, Solidarity, with its functions torn apart between defending workers' interests and serving as a shock-absorber for the government, was clearly unable to accommodate these two entirely opposite policy courses. The union split into several parties and lost much of its political prestige and reputation during 1990-1991. In mid-1989, after the Round-Table Conference, Solidarity enjoyed the support of 65-70 per cent of the Polish population. In the first free parliamentary elections held in October 1991 the union won only 6 per cent of parliamentary seats.

Interestingly, there are historical analogies to this situation. In the late 1920s labour governments in western Europe found themselves in a similar position: having committed themselves to pursue a policy of a stable currency, they were unable to defend workers' interests. The unavoidable result was their removal from power (K. Polanyi, *The Great Transformation*, Second edition, Beacon Press, Boston, 1957).

pears to be in essence *the crisis of "disillusion"* : its symptoms are perhaps most clearly visible in Poland, Romania and Bulgaria, i.e., those countries where living standards prior to the stabilization were already at relatively low levels.

The change in the overall social mood in eastern Europe offers both an opportunity and poses a challenge. An opportunity, as it is only through realistic programmes applied persistently over many years, if not decades, that the east European countries may expect to receive the benefits of the market system and approach the standard of living of the developed market economies. Finally, it is a big illusion to believe that the shift to the market system can transform a backward centrally planned economy overnight and painlessly into an affluent market economy. It is also a challenge, as, after decades of waiting for a better future, the population of the eastern countries may not have the patience and indeed the moral or economic strength to wait long for the tangible improvements in its everyday life, which had been promised both from inside and outside. Thus it is highly important, both for the new leaders in the east as well as (and perhaps even more) for western governments to assess realistically the endurance of the population, to draw adequate lessons from recent experience and to apply them, as soon possible, in future political and economic policies.

(vii) Political lessons

Market-oriented transformation involves some recession in the initial stage and entails a significant redistribution of income and wealth. These reforms affect the living standards of the population and therefore cannot be carried out by governments which lack political legitimacy.[83] *Political approval* for reforms is thus indispensable for a successful transformation. The political space required for transformation can in principle be obtained either through a democratic upheaval (as in Poland, Hungary or Czechoslovakia), or through a kind of "social pact", or (exceptionally) through authoritarian rule.

But the initial political support in most cases proved *short-lived*. The social costs of transition, resulting from the necessary stabilization policies, are bound to erode popular support for the reforms. That is why governments should avoid making overly optimistic statements about reform prospects and should undertake unpopular measures early in the reform programme. On the other hand, the programme should be able to bring about some improvement in living standards soon after its introduction; if it fails to do so, a dangerous expectations gap emerges. In Poland, this critical period lasted for only about nine months; perhaps it would have been longer, had the presidential campaign in the autumn of 1990 not been dominated by highly critical (at times unfair) anti-government propaganda. In Romania, workers' protests and a lack of consensus over the required path of reform led to the fall of Mr. Roman's government less than a year after the beginning of the stabilization programme. In Czechoslovakia, the "grace" period seems to be longer, probably because of relatively better initial economic conditions there. In Hungary too, where the fall in living standards appears to be the smallest, society is demonstrating more patience.

The main social groups (wage-earners, farmers) are likely to be the *main losers* in the first stage of transformation. Their incomes should be protected to some extent, to preserve their support for reforms and to prevent the reform process from being stopped or reversed. But the protection scheme adopted should not interfere with emerging market mechanisms; direct labour subsidies or consumption subsidies would thus be superior to price controls or wage indexation.

An efficient mechanism of solving *social conflicts* has to be established, allowing a consensus on the critical policy issues to be reached between the main social groups. Parliamentary institutions may be too weak and unstable to perform this task; so it may be necessary to establish an institutional framework for direct negotiations between unions, farmers, business groups and the government for solving immediate conflicts. This social-pact type of solution should not be designed to circumvent parliament, but to speed up formal procedures and allow for more efficient bargaining.

Frequent elections at the national level should be avoided, for they induce needless political conflicts and make the people believe that a simple change of government may radically improve the situation.

There is a great danger of *populism* in the course of transformation. Whereas imaginative economic policies may reduce this danger to a point, in no case should populist demagoguery be left unanswered. An efficient information policy and popular economic education should be high on the list of priority actions for governments starting the transformation process.

If the first stage of transformation fails to meet popular expectations, necessary market reforms may be delayed because of a lack of social actors with a strong interest in the transition to the market economy. If the middle class is weak and dispersed, the reform-oriented government will have to represent interests of a "phantom" class, thus acting in the interests of future generations rather than of any existing social group.

This leads to *political instability*. The clash of various interests may not be solved through parliamentary procedures as would probably be the case in western Europe. Democratic institutions and practices are still rudimentary, the new political elites lack experience in solving conflicts and accommodating different positions and no patterns of negotiation and cooperation among the various political parties have yet been established. The parties themselves are weak and lack credibility and their constituencies are unstable and mistrustful. Under such circumstances every government committed to genuine market reforms may expect to come under early popular pressure to ease economic policy or to resign. One implication is that frequent changes of governments in east European countries are quite

---

[83] See: D.M. Nuti, "Economic Inertia in the Transitional Economies of eastern Europe", op.cit.

likely. Another is that economic policies may become less and less restrictive over time. The most ominous threat is that political instability will endanger democratic rule and lead to authoritarian government.

(viii) Short-term prospects: the need for political stabilization

Economic prospects for east European countries for 1992 remain bleak and uncertain. In most countries GDP levels are expected to decline further, although a modest recovery may begin in the second half of the year in Poland and Hungary. A stronger upward trend in output is to be expected only in 1993. In the meantime, however, unemployment is bound to rise steadily and real income levels will continue to fall.

The economic situation will continue to be particularly difficult and complicated in the "southern-tier" countries: Albania, Bulgaria, Romania and Yugoslavia. Not only are they less advanced in institutional reforms (except for Yugoslavia) but their economies are still plagued by imbalances and their populations' living standards are much lower than in the "northern-tier" countries. This makes their socio-political situation very precarious.

But the relatively prosperous and fast-reforming economies of Poland, Hungary and Czechoslovakia are also facing difficult challenges. Probably the most important of these is the spread of "reform fatigue". Prolonged recession, anxiety about declining social security and continued hardships, especially when compared with the rapidly growing fortunes and the ostentatious consumption of the emerging entrepreneurial class, are undermining the credibility of democratically appointed governments and are contributing to popular discontent.

The process of reform in east European countries has entered a critical stage. Economic recovery must come soon in order to reduce social tensions; otherwise the reforming governments will sooner or later be forced to give in to demands for more economic interventionism and social protection, thus obstructing the market mechanism and slowing down the necessary restructuring. As a result, irreparable damage may be inflicted on east European societies through a loss of confidence in market systems and democratic institutions. In this sense, economic recovery is a necessary condition for maintaining political stability in eastern Europe.

On the other hand, political stability is also an essential prerequisite for the continuation of economic reforms in those countries. Free markets do require political democracy but for them to be firmly established, time and patience are needed as well. Reforming governments should be offered both: time is needed to prepare and implement decisions and patience is required before the first positive results appear. Otherwise, no structural reform can succeed. However, at present no economic upturn is seen in the immediate future and time and patience are quickly running out. How can this vicious circle be broken and reversed?

It seems that some relief could come from a concerted effort to boost the economies in transition through a combination of domestic and international measures. First of all, a gradual shift in economic priorities from stabilization to growth has to take place in the transition countries, with a broad range of policy instruments assigned to deal with structural changes and institutional reforms.[84] The role of the state in overcoming recession and enhancing smooth and vigorous restructuring will probably have to be greater than was originally envisaged. Although the danger of excessive and distortionary government intervention cannot be excluded, it would be unreasonable to assume that this type of intervention will always be welfare-reducing, as it was under central planning. The emerging market mechanism should not be inhibited by state intervention but, instead, government actions should strengthen and amplify the market forces in those areas where they are weak or distorted.

However, a change in economic policies alone will not be sufficient. It is clear that the domestic potential for economic recovery in the east European economies is limited, at least in the short and medium run. Investment levels are low and falling, capital resources are meagre and production is not competitive. These constraints can probably only be overcome with the help of a comprehensive external assistance programme, consisting of three key elements: financial assistance for industrial restructuring, technical assistance for institutional remoulding, and enlarged market access to industrialized countries. Several months ago, the ECE secretariat argued for a "Second recovery programme for Europe",[85] which would coordinate the efforts of all providers of international assistance, tailor programmes to the specific needs of the individual east European countries and impose a greater discipline on the transition process. As demonstrated by recent developments in eastern Europe, this call is now even more topical and urgent.

---

[84] This seems to be a thrust of the new economic programme announced by the Polish government in mid-February 1992. The programme marks a departure from the restrictive anti-inflation strategy pursued by two former governments and promises to ease the rigours of market-oriented policies (*Financial Times*, 17 February 1992).

[85] In United Nations Economic Commission for Europe *Economic Bulletin for Europe*, vol.43, New York, 1991.

3.2 OUTPUT AND DEMAND

(i) Output

For eastern Europe as a whole 1991 was the third consecutive year of output contraction. The declines in output are so large that the recession which started in the fall of 1989 could now be described as a depression. In 1991 total output fell on average by 14 per cent in the six east European countries taken together and given a 10 per cent fall in 1990, output has now contracted by almost a quarter since 1988 (tables 3.2.1 and 3.2.2).[86] This represents an enormous loss, equivalent to more than one decade of increments in the pre-recession period. Thus in most east European countries the level of domestic output in 1991 fell to that of 1977-1978, and in Poland, with output falling to its 1974 level (see chart 3.2.1).

Although the fall of output in eastern Europe in 1991 affected all those countries of the region, its magnitude differed widely from country to country, from about 8 per cent in Hungary and Poland to 13-16 per cent in Czechoslovakia, Romania and Yugoslavia and 23 per cent in Bulgaria.[87] The better performance of Hungary in 1991, and also its smaller cumulative output contraction from the start of recession (about 11 per cent), can be explained to a large extent by the earlier start and the more gradual implementation of reforms there. Poland and Yugoslavia felt the burden of stabilization policies in 1990, with Czechoslovakia, Bulgaria and Romania beginning such policies in 1991.

The present low level of output is the consequence of a variety of factors, some of them inherited from the past and some linked to the rapid transformation of the former centrally planned economies into market economies. Together with the external shocks coming from the collapse of former CMEA trade, they produced a recession whose depth is comparable with the economic depression of the 1930s. These developments took many professional economists and national policymakers by surprise. While they assumed that the transition to a market economy would be accompanied by a fall in output, they did not expect such a steep decline. They also demonstrated how feeble the former centrally planned economies can be in the face of market forces and indicated the scale of adjustment facing the economies in transition. A disturbing feature of recent economic developments is the fact that the gap between the economic level and living standards of the developed market economies and east European countries has largely widened as production and consumption have fallen dramatically in the last two years. Since the prospects for narrowing this gap are not so bright as originally believed, this only adds to a disillusion which can compromise the social consensus needed for a continuation of reforms.

In explaining the significant output contraction in eastern Europe, it should be borne in mind that some of the fall is due to the elimination of production lines which did not satisfy the needs of consumers (the over-development of the heavy and defence industries and the stockpiling of unsaleable production are well known examples). In addition, reported statistics in these countries do not often capture fully the output in the private sector and misleading price statistics can overstate the fall in output.[88] However, the fall is of such a magnitude that the above factors can explain only a small part of the decline. The vast majority of the fall is due to demand constraints and a low supply response to changed conditions.

A precise quantification of the reasons for the decline in output is not feasible at the moment. It is even impossible to assess with any precision the extent to which the decline in output was caused by the fall in domestic demand, supply constraints or by external factors. However, given the high share of personal consumption in NMP (or GDP) used and its sharp fall in most east European countries in 1991 (Poland being an exception), a large share of the output fall can be attributed to private consumption. Two other important expenditure components of NMP used — public consumption and investment — also contributed to the output contraction. In part, these falls were the result of the tight fiscal and monetary policies pursued in all east European countries but some of the large falls in investment were caused by the uncertainties of the transition period and the clouded expectations of many enterprises as far as their future development was concerned. Supply constraints of both domestic and external origin played a role in Albania, Bulgaria, Romania and Yugoslavia, where energy and material input supplies were limited by the shortage of foreign

---

[86] Since the eastern countries have completed (Hungary, Poland) or have started the transformation of their traditional system of macroeconomic indicators, based on material product system (MPS) to the system of national accounts (SNA) with GDP or GNP as the basic measure of production (this includes gross value added in both the material and non-material spheres), the reported figures on overall output changes thus reflect a mixture of different indicators. They are not always comparable. NMP produced generally falls faster than GDP because it does not include non-material services and is net of depreciation. Both components grow faster (or decline slower) than net value added in the material sphere (NMP). The difference between the rate of growth of GDP and NMP can be large. Moreover, the transformation of the system of statistics to market economy conditions brings in its initial phase many difficulties, particularly in capturing the economic activities of the private sector and big price changes. Thus, the data on output and demand are not always reliable and mutually consistent, although the situation varies considerably from country to country.

[87] The figures on output changes are expressed in terms of GDP produced for all countries except for Yugoslavia, where value added in the material sphere including depreciation is used as a basic measure of total output.

[88] For example in Czechoslovakia, the price deflators are based on the weights of the year 1989 and the contraction of industrial output in 1991 is believed to have been overstated. See the article by K. Dyba, Czech Minister for Economic Policy and Development, *Hospodarske noviny*, 6 August 1991, p.8.

CHART 3.2.1

Net material product produced
(Indices, 1975 = 100)

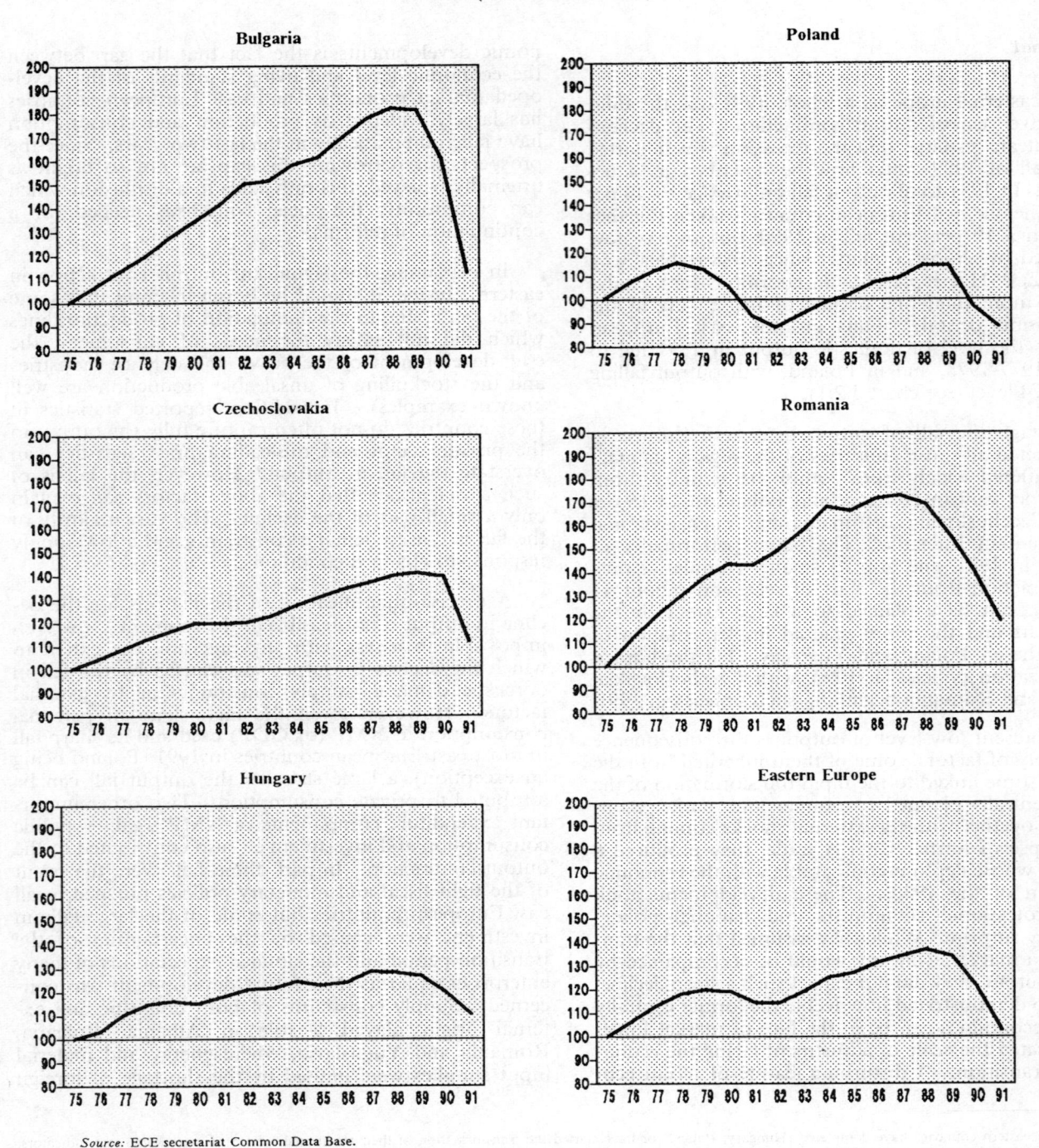

currency and disruptions in domestic production. Overall, it seems that domestic demand and supply factors,[89] coupled with the collapse of trade among the

---

[89] Some studies have tried to quantify the share of internal and external factors in the contraction of aggregate output in 1991. However, their results differ

TABLE 3.2.1
Eastern Europe: Basic economic indicators, 1986-1991
(Percentage change over same period of preceding year)

Country or group, indicator	1986	1987	1988	1989	1990 Jan.-Sept.	1990 Full year	1991 Jan.-March	1991 Jan.-June	1991 Jan.-Sept.	1991 Jan.-Dec.
National product [a]	3.7	1.8	1.2	-1.4	..	-9.5	..	..	..	-14.1
Industrial output [b]	4.4	2.7	2.8	-0.5	-15.5	-14.7	-13.7	-15.6	-17.6	-19.1
Agricultural output [b]	3.9	-3.5	1.5	0.8	..	-3.7	..	..	..	-0.9
Gross investment	4.2	0.8	-	-1.5	..	-13.7	-24.1 [c]	-23.5 [c]	..	-22.7 [c]
Export [c]	0.2	2.0	5.2	-2.8	-11.1	-11.0	-10.7 [d]	-5.7 [d]	-9.9 [d]	-16*
Import [c]	5.5	1.2	2.7	0.7	-3.6	-5.8	0.4 [d]	9.9 [d]	5.8 [d]	-15*

Source: ECE secretariat Common Data Base, compiled from national statistics supplemented with secretariat estimates. Unless otherwise noted, all measures are in real terms.

[a] Net material product in general, but gross material product for Yugoslavia; gross domestic product (SNA) for Hungary, Poland and Romania in 1991 (see notes to table 3.2.2).
[b] Gross output.
[c] Excluding Yugoslavia.
[d] Nominal US dollar values.

TABLE 3.2.2
Eastern Europe: National product,[a] 1988-1992
(Annual percentage change)

	1988	1989	1990	1991	1992 Forecast
Albania	-0.5	11.8	-13.1	..	..
Bulgaria	2.4	-0.3	-11.5	-25.7	..
Czechoslovakia	2.3	0.7	-1.1	-19.5	-(3-6)
Hungary [b]	-0.1	0.4	-3.3	-(7-9)	0-2
Poland [b]	4.1	0.2	-11.6	-(8-10)	-
Romania	-2.0	-8.0	-9.9	-13.0 [b]	..
Yugoslavia [c]	-1.7	0.6	-8.5	-15.0 *	..
Eastern Europe	1.2	-1.4	-9.5	-14.1	..

Source: ECE secretariat Common Data Base, based on national statistical publications or direct communications the ECE secretariat.

[a] Net material product (produced) unless otherwise noted.
[b] Gross domestic product.
[c] Gross material product (value added of the material sphere including depreciation).

former CMEA countries were the main causes of the deep recession.[90]

Although the recession in the east is general, there are large inter-country differences both in its severity and in the forces which are shaping it. This is mainly due to largely differing initial internal and external conditions of the countries concerned and the differences in the transformation process — its start, scope, ways and speed. In this sense each east European country represents a special case with many specific features. Available national statistical reports on economic developments in 1991 enumerate different causes of output contraction. In *Bulgaria* output decline and its unevenenness is linked with supply shortages, insufficient orders and unclear production programmes. In *Czechoslovakia* the transformation process, stabilization policies and unfavourable external conditions are mainly responsible for a sharp drop in output. In *Hungary* the recession stems mainly from structural factors. Some positive signs have appeared in the shift of exports on western markets, in the establishment of growing number of new firms and relatively large inflow of foreign capital. In *Poland* a basic cause of output decline is seen in strongly depressed level of domestic and external demand. In *Romania* the shortage of material and energy inputs, implementation of the economic reforms and certain conjunctural factors affected decisively economic performance in 1991.

Simplifying to some extent, two groups of countries can be distinguished. The first group of countries consists of those where the radical economic reforms were started earlier (although important differences in this respect exist between them too) and where the decline in output reflects the impact of stabilization policies and determined efforts to speed up the pace of economic transformation. Czechoslovakia, Hungary and

---

widely. Thus, the study of Economic Institute of the Czechoslovak Academy of Sciences found that the effects of internal and external factors were roughly in the proportion 70:30. However, after corrections the proportion was 50:50. See *Politicka ekonomie*, No.9-10, 1991, p.727.

[90] It should be noted that the official authorities in Czechoslovakia, Hungary and Poland attributed a very important role in output contraction to external factors. Thus, Czechoslovak Finance Minister V. Klaus mainly blamed external factors for the fall of output. See BBC, *Summary of World Broadcasts*, EE/1262, 23 December 1991, p.B/5. Hungarian Finance Minister M. Kupa in presenting the budget for 1992 emphasized that the collapse of east European trade markedly affected the fall in output in 1991. See BBC, *Summary of World Broadcasts*, EE/1255, 14 December 1991, p.C2/2. In a similar tone, the former Polish Minister of Finance L. Balcerowicz stressed that the Polish economy was exposed to greater than planned external shocks and that their exceptional nature and impact were still not fully appreciated. See his speech in the Polish Sejm, BBC, *Summary of World Broadcasts*, EE/1165, 31 August 1991, p.C1/1.

TABLE 3.2.3

Eastern Europe: Domestic production and absorption,[a] 1989-1991
(Annual percentage change)

Country and period	NMP produced (1)	NMP used[a] (2)	Consumption Total (3)	Consumption Personal[b] (4)	Consumption Social[c] (5)	Accumulation Total (6)	Net fixed capital formation (7)	Changes in stocks (8)	Retail trade turnover (9)	Real income per capita (10)	Gross investment (11)
Bulgaria											
1989	-0.3	2.0	2.9	2.8	3.4	-0.6	-11.2	6.2	0.8	-4.8	-10.1[d]
1990	-11.5	-9.2	-4.9	-8.6	14.1	-22.6	-38.8	-14.4	-9.3	..	-12.0[d]
1991	-25.7	..	..	..	..	..	..	..	-52.8	-45 *	-49.3
Czechoslovakia											
1989	0.7	3.2	3.6	1.8	7.3	0.8	-22.7	79.7	2.3	1.8	1.6
1990	-1.1	4.7	3.4	4.8	0.6	12.0	-12.5	47.3	1.3	-1.3	7.7
1991	-19.5	-32.4	-22.9	-33.1	-1.9	-83.1	..	..	-39.9	-29 *	-36
Hungary[e]											
1989	0.4	0.6	0.8	2.3	-6.3	-0.1	5.1	-25.5	-0.2	2.5	5.1
1990	-3.3	-4.0	-2.7	-3.6	2.6	-7.9	-8.7	-2.3	-7.6	-1.6	- 8.7
1991	-(7-9)	-(7-8) *	-(6-7) *	-(8-10)	(3-5)	-(3-5)	..	..	-28.2	- (2-4)	-(10-12) *
Poland											
1989	-0.2	0.1	-1.7	0.8	-4.2	7.1	-7.4	36.7	-2.7	6.2	-2.4
1990	-14.9	-19.8	-13.0	-15.8	3.4	-45.0	-27.8	..	-17.4	-14.9	-10.1
1991[e]	-(8-10)	..	..	6-8	..	..	..	..	..	..	-8.0
Romania											
1989	-8.0	-5.0*	0.8	..	..	-23.8	-5.8	..	-1.3	2.4	-1.5
1990	-9.9	11.1*	12.0	..	..	7.2	-65.9	..	7.3	17.9	-38.3
1991	-13.0[e]	..	..	..	..	..	..	..	-27.7	..	-16.8
Yugoslavia											
1989	0.6	2.1	..	1.0	-1.8	..	0.5	7.2	..	25.3	0.5
1990	-7.6	-3.6	..	2.5	1.1	..	-7.0	-15.3	..	-21.9	-7.0
1991	-15 *	..	..	..	..	..	..	..	..	-7 *	..

Source: ECE secretariat Common Data Base, based on national statistical publications or direct communications the ECE secretariat.

a "Net material product produced" and "net material product used for consumption and accumulation" (material balance system), unless otherwise specified.
b Volume of consumer goods and material services supplied to the population.
c Consumption of material goods in institutions providing amenities and social welfare services.
d At current prices.
e Gross domestic product.

Poland can be placed in this group. Restrictive fiscal and monetary policies and severe controls on aggregate demand coupled with external shocks were the main causes of falling output in these countries.

In *Czechoslovakia* the introduction of stabilization policies at the beginning of 1991 led to a sharp and much deeper than expected fall in output. After declining by some 1 per cent in 1990, NMP was officially forecast to fall by 5 to 10 per cent in 1991. Actually, in 1991 real NMP produced and GDP fell by almost 20 and 16 per cent, respectively. This abrupt downturn in economic activity can be compared with Polish experience in 1990.

In *Hungary,* the drop of production in 1991 was also greater than expected but nevertheless it was significantly lower than in Czechoslovakia. Forecasts for GDP change made at the beginning of 1991 pointed to a decline of 3-4 per cent, but the outcome was significantly worse (a fall of 7-9 per cent). The earlier start of economic reforms and less tight fiscal and monetary policy, as well as the growing contribution of the private sector, seem to be the main reasons why the fall in output in Hungary was lower.

In contrast to the optimistic expectations of resumed economic growth, *Poland* experienced the second year of a sharp downturn in economic activity, with GDP falling by 12 and 8-10 per cent in 1990 and 1991, respectively. This largely reflects the combined impact of tight domestic policies and the loss of eastern markets due to the collapse of CMEA trade. However, strong private sector activity has helped to soften the downturn.

Albania, Bulgaria and Romania belong to the second group of countries. These countries embarked on the transition from a centrally planned economic system to a market oriented one later (actually in the course of 1991), with highly centralized systems and large structural imbalances. The old centralized supply system has collapsed and has not been replaced by a functioning market system. The fall in overall output thus reflects the interaction of supply side constraints (worsening shortages of industrial inputs, including energy shortages, and import constraints for fuels and material inputs)[91] and the weakening of demand, both at home and abroad. The fall in output is larger than in the first group of countries.

---

91 In 1990 oil supplies from the Soviet Union to five east European countries were more than 23 per cent below the previous year's level. However, Soviet oil deliveries to Bulgaria and Romania in the same year dropped by 32 and 36.6 per cent, respectively. In 1991 Bulgarian oil imports from the former Soviet Union decreased by 60 per cent (in the first three quarters against the corresponding period of the preceding year) and Romanian imports of oil dropped from 16 million tons in 1990 to 8.4 million tons in 1991 and Soviet oil imports have virtually disappeared.

TABLE 3.2.4

Eastern Europe: Gross fixed investment, 1986-1991
(Percentage change from same period of the preceding year)

	1986	1987	1988	1989	1990	1991 Jan.-March	1991 Jan.-June	1991 Jan.-Sept.	1991 Jan.-Dec.
Albania	..	..	..	..	..	..	..	..	..
Bulgaria	13.0	0.3	4.5	-10.1	-12.0	-33.0	-33.0*	..	-49.3
Czechoslovakia	1.4	4.4	4.1	1.6	7.7	-27.7	-28.3	-29.3	-36.0
Hungary	6.5	9.8	-9.1	0.5	-8.7	-15.0*	-15.0*	-15.0*	-11.0*
Poland	5.1	4.2	5.4	-2.4	-10.1	-13.8	-13.0	-11.0	-8.0
Romania	1.1	-1.4	-2.2	-1.6	-35.0	-32.0	-30.1	-24.1	-16.8
Yugoslavia	3.5	-5.1	-5.8	0.5	-7.0	..	..	..	..
Eastern Europe [a]	4.2	0.8	-	-1.5	-13.7	-24.1	-23.5	..	-22.7

Source: ECE secretariat Common Data Base, based on published national statistics and communication to the ECE secretariat.

[a] Excluding Yugoslavia in 1991.

TABLE 3.2.5

Eastern Europe: Volume of foreign trade, 1988-1991
(Annual percentage change)

	Exports 1988	1989	1990	1991 [a]	Imports 1988	1989	1990	1991 [a]
Albania	..	..	..	..	..	..	..	..
Bulgaria	2.4	-2.3	-24.2	neg.	5.3	-4.6	-24.1	neg.
Czechoslovakia	3.2	-2.0	-4.2	-20.0	2.9	2.7	9.7	-35.0
Hungary	5.0	0.3	-4.3	-10.7	-1.9	1.1	-3.4	-2.3
Poland	9.1	0.2	13.7	-1.4	9.4	1.5	-17.9	39.0
Romania	7.4*	-10.8*	-46.0*	neg.	-5.8*	3.7*	4.0*	neg.
Five countries above	5.2	-2.8	-11.0	-16.0*	2.7	0.7	-5.8	-15.0*
Yugoslavia	-1.0	4.8	2.2	neg.	-8.6	13.1	21.9	neg.

Source: ECE secretariat Common Data Base. Where no firm quantification of trade volume change for 1991 was possible, the probable *sign* of the statistic is indicated by *neg.* for (-) or *pos.* for (+). See United Nations Economic Commission for Europe, *Economic Bulletin for Europe*, vol.43, New York, 1991, table 1.3.1 and the discussion in section 2.1 for some very approximate secretariat estimates of the orders of magnitude of the trade volume contraction in 1991.

[a] Preliminary national data or ECE secretariat estimates.

Albania is the poorest country in Europe and the production system of the country has virtually collapsed. There is a severe shortage of energy, material inputs and consumer goods. In 1990 NMP produced contracted by 13 per cent and the fall in output substantially accelerated in 1991. Industrial output in 1991 fell by an estimated 60 per cent.[92] However, comprehensive statistical information is not available.

In *Bulgaria* NMP dropped by about 26 per cent in 1991 (after a 12 per cent decline in 1990), so that output has fallen by more than a third over the last two years. GDP declined by 23 per cent in 1991. It should be noted that the collapse of CMEA trade has hit Bulgaria particularly hard, due to its high previous dependence on trade with the former Soviet Union. In 1991 imports from the east European countries and the Soviet Union decreased dramatically. The availability of fuels, energy and material inputs was thus drastically reduced with large adverse effects on output. Moreover, since Bulgaria was not able to service its large external debt, the inflow of external financing was very limited and imports from the west were severely constrained.

In *Romania* the fall in output started in 1988 and continued for the fourth consecutive year. In 1991, GDP fell by about 13 per cent and the cumulative loss of output was almost one third for the last four years. However, the fall in output in 1991 was not as sharp as in Albania and Bulgaria and domestic output was not so severely constrained by external factors as in Albania and Bulgaria. It is difficult to judge with any precision whether this was caused by differences in economic policies or by more favourable economic conditions. Romania was less dependent on eastern markets, had a very low initial foreign debt and has oil and natural gas resources which can meet a part of its domestic energy needs.

Yugoslavia is a special case since the reforms which were introduced in 1990 were abruptly interrupted by national hostilities and the outbreak of civil war. Output contracted strongly in 1990 and in 1991 it fell by a further 15 per cent. The output level in 1991 thus corresponds to that of 1976. The civil war and the imposition of European Community sanctions on 9 November contributed to disruption in the production system of the country at the end of the year. In contrast, a good agricultural performance in 1991 (a 7.6 per cent growth of agricultural production) partially compensated for the fall of output in other sectors.

---

[92] See *Neue Zürcher Zeitung*, 25 February 1992.

In assessing the sharp fall of output it should be emphasized that the larger than expected drop in output was — beside the impact of stabilization policies, external shocks and disturbances linked with the transformation process — also caused by the low flexibility and adaptability of the supply side. Declining investment, the monopolistic positions of many enterprises, growing uncertainty and management problems were responsible for much of the poor supply response.

(ii) Domestic absorption

Developments in *domestic absorption* reflected the differing extent of domestic and external adjustment in individual countries. Although relevant data on domestic demand are sketchy and not yet available for all countries, it appears that in countries which pursued severe stabilization policies and external adjustment to attain a foreign trade surplus (mainly by squeezing imports), NMP used domestically has fallen faster than total output. This is the case for Bulgaria, Czechoslovakia and probably Romania (table 3.2.3). In Bulgaria appropriate information is limited, but sharp falls in retail sales (a proxy for private consumption) and in investment (by about 50 per cent) suggest that the fall in domestic absorption was larger than in output. Czechoslovakia registered an almost 5 per cent increase in NMP used in 1990 so that the fall of 32 per cent in 1991 was even more abrupt. Romania protected consumption from falling in 1990, but, after the implementation of stabilization policies in 1991, retail sales fell by 27.7 per cent and investment in the public sector by 16.8 per cent. In the above countries, a faster fall of NMP used as compared with NMP produced indicates an improvement in the real foreign balance. In Poland severe stabilization measures implemented in 1990 resulted in a 20 per cent decline of NMP used. For 1991 the picture is different, since incomes policies have been eased and private consumption increased. Since investment declined by 8 per cent, it can be gauged that in 1991 the fall in domestic absorption was less than in domestic output. This is reflected in a substantial deterioration in the foreign balance. In Hungary, the fall in GDP used in 1991 was substantially smaller (about 7 per cent, slightly less than the fall in production) than in the countries which only started to implement stabilization policies in 1991.

Real *gross investment* in 1991 declined by almost 23 per cent in the five east European countries combined, bringing the fall in investment expenditures in the group to more than one third in the last three years. The fall was general, with very sharp declines in Bulgaria (some 50 per cent), Czechoslovakia (36 per cent) and Romania (about 17 per cent). In Hungary and Poland the decline was about 11 and 8 per cent, respectively (table 3.2.4). However, while in Czechoslovakia this was the first recent year when investment has fallen, in the other countries the investment has been falling for several years. Since investment performance was weak in the 1980s, the volume of investment in 1991 is now at a very low level. Thus the process of ageing of fixed assets has continued and even accelerated. Taking into account the fact that the fundamental transformation now under way in east European countries has made a large part of the fixed capital stock technically and economically unviable, the process of restructuring and economic recovery will be slowed down by such strongly depressed investment levels.

The situation in *housing construction* is alarming. The number of new dwellings constructed has fallen to the levels of the end of the 1950s. Thus, for example, in Bulgaria and Romania the number of dwellings constructed in 1991 was respectively 22 per cent (11 months figures) and 50 per cent below the already low level of housing construction in 1990. In 1991 Poland stabilized the housing construction at its level in 1959.[93] The critical situation in housing construction indicates the more general problem of the lack of modern infrastructure. Huge investment will be needed to improve the situation. This can not be fully financed from domestic sources and many projects will have to be financed from external sources.[94]

It seems that investment demand suffered particularly from economic austerity policies. Thus, a restrictive budgetary stance substantially curtailed investment financed from the state budget. Tight monetary policies restricted commercial credits to enterprises and high interest rates made them too expensive for most enterprises. To make things worse, enterprise indebtedness reached historically high levels and business confidence has slumped. The private sector is still small and lacks capital and so cannot significantly change the overall picture.

Large falls in investment in eastern Europe are worrying, since stabilization and structural reforms are mutually intertwined and there is a danger that slow progress in structural changes (due to insufficient investment) may cause difficulties in implementing stabilization policies. The impact of the fall in investment on output and productivity could be partially compensated by further technological progress (linked with the substitution of domestically produced capital goods by technically more advanced imports from the west) and the more efficient use of investment. Limited domestic savings in most countries are coupled with very low direct foreign investments, Hungary being an exception. Privatization may bring some improvement in private capital formation, but in the short to medium term can hardly counterbalance the forces holding back investment activity. Restricted public capital flows thus will probably continue to dominate in the short run.

It should be kept in mind that not only physical investment in machines, but also investment in human capital are necessary for economic recovery. The old system of administrative central planning required in certain fields particular skills not needed in a market

---

[93] The Polish Minister of Regional Economy and Construction A. Diakonow indicated that the satisfaction of adequate housing in Poland will require the annual construction of 360,000 dwellings in the next ten years, while at present the construction is less than one third of this amount. See *Rzeczpospolita*, 20 February 1992, p.1.

[94] Thus in Czechoslovakia the needed inflow of foreign capital is estimated between $12-15 billion in the first half of the 1990s. *Národní hospodárství*, No.7, 1991, p.4.

economy. It is thus likely that some "old" qualifications are now obsolete. The acquisition of new skills, know-how and education necessary for the efficient functioning of a market economy will be a long-term process which will need to be supported by requalification programmes and an increased allocation of resources to training.

Changes in *consumption levels* have not been uniform. While Bulgaria, Czechoslovakia and Romania registered sharp falls in private consumption, the decline was moderate in Hungary and in Poland there was an increase in consumption. The changes in private consumption were mainly determined by the prices and income policies in force. Price liberalization has triggered high rate of inflation (although there were large differences between the countries) which exceeded the growth of wages and incomes with resulting declines in the real incomes of population. These were particularly steep in the countries which have tried to improve their internal balance by squeezing consumer demand. An abrupt fall in real incomes of population in Bulgaria, Czechoslovakia and Romania led to cutting off the spending on all main component parts of private consumption (food, non-food products and services). However, spending on consumer durables was reduced most and services increased their proportion in aggregate consumer spending. Public consumption fell generally less than private consumption in most countries. In contrast, in Poland private consumption increased while public consumption fell significantly. Falling consumption levels and living standards indicate that the costs of the transition to a market economy appear to be high and can result in growing social tensions in most east European countries.

(iii) **Sectoral developments**

A hesitant shift to services?

Any assessment of sectoral developments in east European countries in 1991 can only be tentative since most data on the developments of basic sectors are missing or are incomplete. All the east European countries are in the process of transforming their system of statistics from the material product system (MPS) to the system of national accounting framework (SNA) which gives a broader coverage of economic activities and allows the more comprehensive study of developments in services and/or the so called non-material sphere. Hungary and Poland have progressed furthest in this direction while the other countries have now started to publish selected indicators measured according to the SNA system. Thus a mixture of indicators has to be used in this section.

The development of the *service sector* can be assessed only partially. Available figures on GDP by sector of origin (in current prices) indicate a general shift in favour of services. The share of services in GDP was about 30 per cent in Bulgaria (1989), 38 per cent in Czechoslovakia (1989), 43 per cent in Hungary (1990), 35 per cent in Poland (1991) and 28 per cent in Romania (1990). However, the growth of services has been slower than was originally expected. In Bulgaria, GDP is estimated to have fallen by 23 per cent with the output of the non-material sphere falling by 14 per cent in 1991. In Hungary, the fall in real GDP and gross value added in services (both material and non-material) was more or less the same between 1987 and 1990. In Poland, the output of non-material services grew only moderately in 1985-1989 and stagnated in 1990. In Romania, the output of total services virtually stagnated between 1986 and 1990. In 1991 marketable services rendered to population (including the private sector) fell by 13 per cent in real terms.[95]

The main reasons for the slower than expected shift to services lie in the constraints on the supply side (limited investments particularly as far as the large capital-intensive projects in transport and communications are concerned), and on the demand side, which has been strongly constrained by restrictive budgetary policies and falling real incomes of population. Falling output levels in industry and agriculture have hit the transport and trade sectors, which are closely linked with the performance of the goods producing sectors, particularly hard. Health and education were adversely affected by tight fiscal policies. However, these general trends can hide important differences. It is likely that some services with high growth potential such as communications, banking, finance and insurance, consultancy and business services and tourism, in some east European countries have recently increased. Thus, in Hungary, business, financial and computer services grew rapidly (also due to foreign direct investment in this sphere), while health, education and administration are likely to have declined in real terms. In Poland, communications were the only sector which has registered output growth in recent years.

Industrial slump deteriorates

The contraction of industrial output in most countries was steeper than of NMP produced. After a sharp decline of 15 per cent in 1990, it fell further by about 19 per cent in 1991 (table 3.2.6). Thus, gross industrial production has fallen by almost one third since 1989. The dramatic fall in industrial output in 1991 was mainly due to depressed domestic demand, collapse of former CMEA trade, growing competition from imported industrial goods, particularly in countries which introduced internal convertibility of their currencies, and supply constraints. The deep industrial depression reveals the enormous complexity of the adjustment process in the former centrally planned economies.

In assessing the industrial slump in 1991, two observations are worth noting. *First,* the downturn was much deeper than envisaged, with falls even in those countries which had expected some recovery after the deep contraction in 1990. *Second,* industrial output in most countries weakened as the year went on and thus it is likely that in most countries the decline will continue in 1992, albeit at a decelerating rate.

---

[95] It should be noted that the output of services is still not fully captured in the official statistics given the incomplete recording of private activities in this area and difficulties in the measurement of the output of services which are subsidized.

TABLE 3.2.6

Eastern Europe: Industrial output, 1989-1991

(Percentage change over same period of preceding year)

	1989	1990 Jan.-March	1990 Jan.-June	1990 Jan.-Sept.	1990 Jan.-Dec.	1991 Jan.-March	1991 Jan.-June	1991 Jan.-Sept.	1991 Jan.-Dec.
Albania [a]	8.5	..	..	..	-11.1	..	..	..	-60.0*
Bulgaria	2.2	-8.5	-10.8	-13.0	-14.1	-21.0*	-29.1	-28.1	-27.3
Czechoslovakia	0.8	-2.9	-3.0	-3.7	-3.7	-10.5	-14.3	-19.8	-23.1
Hungary	-2.5	-6.3	-6.8	-6.6	-5.0	-8.7	-14.2	-16.6	-19.1
Poland	-0.5	-27.8	-28.0	-25.0	-23.3	-5.5	-9.3	-11.0	-11.9
Romania	-2.1	-18.4	-18.8	-20.6	-19.8	-17.0	-16.6	-17.7	-18.7
Yugoslavia	0.9	-7.0	-11.0	-10.0	-10.3	-21.1	-17.4	-18.3	-20.7
Eastern Europe	-0.5	-14.5	-16.5	-15.5	-14.7	-13.7	-15.6	17.7	-19.1

Sources: National statistical yearbooks and short-term reports; ECE secretariat estimates.

[a] Net value added in industry.

Although the fall in east European industrial output was general, its extent differed widely. The drop in industrial output was 12 per cent in Poland, almost 20 per cent in Hungary, more than 20 per cent in Czechoslovakia, Romania[96] and Yugoslavia, while in Bulgaria it was close to 27 per cent. In Albania, the least industrialized country in Europe, the contraction was even 60 per cent.

There were a number of common factors behind the fall in industrial output in 1991. Their relative importance however varied from country to country – and, of course, there were additional country-specific reasons for the decline. While restrictive policies depressing domestic demand coupled with the collapse of CMEA trade were the main factors contributing to the fall of output in Czechoslovakia, Hungary and Poland, the collapse of industrial production in the other countries was exacerbated by worsening shortages of energy and material inputs due to disturbances in domestic production and distribution systems and hard currency shortages, which sharply restricted necessary imports of fuels and production inputs.

The dynamic growth of industrial production in the private sector is a positive sign. But given the very low share of the private sector in total industrial output, this could not compensate for the sharp fall of output in the state sector. Developments in this sphere are nevertheless encouraging: in Poland, for example, the production of private industry in 1991 grew by one quarter and its share in total industrial production reached almost 25 per cent.

The decline in industrial production levels in 1991 was accompanied by a slower decline in industrial employment, with consequent falls in industrial labour productivity. These were substantial and exceeded 10 per cent in most countries. Thus, in Bulgaria, Czechoslovakia, Hungary and Romania labour productivity in industry declined by 10, 14, 11 and 12 per cent respectively in 1991.

The interpretation of change in the product mix of industry is difficult since the structural change is taking place under conditions of sharply falling output and various shocks of both internal and external origin. The better than average performance in the energy sector was caused mainly by a substitution of domestic fuels and energy for more expensive and not always available imports, particularly from the former Soviet Union. Metallurgy was hit hard by depressed domestic demand and lost CMEA export markets: in Bulgaria the production of the metallurgy industry declined by more than 40 per cent and in Czechoslovakia, Poland and Romania by more than 20 per cent in 1991. The chemical industry was heavily affected by reduced oil imports, particularly from the former Soviet Union. The decline of engineering was generally steeper than of total industrial output in most countries, reflecting the collapse of the former CMEA market (most of the east European countries were exporters of engineering products, particularly to the former Soviet Union) and a more than proportional fall in investment demand. Difficulties in the conversion of the defence industry to civilian uses worked to the same end. Light and food-processing industries suffered from sharply falling internal demand, particularly in countries adopting restrictive policies and severe controls on aggregate demand, such as Bulgaria and Czechoslovakia. Only in Poland did foodstuffs production increase slightly in 1991, after a sharp decline in 1990. This was mainly due to a revival of domestic demand in 1991. However, output of Polish light industry declined by 13 per cent, as consumers preferred imported consumer goods.

Weak performance of construction sector

The available data on *construction activity*, which are still sketchy and not fully comparable, indicate that the fall in construction output widely differed, from 7 per cent in Poland to about 60 per cent in Bulgaria. In the latter country and in Czechoslovakia (a decline by 31 per cent) the drop was much steeper than in industry. This development resulted mainly from a sharp decline in investment demand, which was caused by restrictive monetary and fiscal policies, a lack of domestic capital, high interest rates, but also by enterprises' uncertainty about the future. In Poland, output

---

[96] Romanian statistical report on economic developments in 1991 contains two figures on industrial output change in 1991: a 18.7 and 22 per cent decline. The former is adjusted for the number of working days.

TABLE 3.2.7

Gross agricultural production, 1986-1991
(Annual percentage change)

	1986	1987	1988	1989	1990	1991
Bulgaria						
Total	11.7	-3.5	0.9	1.2	-8.6	-6.4
Crop	22.7	-8.8	-0.3	5.3	-14.0	3.2
Animal	3.7	-1.9	0.4	-2.7	-3.7	-15.7
Czechoslovakia						
Total	0.6	0.9	2.9	1.8	-3.5	-8.8
Crop	-2.5	1.8	4.0	1.7	-3.6	1.5
Animal	2.9	0.3	2.1	2.0	-3.5	-16.4
Hungary						
Total	2.4	-2.0	4.3	-1.3	-3.8	-3.0
Crop	3.7	-5.5	7.5	0.1	-7.8	9.0
Animal	1.1	1.5	1.5	-2.7	0.2	-(13-15)
Poland						
Total	5.0	-2.3	1.2	1.5	-2.2	-2.0
Crop	6.3	-2.0	-0.3	2.7	0.1	-3.9
Animal	3.2	-2.7	3.2	-0.1	-5.2	-1.0
Romania						
Total	-5.5	-8.9	5.8	-5.0	-2.9	1.2
Crop	-8.5	-14.0	8.5	-1.8	-7.2	2.9
Animal	-1.4	-2.5	3.0	-8.9	2.1	-1.0
Yugoslavia						
Total	11.0	-4.4	-3.6	5.0	-4.8	7.6
Crop [a]	11.0	-12.0	-6.0	10.0	-8.8	..
Animal	2.0	1.0	-4.0	-1.0	-3.0	..
Eastern Europe						
Total	3.9	-3.5	1.5	0.8	-3.7	-0.9
Crop	4.1	-6.4	1.3	3.2	-5.0	0.7 [b]
Animal	1.8	-1.1	1.1	-2.2	-2.5	-6.7 [b]

Source: ECE secretariat Common Data Base, based on national statistics.

a Excluding fruits growing and viticulture.
b Excluding Yugoslavia.

in the construction sector fell by less than industrial output and the first signs of revival have appeared. This is linked with the dynamic performance of private construction firms which increased their output by one third. In Hungary and Poland, the private sector has already gained a strong position in construction and in the latter country it has even become predominant.

Agricultural production continues to fall

In 1991, there was a drop in gross agricultural production in the six east European countries taken together, but the decline of 1 per cent in 1991 was substantially less than a 3.7 per cent decline in 1990 (table 3.2.7). The main reasons for the agricultural slump lie in a collapse of export and domestic demand for food, in sharp shifts in terms of trade against agriculture and in the transformation process now under way in the east European countries. While grain production increased in most countries due to better weather conditions, a sizeable loss of output was registered in animal production. The impact of price liberalization and the elimination of large subsidies for foodstuffs led to sharp price increases which strongly diminished domestic demand, particularly for more expensive food products as meat. In Bulgaria, Czechoslovakia and Hungary, animal production dropped by about 15 per cent in 1991. Poland is an exception due to a revival of domestic demand in 1991. As a result, livestock numbers fell substantially, which may adversely affect animal production in 1992.

Crop production recorded substantially better results, since in all east European countries (except Poland) it increased. Only in Czechoslovakia and Poland was grain production in 1991 below the record level of the preceding year, while in the countries which suffered from the drought in 1990 (Bulgaria, Hungary, Romania and Yugoslavia) grain production in 1991 substantially exceeded its year-earlier level.

It is obvious that the transition of former centrally planned economies to the market economies is strongly affecting agriculture. Although there are large inter-country differences, the agrarian reforms generally have two main objectives. *First,* the transformation of ownership relations through the strengthening of the private sector and the transformation of former state-run agricultural enterprises and cooperatives into private farms or cooperatives of real owners. It is possible that the resulting fragmentation of agricultural production could have adverse effects on the efficiency and competitiveness of this sector. In Poland and Yugoslavia, the private sector in agriculture predominated even in the past. In Albania and Romania, privatization through the distribution of land to private farmers has made significant progress. In the other countries, the necessary legislation (the laws on land, restitution and transformation of cooperatives) has been adopted or are under preparation. However, in Bulgaria, Czechoslovakia and Hungary the establishment of new private farms is moving ahead slowly. According to opinion polls most former owners intend to lease the regained land instead of setting up private farms because of the difficulties facing agricultural producers.

The *second* objective is the adjustment of agriculture to market conditions in order to increase the efficiency of production, which is currently substantially lower than in developed market economies. The relatively large share of agriculture in total employment (greater than 20 per in most east European countries) and relatively low labour productivity show the extent of the changes required. In the near future much of the flow of labour out of agriculture will only add to unemployment.[97] It should be noted that the stabilization policies implemented by east European countries, which have curtailed subsidies and liberalized prices, have adversely affected agriculture. In most countries increases in the prices of agricultural inputs outpaced those of agricultural products with resulting financial losses for agricultural enterprises. In addition, the sales crisis caused by strongly depressed domestic demand has substantially weakened the financial position of agricultural enterprises and has led to falling incomes in agriculture. This has squeezed purchases of inputs required for agricultural production and agricultural investment, with possible negative effects on future agricultural output.[98] It is thus very likely that the stock of fixed assets has deteriorated and that the nutrition content of the soil has diminished so that crop yields will become more dependent on weather conditions. Moreover, increased competition from imported agricultural and food products and difficulties facing agricultural export have weakened agricultural enterprises. In this situation most governments adopted measures or programmes aiming at stabilizing the agrarian sector and helping it to adjust to market conditions. These include such measures as providing more credits, the establishment of agricultural market funds, guaranteed prices for selected agricultural products, increased tariffs on imports of agricultural products and export promotion. However, the economic policies adopted in respect of agriculture differ between countries. Thus, it seems that Hungary and Poland are adopting a policy of greater support for agriculture while Czechoslovakia is trying to pursue a less interventionist approach.

In *Albania*, where agriculture is one of most important sectors, the agrarian reform and the privatization of land is considered to be a priority of the economic reforms now under way. According to some reports, about 60 per cent of agricultural land has been distributed to private owners.[99] However, land distribution on the basis of the adopted Land Law has been accompanied by the rapid disintegration of agricultural cooperatives. Foreign aid has thus become badly needed to overcome acute food shortages.

In *Bulgaria*, gross agricultural production in 1991 fell by 6.4 per cent. Grain production in 1991 (8.3 million tons) was above its 1990 level (7.8 million tons). However, this year's wheat crop is 4.3 million tons, which is 1 million tons less than in 1990, and grain is to be imported to replenish the state stocks. Livestock numbers fell significantly, with a resulting large fall in animal production (by 15.7 per cent). Some of the instability of agriculture stems from ongoing economic reforms, which worsened the financial situation of farmers, and from the transformation process which is now under way. In March 1991 the Parliament adopted a Law on Land Reform. The first phase of land reform provides for a return of a maximum of 30 ha to former owners. However, uncertainty remains as for the restitution and existence of agricultural cooperatives.

In *Czechoslovakia*, gross agricultural production in 1991 declined by about 9 per cent, mainly due to a fall in animal production. Grain production of 11.8 million tons was less than in the preceding year of a record harvest (12.6 million tons) but was more or less at the level of the harvests in 1985-1989. An excess supply of agricultural products appeared as a result of rapidly falling domestic demand and difficulties in finding foreign markets. The financial situation of agricultural enterprises has significantly deteriorated due to unfavourable price movements and sales difficulties. In 1991, the Federal Assembly adopted the Law on Agricultural Land and the Law on the Transformation of Cooperatives. The first law is in fact a restitution law, while the second enables the transformation of large and centrally regulated agricultural cooperatives into smaller and more effective units operating on market principles.

In *Hungary*, gross output declined by 3 per cent, mainly due to a strong fall of animal production (by 13-15 per cent). Hungary registered a harvest of 15.4 million tons of grain in 1991, which compares favourably with the 12.5 million tons produced in the preceding poor year. The country is traditionally a net exporter of agricultural and food products but tough competition and protectionism in international agricultural markets has made selling its agricultural surpluses in foreign markets difficult. The transformation of the agricultural economy into a more efficient and competitive sector is envisaged. However, the policy of state support for agriculture is to continue and financial resources provided to agriculture in 1992 are to increase.

In *Poland*, gross agricultural output in 1991 declined by about 2 per cent, mainly on account of lower crop production. Animal production was on the level of the previous year. Grain production of 27.8 million tons was only slightly below the record harvest in 1990. Due to sales difficulties and relatively low procurement prices for agricultural products, the incomes of farmers fell and their indebtedness increased. Although the private sector clearly predominates, the weakness of Polish agriculture is seen in the small size of agricultural firms (the average size of private agricultural farms is below 7 ha) and in the low efficiency of agricultural production which lowers competitiveness on western markets. Due to emerging foreign competition, Poland has increased tariffs on imported food to protect the domestic agricultural sector.

---

[97] Possible sectoral effects on the potential for migration are discussed in chapter 7.

[98] In Poland agricultural investment in 1991 fell by 50 per cent. *Rzeczpospolita*, 12 February 1992, p.3.

[99] See BBC, *Summary of World Broadcasts*, EE/1271, 7 January 1992, p.B/1.

Romanian agricultural performance in 1991 was helped by good weather conditions. Grain production of 19.3 million tons (mainly due to a bumper harvest of maize) compares favourably to an average harvest of 18.4 million tons in 1986-1990. Animal production declined by 1 per cent. However, the growing shortage of agro-industrial inputs, remaining price distortions and the hasty return of land to the peasants (in 1991 about 80 per cent of agricultural land was in private ownership) will adversely affect agricultural performance in 1992.[100] As a result, Romania had to increase its grain imports to about 1.5 million tons.

For *Yugoslavia*, 1991 was a good agricultural year with gross agricultural production increasing by almost 8 per cent, mainly due to an expansion of crop production. Production of wheat, industrial crops and viticulture increased by 27, 14 and 24 per cent, respectively. In contrast, animal production fell by 3 per cent.

The restructuring of the agricultural sector is to lead to reduced costs of agricultural output, increased efficiency in the use of production inputs and growing competitiveness on the international markets. This will need capital, better management and much better infrastructure, all factors which are now lacking. It is thus likely that in the short run the transformation process will adversely affect agricultural production. The adjustment process, if seen in the perspective of full integration of east European agriculture into the world economy, is likely to be painful and long-term.

(iv) Labour market developments

The deterioration in the labour market situation seen in 1990 in several eastern European countries, notably Poland and the *Länder* of the former GDR, spread throughout the region in 1991. All the countries of the region experienced rapid rises in unemployment and large falls in conventionally measured employment; indicators of stocks of vacancies also fell. These negative trends are likely to continue in 1992 and, even if economic growth resumes, no early fall in unemployment can be expected as the restructuring of large sectors of the economy appears still to be in its early stages.

Labour force developments

As household labour force surveys are still in the process of being set up, there is no direct information available on the size of the overall labour force since open unemployment emerged at the end of 1989 and the beginning of 1990. As table 3.2.8 shows, the fall in total employment in the course of 1990 was higher in Czechoslovakia and Hungary than the rise in official unemployment, though the two changes were about the same level in Poland. The obvious estimate of the active population (the sum of measured unemployment and total employment) therefore shows a considerable fall in apparent participation in Hungary and Czechoslovakia but very little change in Poland.

This disparity between changes in the official employment and unemployment figures may be due to any or all of the three following factors. Firstly, the individuals concerned may be employed (according to the ILO definition) but are not included in official employment statistics. This may be because the employing enterprise is too small to be included in the regular statistical reporting system or because the enterprise is operating in the informal economy and so is unknown to the authorities. The second possibility is that they are unemployed (again according to the ILO definition) but have not registered with a labour office and so do not appear in the unemployment statistics.[101] Finally, they may have become economically inactive and have therefore left the labour force. This final category includes "discouraged workers" who would re-enter the labour force if they believed that jobs were available.

Only the third of these three categories represents withdrawal from the labour force, and the available information does not allow us any distinction between these three possibilities. However, it seems likely that the contrast between the situation in Poland and that in Hungary and Czechoslovakia is related to the relatively generous unemployment benefit system which was initially introduced in Poland, which encouraged a wider range of individuals to register as unemployed than did the more restrictive systems in Czechoslovakia and Hungary.

Unemployment: dramatic rises in joblessness ...

At the end of 1990, unemployment in eastern Europe, although rising rapidly, was still generally lower than in the market economies of western Europe. This is no longer the case and all the countries of the region saw rapid rises in unemployment in the course of 1991. The apparent differences in unemployment rates between the countries of the region narrowed over the year (table 3.2.9).[102]

Bulgaria provides the most dramatic example of this tendency, with unemployment rising over sixfold in the course of the year. In contrast, *Romania* saw the smallest rises in registered joblessness but this reflects postponement or, at most, the only partial effectiveness of stabilization measures rather than better labour market performance. Moreover, the unemployment figures exclude nearly 600,000 workers who are receiving benefits because their factories are idle due to shortages of raw materials.[103] In *Yugoslavia* recorded

---

[100] Romanian Agriculture and Food Minister P. Marculescu speaks of dramatic period in food supplies. See BBC, *Summary of World Broadcasts*, EE 1272, 8 January 1992, p.B/13.

[101] Note that it is also possible that some of those counted as unemployed in official statistics may not fulfil the conditions for belonging to the labour force. See *Employment Gazette*, November 1991, pp.617-624 for an attempt to reconcile the official and ILO measures of unemployment in the United Kingdom.

[102] International comparisons of unemployment rates always should be viewed with caution and this is especially true for the countries of central and eastern Europe. See United Nations Economic Commission for Europe, *Economic Survey of Europe in 1990-1991*, New York, 1991, p.60 for a fuller discussion.

[103] These workers receive benefits amounting to 60 per cent of the indexed basic wage direct from the Ministry of Labour and Social Security. See BBC, *Summary of World Broadcasts*, Third Series, EE/W0123, 16 January 1992.

TABLE 3.2.8

Changes in employment and unemployment 1989-1990
(Thousands)

	Total employment End 1989	Total employment End 1990	Change	Increase in unemployment	Change in "labour force"
Czechoslovakia	7 994	7 674	-320	76	-244 (-3.2%)
Hungary	5 472	5 300	-172	66	-106 (-2.0%)
Poland	17 558	16 474	-1 084	1 126	-14 (-0.1%)

Source: National statistics.

Note: "Labour force" is defined here to be the sum of employment and registered unemployment. As explained in the text, this is not the same as the ILO definition of the labour force.

TABLE 3.2.9

Eastern Europe: Unemployment, 1990-1991
(Thousands and per cent of labour force, end-of-period)

	Unemployed (thousands) Dec. 1990	Mar. 1991	Jun. 1991	Sept. 1991	Dec. 1991	Jan. 1992	Unemployment rate (per cent) Dec. 1990	Mar. 1991	Jun. 1991	Sept. 1991	Dec. 1991	Jan. 1992
Albania	..	..	..	..	419	..	..	..	..	..	..	..
Bulgaria	65.1	134.8	233.7	343.3	523.7	550.6	1.7	3.5	6.0	8.8	10.7	..
Czechoslovakia	76.7	184.6	300.8	446.2	523.7	550.6	1.0	2.3	3.8	5.7	6.6	6.9
Ex-GDR Länder [a]	642.2	808.3	842.5	1 028.8	1 037.7	1343.3	7.3	9.2	9.5	11.7	11.8	15.2 [b]
Hungary	79.5	144.8	185.6	292.8	406.1	440	1.7	3.0	3.9	6.1	8.3	9.2 [c]
Poland	1 126.1	1 322.1	1 574.1	1 970.9	2 155.6	2 230.1	6.1	7.1	8.4	10.4	11.5	11.9
Romania	..	79.2	169.9	260.5	337.5	..	..	0.7	1.6	2.4	3.1	..
Yugoslavia	1 386.5	1 455.0	1 498.8	1 540.4 [d]	2 000.0 [e]	..	13.6	14.2	14.7	15.2 [d]	19.6 [e]	..

Sources: National statistics of "registered unemployed", except where otherwise noted.

[a] Excludes part-time unemployment (involuntary short-time working).
[b] The official reported rate for January 1992 of 16.5 per cent is based on an updated (and considerably lower) estimate of the civilian labour force. To preserve consistency, the unemployment rate for January 1992 shown in the table has been recalculated to be consistent with the reported rates for 1991.
[c] The officially reported unemployment rate of 8.2 per cent for January 1992 is based on a wider definition of the labour force than that used previously. To preserve consistency, the unemployment rate for January 1992 shown in the table has been recalculated to be consistent with the reported rates for 1991.
[d] August 1991.
[e] "Initial estimates show that the number of unemployed in the country has already reached two million." Tanjug report, 6 January 1992. See BBC, *Summary of World Broadcasts*, EE W0213, 16 January 1992.

unemployment continued to increase throughout the year, with the rise accelerating towards the end of the year as the economy weakened under the stresses imposed by the outbreak of civil war.

At first sight, the figures for the *ex-GDR* give some grounds for optimism as the rise in unemployment in the summer (following the expiry of guarantees of job security in several sectors of the economy at the end of June 1991) was lower than expected. The official unemployment rate then fluctuated around a level just below 12 per cent in the second half of 1991. At the same time, the number of part-time workers has fallen steadily from its peak of over 2 million in April 1991 to just over 1 million in December 1991.

However, recorded unemployment has only been kept low by massive expenditures on training schemes (365,000 people were estimated to be on such schemes at the end of 1991), job creation measures (nearly 390,000 people at the end of 1991), provisions for early retirement (some 705,000 people) and for subsidizing part-time work. The recorded unemployment rate rose dramatically in January 1992 (from 11.8 per cent in December to 16.5 per cent in January) as schemes subsidizing part-time working in many enterprises ran out.[104] This should be regarded as bringing previously hidden unemployment into the open rather than signalling any new deterioration in the underlying labour market situation.

In *Czechoslovakia*, unemployment rose particularly fast over the summer but showed signs of slowing towards the end of the year. Vacancies fell sharply at the beginning of 1991 following the introduction of tight stabilization policies and price liberalization but have risen steadily since the middle of 1991. The number of recorded vacancies at the end of January 1992 was higher than in January 1991, giving some grounds for optimism that the labour market is beginning to adapt to the new economic situation. Unemployment in *Hungary* initially rose at about the same rate as joblessness in Czechoslovakia but then rose more rapidly in the second half of 1991. The number of unfilled vacancies remained approximately constant over the year. In *Poland*, where unemployment was at a high level even at the beginning of the year, the rise in unemployment was concentrated in the middle of the year. Stocks of unfilled vacancies declined sharply at the end of the year and finished the year substantially below their levels of the year before.

---

[104] The estimate of the civilian labour force used to calculate the unemployment rate was updated for the January 1992 unemployment figures. This change increased the reported unemployment rate by 1.3 percentage points as from January 1992.

TABLE 3.2.10
Registered vacancies
(Thousands)

	December 1990	March 1991	June 1991	September 1991	December 1991	January 1992
Bulgaria	28.4	11.4	..	..	10	..
Czechoslovakia	72.2	44.6	41.7	52.1	56.6	62.4
Ex-GDR *Länder*	17.5	20.9	31.7	43.0	35.4	39.8
Hungary	16.8	13.6	14.7	15.4	11.5	..
Poland	54.1	45.8	47.4	48.0	29.1	31.5
Yugoslavia	36.2	43.6	43.0	38.7 [a]	..	..

Source National statistics.

[a] August 1991.

It appears that seasonal influences are playing a large role in many of these short-term movements, so that a large part of the sharp increases in unemployment in the summer is probably accounted for by the appearance of school-leavers and university graduates on the unemployment count.

... especially amongst women and in less developed regions

The burden of unemployment is not being shared uniformly. Women are generally far more likely to become unemployed than men. Table 3.2.11 shows unemployment rates by sex in September 1991. In all the countries of eastern Europe, except Hungary, women have significantly higher unemployment rates than men. Anecdotal reports suggest that when jobs have to be shed, women are made redundant in preference to men, often because women's jobs are regarded as being less important to the family budget than those of men.

Unemployment rates also show sharp divergences between different regions of the same country. Table 3.2.12 summarizes some information on the regional variation of unemployment in eastern Europe in September 1991. The table reveals very large disparities in unemployment rates in all the countries, except the ex-GDR.[105] In all the countries with large disparities in unemployment, the regions around capital cities have the lowest unemployment rates, while those regions which are less developed or have high concentrations of heavy industry have been particularly hard hit by high unemployment (for example, eastern Slovakia in Czechoslovakia and north-east Hungary both have particularly high rates of unemployment).

As might be expected, complementary patterns are seen in the regional distribution of vacancies, with areas of high unemployment having relatively low vacancy figures. Czechoslovakia provides a particularly striking example of this tendency. At the end of November 1991, there were more vacancies than registered unemployed in Prague, while in Slovakia as a whole there was one recorded vacancy for every 36 unemployed and one region of Slovakia had over 50 unemployed per notified vacancy.

Information on the distribution of unemployment by age group, skill and duration is more sketchy but does suggest that unemployment is concentrated on the young and less skilled and that the lengths of unemployment spells, though still low, are increasing.

The young appear to be bearing much of the burden of unemployment. Although recent data on the age composition of employment is generally not available, the proportion of unemployment accounted for by the young is far higher than their weight in the population of working age (here taken to be those aged between 15 and 64 years).[106] Thus 48.6 per cent of the unemployed in Bulgaria at the end of 1991 were aged 30 or below (this age group accounted for about 33 per cent of the population of working age) and 33.3 per cent of the unemployed in Poland were aged between 18 and 24 (less than 15 per cent of the population of working age are estimated to lie in this age group). Similar patterns hold in Hungary and Czechoslovakia.[107]

The average duration of unemployment appears to be increasing, though the number of long-term unemployed is still low, especially in relation to the levels prevalent in many countries of western Europe. Thus, the proportion of the unemployed out of work for less than three months in the Czech republic fell from 64.8 per cent to 51.4 per cent between March and September 1991. In Hungary, the proportion of benefit claimants whose claims were of less than 120 days duration fell from 64.1 per cent in January-April 1991 to 47.5 per cent in January-September 1991. Long-term unemployment (defined as unemployment lasting over a year) accounted for 2.3 per cent of the unemployed in the Czech republic in September 1991 but for 8.8 per cent of unemployment benefit claims in Hungary between January and September 1991. Given the short period of time which has elapsed since unemployment

---

[105] There are substantial differences between countries in the size of the administrative units reporting regional unemployment figures. Measures of dispersion (such as the standard deviation) should therefore be interpreted cautiously.

[106] The proportion of the labour force which is young is generally lower than the proportion of the 15-64 population which is young. This is mainly a result of increased staying on rates in education. As a result, the concentration of unemployment among the young labour force is even higher than is suggested by the population figures.

[107] Estimates of the size of population age groups are taken from *The sex and age distribution of population: the 1990 revision*, UN Population Studies No.122, New York, 1991.

TABLE 3.2.11

Unemployment rates by sex
(Per cent of labour force)

Country	Observation	Unemployment rate Total	Male	Female
Bulgaria	December 1991	10.7	9.5	11.5
Czechoslovakia	September 1991	5.6	5.0	6.3
Ex-GDR *Länder*	September 1991	11.7	9.1	14.3
Hungary	September 1991	6.1	6.6	5.5
Poland	September 1991	10.4	9.2	11.8
Romania	September 1991	2.4	1.8	3.2
Yugoslavia	August 1991	15.2	12.5	18.9

Sources: National statistical bulletins, supplemented where necessary with secretariat estimates of male and female labour forces.

TABLE 3.2.12

Regional dispersion of unemployment rates in September 1991
(Per cent of labour force)

Country	Number of areas	Unemployment rate Average	Highest	Lowest	Standard deviation (unweighted)
Czechoslovakia	12	5.6	10.6	1.5	2.9
Ex-GDR *Länder*	6	11.7	14.0	10.4	1.2
Hungary	20	6.1	12.6	1.8	2.6
Poland	49	10.5	17.3	3.9	3.3
Romania [a]	41	2.4	6.0	0.7	1.2
Yugoslavia [a, b]	8	15.2	21.1	9.3	3.4

Source: National statistics, supplemented where necessary with secretariat estimates of regional labour force.

[a] Regional unemployment rates are not available for Romania or Yugoslavia. The estimates in the table assume that the regional distribution of the labour force is the same as the regional distribution of the population.
[b] August 1991.

began to rise, the relatively low levels of long-term unemployment are to be expected. However, in the next year the number of unemployed who will have been out of work for over six or twelve months is likely to increase significantly. Experience from western Europe suggests that once long-term unemployment has become established, it is very difficult to reduce.

Finally, manual workers are generally more affected by unemployment than are those with higher qualifications. Thus in Hungary, for example, manual workers made up two thirds of total employment in 1990 but accounted for about 80 per cent of the registered unemployed in September 1991. In Czechoslovakia manual workers are also more likely to become unemployed than white collar workers, but the disparities in unemployment rates between the two groups are less pronounced.

Employment: large falls in employment in nearly all sectors

Only partial information is yet available on the employment level in 1991. The private sector is now included in principle in the monthly and quarterly statistical reports for most of the countries of the region but only enterprises above a certain size (for example, 100 employees in Czechoslovakia, 50 employees in Hungary, 5 employees in Poland) are covered, so that new private sector enterprises will generally not be included. A full picture of employment developments in 1991 is therefore not likely to appear until the end of 1992, when the results of more comprehensive annual statistical surveys become available.

Table 3.2.13 shows the falls in employment between the first quarter of 1990 (the first period for which comparable figures are available) and the third quarter of 1991, by industrial branch for the four countries for which information is available. Yugoslavia is included for completeness but the unique political situation in Yugoslavia makes the country a special case.

Again, comparisons between countries should only be made with caution as differences in statistical coverage between countries may make simple comparisons unreliable. Thus, the much larger drops in employment in Hungary and Czechoslovakia as compared to Poland may merely reflect the different sizes of enterprises included in statistical reports. Growth in employment in private sector enterprises would appear to be more likely to be recorded in Poland because of its more inclusive statistical reporting system.[108]

There appears to be very little uniformity between the countries in the pattern of employment change across industries. Employment in *finance and insurance* grew strongly in both Czechoslovakia and Poland (unfortunately, figures for Hungary are not available) and was almost unchanged in Bulgaria. All other branches

---

[108] However, Czechoslovak estimates of total employment in all sizes of enterprises show a larger fall than do the figures for employment in large enterprises.

TABLE 3.2.13

Employment change by industrial branch between 1990-QI and 1991-QIII

(Percentage change)

	CSFR a	Hungary b	Poland c	Yugoslavia d
Power and fuels	-15.5	-18.6	-10.1	- 6.4
Metals	-15.7	-24.0	-11.4	-10.4
Engineering	-15.9	-21.7	-17.7	-15.6
Chemicals	- 7.7	-10.8	- 9.8	-10.2
Minerals	-14.0	-14.9	- 6.4	- 9.5
Food, drink, tobacco	- 6.1	- 8.0	4.6	- 7.1
Textiles, clothing	-23.2	-16.6 e	-21.5	-11.3
Wood	-18.8	-24.8 e	0.0	-15.0
Paper, printing	-10.8	-20.5 e	-12.6	-11.9
Other	-12.1	-32.9	-28.9	-14.7
Total industry	-15.3	-17.3	-12.9	-11.9

Source: National statistical bulletins.

a Only enterprises with more than 100 employees are included.
b Only enterprises in the material sector with more than 50 employees are included.
c Only employees (full-time equivalents) in enterprises with 5 or more employees are included.
d State and cooperative sectors only.
e Enterprises with more than 500 employees only. Employment in light industry, which includes these three industries, fell by 25.5 per cent in this period in enterprises with more than 500 employees and by only 16.9 per cent in the larger group of enterprises with 50 or more employees.

suffered falls in employment with particularly large job losses in agriculture (especially in Poland), trade and construction (though to a smaller degree in Poland). Falls in industrial employment (in relation to employment in the branch) have generally been lower than percentage falls in overall employment.

Within industry, food processing and chemicals appear to have had the smallest falls in employment (employment in the food industry in Poland has actually increased) and textiles and engineering the highest. In Poland and Czechoslovakia it is noticeable that mining and energy have had lower than average falls in employment.

However, throughout industry the falls in output have been greater than the falls in employment, so that labour productivity has fallen sharply.[109] This suggests that large scale restructuring and the reduction of overstaffing has not yet begun.

A note on contrasting approaches to the link between wages and unemployment

The simultaneous rapid rises in unemployment and real wages seen in the ex-GDR have led some commentators to propose some public intervention in the wage determination process to improve the trade-off between wage growth and unemployment.[110] Elsewhere in eastern Europe, governments are intervening in the process of wage formation as part of their stabilization policies to keep inflation under control. This note sets out the advantages and problems of the various policy options which have been proposed.

In well functioning labour markets, the relationship between real wage growth and unemployment is taken into account by the parties to the wage bargain, whether they be individual employers and workers ("individualist" systems, with the USA usually cited as the prime example) or strong economy-wide organizations of employers and trade unions (often, somewhat misleadingly, described as "corporatist" systems, with Sweden generally taken as the typical case). Available evidence seems to indicate that both highly corporatist and highly individualist systems produce lower levels of unemployment for given levels of wage inflation than do mixed systems.[111]

The current systems of industrial relations in the ex-GDR and the countries of eastern Europe do not fit easily into either of these typical systems. Instead, the collapse of central planning and the increased autonomy given to enterprise management have led to a situation where the incentives for sensible bargaining between the representatives of capital and labour are often lacking and may even be perverse. In addition, representative organizations of workers and management are still in the process of formation.

The German case

In the ex-GDR, west German unions moved in quickly to organize the workforce. The unions faced weak enterprise management and were able to extract commitments to increase east German wages to west German levels in only three or four years — an unrealistically short period of time for productivity in the east to catch up with that in the west — and this sharp rise in wage costs in the ex-GDR has been cited by

---

[109] The phenomenon of "labour hoarding" is common in western economies during the early stages of economic downturns. It is usually explained by the high costs of hiring and firing labour which lead managers to smooth the level of employment over the cycle. This type of argument seems inadequate for the current situation in eastern Europe.

[110] For proposals to subsidize wages in the ex-GDR, see G. Akerlof et al, "East Germany in from the cold: the economic aftermath of currency union", *Brookings Papers on Economic Activity*, 1991:1 pp.1-105. For alternative views of the problem, see H. Siebert, "German unification: the economics of transition", *Economic Policy*, No.13, October 1991, "Allgemeine Lohnsubventionen: keine Ausweg aus der Beschäftigungskrise in Ostdeutschland", *DIW Wochenbericht*, No.36/91 and M. Neumann, "German unification: economic problems and consequences", *CEPR Discussion Paper Series*, No.584.

[111] See for example United Nations Economic Commission for Europe, *Economic Survey of Europe in 1990-1991*, New York, 1991, chapter 5.

many observers as one of the main causes of the massive fall in employment in eastern Germany since July 1990.

Contrasting explanations have been put forward for this outcome. On the one hand, it has been argued that the German trade unions and employers' organizations have been acting mainly in the interests of their members in the western part of Germany. The rise in wages in the ex-GDR is then seen as a means of forestalling the threat to west German wage levels from lower wage competition from eastern Germany. Higher wages in the east were also proposed as a means of slowing migration from eastern to western Germany.[112] According to this view, the problem lies in the representation of east German workers by predominantly west German unions, who may be acting against the interests of their eastern members, many of whom will become unemployed as a result of the high wage settlements.

Alternative views place the blame on the incentives facing management. It is argued that the existing enterprise management has little inclination to resist high wage increases as it knows that it is likely to be replaced after privatization; it therefore does not bargain in the same way as the management of a private company and, in particular, does not represent the interests of the owners of the capital of the enterprise (the state, at least until privatization). Incentives for an economically warranted bargain are further reduced if the management believes that easy credits will be available from the state (represented by grants from the Treuhand in the ex-GDR) — the familiar problem of the soft budget constraint.

Both these factors are reinforced by the interactions of the wage bargaining process with the unemployment benefit system. In a situation where unemployment benefits are linked directly to the level of final wages and at the same time a large proportion of the workforce expects to be made unemployed, irrespective of the outcome of the wage negotiations, there is a clear incentive to increase the level of the final wage solely to increase benefit entitlements. This mechanism appears to have played a role in the sharp increase in wage levels in the first half of 1990, immediately prior to currency union.

Policy proposals to improve the situation vary according to the view that is taken of the underlying process driving the wage increases. The most basic view is that pressure for rapid convergence between east and west German wage levels is inevitable. The high level of east German wage settlements ensures that the restructuring of the economy in the ex-GDR will take place quickly and high transitional unemployment is viewed as the price that has to be paid for rapid increases in productivity. Hence no specific policy action is called for to reduce unemployment. According to this view, unemployment is expected to fall as physical and human capital flow into eastern Germany, increasing the feasible level of employment at west German wages. The problem with this view is that with wages at near-west German levels, the incentives for a large flow of capital into the GDR are much lower, so that prospects for a rapid decline in unemployment are reduced.[113]

If the view that west German unions and employers are mainly responsible for driving up wages in the ex-GDR to above "equilibrium" levels is accepted, a wage subsidy would appear as a feasible policy. A subsidy would introduce a wedge between labour costs to employers and workers' wage income and thus increase the price competitiveness of firms in the ex-GDR at a given level of wages.[114] If such a subsidy did not alter the bargaining behaviour of management and unions then it seems likely that it would indeed improve the employment situation in the east, although at considerable cost to the government budget.

However, the introduction of a flat-rate wage subsidy, which would not reduce the incentives for increasing productivity, is likely to increase the bargaining position of the workers relative to management. The main result of such a uniform wage subsidy would then be an even faster convergence between wages in the two parts of Germany, rather than higher employment. On the other hand, a wage subsidy which depended positively on the difference between east and west German wages (as proposed by Akerlof et al.) would reduce workers' desire to press for immediate wage parity between east and west but at the cost of reducing incentives to increase productivity as well. As a result, although employment losses would be lower, the existing inefficiencies of east German industry would take longer to remove and subsidies would have to be kept in place for longer.

In contrast, if weak management is seen as the culprit, the solution is to be found in rapid privatization and the installation of real owners of capital who will bargain realistically with the workforce over wage levels. According to this view, interventions by government in the wage bargaining process will then not be needed, though unemployment would still be high during the transitional period of restructuring.

Additional proposals to accelerate movement in this direction have included giving existing management an equity stake in the enterprise, thus providing them with a material interest in preserving the value of the firm and its capital or giving the workforce the same kind of stake. Giving management an equity stake puts the correct incentives in place but at the cost of severe distributional problems. Granting the workforce a stake increases the long-term interest of workers in the firm, thus lowering the pressures for immediate wage increases, but this is at the cost of giving existing

---

[112] The assumption here is that the combination of high wages and higher unemployment is less likely to lead to a flood of migrants from eastern to western Germany than are lower wages and lower unemployment. Akerlof et al., op cit., provide some evidence challenging this view.

[113] Producers of traded goods who are able to expand their operations relatively easily in western Germany are the most likely to scale down investments in the ex-GDR because of the rapid growth in wage costs there.

[114] Of course, the poor quality of goods produced in the ex-GDR may mean that the effective competitiveness of firms there may still be low even with a wage subsidy.

workers an additional interest in restricting new employment in the firm.[115]

It has been proposed that enterprises which are still under the control of the Treuhand but can obtain a large degree of private sector finance for their restructuring plans, could receive a combination of investment aid and grants towards paying their wage costs from the government for a strictly limited period of time.[116] This proposal has the advantages of subsidizing only enterprises which appear to have a realistic chance of being viable and of increasing the pressures on incumbent management to improve the enterprise's competitiveness. However, because of the selective nature of the subsidies, firms in the ex-GDR which do not benefit from such grants (for example firms which have already been privatized), would be put at a competitive disadvantage.

The current policy of the German government is to rely on rapid privatization to introduce the correct incentives for management. West German governments have traditionally avoided interfering in the wage bargaining process and general wage subsidies are very unlikely to be introduced. Instead, the government is spending heavily on a wide variety of measures to retrain the unemployed and to encourage employers to take on jobless workers.

Experience elsewhere in eastern Europe

In the other countries of eastern Europe, the government has taken a far more active role as, in the absence of "real" employers in the state-owned sectors of the economy, bargaining between workers and management alone was expected to lead to higher wages and rising inflation, thus endangering the success of stabilization policies. National tripartite agreements between governments, employers and unions on permitted levels of wage increases have been adopted by several of the countries of the region, though the commitment of the agents to such agreements can often be more nominal than real.

In Poland, Czechoslovakia and Hungary, tax-based income policies (TIP), where penal rates of taxation are imposed on wage increases which are above a certain predetermined level, have been introduced.[117] This cut-off level is usually set so that the maximum permitted level of wage increases is below the level of price increases and, as a result, real wages are intended to decline over time.

The effectiveness of such schemes has been varied between countries. For example, in *Czechoslovakia*, the economic climate has been so harsh that actual wage increases were below the permitted level in 1991 whereas, in *Poland*, management in several sectors of industry was so weak that wage increases substantially above the cut-off point were awarded from the second half of 1990, despite the resulting high tax bills. In *Romania*, controls on individual wage rates have proved almost completely ineffective (workers are continually regraded to higher paying jobs to evade the controls) and the government intends to introduce a TIP for state owned enterprises.

In the longer term, tax-based incomes policies with such very high rates of taxation are likely to retard the workings of the labour market and impair the efficient allocation of labour. TIPs tend to discourage the adjustment of wage differentials, as increasing the relative wages of workers with skills in short supply attracts an extra tax charge. The detailed provisions of a TIP may also cause additional distortions. Thus where the tax is based on the increase in the total wage bill, enterprises may still award high wage increases but may avoid the tax charge by reducing the workforce. Where the tax is imposed on the increase in average wages in a firm, there is a tax-induced incentive to take on lower paid workers.

In addition, TIPs are increasingly regarded as being unfair to workers in state-owned enterprises. Foreign-owned and private firms are generally exempted from the excess wages tax as these firms' managements are regarded as being more subject to market disciplines. Wage differentials between the private and socialized sectors are therefore increasing rapidly and, although this will tend to speed up the reallocation of labour to more efficient enterprises, such a high degree of wage inequality is proving very unpopular.

For these reasons, the governments of eastern Europe which have adopted TIPs have viewed them as temporary policy instruments for the period of macroeconomic stabilization which will be replaced by (more or less) decentralized bargaining between management and workers once economic conditions allow and the necessary institutions (for example, a sufficient degree of privatization; the existence of representative trade unions and employers associations) are in place.

Possible lessons

Experience since these policies were introduced suggests that, while a tax-base income policy may be a useful tool of stabilization policy, even very high rates of taxation on excessive wage increases cannot compensate for weaknesses in enterprise management or a basic lack of credibility in the tightness of domestic policies. Installing an independent management team, accountable for the management of the enterprise's capital, and ensuring that both management and workers face sensible incentives (including "hard budget constraints") when bargaining over wages is therefore urgently required if macroeconomic stabilization is to succeed and broad based growth is to resume.

---

[115] These schemes have obvious parallels with the various options for privatization discussed elsewhere in this *Survey*.

[116] See "Subventionierung und Privatisierung durch die Treuhandanstalt: Kurswechsel erforderlich", *DIW Wochenbericht*, No.41/91.

[117] See R. Layard, "Wage bargaining and incomes policy: possible lessons for eastern Europe", *Centre for Economic Performance Discussion Paper No.2* for arguments in favour of tax-based income policies.

3.3 FOREIGN TRADE AND EXTERNAL BALANCE

(i) An overview

The situation in the foreign trade of the eastern countries in 1991 has been shaped by a unique combination of various unfavourable internal and external factors.[118] The impact of *domestic recession*, whether attributable to stabilization measures, balance-of-payments constraints, or a general falling apart of the economic control mechanisms, was perhaps the most significant. The fall of domestic demand exerted a downward pressure on import levels, which generally declined in volume terms (though not in all countries), and led to a significant change in import structure. While the same factors should have worked to stimulate exports, in most eastern countries this reaction was still hampered by the feeble working of market forces, inadequate institutional infrastructure, frequent production stoppages and political instability.

Foreign trade flows, especially among the eastern countries themselves, have been also hit hard in 1991 by various *external developments*, with the dissolution of the CMEA trade and payments system and the collapse of the Soviet market being probably the most important ones. The shift to convertible currency settlements and world market prices in mutual trade is considered to have led to a spontaneous destruction of intra-eastern trade; this in turn certainly contributed to further aggravating the domestic economic situation of the former CMEA-member countries. On the other side, expansion of exports to industrialized countries was boosted by relatively strong import demand in the markets most relevant to the east European countries (see section 3.3(ii) below).

The analysis of trade developments in eastern countries in 1991 has become a difficult task because of problems with data classification, measurement and aggregation. While part of them date back to CMEA times, some new difficulties have emerged recently in the wake of transition process. Nevertheless, the overall picture of broad changes is quite clear. The four most pronounced tendencies in trade of east European countries in 1991 were: (a) the change in the territorial structure of trade in favour of western countries, resulting from the sharp contraction of intra-CMEA trade[119] and the rapid expansion of trade with developed market economies, particularly with the EC, (b) the change in the traditional commodity structure of eastern trade, with falling shares of capital goods, (c) the significant deterioration of eastern Europe's terms-of-trade, especially *vis-à-vis* the former Soviet Union, and (d) the marked worsening of the overall trade balance of eastern Europe, resulting from the fall of the area's exports and increase of imports.

While the value of *total trade* of five east European countries remained broadly at 1990 levels, their *mutual trade* declined considerably for the second year in a row, both in absolute terms and in relation to total trade turnover. On the other hand, their trade with the former Soviet Union, while declining sharply in *volume* terms, has generally increased in *values*, especially on the import side. Two principal phenomena were behind this asymmetric behaviour of intra-CMEA trade flows: the elimination of the traditional CMEA trading system based on transferable rouble settlements and largely artificial prices (which as a rule were inflated for industrial products and very low for fuels and other commodities), and the rapid disintegration of the Soviet Union, resulting in a deep economic recession and political falling apart of the Soviet state structures. While the change in the trading rules was responsible for the drastic deterioration of *terms-of-trade* of east European countries and provided strong incentives to shed superfluous trade flows, the massive crisis in the Soviet economy further reinforced the trade contraction, sharply reducing import possibilities of the ex-Soviet republics. The result was a much steeper fall of east European exports to the ex-Soviet market. The share of intra-eastern trade in total trade of the group (excluding trade with the ex-USSR) declined further from 13 per cent in 1990 to less than 10 per cent in 1991.

The remarkable growth of trade with *western countries* was also much stronger on the east European import side. While exports to industrialized countries increased by 6 per cent in value in January-September 1991 over the corresponding period of 1990, east European imports increased over the same period by 18 per cent.[120]

Changes in foreign trade of the eastern countries have not however followed a uniform pattern, but rather reflected the varying speed of systemic reforms and differences in economic policies pursued in individual countries. *Hungary and Poland,* in spite of falling overall export levels in volume terms, managed to maintain high growth rates of exports to developed market economies, but their imports increased at a much faster pace (by 81 per cent and 67 per cent in current prices, respectively). The observed import expansion in both countries appears to have been trig-

---

[118] This section updates the more detailed treatment of east European trade and finance in the United Nations Economic Commission for Europe, *Economic Bulletin for Europe*, vol.43, New York, 1991, chapter 3.

[119] The term "intra-CMEA trade" as used in this publication is applied for convenience reasons, and indicates trade among the former European CMEA member countries (including the Soviet Union), although the organization itself was formally dissolved at the end of June 1991.

[120] Eastern data: somewhat higher growth of east European exports is suggested by western statistics.

TABLE 3.3.1

Eastern Europe: Foreign trade, by direction, 1989-1991
(Value in billion US dollars; growth rates in percentages) a

Country or country group b	Exports Value 1990	Exports Growth rates 1989	Exports Growth rates 1990	Exports Growth rates 1991 c	Imports Value 1990	Imports Growth rates 1989	Imports Growth rates 1990	Imports Growth rates 1991 c
Eastern Europe, d *to or from:*								
World	64.8	-3.2	-3.3	-9.9	65.1	-2.2	2.9	5.8
"Socialist countries"	26.8	-8.6	-14.4	-29.1	24.0	-9.4	-16.9	-10.6
Eastern Europe	8.1	-8.4	-18.6	-22.0	8.1	-8.9	-18.2	-25.9
Soviet Union	14.5	-9.3	-11.4	-32.9	11.9	-12.5	-13.9	2.6
Developed market economies	31.9	6.5	11.6	6.0	34.6	4.8	24.2	18.0
Developing countries	6.2	-12.5	-14.3	-14.7	6.5	5.5	-	6.5

Source: Secretariat of the United Nations Economic Commission for Europe, based on national statistical publications, direct communications to the ECE secretariat from national statistical offices and (for 1991) in part on trade partner data.

a Both export and import values are expressed f.o.b., except for Hungarian imports which are shown c.i.f. in the national returns. Growth rates are calculated on values expressed in US dollars. Trade with "socialist" and east European countries in the years prior to 1991 was valued in an adjusted dollar measure reflecting consistent rouble-dollar crossrates. For details of the revaluation, see the note to table 2.1.4 and the discussion in box 2.1.1 and section 2.1(iii) below. All trade values for 1991 were converted to dollars at the appropriate national conversion coefficient (usually the "commercial" rate quoted by national banks).
b "Eastern Europe" refers to the east European former member countries of CMEA (Bulgaria, Czechoslovakia, German Democratic Republic through 1990, Hungary, Poland and Romania). The partner country grouping follows the practice until recently prevalent in the national statistical sources, which differs from the breakdown usually employed in United Nations publications. Thus, "socialist countries", in addition to the east European countries, the Soviet Union, and the Asian centrally planned economies, includes Yugoslavia and Cuba. "Developed market economies" differs from the aggregate used in chapter 5 below by the exclusion of Turkey and the inclusion of Australia, New Zealand and South Africa.
c January-September 1990 to January-September 1991.
d Excluding Yugoslavia. The former German Democratic Republic is included in the data for 1989-1990, but not in those for the first semesters of 1990 and 1991.

TABLE 3.3.2

Eastern Europe: Trade balances, 1988-1991
(Billion US dollars or transferable roubles)

Country group	1988	1989	1990 a	1990 b	January-September 1990 b	January-September 1991 b
Eastern Europe c						
World	4.6	3.8	-0.2	2.9	3.2	-1.7
"Socialist" countries	2.3	2.4	2.8	0.9	1.7	-0.8
Developed market economies	0.2	0.7	-2.7	2.5	1.9	-0.3
Developing countries	2.1	0.7	-0.3	-0.5	-0.4	-1.2

Source and country groups: As for table 3.3.1. Conversion of national currency data to dollars as in table 3.3.1.

a Including the former German Democratic Republic.
b Excluding the former German Democratic Republic.
c Excluding Yugoslavia.

gered primarily by a substantial real appreciation of domestic currencies in the first half of 1991. As a result, Hungary's balance of trade turned from $0.9 billion surplus in 1990 into a deficit of $1.5 billion 1991; similarly, Poland's huge trade surplus of $4.7 in billion in 1990 vanished almost completely, to a mere surplus of $200 million. Poland and Hungary were the only countries in the region where imports levels in 1991 exceeded those of 1990, in both cases rather substantially (table 3.3.1).[121]

Three "southern-tier" countries, *Bulgaria, Romania* and *Yugoslavia,* registered substantial declines in their trade in 1991, with shrinking export earnings having a negative feedback effect on import possibilities. In Yugoslavia the contraction of exports by 21 per cent and imports by 27 per cent (in volume terms) was a direct result of the fall of production, disintegration of the Yugoslav state and the subsequent civil war. By contrast in, Bulgaria the unprecedented contraction of exports and imports by 60 and 70 per cent, respectively, was the combined outcome of the collapse of sales to the ex-Soviet market, serious difficulties in convertible currency payments caused by foreign debt problems, and of drastic stabilization measures (including the steep devaluation of the lev against the dollar by the factor of 20 between mid-1990 and mid-1991). In Romania, the foreign trade fall was partly linked to the fall of domestic output, and partly reflected balance of payments problems and the depletion of international reserves.

By contrast, the decline of trade levels in *Czechoslovakia* was an outcome of strict austerity measures introduced within the framework of the IMF-sponsored stabilization programme at the beginning of 1991. While imports fell steeply already in the first half of 1991, and remained at low levels throughout the year, exports also declined initially and recovered only in the second half of the year. As a result, the Czechoslovak imports in 1991 were 20 per cent lower than in 1990, while exports declined by 7 per cent.[122] A similar re-

---

[121] Eastern data. See footnote (125) below for a discussion of differences from western mirror data.

[122] The stabilization package implemented in Czechoslovakia in January 1991 was essentially similar to the Polish programme introduced a year earlier. But the

TABLE 3.3.3

Eastern Europe: Change in foreign trade value and trade balances by partner region, 1989-1991

(Growth rates in percentages; trade balances in billion US dollars)

		Growth rates					Trade balance, in billion US dollars		
		Exports			Imports				
Country and trade partner groups [a]	1989	1990	1991 QI-III	1989	1990	1991 QI-III	1989	1990	1991 QI-III
Bulgaria									
World	-12.0	-22.4	-29.5	-9.9	-25.1	-54.8	-0.7	-0.3	0.6
"Socialist countries"	-10.6	-32.0	-22.3	-16.7	-24.8	-44.8	0.8	0.3	0.6
Developed market economies	17.2	-12.4	-32.5	0.6	-26.7	-59.3	-1.3	-0.8	-0.1
Developing countries	-35.8	4.5	-45.3	-8.7	-22.6	-68.2	-0.2	0.2	0.2
Czechoslovakia									
World	-3.2	-10.5	2.3	-2.4	0.3	-8.8	0.2	-1.3	0.3
"Socialist countries"	-11.7	-27.4	5.2	-6.9	-17.3	3.6	-0.1	-0.7	-0.1
Developed market economies	10.9	13.4	1.3	-1.6	28.1	-20.2	0.1	-0.6	0.5
Developing countries	0.1	-10.9	-4.5	17.0	-11.9	8.4	0.2	0.2	-
Hungary									
World	-3.3	-1.3	5.7	-5.4	-2.7	44.8	0.8	0.9	-1.9
"Socialist countries"	-9.5	-21.4	-26.4	-14.4	-19.1	18.9	0.6	0.4	-0.6
Developed market economies	5.6	20.6	26.5	7.7	3.8	48.8	-0.2	0.5	-0.4
Developing countries	-6.8	-0.2	-1.1	-22.0	60.9	114.8	0.4	-	-0.5
Poland									
World	0.6	24.7	-18.7	-1.1	-2.5	42.7	1.7	5.7	-
"Socialist countries"	-2.5	14.9	-61.0	-5.7	1.6	-27.2	0.9	1.8	-0.3
Developed market economies	5.3	40.0	12.5	7.1	-4.7	82.5	0.3	3.1	0.6
Developing countries	-3.6	3.2	-12.6	-8.8	-17.1	260.2	0.5	0.7	-0.2
Romania									
World	-10.0	-43.4	-12.9	8.8	18.1	-15.1	2.2	-2.3	-1.2
"Socialist countries"	-14.7	-45.5	11.0	-2.3	-13.7	-2.1	-0.2	-0.9	-0.4
Developed market economies	-3.9	-38.4	-27.5	1.7	116.7	-8.7	2.9	0.2	-0.2
Developing countries	-15.2	-51.0	-5.7	29.0	10.1	-31.4	-0.4	-1.6	-0.7
Yugoslavia									
World	6.1	5.5	..	12.6	25.8	..	-1.4	-4.6	..
"Socialist" countries	3.1	-8.6	..	..	5.4	..	0.1	-0.5	..
Developed market economies	10.4	19.6	..	..	42.9	..	-1.2	-3.4	..
Developing countries	-2.5	-4.2	..	..	11.2	..	-0.3	-0.6	..

Source: Secretariat of the United Nations Economic Commission for Europe, based on national foreign trade statistics.

Note: Growth rates and trade balances are based on trade values in terms of US dollars. As an approximation to a consistent dollar valuation of rouble-denominated intra-group trade flows here and for the longer time series in Appendix tables C.4 and C.5, the pre-1991 national-currency data on trade with the market economies were revalued, in national currency terms, at a common rouble-dollar crossrate and reaggregated with the data on trade with the "socialist countries" to obtain new trade totals (see *Economic Bulletin for Europe*, vol.43, New York, 1991, box 2.1.1 and the discussion in section 2.1(iii) there). All 1991 trade flows were converted to dollars at the relevant national conversion coefficient. Both procedures must be considered approximations to the desired standard of consistent valuation because (i) pre-1991 intra-group trade flows contained convertible-currency components (which in 1990 were significant), and (ii) 1991 trade flows still comprise some rouble-denominated trade.

[a] The partner country grouping follows the past practice of the national statistical sources, which differed from the breakdown usually employed in United Nations publications. Thus, "socialist countries" includes Yugoslavia and Cuba, in addition to the east European countries, the Soviet Union, and the Asian centrally planned economies. "Eastern Europe" refers to the six east European country-members of the CMEA shown separately in the table.

---

action pattern could have been observed in Bulgaria: after a significant slow-down in the first half of 1991, the export performance improved towards the end of the year, in a marked response to domestic austerity policies and trade liberalization measures, which sharply reduced internal demand while changing the incentives structure for domestic producers in favour of exports and import substitution. The policy of deep real depreciation of domestic currencies at the beginning of 1991 appears to have been essential in obtaining an overall trade surplus in both countries.[123]

Trade balances of the east European countries in the first half of 1991 were essentially outcomes of specific policy measures aimed at domestic price stabilization and restoring internal balances (e.g., the policy of fixed exchange rate in Poland and Czechoslovakia), or efforts to protect precarious international liquidity positions (e.g., import cuts in Bulgaria and Romania). Sizable trade deficits were registered in Romania ($1.6 billion), Hungary ($1.5 billion), and Yugoslavia (the exact figure is unknown in the time of writing). The trade was relatively balanced in Poland and in Bulgaria (a small surplus of $160 million over January-September 1991),

---

early adjustment in the external sector displays some differences. While the fall of imports in Poland in 1990 was accompanied by a strong export expansion to the west, spurred by the fall of domestic demand and deep devaluation of the zloty, in Czechoslovakia the response of the export sector in 1991 was weaker and more sluggish, especially in the first half of the year. This delayed response probably reflects a greater structural rigidity in the Czechoslovak economy, which was much more oriented towards the Soviet market and thus needs more time and effort to shift sales to other markets, but may also result in part from the slackening of demand in the west in 1991.

123 The real depreciation of the Czechoslovak *koruna* was obtained essentially during the last quarter of 1990, when the currency was steeply devalued from 16 Kcs per dollar to 28 Kcs per dollar. After the rate had been fixed in end-December 1990, the inflation accelerated and the real exchange rate appreciated gradually during the 1991, but in December 1991 its level was still lower than in 1990.

TABLE 3.3.4
Eastern Europe: Foreign trade with the west, 1989-1991
(Growth rates in percentage: Trade balances in billion US dollars)

	Exports 1989	Exports 1990	Exports 1991[a]	Imports 1989	Imports 1990	Imports 1991[a]	Trade balances 1989	Trade balances 1990	QI-III 1990	QI-III 1991
Albania										
Value ....(W)	15	-10	-24	45	20	11	-	-0.1	-	-0.1
Volume ....(W)	..	-14	-21	..	8	11	..	..	..	..
Bulgaria										
Value ....(E)	17	-12	-32	1	-27	-59	-1.3	-0.8	-0.8	-0.1
........(W)	7	25	26	1	-35	-1	-1.6	-0.6	-0.4	-0.3
Volume ....(W)	10	11	26	1	-42	-	..	..	..	..
Czechoslovakia										
Value ....(E)	11	13	2	-2	28	-20	0.1	-0.6	-0.4	0.5
........(W)	8	18	24	2	34	27	0.4	-0.1	0.2	0.1
Volume ....(W)	8	5	24	2	19	28	..	..	..	..
Hungary										
Value ....(E)	6	21	27	8	4	49	-0.2	0.5	0.2	-0.4
........(W)	10	27	18	17	17	23	-0.3	0.1	-	-0.2
Volume ....(W)	13	12	17	21	3	23	..	..	..	..
Poland										
Value ....(E)	5	40	13	7	-5	81	0.3	3.1	2.7	0.6
........(W)	7	46	12	27	26	79	-0.2	0.9	1.2	-1.9
Volume ....(W)	8	32	12	25	13	82	..	..	..	..
Romania										
Value ....(E)	-4	-38	-27	2	117	-9	2.9	0.2	0.2	-0.2
........(W)	-4	-29	-17	-4	103	-6	2.6	0.3	0.3	-
Volume ....(W)	-8	-39	-19	-6	89	-5	..	..	..	..
Yugoslavia										
Value ....(E)	..	..	..	..	..	..	..	..	..	..
........(W)	9	22	-1	13	38	-13	-0.4	-2.1	-0.9	0.3
Volume ....(W)	..	9	-1	..	23	-12	..	..	..	..
Eastern Europe										
Value ....(E)	5	12	6	4	9	18	1.8	2.5	1.9	0.3
........(W)	7	20	8	13	28	17	0.4	-0.5	0.2	-2.0
Volume ....(W)[b]	5	7	8	11	14	18	..	...	..	..

Sources: For western data, United Nations commodity trade data base (COMTRADE); OECD, *Statistics on Foreign Trade*, Series A, Paris; IMF; *Directions of Trade and International Financial Statistics*, Washington, D.C.; national statistics; and ECE secretariat estimates based upon western data. These data reflect the trade of 23 western reporting countries (Appendix table C.6 contains a list of the countries included).

Note: (E) eastern data, see table 3.3.3; (W) western data as above; volume changes are calculated on western value data. For the methodology and derivation, see United Nations Economic Commission for Europe, *Economic Bulletin for Europe*, vol.31, No.1, New York, 1979.

[a] January-September.
[b] Excluding Yugoslavia, 1989.

but underlying causes for these broadly similar results were different in both countries. The significant surplus in Czechoslovakia (nearly $1 billion) was obtained mostly through a sharp reduction of imports. As a whole, the region registered a net trade deficit of $1.5 billion in 1991 (table 3.3.2).

(ii) Trade and payment relations with the west

(a) Development of trade

Eastern Europe's trade with the west[124] developed relatively dynamically during the first three quarters of 1991.[125] The volume of the area's western *exports* continued to expand by some 7-8 per cent (table 3.3.4), considerably faster than the growth of western import demand (2 per cent during the same period). Eastern Europe's *imports* grew even more quickly (by 18 per cent), and faster than in the previous year. The area's trade balance with the west deteriorated, chiefly because of the sharp worsening of Poland's trade position.

This rather favourable outcome conceals very positive performances by Czechoslovakia, Hungary and Poland, which more than offset the faltering trade of Albania, Bulgaria, Romania and Yugoslavia. The exports of the former group — the countries which have been in the vanguard of economic reform — continued

---

[124] The terms "west", "western", or "developed market economies" as used here refer to the countries of western Europe (including Turkey), North America and Japan. The term "eastern Europe" refers to Albania, Bulgaria, Czechoslovakia (the Czech and Slovak Federal Republic), Hungary, Poland, Romania and Yugoslavia taken together.

[125] This analysis of the trade of the east European (and in chapter 4, ex-Soviet) trade with the developed market economies is analysed in terms of western reported ("mirror") statistics. (See table 3.3.4. Comparable eastern national statistics are presented in the same table.) Such a comparison is useful, indeed essential, given the numerous problems associated with eastern statistics in 1991. The major divergences (i.e., those which give a totally different picture of developments in trade) occur in Bulgaria and Czechoslovakia. In both cases western statistics show considerably more favourable trade results than their national statistics do. Since western statistics have in the past correlated quite closely with Czechoslovak national data (this has not been the case for Bulgaria), it is assumed throughout the discussion that in 1991 the western data more accurately reflect the development of the country's trade than national statistics do. For Bulgaria, national statistics are given more weight.

CHART 3.3.1

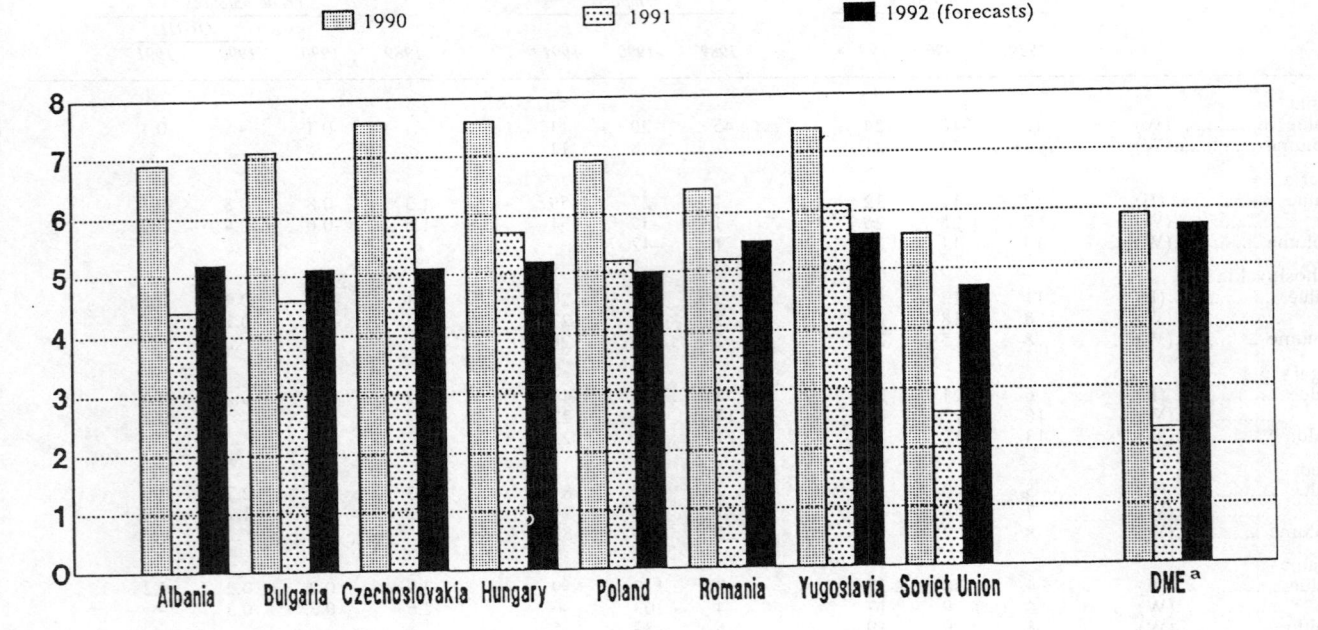

Effective western market demand facing eastern Europe and the Soviet Union, 1990-1992

(Per cent, volumes)

▨ 1990   ▦ 1991   ■ 1992 (forecasts)

Source: ECE secretariat estimates based upon COMTRADE and OECD, *Economic Outlook*, Paris, July 1991.

Note: These are changes in the import volumes of western countries weighted by the shares of those countries in the exports of eastern countries to the west.

[a] Import growth of developed market economies.

to expand strongly in the first three quarters of 1991. At the same time the imports of the three countries boomed, the pace picking up sharply in Poland and, to a lesser extent, in Hungary. The growth in the volume of Czechoslovak exports appears to have quickened during the course of the year, while the opposite was true of Poland's deliveries to the west. All three countries have managed to boost exports during the past 4-5 consecutive years. It appears that exporters have been able to shift the sales of certain goods from their traditional, but collapsing, ex-CMEA market to the west. This reorientation was presumably reinforced by the contraction in domestic demand. Indeed exports to the western market provided the only support for domestic demand in these economies during the past two years.[126]

In recent years, Czechoslovakia, Hungary and Poland have benefited from a particular pattern of market growth among the western countries (chart 3.3.1). While the volume of overall western import demand grew by 5 per cent in 1990 and 2 per cent in 1991, the specific western demand facing the eastern countries expanded by 7 per cent and 5 per cent, respectively. The explanation for these differences lies in the fact that eastern exports are concentrated in western countries, above all Germany, which experienced relatively high import growth rates.

The results in chart 3.3.2 indicate that the exports of Czechoslovakia, Hungary and Poland to the rapidly growing German market accounted for some 40-50 per cent of the increment in their total exports to the west during 1988-1991. Smaller but still important increases in exports to Italy, France, Austria, the Netherlands and Turkey were also achieved.

The western trade of Albania, Bulgaria,[127] Romania and Yugoslavia, by contrast, has been disappointing. In general trade values and volumes declined in the first three quarters of the year, weakened by various domestic supply constraints and shortages of convertible currencies.

(b) Exports by commodity, 1988-1990

Given the large sustained increase in the exports of Czechoslovakia, Hungary and Poland over the past several years, it may be of interest to examine, in a cursory and preliminary fashion, the role of individual commodity categories. Special attention attaches to the so-called "sensitive products" (textiles and clothing, iron and steel, and agriculture), which in western markets are subject to the most comprehensive import regulations.

During the period 1988-1990 covered here, *total* exports to the west from Poland increased by 81 per cent, from Hungary by 54 per cent, and from the Czech and

---

[126] Domestic policy changes affecting trade in 1991 have been discussed in more detail in United Nations Economic Commission for Europe, *Economic Bulletin for Europe*, vol.43, New York, 1991, chapter 3.

[127] See footnote (125) above.

CHART 3.3.2

Exports of Czechoslovakia, Hungary and Poland
to the developed market economies, by destination, 1988-1991[a]
(Cumulative changes; million US dollars)

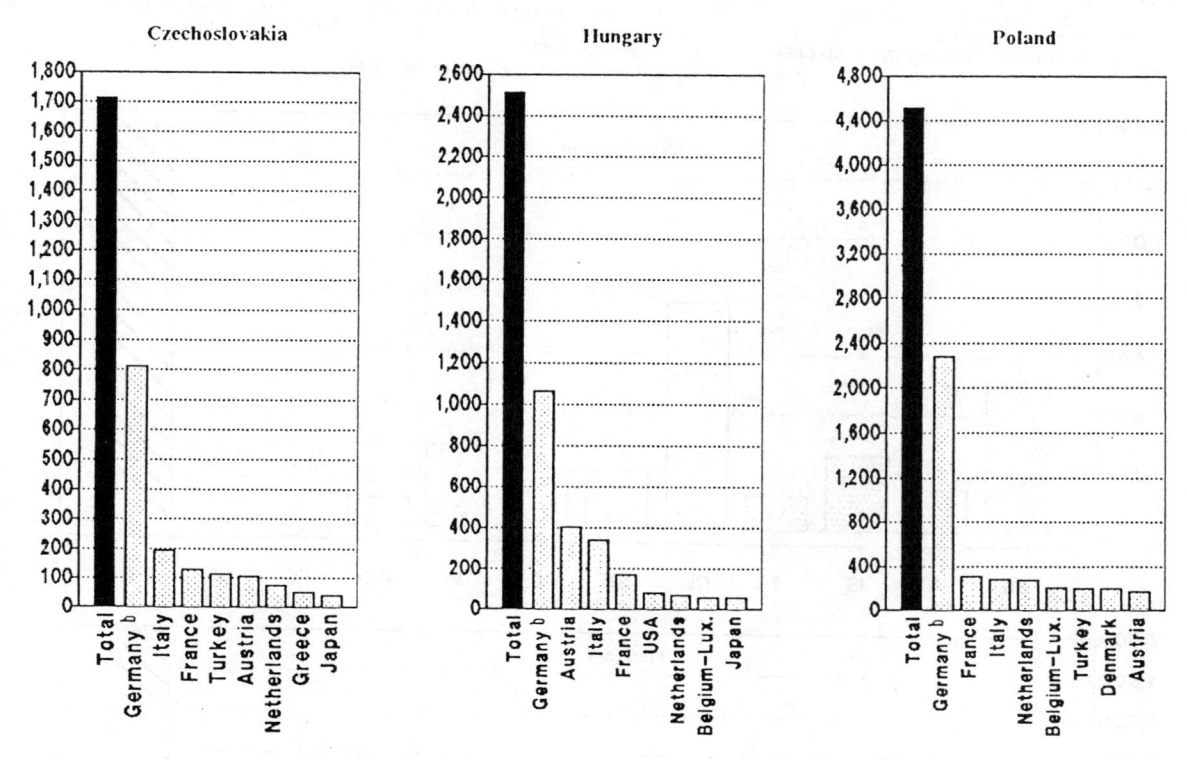

Source: ECE secretariat based upon COMTRADE. For January-June, see table 3.3.4.
[a] 1988-June 1991.
[b] Germany excluding the ex-GDR.

Slovak Federal Republic by 39 per cent (chart 3.3.3).[128] Czechoslovak, Hungarian and Polish exports of *manufactured goods* other than those included in the "sensitive" category outpaced the growth of these countries' total western exports. They account for some 44-56 per cent of the incremental value of total exports. Sales of *semi-manufactures*[129] and *engineering goods* grew at relatively rapid rates.

In 1990 the combined export shares of the *"sensitive products"* ranged from 32 per cent for the Czech and Slovak Republic to 41 per cent for Hungary (see table 3.3.5). Agricultural goods exports were most important for Hungary and Poland, accounting for over 20 per cent of total exports. The iron and steel sector was important for Czechoslovakia (12 per cent of total exports), but less so for Hungary and Poland. The textile sector held almost equal importance for the three countries, accounting for between 10 and 13 per cent of total exports.

Czechoslovak and Polish exports of *"sensitive goods"* rose faster than their total western exports (chart 3.3.3). This was not the case in Hungary, but none the less Hungarian sales of these goods increased by an impressive rate of 47 per cent. In all three cases, however, exports of sensitive goods accounted for around 40 per cent of the incremental value of total exports. *Textile and clothing* exports grew faster than total exports in Poland; similarly, *agricultural products* in Czechoslovakia; and *iron and steel* in all three countries. Even in the cases of those products which grew more slowly than total exports, the increases were substantial.

These finding should be considered tentative. The analysis has not separately considered specific goods for which market access in some western countries is virtually foreclosed. However, in the aggregate, the results indicate that the trade restrictions faced by these eastern countries were not entirely binding during this period. Due to the collapse of the eastern market and internal policy changes discussed above, exporters in these three countries may have become more responsive to existing sales opportunities, using available quota allocations in traditional markets and/or seeking them in other mar-

---

[128] A part of these increases reflects the depreciation of the US dollar in 1990, which tended to raise the US dollar value of those eastern exports denominated in other currencies.

[129] SITC 6-65-67-68.

CHART 3.3.3
Exports of Czechoslovakia, Hungary and Poland
to the developed market economies, by commodity, 1988-1990
(Cumulative changes, million US$ and per cent)

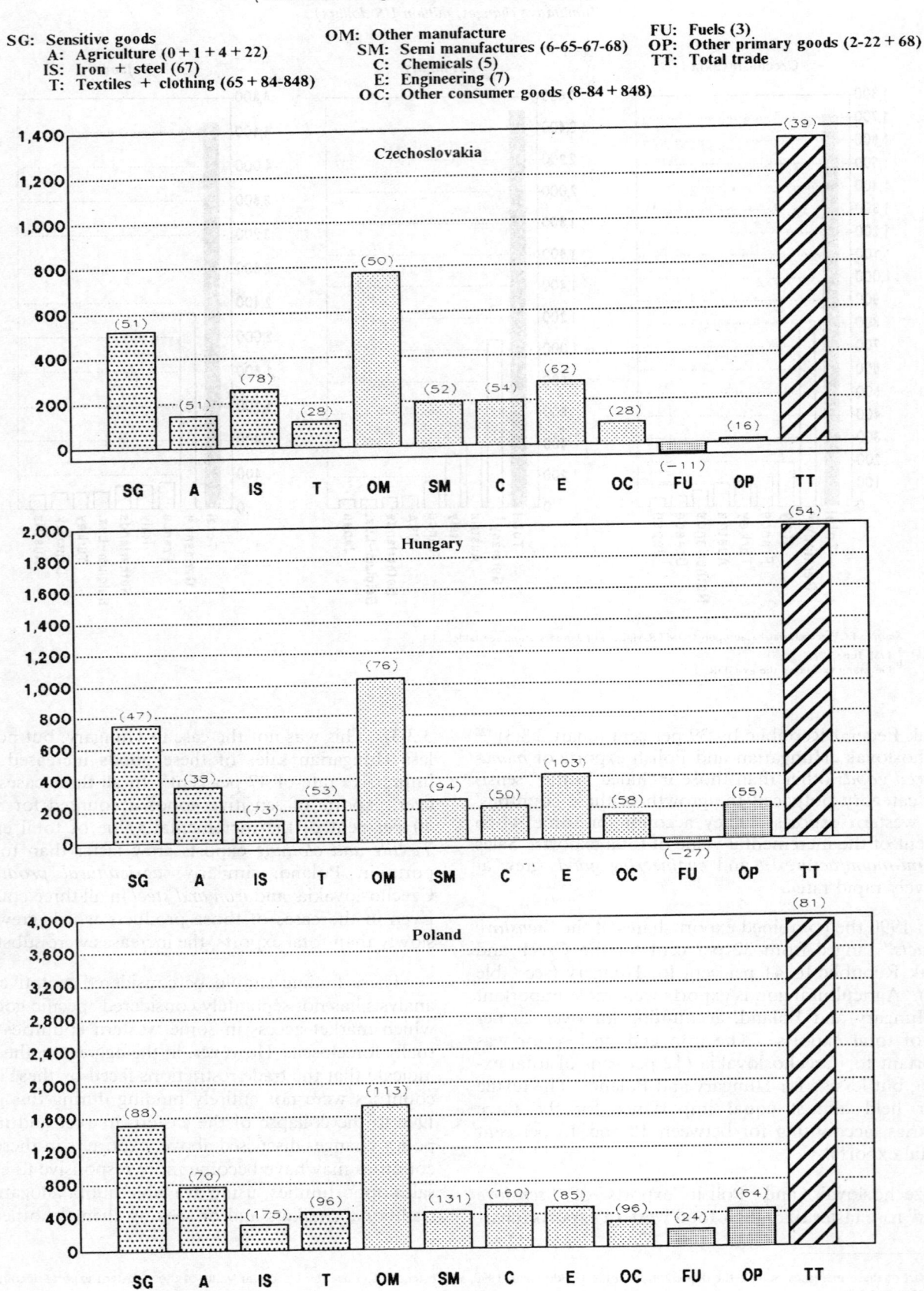

SG: Sensitive goods
  A: Agriculture (0+1+4+22)
  IS: Iron + steel (67)
  T: Textiles + clothing (65+84-848)

OM: Other manufacture
  SM: Semi manufactures (6-65-67-68)
  C: Chemicals (5)
  E: Engineering (7)
  OC: Other consumer goods (8-84+848)

FU: Fuels (3)
OP: Other primary goods (2-22+68)
TT: Total trade

Source: COMTRADE, United Nations Trade Data Base.
Note: In the charts percentage changes 1988-1990 are in parenthesis. Commodities are defined above in terms of SITC Rev.2 (in parenthesis).

TABLE 3.3.5

Exports of Czechoslovakia, Hungary and Poland to the west by commodity, 1990
(Shares in per cent)

	CSFR	Hungary	Poland
Sensitive goods	31.9	41.0	36.7
Agricultural products [a]	8.9	22.2	20.9
Iron and steel (67)	12.2	5.6	5.4
Textiles and clothing [b]	10.8	13.2	10.4
Other manufactures	48.0	42.5	37.0
Other semimanufactures [c]	11.8	9.5	8.7
Chemicals (5)	11.8	11.3	9.4
Machinery (7)	15.3	14.3	11.9
Other consumer goods [d]	9.1	7.4	7.0
Fuels (3)	7.2	4.9	12.2
Other primary goods [e]	11.5	10.8	13.3
Other	1.5	0.8	0.8
Total	100.0	100.0	100.0
Memorandum item:			
Value of exports (million US dollars)	4 830.0	5 691.0	8 817.0

Source: United Nations Trade Data Base (COMTRADE). Commodities are defined in terms of SITC Rev.2.

a SITC (0 + 1 + 4 + 22).
b SITC (65 + 84-848).
c SITC (6-65-67-68).
d SITC (8-84 + 848).
e SITC (2-22 + 68).

TABLE 3.3.6

Eastern Europe and the Soviet Union: Convertible currency current account balances in 1990-1991
(Million US dollars)

	1990	1991 Initial projection	1991 Actual	1992 Outlook
Bulgaria	-1.2	-2.0	-0.5 [a]	-1.7
Czechoslovakia	-1.1	-2.5	0.1 [b]	-1.5
Hungary	0.1	-1.2	0.3	-0.3
Poland	0.7	-2.7	-1.7 [b]	-0.9
Romania	-1.7	-1.7	-1.3	-1.8
Yugoslavia	-2.7	-3.5	-1.1 [c]	..
Soviet Union [d]	-5.1	..	-1.8	..

Source: National sources; IMF (see table 3.3.14), ECE estimates ; table 4.1.7. Also see Appendix table 10.

a January-September.
b January-November.
c January-October.
d Includes gold sales of $2.7 and $3.8 billion in 1990 and 1991 respectively.

kets.[130] For example, it appears that eastern exports of iron and steel remained below ceilings set in "voluntary export restraints" established with the EC and the United States. The EC progressively increased quota allocations for these countries during this period. It also seems that quotas allocated to the eastern countries for textile and clothing products were not fully utilized, and that the role of re-exports had increased.

The rapid growth of eastern exports in recent years (including in 1991) gives rise to the question whether some countries may not now approach full utilization of their quotas, which would curtail the scope for any further growth of sales. While this question is not examined in detail here, there are some indications that this has occurred in certain markets. For example, iron and steel quotas allocated by the EC to Czechoslovakia and Poland are reported to have been used up to 98 and 95 per cent, respectively, in 1991.[131] It is against this background of tightening constraints that the recent initiatives granting further market access benefits to the eastern countries take on additional importance (see chapter 5). It should be borne in mind, however, that the restructuring of eastern industry (above all of iron and steel) is likely to result in the reduction of some export capacity.

(c) Financial relations

In 1991, all east European countries posted better results on *current account* in convertible currencies than had been expected at the beginning of that year (tables 3.3.6 and 3.3.7). Czechoslovakia and Hungary posted small surpluses, this representing a considerable improvement for the CSFR. Only Poland's position worsened, due to a deterioration in its trade balance and the virtual disappearance of its traditional large surplus on transfers. The appreciating real exchange rate fuelled an import boom and braked the growth of exports.

The better than expected performance was due to a number of factors, the importance of which varies considerably from country to country. All benefited from the decline in oil prices to levels considerably below the $25-28 per barrel assumed in their programmes for 1991. Second, internal demand declined, in some cases considerably more than anticipated, reducing pressure on imports (certain countries were actually counting on an upturn in economic activity). Third, a number of countries did not receive the agreed quantities of fuels from the ex-Soviet Union. In Bulgaria and Romania shortfalls in official financing[132] and the absence of reserves led to declines in imports, which exacerbated the contraction in domestic output.

In 1991, the overall *financing* of eastern Europe's balance of payments involved the coordination of G-24 creditors and the international financial organizations (see chapter 5). The resulting arrangements were designed to cover the projected current account deficits and to rebuild depleted foreign currency reserves. Aside from Czechoslovakia and Hungary, little private capital was expected owing to private creditors' general loss of confidence in the eastern countries after the revolutions in late 1989.[133]

---

[130] It is doubtful that the trade liberalization initiatives launched by the G-24 in support of the east's transition programmes explain much of the change in the east's exports of sensitive goods during this period. (The changes in trade policy are discussed in chapter 5.)

[131] "L'acier de l'Est, bouc emissaire de la crise", *Siderurgie Européenne et Internationale*, 3 January 1992.

[132] On this point see chapter 5.

[133] The reasons for changes in creditors assessments of the eastern countries have been discussed in the United Nations Economic Commission for Europe, *Economic Bulletin for Europe*, vol.43, New York, 1991, and in the United Nations Economic Commission for Europe, *Economic Survey of Europe in 1990-1991*, New York, 1991.

TABLE 3.3.7

Eastern Europe and the Soviet Union: Balance of payments in convertible currencies, 1990-1991

(Million US dollars)

	Bulgaria 1990	Bulgaria 1991 [a]	Czechoslovakia 1990	Czechoslovakia 1991 [b]	Hungary 1990	Hungary 1991	Poland 1990	Poland 1991 [b]
Current account balance	-1 206	-503 *	-1 104	112	127	267	668	-1 749
Trade balance	-797	169	-785	-100	348	189	2 214	94
Exports	2 488	2 302	5 994	7 633	6 346	9 258	10 863	11 386
Imports	3 285	2 133	6 779	7 733	5 998	9 069	8 649	11 292
Services balance	-518	-712 *	-279	208	-948	-781	-3 479	-2 147
of which:								
Transport	51	-13	259	461	-164	-80	..	..
Travel	78	-85	-71	133	345	560	..	..
Investment income	-750	-600 *	-316	-321	-1 438	-1 331	-3 329	-2 343
Transfers	108	40	-40	4	727	861	1 933	304
Capital account [c]	-3 395	..	326	1 485	-689	2 473	-6 678 [d]	-3 993 [d]
of which:								
Long-term capital (net)	-3 341	..	899	1 439	204	3 090	-4 153	-2 771
Assets	297	..	-40	95	-76	-57	42	49
Liabilities	-3 638	..	758	1 345	280	3 147	-4 205	-2 820
Short-term capital (net)	-58	..	-573	-481	-893	-617	-2 525 [d]	-1 222 [d]
Errors and omissions	149	..	-324	393	..	..	..	..
Overall balance	-4 454	..	-1 102	1 990	-562	2 740	-5 650 [e]	-5 967 [e]
Exceptional financing (net)	3 576	..	-	-	-	-	7 803	5 148
Reserves (net) [f]	862	..	1 102	-1 990	562	-2 740	-2 153	819

	Romania 1990	Romania 1991	Yugoslavia 1990	Yugoslavia 1991 [h]	Soviet Union [g] 1990	Soviet Union [g] 1991
Current account balance	-1 656	-1 311	-2 664	-1 092	-5.1	-1.8
Trade balance	-1 743	-1 230	-4 670	-496	-1.6	1.1
Exports	3 364	3 520	11 834	12 268	33.5	31.8
Imports	5 107	4 750	16 504 [i]	12 764	35.1	30.7
Services balance	97	-181	986	-48	-4.7	-4.2
of which:						
Transport	..	-196	1 090	690	-0.9	-0.7
Travel	..	2	2 708 [j]	325	0.2	0.2
Investment income	137	-25	-822	-632	-4.0	-3.7
Transfers	..	100	1 020	-644	-1.5	-2.5
Capital account [c]	47	488	-1 177	..	-6.9	0.4
of which:						
Long-term capital (net)	..	250	906	..	2.7	3.8 [k]
Assets	..	157	240	..	..	..
Liabilities	..	93	-1 146	..	..	..
Short-term capital (net)	..	202	-271	..	-10.1	-5.6
Errors and omissions	-35	-	4 784 [l]	..	-0.9	-0.7
Overall balance	-1 664	-789	943	..	-12.9	-2.1
Exceptional financing (net)	-	-	-	-	4.5	-0.5
Reserves (net) [f]	1 664	789	-943	..	8.4	2.5

Sources: National statistics and direct communications to ECE secretariat.

a January-September.
b January-November.
c Excluding changes in reserves.
d Includes errors and omissions.
e Includes valuation changes.
f A negative sign indicates an increase in reserves.
g Includes gold sales of $2.7 billion and $3.8 billion in 1990 and 1991 respectively.
h January-October.
i Imports c.i.f.
j Receipts only.
k Includes grants of $1.9 billion.
l Includes "other" and errors and omissions.

In general, the east's access to the international (publicized) markets continued to diminish in 1991, contributing to the overall decline in funds raised (table 3.3.8). The market for *syndicated loans* has been virtually closed to eastern governments for some time, while *bond* issues, one of the few alternative sources of finance, are now foreclosed to all countries except Czechoslovakia and Hungary. The latter raised over $1.3 billion, the bulk of which was in the DM and ECU markets. However costs for both countries were high — some 2-3 percentage points above the rates paid by most west European governments.

In general, *private bank financing* was unsupportive in 1991. Data for the first three quarters of the year indicate that banks continued to reduce their commercial exposure *vis-à-vis* eastern Europe (table 3.3.9), which is also reflected in the outflow of short-term capital from most eastern countries in 1991 (see table

TABLE 3.3.8

Eastern Europe and the Soviet Union: Medium- and long-term funds raised on the international financial markets, 1988-1991
(Million US dollars)

	1988	1989	1990	1991
Bulgaria	194	580	-	-
Czechoslovakia	330	334	438	278
Hungary	1 016	1 708	987	1 378
Poland	-	163	-	5
Romania	-	-	-	-
Eastern Europe	1 540	2 785	1 425	1 661
Soviet Union	2 679	1 858	3 250	-
CMEA Banks	75	75	-	-
Total above	4 294	4 718	4 675	1 661
of which:				
Bank loans [a]	1 050	2 047	2 993	86
Foreign bank loan [b]	1 652	358	-	60
Other [c]	232	75	-	-
Bonds	1 360	2 239	1 682	1 516

Source: OECD, *Financial Statistics Monthly, Part I*, January 1992 and previous issues.

[a] International bank loans in Eurocurrencies, excluding officially guaranteed loans and rescheduled debt.
[b] In domestic currency of lending countries, excluding guaranteed loans.
[c] Other bank facilities, including bankers' acceptances.

3.3.7).[134] In consequence, all eastern countries resorted to *guaranteed bank and official trade credits*, after years of shunning these facilities, but the amounts taken up were not large. *Foreign direct investment* considerably bolstered resources available to Hungary and, to a lesser extent, to Czechoslovakia (table 3.3.11). Inflows into the other countries remained disappointing. The bulk financing obtained by Bulgaria was in the form of a moratorium on the payments of most interest and principal. Poland was in a similar position benefiting from exceptional financing: debt rescheduling, forgiveness and capitalization of interest.

The combination of small current account surpluses, international assistance, some private credits and inflows of foreign direct investment enabled Hungary and Czechoslovakia to substantially strengthen their *foreign currency reserves* (table 3.3.12). By contrast, those of Bulgaria and Romania remained inadequate and below target levels agreed with the IMF. Although Poland drew upon reserves to finance its current account deficit, their level remained adequate.

The *gross indebtedness* of the east European countries tended to rise in 1991 (table 3.3.13). In the case of Czechoslovakia, the rise was due primarily to official borrowing for the purpose of boosting reserves. By contrast, financing of current account deficits raised the debts of Bulgaria and Romania. Poland's debt fell as a result of exchange rate movements and actions taken by the Paris Club, which called for an eventual reduction of the country's official debt by 50 per cent.[135]

(iii) Eastern trade

(a) Data and measurement problems

The statistical analysis of eastern trade has always been plagued by severe data and measurement problems, stemming from differences in units of payments and accounting, commodity classification, and reporting rules for statistical purposes. The dismantling of the CMEA regime and the gradual transformation of former centrally planned economies into market-oriented economies, while not immediately washing out the old difficulties, actually added some new serious problems. As a result, not only does the aggregation of trade flows denominated in roubles and in dollars pose as difficult a task as before, but also meaningful comparisons of eastern trade flows in 1990 and 1991 have become virtually impossible.

The "old" problems with converting rouble and dollar trade flows into a common denominator have been extensively discussed in the last issue of the *Economic Bulletin for Europe*.[136] Essentially, they arise from using various national implicit cross rates between roubles and dollars by different countries. The "first best" solution to this problem would be to apply an appropriate, "realistic" rouble/dollar cross-rate to all rouble trade flows. Unfortunately it is impossible to determine a proper — whether equilibrium or purchasing power parity — conversion coefficient for the transferable rouble. Moreover, different commodity and price structures of imports and exports of eastern Europe on the one side and of the Soviet Union on the other side, suggest that the "realistic" cross-rate would probably be different for export and import transactions.

Thus, the "second best" solution to overcome the problem of divergent values of the national TR/dollar cross-rates is to select a reasonable approximation of the "realistic" rate and to apply it in a uniform way for all intra-eastern trade flows. This at least would ensure consistency and allow the elimination of extreme cases of undervaluation or overvaluation of trade flows among the former CMEA countries.

The switch to dollars, without a complete elimination of the rouble, and the coexistence of various payments means in intra-eastern trade, added new measurement and statistical problems. Individual countries report data on dollar and rouble trade flows in 1991 in value terms; but their aggregation has become even more difficult than before.

First, trade is now conducted at world market prices for commodities and individually negotiated prices for manufactures; these prices, expressed in dollars, have little or no connection with former rouble prices. Thus, the same quantity of certain goods may now have lower value expressed in dollars than formerly in roubles (the

---

[134] Data for mid-1991 indicate that banks' undisbursed commitments of credits to the east European countries continued to decline (table 3.3.10), which suggests that a revival of bank lending to the east is not imminent.

[135] Exchange rate movements reduced Poland's debt by $2.1 billion and the forgiveness of its obligations by Paris Club members by $1.7 billion (by Finland, the Netherlands and the United States). The capitalization of interest ($1.5 billion) was the main factor tending to increase the debt. *Rzeczpospolita*, 6 February 1990.

[136] United Nations Economic Commission for Europe, *Economic Bulletin for Europe*, vol.43, New York, 1991, p.58-62.

TABLE 3.3.9

Eastern Europe and the Soviet Union: Gross debt vis-à-vis BIS and OECD reporting institutions, by type of debt: 1989-1991

(Changes in million US dollars at constant exchange rates)

	Type of debt	1989	1990	1991 Q1-II	1991 Q-III [a]
Albania	Commercial	270	-18	-107	8
	Guaranteed	-9	3	10	..
	Total	261	-15	-97	..
Bulgaria	Commercial	952	-216	-387	-144
	Guaranteed	-339	-277	73	..
	Total	613	-493	-314	..
Czechoslovakia	Commercial	772	-226	-513	-266
	Guaranteed	-80	-204	261	..
	Total	692	-430	-252	..
Hungary	Commercial	881	-1 827	-825	-261
	Guaranteed	-331	4	117	..
	Total	550	-1 823	-708	..
Poland	Commercial	572	124	-68	174
	Guaranteed	398	703	654	..
	Total	970	827	586	..
Romania	Commercial	-294	26	292	98
	Guaranteed	-450	-24	591	..
	Total	-744	2	883	..
Yugoslavia	Commercial	..	..	..	-211
	Guaranteed	..	..	..	..
	Total	..	..	..	..
Soviet Union	Commercial	7 368	-11 170	-2 389	1 636
	Guaranteed	240	4 998	2 539	..
	Total	7 608	-6 172	150	..

Source: BIS and OECD, *Statistics on External Indebtedness*, Basle and Paris, January 1992 and previous issues. BIS, *International Banking and Financial Market Developments*,, Basle, February 1992.

[a] Commercial and guaranteed bank debt.

case for most industrial goods) or higher dollar value (as in the case of fuels). *Second*, because of changing proportions of dollar and rouble components in total trade in 1990 and 1991, and their valuation at different cross-rates, the total value trade figure in dollar terms for 1991 (first quarter or first half) has practically no meaningful relation with the last year figure. *Third*, all countries in the region devalued substantially their national currencies against the dollar, thus further differentiating the implicit rouble/dollar cross rates. This effect was perhaps the most conspicuous in Bulgaria: the devaluation of the leva from 0.78 leva per dollar in 1990 to 14 leva per dollar in the second quarter of 1991 (i.e., 18 times over less than a year) with no devaluation against the rouble had a dramatic impact on trade statistics, boosting the dollar component of trade and diminishing the rouble component.

The implications for statistical analysis are perplexing. Since the reported changes in trade values between 1990 and 1991 reflect: (a) changes in national cross-rates, (b) changes in transaction prices, (c) changes in rouble-dollar composition of trade and, finally, (d) changes in volumes traded, the real picture of changes in trade is inevitably blurred. The technique used by the ECE secretariat to cope with these difficulties and to obtain a reasonably clear view of main tendencies in eastern trade has been discussed in the last issue of the *Economic Bulletin for Europe*.[137] It involves using a uniform, "consistent" dollar/rouble cross rate for revaluing rouble trade flows and obtaining aggregate trade figures expressed in dollars.

(b) The collapse of intra-CMEA trade

Intra-eastern trade declined sharply in all ex-CMEA countries not only in absolute terms but also as a proportion of their total trade turnover. The share of intra-group trade in total trade of eastern Europe (including trade with the former Soviet Union), shrunk from 39 per cent in 1990 to 32 per cent in 1991, with trade among five east European countries falling even more steeply, from 13 per cent to 10 per cent. Again, the pattern of intra-group trade changes was dissimilar in different countries. Trade flows between Poland and Czechoslovakia actually increased as compared with 1990, while trade of the two countries with Hungary declined only marginally; on the other hand, intra-group trade with Bulgaria and Romania collapsed almost completely, reduced only to 20-30 per cent of the corresponding 1990 levels.

The most important was, however, the unprecedented *collapse of the Soviet market*. Faced by the serious balance-of-payments crisis, generated by falling oil export revenues and accumulation of foreign debt,

---

[137] United Nations Economic Commission for Europe, *Economic Bulletin for Europe*, vol.43, New York, 1991.

the Soviet Union reduced total imports by 44 per cent, and imports from its former CMEA partners by 62 per cent. Given the large share of the Soviet market in intra-group trade (more than 60 per cent), this sudden destruction of export links put hundreds of enterprises in eastern Europe on the verge of bankruptcy. Even though the fall of deliveries to the Soviet market had been reckoned with, the scale and the depth of the collapse came in fact as a surprise. Not only has domestic contraction in the Soviet Union naturally reduced import demand, but also the shortage of convertible currencies, coupled with an apparently highly chaotic system of allocation of foreign exchange for imports to enterprises, resulted in indiscriminate cuts of imports on a massive scale.

Payments difficulties and decentralization of decision making to enterprise levels brought about a substantial change in the *commodity structure* of intra-group trade. The share of machinery and equipment, erstwhile prominent in the CMEA trade, declined dramatically in 1991, affected not only by the cuts in domestic investment programmes in all countries of the group, but also by the apparent diversion of purchases of machinery and equipment to western markets (Poland, Hungary). The share of industrial machinery, equipment and transport means in total exports declined from 60 per cent in 1990 to 29 per cent in 1991 in Bulgaria, from 52 per cent to 28 per cent in Czechoslovakia, from 18 per cent to 12 per cent in Hungary, and from 29 per cent to 22 per cent in Poland. The fall is even more dramatic in intra-group trade because of the high concentration of capital goods exports in the CMEA markets. On the other hand, the share of fuels and commodities soared, reflecting the switch to higher dollar prices and the relatively price-insensitive domestic demand.

The *terms-of-trade* changes in eastern Europe in 1991 directly reflected the demise of the preferential CMEA system of trade and payments. The elimination of the transferable rouble and the switch to world market prices in mutual trade have led to a massive terms-of-trade deterioration for net importers of fuels and commodities (smaller east European countries), and a symmetrical terms-of-trade improvement for net exporters (the Soviet Union). The f.o.b. prices for imported fuels from the Soviet Union jumped from TR 97 per ton of crude oil and TR 76 per 1,000 cubic meters of natural gas in 1990, to an average of $140 per ton and $80 per 1,000 cubic meters of gas in 1991, respectively.[138] Thus, the effective price increase for imported fuels ranged broadly between 200 and 500 per cent, depending on the national dollar/rouble cross rate applied. As a result, the terms-of-trade of fuel-importing countries deteriorated in 1991 by some 15-20 per cent for total trade, and by 30-35 per cent in trade with the former Soviet Union.[139]

TABLE 3.3.10

Undisbursed credits commitments [a] of BIS Reporting Banks vis-à-vis eastern Europe and the Soviet Union
(Million US dollars, end of period)

	1989	1990 June	1990	1991 June
Albania	24	24	39	38
Bulgaria	1 116	652	547	358
Czechoslovakia	1 110	1 174	1 149	892
Hungary	1 268	1 079	1 003	855
Poland	427	694	853	553
Romania	330	..	262	272
Yugoslavia	536	583	385	290
Soviet Union	7 253	7 206	5 781	6 806

Source: BIS, *The Maturity and Sectoral Distribution of International Bank Lending*, Basle, January 1992.

a Includes back-up facilities.

TABLE 3.3.11

Eastern Europe and the Soviet Union: Joint ventures and foreign direct investment: 1990-1991
(Number of projects; million dollars)

	Joint ventures [a] 1990	1991 [b]	Net flows of FDI 1990	1991
Bulgaria	140	800	4	50 [c]
Czechoslovakia	1 600	3 700	188	526 [d]
Hungary	5 693	9 100	300	1 459
Poland	2 799	4 350	88	..
Romania	1 501	4 196	-18	36
Yugoslavia	3 918	4 900	189 [e]	137 [e]
Soviet Union	2 905	3 700	..	..
Total	18 556	30 746	..	..

Sources: ECE joint venture data base; national statistics; IMF, *International Financial Statistics*, various issues.

a Number of foreign direct investment projects registered.
b End-September.   c January-September.
d January-November.   e January-October.

(c) Settling rouble accounts is not easy

The first half of 1991 witnessed the almost complete disappearance of *rouble trade*. Once the dominant means of exchange in the region, the transferable rouble had already lost much of its significance in 1990, when it became clear that the traditional CMEA trading system would be soon replaced by a market trade regime. While in 1985-1988 rouble trade accounted for 90-95 per cent of total intra-CMEA trade, its share diminished to 60-65 per cent in 1990, and to 8-10 per cent in the first half of 1991.[140]

The fading away of the transferable rouble has left behind a plethora of old unsettled credit and capital transaction accounts among former CMEA countries, which for various reasons could not be cleared during 1991, and are now the subject of difficult negotiations

---

[138] Prices effectively paid by Poland for imported oil and natural gas from the USSR in 1990 and in 1991 (Central Statistical Office (GUS), *Handel zagraniczny*, various issues).

[139] Terms of trade worsened for Hungary by 16 per cent (National Bank of Hungary, *Quarterly Review*, No.3, 1991), while in Poland by 4.8 per cent for total trade and by 32.5 per cent for ex-CMEA trade (GUS, *Handel Zagraniczny, Informacje statystyczne*, No.12, 1991).

[140] Officially abolished on 1 January 1991, the transferable rouble has nevertheless been used for settling old contracts and deferred payments for deliveries among ex-CMEA countries. Rouble-denominated transactions in 1991 accounted for less than 2 per cent of total trade turnover in Hungary and Poland, and 5-7 per cent in Bulgaria and Czechoslovakia.

TABLE 3.3.12

Eastern Europe and the Soviet Union: Foreign currency reserves, 1988-1991

(Billion US dollars, end of period)

	1988	1989	1990	1991
Albania [a]	0.14	0.31	0.22	0.03 [b]
Bulgaria	1.78 [a]	1.18 [a]	-	0.15 [c]
Czechoslovakia	1.58	2.16	1.10	2.23 [d]
Hungary	1.47	1.25	1.07	3.93
Poland	2.06	2.31	4.49	3.99 [e]
Romania	0.78	1.76	0.52	0.32
Yugoslavia	2.30	4.14	5.46	3.27 [d]
Soviet Union [a]	15.31	14.70	8.63	7.64 [b]

Source: BIS, *International Banking Development* - Quarterly Reports, Basle. IMF, *International Financial Statistics;* national statistics.

[a] Country deposits held with BIS reporting banks.
[b] September. [c] June.
[d] October. [e] November.

TABLE 3.3.13

Eastern Europe: External debt in convertible currencies, 1989-1991

(Billion US dollars, end of period)

	Gross debt			Net debt [a]	
	1989	1990	1991	1990	1991
Albania	0.4	0.4	0.6	0.2	0.6
Bulgaria	10.7	11.1	11.2	11.2	10.9*
Czechoslovakia	7.9	8.1	9.3	7.0	6.3*
Hungary	20.6	21.3	22.7	20.2	18.7
Poland	40.8	48.5	46.5 [b]	44.0	42.5 [b]
Romania	0.7*	1.2*	3.1*	0.7*	2.8*
Yugoslavia	17.3	16.5	14.5	11.0	11.2
Eastern Europe	98.4	107.1	107.9	94.3	93.0

Source: National statistics; ECE secretariat estimates.

[a] Gross debt less foreign currency reserves or BIS deposits.
[b] End-November.

between the countries. The biggest "rouble" debtor seems to be the former Soviet Union, but the conditions of repayments, and even the size of the debt, are controversial. Hungary managed to sign an agreement in 1991 with the then Soviet Union, under which the TR 2 billion debt would be repaid at 92 cents per rouble; a similar deal has been struck by Czechoslovakia, with the rate 1 dollar for 1 rouble.

Poland's net position *vis-à-vis* the ex-USSR is more ambiguous: its long-term debt includes TR 4.9 billion and $2 billion accumulated in the first half of 1980s, but it may be easily outweighed by huge short-term claims, which raised to TR 8 billion and $300 million during 1990-1991 only. Negotiations to settle these accounts seem to be in a deadlock, with both sides deeply divided over the inextricable tangle of mutual claims and pretensions.[141]

Bulgaria in turn is a net debtor to other east European countries: it has partly repaid its huge debt to the Soviet Union with deliveries of goods in 1991, with the balance to be settled in convertible currencies in the first half of 1992. But the rate of rouble/dollar conversion has not yet been decided. Romania has successfully repaid its commitments to the ex-USSR in 1991 (TR 367 million) through deliveries of subsidized exports, and has left with relatively minor debt obligations to Czechoslovakia.

One more troubling sequel of the east European revolutions is the still unsettled deficit of ex-CMEA countries with the former GDR, accumulated over years and estimated in end-1991 at DM 22 billion. The suggestion by east European countries to cancel this debt as a "sunk cost" of the unification has little chance of winning an unqualified acceptance from Germany.[142]

(d) Energy supplies from the Soviet Union to eastern Europe

The uncertainty about the continuity of energy supplies from the Soviet Union to east European countries was one of the major concerns for these countries in the eve of the switch-over to the market trade system. Fears were expressed that the curtailment of Soviet oil and gas deliveries would result in substantial adjustment costs connected with shifting to alternative sources of supply, or might even lead to rationing of energy.[143] These gloomy prospects led some east European countries to undertake precautionary measures to protect themselves against possible energy shortage. Some countries (Poland, Czechoslovakia, Hungary) obtained special credit lines from the IMF to compensate for higher energy prices in 1991 (CCFF), and the European Community was apparently prepared to provide a special reserve fund of credits in case the need arises.[144]

While prices of imported fuels increased indeed, there was no major interruption in deliveries, although frequent delays were reported by some countries (Poland). Soviet supplies of fuels to east European countries continued in 1991 at levels generally lower by one third than in 1990, except for Bulgaria where fuel imports fell by half. Part of the decline of oil and gas deliveries may be plausibly attributed to lower domestic demand in importing countries, and also to a gradual shift of purchases to other sources (Norway, Italy, Iran). But an increasing proportion of the decline appears to have been due to falling output levels in the former Soviet Union and growing difficulties in obtaining export licences for fuels.

---

[141] See *Világgazdaság*, 31 December, 1991; *Rzeczpospolita*, 15 January, 1992.

[142] Since the biggest debtor is the Soviet union (DM 15 billion), the problem may however be solved within a larger framework of a more general cooperation agreement, involving also issues like the financing of the withdrawal of Soviet troops from east Germany.

[143] Czechoslovak Minister of Finance V. Klaus warned even about the possibility of introducing a "war economy" (drastic cuts in energy supplies and widespread rationing) if Soviet oil deliveries drop below 10 million tons in 1991 (*Eastern Europe Newsletter*, December, 17, 1990). See also the United Nations Economic Commission for Europe, *Economic Survey of Europe in 1990-1991*, New York, 1991, p.81.

[144] *Eastern European Newsletter*, 24 September, 1990.

While an energy crisis on a large scale has been apparently avoided so far, the prospects for 1992 seem to be again very uncertain. The two most alarming tendencies are the continuous fall of oil output in the former Soviet Union and ceaseless changes in central regulation of oil and gas exports by individual ex-Soviet republics.[145] Some countries in the region already face increasing difficulties in securing energy supplies. Bulgaria stands out as a special case, as it received in the first three quarters of 1991 58 per cent less of oil and 25 per cent less of natural gas as compared with the corresponding period of 1990, and energy rationing had to be introduced subsequently. The main reason behind the fall were the sharp import cuts due to the acute shortage of foreign exchange, occasionally exacerbated by delays in deliveries.[146]

(e) The new trading regime and return to bilateralism

The traditional CMEA system of trade and payments was dismantled in 1990. The political and economic changes which swept through the region paved the way for abandoning the centralized state-trading system and adopting market rules in mutual trade relations. While there seems to be a general agreement among economists and policy-makers that the switch to the market system will ultimately bring about substantial efficiency gains through better allocation of resources, it is also recognized that short-term costs of the transition are likely to be high, adversely affecting levels of trade, output, income and employment in the CMEA countries.

The new trading system, based on convertible currency settlements and world market prices, was introduced in January 1991. Early results proved to be disappointing. Preliminary estimates indicate that the volume of intra-CMEA trade fell by some 40 per cent in 1991 (adding to a decline of 15 per cent in 1990), and the drop was particularly strong in east European exports to the former Soviet Union. The sudden collapse of the Soviet market put hundreds of enterprises in a deep financial crisis; furthermore, all ex-CMEA countries inevitably developed large trade deficits with the former Soviet Union (except for Bulgaria, where the trade surplus was an outcome of drastic import cuts). Faced by the trade destruction, some countries resorted in the second quarter of 1991 to various bilateral barter agreements in order to contain losses from abrupt cuts in mutual trade links.

The new institutional framework for trade which emerged immediately after the demise of the CMEA, was based on the series of bilateral trade agreements concluded at the end of 1990. But these agreements were essentially not more than mutual declarations of intentions to shift trade to market rules. In the absence of key market mechanisms and institutions in eastern Europe, this framework proved to be largely inadequate to avoid the crash. With early results of the switch-over to a market system in mutual trade having appeared nearly catastrophic, former CMEA member countries rushed for searching of "second" and "third best" solutions. Faced by the abrupt loss of markets and apparently incapable of an instantaneous shifting of their sales to the west, east European enterprises put growing pressures on their governments to find ways and means to secure export markets and support dying trade links within the group. With the USSR accounting for 60-70 per cent of all eastern trade, the key issue was to revitalize exports to the Soviet market.

The rapidly deteriorating economic situation in the Soviet Union, and especially widespread production stoppages due to shortage of imported inputs necessary for production, have clearly demonstrated, however, that earlier hopes for a smooth working of the market mechanism were premature and that more flexibility is required in the new trade regime. Between April and June 1991, the Soviet government relaxed the strict trade regulations, lifting the ban on barter operations with its former CMEA partners. This has brought about a proliferation of various bilateral trade agreements in the form of barter deals, convertible currency clearing arrangements, countertrade, agreements on using national currencies in trade, etc. On a parallel track, similar deals were negotiated with individual Soviet republics, which eventually emerged during the course of 1991 as independent states.

A mosaic of bilateral deals all relying on some kind of countertrade, and linking east European countries with Soviet successor states, is probably something nobody expected only a year ago. Clearly, the radical and precipitated shift to market rules in east European trade has not been successful so far. In fact, it contributed to the trade collapse and return to bilateralism rather than helped in establishing a genuine multilateralism. But the bilateralism is clearly a sub-optimal solution. Not only will a growth of barter deals lead to substantial welfare losses because in many instances the implicit prices do not cover costs of production, but also clearing arrangements, though more comprehensive than barter transactions, tend to reduce trade flows to levels acceptable for the weaker partner and greatly distort prices. The traditional trade pattern inherited from the past can thus be restored and necessary structural adjustment postponed.

It seems that the core of the problem is essentially of an internal character: inadequate market institutional framework, deep domestic contraction, and lack of capital do not allow countries in the region to adjust smoothly to new trade conditions. The emerging threat of renewed bilateralism calls for a concerted effort to provide urgently stronger support for market-oriented

---

[145] Many reports point out to an aggravating situation with fuel supplies in the former Soviet Union, which may not only hit energy exports but also domestic market situation (*Financial Times*, 6 January 1992, p.2). According to some sources, the ever-spreading oil crisis in the main producing region of Tyumen in Western Siberia may dry up Soviet oil exports next year (*Komsomolskaya Pravda*, 24 October 1991). The review of export licenses by the Russian government in January 1992 resulted in a sharp drop of daily oil exports from 1 million barrels in December 1991 to some 600,000 barrels in the first quarter 1992 (*Financial Times*, 6 February 1992, p.20).

[146] Poland may be next in line: while it signed a barter agreement with Russia on 24 December 1991 on deliveries of 8.1 billion cubic meters of natural gas in exchange for coal, sulphur, food and medicine, the $2.8 billion deal was invalidated in early January 1992 by President Yeltsin's decree. Subsequently, daily gas deliveries to Poland dropped by 60-70 per cent, and resumed only in February, after repeated interventions by the Polish government led to signing a new agreement. But planned deliveries were reduced in the new agreement to 6.6 billion cubic meters, i.e. 7 per cent less than in 1991 (*Financial Times*, 30 January 1992, p.3, *Rzeczpospolita*, 28 January 1992).

reforms in eastern Europe. While bilateral deals may perhaps be an acceptable emergency measure, and are certainly better than a total trade collapse, they are clearly incompatible with the market system and do not ensure the optimal trade structure.

(f) Possible multilateral solutions

The essential problem of eastern Europe is probably not that the intra-trade declines, but that it declines so abruptly, with no time and resources available for an orderly adjustment. Not only sudden cuts in production and trade involve unnecessary economic costs, but they may be also politically dangerous. Various schemes have been contemplated to alleviate the transition costs: one of the most vividly discussed has been the concept of the Central European Payments Union, modelled after the European Payments Union of 1950-1958.

The payments union would allow, at least in theory, an increase in the trade potential of participating countries through extension of their budget constraints, rooted in very scarce convertible currency resources. It could also be expected to introduce some degree of coordination of national economic policies of member countries and to facilitate the convertibility of domestic currencies.[147] But the critics of the idea point out that analogies between the situation of western Europe in the 1950s and the current situation of eastern Europe are deceptive, and that there is only limited potential for a balanced and economically justified trade expansion within the ex-CMEA group at present. What is needed in the region, they argue, is not a scheme for preserving existing trade patterns, but rather a mechanism allowing for a smooth restructuring of eastern economies and their integration with the European and world markets.[148]

To this end, the payments union may be of little help, as it is essentially a short-term, "lubricating" mechanism. Furthermore, the EPU-type of arrangement is a "trade-protecting" mechanism, whereas what is needed in eastern Europe is rather a "production-shifting" mechanism. Intra-CMEA trade patterns reflect distorted production structures and should not be supported across-the-board; instead, the fundamental distortions should be addressed at source, i.e. in the production sector.

On the other hand the current trade collapse reflects *the foreign exchange liquidity crisis* in several former CMEA countries (the ex-USSR, Bulgaria, Romania, Albania), and may be responsible for destroying also economically sound trade flows.[149] This in turn is a *short-term issue*, which could be addressed through trade and financial measures.

The problem can be overcome by a comprehensive programme of external financial and technical assistance, involving an infusion of funds geared to market-oriented reconstruction of particular industrial sectors and enterprises in eastern Europe. This solution would combine an immediate relief with the necessary structural measures. Such programme of external assistance to eastern Europe should aim at filling the gap left by the absence of flexible capital markets in the region: while based on commercial criteria, adjustment loan allocation should concentrate in areas where market mechanism fails to attract private capital, but substantial externalities exist. The essential requirement is to assure the appropriate conditionality for external assistance. Western credits have to be accompanied by a mutually agreed system of domestic policy monitoring and surveillance in debtor country, allowing for efficient targeting and optimal use of funds.

To alleviate the costs of the restructuring and to reduce requirements for financial resources, various supportive measures of industrial and trade policies should be also applied. One of them could be an open-end *free trade area* covering selected east European countries with most compatible market economic systems and relatively balanced economies (Poland, Czechoslovakia and Hungary). The Central European Free Trade Area (CEFTA) would expose local producers to an international, albeit moderate competition, while maintaining some degree of temporary protection against more competitive western firms. The CEFTA could be extended in the future, to include also other economies in transition, like Yugoslavia and the Baltic states.[150] This would increase the competitive pressure on east European producers while still leaving them with relatively large shares of their domestic markets. The restructuring process would be accelerated without necessarily ruining entire industrial sectors in the post-CMEA countries, which might be the case if the region opened rapidly to the EC (as was the case in the eastern part of Germany).

Perhaps not surprisingly, one could not observe a particular willingness among east European countries to preserve their existing trade links through establishing some forms of regional cooperation. The dismantling of the CMEA was done in an aura of euphoria rather than grief. Having eventually wrested their economic and political independence from the Soviet Union, east European countries seem to be in no hurry to enter any new multilateral arrangement which would possibly limit their policy options. But the soundness of that strategy has yet to be proven. Indeed, while

---

[147] See United Nations Economic Commission for Europe, *Economic Survey of Europe in 1989-1990*, New York, 1990, pp.147-150; J.M.van Brabant "On Reforming the Trade and Payments regimes in the CMEA", *Jahrbuch der Wirtschaft Osteuropas*, vol.14, No.2, 1990.

[148] See for example P. Kenen, "Transitional Arrangements for Trade and Payments Among the CMEA Countries", *IMF Staff Papers*, vol.38, No.2, 1991; D.Rosati, "After the CMEA collapse: Is the Central European Payments Union Really Necessary?", *FTRI Discussion Paper*, No.18, May 1991.

[149] It is often argued that the reduction of the intra-CMEA trade, due primarily to the apparent shortage of foreign exchange, may also lead to a discontinuation of (or sharp fall in) economically justified trade, thus resulting in a loss of welfare. Although that possibility cannot be dismissed, it is difficult to explain why this should not happen also in trade with the western economies – which after all has always been settled in convertible currencies – and therefore why one should not envisage a similar trade-supporting mechanism for trade with the west as well.

[150] An alternative solution would be to extend EFTA to include some east European countries. The Secretary General of EFTA Georg Reisch declared recently that his organization is already prepared to accept new members, specifically Hungary, Czechoslovakia and Poland, while other countries may become candidates in the future (see the interview in *Le Nouveau Quotidien*, 3 October, 1991).

being right in breaking away with the past, the east European countries perhaps should not ignore existing natural prerequisites for mutual cooperation. Not only geographical proximity, but also established trade and business contacts, and above all common problems faced by all these countries on the road to a market economy and to a united Europe, offer a solid background for closer multilateral cooperation. A Second European Recovery Programme, supported by the Group of 24, could certainly be helpful in promoting trade and cooperation among the transition countries themselves and also between them and the west European countries.

(iv) Short-term prospects

No fundamental reversal of observed tendencies can be expected in east European countries in the first half of 1992. The region's foreign trade will be determined primarily by internal developments, especially by the scale of recession, domestic macroeconomic policies and balance of payments situation in east European countries, and conditions of trade in the CIS markets. Factors external to the group (like the recession in the West, market access to the EC) will be of lesser significance.

The major impact on *intra-group* trade will undoubtedly stem from developments in the CIS. Exports of east European countries to the ex-Soviet market will probably increase in 1992, provided the new possibilities open under barter contracts will be extended over the whole 1992. Import potential of the CIS economies may further be increased by assistance schemes provided by western countries. If barter and clearing arrangements are not extended, problems with exports to the USSR will continue through 1992, as it seems unlikely that the observed acute deficit of convertible currencies in the Soviet Union could be alleviated to any considerable extent.

Trade within the advanced reform "triangle", i.e., among Czechoslovakia, Hungary and Poland, does not face similar difficulties and the level of mutual trade in 1992 is likely to increase. Foreign exchange regulations in all three countries assure *in practice* unrestricted currency convertibility for current trade transactions, and the level of mutual trade does not seem to be limited by the lack of foreign exchange or inadequate production capacities.

Trade levels of Bulgaria and Romania will remain low throughout 1992, reflecting the slow and painful adjustment process taking place in both economies. If the governments persevere with restrictive macroeconomic policies as planned, falling domestic demand may lead to some expansion of exports and an improvement of external balances. The situation in Bulgaria seems to be particularly difficult, because the country is practically cut off from international financial markets because of the unilateral suspension of foreign debt servicing declared in March 1990.

In 1992, the growth of effective *western* demand facing the eastern countries is expected to remain roughly unchanged at about 5 per cent (chart 3.3.1). According to current prospects these countries cannot expect a sharp increase in the demand for their goods, in parallel with the foreseen doubling in the growth of total western import demand to nearly 6 per cent. The major reason for this lack of expected improvement in market prospects is that the expansion of imports into Germany, the east's major western customer, is expected to halve to 6 per cent in 1992. A pickup in the import growth of several other large western markets (table 2.1.10) would only compensate, since their individual importance for east European goods is comparatively small.

Further adaption to improved access to western markets could strengthen the export performance of some east European countries. Czechoslovakia, Hungary and Poland will gain additional access with the coming into force of the trade provisions of the association agreements with the EC (on 1 March 1992) and of the free trade agreements with EFTA (section 5.3).[151]

As regards the supply of east European goods, the same factors which prevailed during the past two years — declining domestic economic activity, generally weak market prospects in the ex-Soviet republics and several east European countries, and the ongoing domestic reforms — should continue to motivate eastern producers to export to world markets. However, the impact of falling or stagnating domestic output on export capacity is uncertain. Hungary and Poland devalued in November 1991 and February 1992, respectively, to give impetus to exports; other countries may have to follow suit. Supply side difficulties in Albania, Bulgaria and Romania, exacerbated by severe constraints on imports, have and may continue to restrain their export capacity.

The outlook for eastern Europe's balance of payments and financing in 1992 is mixed (table 3.3.14).[152] The financing requirements of the individual countries reflect current account deficits and further strengthening of foreign currency reserves.

Adequate resources would be available to Hungary and Poland to cover their financing requirements. In both cases this would include disbursements from the IMF under the multi-year extended arrangements approved in 1991. Hungary is counting on further sales of bonds and buoyant foreign direct investment. Reduction of official debt and lending from the development banks is to provide the bulk of assistance to Poland. There would be no need of additional exceptional financing from the G-24 for either country.

As regards the other east European countries, a critically important financing role for the G-24 is foreseen. Preliminary estimates of financing gaps range from $0.6 billion for Czechoslovakia to $0.8-0.9 billion

---

[151] The trade provisions of the association agreements with the EC went into effect 1 March, 1990.

[152] It should be noted that these perspectives may be somewhat dated. They are based upon preliminary estimates submitted jointly by the Commission of the European Communities and the IMF to the meeting of senior Finance Ministry officials of the G-24 countries and representatives of the international financial institutions in Bangkok, October 1991.

TABLE 3.3.14
Eastern Europe: Preliminary balance of payments outlook and financing needs in 1992
(Billion US dollars)

	Bulgaria	CSFR	Hungary	Poland	Romania
Financing requirement	2.7	2.3	3.7	5.9	2.3
of which:					
Current account	-1.7	-1.5	-0.4	-0.9	-1.8
Change in reserves [a]	-0.3	-0.6	-0.6	-0.2	-0.3
Financing committed	1.8	1.7	3.7	6.2	1.5
of which:					
Private capital [b]	1.3	0.9	2.2	3.9	0.9
Official capital	0.5	0.8	1.4	2.3	0.6
of which:					
IMF resources [c]	0.1	0.1	0.4	0.6	0.2
Remaining financing gap [c]	0.9	0.6	-	-	0.8

Source: Commission of the European Communities, *Exceptional Balance of Payments Assistance for Central and Eastern European Countries: Review of experience in 1991 and preliminary financing needs for 1992*, Brussels, 28 October 1991.

[a] A negative sign indicates an increase in reserves.
[b] Includes officially supported export credits.
[c] Before new arrangements from the IMF and new disbursements from the G-24.

for Bulgaria and Romania (table 3.3.14).[153] Only part of this could likely be met through disbursements under new arrangements from the IMF. Assembly of the required funds for Bulgaria and Romania is particularly crucial since the failure to reach the targeted amounts in 1991 caused much more severe adjustment than had been foreseen in their agreements with the IMF (chapter 5). Balance of payments financing for Albania awaits an arrangement with the IMF, which appears to have been delayed.

---

[153] The financing gaps are calculated allowing only for remaining disbursements under IMF arrangements concluded in 1991 and assuming full disbursement of G-24 assistance pledged for 1991. As regards the latter, the amounts not actually disbursed in 1991 (chapter 5) will spill over into 1992.

3.4 MACROECONOMIC STABILIZATION: EFFORTS AND RESULTS

This section reviews certain aspects of the macroeconomic stabilization programmes carried out by the countries of eastern Europe. The objective is to provide some details by country, as a comprehensive assessment for the group was already given in section 3.1.

(i) Price liberalization and the fight against inflation

The previous edition of this publication described price liberalization as a "bold jump" into the dark, the precise effects of which were almost impossible to forecast. It was suggested, however, that given the deep roots of the underlying imbalances, there was no ground for believing that these policies would be successful quickly. When this comment was made a year ago — 12 months after the inception of the *Yugoslav* and the *Polish* programmes — inflation in these two countries was still running at an annualized rate of 40 and 100 per cent, respectively. In the subsequent 12 months, the tendencies in the two countries were reversed: in Poland price rises continued to slow, while in Yugoslavia the Federal government has completely lost control of inflation.

By the beginning of 1991, the *Bulgarian* economy had come close to collapse. Uncontrolled price increases approached hyper-inflationary proportions (almost 300 per cent at the annualized rate of January 1991). Industry and trade had reduced their deliveries to consumer markets to a minimum in the anticipation of the price liberalization; the weak lev almost disappeared from circulation as a "parallel" hard-currency system became established.[154] The decisive step was taken on 1 February 1991, when the situation was very similar to that which had prevailed in Poland and Yugoslavia before the launch of the stabilization programmes there. Therefore it was understandable that the Bulgarian authorities chose policies partly modelled on the Polish and Yugoslav programme.

The main idea of the Bulgarian programme was the elimination of inconsistencies and the reduction of excess liquidity within a very short period of time. During implementation the programme lost some of its radicalism, and some U-turns could not be avoided.

As a first step of decontrol, prices of energy were raised substantially, which allowed a large initial reduction in subsidies. Prices in the rest of the economy were entirely deregulated and all subsidies abolished.[155] The targets for the curtailment of inflation set by the Bulgarian government were very ambitious both in themselves and in comparison to the Polish experience (table 3.4.1). It was envisaged that after decontrol, the rise of CPI would be no more than threefold and that it would take 6-12 months to remove inflation almost completely from the economy.[156]

The initial leap in prices after 1 February was large — prices more than tripled in the first two months (table 3.4.2). Within a few weeks, the Government started to monitor the fluctuation of prices of 14 basic goods and necessities,[157] which on the average had risen more than five times from their previous fixed level. In June, subsidies for oil products and natural gas were abolished, though their prices remained regulated. For these goods a system of ceiling prices was introduced which was determined on the basis of current world market prices, but converted into domestic prices at an exchange rate fixed for a month at a time. In early August, the prices of the above-mentioned 14 basic necessities were put under administrative control,[158] but this only slightly slowed the pace of consumer price inflation.

When *Czechoslovakia* opted for price liberalization on 1 January 1991, the country's starting position was much better than those of the other fast-reforming countries. It is also noteworthy that price reform was to some extent gradual. The abolition of direct subsidies on foodstuffs (July 1990) and the devaluation of the crown (October 1990) had already set in motion the adjustment process and thus eased the tensions. The new price law did not fully abolish price regulation. The range of goods still under price regulations initially comprised 15 per cent of total transactions. In the course of the year, however, the authorities were able to reduce this to 10 and then to 5 per cent. Thus, from early 1992 prices remained regulated only in the strongly monopolized sectors such as transport, communication, fuels and energy as well as in some politically sensitive service areas (housing and health).

---

[154] V. Karabashev, "The economic reform in Bulgaria — first results and prospect for development", *Bulgarian Quarterly*, August 1991, pp.73-84.

[155] *Bulgarian Economic Review*, September 1991, p.14.

[156] According to the government's *Letter of Intent* sent to the IMF, the aim was to reduce inflation to a monthly 1-2 per cent in the second half of 1991 (*Bulgarian Economic Outlook*, No.3, 1992).

[157] White flour, bread (two sorts), meat, meat preparations, milk, yoghurt, butter, cheese (two sorts), sunflower-seed oil, crystallized sugar, pasta, intercity and urban bus fares, rail passenger fares (*Bulgarian Economic Outlook*, 1992, No.2, p.8).

[158] See Bulgarian National Bank, *News Bulletin*, No.6, 1991, p.26. These control measures were still in force in February 1992. According to Prime Minister F. Dimitrov, these measures are "anti-market but inevitable". (BTA in English, reporting on the Mr. Dimitrov's press conference on 10 February 1992. BBC, *Summary of World Broadcasts*, 13 February 1992.)

TABLE 3.4.1

Rapid price liberalization: Forecasts and reality

	Increase in the overall price level during the first 12 months after liberalization		Monthly rate of inflation 12 months after liberalization	
	Planned	Actual	Planned	Actual
	(Annual percentage change)		(Percentage)	
Bulgaria	288 [a]	474 [a]	1-2	4.8
CSFR	30	58	1.0	1.2
Poland	90-100	250	1.0	5.9
Romania	120	291	..	10.4
Yugoslavia	..	123	1.0	2.6

Source: National statistics

[a] December 1990 = 100.

TABLE 3.4.2

Price liberalization and the fight against inflation: The radical approach
(Monthly rates of CPI, in percentages)

	Price decontrol started	Last month preceding liberalization	First month after liberalization	6 months after liberalization	12 months after liberalization	18 months after liberalization	24 months after liberalization
Bulgaria	1 Feb. 91	13.6	122.9	8.4	4.8	..	..
CSFR	1 Jan. 91	..	25.8	1.8	1.2	..	..
Poland	1 Jan. 90	17.1	79.6	3.4	5.9	4.9	3.1
Romania	15 Nov. 90	..	23.4	26.5	10.4	..	..
Yugoslavia	Dec. 89	40.0	60.0	2.1	2.6	12.7	17.7 [a]

Source: National statistics

[a] Excluding Croatia.

In contrast to these four countries where sweeping price liberalization was introduced in one single step, in *Romania* price liberalization was introduced in four phases. The *first* round started on 1 November 1990 and concerned manufactured goods and services, but not food. Rents and fuel prices also remained unchanged. According to official accounts, about half of the prices were freed, but if weighted by the volume of transactions, the actual scope of liberalization was much smaller.[159] The start of the *second* round was postponed from 1 January 1991 to April 1991 as a result of protests after the first liberalization measures. It brought the abolition of comprehensive controls on basic food items. However, controls in terms of indicative ceilings remained. In addition, at the wholesale level prices of 88 products, chiefly raw materials, continued to be controlled. The *third* round of price liberalization began on 1 July 1991. The indicative ceilings were abolished and only a group of 15 mining products, as well as 14 basic goods and services remained under control and continued to be subsidized from the state budget.[160] The *fourth* stage of price liberalization was implemented in November 1991, with the elimination of the official exchange rate used to establish domestic prices of a number of imported goods. That rate had been significantly below the market rate.

As devaluation effects worked through the economy, it was expected that price level would double.[161]

Altogether, the track-record of the radical anti-inflationary strategies in the countries reviewed above is far from satisfactory (tables 3.4.3 and 3.4.4). At the turn of 1991/92 the monthly rate of inflation was still dangerously high in four countries – ranging from 5 per cent per month in Bulgaria to 26 per cent in Yugoslavia. By contrast, in Czechoslovakia the rate of inflation was fairly moderate at the end of the year. In most cases the initial jump in price levels had been much greater than anticipated, producing greater falls in real incomes and savings stocks than envisioned, which in turn evoked popular resistance. In the worst cases, when governments were unable to resist the popular pressure, they resorted once again to administrative price control measures (Bulgaria, Romania).

Hungary has been living with double-digit inflation since 1988. When the new democratically elected government assumed office in May 1990, the economic profession was divided in its counsels. Some academic circles argued for a Polish-type anti-inflationary onslaught, while pragmatists working closer to the state bureaucracy made a strong case for gradualism. The discussion can be summarized as follows. In the view

---

[159] *Romania – the transition to a market economy* (statement of Mr. Negritoiu, President of the Romanian Development Agency), 3 December 1991, manuscript.

[160] In early February 1992, the government endorsed a resolution meant to avert monopoly prices and profiteering. This was directly addressed to companies producing meat, meat preparations and staple dairy products. The newly elaborated normative act stipulates that as long as these items are subsidized, prices should be established through negotiations between suppliers and end-users, under the control of the Ministry of Economy and Finance and the Ministry of Commerce and Tourism. (Rompress in English, quoted by BBC, *Summary of World Broadcasts*, Third Series, EE/1302, 12 February 1992.)

[161] *Romania: Economic Newsletter*, October-December 1991.

TABLE 3.4.3
Rate of inflation, 1990-1991, month over preceding month
(Percentage change)

	1990 Dec.	Jan.	Feb.	Mar.	Apr.	May	1991 June	July	Aug.	Sep.	Oct.	Nov.	Dec.	1992 Jan.
Bulgaria	10.4	13.6	122.9	50.5	2.5	0.8	5.9	8.4	7.5	3.8	3.3	5.0	4.9	4.8
Czechoslovakia	..	25.8	7.0	4.7	2.0	1.9	1.8	-0.1	-	0.3	-	1.6	1.2	1.0
GDR	1.2	6.9	0.7	1.5	1.1	0.7	0.6	0.9	0.1	0.2	..	..	..	..
Hungary	1.7	7.5	4.9	3.7	2.4	2.2	2.1	0.9	0.2	1.5	1.3	1.4	1.6	3.2
Poland	5.9	12.7	6.7	4.5	2.7	2.7	4.9	0.1	0.6	4.3	3.2	3.2	3.1	7.5
Romania	11.6	8.6	7.0	6.6	26.5	5.1	2.0	9.5	11.2	7.3	10.4	10.9	13.7	..
Yugoslavia	2.7	5.6	9.2	3.2	4.9	10.9	10.3	5.8	8.0	14.4	18.8	18.9	18.2	26.1

Sources: National statistics.

Notes: Bulgaria: Retail prices, goods and services. *CSFR:* Retail prices, goods and services. *GDR:* Cost of living of all employee households, new series. *Hungary:* Cost-of-living index. *Poland:* Retail prices, goods and services, 1989 weights. *Romania:* Consumer prices (goods and services). *Yugoslavia:* Retail price index.

TABLE 3.4.4
Rate of inflation, 1990-1991, period-over-period of preceding year
(Percentage change)

	1990 Jan.-Dec.	1991 Jan.-Dec.
Bulgaria	20.0*	249.8 a
Czechoslovakia	10.0	57.9
Hungary	28.9	35.0
Poland	584.7	70.3
Romania	13.0*	344.5 b
Yugoslavia	587.6	118.1

Source and notes: As for table 3.4.3.
a Socialist sector.
b Last month of period, change from October 1990.

of the first camp, inflation is a deadly disease under all circumstances, but it is particularly damaging in a shortage economy. Radical reform surgery is needed, but once this is done, inflation can be arrested within a year.[162] The moderates were less concerned about the current rate of inflation and suggested that for 2-3 years the country could continue to live with 20-40 per cent annual price rises without dramatic consequences. In their view, the impending institutional changes (democratization, trade liberalization, privatization, etc.) coupled with the costs of the rouble/dollar switch, would entail such a blow to the economy, that a radical anti-inflationary programme would rock the boat. The advocates of gradualism pointed out that shortages had practically disappeared by late 1989 and — as a result of the 20-year long reform process — relative prices already conformed with market-economy criteria.[163]

This more cautious line was finally adopted by the government. For 1991, policy makers accepted a small but discernable acceleration of inflation (from 29 per cent to 35-37 per cent), in the hope that inflation would eventually decelerate from 1992 onwards.[164]

So far the track record of the Hungarian approach to inflation appears to be favourable. Between January and August 1991, the monthly rate of inflation was slowing despite further liberalization measures in industry and related services.[165] Inflation picked up somewhat later in the year, but, even so, the annualized average monthly rate remained under 30 per cent during the last four months of 1991.

(ii) Fiscal and monetary performance in 1991

Fiscal consolidation and tight control on the money supply were the cornerstones of all IMF-sponsored stabilization packages. As the year 1991 ended and preliminary estimates on revenues and expenditure became known, it turned out that fiscal *deficits* had significantly exceeded the planned levels in all countries but Bulgaria. The degree of excess varied to a considerable extent.

In Yugoslavia, the central government was totally unable to ensure the inflow of revenues from the component republics, especially once civil war broke out. As table 3.4.5 shows, the actual central budget revenues were less than half of the planned level even in nominal terms. Realized federal fiscal revenues from tariffs, taxes and contributions from republics were lower than planned due to the fact that Slovenia, Croatia, and to some extent three other republics, stopped financing the

---

[162] According to J. Kornai, "The gist of the operation is fairly simple. There is a given macro-supply, and facing it is a given macro-demand. On the whole, we allow free play to prices. In this situation an equilibrium would come about at some price level. (...) In all likelihood the operation would finally bring about a considerable rise in the average price level as compared with the current level. This, however, could remain a non-recurrent development, provided that from the very beginning the government stick to a steadfast anti-inflationary policy." (*The Road to a Free Economy*, W.W. Norton & Company, New York, 1990, pp.112-114.)

[163] Price liberalization had proceeded quickly during the second half of the 1980s. In 1985 the share of market-determined prices had been 40-44 per cent of he total; by 1990 it covered 89 per cent of transactions, and now more than 90 per cent. (OECD, *Economic Surveys: Hungary*, Paris, 1991, p.35.)

[164] The IMF-backed stabilization programme reckoned with a 21 per cent inflation rate in 1992, followed by 13 per cent in 1993 and 8-9 per cent in 1994. (See *Programme of Conversion and Development for the Hungarian Economy — Stability and Convertibility*, Appendix, Budapest, March 1991.)

[165] Currently the scope of price regulation pertains to some 13 per cent of total industrial output. Prices are totally free in the case of engineering goods, building materials and light industry products. Among the products of the food industry, price control affects only low-fat milk and the cheapest type of bread. Some 90 per cent of chemicals and 96 per cent of metallurgical products are also free from price control if they are produced by domestic enterprises. As from 1 June 1991, the price of fuels (except for central heating) was completely liberalized after state subsidies had been abolished. At the start of the heating season, even the subsidy for central heating was eliminated. (*Magyar Hirlap*, 14 October 1991.)

TABLE 3.4.5

Fiscal revenues and expenditures in 1991

	Revenues Planned (billions of national currencies) (1)	Revenues Actual (billions of national currencies) (2)	Fulfilment (2):(1)* 100 (3)	Expenditures Planned (billions of national currencies) (4)	Expenditures Actual (billions of national currencies) (5)	Fulfilment (5):(4)* 100 (6)	Deficit Planned (billions of national currencies) (7)	Deficit Actual (billions of national currencies) (8)	Deficit Actual per cent of revenues (9)	Deficit Actual per cent of GDP (10) [a]	Addendum GDP (billions of nat currencies) (11)
Bulgaria	63.0	54.7	102.4	70.5	61.4	81.3	-7.5	-6.7	-12.3	-5.8	115
Czechoslovakia	472.0	466.3	98.8	464.0	484.9	104.5	8	-18.6	-4.0	-1.9	978
Hungary	852.9	716.5	84.0	931.7	830.6	89.1	-78.8	-114.1	-15.9	-4.7	2 450
Poland	289100.0	211800.0	73.3	293400.0	242400.0	82.6	-4300.0	-30600.0	-14.4	-3.4	900000.0
Romania	332.0	290.0	87.6	367.0	356.4	97.1	-35.0	-65.5	-22.3	-3.1	2 100
Yugoslavia	116.8	47.8	40.9	..[b]	102.7	..	..	-54.9	-114.8	-17.5	314

Sources: National bank publications and press reports on legislative developments.

Notes: Bulgaria: On cash basis. *Poland:* Central budget. *Romania:* Actual data are secretariat estimates, based on 9 month returns. *Yugoslavia:* Actual revenue data refer to the situation as of 11 December 1991.

[a] These figure are of a highly provisional character, due to the absence of accurate GDP data for 1991. Moreover, they cannot be directly compared to official statements made by national governments or the IMF, since their numbers are usually based on country-specific definitions of budgetary outlays and revenues, which do not necessarily coincide with the provisions used in the legislation of the respective countries.
[b] The federal parliament did not adopt a budget for 1991.

expenses of the federal government. (Strictly speaking, this was not a breach of promise, since the country's economy was run from the beginning of the year without an approved budget.) In the absence of alternatives, money printing became the main source of federal budget financing. At the time of writing, expenditure data for 1991 are still not available, but according to newspaper reports the government borrowed more than 50 billion dinars from the central bank,[166] which is more than the sum of revenues raised through the normal channels. Overall, the deficit absorbed almost 18 per cent of GDP.

At the other extreme of the spectrum, Czechoslovakia moved from a planned surplus (less than 1 per cent of GDP) to a small deficit (2 per cent of GDP). On the basis of preliminary information it appears that this deterioration occurred in the last two months of the year. Apparently the built-in reflexes of the "old" economic system still worked: budgetary institutions remained cautious for 10-11 months, but then depleted their accounts at the end of the year. Apart from this year-end loosening of fiscal control the budgetary situation of this country gives no reason to worry.

Other east European countries registered fiscal deficits ranging from 3 to 6 per cent of GDP (table 3.4.5).

When assessing the impact of fiscal policy, it is customary to focus on the size of the expenditure and revenue sides of the budget and the deficit relative to a measure of overall economic activity. Under present circumstances this is not easy to do. First, inflation makes GDP estimates very unreliable indeed, so any indicator where GDP appears in the denominator is subject to a large margin of uncertainty. The second source of confusion arises from the lack of standardized accounting methods (see below). However, in spite of these caveats, divergent patterns among countries can be noted.

Amidst rapidly changing relative and absolute prices, the ratio of budgetary expenditures to GDP tends to change quite substantially from year to year, but it is not always certain whether these measured

TABLE 3.4.6

Changes in standard of living, 1988-1991
(Annual percentage change)

	1988	1989	1990	1991
Albania				
Real wages	1.3	3.7	4.7	..
Real incomes [a]	..	..	..	..
Retail sales (real) [b]	2.1	..	..	..
Bulgaria				
Real wages	5.5	2.5	6.9	-45 [c]
Real incomes [a]	3.4	-4.8	..	-45
Retail sales (real)	1.9	0.8	-9.3	-52.8
Czechoslovakia				
Real wages	1.9	0.7	-5.6	-24
Real incomes [a]	3.7	1.6	-1.3	-28.6 [d]
Retail sales (real)	4.8	2.3	1.3	-39.4
Ex-GDR: *Länder*				
Real wages	0.7	0.2	..	23.2
Real incomes [a]	..	..	..	..
Retail sales (real)	3.9	1.4	..	..
Hungary				
Real wages	-4.9	0.9	-5.1	-5 *
Real incomes [a]	-1.0	2.5	-1.6	-(2-4)
Retail sales (real)	-5.3	-0.2	-7.6	-28.2
Poland				
Real wages	14.4	9.9	-24.4	2
Real incomes [a]	13.2	6.2	-14.9	..
Retail sales (real)	3.9	-2.7	-17.4	..
Romania				
Real wages	-0.2	2.1	5.6	-25.5 [e]
Real income [a]	0.5	2.4	17.9	..
Retail sales (real)	0.8	-1.3	7.3	-27.3
Yugoslavia				
Real wages [b]	-7.8	25.3	-22.0	-16.9
Real incomes [a]	-7.9	25.3	-21.9	-7.0
Retail sales (real) [b]	-3.7	-13.0	-5.9	-12.3

Sources: National statistics.

[a] Per capita.
[b] Socialist sector.
[c] State sector.
[d] January to November.
[e] Change from October 1990.

changes reflect any significant "real" change. Thus in Romania this ratio dropped from 37 per cent in 1990

[166] *Ekonomska politika*, 30 December 1991.

TABLE 3.4.7

Minimum wages, average wages and consumer prices
(Growth in per cent; levels in national currency units)

	Bulgaria June 90-June 91	Czechoslovakia Jan. 91-Dec.91	Hungary Feb. 90-April 91	Poland Jan. 90-Jan. 91	Romania Feb. 91-Dec. 91
Growth between given dates:					
Minimum wage	275.8	-	45.8	362.5	122.2
Average wage	135.3	16.4	46.4	128.0	194.0
Consumer prices	503.0	53.6	41.4	119.2	162.7
Levels at end of given period (national currency units per month):					
Minimum wage	620 lev	2 000 Kcs [a]	7 000 Ft	555 000 zl	7 000 lei [b]
Average wage	2 181 lev	3 775 Kcs	15 501 Ft	1 656 000 zl	11 394 lei

Sources: National statistical bulletins; various newspaper and other reports.

Notes: The dates shown are approximate dates when changes in minimum wage rates came into force, providing such changes took place before the end of 1991. It should be noted that the growth in the minimum wage, when calculated over different periods of time, can differ significantly from the figures shown in the table. For example, minimum wages in Czechoslovakia remained at 2,000 Kcs throughout 1991 and were only increased to 2,200 Kcs at the beginning of 1992. A comparison ending in early 1992 would therefore show an increase of 10 per cent in the minimum wage. Average wage levels are generally available on a quarterly basis, while price indices are published monthly. Because of these problems with the periodicity of the figures, the comparisons in the table should be treated with considerable caution.

[a] The minimum wage in Czechoslovakia was raised to 2,200 Kcs at the beginning of 1992.
[b] The minimum wage in Romania is to be raised to 8,500 lei for January-April 1992.

to 17 per cent in 1991, which may imply an an equally substantial retreat of the public sector from the management of the economy. In Bulgaria and Poland, the drop amounted to 8 and 5 percentage points, to 53 and 27 per cent of GDP, respectively. By contrast, in Czechoslovakia and Hungary — i.e., the two countries where political stability was better preserved — the public-sector spending ratio actually appears to have *risen* in 1991. In the first case, the share of public expenditures rose by 9 percentage points (from 42 per cent to 49 per cent), while in Hungary the increment was smaller (from 31 per cent to 34 per cent).

Monetary policy throughout the region was encumbered by the need to finance large government deficits. How to finance the uncovered part of budgetary outlays in a non-inflationary manner remains an unsolved problem everywhere. This burden was extremely high in Yugoslavia where, in the second half of 1991, the federal deficit has been almost entirely monetized,[167] but — broadly speaking — the problem was similar everywhere. Within the tight money supply targets agreed with the IMF, the government sector's excessive borrowings left central banks with very little room for manoeuvre for lending to enterprises. Thus, enterprises were confronted with indiscriminate credit squeezes — sometimes with centrally-set credit ceilings too, as in Czechoslovakia and Romania — and increasingly high nominal interest rates.

To alleviate the crowding-out effect of fiscal borrowing from the banking system, all countries have been experimenting with raising revenues through the commercial issue of bonds and other securities, but these instruments are still unable to fill the budgetary gaps. Besides, in most cases these methods do not differ much from direct bank financing since the holders of these bills are chiefly the central banks themselves or the state-owned commercial banks.

Amidst wildly fluctuating monthly inflation rates, it proved impossible to fine-tune the interest rate structure. In some months these rates were positive (in Poland especially), but most of the time they were actually negative in real terms. Under such circumstances, a rise in the level of inter-enterprise indebtedness was virtually unavoidable, since for enterprises this was the most "cost-effective" way of borrowing (see below).

(iii) The social burden of inflation

Most stabilization programmes applied in eastern Europe were based on the conviction that rapid price liberalization was a pre-condition for further reform steps. It was assumed that the size of the initial adjustment was not a major concern in the light of the urgency of restoring equilibrium on product markets. The experience gained so far, however, may necessitate a correction of this view: the release of pent-up pressures resulted in much higher-than-planned increases in prices, and this generated difficulties not only for the population but also for the orderly continuation of the entire transformation process.

Firstly, these unexpectedly large price surges entailed steep falls in *real wages* (table 3.4.6), with especially large reductions in Poland and Yugoslavia in 1990 and in Bulgaria, Czechoslovakia and Romania in 1991. The fall in real wages in Bulgaria has been particularly drastic, with purchasing power of wages falling by over 40 per cent within the year of 1991. Only in Hungary has the fall in the purchasing power of wages been relatively small. The contrast with the strong growth of real wages in the ex-GDR is stark and the reasons for this are discussed in section 3.2(iv).

All the countries of the region have set statutory *minimum wages* to protect vulnerable workers, and most governments initially committed themselves to

---

[167] The introduction of new currencies in Croatia (Croatian dinar) and Slovenia (tolar) presented a further challenge to the National Bank of Yugoslavia through anticipated and real "cross-border" flows.

TABLE 3.4.8

Average pensions in 1990

	National currency unit per month	As per cent of monthly wage
Bulgaria	143	39.6
Czechoslovakia	1 636	50.5
Hungary	6 683	52.7
Poland	562 107	54.5
Romania	1 575	46.5
Memorandum item:		
GDR [a]	447	34.4
USSR	88.7	32.2

Source: National statistics. Monthly wage data are taken from Appendix table B.3.

[a] 1989.

index these minimum rates in line with increases in prices, often as part of tripartite agreements with trade unions and management organizations (table 3.4.7). In turn, many social benefits such as pensions, family allowances and unemployment benefits are linked to the level of the minimum wage. The deteriorating economic situation has forced some countries to weaken their commitments to increase the minimum wage in line with prices.

Thus, in Czechoslovakia, for example, the minimum wage newly established at the beginning of the year remained unchanged in nominal terms throughout 1991 despite the rapid (and much faster than expected) rise in prices. The minimum wage therefore not only declined in real terms but also relative to the average level of wages. This would be expected to lead to an increase in the incidence of poverty both amongst workers on low wages and among recipients of social benefits linked to the minimum wage rate. In Hungary, minimum wages rose virtually in line with average wages. In Bulgaria, in contrast, minimum wages rose faster than average wages in 1991 (although not as rapidly as prices), compressing the structure of wage differentials. The same situation appears to have been present in Poland in 1990, though problems with the choice of time period may make this observation misleading.[168]

Secondly, the removal of the monetary overhang, which was intentional to a certain degree, turned out to be painfully successful. *Savings* were wiped out so thoroughly that an important part of the population, chiefly the elderly, were deprived of the fruits of their working lives and left without any financial cushion.

As underlined earlier, the prime objective of the stabilization programmes was to rectify the distorted price system and to restore basic macroeconomic balance. It was obvious from the very outset that this goal cannot be achieved without a substantial hardening of the *ultimate* budget constraint — i.e., that on the central government. Hence a third consequence of the higher-than-planned increases in the overall price level was to accentuate the budgetary dilemma. The governments of the countries concerned had to make painful compromises on all fronts: expenditures were adjusted, tax burdens were increased and larger-than-planned deficits were covered by diluting the money supply. One of these compromises involved the acceptance of a drastic breach with deeply rooted social norms. The volume and the quality of state services were cut in such critical areas as health, education, law and order, etc. It can be argued, of course, that the defunct system had created vastly inefficient networks and practices, but the sharp cuts in the real level of state funding are not a remedy to that problem.

This conflict seems to have surfaced especially in Poland, where constraints on budget funding caused teaching time in elementary schools to be reduced by 10-20 per cent, hospital wards and court rooms to be closed, and the like.

The plight of *pensioners* would deserve a separate analysis. In the absence of final data for 1991, only an approximate overview can be provided here. It appears that in Czechoslovakia and Romania the continuous revaluation of pensions during 1991 meant that the decline of average pension incomes was noticeably smaller than that of real wages. In Poland, where the big fall in real wages and incomes had occurred during the previous year, 1991 saw a 15 per cent rise in the real value of pensions, as against the 2 per cent increase registered for real wages. In Hungary, the erosion of these two types of incomes were quite similar in 1991: 7.5 per cent in the case of wage earners and 5.5 per cent for pensioners.[169] (No comparable information is available on Bulgaria or Yugoslavia.) But it has to be stressed that in all countries the method chosen to revalue pensions led to their levelling out. In Czechoslovakia, for example, the real value of the lowest pensions stagnated, while that of the higher pensions went down by almost 20 per cent.[170]

But these data on year-to-year relative changes are somewhat misleading. The situation of pensioners is very grave in all transition economies, because the absolute level of their incomes is insufficient to maintain a socially acceptable way of living for many of them. The pension systems of these countries had never been equipped with legal and financial instruments to cope with the twin problem of recession and inflation. Historically, the pensions were deliberately calibrated at a relatively low level compared to the going wage rate, because planners' objective was to free the maximum amount of resources to stimulate the working cohorts (table 3.4.8). This was part and parcel of the overall industrialization drive and taut planning. As long as

---

[168] In periods of high inflation, comparing the levels of infrequently altered quantities, such as minimum wages, with prices or wages which are continually increasing is particularly problematic. In such circumstances small changes in the choice of starting and finishing dates may significantly affect the results of comparisons.

[169] Calculated from cumulative monthly data, reflecting total wage bill and the total pension outlays. The erosion of the relative purchasing power of average pensions has certainly accelerated in 1991, since the number of pensioners and the number of wage earners changed in the opposite direction. In fact, this caveat has to be born in mind in the case of all other countries too.

[170] Kamil Janacek et al., *Transformation of the Czechoslovak Economy: Macroeconomic and Social Problems and Perspectives*, Institute of Economics of Czechoslovak Academy of Sciences (mimeo), December 1991, p.33.

high growth rates were maintained, this strategy brought fruits to the elderly as well, since their pensions grew along with wages, while the price level of basic goods and services remained constant thanks to the budgetary subsidies. Over the past two years, however, output growth rates turned into negative, prices rose faster than pensions and — given the low *level* of average pensions — a relatively short period was enough to plunge many pensioners into or very close to absolute poverty.[171]

A fifth consequence (at least in part) of higher-than-planned inflation was the adverse change in the relation between *labour* and *non-labour (largely transfer)* incomes. In a very short time — between January and September 1991 — the weight of labour incomes[172] went down from 69 per cent of household money incomes to 63 per cent in Czechoslovakia[173] and from 58 per cent to 49 per cent in Bulgaria.[174] In Poland, where meaningful comparisons can be made for a longer period (December 1989-June 1991), the share of earned incomes[175] eroded from 63 per cent to 52 per cent of household money incomes. The rising share of transfer incomes of course runs rather against the spirit of the transition to the market economy. As some critical observers noted, with some exaggeration perhaps, price liberalization lead to the replacement of production subsidies by social subsidies through the social security system.

(iv) Spending and saving behaviour of households

In 1991 households were confronted by an environment profoundly different from that of previous decades. The dynamics of households' behaviour was determined by five main factors which acted in different directions:

— falling real incomes,

— large changes in relative prices,

— improved availability of consumer goods,

— volatile changes in interest rates and currency exchange rates, and

— appearance or enhancement of alternative forms for saving.

Firstly, *retail sales* fell spectacularly in volume, ranging from 12 per cent to 53 per cent in those countries for which data are available (table 3.4.6). However, some reservations are in order. The figures reported in the table probably tend to overstate the fall because the shift, especially strong in retail trade, towards transactions in the private sector probably has not been fully captured by statistical data collection systems. There was also a change in the traditional division between wholesale and retail trade. As a result of privatization and the increased financial pressure on industrial enterprises, firms engaged in wholesale trading have been shifting their activities towards retailing, but this change too, may not yet be correctly reflected in official statistics.[176]

In response to changes in real incomes and relative prices, the most important modification in spending patterns was the sudden growth of the share of spending on *basic food*. This was clearly the case in Poland in 1990 and in Bulgaria, Czechoslovakia and Hungary in 1991 (table 3.4.9), and is likely to have happened in other countries also. The evolution of the changes is particularly well documented in the case of Bulgaria, where information on household spending behaviour is now available on a monthly basis.[177] Judging by the Polish experience, it can be assumed that the increase in the share of food expenditures is a temporary phenomenon, and that as soon as real incomes start to move upward there will be a tendency to restore previous consumption patterns. Interestingly, the available statistical information for Romania suggests that so far no increase in the share of food expenditures has occurred. This may be related to the fact that this share was already very high in 1990 (food accounted for 49 per cent of expenditures for all households and 59 per cent for pensioners), but it is also possible that the more recent information is simply not accurate enough.[178]

One of the early benefits of the radical shock therapy programmes was expected to be the restoration of *equilibrium on consumer markets* — i.e., the elimination of shortages. On this score the situation has improved in all countries except Yugoslavia,[179] although some problems remain. In Romania, improvements in the

---

[171] At then end of 1991, 2.3 million pensioners in Bulgaria received pensions of 430 leva or less, which was one third of the calculated poverty line. (See N. Krysteva, report commissioned by the ECE secretariat.)

[172] Including a rough estimate of private sector incomes.

[173] Janacek, op.cit., p.30.

[174] "Macroeconomic situation in Bulgaria in 1991" (Report prepared by the Agency for Economic Projections and Development), *Bulgarian Economic Outlook*, No.5, 1992. In Bulgaria, a substantial rise in the share of income from interest on bank deposits played a substantial role in this change: these rose to 12 per cent of personal incomes, from less than 1 per cent in 1990, owing to a sharp rise in deposit rates (ibid., p.15).

[175] Including incomes of private farmers and private industrial entrepreneurs.

[176] This was the case notably in Hungary, but presumably also in other countries.

[177] In January 1991 — i.e., one month before price decontrol — the average share of food in total outlays was 35 per cent. In February, this share rose to 53 per cent, but fell to 50 per cent by August 1991. (*Bulgarian Economic Outlook*, No.2, 13 January 1992., p.4.)

[178] According to a report prepared for the ECE secretariat, the proportion of expenditures for foodstuff in the first 9 months was around 50 per cent for employee households and 60 per cent for pensioners.

[179] At the end of 1991, six months after the outbreak of hostilities, the situation was generally better than one would expect under such circumstances, but varied greatly from one part of the country to another. In Croatia, electricity, water and food shortages became part of daily life during the months of intensive fighting, but quickly normalized soon after that. In Slovenia, market shortages appeared to be less intensive throughout the year and the supply problems were generally translated into exorbitant prices (occasionally 3-4 times higher than in Serbia). The worst situation was reported from Bosnia and Hercegovina. In Serbia, Montenegro and Macedonia, shortages were generally not felt in 1991.

TABLE 3.4.9
Share of food expenditures in total outlays of workers' and employee households and in total retail sales
(Per cent)

	1985	1989	1990	1991
Albania				
Household surveys	63.5 [a]	..	..	..
Bulgaria				
Household surveys	44.2 [b]	40.5 [b]	41.0 [b]	49.8 [c]
Czechoslovakia				
Household surveys	..	..	28.2	31.5
Retail sales [d]	47.5	44.9	42.9	..
Former GDR				
Household surveys [e]	-	38.9 [f]	..	30.0 [f]
Retail sales [d]	50.3	47.3	..	..
Hungary				
Household surveys [g]	27.8 [h]	31.5	..	..
Retail sales [d]	41.6	39.8	39.2	39.8
Poland				
Household surveys	46.6	45.8	49.9	43.4
Retail sales [d]	32.3	31.5	37.9	..
Romania				
Household surveys [g,i]	50.1	51.1	49.4	50.0 [j]
Retail sales [d]	54.4	53.3	51.5 [k]	..
Memorandum items: [l]				
Greece	32.0			
Ireland	25.0			
Portugal	46.0			
Spain	34.0 [m]			
Turkey	36.0 [n]			

[a] 1986.
[b] Estimated retail trade statistics.
[c] August 1991.
[d] Includes public catering.
[e] Includes beverages and tobacco.
[f] Weighting patterns used in 1989 and in 1990-QI-II, 1991-QI-II, respectively.
[g] Includes consumption from own production.
[h] All households.
[i] Includes beverages.
[j] September 1991.
[k] Excludes sales in private sector.
[l] 1985 weights used by OECD for the aggregation of consumer prices.
[m] Includes beverages and tobacco, excludes restaurant meals.
[n] Excluding restaurant meals.

supply situation have permitted the scrapping of rationing for all food items (except sugar). There was also a noticeable improvement in Bulgaria, but electricity is still rationed and certain basic food items (e.g., cooking oil) are occasionally in short supply. In Czechoslovakia, price liberalization and tough anti-inflationary measures were able to bring markets to equilibrium within a few months. It appears that the change in consumers' expectations has played an important role in this turnround. In the case of textiles, furniture and other durables, households tended to postpone purchases, as they were confronted with very high prices for imported goods but hoped that these prices would fall very soon.[180] In Hungary, consumer shortages had already ceased to be a major problem before 1991 — with one notable exception. In the absence of domestic production, the demand for imported automobiles had always been much higher than supply, and this had led to various rationing schemes and the appearance of queues. With the liberalization of western imports during 1990 and 1991 and the two- to threefold rise in the price of eastern cars in consequence of the switch from rouble to dollar trade, these shortages were quickly eliminated.

It is very difficult to make general statements on changes in *savings behaviour* which encompass all countries of eastern Europe, partly because of a lack of information, but partly also because the available data indicate markedly different patterns in the countries concerned.

There are two features, however, which appear to apply to all countries. Firstly, persistent inflation and rapidly changing conditions on savings instruments (large differentiation both in nominal and real interest rates, in degrees of liquidity and security, etc.) have compelled households to pay much greater attention to savings decisions. Households in response have tended to reduce their cash balances to a minimum and to diversify their portfolios. The second observation is that privatization — direct purchases of state assets or of equity in corporatized firms — so far has not become a major factor in shaping savings behaviour. Relative to the total stock of savings, the flows mobilized for buying state assets remained insignificant in all countries. Czechoslovakia, might appear to be an exception, since the small privatization programme and the implementation of the first round of voucher issues have channelled 14 billion crowns[181] and 9 billion crowns, respectively, into state coffers. Nevertheless, these

---

180 See Janacek et al., op.cit., p.47.

181 This figure refers to state revenues obtained in the first three quarters of 1991 from auctioning shops in the retail trade sector (Federalni Statisticky Urad, *Bulletin*, vol.18., No.11, 1991, pp.A35, A37).

TABLE 3.4.10

Households' savings on convertible currency accounts
(Million US dollars, end of period)

	1989	1990	1991 June	1991 September	1991 December
Bulgaria	..	..	..	354	..
Czechoslovakia	59	338	603	735	848
Hungary	400	1 164	1 153	1 522	1 750
Poland	4 834	5 800	5 025	5 180	5 940
Romania	..	..	..	..	..
Yugoslavia	12 000	13 633	..	12 000	..

Source: National statistics, bank bulletin and daily press reports.

amounts are still rather small if compared to the total stock of households savings deposited on traditional bank accounts (360 billion crowns in November 1991). The rapid rise of new private ventures must have absorbed some savings in all countries, but information is still insufficient to permit quantification of these flows.

In Yugoslavia, the most important development pertaining to the savings behaviour was the de facto confiscation of foreign currency savings deposits, which prevented any further increase of these assets. Foreign currency deposits worth $12 billion were blocked already in April 1991, and it is not likely that households will be able to regain access to them in the foreseeable future. It is very likely that they will be compensated in one way or another through privatization bonds instead.[182] The banking authorities' unilateral decision was reinforced by the federal government's decision to suspend the convertibility of the dinar in autumn 1991, while it remained committed to continuing to service the foreign debt.

The increased tendency for savings to be held in hard currency form ("dollarization") has been a general phenomenon in the remaining east European countries (table 3.4.10). The case of Poland, however, is different, because the zloty was made convertible on 1 January 1990 and remained so throughout 1991. Thus, Polish households are legally entitled to buy convertible currencies at practically stable exchange rates, and as long as this access is not perceived to be threatened, there is no reason to convert zloty savings or cash holdings into dollars. Nevertheless, the levels of dollar-denominated savings remained very high in Poland throughout 1991. In all other east European countries, households' access to foreign currency is strictly limited by the law.[183] At the beginning of March 1992, citizens of these countries were entitled to buy (once a year or cumulatively within a year) the following amounts of hard currency: $500 in Bulgaria, $250 in Czechoslovakia, $50 in Hungary, $150 in Romania.

The behaviour of households also changed on the borrowing side. In Bulgaria, Czechoslovakia and Hungary the combined effect of rising interest rates, the tendency to postpone purchases of consumer durables, and the dramatic decline in new housing starts all contributed to a marked contraction of new borrowing, even in nominal terms. In addition, in at least in two countries (Bulgaria and Hungary) there was large-scale advance repayment of housing loans. All in all, in these two countries the net indebtedness of the household sector dropped quite substantially, which in turn helped to finance the government's budgetary deficit through the intermediation of the state-owned commercial banks.[184]

(v) A note on comparability of budgetary and monetary statistics

Under central planning, budgetary and monetary policies used to be simple technical means to implement party, government and ministerial decisions formulated in non-monetary terms. Once such decisions were made, it was up to the Ministry of Finance and the central bank to translate these instructions into executable fiscal and monetary policy steps. These implementation procedures were never fully formalized, and this gave rise to randomly changing practices even within a country itself, but even more between the countries. This was in sharp contrast to the relatively high degree of region-wide standardization in the systems of production planning and the management of foreign trade. This great diversity in the operation of various fiscal and monetary systems is often overlooked by Western observers and advisers.

The difficulties start with statistics. The lack of unambiguous delineation of ownership rights generates measurement problems everywhere: government functions are not clearly separated from the functions of the central bank; the border lines between the central bank on the one hand, and the commercial banks on the other are blurred; banks and their industrial clients are

---

[182] BBC, *Summary of World Broadcasts*, Third Series, EE/W0218, 20 February 1992.

[183] The Romanian leu was declared fully convertible for households in November 1990. This decision, however, remained on paper, as the banking system was not in the position to secure the supply of foreign exchange. In early March 1992, convertibility was formally suspended.

[184] In Bulgaria, the difference between loans repaid and loans contracted in 1991 was 2.1 billion leva, as against *minus* 1.5 billion leva in 1990. (*Macroeconomic Situation ...* op.cit., p.15.) The Hungarian statistics, not directly comparable to the previously quoted Bulgarian one, show a decline in the stock of outstanding debt of the household sector. Between December 1990 and December 1991 this amount went down from Ft 330 billion to Ft 215 billion. (See Központi Statisztikai Hivatal, *Tájékoztató*, Budapest, 20 February 1992, p.29.)

TABLE 3.4.11

Inter-enterprise credits, as a non-registered component of the money supply in 1991

	Inter-enterprise credits	Bank credits granted to enterprises [a]	Inter-enterprise credits as per cent of bank credits
	as reported in the official bank statistics (Billion national currency units)		
Czechoslovakia [b]			
March	76.4	..	..
June	123.5	489.7	25.2
September	147.0	500.5	29.4
Hungary			
March	119.4	432.5	27.6
November	160.0	486.0 [c]	32.9
Poland [d]			
March	109 100	65 588	166.3
June	126 200	78 180	161.4
September	143 100	87 326	163.9

[a] In Hungary and Poland bank credits granted to enterprises refer to credit for working capital only.
[b] State sector only. Only arrears, including an unspecified amount of debt held by the commercial banks.
[c] October 1991.
[d] Inter-enterprise credits include loans not in arrears.

unhealthily dependent on each other, etc. Ultimately, of course, all transactions are recorded somewhere, but not necessarily under the same category as they were the year before, or as they are in the same year in another east European country. As long as ownership rights are not clearly defined, governments are not subject to relentless parliamentary supervision (i.e., control by the taxpayers), and accounting practices are not brought in line with world standards, such measurement problems will confound analysis over time or across countries. A few examples may help to indicate the nature of the issue.

Czechoslovak enterprises traditionally paid *taxes* at the moment of production — thus taxes were collected without regard to whether the product had been sold or not. This practice remains in force even today.[185] By contrast, the Hungarian practice has been for decades to collect taxes on the basis of realized (after-sale) profits.[186] A well-informed observer of the Romanian economy has recently provided an explanation to a puzzle that bewildered users of that country's official data.[187] Romanian budget statistics suggested that the Government had the budgetary process well under control throughout the 1980s — 1990 included — and that a budget deficit appeared only in the second half of 1991.[188] However, this does not give a correct picture of the impact of government decisions on macro-economic balance, principally because the enterprise sector as a whole was forced for years to accumulate deficits which were presumably carried by the banking sector.

TABLE 3.4.12

Domestic state debt, as of end-1991

	In billion national currency units	As a per cent of GDP
Bulgaria	22.1	19.2
Czechoslovakia [a]	57	7.0
Hungary	1535.7 [b,c]	62.7
Poland	993 2	1.1
Romania	245 [d]	11.7

Source: National statistics and OECD estimates (Bulgaria, Czechoslovakia).

[a] 1990.
[b] September 1991.
[c] Includes the impact of forint devaluations debited to the budget.
[d] Forecast.

Another distortion, which to a varying degree applies to all east European countries, is that interest payments on *domestic government debt* held by the central bank are not made at market rates. In the current high-inflation environment, the size of this unrecorded subsidy to the government carried by the rest of the economy and the ensuing statistical distortion can be quite substantial when (a) the stock of debt is already large and (b) the external component of the debt is periodically revalued in line with the depreciation of the national currencies. In Hungary, both conditions are met, and the size of this interest rate subsidy is as much as 10 per cent of GDP.[189] By contrast, this issue has attracted little attention in Poland, mainly because the high inflation rates of the recent past have reduced the value domestic debt to relative insignificance (table 3.4.12).[190]

---

[185] *PlanEcon Report*, Vol.VII, Nos.40-41, 8 November 1991.

[186] Thus, in the first case, *ceteris paribus*, the budget can easily display a surplus in the presence of wide-spread insolvency among enterprises, while in the second one the budget performance may be poor, when companies are proud of their good bill of health.

[187] See J.M. Montias, "The Romanian economy: a survey of current problems", *European Economy*, Special edition No.2, 1991, pp.177-198.

[188] The official data show, for example, that in 1989, the last almost full year of communist rule, the budget had a surplus equivalent to 8.2 per cent of GDP. (IMF, *International Financial Statistics*, January 1992., p.446, 507.)

[189] For a detailed analysis of the history of the "old debt", see OECD, *Economic Surveys: Hungary*, Paris, 1991, p.131. As from 1991, the new debt to the National Bank are contracted at unsubsidized rates and efforts are made to increase the role of public borrowing through the bond market.

[190] No information is available on domestic debt in Yugoslavia, perhaps because it does not even exist as an accounting category within the federal fiscal system.

Fiscal decentralization is often a source of statistical confusion. There is a proliferation of extrabudgetary funds — mostly money spenders, like housing, export promotion, debt service, but in some cases money earners, such as privatization funds. Unfortunately, internationally recommended accounting methods are gaining ground only slowly, and to the extent this happens, the immediate result is not an increase in cross-country comparability, but rather a decreasing comparability between budgetary data of subsequent years within the same country.[191]

Consequently, every east European country probably has had its own specific arrangement with the IMF on the statistical definition of the fiscal deficit.[192] In the case of Hungary, the 1991 deficit target approved by Parliament was Ft 78.8 billion. When the budget was presented to the IMF, it was corrected for not less than five factors (social security fund, housing fund, employment fund, amortization costs of the domestic and the external debt). After making allowance for all of them, the original figure was reduced to Ft 38.3 billion.[193] For Poland, the difference between the two deficit numbers was much smaller. The figure approved by Parliament was zl 4.3 trillion, while the target figure negotiated with the IMF, which covers the entire public sector, was zl 5.5 trillion. In Bulgaria, the relatively small budgetary deficit (leva 6.7 billion) is also deceptive, but for another reason. It is small only because no interest was paid on the foreign debt and only partial payments are effected on the domestic debt.[194]

The transparency of monetary statistics is weakened by a relatively new phenomenon, called *"queuing"* or *"payment incapability"*. This occurs when enterprises run up large payments arrears with each other, but none of them goes into bankruptcy. Under central planning, this was not a significant problem, since it was strictly forbidden for enterprises to provide credits to one another. In a fully-fledged market economy, where enterprises have real owners, there are strong economic incentives for creditors to force non-paying debtors into bankruptcy, or for the debtor to voluntarily declare himself bankrupt.[195] But today, the east European economies are in a transitional situation where the discipline of bankruptcy mechanisms is not yet effective. This gives rise to the inter-enterprise credit chains, which have the effect of insulating the enterprise sector from the impact of monetary policy.

The problem of queuing is a widely discussed issue in Czechoslovakia,[196] as well as in Hungary,[197] but sporadic evidence suggests that to some extent all countries are plagued by it (table 3.4.11).[198]

Quantitatively speaking, the problem appears to be the most pervasive in Poland.[199] Although official banking statistics do keep a very detailed record of inter-enterprise loans, there is no systematic effort to assess how many of these loans are non-performing. However, the mere fact that the total value of these inter-enterprise loans is almost twice as high as the stock of conventional credits is an alarming signal in itself, even if allowance is made for a certain proportion of "good" loans: two thirds of the credit transactions takes place outside of the financial system. The situation is better in Czechoslovakia, partly because the relative weight of these inter-enterprise credits is much smaller. Nevertheless, there is a rapid rise in these debt figures. In Hungary, the commercial banks report to the central bank any companies which are grappling with permanent severe insolvency problems.[200] According to their figures, the problem is of manageable dimensions. However, the official figures on payment arrears are surrounded by a great deal of uncertainty and even the National Bank acknowledges that it may have underestimated them by a considerable margin.[201]

---

[191] In Hungary, for example, privatization revenues of 1991 (Ft 35-40 billion) were used to reduce the domestic debt. The 1992 budget, however, has brought a turnround with the government devoting two thirds of the targeted Ft 35 billion of privatization revenue to cover the current deficit.

[192] This explains why the numbers presented in column 10 of table 3.4.5 differ from the figures accepted by the IMF.

[193] *Világgazdaság*, 29 November 1991.

[194] See *Bulgarian Economic Outlook*, No.4, January 1992, p.4. The magnitude of this deferred burden is variously estimated as ranging from 12 to 40 billion leva (*Hospodárské noviny* reporting from Sofia, 7 January 1992, and direct communication to the ECE secretariat.)

[195] See P. Marer, "Pitfalls in transferring market-economy experiences to the European economies in transition", in OECD, *The Transition to a Market Economy*, Paris 1991, Vol.I, pp.38-56.

[196] V. Klaus, "Monetary policy in Czechoslovakia in the 1970s and the 1980s and the nature of problems of the current economic reform", *Communist Economies*, vol.2, No.1, 1990.

[197] See *Jelentések az alagútból* (Reports from the tunnel), No.3, 1990, pp.49-53, published by Finance Research Limited.

[198] In Bulgaria, a report of the Agency for Economic Projections and Development noted that as soon as the stabilization programme was put into effect ensuing a dramatic shrinkage of real-terms credits, this was massively circumvented by the expansion of inter-company liabilities. In three months, such indebtedness grew by 5 billion leva. (For the full text of the report, see *The Insider*, No.10, 1991, p.7.) No recent information is available on Yugoslavia, but time series covering 1980-1988 suggests that the relative weight of inter-firm debt rose from 38.8 to 44.8 per cent of bank credits already then. (OECD, *Etudes Economiques de l'OECD: Yougoslavie*, Paris 1990, p.38.)

[199] In the view of an influential observer, "credit of this type is an illiquid monetary asset and is, therefore, of limited danger to the overall effectiveness of monetary policy". (S. Gomulka, "Poland", in OECD, *The Transition ...*, op.cit., pp.65-69).

[200] The National Bank refuses to rediscount the bills of exchange issued by these organizations as direct debtors. For this reason, the commercial banks also refrain from discounting such bills. (National Bank of Hungary, *Quarterly Review*, No.2, 1991, p.13.)

[201] The 1989 Annual Report of the bank put the amount of company arrears to Ft 127.6 billion (as of end-1989), but noted some expert believed that the true number was around Ft 200 billion. (National Bank of Hungary, *Annual Report 1989*, p.52.) The problem is that firms are hesitant to report the payment incapabilities of their clients, because they only know too well that they can be in a similar situation at any moment. In Hungarian jargon, this is called "queuing hidden in drawers".

Chapter 4

THE ECONOMIES OF THE FORMER SOVIET UNION

This chapter provides an account of the principal macroeconomic developments in the USSR in 1991 and discusses the prospects for the economies of the new Commonwealth of Independent States (CIS) in 1992. The first section, 4.1, reviews the macroeconomic evolution in the territories of the former Soviet Union in 1991. Section 4.2 focuses on the processes leading to the break-up of the Union and section 4.3 on some of the key macroeconomic issues which must be solved by the new Commonwealth of Independent States or the successor republics separately. In sections 4.4. and 4.5, recent developments in the CIS republics and the Baltic countries are discussed. The chapter closes with a brief outlook in section 4.6.

4.1 THE SOVIET ECONOMY IN 1991

(i) Introduction

The economy of the Soviet Union went into the downspin in 1991 which had long been feared, with a two-digit rate of contraction and three-digit inflation. Probably this would have occurred in any case, but the fact that the long search for agreement on a policy for transformation and stabilization, which had occupied most of the preceding year, had failed to produce a result by the autumn of 1990, certainly contributed to this outcome. Disastrous fiscal and monetary policies did the rest. In 1991, the efforts to formulate radical transformation programmes shifted from the all-Union to the republican plane, and at the same time intense attempts continued to define a new relationship between the Union centre and the republics. A compromise appeared to have been reached in the Union Treaty that was to be ratified in the fall, involving a much weakened central state, when the conservative *coup* in August tried to roll the wheel back. With its failure, the goodwill and trust necessary for maintaining any kind of centralized administration — economic or otherwise — was gone. One after another, the republics asserted the independence which many had earlier declared. The new *Commonwealth of Independent States (CIS)* proclaimed in December in Minsk, and later that month in an expanded form in Alma Ata, paid lip service to the need for policy coordination among the 11 member states and indeed avowed the desire to maintain a common currency sphere, but did not provide for institutions that would make this possible. By the end of the year, the *Union of Soviet Socialist Republics*, one of the largest and certainly the most centralized of economic entities, had disappeared.

Among the many factors impinging on the course of economic developments in 1991, three may be singled out because of their impact on the macroeconomic disequilibria which deepened as the year went on: the bungled attempt at reform in the sphere of prices, the general waning of authority at the centre, and the policies employed to face the foreign trade and external debt problems the country had to deal with in 1991.

The need for price changes was the aspect of the reform policy debates of 1990 on which all parties agreed and which survived the debacle of the search for a radical reform programme. However, the price "reform" eventually implemented retained the administered price system. Producer prices were raised by fiat and almost doubled at the beginning of the year, but the politically sensitive adjustment of consumer prices was postponed until April (with a much smaller rise of the average price level). The consequences were an aggravation of monetary-fiscal disarray (the difference between the two price levels had to be financed out of budget subsidies, and the fiscal deficit already in the first quarter exceeded the figure planned for whole year) and of market imbalance (consumers hoarded in anticipation of price rises while producers withheld goods from the market, if they produced them at all).

The capacity of central institutions to control developments in the economy has been weakening for some time. For the macroeconomic development in 1991 certain aspects were especially important.

First, the weakening and virtual disappearance of the control of central institutions over the activities of enterprises. Because of the highly monopolistic production structure, in combination with the partial freeing of producer prices in 1991, this had a highly inflationary impact.

Second, the increasing autonomy of republican and regional *political* authorities which yet retained considerable *economic* responsibilities within their jurisdictions. One typical use of this autonomy under the conditions of shortages which developed in 1991 was the resort to "mercantilist" policies of supply protection (local export barriers), which in turn worsened Union-wide shortages and aggravated that part of the production fall which stemmed from lack of inputs.

Third, the waning of central authority, even while many functions remained centralized, had particularly deleterious consequences in the fiscal-monetary sphere. This is evident in the reported shortfalls in the transfer of all-Union tax revenues to the central budget, which contributed to the fiscal deficit. At the same time, control of the money supply remained a central function, but one exercised passively by a weak centre. This is evident in Gosbank's accommodative financing of fiscal deficits wherever they arose (see section 4.3 for a discussion of monetary issues).

In external economic relations, the course of developments in the year was particularly affected by the dissolution of the CMEA trading system at the close of 1990 and the policies set to deal with a bulge in debt service payments due in 1991.

The breakup of the CMEA system and its special pricing rules was to yield terms-of-trade gains, but its main effect was a breakdown of customary supply links, in part simply for lack of arrangements prepared beforehand for payments and other aspects. On balance the Soviet economy was hurt more than it gained.

In the relation with the market economies, the authorities attempted to deal with a bunching of debt service payments due in 1991 through a high degree of centralization of import decisions to hold down domestic claims on foreign currency resources and a near-confiscation of economic agents' export earnings to obtain funds for debt service. The latter appears not to have been very successful (foreign-currency earnings declined, partly because of supply problems and perhaps because the measure killed incentives; but also, apparently, because "tax honesty" declined — enterprises hid their earnings, in some cases abroad, and/or regional authorities withheld transfers to the centre), but the former on the whole was: imports were reduced sharply, and the trade balance swung into a large surplus. However, the lack of imported resources, especially intermediate goods, further depressed production activities, especially because the process undoubtedly worked in a very irrational (sub-optimal) manner.

By the end of 1991, even before the demise of the Union, the focus of economic policy-making had shifted to the republics, both for the transformation to a market economy (the transition agenda) and for current macroeconomic policy. Thus there now are 15 policy-making entities where formerly there was one. Indeed the one did not know its own mind, but the danger of policy conflicts obviously rises with the number of entities. However, there still is in existence an all-USSR "economic space", at least in a "structural" sense (long-standing economic interdependence does not disappear overnight because of political change) and even if of diminished permeability. Because of this and the very uneven size of the successor states acting in that space, the policies and actions of the Russian Federation will continue to have major repercussions on the entire "space". This is already evident in the impact of the price reforms enacted throughout the region at the beginning of 1992.

(ii) Output and demand

Output declined steeply in 1991. Gross national product of the 11 members of the Commonwealth of Independent States (CIS) fell by 17 per cent, after a 2 per cent decline in 1990, and net material product by 15 per cent.[202] Quarterly data show that the downturn gathered pace during the year and accelerated substantially in the last quarter (table 4.1.1). The fall is expected to steepen in 1992.

While the recession touched all parts of the former Soviet Union, the impact appears to have differed among republics. Thus, the fall of NMP produced was reported to be about 11 per cent in the Russian Federation, Ukraine and Moldova. But Belarus reported a decline of only 3 per cent, and contractions of less than 1 per cent in NMP produced were registered in Azerbaijan, Turkmenistan and Uzbekistan.[203]

A number of factors contributed to the output decline. Most of them were attributable to disruptions on the supply side. The *traditional supply links* between enterprises and between republics have been broken by the collapse of the state procurement system.[204] It has not been possible to put into place a new system of coordination of activities of economic agents. *Falling exports* to western markets reduced the hard-currency resources available to *import industrial inputs and consumer goods*. Plummeting external trade with eastern Europe also played a role, restricting the supply of production inputs and investment goods and sales of output for the Soviet enterprises. However, the collapse of the former CMEA trade, which hit the east European countries hard, affected the Soviet Union differently since the transition to world prices and payments in convertible currencies improved Soviet terms

---

[202] Goskomstat, "Ekonomika stran-chlenov Sodruzhestva Nezavisimykh Gosudarstv v 1991 godu" (The economy of member-countries of the Commonwealth of Independent States in 1991), *Ekonomicheskii obzor*, 1992, No.12, p.5. The report of the State Committee for Statistics on 1991 in general covers developments only in the 11 states which joined the CIS. However, data on monetary and financial variables cover also the Baltic republics and Georgia, as these states were still part of the common rouble monetary system as of the end of the year.

[203] Ibid., p.7. In fact, the aggregate contraction in NMP produced of 15 per cent is larger than that reported for *any* of the individual republics. The report provides no explanation for this discrepancy. Perhaps it stems from the impact of foreign trade, which declined more steeply than production and which may have been reflected only in the all-CIS aggregate. Another source for the difference may be inadequate deflation of the data reported by the republics which was corrected in the calculation of the CIS aggregate. This of course raises the question what purpose is served by the publication of the unadjusted component data, and what information they carry about real differences between the republics.

[204] In 1991, inter-republican goods flows fell considerably and agreed contracts (15 per cent below their level in 1990) were not fulfilled. Serious shortages of fuels and energy, material inputs and consumer goods in the republics appeared because of their dependence on monopolistic producers in other republics. This created a chain reaction, and since imports could not be called upon to substitute for products in short supply, the disruptions in the production process have become general. Thus the failure to agree on a new mechanism for inter-republican economic coordination was among the main factors of the worsening economic situation. For a discussion of economic relations among successor states, see section 4.3(vi).

TABLE 4.1.1
USSR/CIS: Output, employment, costs and prices, 1987-1991
(Annual percentage change)

	1987	1988	1989	1990	1991, over same period of 1990			
					QI	QI-QII	QI-QIII	QI-QIV
GDP	2.9	5.5	3.0	-2.3	-8.0	-10.0	-12.0	-17.0
NMP	1.6	4.4	2.5	-4.0	-10.0	-12.0	-13.0	-15.0
Population	1.0	0.9	0.5	0.7	..	..	..	0.5
Employment [a]	0.4	0.1	0.5	-0.6	-0.1	-2.6	-1.8	-1.7
Labour productivity [b]	1.5	4.8	2.3	-3.0	-9.0	-11.0	-12.0	-14.0
Money wages [c]	3.7	8.3	9.4	14.2	10.0	30.0	54.0	70.0*
Unit labour costs [d]	2.0	1.1	5.7	20.5	-	-	-	139.0*
Industrial wholesale prices	0.5	0.9	1.7	3.0	83.0	100.0	117.0	138.0
Agricultural procurement prices	2.9	12.1	6.7	11.7	61.0	56.0	63.0	63.0
Enterprise profits [e]	6.9	12.3	9.0	3.9	-	80.0	78.0	75.0
Gross industrial production	3.8	3.9	1.7	-1.2	-5.0	-6.2	-6.4	-7.8
of which:								
Consumer goods	4.8	6.2	7.5	6.1	-2.0	-4.5	-3.7	-4.5
food	5.8	1.2	3.2	0.9	-6.0	-8.5	-8.3	-8.7
non-food	5.2	7.7	7.7	9.1	-2.0	-3.0	-1.6	-3.0
alcoholic drink	-0.8	16.7	21.1	7.6	5.0	0.7	4.0	5.0
Gross agricultural production	-0.6	1.7	1.3	-2.9	-13.0	-11.0	-10.0	-7.0
Goods transport [f]	2.0	1.3	-1.9	-4.9	-7.8	-8.4	-7.7	-7.5

Source: Narodnoe khozyaistvo SSSR v 1990 g., Moscow 1991, pp.5, 7, 36, 67, 100, 102, 159-160, 527, 582; USSR Goskomstat, *Ekonomicheskii obzor*, No.12, 1992; ECE secretariat estimates. Data refer to the Soviet Union through 1991 QII and, in principle, only to the 11 CIS member republics for the last two quarters of 1991.

a Workers and employees and collective farmers. Excludes armed forces and private sector.
b As given in official series.
c Money wages through 1990 in current prices. The increase between 1990 and 1991 is given on the basis of a new official series "average funds committed to consumption per worker and employee per month". This covers payment in money and kind, i.e., including food supplies at the workplace, etc.
d Based on GDP.
e 1987-1990: excluding collective farms and joint agricultural enterprise units, current prices.
f Based on ton/kilometres.

---

of trade. The origin of Soviet difficulties thus is falling domestic output in the sectors supplying the main exportables. Damaging effects came also from the disorder in the *financial and credit* system. The *conversion of the defence industry* from military to civilian production has run into many difficulties. Moreover, general uncertainty, as well as increasing labour unrest and growing social tensions added to the above factors. Thus, the parallel influence of many negative factors was reflected in sharply deteriorating economic performance of the ex-Soviet Union.

In many respects, Soviet developments have been *sui generis*, differing from those in eastern Europe. The decline of output in 1991 is a feature shared with the other countries of the region, but its causes lay mainly in a general falling apart of the country and not in market-oriented reforms and stabilization policies which were implemented to different degrees by all east European countries. The Soviet Union lagged behind most of its former European allies both in designing economic reforms and in their implementation.

Domestic absorption contracted more steeply in 1991 than production, reflecting the external "adjustment" based mainly on sharply reduced import volume (exports also fell, but less), and perhaps increased wastage of output. This contrasts with the development in 1990, when the external sector was permitted to mitigate the impact of reduced production on final uses, at the expense of a sharp rise in the external deficit. In 1991, domestic absorption (NMP used) fell by 16 per cent, slightly more than NMP produced. *Consumption* contracted 13 per cent and *accumulation* 25 per cent (table 4.1.2). The Soviet consumer has certainly suffered, but the aggregate decline may underestimate the real drop in living standards because it is widely believed that official consumer price index may underrepresent price inflation. Moreover, disturbances on the domestic consumer market and widespread shortages of foodstuffs and consumer goods were exacerbated by household inventory purchases in anticipation of price rises. Thus the domestic market virtually collapsed. The fall in private consumption in 1991 (by 15 per cent) further reduced living standards which were already low; in early 1992 it was followed by an even more pronounced fall after the price liberalization at the beginning of the year. There are fears that this could undermine the fragile political and social consensus on the necessity of introducing market-oriented reforms and stabilization policies.

No aggregate data were reported on *investment* change in 1991. Scattered investment data reported by individual republics register declines roughly in step with the fall of output (e.g., by 11 per cent in the case of the Russian Federation). This would indicate a surprising robustness of investment demand, or perhaps rather illustrate the surviving capacity of economic agents to lay claim to resources outside of market channels. However, other estimates also point to a much steeper contraction of investment spending.[205] In any case, it seems that long-lasting problems of inefficiency in the investment process, construction delays and the growing disparity between investment expenditure and the value of completed and commissioned investment projects, have not improved. The decline in investment, accompanied by a further downturn in in-

---

[205] In August 1991, the head of *Gosstroi*, the state construction agency, estimated that investment in 1991 would fall by "at least 23-25 per cent". *Izvestiya*, 28 August 1991.

TABLE 4.1.2

USSR/CIS: Incomes, prices and expenditure, 1987-1991
(Per cent annual change)

	1987	1988	1989	1990	1991 QI	QI-QII	QI-QIII	QI-QIV
Money incomes	3.9	9.2	13.1	17.3	24.0	43.5	69.8 [a]	90 [a]
Consumer prices [b]	1.0	-0.2	3.2	6.9	..	5.9	81.0	96
Real incomes [c]	2.9	9.4	9.6	8.9	..	..	..	-3
Retail sales	1.1	6.9	8.4	10.3	0.2	-12.5	-11.7	-7.1
Retail prices	1.0	1.0	1.9	4.7	23.8	55.5	70.6	86
NMP used	0.7	4.6	3.4	-1.8	..	..	..	-16
Consumption	2.4	5.5	5.0	3.1	..	..	..	-13
Accumulation	-4.2	2.0	-1.8	-18.4	..	..	..	-25
Gross fixed investment	5.6	6.2	4.7	0.6	-16.0	-6.0	-4.0	..

Source: IMF, *Narodnoe khozyaistvo SSSR v 1990 g.*, Moscow 1991, pp.7, 13-14, 166, 546; USSR Goskomstat, *Ekonomicheskii obzor*, No.12, 1991. Data refer to the Soviet Union through 1991-QII and, in principle, only to the 11 CIS member republics for the last two quarters of 1991.

[a] Excluding the "compensation" payments to personal savings made by the state to reduce the impact of state-decreed price rises in April 1991.
[b] Implicit deflator of consumption within NMP. For 1990, the deflator for consumption is given as 6.5 per cent (*Narodnoe khozyaistvo SSSR v 1990 g.*, op.cit., p.10).
[c] Money incomes deflated by consumer prices.

vestment efficiency and a rise in unfinished construction, meant that virtually no new capacity came into operation in 1991. This will seriously constrain any supply response from industrial branches with growth and export potential. The modernization of these branches will need huge investment and increased imports of capital goods from abroad.

(iii) Sectoral developments

The fall of output levels in 1991 affected all main sectors of the national economy. The fall in *material production* is reflected in the NMP data already cited. In contrast to most east European countries, GDP fell more steeply than NMP produced in the CIS economies, which may indicate an even sharper decline of output and a diminishing role of *non-material services*. This could be caused by serious difficulties in financing the activities of the non-material sphere from the state budget and a worsening situation in providing such services as health, education, housing, communal services and administration. However, private demand for services must have also fallen, presumably in consequence of the real income loss associated with consumer price inflation (see below), since "paid services" (i.e., consumer services purchased out of personal incomes) registered an 18 per cent decline in 1991.

A fall of 7.8 per cent in real *gross industrial production* is reported for the CIS republics. This is a surprisingly moderate decline in view of the 15 per cent fall in NMP produced. One explanation might be that net industrial output was falling more than gross output due to substantially rising material intensity of industrial production. However, given the existing acute supply constraints this interpretation does not seem to fit. Inadequate deflation of the underlying nominal gross output data must therefore also be considered a possibility, but cannot be verified because of the very small range of physical output data published for 1991.

The rate of industrial output decline accelerated considerably during the course of the year (table 4.1.1). The contraction in output affected virtually all industrial branches. With an overall fall of industrial production of almost 8 per cent, the output of consumer goods was down 4½ per cent in 1991 and there was a nearly 9 per cent contraction in food-processing. The production of investment and intermediate goods (group "A") must therefore have contracted at above-average rates — a conclusion which is confirmed by branch and product data. In the fuels and oil industry, metallurgy, some engineering sub-branches, wood-processing, and the pulp and paper branch the output contraction was much larger than in total industry.

In 1991, Soviet *primary energy production* fell for the third consecutive year. Electricity, coal, oil and gas declined by 2, 10, 10 and 0.5 per cent, respectively. Oil production in 1991 (515 million tons) was at the level of 1976. This resulted in substantially reduced oil deliveries both for the domestic market and for exports. Total oil exports declined by 52 per cent in 1991. There were many reasons for the poor performance in the Soviet fuel and energy sector: shortages of material inputs and equipment, mismanagement, labour unrest, transport bottlenecks and the deplorable state of the infrastructure. The effect of the production fall was aggravated by trade barriers imposed by individual republics and regions to protect local supplies. These conditions, coupled with the absence of serious conservation measures, led to domestic energy shortages in the largest oil-producing country in the world.

Gross agricultural output declined by 7 per cent, mainly because of declines in the sown area, falls in the number of livestock and declining yields of land and animals. The overall output drop included a fall of 27 per cent in grain production, to 155 million tons in 1991, and 7 and 6 per cent falls in meat and milk output. The output drops were accompanied by substantially stronger declines in state purchases of these products. Thus, state purchases of grains in 1991 reached only 40 million tons (41 per cent less than in the preceding year).

The falling proportion of output delivered to the state has several causes. Some produce is reportedly being retained in rural areas, or even not harvested, because of the deterioration of the farm sector's terms of trade with the rest of the economy. Probably more important in practice is the diversion of farm output to

TABLE 4.1.3

USSR/Successor states: Money supply, 1987-1991
(Billions of roubles)

	\multicolumn{5}{c}{1 January}	1 July	1 January
	1987	1988	1989	1990	1991	1991	1992
A. Cash							
Population	73.0	78.9	88.1	104.7	131.9	15.0	252.6
Other	1.8	1.7	3.5	4.8	4.2	7.6	10.8
Total	74.8	80.6	91.6	109.5	136.1	157.6	263.4
B. Bank deposits							
Population	242.8	266.9	297.8	340.5	386.8	572.0	662.1
Enterprises [a]	93.3	124.4	146.1	163.7	210.2	328.9	396.7 [b]
Total	336.1	391.3	443.9	504.2	597.0	900.9	1 058.8
C. Short term government securities							
Total	35.0*	38.0*	41.0	45.0	54.0	65.0* [c]	100.0* [c]
D. Total broad money	445.9	509.9	576.5	658.7	787.1	1 123.5*	1 422.2

Sources: Narodnoe khozyaistvo SSSR v 1990 g., Moscow 1991, pp.28, 45. V. Gerashchenko, "Dlya chego nuzhna kreditnaya ekspansiya?", *Ekonomika i zhizn'*, No.45, September 1991, p.4 and No.47, November 1991, p.5. USSR Goskomstat, *Ekonomicheskii obzor*, No.12, 1991, and direct communication to the ECE secretariat. Data refer to the Soviet Union or the aggregate of the 15 successor states (CIS republics, Georgia and the Baltic republics) included in the rouble monetary system.

a Gerashchenko op.cit.
b Estimated on the basis of a continuing slight rise in enterprises' share of the total.
c Crude estimates based on a figure of R77 billion on 1 October 1991.

---

other channels: to private trade, which offers higher prices, and into barter deals with enterprises in other sectors. Transactions on commodity exchanges (*birzhy*) in agricultural bulk commodities also increased rapidly. However, these new marketing channels do not yet appear to be able to replace adequately the distribution functions of the state procurement system. Problems are compounded by what amount to regional or local trade wars. As a result, areas that are major net food importers have suffered substantial reductions in supplies. Thus, a poor agricultural performance coupled with disturbances in distribution led to supply problems in some areas and increased import of agricultural products. Foreign aid has become necessary to improve the situation.

The *transport* sector registered a 7.5 per cent fall in tons carried, reflecting the deteriorating performance in the main goods-producing sectors. Falling investment volume must have been reflected in reduced *construction* output, but no aggregate data are available.

(iv) Internal balance

Fiscal, monetary and income policies were in 1991 in disarray and the crisis of financial and monetary systems has deepened. The Union and republic budgets reflected independent (and competing) policy objectives, with no effective coordination between them. These fiscal policies generated large and increasing deficits which were funded by an expansion of bank credit that has led to an explosive growth of the money supply.

An assessment of developments in government finances is complicated by the fact that for 1991 no consolidated general government budget for the Union and the republics is available. In the statistical communiqué on 1991 economic developments in the 11 CIS member states, two different figures on the budgetary deficit in 1991 are reported.[206] The Union deficit narrowly defined amounted to R150 billion (some 8 per cent of GDP).[207] A more broadly defined fiscal aggregate comprising the "budget system and economic stabilization funds" recorded a deficit of R200-240 billion (11-13 per cent of GDP). This reflects a five- to sixfold increase from 1990, when share in GDP was only 4 per cent. However, neither measure includes the budgetary deficits of the republics. These are estimated at R175-R180. Thus, the broadly defined consolidated (Union and republics) deficit could reach R375-R420 billion (equal to 21-23 per cent of GDP).[208]

The dramatic growth of budgetary deficits was mainly due to higher than foreseen expenditures and lower than expected revenues on account of the sharp downturn in economic activity. Revenues were also constrained by the declining fiscal authority of the central state and the virtual absence of an effective revenue collection mechanism once ministerial control over the state enterprises waned. Thus the tax shortfalls totalled 47 per cent of Union expenditures budgeted for the year. Part of the Union deficit stemmed from the fact that most of the republics, above all the Russian Federation and Ukraine, did not meet their obligations for

---

[206] See *Ekonomicheskii obzor*, 1992, No.12, pp.9-10.

[207] The 1991 GDP at current prices of the 11 CIS members is estimated at 1,800 billion roubles. Ibid., p.5.

[208] This order of magnitude was largely anticipated at an early date. In his report to the IMF and World Bank meeting in Bangkok on 15-17 October 1991, G. Yavlinskii estimated the consolidated budgetary deficit for the year at R320 billion. The figures are also consistent with data on the evolution of the domestic state debt of the ex-USSR, which at the end of 1990 was R628 billion and rose to over R1,000 billion by end-1991 (Goskomstat communiqué, op.cit.). Some 90 per cent of this consisted of bank credits to cover the budgetary deficit. Recently, Egor Gaidar, Deputy Prime Minister of the Russian Federation, confirmed a budget deficit of more than 20 per cent of GDP. See his article in *Financial Times*, 4 March 1992, p.11.

TABLE 4.1.4

USSR/Successor states: Incomes and credit, 1987-1991
(Billions of roubles, current prices)

	1987	1988	1989	1990	1991
Personal sector					
Money incomes	452.1	493.5	558.0	652.5	1 242.0 [a]
Money expenditures	420.1	451.6	496.2	572.0	961.0
Excess of incomes	32.0	41.9	61.8	80.5	281.0
Bank credit outstanding (1 January)					
Long-term	3.1	5.8	7.4	11.6	12.0*[b]
Short-term	-	-	-	-	-
Enterprise sector [c]					
Profits	209.0	240.2	268.2	282.4	494.0
Depreciation	118.1	125.6	134.5	137.5	..
Bank credit outstanding (1 January)					
Long-term	94.3	96.5	96.6	80.3	95.0*
Short-term	334.7	302.3	287.1	272.5	656.2*[b]
Memorandum items (1 January):					
Total bank credit outstanding	432.1	404.6	391.1	364.4	762.4 [b]
Overdue credits	12.5	21.9	21.9	42.0	78.7
Banks	8.5	6.3	4.4	9.2	..
Enterprises	4.0	15.6	17.5	32.8	..
State internal debt	219.6	311.8	398.6	627.7 [c]	over 1 000 [d]
percentage of GNP	26.6	35.6	43.1	56.6	57.0*

Sources: Narodnoe khozyaistvo SSSR v 1990 g., Moscow 1991, pp.19-20, 25, 29-31 and 36; USSR Goskomstat, Ekonomicheskii obzor, No.12, 1992. Data refer to the Soviet Union or the aggregate of the 15 successor states (CIS republics, Georgia and the Baltic republics) included in the rouble monetary system.

[a] Goskomstat, *Ekonomicheskii obzor* reports a 90 per cent rise.
[b] 1 December.
[c] Data for 1987-1990 excludes collective farms and agricultural joint enterprise units. The data for 1991 may include them.
[d] Includes food subsidies, given as R61.6 billion in 1990 and R74.6 billion in the first 10 months of 1991.

transfers to the Union budget laid down in the interrepublican agreement for 1991.[209]

On the expenditure side, the scanty data suggest that subsidies of various kinds continued at high levels. Food subsidies were reported to have totalled some R75 billion — over 20 per cent higher than in 1990. Subsidies to enterprises to cover the cost of certain social initiatives taken by the government but financed through enterprises (wage indexation, etc.) also remained high. Calls on the budget for higher payments under existing social programmes, and also for new kinds of welfare needs stemming from the transition process, also increased. These included unemployment benefits, higher pensions and payments to compensate vulnerable groups of the population for rising prices and other losses. Against this, some other expenditures were reduced. Defence spending in particular decreased. In addition, the withdrawal of the state from direct involvement in productive activity tended to reduce investment allocations formerly funnelled through the budget.

Monetary and credit policy was another source of inflationary pressures. The expansion of the money supply has been largely the result of the passive accommodation of the state budget deficits by the banking system. Developments in this sphere, however, are rather difficult to assess with any precision because of the limited range and varying coverage of monetary statistics.[210] Available data on money supply are summarized in table 4.1.3. They indicate that all the main component parts of money supply (cash, bank deposits and bonds) registered rapid growth. The increase in the money supply broadly defined appears to be around R653 billion — a rise of more than 80 per cent over its year-earlier level. Most of the rise in the money supply appears to have occurred in the "personal" sector (see table 4.1.4). According to the end-year Goskomstat report, money in the hands of the population and in current account deposits, together with short-term government securities, rose by 49 per cent or R277 billion between the end of 1990 and 1991. This was nearly 5 times higher than in 1990, the last near-normal year under the old system.

The "passive" role of the banking system was reflected in the expansion of credit to the government sector and to enterprises. In the first 11 months of the year credits increased by 110 per cent and reached R762 billion on 1 December 1991. Interest rates on loans from Gosbank USSR and the Russian Central Bank remained well below the rate of inflation in 1991.[211] Some of the large number of new private commercial

---

[209] *Ekonomika i zhizn'*, No. 25, June 1991 and *Izvestiya*, 3 June 1991.

[210] While data on monetary stocks and flows were always compiled, they were not until recently published. Moreover, data geared to the purposes of the administrative planning system proved quite inadequate to the purposes of a market system. The construction of an appropriate accounting and data collection system is only under way, with the help mainly of the international financial institutions.

[211] At the beginning of 1992, an official of the Russian Savings Bank indicated that the bank now paid interest of 15 per cent on deposits and charged a rate of 20 per cent on loans.

TABLE 4.1.5

USSR/CIS: Foreign trade, by direction, 1989-1991

(Value in billion US dollars; growth rates in percentages) [a]

Country or country group [b]	Exports Value 1990	Growth rates 1989	Growth rates 1990	Growth rates 1991	Imports Value 1990	Growth rates 1989	Growth rates 1990	Growth rates 1991
World	59.1	0.4	-5.2	-25.2	65.0	12.0	-	-37.3
"Socialist countries"	15.3	-8.7	-24.3	-36.5	19.1	-4.5	-10.6	-45.3
Eastern Europe [c]	11.1	-11.1	-26.9	..	15.0	-5.7	-12.1	..
Developed market economies	29.2	7.8	12.3	-16.0	34.4	21.1	5.6	-31.9
Developing countries	14.5	2.0	-9.5	-30.1	11.5	26.0	3.8	-36.9

Source: Secretariat of the United Nations Economic Commission for Europe, based on national statistical publications and direct communications to the ECE secretariat from USSR Goskomstat. Data for 1989-1990 refer to the former Soviet Union; those for 1991 in principle should refer only to the 11 republics which joined the Commonwealth of Independent States (CIS), but in fact probably also include the foreign trade of the remaining successor states (the Baltic countries and Georgia), at least through the third quarter of 1991 and perhaps through the rest of the year.

[a] Both export and import values are expressed f.o.b. through 1990. Import values in 1991 should in principle have been valued on c.i.f. basis, but in fact represent a mixture of f.o.b. and c.i.f. valuation. Growth rates are calculated on values expressed in US dollars. Trade with "socialist" and east European countries in the years prior to 1991 was valued in an adjusted dollar measure reflecting consistent rouble/dollar crossrates for the eastern trading region. For details of the revaluation, see United Nations Economic Commission for Europe, *Economic Bulletin for Europe*, no.43, New York, 1991, section 2.1(iii), box 2.1.1, and note to table 2.1.4. All trade values for 1991 were converted to dollars at the "commercial" rate quoted by USSR Gosbank.
[b] "Eastern Europe" refers to the east European former member countries of CMEA (Bulgaria, Czechoslovakia, German Democratic Republic through 1990, Hungary, Poland and Romania). The partner country grouping follows the practice until recently prevalent in the Soviet statistical sources, which differs from the breakdown usually employed in United Nations publications. Thus, "socialist countries", in addition to the east European countries, and the Asian centrally planned economies, includes Yugoslavia and Cuba. "Developed market economies" excludes Turkey and includes of Australia, New Zealand and South Africa.
[c] Excluding Yugoslavia. The former German Democratic Republic is included in the data for 1989-1990, but not in those used for the comparison between 1990 and 1991.

TABLE 4.1.6

USSR/CIS: Trade balances, 1988-1991

(Billion US dollars)

Country group	1988	1989	1990 [a]	January-December 1990 [b]	January-December 1991 [b]
World	4.0	-2.7	-5.9	-6.1	3.6
"Socialist countries"	-0.3	-1.2	-3.8	-3.4	-
Eastern Europe [c]	-1.1	-1.9	-3.9	..	..
Developed market economies	-2.7	-6.5	-5.1	-4.7	1.8
Developing countries	6.9	5.0	3.0	2.0	1.8

Source and country groups: As for table 4.1.5. Conversion of national currency data to dollars as in table 4.1.5.
[a] USSR.
[b] CIS republics and Georgia.
[c] Including the former German Democratic Republic through 1990.

---

banks (most of which are, however, very small) have been charging much higher rates.[212]

Inflationary pressures were also fuelled from the side of rapidly growing personal money *incomes* which did not meet with enlarged or improved supplies of consumer goods. In 1991, total personal money incomes increased by 90 per cent (table 4.1.2). Given a 96 per cent rise in living costs, *real* incomes thus fell by 3 per cent. Nominal expenditures of the population rose substantially more slowly (by 68 per cent). Owing to acute shortages of consumer goods, the additional personal incomes could not be realized in the market; the resulting savings thus had a forced character. The total money stock in the hands of the population at the end of 1991 in the form of cash, bank deposits and bonds amounted to R846 billion (R976 billion if compensation payments on special accounts are included), almost 50 per cent more than at the beginning of the year. The main impetus to the growth of incomes were compensatory increases in wages and pensions to mitigate the impact of administrative price changes.

Consumer prices increased by 86 per cent on average in 1991 (in a year-over-year comparison), and by 140 per cent if their level in December 1991 is compared with December 1990. The price reform from April 1991 was supposed to improve the balance on domestic market and reduce the shortages. However, due to a large monetary overhang, accelerating income rises and falling output levels, the shortages have persisted and even worsened. Price rises accelerated in the final months of the year. This occurred under a system of largely administered prices which continued in operation until it was abolished by the Russian Federation on 2 January 1992, a measure followed — in some cases involuntarily — by the other constituent republics of the Commonwealth. The price liberalization in January 1992 led to dramatic price rises. Thus, food prices in January 1992 were generally five- tenfold higher than in December 1991. However, even such a steep price increases appear so far to have resulted only in a rather slow improvement of supplies.

---

[212] By the end of 1991 more than 1,600 private commercial banks had been set up. It might be observed that this is not an indication of any notable increase in the efficiency of the financial sector since most of the new establishments are "pocket" banks which accept deposits from, and make loans to, a small number of enterprises which often own shares in these banks. There is little effective regulation of these activities on the part of the central bank, limited expertise and poorly functioning inter-bank settlement system.

TABLE 4.1.7
USSR/Successor states: Balance of payments, 1990-1991
(Billion US dollars)

	1990			1991		
	Hard currency	Other	Total	Hard currency	Other	Total
Exports	33.5	70.3	103.8	31.8	38.4	70.2
Imports	-35.1	-85.6	-120.7	-30.7	-37.5	-68.2
Trade balance	-1.6	-15.3	-16.9	1.1	0.9	2.0
Other current account	-6.2	-1.0	-7.2	-6.7	-1.0	-7.7
of which:						
Net interest	-4.0	-	-4.0	-3.7	-	-3.7
Gold sales [a]	2.7	-	2.7	3.8	-	3.8
Current account + gold	-5.1	-16.3	-21.4	-1.8	-0.1	-1.9
Capital account	7.8	16.3	8.5	-0.3	0.1	-0.2
of which:						
Long-term net	2.7	-	2.7	3.8	-	3.8
Short-term net	-10.1	17.0	6.9	-5.6	0.4	-5.2
Grant aid	-	-	-	1.9	-	1.9
Other	0.5	-0.7	-0.2	0.3	-0.3	-
Errors	-0.9	-	-0.9	-0.7	-	-0.7
Overall balance	-12.9	-	-12.9	-2.0	-	-2.0
Financing: changes in:[b]						
Reserves	8.4	-	8.4	2.5	-	2.5
Arrears	4.5	-	4.5	-0.8	-	-0.8
Rescheduling	-	-	-	0.3	-	0.3

Source: Ekonomika i zhizn', No.6, 1992, p.11. Data for 1990 refer to the Soviet Union; coverage for 1991 probably is the aggregate of successor states (CIS republics, Georgia and the Baltic republics). Dollar values for trade flows in 1990 are obtained from *valuta* rouble data converted at the "official" exchange rate (approximately 0.58 roubles per dollar). Dollar values for trade flows in 1991 are obtained from data recorded in *invalyutnye* roubles, converted at the "commercial" exchange rate (approximately 1.75 roubles per dollar).

a Excluding movement of gold into swaps.
b Reduction (+), increase (-).

(v) Labour market

Total *employment* in the CIS republics in 1991 averaged 130 million. This represents a decline of about 2 per cent from 1990. The slight decline in employment in the face of the 15 per cent fall in NMP produced indicates that labour hoarding in enterprises still continues, with probably a significant rise in hidden unemployment.

There was a marked shift away from employment in the state sector. The share of the state sector in total employment in 11 CIS republics fell from 78 per cent in 1990 to 72 per cent in 1991. At the same time employment in the agricultural cooperatives decreased from 14 to 13 per cent of the total. While employment in the independent (including private) sector has been growing fast, it thus remains still small as compared with the state and cooperative sectors.

There has been much discussion on *unemployment*, but the available data are not very helpful in assessing its extent. By the end of 1991, 1 million people had been registered as non-employed job-seekers at labour offices of the CIS republics since unemployment registration and assessment for benefits had started at the beginning of July. However, only 77,000 of these had been formally assigned the status of "unemployed". It is widely believed that an internationally comparable figure for unemployment would be substantially larger. Figures of between 4 and 12 million have been cited.[213] Figures in upper end of this range appear not to be very likely. Judging from the pace at which unemployment developed in the east European countries during the early phase of the transformation process, unemployment rates of 2-3 per cent (2.5-4 million) could be expected for the near future.

So long as total number of unemployed remains small and only a small fraction of them qualify for unemployment benefits, the budgetary spending in this respect are very modest. However, both the numbers unemployed and the ratio of those qualified for benefit are likely to rise substantially in 1992.[214]

The social safety net arrangements in place differ between republics, and provide varying incentives and disincentives to register as unemployed. In the Russian Federation, under legislation enacted in April 1991,[215] the state only guarantees redundancy compensation, unemployment benefit and re-training allowances to people who have been made redundant or are entering

---

[213] Viktor Supyan: "Predupredit' bazar na rynke truda", *Izvestiya*, 3 January 1992, p.2. See also section 4.4(ii) for estimates for the Russian Federation alone.

[214] Deputy Prime Minister Aleksandr Shokhin, who is responsible for social affairs in the Russian Federation, recently argued that with correct policies, including rapid privatization and public works programmes, unemployment in the republic could be capped at 2 million. *Financial Times*, 25 February 1992, p.3.

[215] "Zakon RSFSR o zanyatosti", *Ekonomika i zhizn'*, No.22, 1991, pp.18-20. This law was approved on 19 April and came into effect from 1 July 1991.

TABLE 4.1.8

Soviet Union: Foreign trade with the west, 1989-1991
(Growth rates in percentage: trade balances in billion US dollars)

		Exports 1989	Exports 1990	Exports 1991 a	Imports 1989	Imports 1990	Imports 1991 a	Trade balances 1989	Trade balances 1990	QI-III 1990	QI-III 1991	1991
Value	(S)	8	12	-11	21	6	-33	-6.5	-5.1	-5.5	-1.2	1.8
	(W)	10	20	3	15	-5	-21	-3.6	2.4	0.2	5.1	..
Volume	(W)	7	1	-3	15	-13	-19	..	..	..	..	..

Source: Western data, see United Nations commodity trade data base (COMTRADE); OECD, *Statistics on Foreign Trade*, Series A, Paris; IMF, *Directions of Trade and International Financial Statistics*, Washington, D.C; United Nations, *Monthly Bulletin of Statistics* (volume indices of total western exports to and imports from the world); national statistics; and ECE secretariat estimates based upon western data. These data reflect the trade of 23 western reporting countries (Appendix table C.6 contains a list of the countries included). Soviet data: as for table 4.1.5.

Note: (S) = Soviet data; (W) = western data; volumes changes are calculated on western value data. For the methodology and derivation, see United Nations Economic Commission for Europe, *Economic Bulletin for Europe*, vol.31, No.1, New York, 1979.

a January-September.

the labour market for the first time, and only on condition that they do not refuse more than two offers of "suitable" employment. In some other republics, the availability of unemployment benefits is not clearly defined, and under-reporting may be correspondingly greater. In addition, there are appreciable numbers of inter-state refugees, who may not qualify for unemployment benefit in the republic where they now are.

(vi) Trade and payments

The disarray in the foreign economic relations of the Soviet successor states matched the disarray in their domestic economies. Both imports and exports fell heavily, but particularly severe import cuts yielded a trade surplus at a reduced level of activity. The financial benefits of this were more than offset, however, by other factors.

The value of *exports* from the CIS states fell by 25 per cent, and that of *imports* by 37 per cent in 1991, measured in "adjusted" dollar terms.[216] A shift of trade flows in favour of developed market economies at the expense of the former CMEA trade partners is clearly observable. In 1991 exports from the CIS countries to developed market economies fell by 16 per cent while those to former CMEA countries dropped 36 per cent in value. On the import side, the corresponding falls were 32 per cent and 45 per cent (table 4.1.5).

In consequence of these large changes, the *balance of trade* (on a trade returns basis) swung from a $5.9 billion deficit in 1990 to a $3.6 billion surplus in 1991 (table 4.1.6).

Full balance-of-payments estimates for the former Soviet Union and for Russia were published for the first time in February 1992 (see table 4.1.7).[217] They were prepared to meet IMF requirements in connection with Russia's application for membership. They do not seem to conform entirely to the IMF methodology, however, and they leave several unanswered questions.

The data confirm part of the picture of developments in 1991 that analysts had built up: a modest merchandise trade surplus in hard-currency transactions ($1 billion – somewhat smaller than that cited above presumably because trade flows are registered on a payments basis), large net interest payments, substantial revenue from goldsales, and a net withdrawal of short-term credits. On the other hand, the hard currency trade surplus is shown as less than the surplus in trade with developed market economies that appears in the western mirror trade data (table 4.1.8), the balance in services is less favourable than was generally thought, and errors and omissions are, under all the circumstances, surprisingly small.

Broadly speaking, these pioneering estimates tell a story that is not widely at variance with existing western assessments. The questions that remain about these figures are none the less troubling. The total export and import values in dollars are not easy to reconcile with the *valuta* rouble figures given in the Goskomstat report for the year.[218] Transactions with former CMEA partners have been treated in the new balance of payments figures as though none of them were settled in convertible currency, though some almost certainly were.[219]

---

[216] In *valuta* rouble terms, the fall was even more pronounced: 33 per cent for exports and 44 per cent for imports. Volume changes are extraordinarily difficult to determine in 1991 because the switchover from rouble-denominated trade to convertible currencies in transactions with the former CMEA countries (see *Economic Bulletin for Europe*, vol.43, New York, 1991, chapter 2). Their broad order of magnitude, however, is probably quite similar to the value changes cited in the text.

[217] *Ekonomika i zhizn'*, 1992, No.6 (February), p.11. The estimates were prepared by an expert group of the Russian State Committee for Foreign Economic Relations, working together with IMF specialists.

[218] The Goskomstat figures for exports and imports in *valuta* roubles, said to be converted at the commercial rate (1.748 roubles/dollar on average in 1991) are 80 and 74 billion roubles, respectively (*Statisticheskii obzor*, No.12, 1992, op.cit., pp.30-32, and direct communication from Goskomstat to UN ECE). Clearly a large segment of transactions were not in fact converted at the commercial rate. It appears that transactions with CMEA partners were converted at about $1.3 to the rouble, for both exports and imports.

[219] The text accompanying the estimates justifies the continued treatment of trade with former CMEA partners as non-convertible currency trade by saying that "neither in 1990 nor in 1991 was there any real success in transferring settlements with them onto the basis of freely-convertible currency".

There is more doubt than has been usual in the past, moreover, about the reliability of the recording of total exports and imports. The recording system was in transition during 1990-1991 between the old administrative system of obligatory reporting by foreign trade organizations and the collection of data at border crossings by the customs service; there have been difficulties in implementing the latter. Therefore the differences already mentioned from the picture derived from western trade data may well be due to factors other than the difference in the set of trade partners involved. It is widely believed that there has been a strong tendency for exporters to deposit hard-currency revenues offshore, in order to avoid the compulsory sale of a large slice of it to the authorities at the punishingly low commercial rate, and the possibility of substantial under-recording of exports cannot be ruled out. This question arises not only for merchandise exports but for other items as well; for example, the balance on services (chiefly shipping and tourism) is weaker than some observers had expected.[220]

During the course of the past year, official (Soviet) estimates of the ex-Soviet Union's foreign *debt* have ranged from $57 billion to $77 billion.[221] A figure of $65.1 billion was recently given by Vneshekonombank to a group of western creditor banks, of which $53 billion is medium- and long-term obligations.[222] For comparison, Soviet debt *vis-à-vis* BIS/OECD reporting institutions stood at $51.1 billion in mid-1991. This figure comprises bank and non-bank debt, but is not comprehensive.

As regards foreign currency *reserves*, recently published data for end-September 1991 show Soviet deposits with BIS reporting banks at $7.6 billion, down from $8.6 billion at the end of 1990, but up by nearly $0.9 billion over the previous quarter. It is probable that this increase reflected a refunding of the foreign establishments of Soviet banks located in the BIS reporting area to compensate for sharp withdrawals by their depositors in the third quarter of 1991.[223]

Reports during 1991 that Vneshekonombank was on the verge of bankruptcy were supported by the text that accompanied the balance of payments estimates discussed above. In 1991, the country was unable to raise any funds in the *international financial markets* (see table 3.3.8 in chapter 3 above). During 1990, international banks had reduced their commercial exposure by over $11 billion, a trend which continued during the first three quarters of 1991 (measured at constant exchange rates; see table 3.3.9).[224]

In this situation the Soviet Union resorted to *guaranteed credits* (bank and nonbank), its net borrowing amounting to some $7.5 billion from the beginning of January 1990 to end-June 1991. However this was insufficient to make up for the loss of access to non-guaranteed bank facilities. Undisbursed credit commitments of BIS reporting banks to the Soviet Union partially recovered in mid-1991 (to $6.8 billion; see table 3.3.10), but this presumably reflects new credit lines guaranteed by western governments.

With the deteriorating financial position, issues of *debt servicing* came to the forefront towards the end of 1991. A key question in this regard was who would take responsibility for the outstanding Soviet debt and in what form. Western creditors insisted on a joint responsibility of the successor states for the debt and its servicing. In several rounds of negotiations stretching from October through December 1991, partly with the participation of representatives of the G-7, a number of republics agreed in principle to assume this obligation "jointly and severally" and to authorize Vneshekonombank (or a successor organization) to act, under the supervision of an Interstate Council, as their agent in this respect. However, many details — especially regarding the distribution of powers in the Interstate Council — were left for further negotiations, and over the next several months the agreement often seemed to be falling apart. Ukraine, in particular, was hesitant to entrust the debt service responsibility to Vneshekonombank as an essentially Russian institution and preferred a less centralized solution. A settlement of these issues appears to have been reached with the conclusion of a supplementary agreement and additional rules and protocols in mid-March 1992, but even then only 8 of the 12 successor states signed all parts of this package.[225]

---

[220] There are other queries about these figures which require further explanation of how the published table was derived. It appears that the table shows only payments flows that actually took place; the convention, for example, of entering interest payments due in the current account, with an offsetting entry in the capital account for payments due but not made, has probably not been followed. Thus there is no record of interest due on the substantial debt owed to the Soviet Union by developing countries and certain CMEA countries.

[221] This comprises $60 billion described as USSR debt to the west and an additional $17 billion, probably at least in part in non-convertible currencies, owed to eastern Europe, China, India and other countries. These figures were quoted in a discussion paper circulated at a meeting on foreign economic relations attended by representatives of the 15 republics in September. *Izvestiya*, 24 September 1991. At least some of the non-convertible currency obligations have been converted to hard currency debt, a process in which the choice of exchange rates plays a key role.

[222] BBC, *Summary of World Broadcasts*, SU/W0214, 24 January 1992. Presumably this is only convertible currency debt, but the statement does not make this clear.

[223] BIS, *International Banking and Financial Market Developments*, Basle, February 1992.

[224] Data for the third quarter of 1991 indicate that Soviet debt to BIS banks rose by $1.6 billion. However, this was accounted for by officially guaranteed new credits by German banks. BIS, op.cit.

[225] The principle of "joint and several" responsibility was established in a "Memorandum of mutual understanding concerning the debt of foreign creditors of the USSR and its successors in law" of 28 October 1991 (*Izvestiya*, 29 October 1991) which was signed by 8 successor states (without Azerbaijan, Georgia, Ukraine and Uzbekistan). The same group participated in the adoption of the Communiqué on the discussions with the G-7 of 21 November 1991. As part of the agreement with the G-7, a "Treaty on the legal succession regarding the external debt" was adopted on 4 December 1991, to which only Uzbekistan refused to adhere (though not all states may actually have signed). This Treaty set up an allocation key which distributed the debt of the former USSR as follows: Russian Federation, 61 per cent; Ukraine, 16 per cent; Belarus and Kazakhstan, about 4 per cent each; with smaller shares for the remaining republics. The "Agreement on additions to the Treaty on the legal succession regarding the external debt" of 13 March 1992 was signed by 8 CIS member states, with Azerbaijan, Turkmenistan and Uzbekistan standing aside (BBC, *Summary of World Broadcasts*, 17 March 1992, SU/1331, pp.C2/1-3). By this agreement, Ukraine gained one of the permanent chairmanships of the Interstate Council, together with the Russian Federation and a rotating third member, as well as a blocking vote on the Council since 80 per cent of the voting power is required for a decision.

The underlying issue, apart from the mistrust between successor states, was their inability to meet debt repayments. In consequence, the Paris Club of creditor governments formally agreed in early January 1992 to defer repayment of about $3.3 billion in principal.[226]

Commercial banks agreed to defer payments on debt as well.[227] Although the amounts involved have not been officially announced, it has been reported that principal and interest payments of $3.4 billion and $130 million, respectively, were due in December 1991 alone. In both cases, a grouping of successor states pledged to remain current on interest payments.

Clarity on the issue of responsibility for debt is central to the republics' chances of obtaining new credits, including those under consideration in association with humanitarian assistance (see chapter 5 below).

It is possible that large scale capital flight — between $14-19 billion according to one estimate — may have precipitated the cessation of Soviet debt repayment in 1991.[228] During that year exporting enterprises are understood to have repatriated only part of the convertible currency earnings as they were obliged to do under existing regulations. These required them to sell 40 per cent of their foreign currency earnings to Vneshekonombank at the overvalued "commercial" exchange rate (which ranged from about R1.65 to 1.83 per dollar during 1991).[229] Loose controls over the currency management of enterprises undoubtedly facilitated such leakages.

New exchange measures which went into effect in the Russian Federation in 1992 are intended to channel more convertible currency from enterprises to the center and discourage capital flight. Exporters of non-staple export items will have to sell at least 10 per cent of their foreign exchange earnings to the government at the market rate. Importers must buy foreign currency from banks at the same rate. For exporters of oil, natural gas, timber and precious metals, 40 per cent of earnings are to be relinquished at half the market exchange rate.

Russia's stabilization programme elaborated with the help of the IMF provides for further liberalization of prices, tax reform, stabilization of the rouble at a unified realistic exchange rate and restrictive fiscal, monetary and income policies (see section 4.4(ii) below).

---

[226] At stake is medium- and long-term debt contracted before 1 January 1991 and due between 5 December and end-1991. The rescheduling of debt was made conditional upon the pursuit of economic reforms and tough stabilization programmes in the republics. Progress in implementing these policies is to be reviewed by creditor governments prior to 31 March 1992.

[227] Their agreement referred to debt contracted before 1 January 1991 and falling due between 5 December 1991 and 31 March 1992. Repayment was postponed to the latter date. The accord was reached between representatives of 12 major commercial banks, Vneshekonombank and the new central bank of the Russian Federation. The agreement excludes public and private securities, bonds and short-term credit facilities at financial institutions. *International Herald Tribune*, 18 December 1991.

[228] Estimate of the International Institute of Finance, as reported in the *Financial Times*, 13 February 1992.

[229] By comparison, the auction price of the dollar rose steadily during the year, from some R22 per dollar in January to R170 per dollar in December.

4.2 POLITICAL DISINTEGRATION AND ECONOMIC FRAGMENTATION

(i) Legislation and current developments before August 1991

The main legislative acts of the union government affecting the economy up to the early months of 1991 were summarized and listed in the last edition of this publication. Legislative activity to underpin the transformation process continued during the spring and summer of 1991 at a considerably faster rate than in the previous year. The legislation was mainly aimed at establishing some of the less controversial elements of a market economy — procedures, regulations and in some cases courts or other institutions for the settlement of disputes of various kinds, the regulation of intellectual property rights, trademarks, customs duties, social security and unemployment, new types of taxation, licensing procedures for foreign trade, foreign exchange retention quotas for enterprises, basic regulations on foreign investment in the economy, etc. (see box 4.2.1).

Land legislation early in the year clearly did not conclusively settle the all-important ownership question. More progress was made in the privatization (in its broadest sense) of non-agricultural activities, where new enterprises leased from the state gave private operators the right of independent activity under conditions where property rights none the less remained ill defined. But important lacunae remained in the development of regulatory instruments, notably with regard to money and banking. This paralleled the failure of short-term economic policy to address the fundamentals of privatization, price liberalization, the imposition of tight monetary, credit and public finance policies or the pursuit of currency convertibility. The pause in the transformation effort from the beginning of the year accompanied the appointment of V.S. Pavlov, later a leader of the August *coup*, as prime minister following a resolution of the Supreme Soviet of 26 December 1990. But it also owed something to the persistent uncertainty with regard to relationships between the union and the republics which occupied a large share of the president's attention both before and after the *coup* as discussed in the next section.

The bulk of business activity remained in the hands of the state and its agents. However, this no longer meant the industrial and other branch ministries. Although the sale (full privatization) of the bulk of state-owned firms has not yet proceed very far, their status — varying between employee- or management-owned joint stock companies, cooperative concerns leasing building or equipment from these and a number of still wholly state-owned enterprises — probably represents a transitional form on the road to privatization of a kind and via procedures which are as yet unknown. The marketization of the economy took off during 1991 in certain sectors — the spontaneous creation of a large number of commodity exchanges, the growth of private markets for food and other consumer goods, the setting up of a large number of privately-owned banks and other institutions and the floating of new private companies on a more limited scale. However, only the Russian price liberalization at the beginning of 1992, which pulled the other republics along the same path whatever the preferences of their governments, was the first clear indication of the introduction of market forces in the traditional consumer trade network.

(ii) The abortive Union Treaty of August 1991

No less than four draft versions of a new union treaty were presented in 1991[230] including a version published in late 1990. Before the August *coup*, these long drawn out negotiations on a new form of union between the republics and Mr. Gorbachev culminated in what appeared to be a generally acceptable draft, although the Baltic states refused to accept even a much looser arrangement than in the past or even to participate in the negotiations at Novo Ogarevo. Moldova, Armenia and Georgia also held back. The date of 20 August was set for signature by Mr. Gorbachev and the remaining nine republican presidents (excluding the above three and the Baltic republics).

The final document, accepted in principle by the representatives of these nine republics, was basically an agreement on political union. The relationships agreed between the republics and the union proceeded from the principle that the republics were sovereign states with the right to withdraw from the union. The treaty[231] limited activity by the centre in the political sphere to certain common services in the realms of defence, security, law enforcement and diplomatic representation. In addition to representative assemblies such as the Supreme Soviet, union organs included a federal presidency, vice-presidency, cabinet of ministers, a constitutional court and also supreme courts of appeal and of arbitration. The sphere of joint union and republican competence included protection of the constitution and of the rights and liberties of individuals, military policy and security strategy, environmental principles and standards (including nuclear).

Of the treaty's 26 articles, only five tackled economic matters and then only cursorily: article 5 on the jurisdiction of the USSR, article 6 on the sphere of joint

---

[230] See *Izvestiya*, 9 March, 27 June, 15 August and 27 November 1991.

[231] *Sovetskaya Rossiya*, 15 August 1991.

> **BOX 4.2.1**
>
> *Selected instruments of economic institutional change in the Soviet Union, early 1991-August 1991*
>
> Presidential decree on the first-priority measures to implement land reform (5 January).
> Law on the state budget for 1991 (11 January).
> Law on employment (15 January).
> Resolution of the USSR Supreme Soviet on the all-Union economic forecast for 1991 and on the 1991 state plan (12 January).
> Resolution of the USSR Supreme Soviet to hold a referendum on 17 March 1991 on the question of preserving the Union (16 January).
> Resolution of the USSR Council of Ministers on setting the rates of turnover tax (19 January).
> Presidential decree on withdrawal of 50- and 100-rouble banknotes (22 January).
> Presidential decree on economic sabotage (26 January).
> Resolution of the USSR Cabinet of Ministers on the method of calculating and paying turnover tax (31 January).
> Law on the protection of the rights of consumers (27 February).
> Law on hard currency regulation (1 March).
> Law introducing an amendment to the basic legislation on land (16 March).
> Draft treaty on a Union of Sovereign States (published in Izvestiya, 9 March 1991).
> Law on the resolution of labour disputes involving individuals (11 March).
> Presidential decree on retail price reform and the protection of the population (19 March).
> Resolution of USSR Cabinet of Ministers on the reform of retail prices and social protection (19 March).
> Presidential decree on income taxation (amendment to the law of 14 June 1990) (19 March).
> Presidential decree on compensating savings deposits following retail price increases (19 March).
> Resolution of the USSR Supreme Soviet on the introduction of the USSR customs codex (26 March).
> Law on the general principles of entrepreneurship (2 April).
> Presidential decree extending favourable rates of turnover tax to the population (5 April).
> Resolution of USSR Cabinet of Ministers on social safeguards in connection with the reform of retail prices (6 April).
> Resolution of USSR Cabinet of Ministers on measures to ensure external economic relations in 1991 (8 April – not published until August 1991).
> Presidential decree on extraordinary measures to ensure material resources for enterprises, units and organizations (12 April).
> Law on railway transport (15 April).
> Presidential decree on compensation for losses arising from citizens' long-term savings agreements with the USSR State Insurance (6 May).
> Presidential decree on compensation for retail price increases (13 May).
> Presidential decree on stability in basic industries (16 May).
> Law on the auditing chamber of the USSR (16 May).
> Law on the USSR high court of arbitration (17 May).
> Law on the system of arbitration of disputes in the USSR high court of arbitration (17 May).
> Law on the resolution of collective labour disputes (20 May).
> Presidential decree on minimum consumption budget (21 May).
> Law on protection of the rights of consumers (22 May).
> Resolution of the USSR Supreme Soviet on the legal basis of land legislation in the USSR and in the Union-republics (27 May).
> Resolution of the USSR Supreme Soviet on types of activity which enterprises can undertake only on the basis of special permits (licences) (28 May).
> Resolution of USSR Cabinet of Ministers on compensation in 1991 for the supplementary payments made by enterprises and organizations of the agro-industrial complex in connection with the reform of price formation (31 May).
> Law on inventions in the USSR (31 May).
> Law on the income tax of USSR citizens, foreign citizens and stateless persons (containing amendments to the 23 April 1990 law) (11 June).
> Draft law on the protection of labour (published on 18 June).
> Resolution of USSR Cabinet of Ministers on creating supplementary conditions for state enterprises, units and USSR organizations for the development in 1991 of foreign trade and economic links (23 June).
> Basic legislation on the indexation of the incomes of the population (25 June).
> Draft treaty on a union of sovereign states (published on 27 June).
> Presidential decree on changes in the methods of using the foreign currency resources held by enterprises, organizations and units of the agro-industrial complex (27 June).
> Law on the basic principles of de-statization and privatization of enterprises (1 July).
> Law on trademarks (3 July).
> Basic legislation on foreign investment in the USSR (5 July).
> Law on the limitation of monopoly activity in the USSR (10 July).
> Law on industrial models (10 July).
> Amendments to the law on enterprise taxation of 14 June 1990 (10 July).
> Presidential decree confirming the regulations governing the USSR state property fund (10 August).
> Treaty on a Union of Sovereign States (initialled on 23 July 1991 and published on 15 August 1991).
> Treaty on a Union of Sovereign States (initialled on 14 November and published on 27 November 1991).

competence of the union and the republics, article 7 on the exercise of the powers of state bodies of the union and the joint powers of state bodies of the union and the republics, article 8 on ownership and article 9 on union taxation and levies. The central organs would have been responsible for the "pursuit" of the unions's foreign economic activity by coordinating that of the republics, by ensuring the union's representation in international organizations and the conclusion of foreign economic agreements. The union would also have been responsible for the ratification and implementation of the union budget and control of the money supply and would hold the union's reserves of gold and diamonds. It would also lead the space research programme, manage all-union transport and communications networks and the geodesic, cartographic, weights and measures, standardization and meteorological services. To finance these activities, union taxes and other levies were to be set at fixed rates as agreed with the republics and monitored by the parties to the treaty. A number of special Union-wide programmes, whose size and purpose were to be determined by agreement with the republics, would be funded by proportional contributions from those republics participating and managed taking into account the republics' socio-economic development indicators.

The union treaty initialled in midsummer 1991 represented a considerable further dilution of central government power *vis-à-vis* the republics. The basis of the treaty was that union powers in the economic, and indeed all other spheres, would be limited to implementing decisions agreed between all participating republics and the appropriate union bodies. As such it would have been an unwieldy instrument, offering unlimited opportunities for delay without rapid agreement between all of the parties. Subsequent events — the lack of agreement between Russia and other republics on control of the money supply, as well as the pace of price reform and privatization — suggest that the necessary measure of agreement would not have been possible in the economic sphere at least. In the event, the treaty was not put to the test. Indeed, it is likely that the treaty was the proximate cause of the *coup*, as the breakdown of centralized power was, for its leaders, one of the most unwelcome features of the transition process.

(iii) Last attempts to save the Union

President Gorbachev spent the just under four-month period between the *coup* and his resignation in December 1991 attempting to find a new formula to underpin the maintenance of the union structure. Previous treaties to regulate relations between republics, and between them and the union authorities, contained little on purely economic questions and that in very general terms only. Increasing disquiet among western aid donors as to the division of responsibility between the increasingly independence-minded republics for Soviet-incurred debt as well as the need to respond to the increasing pace of economic collapse, led to the preparation of a "treaty on an economic community"[232] in advance of another revised union treaty. This occurred immediately after a meeting of the leaders of eight republics, lower ranking delegations from four republics and a Latvian observer, set up by the Kazakhstan president Nursultan Nazarbayev in Alma Ata at the beginning of October 1991.

The change-over in nomenclature from "union" to "community" in the treaty was a concrete indication that the concept of centralized economic, as well as political, power was henceforth ruled out. A number of principles important for the marketization of the economy were also incorporated into the final version. Attempts were made, for instance, to dilute or remove references to private ownership and the role of the market during the discussions, but they were successfully resisted.[233] Provisions to preserve central allocation of resources through inter-state agreements at centrally determined prices were cut out, as were clauses preserving the state's ability to control output decisions through "state orders". The main points defining relations between the union and the republics provided for free movement throughout the community of goods, services, capital and labour; a common monetary system and a community-wide central bank; uniform taxation rates; a union budget, which must be balanced and used only to finance the limited number of common services together with any joint projects financed by transfers from republican budgets; limits on republican budgetary deficits; inter-republican coordination of price liberalization.

Eight republics signed the treaty by 18 October 1991 and Moldova and Ukraine on 6 November. Azerbaijan and Georgia, both of which were inhibited by internal domestic strife, and the three Baltic states were the only former Soviet republics not to sign.

A new draft union treaty was published at the end of November.[234] The new draft repeated the commitment to democratic rights and freedoms. But a powerful symbolic difference between this draft and the previous variant was the transformation of the union from a federal to a confederal state — the Union of Sovereign States — and the abandonment of a union constitution of any kind. Constitutional forms and their protection devolved entirely upon constituent republics. The union presidency and vice presidency were maintained, together with a state council, consisting of the supreme leaders of the republics and the union president, and an inter-state economic committee. The supreme courts of appeal and arbitration were also continued but not the constitutional court. The new union lost its right to own property. The definition of union budgetary and other economic functions was reserved to 24 special agreements which were to be incorporated in annexes to the economic community treaty. Only the one on ensuring food supplies in 1992 was actually signed (by all 10 signatory republics plus Georgia and Azerbaijan). The other drafts submitted to the heads of republican governments at the end of November were never published.[235] No mention was

---

[232] Published in *Izvestiya*, 19 October 1991.

[233] *Izvestiya*, 5 October 1991.

[234] *Izvestiya*, 26 November 1991.

[235] *Izvestiya*, 29 November 1991.

made of macroeconomic management at the union level.

(iv) The birth of the Commonwealth of Independent States

Less than two weeks after the final draft Union treaty was published, and less than five weeks after the economic community document was accepted by the last two signatory republics (Ukraine and Moldova), the presidents of Russia, Ukraine and Belarus met in Minsk. In effect, the latest union treaty draft was rejected — as also the treaty on the economic community. The three declared their republics to be fully independent and, by a declaration signed on 8 December, created a new political entity — the Commonwealth of Independent States.[236]

The declaration took as its starting point the fact that negotiations on a new union treaty were deadlocked as a result of the policies of a "myopic" centre. The objectives of the new entity was stated to be the strengthening of peace and security and preliminary assurances were given concerning non-proliferation and control of nuclear weapons. Membership was invited by any other state which wished it. In contrast with the various union treaty drafts, no mention was made or implied concerning the type of political regime or economic system aimed at by member countries.

The declaration establishing the Commonwealth was ratified by the Supreme Soviets of Belarus and Ukraine on 10 December and by the Russian Parliament two days later. The second meeting of the original three republican heads of state, in the Kazakh republic's capital Alma Ata, was also attended by those of all other republics except Georgia, which sent an observer, and the Baltic states. The other eight heads of state announced their accession to the Commonwealth in a joint declaration[237] with the original three heads of state dated 21 December 1991. This expanded the aims of the Commonwealth to include "seeking to build democratic law-governed states". It also announced that "cooperation ... will be carried out ... through co-ordinating institutions formed on a parity basis and operating in the way established by the agreements established by members of the Commonwealth, which is neither a state nor a super-state structure".

On 25 December 1991 the last president of the Union of Soviet Socialist Republics, Mr. Mikhail Sergeevich Gorbachev made his resignation speech. By proclamation of the USSR Supreme Soviet on 26 December, the USSR, the state set up in 1922, ceased to exist.

The two above-mentioned declarations concerning the setting up of the Commonwealth were much shorter than the already brief drafts prepared as a basis for the abortive last union treaty. Neither of them contained any description of the institutions or mechanisms to be used in the process of inter-republican consultation and coordination nor indeed any indication of how far these are expected to be taken nor what spheres they are to cover. It is thus no surprise that, while the rights of individual republics to go their own way appears to have been readily accepted as a principle, the actual consequences of exercising their right of independent action has given rise to friction in a number of fields, including the division of the defence forces between republics which dominated the agenda of the third meeting of the Commonwealth heads of state in Minsk on 30 December.

On the economic side, frictions arose from the Russian decision to liberalize prices at an early date with or without the agreement of the other republics, and from the trade war in the form of export barriers to retain goods in short supply within their republic of origin.[238] While these phenomena bear witness to the genuine independence of Commonwealth members, the motives underlying the refusal of Ukraine in particular to sign any of the agreements proposed so far limiting its rights to complete economic freedom must be set against the fact that economic developments in Russia, by virtue of the latter's very size and economic weight, will inevitably play the predominant role in determining economic policy in the successor states. This applies not least to the agenda for economic reform — as well as to the shaping of short- and medium-term economic policies in all the republics.

The republics' desire to retain their steadily increasing but newly-won independence has generally outweighed any perceived positive trade-off between the coordination of economic transformation and the partial surrender of economic sovereignty which this could involve. Hence the areas of disagreement between the republics have remained remarkably constant since the first decisions to recast relations between the centre and the periphery were taken at the end of 1990. They appear to relate both to the *principle* of coordination and to the different views held in the republics with regard to the *substance* of policies in various fields.

The main areas in which inter-republican agreement was considered necessary and which were listed in Chapter X of the economic community treaty are as follows:

Common institutions

Banking union

---

[236] *Izvestiya*, 9 December 1991.

[237] *Izvestiya*, 23 December 1991.

[238] Pressure to erect Russian export barriers have had a somewhat different motivation. Although Russia was responsible for the output of 90 per cent of crude oil and 56 per cent of coal output in 1990, the export structure by republic was very different. In the first six months of 1991 Russia exported 59 per cent of crude oil and 21 per cent of refined products while the figures for Latvia alone were 33 and 23 per cent. Ukraine exported 45 per cent of refined petroleum and 74 per cent of coal. It may be that some of these statistics result from reporting transit items from Russia to abroad as exports by the republics through whose ports they passed and for which all, or nearly all, the export earnings accrued to Russia (i.e., through Ventspils in Latvia). But some of the republics paid Russia for purchases of these products in roubles and then exported them for hard currency. See an interview with Aleksandr Rutskoi, vice-president of Russia, on Russian television on 1 October 1991, BBC, *Summary of World Broadcasts*, SU/1193, p. C1/4, 3 October 1991.

- Common foreign bank
- Ownership legislation
- Harmonization of economic legislation
- Migration
- Regional development and social support
- Creation of non-budgetary funds
- Settlement of obligations on withdrawal from the community
- Capital movements
- Anti-monopoly policy
- Reciprocity with respect to pensions and social security
- Patents
- Introduction of national currencies
- Relations with states previously members of USSR but not of the Community
- Internal state debt service
- Foreign state debt service
- Resolution of property and other disputes.

A number of other areas were to be covered by one-year agreements:

- Community budget
- Tariff and customs policy
- Agreed taxation policy
- Republican budget deficit limits
- Prices and volumes of goods shipped under interstate contracts;
- Limits on the growth of member-republic debt, debt settlement
- Cooperation in emergencies.

As noted above, no agreement was reached on any of them (except one on food supply in 1992) before events overtook the accord on an economic community and the final version of the union treaty. At the time of writing, however, the Commonwealth still had no written legal basis other than the very broad declarations published following the two meetings in Minsk and the one in Alma Ata, though a draft treaty was published in January.[239] However, agreement of some kind in most of these areas is necessary if the successor states are to preserve the advantages of mutual free trade. At the same time, some mechanisms are needed to ensure that the less developed regions of the country are offered options to offset the cessation of the centralized transfer of resources to the outlying regions from which they have benefited in the past. The dilemma is that if no accord can be reached, then impermeable borders must be erected and policed. If they are not, there can be no coherent national economic policy. Attempts to carry out independent economic policy initiatives will in practice need to be consistent with those of Russia, which would, by its sheer size and the strategic nature of its raw material exports, largely determine the pace of economic transformation and future economic developments in the Commonwealth. The options available are evaluated in more detail in section 4(iv) below.

(v) Trade between independent states

At the beginning of 1992 inter-republican economic relations were still mainly conducted on the basis of predominantly ad hoc arrangements. The provisions of these agreements indicate that they are essentially a hold-over from state participation in central planning which will inevitably involve state interference in the production and marketing processes. This is of course to be expected given that marketing structures are still undeveloped and that market price signals are not yet functioning. Bilateral trade and other economic agreements between republican governments began in 1990. They continued into 1991 but were accompanied by the growth of special and often restrictive unilateral measures of the kind mentioned above.

As noted in the last edition of this publication,[240] by early 1991 the number of bilateral inter-republican economic agreements signed by the 15 constituent republics of the Soviet Union had reached 40 out of a possible 105. By the February 1992, 35 out of a possible 55 had been signed between the 11 members of the Commonwealth to cover the year 1992. A typical agreement, between Belarus and Kazakhstan, involves the placing of orders for specific types of goods, achieved in part by the governments concerned urging "ministries and departments, associations, enterprises and organizations to take the necessary measures for maintaining economic ties and to create a favourable regime for concluding agreements for 1992 by 31 December 1991". Another, between Tajikistan and Moldova, agrees to preserve mutual shipments in 1992 at the 1990 level and envisages mutual assistance to "maintain and expand direct economic contacts between enterprises and organizations". The two sides also agree to notify each other about steps to alter retail or procurement prices. Another, between Tajikistan and Kazakhstan, included statements that both republics would refrain from actions which may cause harm to the other.[241] This undertaking, of course, is a safeguard against the unilateral restrictions on trade and other economic activities which have accompanied the deterioration in supply. The number of these restrictions is unknown but they have clearly caused

---

[239] *Izvestiya*, 11 January 1992.

[240] United Nations Economic Commission for Europe *Economic Survey of Europe in 1990-1991*, New York, 1991, p.175.

[241] Details taken from BBC, *Summary of World Broadcasts*, SU/W0207, 3 October 1991, ibid., SU/1246, 4 December 1991.

considerable bad will between some republics and provoked retaliation. Frictions have been clearly apparent in trading relations between Russia and Ukraine and between Russia and the Baltic States. Steps taken by Ukraine to preserve its relatively favourable food supply situation from buyers from other republics took the form of a temporary ban[242] in mid-1991 on exports of food to other republics. This hit Russia particularly hard. The Baltic states imposed similar restrictions. At the beginning of 1992 Russia reacted by banning the export of 60 commodities in short supply (including food, alcohol, tobacco, electrical appliances, building materials and bicycles) to certain other republics.[243]

---

[242] BBC, *Summary of World Broadcasts*, SU/W0189, 26 July 1991, p. A/7.

[243] *Rossiiskaya gazeta*, 10 January 1992.

4.3 THE TRANSFORMATION PROCESS AFTER THE AUGUST COUP

(i) Introduction

After the August *coup*, economic decision-making began to devolve to the republics. Their policies and legislation relevant to macroeconomic stability, price liberalization, openness to the outside world, property rights — in other words, to the main elements of the transformation process — became more diverse. They also became much harder for observers to follow. At the same time, some relevant statistical reporting (e.g., of employment by type of enterprise) continued to be published on an "all-Union" basis. The overall picture that is given here is therefore rather patchy in coverage.

Any assessment of the transformation process must take into account political circumstances, and also the effectiveness of state administration. A policy measure or a piece of commercial legislation may make economic sense; but if it is widely expected to be changed soon, or to remain in force but only on paper, it will have no useful economic consequences. For the Soviet successor states at present, the requirements of political stability and a certain minimum administrative effectiveness in state institutions must be met if any programme of economic transformation is to have a chance of succeeding. They are a great deal further from being met than they are in Bulgaria, Czechoslovakia, Hungary and Poland.

(ii) Monetary stabilization

All the Soviet successor states formally remain, in February 1992, within a single monetary area. The monetary system was in disarray before the coup. Afterwards, the situation got worse. One of the few money-supply measures for which data at different times in the year are available is basic money: notes and coins in circulation. The quantity of cash increased by 15.8 per cent between 1 January and 1 July,[244] but by a further 67.1 per cent over the second half of the year.[245] The contrast between first-half and second-half monetary expansion was less marked for a broad-money measure, but there is little doubt that money-supply growth on all definitions continued to be rapid throughout the year (see table 4.1.3).

Inflationary pressure increased in the Soviet economy in the early years of *perestroika*, primarily because of a mixture of policy errors and the side-effects of partial decentralization.[246] In 1990-1991 budgetary policy devolved to republics, without anybody having effective control of the total deficit. At the same time, there was no matching devolution of monetary policies. There has continued to be not only a single monetary authority, but a single monetary authority that responds permissively to the sum of Union and republic budget deficits by creating more roubles. This monetization of budget deficits, through both cash and credit expansion, has been assisted by the rapid growth of commercial banking without effective regulation.

Two institutional changes had to be made, if this inflationary process was to be brought to a halt. The inflationary mismatch between republic-level budgetary decisions and central monetary decisions had to be eliminated, and banking institutions had to be made capable of controlling the money supply — whether of individual republic currencies or of a surviving common currency.[247] With those difficult institutional changes made, policies of budgetary and financial stringency would have to be maintained to stabilize the rouble or any of its successor currencies.

Amongst the CIS states, there has been some movement on all these fronts, but not enough.

So far as the mismatch of levels of budgetary and monetary decision-making is concerned, the indications are that a solution of several separate currencies is more likely than a solution entailing joint control of budgetary totals and of a single currency.[248] The introduction of separate national currencies is a declared objective in several successor states, including Belarus and Ukraine, as well as the three Baltic states (see sections 4.4 and 4.5 below). But it is doubtful whether the skills and institutional arrangements in the banking system that would be needed to maintain the values of these new currencies are yet available.

The development of effective banking systems can be accelerated by technical assistance. The IMF and some western central and commercial banks are already providing such assistance through a number of channels. But establishing effective registration and regulation of commercial banks, installing modern

---

[244] V. Gerashchenko, "Dlya chego nuzhna kreditnaya ekspansiya?", *Ekonomika i zhizn'*, 1991 No.38, p.4. Gerashchenko also gives a measure of broad money supply (cash plus demand deposits plus short-term deposits) that grew more rapidly, by 44.4 per cent.

[245] Goskomstat USSR communication to United Nations Economic Commission for Europe.

[246] See section 4.3(vi) below.

[247] The issues are discussed and possible solutions, including payments-union arrangements between republics and currency boards for republics, are assessed in sections 4.3(vi)-(vii) below.

[248] In January 1992, *Izvestiya*'s financial correspondent observed that none of the leaders of CIS states appeared to be interested in the maintenance of a single financial system. I. Zhagel', "Finansovaya svoboda ili finansovoye bezumie?", *Izvestiya*, 3 January 1992, p.2.

payments systems, clarifying the rules of the game for central banks' control of the money supply, are all processes that have started only recently, and from low initial levels of banking development. Thus the short-term prospects for any new republic currencies, as for the rouble, are doubtful.

The introduction of new currencies will have to be carried out in conjunction with the withdrawal of appropriate quantities of roubles from circulation. The introduction of new currencies and their stabilization are likely in practice also to be closely linked with moves to make them internally and externally convertible for current account transactions, facilitating the maintenance of transactions among Soviet successor states.

In general, it is hard to envisage these changes being carried through successfully without substantial western financial assistance, in addition to the technical assistance that has already begun to flow to the financial sector. A number of institutional arrangements are possible that could facilitate macroeconomic stabilization, the maintenance of trade amongst successor states and the transition to convertibility: currency stabilization funds, an intra-CIS (or broader) payments union, a rouble zone analogous to the franc zone, and such radical departures from conventional banking systems as the use of currency boards.[249] All would entail significant sums of western financial assistance. So far, these are not available.

The current stabilization programme of the Russian government illustrates the difficulties.[250] The Deputy Prime Minister and Finance Minister, Egor Gaidar, has presided over an attempt simultaneously to decontrol prices and to impose financial stabilization. This politically risky manoeuvre has been embarked upon in the absence of significant foreign exchange reserves or significant western financial assistance apart from debt rescheduling, without an effective system of tax collection, ahead of any systematic process of demonopolization, with a parliament and a Vice-President (Aleksandr Rutskoi) who are publicly critical of the policy, and with a central bank president (Georgy Matyukhin) who was also known to be opposed to it, at least initially. Gaidar and his economic-policy team were aware of the adverse circumstances, but considered that they had no choice but to launch a radical liberalization and stabilization attempt in December 1991 or January 1992.

The Russian Federation budget that was adopted on 24 January 1992 was for the first quarter of 1992 only, and projected a substantial reduction of the deficit from 1991 levels.[251] It was anticipated that the initial explosion of consumer prices would slow down markedly in February. Prices would level off in February-March provided the line was held on the budget and the money supply. The Russian reform team continued to ask publicly for Western assistance with a stabilization fund and balance-of-payments support,[252] but the response of the US Administration and the G-7 nations as a group has been that any such assistance will come best through the IMF and World Bank, conditionally on convincing reform programmes.[253]

The Gaidar reform team has as a result been counting heavily on the capacity of its tax collection system to raise targeted revenues by partly untried means, and in particular by the new value-added tax, on the ability of the Russian financial system to collect enough of the hard currency earnings of Russian exporters to build up reserves, and on the parliament and the central bank to support their policies.

There are doubts on all these scores. The absence of a professional tax inspectorate and, in general, of a normal tax collection system, in a situation where privatization is under way, makes it unlikely that the projected tax yields will materialize. The objective is to collect taxes to the value of 40-42 per cent of net material product, with a tax base that would outpace a once-for-all price hike estimated at 350-580 per cent between the beginning and the end of the year.[254] This would be a tall order for a properly functioning tax system.

Similarly, the ability of the state to appropriate targeted amounts of convertible currency from exporters has declined. The International Institute of Finance estimates that in 1991 exporters from the successor states placed some $14 billion of hard currency revenues in foreign banks, beyond the scope of monitoring and control by the central authorities, and that this will continue, though on a smaller scale, in 1992.[255] This assessment covers the whole of the former USSR, but is chiefly a Russian problem, since the Russian Federation has been the source of about 80 per cent of the convertible currency earnings of the former Union.

The predicted levelling off of many consumer prices began to be reported in mid-February, together with some improvement in quantities supplied to shops and available for purchase in them.[256] But on 13 February

---

249 For a discussion on this, see section 4.3(vii) below.

250 "Stabilizatsiya i vykhod iz krizisa. Osnovnye napravleniya ekonomicheskoi politiki pravitel'stva RSFSR", programme outline written at the end of November 1991. This document already notes that the $6-7 billion stabilization fund sought from the west was unlikely to be available, so that a simultaneous transition to convertibility was not possible. See also an interview with Deputy Prime Minister Gaidar by Mikhail Berger, "Budushchee prineset nam novye tseny i zabytye tovary", *Izvestiya*, 2 January 1992, p.2.

251 See section 4.4(ii) below.

252 Egor Gaidar, "Russia needs three kinds of aid − and quickly", *Financial Times*, 22 January 1992, p.11.

253 Reuters from Washington, 5 February 1992, citing US Treasury Under-Secretary, David Mulford.

254 "Stabilizatsiya ..." op.cit. The price increases over the year are derived from the month-by-month projections in the programme.

255 *Neue Zürcher Zeitung*, 13 February 1992, p.37.

256 Reuters from Moscow, 13 February 1992. The distinction is not trivial; in the past, much of the supply of consumer goods to the retail system was syphoned off for sale elsewhere at black market prices.

President Yeltsin was already telling the Russian parliament that some shift of policy was being contemplated.[257] The widespread belief that Yeltsin might change policies and government teams has not been the least of the handicaps faced by the Gaidar reform team.

A softening of budgetary and monetary stance at this stage would undermine the already shaky prospects of macroeconomic stabilization in the course of 1992.

The final difficulty facing the Russian stabilization effort is that it is being attempted in a rouble zone shared with states that have independent fiscal policies and that might introduce currencies of their own without coordinating the withdrawal of appropriate amounts of roubles from circulation, exacerbating Russian monetary disequilibrium. Conversely, macroeconomic stabilization for the other successor states remains conditional on a successful Russian stabilization, so long as they stop short of substituting fully-fledged currencies of their own for the rouble.

(iii) The decontrol of prices

Only the Baltic states preceded Russia in decontrolling the great majority of consumer and wholesale prices. The non-Russian CIS states were compelled, as lesser regions within a single monetary area, to follow the Russian decontrol that was implemented on 2 January 1992.

At the time when the price liberalization took effect, many prices were already behaving in a "liberalized" way. According to unofficial estimates, the general rate of price inflation at the end of 1991 was, on an annual basis, about 600-700 per cent.[258] However, price controls were at least nominally in place for a wide range of consumer items, especially food. The chief practical results of the relics of the old price controls were two: some of the population for some part of the time could obtain some items at subsidized prices; and for many people for much of the time price-controlled items could not be found in state shops and were either not obtained at all or were obtained through different channels and on different terms.

The other channels consisted mainly of private or semi-private purchases at above-state prices. Such channels often involved corrupt diversion of goods intended for the state retail network. They are also often connected with a quite different channel: that of supplies to employees through their workplaces. In neither case does the removal of official retail price controls necessarily lead to a unification of the flows of goods from producers to consumers through "normal" retail channels. The interests of corrupt employees of the distribution system are one reason, often cited in the Russian press, why this is so. There is more to the informal exchange process than this, however.

One impediment to a ready response of shop supplies to the decontrol of retail prices is that much of the existing distribution of goods is managed through transactions in which *money* (even convertible currency) is not the *only* medium of exchange. This phenomenon has become more important in the recent inflationary period.

With the collapse of central control, the movement of consumer goods in most areas of the former Soviet Union is now managed, to a greater extent than before, by what one anthropologist has called local "suzerainties".[259] These are the political and managerial establishments of the old order, in which state-enterprise managers and local party and state officials have long-established networks through which they can exchange favours and assist one another in resolving production and supply problems.

The informal, traditional arrangement of patron-client relations between officials, between officials and managers, and between managers and their employees has always involved exchanging bundles of favours, in which goods are only part of the bundle; promotion, protection from prosecution, bureaucratic goodwill of assistance in future operations, selection for travel abroad, and numerous other benefits may be included in the deals. The supplies of food and other consumer goods on special terms at the workplace are in part an offshoot of this system, helping to tie employees to particular enterprises whose management has particular influence in the various networks, or is particularly skilful at arranging barter deals with other enterprises.

The effect of this system is that consumer-goods producers will weigh up many non-price considerations before switching output from existing channels of this kind. A very large increase in the price legally obtainable from the distribution network may not be enough to compensate for the non-price benefits derived from the existing informal network. This is a factor that is separate, in principle, from the influence of existing black market prices.

To these impediments must be added the often high degree of market power, e.g., of regional or city wholesaling organizations, and the standard organizational structure of state retailing, in which individual shops are merely the instruments of local retail organizations (*torgi*), specialized by product-group, that are themselves often local monopolists. The Yeltsin-Gaidar reform package includes provisions to change the status of state retail outlets so that they become separate legal persons. This is an example of the way in which changes in property rights may help price liberalization to work; but the speed with which the price liberalization was introduced has meant that even such small steps in the privatization process had not been taken when the price controls were lifted.

In all these circumstances, the extremely high increases initially made in many decontrolled prices are

---

[257] He also announced that he was putting Aleksandr Rutskoi in charge of agriculture, as Gorbachev had done earlier with Ligachev.

[258] *Le Monde*, 21 January 1992, pp.1, 20. Even on the official measure prices were rising at an annualized rate of 200-250 per cent in November-December.

[259] Caroline Humphrey, "Obstacles to Reform: the Siberian Dimension", in Catherine Merridale and Chris Ward (eds,), *Perestroika: The Historical Perspective*, London, Edward Arnold, 1991, pp.183-202.

not surprising. In some cases, such as the internal rouble price of aluminium, which had risen by early February from R1,800-4,000 a ton to R30,000-50,000 a ton,[260] the rouble price is strongly influenced by the current rouble exchange rate and the dollar price for a readily tradable good. In others, such as flour (a 600 per cent increase, reportedly, in January), yeast (800 per cent) and sugar (1,300 per cent),[261] a combination of monopoly power and the influence of black-market and non-price terms of alternative deals, is the most likely explanation.

Some subsequent stabilization and reduction of prices was to be expected, for a variety of reasons: the emergence of competition in at least some markets, for example; the correction by monopolists of price increases that overshot their profit maximizing level; and perhaps, in some cases, the imposition of stronger export controls. But in the meantime, pressures generating a price spiral are accumulating. Thus, the flour, yeast and sugar price increases mentioned above have been cited by Russian bakeries as reasons for raising further the price of bread. Bread prices have continued to be subject to ceilings, and were administratively raised some threefold in January. If popular and parliamentary pressure leads to a large increase in state expenditure on "social protection", increasing the budget deficit, second round increases in money supply will turn what was supposed to be a once-for-all price adjustment into continued inflation.

(iv) The privatization process

So far as changes in property rights are concerned, the public debate, the developments from below, the legislation, and the implementation of legislation during the 1987-1991 period exhibited both rapid ideological change and extreme confusion. The public debate was thin on serious discussion of the economics of property rights. There was, and still is, little systematic discussion of just how different property rights arrangements might affect economic behaviour. Discussion of how to introduce changes (free vouchers versus asset sales, etc.) has been clamorous but rather generalized. The Union legislation was often defective, though it tended to improve in quality between 1989-1990 and 1991. Land ownership issues remained unresolved, even on paper.[262]

In addition, the relationship between legislation and practical changes was tenuous. There are a number of obvious reasons for this: lack of a strong machinery of government administration and a low general regard for the law; lack of capital market institutions and banking, accounting and commercial law expertise; resistance to change by the Party-state apparatus at the local level;

the continuation of price and quantity controls; an environment of accelerating inflation – all of these things made for a yawning gap between legislation and practice. Above all, the uncertainty and conflict over jurisdiction between republics and the centre hampered change.

At the same time, a process of change in property rights had got under way before the *coup*. As in Hungary and Poland, the process of creation of new firms *ab initio* together with (and often closely intertwined with) "spontaneous privatization" of existing state assets has been more dynamic than many people expected. Unlike eastern and central Europe, Russia and most of the Commonwealth of Independent States do not appear to face the complication of claims by former owners (though the Baltic states do).

There were at the end of 1989 well over a million basic management units, if retail and catering establishments are included as individual businesses. Outside the distribution sector, however, the number of state enterprises is tiny (and their average size correspondingly huge) by western standards. This is a normal feature of centrally planned economies.[263]

Data on numbers of different organizational and property rights types of enterprise have been published from time to time, but perhaps the most internally consistent data available for 1991 come from information on employment by form of organization of the workplace. This is summarized in table 4.3.1.

The role of an independent, non-state sector in the former USSR was considerably smaller than the proliferation of categories in table 4.3.1 might suggest.

State enterprises, in that table, are state-sector workplaces that have neither been moved to an *arenda* or other new form of organization nor been incorporated in a "concern" or association.

Arenda enterprises in industry or construction are typically leased for a period of 8-10 years, with the branch ministry as the lessor (*arendodatel'*) and the work collective as the lessee (*arendator*). Leasing arrangements made in 1989 and 1990 generally incorporated a commitment on the part of the work collective to meet delivery requirements under state orders, and the payments for the lease were very often based on the level of profit transfers from the enterprise to its superior body in the recent past, with much depending on deals struck between enterprise management and ministry. Insofar as these arrangements increased confidence at the enterprise level about the rate of transfers to higher authorities that could be expected for several years ahead, they provided more encouragement than the traditional system for initiative from below, but dependence on the state was still high.

---

[260] *Financial Times*, 13 February 1992, p.26.

[261] Examples from Reuters from Moscow, 10 February 1992.

[262] See section 4.2 above; also Philip Hanson, "Ownership Issues in Perestroika", in John Tedstrom (ed.), *Perestroika and the Private Sector of the Soviet Economy*, Boulder, CO, Westview Press, 1990, pp.67-99; ibid., "Property Rights in the New Phase of Reform", *Soviet Economy* vol.6 No.2 (1990).

[263] For an empirical analysis covering a large number of countries see F.L. Pryor, *Property and Industrial Organization in Communist and Capitalist Nations*, New York, 1973; see also Peter Temin, "Soviet and Nazi economic planning in the 1930s", *Economic History Review*, vol.XLIV, No.4 (1991), pp.573-593. For arguments about the central importance in transformation of creating much larger numbers of firms, see David M. Newberry, "Sequencing the Transition", London, *Centre for Economic Policy Research Discussion Paper No.575*, August 1991.

TABLE 4.3.1

USSR: Employment by form of organization of the workplace, January-September 1991 [a]
(Million persons)

State enterprises	98.9
Arenda enterprises [b]	9.0
Joint-stock companies	1.0
Concerns, associations [c]	0.7
Social organizations	1.8
Joint ventures	0.2
Kolkhozy	14.4
Cooperatives	3.2
Individual sector [d]	6.5
Total	135.7

Source: USSR Goskomstat report, *Ekonomika i zhizn'*, No.43, 1991, pp.7-10. Data exclude the Baltic republics unless otherwise noted.

[a] For all 15 former Soviet republics; probably the average of monthly employment figures during the nine-month period.
[b] Enterprises leased, nominally by their entire workforce, from "the state".
[c] Often groupings of enterprises that have replaced former branch ministries or sub-branch main administrations of branch ministries.
[d] Includes persons wholly engaged in household subsidiary plot work, individual family farms (fermy) and persons registered as engaged in individual (one-man or family) businesses.

Joint stock companies are typically a development "from below", with shares held by some mixture of the superior branch ministry or its successor entity, local or republic government, workers and managers in the enterprise itself, one of the new commercial banks (see below), and other enterprises that are either major suppliers or major customers. This form approximates the kind of cross-ownership arrangements associated with spontaneous privatization in Hungary.[264] Thus, with worker-shares usually forming a minority stake and often not saleable outside the workforce, this sort of corporatization represents a pluralization of state ownership; there begin to be identifiable proprietors, and some scope for the disposal of shares amongst them, and hence for a rudimentary and limited capital market, but the process does not by itself create an open capital market, on which the players themselves have hard budget constraints.

Concerns and associations are typically the old administrative structures or, more precisely, the old administrative structures plus their subordinate enterprises, under a new name. They may themselves be shareholders in some or all of the "companies" in question. They may also themselves be made into corporations.

Joint ventures and *collective farms* (*kolkhozy*) are well-known categories. A *cooperative*, under the 1988 legislation, could be a partnership of a small number of cooperative members, employing non-member contract labour. It was therefore legally possible (though by no means necessary) for a Soviet cooperative to embody the distinction between owners and hired labour that is characteristic of capitalism — with the proviso that under this law the co-owners have themselves to be working members of the firm. And cooperatives could issue shares, which could be traded.

In practice, more than 80 per cent of cooperatives have been spun off by state enterprises. They are often a former subunit of the state enterprise, transferred to an arms' length relationship because of the weaker financial controls to which cooperatives are subject. As control over state enterprises has itself weakened, and as more permissive legislation on privatization comes into effect, cooperatives may prove to have been, in most cases, a temporary, transitional form of organization.

Finally, the *individual* sector is mainly composed of the traditional private plots. Various forms of family business can now exist under different successor states legislation, but as a statistical reporting category, the individual sector at present is primarily agricultural.

The so-called private plot sector, though long-established, is an important part of the independent sector. If urban allotments and orchards are included (and if there is no double-counting of families), a remarkable 56.5 million Soviet households were estimated to have some sort of subsidiary household plot in 1990.[265] These plots of land housed 22 per cent of all cattle at the start of 1991, the same percentage of pigs and 35 per cent of poultry. In 1990 they are estimated to have produced 31 per cent of all meat, 28 per cent of milk, 27 per cent of eggs, 65 per cent of potatoes, 33 per cent of green vegetables and 54 per cent of fruit.[266]

One part of the picture that is not represented in table 4.3.1 is the development of commercial banks. The first banks to be described in this way in the USSR were the small number of specialized state banks that were originally, in effect, divisions within the traditional monobank system. More recently, there has been a proliferation of new commercial banks. At 1 December 1991 there were 1,616 of them.[267] A small number were cooperatives; most were jointly owned and founded by groups of state enterprises, either local groupings or branch or sub-branch groupings. The term "pocket bank" is in most cases appropriate, since they operate with both deposits from and loans to a restricted group of businesses. In the absence so far of effective banking regulation (though USSR legislation of December 1990 envisaged such regulation) and of efficient payment systems, their contribution to the development of market institutions is questionable.

So far as property rights reform is concerned, then, the situation on the territory of the former USSR in late 1991 was that there was still only a small independent sector. If, for the reasons indicated above, only one tenth of *arenda* employment and one third of cooperative employment is allotted, arbitrarily, to the independent sector, along with the individual enterprise

---

[264] See chapter 6 below.

[265] There were 73.1 million families in the USSR in January 1989, according to the census, though this number might be raised to 89.5 million if people recorded as living alone are counted as households.

[266] Private plot data are USSR Goskomstat assessments from *Statisticheskii press-byulleten'*, 1991, no.18, p.28. Household numbers cited from Aaron Trehub, "Soviet Housing Policy: Perestroika and Beyond", paper presented at the 23rd National Convention of the American Association for the Advancement of Slavic Studies, Miami, November 1991.

[267] USSR Goskomstat information.

sector, one gets a figure of 6.3 per cent. The unregistered private sector making up the black economy might be added to this. USSR Goskomstat put personal income from the black economy in 1990 at R99.8 billion, or 13 per cent of household income,[268] but value added by labour in the black economy would be a smaller share of total value added by labour than this.[269]

The tiny numbers of leased or privately purchased shops and restaurants reflect three things: first, that programmes of petty privatization in Moscow and St. Petersburg were only just getting under way, and even then amidst considerable difficulties, towards the end of the year; second, the fact that cooperative and joint venture cafes and restaurants are for some reason simply not included in the figures; and, third, that the very considerable growth of informal street trading is not captured in the statistics.

The rapid rise of commodity exchanges has been widely commented on. In the first nine months of 1991 they employed 4,850 people,[270] and officially recorded sales of R20 billion..[271] The value of turnover on these exchanges has been rising fast. This probably reflects both strong inflation and rapid volume growth. A crude impression of their relative importance can be suggested by the report that November turnover on one of the largest of the exchange systems, the Russian Goods and Materials Exchange (RTSB in its Russian acronym) was R4 billion, and this was twice the October level.[272] On the assumption — generous so far as the scale of RTSB operations over the year are concerned — that turnover in the first 10 months was at a monthly rate of R2 billion, and that business doubled again in December, the year's transactions would have totalled R34 billion. There are a great many *birzhy*, but RTSB is one of the largest. If total exchange turnover in 1991 was five times that of the RTSB, i.e., R170 billion, it would have been equivalent to about 5 per cent of the probable total of current price goods transactions in the economy.[273]

The indicator of privatization of housing in table 4.3.2 shows a flow that is tiny in relation to the total stock of housing in the Russian Federation. It should however be borne in mind that the housing stock in the countryside is substantially privately owned to begin with, and so is a modest portion of the urban housing stock, as well.[274]

TABLE 4.3.2

Russian Federation: Non-state entities outside agriculture

Panel A: Industrial sector
(Number of enterprises at 1 October; per cent of output in January-September 1991, current prices)

	Number	Output share
Arenda enterprises	2 558 [a]	10.6 [a]
Collective enterprises [b]	264	0.2
Joint-stock companies	94	0.9
Private	44	-
Small enterprises [c]	10 696	5.3

Panel B: Construction
(Per cent of turnover, January-September 1991)

Arenda enterprises	23
Cooperatives	11
Joint-stock companies	5

Panel C: Retail and catering
(Number of enterprises, on 1 January 1992)

Arenda shops	3 100
Private shops	127

Panel D: Commodity exchanges (birzhy)
(Numbers registered on 1 January 1992)

Exchanges	110

Panel E: Housing
(Area of apartments sold in 1991, m²)

Area (m²)	5,000,000 [d]

Sources: Panels A-C: *Ekonomika i zhizn'*, No.49, 1991, Supplement p.1; Panel D: op.cit., No.40, 1991, p 17; Panel E: *idem* No.28, p.7; Russian Federation Goskomstat, *Ob itogakh fur..tionirovaniya narodnogo khozyaistva Rossiiskoi Federatsii v 1991 godu*, Moscow, 1992, pp.17-19, 28.

a By 1 January 1992 these numbers had risen to 3,000 and 13.4 per cent, respectively.
b Owned by the workforce; the distinction between these and producer cooperatives, in current Russian terminology, appears to be largely to do with how they were initially established.
c Small enterprises are said to be mainly (9,299) state-owned, with 39 private and 1,358 collective. In sectors other than industry, a larger share are probably private. The small enterprises are probably included in the other categories in Panel A.
d In 1990 some 43,000 apartments were sold with an average size of 46m².

Developments in the farm sector are illustrated in table 4.3.3. Private plots of the traditional type are not covered here (see the discussion above of private plots in the USSR/CIS as a whole); the creation of new family farms indicated in the table represents a new and non-state element in agriculture.

---

[268] *Statisticheskii press-byulleten'*, 1991, No.17, p.10; total personal income (assumed to exclude black economy income) from the Goskomstat report for 1990, *Ekonomika i zhizn'*, 1991, no.5, pp.9-13.

[269] Table 4.3.2 gives some more detailed information on the numbers of non-state entities in the Russian Federation, outside the farm sector, in 1991.

[270] On a full-time equivalent basis, assuming the 700 part-timers to be working half-time. This is probably an average of monthly figures, understating the position at the end of the period.

[271] *Ekonomika i zhizn'*, 1991, No.49, supplement p.1.

[272] *Kommersant*, 2-9 December 1991, p.11.

[273] The gross social product (GSP) in 1991 is guesstimated here at about R2,900 billion in current prices. Goskomstat reports CIS GDP as 17 per cent down on 1990 in constant prices, i.e., R830 billion in 1990 prices. Taking the unweighted average of official 1991/1990 consumer and wholesale price indexes as a proxy for a GDP deflator gives a 1991/1990 deflator of 2.12, and therefore a guesstimated current price GDP in 1991 of R1,760 billion. The ratio of current price GSP to current price GDP in 1990 was 1.632 (from *Narodnoe khozyaistvo SSSR v 1990 g.*, pp.5, 10). Hence guesstimated current price 1991 GSP of R2,872 billion.

[274] Close to two fifths of all Soviet households (excluding persons living on their own), were in privately owned housing at the time of the 1989 census, and this excludes occupants of cooperative apartments. However, the proportion was around a fifth in urban areas and almost three quarters in the countryside. Trehub, op.cit., Table 1.

TABLE 4.3.3

Russian Federation: Development of family farms, 1991
(Number of farms, total hectares, hectares per farm)

Date	Number	Total hectares	Hectares/farm
1.1.1991	4 432	200 000	45
1.3.1991	8 931	395 187	44
1.7.1991	25 159	..	..
1.11.1991	34 700	1 400 000	40
1.1.1992	50 000	2 100 000	42

Sources: (in order of rows): *Ekonomika i zhizn'*, 1991, no.6, pp.25-27; *Statisticheskii press-byulleten'*, 1991, No.16, p.34; Supplement, p.1; Reuters from Moscow (interview with the Russian Federation Minister of Agriculture), 6 January 1992; Russian Federation Goskomstat, *Ob itogakh funktsionirovaniya narodnogo khozyaistva Rossiiskoi Federatsii v 1991 godu*, Moscow, 1992, p.18.

By the end of 1991, despite this very rapid growth, only about 1 per cent of Russian farmland had been transferred to the new family farms. None the less, the rate of growth is more than many observers had expected to see, given the continuing uncertainties about land ownership and the resistance of many local officials and state and collective farm directors. Moreover, the size of these farms, though the mean size is still small, is an order of magnitude larger than the traditional private plots (which have, in addition, been allowed some expansion); and some individual farms in the black earth areas are 300-400 hectares in size.[275]

In Russia, and in the CIS states generally, there was clearly some development from below during 1991 of new and more independent forms of business organization. The creation of new large firms, even with foreign capital participation, was, however, a rare occurrence, if it happened at all.

Unlike, say, Hungary, Russia as yet shows no *extensive* development, whether formally organized or spontaneous, of either cross-ownership patterns in large firms or leasing arrangements in so-called petty privatization. What it does show is a rapid early development, from a very low level, of several forms of business organization new to the country: cooperatives in the business services sector, family farms, and commodity exchanges. At the same time there is widely believed to be a considerable amount of spontaneous, *nomenklatura* entrepreneurship, creating new commercial banks, holding companies and the like, that does not seem to show up very clearly in the available statistics.

Nevertheless, the transformation of property rights with respect to existing capital assets has been limited: as the tables show, even the pluralized state ownership or cross-ownership form represented by joint stock companies has not spread very widely; and no programme of state directed petty privatization, whether of housing or of trade, catering and services establishments, had got off the ground by the end of the year.

In comparison with Hungary or Poland, Russia and the other CIS states face four major difficulties in the way of rapid and extensive changes in the prevailing regime of property rights.

First, the degree of political turmoil is such that everyone — policy makers, *nomenklatura* privatizers and potential members of a new business class, in particular — is conscious of exceptional uncertainty about the future. This arises partly as the aftermath of the struggle with the old Union authorities, partly as a result of the uncertainty about future relationships with other CIS member states, and in the case of Russia, partly because of the divisions within the leadership.

The second disadvantage is that, even in the absence of this turbulence, the process of creating an appropriate legislative and institutional framework, and building up the relevant skills, would be at an earlier stage than it is in Hungary, or even in Poland. The scope available in Hungary for drawing on pre-communist commercial legislation[276] or for drawing on the market expertise acquired over 20 years of incremental reform and relative openness to the west, is simply not present in Russia.

Thirdly, during 1991 the continuation of both price controls and rapid, uncontrolled money supply growth had led to an early development of an independent sector whose activities are strongly concentrated on profiting from arbitrage between controlled and uncontrolled markets, and the pursuit of short-term profits in that activity. An effective decontrol of prices would undermine much of the activity on which the embryonic independent sector has hitherto thrived. A substantial opening to import competition and a shift to resident, current account convertibility of the rouble are also still to come, and also make for great uncertainty. In contrast to the unrealistic view that price decontrol should have been delayed pending substantial privatization, it might more plausibly be argued that the early development of an independent sector, however limited in scale it may be, has already run uncomfortably far ahead of liberalization, macroeconomic stabilization and internationalization.

Fourthly, the power and propensity of former members of the Party-state apparatus to impede the implementation of changes in property rights is probably greater than in Hungary or Poland, since they have been able either to retain local political power (often by winning elections) or to stay in key executive positions on a larger scale in Russia.

In the Russian Federation an ambitious programme of privatization from above was launched on 1 January 1992. The main documents that set out the programme are a presidential edict, and a set of guidelines, all approved on 29 December 1991.[277] This had been preceded by a failed attempt at a comprehensive programme of very rapid privatization in the city of

---

[275] Yu. Chernichenko (chairman of the Peasant Party of Russia), "Sindrom antilopy, ili za chto sidit Starodubtsev", *Argumenty i fakty*, 1991, No.39, p.2.

[276] See chapter 6 below.

[277] Respectively, edict No.341, "Ob uskorenii privatizatsii gosudarstvennykh i munitsipal'nykh predpriyatii", *Rossiiskaya gazeta*, 10 January 1992; and "Osnovnye polozheniya programmy privatizatsii gosudarstvennykh i munitsipal'nykh predpriyatii v Rossiiskoi Federatsii na 1992 god", *Ekonomika i zhizn'*, 1992, No.2, pp.18-20.

Moscow under the auspices of the mayor, Gavriil Popov.[278]

The Moscow programme, led by the independent economist Larisa Piyasheva, aimed at the divestment of all shops, restaurants, factories and other production units in Moscow by offering them at low prices to their workers, and subsequently selling by public auction those assets not taken up by the workers associated with them. So far as the smaller units in the service sector were concerned, the entire process of divestment was to be carried out in two months. Hitherto, only eight shops had been sold off by public auction in Moscow, and in St. Petersburg only 17 out of 2,500, in the course of 1991. This programme was blocked by the Moscow city council, and Piyasheva's attempts to mobilize both Popov's and Yeltsin's authority to override the city council did not elicit sufficiently clear and forceful support to allow the programme to proceed. Piyasheva resigned.

This episode illustrates in an extreme form the instability of the transformation process in Russia. The programme was criticized for amounting to give-aways, for depriving the state of revenue, for putting an emphasis on worker ownership that was unwise in the light of experience in other countries, and in general for the attempt to move so fast that many errors were bound to be made. The main argument put forward in its defence was that there had to be very rapid movement to create the momentum needed to break down the existing networks of informal dealings that hindered change. It was also argued that inflation was so rapid that asset sales at any currently attainable price would soon appear to have been equivalent to free gifts. It is the conflicts between Moscow's elected executive mayor and his city council, and some implicit conflicts between Popov and Yeltsin, that illustrate the political complexities of radical economic reform.

The Russian Federation's privatization programme is somewhat less drastic than the Moscow one, but is none the less highly ambitious and problematic.

In many respects, the general approach is one that is familiar in the reform triangle of eastern and central Europe.[279] Privatization is seen as part of a transformation attempt that includes financial stringency, price liberalization, a move to limited currency convertibility, opening to the world economy and eventual reshaping of the structure of production. It is also seen as the transfer of full ownership rights from "the state" to private citizens and legal persons. The programme distinguishes between petty privatization and large-scale privatization, and there is some acceptance of the fact that neither can be done overnight. An outright give-away of large amounts of state assets is not on the agenda, at least in 1992.

The aims of the Russian privatization drive are said to be chiefly to do with financial balance in the short run (up to late 1992), and in the longer run with the achievement of more efficient use of resources. Because of the emphasis on asset sales as a means of reducing the monetary overhang and balancing the state budget, share vouchers will not be issued in 1992. If macro-economic stabilization is carried through successfully, such vouchers (personal privatization accounts, *imennye privatizatsionnye scheta*) will be issued later. Meanwhile, reliance will be on open auctions and offers for sale. Preferential terms will be offered to work collectives, and local authorities will retain a share of the sales proceeds; both these arrangements are explicitly aimed at providing incentives to get assets sold rapidly.

In the same spirit, the Gordian knot of asset valuation will be sliced through by offering assets at their *book value,* and not attempting to assess present value from expected yields. This can be guaranteed to produce an anomalous mix of bargains and anti-bargains, and therefore cries of foul play; but the valuation problem in general is so intractable that it is not obvious that this will generate more discontent than theoretically superior approaches. It will, however, be difficult to find buyers for large assets at historically based book values, in the current atmosphere of uncertainty, unless holders of hard currency can purchase assets freely at the market rate.

The reform's designers expect the market rate to stabilize at around R200 to the dollar later in 1992.[280] They do not, however, envisage assets sales to foreign investors at rates of that order. Government ministers have been referring to a special rate, substantially more favourable to the rouble, to be applied in asset sales for convertible currency.[281]

The time-scale envisaged is heroic: petty privatization to be concentrated in the first half of 1992 and large-scale privatization in consumer industries apparently envisaged as being largely carried through in the second half of the year, and some 25 per cent of state assets to be divested before the end of 1992. The detailed guidelines, with specified numbers of enterprises in particular regions and industries to be sold off by specified dates,[282] is uneasily reminiscent of communist era campaigns.

In the medium term, success in changing the organizational structure of the farm sector and related branches is of special importance. The farm sector element in the current Russian reform programme apparently includes serious moves towards land reform.

---

[278] See *International Herald Tribune*, 29 November 1991, p.2, and an assessment of the programme by Yevgenii Yasin, "Privatizatsiya pomoskovski produmana ne do kontsa", *Izvestiya*, 2 January 1992, p.2.

[279] The following observations on the general strategy governing the privatization programme are taken mainly from "Stabilizatsiya i vykhod iz krizisa", op.cit..

[280] First Deputy Finance Minister Andrei Nechaev, writing in *Trud*, 3 January 1992, cited by Reuters from Moscow of the same date.

[281] Anatoly Chubais, the Russian Federation Minister in charge of privatization, envisages central bank intervention to bring the market rate down to R30-35 per dollar, at which level foreign investors would be allowed to buy assets more freely at the market rate. This intervention would have, as Chubais acknowledges, to be backed by a stabilization fund provided by the west. Reuters from Moscow, 7 February 1992. It is, however, unlikely that such support, probably through the IMF, would be available before the end of 1992.

[282] *Rossiiskaya gazeta*, 10 January 1992.

In February-April 1992, state and collective farms will be required to hold meetings of their workforces to discuss future organization. Farms that are currently making losses will have no choice but to be broken up into family farms, small cooperatives, etc. In profitable collective farms, the option for members of trading their notional shares in farm property into claims on land, with the land then becoming saleable, will be put on the agenda. At the same time, obligatory state orders to all types of farms are supposed to be reduced to around 20-25 per cent of output (but up to 50 per cent for some livestock products from state and collective farms only).[283]

The move towards private land ownership that is apparently entailed is of great potential importance for the reform of property rights in general in Russia. Hungarian experience, however, illustrates the risks that are involved in devolving implementation decisions of this sort to the people involved in operating the existing system. There is, however, a more urgent problem: the uncertainty hanging over the future status and operation of existing large farms may well undermine planting and other preparatory work in the farms, cutting farm output in 1992 to levels still lower than it would otherwise have reached, with serious consequences for food supplies in 1992-1993, greatly increasing the strain on the electorate's patience.

In general, the programme seems bound to produce confusion and disappointment. There are, however, a number of institutional changes that will be attempted in order to facilitate the privatization process; if they are in fact carried out, the whole privatization drive can hardly be carried out as fast as is envisaged, but the outcome might be a delayed but better prepared process than the reform planners appeared to envisage in late November 1991.

The most important of these preparatory institutional changes are the following: the establishment of local privatization bodies reporting both to local authorities and the Russian Federation State Property Committee (*Goskomimushchestvo*); the corporatization of all enterprises with capital assets above R100,000; making all shops and restaurants separate legal persons prior to petty privatization, instead of their present status as subunits of local trade organizations (*torgi*) and catering trusts; the allocation of assets between state and municipal ownership and between different levels of "the state" (presumably distinguishing, *inter alia*, property of autonomous republics from property of the Russian Federation — which is a minefield); the repeal of earlier USSR and RSFSR legislation governing workforce leasing (*arenda*) and the delegation of the management of state assets to branch ministries; the introduction of effective legislation on bankruptcy, loan collateral, etc; and in general to remove anomalies and ambiguities from the relevant legislation.

If all this is done at a great pace, it will probably be done badly, with corresponding consequences for the privatization process. If it is done carefully, on the other hand, there is unlikely to be much progress in asset sales during 1992. The fact that some of the preparatory measures involve scrapping quite recent legislation under which some independent or semi-independent enterprises had begun to take shape, will not promote confidence in the stability of the institutional framework. On the other hand, some of the later USSR legislation may be more serviceable than it is generally given credit for, as noted above. If this is so, simply re-labelling some of it Russian Federation legislation may both save time and limit the legislative turbulence. It might also help towards the long-run aim of making the reform legislation of the CIS states mutually compatible, since all have a common heritage in the legislation of the former Soviet Union.

(v) Internationalization

The Russian Federation and a number of other CIS states have in the recent past adopted new foreign investment laws and other legislation affecting their openness to international transactions. Their most immediate concerns, however, are with their own interstate (intra-CIS) transactions.[284] In general, trade between the CIS states as well as between them and some other states will be settled for the time being in roubles, though pricing is supposed to shift to a world market basis. The rouble remains inconvertible for most business purposes. The Russian Federation and other CIS states at present lack the funds to back up convertibility at significantly higher rates. Making the rouble convertible at the extremely low internal market rate of early 1992 would create still stronger inflationary pressures than already exist.

In these circumstances, the Russian government's present programme understandably relies on continued trade controls.[285] The idea is to move towards a limited array of export licences on selected products, and to make the 40 per cent compulsory sale of convertible currency earnings by exporters obligatory only for energy, basic chemicals and other raw materials exporters, and the sale conducted at half the market rate, as against the previous use of the very low "commercial" rate in these compulsory sales. Other exporters would be obliged to surrender to the central authorities only 10 per cent of their hard currency earnings, and would do so at the market rate.

These limited short-term objectives are reasonable in the current situation, but still leave the Russian economy substantially insulated from the outside world.

---

283 V. Konovalov in *Izvestiya*, 31 December 1991, p.2; Reuters from Moscow 6 January 1992; both based on interviews with Russian Federation Agriculture Minister Viktor Khlystun.

284 See section 4.2(v) above.

285 See the presidential edict, "O liberalizatsii vneshneekonomicheskoi deyatel'nosti na territorii RSFSR", *Izvestiya*, 18 November 1991, pp.1-2; M. Berger, "Svoboda vneshnei torgovli pridet vmeste so svobodnymi tsenami, no budet bolee skovannoi", *Izvestiya*,, 2 January 1992, p.2, quoting Petr Aven, the chairman of the Russian government's Committee for External Economic Relations.

(vi) Economic relations among successor states: issues and options

As noted, relations between the various successor states were, by the end of 1991, a fundamental economic policy concern of all of them. The tendency during 1990 and 1991 was towards loosening integration links. This has often been contrasted with the predominant tendency in western Europe and in several other regions of the world towards economic integration, with the accompanying judgement, implicit or explicit, that what is happening in the former USSR is manifestly economically undesirable.

It is true that the disadvantages of breaking up an existing "single economic space" are easily listed. The momentum of political change in the former USSR, however, makes the circumstances there quite unlike those in western Europe or North America. The levels of economic integration that can be attained in the former Soviet Union in the near future can only sensibly be discussed with this in mind. It is also important to take into account the ways in which the preservation of a single monetary area with separate successor state budgetary policies is now hampering the control of inflation.

The local and republic elections of 1990, which were more open and genuinely contested than the earlier all-Union elections, made the issue of the republics' autonomy more salient, because republic governments with some democratic legitimacy faced a Union leadership that had not issued from direct elections. The general resentment towards the old economic and political system was focused on Moscow, as the all powerful centre of that system, so that the desire for social change and long suppressed feelings of national and local identity formed a powerful combination of pressures towards regional devolution. During 1990 and 1991, these pressures reinforced other factors that were contributing to accelerating inflation and reduced output levels.

In 1991 the economic decline of the ex-Soviet Union was attributable above all to disruptions on the supply side. In the most general sense, what has been happening is that a highly developed division of labour between different production units has tended to break down. This is not to be blamed wholly and directly on breakdowns in inter-republic transactions (see below). It is none the less closely bound up with the problems of inter-republic relations.

Box 4.3.1 gives a cross-classification of some recent supply breakdowns, according to whether they were within or between republics and whether their primary motivation was economic or political. The latter distinction is unavoidably rather crude. The two-by-two matrix of box 4.3.1 omits two additional categories. One is supply breakdowns affecting deliveries across successor state boundaries but motivated by the political objectives of governments of entities within one successor state.[286] The other is supply breakdowns of a type that affect *both* inter- and intra-successor state deliveries. The most conspicuous example of the latter is the widespread non-delivery of "contracted" amounts of grain and other farm products to state procurement agencies.[287]

The latter phenomenon is the result primarily of the deteriorating terms of trade for the farm sector, in conditions of rapid inflation with partial price control. Shortfalls in inter-republic deliveries by state agencies of grain and grain-based items (e.g., of animal feed from Russia to the Baltic states) are often interpreted as deliberate acts designed to promote "political" aims; under the circumstances, they must at least in part be understood as secondary effects of the farm sector's response to its current economic environment.

The examples in box 4.3.1 illustrate the epidemic nature of supply breakdowns in the former Soviet Union. As the examples suggest, the disruptions to supply links are by no means confined to transactions across successor state boundaries, and they are typically the result of economic pressures that reflect the prevailing environment of rapid inflation and shortages.

In general, the relationship between declining output and inter-republic relations takes two forms. There is a direct link, in that some substantial proportion of the supply breakdowns are breakdowns in goods flows across republic boundaries brought about by the actions of republic authorities — usually motivated by economic considerations. There is also a more fundamental and less direct connection, in that many supply breakdowns in both inter- and intra-republic transactions arise from the rouble's rapid loss of value, and that in turn has been accelerated by problems in inter-republic economic relations.

It is useful to focus first on the links between supply breakdowns, inflation and the erosion of a single monetary and fiscal system covering all the states that were previously part of the USSR.

Both enterprise and regional autarky have increased. As the collapse of central control and the process of inflation both gathered pace, barter transactions within the enterprise sector tended to replace centrally planned inter-enterprise flows with rouble settlement. Moreover, the commodity composition of inter-enterprise transactions has shifted towards consumer goods, at the expense of producer goods. Exercising their own priorities under conditions of shortage, weak central control, and continuing soft budget constraints, enterprise managers sought to maintain "their" work forces by providing consumer goods for them, seeking new partners and, where possible, a new product mix in the process. Given the low efficiency of barter arrangements, this attempted shift has been accompanied, it seems, by a shrinking of inter-enterprise transactions

---

[286] For example, the halting of hydrocarbon deliveries to Georgia from Chechen-Ingushetia (which is within the Russian Federation) because of the Chechen leadership's desire to penalize the new Georgian government for ousting President Zviad Gamsakhurdia. See Vladimir Fedorovski, "Après la fin de l'URSS, la fin de la Russie?", *Le Nouveau Quotidien* (Lausanne), 22 January 1992, p.3.

[287] As at 4 November 1991, in the CIS territory, only 68 per cent of the contracted grain deliveries had been purchased, against 86 per cent on 4 November 1990 for the USSR. As proportions of the original state order (*goszakaz*), these purchases were even more markedly down (51 per cent, against 77 per cent in 1990). The corresponding percentages for the Russian Federation alone in 1991 were 78 and 52. *Ekonomika i zhizn'*, 1991, No.49, p.10.

> **BOX 4.3.1**
>
> **Supply breakdowns in the ex-Soviet economy: a classification**
>
> *Reductions in output in the Soviet successor states in 1991-1992 have been the result of supply-side difficulties. Numerous examples of specific supply disruptions can be cited. To ascribe them to disputes between successor states is to explain very little, and to put a misleading emphasis on the direct effects of such conflicts. The examples given below illustrate the wide variety of supply breakdowns that have been occurring. The institutional and macroeconomic environment that generates them is discussed in the text.*
>
> *Examples of supply breakdowns are classified below as "political" or "economic", and as occurring between or within successor states. "Political" here denotes supply cut-offs deliberately imposed in the pursuit of a primarily political aim. "Economic" denotes cut-offs imposed to economic stimuli, such as the supplier's desire to obtain better terms of trade or to "protect" local consumer supplies; an economically motivated cut-off may be imposed by regional government, by state enterprises or by private agents. Successor states here are former Union republics.*
>
> | Motive | Within a successor-state | Between successor-states |
> |---|---|---|
> | Political | Estonian government halts bread supplies to CIS troops in Estonia. | Russian authorities redirecting cargoes from Baltic ports to St. Petersburg.[a] |
> | Economic | City heating cut off in Saratov since defence plants that normally operate it are in financial trouble. Karelia imposes controls on its staple deliveries to other regions. Stavropol' region does the same. | Steel production in Chelyabinsk halted by interruption of coking coal supplies from Donbass because of a miners' strike. Kazakhstan halting all deliveries by road to neighbouring regions of Russia. |
>
> Source: Vladimir Fedorovski, "Apres la fin de l'URSS, la fin de la Russie?", *Le Nouveau Quotidien*, 22 January 1992, p.2; Duncan Robinson, "Cargo Overwhelms Key Russian Port", *Journal of Commerce*, 7 November 1991; Vladimir Capelik, "Yeltsin's Economic Reform: a Pessimistic Appraisal", *RFE/RL Research Report* vol.1, No.4, p.27; Fedorovski, op.cit.; Radio Moscow, 6 January 1992; Russian Radio, 19 September 1991; Tass in English, 18 November 1991.
>
> [a] Arguably economic (negotiating terms for Baltic transit); but the action was apparently unconnected with talks.

overall.[288] At the same time, a tendency towards regional autarky also developed. These two tendencies are closely related.

In the case of the 15 former Union republics and of a number of other regions with a strong sense of regional identity,[289] the tendency towards autarky has been strengthened by political change. Newly elected local leaders, unlike their predecessors, have been sensitive to the demands of the local population. They therefore seek to assert their region's identity, and try to defend the short-term material interests of their electors. Accordingly, they have tended to restrict the outflow of consumer goods to other regions. The latter policy has been a logical response of local leaders to conditions of severe but partly repressed inflation, in the absence of effective central economic controls.

The inflationary process itself has been fed by the growing fiscal autonomy of republics. Open inflation first developed after 1985 because of a mixture of policy errors and the side effects of partial decentralization.[290] After 1989, and particularly in 1991, the control by republics of their own budgets increased. Under certain conditions, this need not have been an inflationary development. In practice, the single rouble currency remained, with a soft monetary centre passively responding to the sum of Union and republic budget deficits by expanding the money supply. For republics it has therefore been rational to run deficits, have them almost automatically financed by increased monetary emission, and avoid the full inflationary consequences because the latter are diffused across all republics.[291]

During 1991, there was not in fact an out-and-out monetary war between republics, with each one trying to increase its deficit faster than the others. The Baltic states, for example, had balanced budgets (see section 4.5). One explanation for this may be that several republics were aiming to introduce currencies of their own, and were attempting to gain control of their budgets in order to facilitate the stabilization of these currencies. A more cynical explanation may be that few officials in the republics understood the workings of the fiscal and monetary system; they therefore did

---

[288] The valuation of these flows is of course highly problematic. What is clear is that enterprise behaviour that tended in aggregate to shift the final use composition of output towards consumer goods was not supported by adjustments of flows of intermediate products that have been sufficient to maintain the aggregate level of final output. On Goskomstat estimates, some growth of consumption was maintained in 1990 despite the modest fall in total output, and this does not seem to be explicable entirely by a growth of net imports of consumer items; in 1991, both total output and consumption fell, but the latter by less than the former (*Narodnoe khozyaistvo SSSR v 1990 godu*, pp.5-13; Goskomstat, *Itogi raboty otraslei ekonomiki i sotsial'noi sfery Sodruzhestva nezavisimykh gosudarstv*, mimeo, 1992).

[289] The sense of regional identity is most often, but not always, connected with ethnic identity. And it is not necessarily identified only with autonomous republics. The city of Leningrad/St. Petersburg, under the leadership of its mayor, Anatoly Sobchak, has pursued independent policies, often including autarkic elements.

[290] The policy errors included the 1985-1987 drive for higher investment spending, the anti-alcohol campaign (diverting income from the budget to bootleggers), and the sharp cuts in consumer imports to adjust to reduced export earnings. The limited extension of enterprise autonomy meant that price and product mix controls were loosened and less enterprise net income was channelled to the state budget, while there was no significant hardening of the budget constraints of enterprises. The net result was a large increase in the state budget deficit, which was monetized.

[291] For an extended discussion, see Oleh Havrylyshyn and John Williamson, *From Soviet disUnion to Eastern Economic Community?*, Washington, D.C., Institute for International Economics, October 1991.

not see that fiscal extravagance was rational. At all events, the situation has been one in which the incentives for republics to embark on macroeconomic stabilization were weak. With the possible exception of the Russian Federation, fiscal prudence would be penalized, and its potential disinflationary effects would be undermined by an inflow of roubles from less prudent republics.

It is in this situation that the Soviet successor states are seeking to stabilize their mutual economic relations. The most urgent short-term objective must be to halt the erosion of inter-enterprise supply links generally, whether they cross successor state boundaries or not. This requires macroeconomic stabilization. That in turn requires a stable solution to the present conflict between decentralized fiscal authority and the continued existence of a single currency with a soft monetary environment. There are a number of proposed solutions (see section 4.3(vii) below). In the meantime some makeshift, but inadequate, arrangements are being used.

Goods and services flow at present across the boundaries between the former Soviet republics under a variety of different arrangements. There are bilateral inter-republic agreements (see section 4.2(v) above), transactions between enterprises outside the framework of inter-governmental agreements, transactions by private citizens and sales through the burgeoning network of commodity exchanges. Despite the fact that the entire territory of the former Soviet Union is still nominally a single currency area, there is a proliferation of controls on these flows. One of the many anomalous features of the present situation is that cross-border flows of labour and capital are probably less restricted than goods flows.[292] The extent of any decline in the aggregate volume of cross-border goods flows cannot be assessed from available data, but the presumption must be that there has been some decline.[293] As was noted above, there are also many similar controls limiting cross-boundary flows between jurisdictions below the former Union republic level, as well.

The controls currently used by successor state governments are predominantly on *exports* of consumer items and key raw materials saleable for hard currency. These controls include export licensing and quotas, the use of one-time or reusable coupons issued only to residents, and requirements that customers show residence permits when buying specific items in the shops.

The allocation mechanisms used include what remains of centralized supply allocation, in the form of republic level state purchase orders (*goszakazy*) that are binding on enterprises; direct inter-enterprise bargaining, circumscribed by licensing and quotas; and transactions on the commodity exchanges (*birzhy*). The last of these is also subject, in principle and for some products, to licensing of the amounts that can be allocated for sale through *birzhy*, but the commodity exchanges probably represent the clearest institutional development of market relations, since direct inter-enterprise deals are more likely to be barter transactions.

The *birzhy* are important as an institutional innovation capable of facilitating transactions throughout the rouble area. Several of them are networks of exchanges in different places, often in more than one of the successor states. Their role, however, is still limited in scale, though rising rapidly (see section 4.3(iv) above).

Inter-republic supply agreements form at present a network of bilateral arrangements. One of the immediate difficulties with these agreements, even as a stopgap arrangement, is that they are unfulfilled. Mobilizing the remnants of the centralized supply system does not in fact work very well. In addition to the traditional explanations, such as supply difficulties further back in the production chain affecting the enterprise instructed to make the cross-border delivery to the designated recipient in the partner state, there is the more recent phenomenon of enterprises simply disregarding instructions "from above". The fact that those instructions now come from a republic centre rather than the former Union centre seems often to make little difference.

From anecdotal evidence, it appears that a growing proportion of these cross-border flows are arranged on a *barter* basis. This applies both to inter-governmental arrangements and to inter-enterprise deals.[294]

In general, current arrangements governing inter-republic goods flows are highly inefficient. The obstacles to efficiency in these flows are not, however, fundamentally different in kind from the obstacles to efficient flows of goods between production units within each of the successor states. The introduction of separate republic currencies will exacerbate the problem if efficient settlement arrangements are not developed. But the underlying source of trouble is the failure to control inflationary pressure.

---

[292] So far as labour flows are concerned, the near absence of a housing market and the continued presence of at least part of the old residence permit system inhibit flows. And the same difficulty in distinguishing between economic and political migrants now arises in Soviet successor states as it does elsewhere — though the distinction is so far relevant to analysis rather than to any programmes of enforced repatriation. Net inwards migration into at least two of the Baltic states has turned into out-migration, and there are relatively large numbers of refugees in the Transcaucasus. So far as capital flows are concerned, new foreign investment legislation is being used in some successor states to exclude or limit Russian direct investment as well as direct investment from outside the rouble area. This tendency may well spread amongst the non-Russian successor states, since there are fears of a reassertion of control "by Moscow" by new means in most republic capitals.

[293] The USSR Goskomstat report for the CIS states in 1991, *Itogi raboty otraslei* ... cited earlier, says that in January-September 1991 interregional goods flows in comparable prices were 46 per cent less than in the previous year (presumably in January-September 1990). This, however, probably refers only to officially managed exchanges, and therefore overstates the decline. The same source also gives, for the same period, the share of "inter-state" deliveries amongst the total of consumer supplies as 12 per cent, compared with 19, 18 and 17 per cent in the years 1988, 1989 and 1990, respectively. Again, these data probably omit a growing volume of private and other supplied not administered by the government, and thus once more overstate the decline. What is striking is that, on this measure, the mutual dependence of successor states for food and other consumer goods is only modest. The measure presumably captures only shares in deliveries from final stage production to internal trade; however, the share in total consumption in one republic of value added in other republics will be higher. (The share of imports from outside the former USSR in the total value to final consumption is also significant.)

[294] Deals by private citizens are partly, and commodity exchange deals very largely, monetized.

(vii) Some possible ways forward

From the picture presented above, it follows that measures to maintain inter-republic trade must be closely linked with measures aimed at macroeconomic stabilization.

The case for measures based on the maintenance of a *single currency area,* with stabilization of the rouble as the central element, is at first sight strong. The advantages of preserving a single currency where one has hitherto been in use will usually be considerable. By lowering transaction costs, compared with several currencies, within the area concerned, a single currency should produce gains in efficiency. Furthermore, where an existing monetary regime is devolved into several currencies, and efficient payments arrangements between them are not put in place, there could be a rapid shift towards autarky, with large losses of existing gains from trade. For the ex-Soviet Union, the first question is whether the conditions for maintaining a single currency hold. If not, there is a second question: what are the best attainable arrangements that could be installed to prevent a general breakdown in inter-state trade?

Four main criteria have been suggested by economists for identifying an appropriate currency area: that there should be a relatively free flow of labour and capital within it; that there should be a high degree of openness to mutual trade within the region; that there should be considerable diversification of production amongst the countries, and that there should be a high degree of fiscal integration.[295] Adjustment through factor movements, production and trade shifts and fiscal coordination will be severely tested, in the absence of separate currencies, if the component parts of a monetary area have very different development levels and growth potential. One might therefore add a fifth criterion: that development levels should not differ very greatly.

These criteria are not conveniently measurable; nor can they be weighed against one another. But as a check-list of attributes to consider, they are useful. The first two, despite the limitations to factor mobility mentioned above, obtain, by and large, in the ex-Soviet Union. Any attempt to apply the criteria of diversification and openness, however, for the Soviet successor states, raises problems. Moreover, development levels do indeed vary widely amongst the Soviet successor states: in a ratio of almost 1:3 between least- and most-developed (see table 4.4.1). The existing patterns of production specialization and intra-regional trade are the product of a highly inefficient economic system from which the successor states are trying to escape. Preserving existing patterns of production and trade is not the policy makers' objective for the medium term and beyond.

The product mix of Soviet final output has thus been substantially different from that which would be expected to emerge in a group of market economies that have the successor states' present resource endowments and development levels, are open to the world economy and are not jointly aiming at the status of a military superpower. Moreover, the pattern of input-output flows required to support any given line of final output will be subject to substantial change in a successful market reform: there should be large gains in X-efficiency, better location and transport decisions, and so on. Therefore patterns of production and trade that should emerge in the longer run will be substantially different from those inherited from the old system.

If the transformation of the system were broadly successful, there might well be, for these reasons, a substantial shift away from inter-successor state trading to trading with countries outside the former USSR. In the 1920s and 1930s, when they were independent, the three Baltic states traded more heavily with the west than with the USSR. A reorientation of the trade of the eastern part of the former Soviet Union towards the Pacific region is widely expected. Against this must be balanced the obvious complementarity of Siberian raw material extraction and European CIS industrial production, which would suggest continuing close links between east and west within the former USSR. In general, however, the patterns of economic activity that policy makers in several successor states hope to achieve in the long term might well be such that the ex-Soviet Union would no longer seem an appropriate currency area on grounds of mutual openness to trade.

It is the criterion of fiscal integration that has aroused the most doubt about the appropriateness of maintaining a single currency among the successor states. There is a great deal of suspicion between successor state governments. Amongst the non-Russian successor states there is a special fear of Russia's propensity to reassert control from Moscow. The general lack of trust, together with the exhilarating effects of newly asserted national identity, make any restoration of close budgetary cooperation unlikely in the near term. As was argued above, the present coexistence of a single but weak monetary centre with independent successor state fiscal policies is a recipe for inflation; and the inflation in turn leads to inter-republic export controls and other forms of autarkic behaviour. Thus the gains from trade are being lost anyway.[296]

The logic of devolved currencies is therefore accepted by many economists inside and outside the ex-Soviet Union. The conclusion they have come to is that the best chance of achieving macroeconomic stabilization within the present rouble area lies, not in attempts to restore and strengthen a single monetary and fiscal centre, but in moves to create *separate successor state currencies*. That would bring the governments of the former Soviet republics face-to-face with the monetary consequences of their fiscal imprudence. To put it another way: the moral hazard or free rider problem embedded in the present arrangements would be elimi-

---

[295] For a summary of the literature, see Peter Robson, *The Economics of International Integration*, third edition, London, Allen and Unwin, 1987, chapter 9.

[296] See Havrylyshyn and Williamson, op.cit., and United Nations Economic Commission for Europe, *Economic Bulletin for Europe*, vol.43, New York, 1991, pp.85-86.

nated. A Ukrainian budget deficit would weaken the *grivnya*, an Estonian deficit the *kroon*, and so on.[297]

The move towards separate currencies is already under way. Reported agreements in early February 1992 between Russia, Belarus and Kazakhstan about a "common rouble space" envisage either the joint maintenance of the rouble as a common currency or close coordination in the introduction of separate currencies, e.g., by agreement on the withdrawal of appropriate quantities of roubles from circulation.[298] The reference to the second, weaker version of a single rouble space is striking. This is, after all, an agreement with two republics that are especially closely tied to Russia. If separate currencies can be envisaged amongst these three, the general tendency towards separate currencies is indeed strong.

Clusters of former Soviet republics, such as Russia and Belarus, or Kazakhstan plus the four Central Asian republics, may none the less, in the end, each opt for shared currencies. If so, they will have to accept close coordination of fiscal policies within their cluster. What is clear is that a single currency shared by 11 or 12 CIS states is unlikely to survive. Ukraine is apparently committed to introducing its own currency soon, and has already taken the preliminary step of issuing near-money in the form of reusable coupons (see section 4.4(iii) below).

Three requirements for the creation of an open trading area amongst the Soviet successor states with several separate currencies can be identified: the introduction of the new currencies needs to be carried out in a way that is not itself destabilizing; they must then be managed in such a way as to facilitate macroeconomic stabilization and a move to convertibility; and, pending the achievement of external convertibility, efficient payments arrangements between the successor states must be available. The paragraphs that follow review these requirements in turn.

First, the introduction of the new currencies must be managed as an effective currency reform. This means that the conversion rates between new and old currencies (perhaps differentiated between wages, social benefits and financial assets) must be chosen in such a way that, in conjunction with the withdrawal from circulation of the roubles thus replaced, the transition is politically acceptable within the state concerned and also does not destabilize other successor states by releasing large, additional flows of roubles into their territories.

Second, the new currencies must be part of separate macroeconomic stabilization measures in each new currency area, followed by a move to convertibility as soon as possible. Exchanging a rapidly depreciating rouble for several rapidly depreciating new currencies will hardly be an improvement. The advantage of the devolution to separate currencies is that it improves the incentives for governments to introduce strong anti-inflationary policies. But implementing the policies requires skills and institutions that are still thin on the ground, and it requires those skills and institutions to be available in more places than are needed in a single currency area.

The prime institutional requirement is effective bank regulation and credit control by the central bank. The absence of these so far in the Baltic states has been a major factor leading to delay in the introduction of Baltic currencies. If the Baltic states' banking institutions have been judged to be unready, it is likely that the CIS states are still less prepared institutionally.

Part of the problem is the central bank's relationship to the state. The arrangement in Russia and several other successor states is that the central bank is responsible to parliament, not to the government. Initially proposed when the state in question was still the Soviet Union, this arrangement had the attraction of seeming to increase the independence of the central bank.[299] So far, however, the tendency in the successor states has been for parliaments to be softer on inflation than governments.[300]

One method of monetary control that might be adopted is the management of a new currency by a *currency board*. This is in effect an alternative to a central bank; once instituted, it leaves no room for discretionary monetary policy. A currency board issues notes and coins that are convertible on demand and at a fixed rate into a foreign currency, the latter constituting the reserve for the local currency.[301] Thus the money supply in the form of cash is tied to the balance of payments, expanding with a surplus and contracting with a deficit. The currency board's notes and coins are held by the public, and by the commercial banks as their reserves. Commercial bank credit varies with the supply of currency-board notes and coins, given the public's desired ratio of cash to bank deposits. Currency boards have maintained stable and convertible currencies in North Russia during the Russian civil war of 1918-1919, in Danzig in 1920-1924, in British colonies when they were under British rule, and latterly in Hong Kong and Singapore.

For the CIS and Baltic states, the introduction of currency boards would require two principal conditions that may be hard to meet. One is the availability of convertible currency to form the currency board re-

---

[297] In the near future, budget deficits will continue to be monetized more or less fully and automatically, pending the development of financial institutions that might allow funding of deficits with bond issues on a significant scale.

[298] *Le Monde*, 5 February 1992, p.4.

[299] This was, for example, one of the recommendations of the Shatalin "500 Days" Programme. See *Perekhod k rynku. Kontseptsiya i programma*, Moscow, Arkhangel'skoe, 1990.

[300] This is reflected in the resignation of the Lithuanian Prime Minister, Mrs Kazimira Prunskiene, in early 1991, in the face of parliamentary opposition to price increases; the resignation of the Estonian Prime Minister, Mr Edgar Savisaar a year later, after he had received inadequate parliamentary support for his assumption of special powers to cope with the strains of economic austerity generated in part by his policies; and the initial open opposition of the President of the Russian central bank, Mr Georgy Matyukhin, backed by the Russian parliament, to Prime Minister Gaidar's abrupt price liberalization.

[301] For a systematic exposition, see Steve H. Hanke and Kurt Schuler, *Monetary Reform and the Development of a Yugoslav Market Economy*, London, Centre for Research into Communist Economies, 1991. The rest of this paragraph and part of the next summarize parts of this account.

serve.[302] As an illustrative figure, a requirement of $50 billion to provide 100 per cent backing for a USSR basic money supply of R200 billion, at R4 per dollar was suggested last autumn.[303] At the end of 1991 the quantity of rouble notes and coins in circulation was 263 billion, according to the Goskomstat report for the year, up from R158 billion at mid-year. The introduction of currency boards in, say, late 1992 would occur in the context of substantially higher prices and a larger monetary base.

The order of magnitude of the sum of currency boards' reserves could still be similar to that suggested, with a corresponding adjustment of the fixed exchange rate to be used (different rates for different successor currencies, if they are introduced at other than one-for-one rates to the old rouble). Provided that price levels for tradable goods had not by that time diverged significantly between successor states, 1990 NMP shares in the Soviet total could serve as a proxy measure for dividing the reserve requirement amongst successor states.

The currency board solution thus requires substantial western support for the successor states, well above the amounts of $5-10 billion that have been mentioned for stabilization funds to assist rouble convertibility. On the other hand, the currency board system, subject to one major proviso, is a more reliable means of securing the initial domestic financial stabilization that is needed.

The proviso is that the commercial banks are subject to the minimum amount of regulation and have the minimum necessary know-how to ensure that they will in fact prudently regulate their lending in the light of their available reserves of currency board cash. This is the second of the two principal conditions for successful working of a currency board system referred to above. It is doubtful whether it is met at present.

This may not, however, be a fatal objection. Many people in Moscow expect soon to see a drastic thinning out of the 1,600-plus commercial banks that have mushroomed in the ex-USSR in the past two to three years.[304] And a currency board system, by removing exchange risk for investors from the reserve currency nation and reducing it substantially for others, allows a rapid development of banking links with banks from abroad, including their extension of branch networks to the region, and a correspondingly rapid growth of banking skills.

The third requirement for the successful establishment of several successor state currencies is that efficient payments arrangements must be made between the separate currencies.

The issues here are similar to those that have been discussed in connection with the idea of a payments union among former CMEA countries. The prime purpose of a *payments union* would be to avoid excessive trade contraction amongst the successor states during the transition of their currencies to non-resident current account convertibility.

In outline, such a scheme would require the successor states to accept one another's currencies in payment for exports, deposit the proceeds with the central payments union institution, which then periodically clears imbalances, settling the inter-state balances partly in convertible currency and partly in credits. The availability of the latter provides an incentive to favour inter-successor state trade over external trade; in other words, to maintain the former, avoiding the collapse of mutual trade that followed the termination of CMEA. Again, a sum of hard currency is needed for payments union operations, but it is relatively modest.[305]

The lesson of the CMEA trade collapse has not been lost on Russian economists and politicians. Thus, a 1991 article proposes a payments union type of arrangement between successor states;[306] in the important area of fuel and energy, a Russian minister has recently invoked the need to avoid a similar trade collapse and therefore to avoid an abrupt shift to world prices and hard currency settlement.[307] It is therefore plausible to argue that the Russian government, whose inclinations on this matter are crucial, could favour payments union arrangements if and when separate currencies begin to be established.

There remains a doubt, however, about the viability of payments union arrangements within the former Soviet Union. This doubt arises from the imbalance between the different successor states' hard currency earning capacities in the short run. Faced with settlement in a mixture of convertible currency and payments union credits, Russia would be strongly tempted to continue its reorientation of energy exports towards the west, and the distinction between "hard goods" (readily saleable for convertible currency) and "soft goods" that characterized the operations of the former CMEA could emerge again, along with continuing barter deals.

In general, it may well be that the requirements for macroeconomic stabilization and for halting the development of autarky on the part of Soviet successor states are best addressed through the development of separate currencies, with the accompanying conditions described above.

---

302 The currency board would in fact hold interest-bearing, low-risk securities denominated in the reserve currency. The interest on these securities less the cost of maintaining the currency supply would be its net income (seigniorage). To offset the risk of a fall in prices of the underlying securities, in a strict version of the currency-board system, the value of the reserve would be somewhat more than the value of the domestic currency times the fixed exchange rate.

303 Havrylyshyn and Williamson, op.cit.

304 David Fairlamb, "Moscow's Financial Crisis", *Institutional Investor*, January 1992, pp.81-88.

305 For discussion of possible arrangements in detail and an estimate of the hard currency requirement, see Havrylyshyn and Williamson, op.cit., pp.50-58.

306 A. Barkovsky and L. Krasnov, "Ni tsentra, ni periferii", *Ekonomika i zhizn'*, 1991, No.41, p.5.

307 Interview with the Russian Federation Minister for Energy Vladimir Lopukhin, *Le Monde*, 5 February 1992, p.3.

Significant western assistance is required for those conditions to be met. This would include both large-scale technical assistance in banking and payments un-ion arrangements,[308] and also significant financial assistance.

---

[308] Aglietta, op.cit., suggests the BIS as the best source of expertise in setting up the payments union.

4.4 THE SUCCESSOR STATES OF THE SOVIET UNION

(i) Introduction

This section attempts to highlight differences between the successor republics of the former Soviet Union. A number of structural distortions, some of which resulted from conscious policy decisions (the excessive share of defence in total output and resource use) and some from the similarity of behavioural responses to central planning in all areas of the country (wasteful resource use) have affected all the successor states – but not always in the same way. These, different resource endowments and variations in past resource allocation patterns have led to considerable differences between the republics in terms of economic development levels and output structures. Many of these have only been revealed in recent months.

The section begins with a brief description covering all 15 successor states which aims to compare their size and relative position in the former Soviet Union. Russia, Ukraine and Belarus, the three biggest European members of the Commonwealth of Independent States, are analysed in more detail in sections (ii) to (iv) below. The economies of the three Baltic states which did not join the CIS, Estonia, Lithuania and Latvia, are reviewed in greater detail in section 4.5.

Russia, Ukraine and Belarus together accounted for 80 per cent of the land area and of the GDP, as well as over 70 per cent of the 290 million population, of the former Soviet Union (table 4.4.1). Russia and Ukraine, with populations of 149 and nearly 52 million, have an economic potential equal to or bigger than the larger west European countries.

In terms of population, Uzbekistan is the biggest of the other 12 republics (nearly 21 million or 7 per cent of the former Soviet population), followed by Kazakhstan with 17 million. Only two of the other republics have populations exceeding 5 million – Georgia (5.5 million) and Tajikistan (5.4 million). In terms of land area, Kazakhstan comes second after Russia, with 12 per cent of the total. Ukraine, Uzbekistan and Turkmenistan are the next most extensive republics, but none of these three holds more than 2-3 per cent of the former Soviet territory and none of the rest more than 1 per cent.

A high share of the population of most republics consists of ethnic groups other than the basic nationality (table 4.4.2). Altogether nearly 20 per cent of the population of the former Soviet Union were domiciled outside their republic of national origin. National homogeneity is most complete in Armenia, where 90 per cent of the population is of Armenian origin. All but about a fifth of the Russian population is of Russian national origin. Of the 54 million people on the territory of the former Soviet Union living outside their republic of origin, just under half of whom are Russians and about 12 per cent Ukrainian – respectively equal to 17 and 15 per cent of the two republics' own populations. Past Russian migration was the principal reason for the minority share of Kazakhs in Kazakhstan and for the low share of the original nationalities in Moldova, Latvia and Estonia. A majority of the roughly 20-30 per cent non-ethnic population of Belarus, Ukraine and Lithuanian are also of Russian origin. The importance of individual republics in terms of their share in total output by major products is shown in table 4.4.3.

There is a nearly 3:1 spread between GDP per capita in Tajikistan, the poorest republic with half the Soviet average, and Estonia (40 per cent above the average). The other central Asian republics of Kyrgyzstan and Uzbekistan, as well as Azerbaijan, are only slightly higher than Tajikistan while the other two Baltic republics of Lithuanuia and Latvia are 20-30 per cent above the average. The European republics of the Ukraine and Moldova, together with Georgia, Turkmenistan and the resource rich Kazakhstan, fall 10-25 per cent below the average while Russia itself, Belarus and Armenia are 5-20 per cent above it (see table 4.4.1, panel B).

Per capita GDP is, of course, closely correlated with the wealth accumulated in different republics. Wealth is defined in the Soviet statistical sources as the total value of assets (including farm animals) built up by human effort – including the capital stock, working capital, dwellings, other buildings serving an economic purpose and consumer durable goods. The value of land, forests and mineral resources is excluded.[309] Except for Armenia, all the republics which have respectively above or below average GDP per head have correspondingly above- or below-average wealth per capita. However, if the value of natural resources could be included in the calculation, it would appear that Russia, Kazakhstan and, to a lesser extent, Uzbekistan, where the bulk of base metals, precious metals and stones and fuel deposits are located, have not created a productive base proportionate to their natural endowment.

High output per head is also associated with high factor productivities. Only Belarus and the Baltics combine average or higher than average productivities for both labour and capital. These are the countries with the highest per capita GDP. In the Russian Federation, GDP per capita is held back by low capital productivity. In Ukraine and Kazakhstan, lower than average labour productivity, and in the latter lower than

---

[309] See *Narodnoe khozyaistvo SSSR v 1990 g.*, pp.287, 695-696.

TABLE 4.4.1
Soviet successor states: Selected economic data, 1990
(Percentage)

	Russia	Ukraine	Belarus	Uzbekistan	Kazakhstan	Georgia	Azerbaijan	Moldova	Kyrgyzstan	Tajikistan	Armenia	Turkmenistan	Lithuania	Latvia	Estonia
Panel A: Share in Soviet macroeconomic aggregates
Area	76.2	2.7	0.9	2.0	12.1	0.3	0.4	0.2	0.9	0.6	0.1	2.2	0.3	0.3	0.2
Population	51.3	18.0	3.6	7.0	5.8	1.9	2.5	1.5	1.5	1.8	1.1	1.2	1.3	0.9	0.5
Employment	53.6	18.2	3.7	5.7	5.5	2.0	2.0	1.5	1.3	1.4	1.2	1.1	1.3	1.0	0.5
NMP [a]	61.3	16.2	4.2	3.2	4.2	1.5	1.7	1.3	0.8	0.7	1.0	0.7	1.4	1.1	0.7
GDP	58.7	16.5	3.8	4.0	5.3	1.7	1.4	1.2	0.9	0.9	1.3	0.9	1.6	1.2	0.7
Investment	62.8	13.5	4.1	3.7	5.7	1.1	1.2	1.1	0.8	0.8	1.6	1.0	1.2	0.8	0.6
Fixed assets	61.9	15.4	3.4	3.3	5.7	1.4	1.5	1.1	0.8	0.7	0.8	1.0	1.4	1.0	0.7
Output of
Industry	66.4	16.0	4.1	1.7	3.5	1.2	1.7	0.8	0.5	0.4	0.8	0.4	1.2	0.8	0.7
Agriculture	46.2	22.5	5.9	4.6	6.9	1.4	1.8	2.2	1.3	1.0	0.6	1.1	2.2	1.4	0.9
Imports [b]	67.5	13.4	4.1	1.9	2.7	1.5	1.3	1.3	0.8	0.6	1.0	0.5	1.5	1.4	0.5
Exports [b]	69.7	15.4	4.0	3.2	1.8	0.8	1.0	0.6	0.2	0.8	0.2	0.4	1.0	0.8	0.4
Panel B: Relative development level (Soviet Union = 100), per capita measures
GDP	114	92	106	56	90	90	56	80	60	50	118	75	123	133	140
Consumption	108	97	108	59	84	95	57	85	66	48	93	66	127	137	151
National wealth	117	93	103	50	91	84	64	80	53	40	82	67	108	122	140
Labour productivity [a]	114	89	113	56	78	75	85	87	86	50	87	66	108	111	113
Capital productivity	98	104	124	93	75	110	124	124	110	103	122	85	102	109	101

Source: Narodnoe khozyaistvo SSSR v 1990 g., Moscow, 1991, pp.67, 68, 102, 290, 459; *Argumenty i Fakty*, No.39, November 1991; USSR Goskomstat, *Soyuznye respubliki: osnovnye ekonomicheskie i sotsial'nye pokazateli*, Moscow 1991, pp.5, 173.

[a] 1989.
[b] Foreign, at domestic prices, 1989.

average capital productivity as well, is associated with relatively low per capita GDP.

The effects of factor productivities on output per capita are modified by the size of employment relative to population. In Russia, Ukraine, Belarus, Kazakhstan, Georgia, Armenia and the Baltic republics, the share of employed persons (excluding collective farmers) in the total population averages 42 per cent. In the four Central Asian republics, Azerbaijan and Moldova taken together, high birth rates and the large share of children below working age bring the ratio down to about 27 per cent, hence pushing down GDP per head relative to a given level of labour productivity.

The very large share of defence and the low level of services relative to total output in the Soviet Union are structural distortions which resulted from conscious political decisions. The share of defence in total output is difficult to estimate partly because of definitional and coverage problems (the defence sector is a major producer of consumer goods) and also by the lack of appropriate prices in which to value output. Looking from the input side, it has been estimated that the defence sector employed 21 per cent of the former Soviet industrial work force in 1985 or about 8.1 million workers. The corresponding numbers for Russia and the Ukraine were 25 and 19 per cent, equivalent to 5.2 and 1.3 million workers respectively.[310] Thus it seems that relative to population a disproportionate share (64 per cent) of defence employees were concentrated in Russia and a less than proportionate share in the other republics.

With regard to services, a comparison of GDP and NMP levels in 1990 suggests that the share of services in total output was less than 30 per cent in the 15 republics taken as a whole. The contribution is lower in Russia (27 per cent) and the other European republics, and thus must have been higher in Central Asia and Kazakhstan. It may reflect the low value-added of these republics' largely agricultural and raw material based output structure relative to the price of services.

Other distortions derived from the high factor and overall input intensity of economic growth under central planning. One example is the large (20 per cent) share of the labour force employed in agriculture to offset low agricultural labour and capital productivity resulting from poor land and livestock yields and enormous post-harvest losses. The situation varies between republics, however. The European states of the former Soviet Union (except Moldova) and Armenia, in which at least two thirds of the population are urban dwellers, are the least disadvantaged by large numbers of the labour force working in a low productive sector. But in Central Asia and Moldova, well over half the population is rural and agricultural employment is high — and this is true to only a slightly lesser extent for Kazakhstan, Georgia and Azerbaijan.

---

[310] See "Industrial Conversion in the Ukraine: Policy and Prospects", J. Tedstrom, *RFE/RL Institute*, August 23 1991, p.14 (table 1). The source refers to unpublished Goskomstat information. An estimate for a more recent year, referring to employment in the former Soviet military-industrial complex (VPK) in 1989, gives a figure of 14.4 million or slightly more than 10 per cent of total employment. This figure probably includes workers in defence industry plants who are engaged in the manufacture of consumer goods, which constitute about half of the total output of the industry. It does not include a further 9.6 million members of the KGB, the MVD or the armed forces. *Ogonyek*, No.24, June 1991, p.8.

Another example is the wasteful use of investment resources.[311] This has been accompanied by a degree of investment starvation in some republics. The distribution of investment by republic in the 1980s has been rather stable and has thus tended to perpetuate past republican economic differentials. Investment per capita was 12-40 per cent above the Soviet average (R792 per person in 1990) in Estonia, Belarus, Russia, Latvia and Armenia. It averaged just over half the all-Union level in the three Central Asian republics, Azerbaijan and Moldova and approached three quarters in the Ukraine and Turkmenistan. Kazakhstan and Lithuania were not far below the average.

Despite differences in developmental levels noted above there have been many similarities in the republics' recent economic performance. The main divergences appear at first sight in output growth. The former Soviet Union recorded a moderate output decline in 1990 and a much stronger one in 1991 (table 4.4.4). This pattern was repeated in Russia, Ukraine, Kazakhstan and also, at least in 1991, in Moldova, Tajikistan and Armenia. Other republics, and notably Belarus, the other Central Asian republics and Azerbaijan, reported only small contractions in 1991. The central statistical authorities have, however, indicated that data for the republics are based on enterprise level returns and may not have been fully adjusted for inflation in all republics. This may explain why NMP in no republic declined by more than 12 per cent, even though the aggregate contraction reported by the CIS Statistical Service was 15 per cent. On the other hand, the individual republics' industrial and agricultural statistics seem consistent with global aggregates showing a nearly 8 per cent and a 7 per cent decline, respectively. But given the supply breakdowns experienced in the European republics, which are the main sources of supply for the others, the relatively more stable performance reported by some republics may be more apparent than real.

This would be partly confirmed by the fact that rapid inflation due to lax monetary and budgetary policy was common to all the republics. Inflation indicators reported by individual republics differed from the 86 per cent rise in retail prices only by a few percentage points. Moreover, the effects of political uncertainties and the dismantling of traditional inter-enterprise and inter-republican supply links also appears to have affected all republics to similar degree. Other monetary and financial indicators also moved in parallel.

Foreign trade with countries outside the territory of the former Soviet Union has traditionally been a preserve of the European republics. Russia, Belarus and Ukraine accounted for 94 per cent of Soviet exports and over 80 per cent of imports in 1991 (table 4.4.5). Little other up-to-date information is available on foreign trade in republics other than Russia for 1991. However, the declining trade deficit recorded in 1991 for the successor states as a whole was paralleled in all of the republics but Armenia, Turkmenistan and Ukraine. The overall improvement resulted from the even steeper cuts in imports which accompanied falling exports.

(ii) Russia

The preponderance and economic weight of *Russia*, now as in the former USSR, reflects its just over half share of the population (some 149 million inhabitants), abundant land resources and a large share, relative to population, of natural resources and industrial and other productive capital (table 4.4.1). Just over 80 per cent of the population are ethnic Russians. The rest consists of 32 non-Russian ethnic groups accounting for about 18 per cent of the population (table 4.4.2). Most of them are concentrated in enclaves designated as autonomous republics or regions, some of which aspire to an enlarged degree of independence.[312]

TABLE 4.4.2

Soviet successor states: Selected population indicators

	in total population [a]	domiciled outside republic of origin [a]	urban in total population	Population density (Inhabitants per km²) [b]
Russia	81	17	74	9
Ukraine	72	15	68	86
Belarus	78	21	67	49
Uzbekistan	71	15	40	46
Kazakhstan	40	20	58	6
Georgia	70	5	56	78
Azerbaijan	83	14	54	82
Lithuania	79	5	69	57
Moldova	65	17	48	130
Latvia	52	5	71	42
Kyrgyzstan	52	12	38	22
Tajikistan	62	25	31	37
Armenia	94	33	68	113
Turkmenistan	72	7	45	8
Estonia	61	6	72	35
Total, 15 republics	..	19	66	13

Source: *Narodnoe khozyaistvo SSSR v 1990g.*, pp.67-73, 81.

[a] 1989 census data.
[b] On 1 January 1991.

Russia is one of the few of the former Soviet republics which can make a claim to self-sufficiency. In the late 1980s it was the source of about four fifths of the former Soviet Union's merchandise exports, if the latter are valued in world prices.[313]

---

[311] See United Nations Economic Commission for Europe, *Economic Survey of Europe in 1985-1986*, New York, 1986, pp.209-223, for a discussion of the declining capital intensity and decelerating labour productivity.

[312] During 1991 several of the enclaves issued sovereignty declarations. *Izvestiya*, 25 October 1991 (Tatarstan); *Izvestiya*, 4 November 1991 (Chechen-Ingushetia). A referendum on independence of Tatarstan is scheduled for late March 1992.

[313] Official data Russian merchandise trade deficit in inter-republic and foreign trade combined, in domestic prices, are misleading because Russian's key exports, such as oil and gas, are under priced relative to other products in the domestic price system.

TABLE 4.4.3
Soviet successor states: Shares in Soviet output by products, 1990
(Per cent)

	Russia	Ukraine	Belarus	Uzbekistan	Kazakhstan	Georgia	Azerbaijan	Moldova	Kyrgyzstan	Tajikistan	Armenia	Turkmenistan	Lithuania	Latvia	Estonia
Industrial products															
Electricity	62.7	17.3	2.3	3.3	5.1	0.8	1.3	0.9	0.8	1.1	0.6	0.8	1.6	0.4	1.0
Oil	90.4	1.0	0.4	0.5	4.5	-	2.2	-	-	-	-	1.0	-	-	-
Gas	78.6	3.5	-	5.0	0.9	-	1.2	-	-	-	-	10.8	-	-	-
Coal	56.2	23.5	-	0.9	18.7	0.1	-	-	0.5	0.1	-	-	-	-	-
Iron-ore	45.2	44.5	-	-	10.1	-	0.2	-	-	-	-	-	-	-	-
Steel	58.0	34.1	0.7	0.7	4.4	0.8	0.4	0.5	-	-	-	-	-	0.4	-
Timber	91.6	3.3	2.3	-	0.7	0.1	-	-	-	-	-	-	0.7	0.8	0.5
Paper	85.2	6.0	3.2	0.4	0.1	0.4	-	-	-	-	0.1	-	1.6	1.7	1.3
Machine tools	47.2	23.6	9.8	-	1.6	1.0	0.4	-	0.9	4.3	5.5	-	5.5	0.2	-
TV sets	44.8	35.8	12.3	-	-	0.5	-	1.3	-	-	-	-	5.3	-	-
Refrigerators	58.1	13.9	11.2	3.1	-	-	5.1	2.0	-	2.6	-	-	4.0	-	-
Footwear	45.7	23.3	5.5	5.5	4.3	2.0	1.8	2.8	1.4	1.3	2.2	0.6	1.4	1.3	0.9
Cotton cloth	71.7	7.2	1.8	6.0	1.9	0.4	1.3	2.2	1.2	1.5	0.4	0.4	1.2	0.6	2.2
Woollen cloth	66.1	10.3	6.6	0.1	4.8	1.4	1.5	-	1.6	0.3	0.7	0.4	3.1	2.1	1.0
Farm products															
Grain	53.3	26.0	3.8	0.8	9.6	0.3	0.4	1.7	0.8	0.2	0.1	0.2	1.7	0.8	0.5
Meat	51.3	21.3	6.9	2.0	6.9	0.6	0.5	2.0	0.9	0.5	0.4	0.3	3.3	1.8	1.3
Milk	51.4	22.6	6.9	2.8	5.2	0.6	0.9	1.4	1.1	0.6	0.4	0.4	3.0	1.8	1.1
Eggs	58.1	20.0	4.4	3.1	5.1	1.0	1.2	1.3	0.9	0.7	0.6	0.4	1.6	1.0	0.7
Fish	74.1	10.1	0.2	0.2	0.8	1.3	0.5	0.1	-	-	0.1	0.5	3.7	4.9	3.6
Sugar	30.2	54.4	2.8	-	2.6	0.3	-	3.5	3.0	-	-	-	1.3	1.9	-
Butter	47.9	25.5	9.2	0.9	4.9	0.1	0.2	1.6	0.7	0.3	-	0.3	4.2	2.5	1.7
Oil	35.5	32.8	0.8	15.7	2.9	0.5	1.2	3.9	0.4	2.5	0.2	3.2	-	0.4	-
Cotton	-	-	-	62.4	3.8	-	6.4	-	0.7	10.8	-	15.9	-	-	-

Source: Data in *Narodnoe khozyaistvo SSSR v 1990g.*, Moscow, 1991, p.358.

The Russian economy in 1991

The official data[314] show the Russian economy declining less dramatically in 1991 than that of the CIS states in the aggregate.[315] Even so, the recorded output decline was severe: GDP contracted by 9 per cent, national income produced by 11 per cent, industrial output by 8 per cent and agricultural output by 5 per cent (table 4.4.6).

The situation was especially acute with regard to food supplies. The grain harvest was considerably smaller than that of 1990. Moreover, collective and state farms have been withholding output deliveries to the state distribution system, which contributed to supply shortages in urban areas. The situation with non-food goods has been little better. The limited price reform introduced in April 1991 by the Union government did not have much impact on the pervasive shortages, and the tendency to resort to barter transactions continued to grow.

In both *industry* and *agriculture*, the decline affected most products and product groups. The immediate reason for falling output was the worsening supply of material inputs, owing in part to the erosion of traditional, centrally imposed inter-enterprise supply arrangements.[316]

Foreign trade contracted much more steeply than production in "valuta" rouble value in 1991, and probably even more so in volume.[317] Russian *exports* in 1991 came to R64 billion ($37 billion), down 29 per cent from 1990, while imports of R45 billion ($26 billion) had fallen by 46 per cent. The resulting trade surplus of R19 billion ($11 billion) was two-and-a-half times larger than that of 1990. (Attention may be drawn to the fact that Russian foreign trade was in surplus in that year, when the Union as a whole had incurred a $6 billion deficit.)

Exports of oil amounted to 48 million tons and decreased by more than half as compared with 1990, coal exports were 17 million tons (a 16 per cent decrease), and natural gas exports of 90 billion cubic metres were down 7 per cent. *Imports* of machinery and equipment decreased by 42 per cent and those of most foodstuffs more than halved, but grain imports remained at their 1990 level of some 20 million tons.

---

[314] Unless otherwise indicated, the data quoted for 1991 in the text are taken from the communiqué of the Russian Federation State Committee for Statistics, "Sotsial'no-ekonomicheskoe polozhenie Rossiiskoi Federatsii v 1991 godu" (The socio-economic situation of the Russian Federation in 1991), *Ekonomika i zhizn'*, 1992, No.4 (January), pp.4-5.

[315] See footnote (203) above for some observations on the relation between all-CIS and republican data for 1991.

[316] This is reflected in the fact that by mid-December 1991 only 14 per cent of the expected number of delivery agreements for 1992 had been concluded. *Rossiiskaya gazeta*, 13 January 1992.

[317] Values in *invalyutnye* roubles are obtained by converting trade values in external prices at the "commercial" exchange rate (about R1.8 per dollar in both years). Thus they do not reflect the inflation which raised domestic prices in domestic prices, are misleading because Russia's much in trade with the market economies, but they may have risen significantly in trade with the former CMEA countries. Because of the latter element, the fall in volume may have been larger than that registered in value terms.

TABLE 4.4.4
Soviet successor states: Economic performance in 1990 and 1991
(Annual percentage change)

	USSR or CIS	Russia	Ukraine	Belarus	Uzbekistan	Kazakhstan	Georgia	Azerbaijan	Moldova	Kyrgyzstan	Tajikistan	Armenia	Turkmenistan
1990 over 1989													
NMP [a]	-4.0	-5.0	-1.5	-1.4	..	..	..	..	..	..	..	..	..
Employment [b]	-2.2	-2.6	-3.8	-1.4	1.9	-0.4	-3.2	-0.2	-4.6	0.3	-0.2	-1.6	0.9
Industrial output	-1.2	-0.1	-0.1	1.6	1.8	-0.8	-5.7	-6.3	3.2	-0.6	1.2	-7.5	3.2
Agricultural output	-3.0	-3.6	-3.7	-5.9	6.0	7.0	7.0	-0.1	-13.0	1.0	3.0	-11.0	7.0
Gross investment	0.6	0.1	-1.5	1.0	13.0	-2.9	-14.4	-4.2	-0.5	11.3	0.7	-4.6	7.5
Retail sales	10.0	16.0	11.5	15.4	9.0	9.0	11.0	7.0	14.0	9.0	10.0	7.0	9.0
Retail prices	6.8	5.6	4.0	5.3	..	..	..	..	..	..	..	..	..
1991 over 1990													
NMP [a]	-15.0	-11.0	-11.0	-3.0	-0.9	-10.0	..	-0.4	-11.9	-5.0	-9.0	-11.0	-0.6
Employment	-1.7	-1.1	-2.0	-	2.5	-1.3	..	-	-4.8	-	10.5	-6.3	6.7
Industrial output [c]	-7.8	-8.0	-4.5	-2.1	1.8	0.7	-19.3 [d]	3.8	-7.0	0.1	-2.0	-4.6 [d]	4.1
Agricultural output	-7.0	-5.0	-12.0	-3.0	-5.0	-8.0	..	-	-11.0	-8.0	-10.0	11.0	-2.0
Gross investment	..	-11.0	..	..	..	..	..	..	..	..	..	..	..
Retail sales	-7.1	-6.0	-10.1	-2.7	-8.8	-14.2	-25.1 [e]	-12.7	-16.1	-16.8	-21.9	-24.8	-11.8
Retail prices [f]	86.0	89.1	82.5	81.3	82.9	82.9	121.8 [e]	86.5	97.4	88.2	83.5	90.7	84.6
Exports [g]	-32.6	-29.4	-46.3	-41.8	-34.5	-38.4	-37.0	-37.9	-41.3	-38.7	-40.4	-40.6	-30.8
Imports [g]	-43.9	-45.6	-38.8	-46.9	-42.1	-39.4	-41.6	-43.6	-50.6	-42.6	-48.5	-19.4	-36.8

Source: As for tables 4.4.6, 4.4.8 and 4.4.9.

[a] NMP produced.
[b] State sector, workers and employees only, which account for 82-85 per cent of total employment.
[c] The data for the total (11 republics) are adjusted for inflation. Data for individual republics (except Russia) are based on enterprise-level information with only partial adjustment for inflation.
[d] January-November.
[e] November 1991 over November 1990.
[f] Consumer goods and services.
[g] Nominal values in roubles at the commercial exchange rate.

TABLE 4.4.5
Soviet successor states: Foreign trade, 1991
(Billions of roubles; [a] *percentages)*

	Russia	Ukraine	Belarus	Uzbekistan	Kazakhstan	Georgia	Azerbaijan	Moldova	Kyrgyzstan	Tajikistan	Armenia	Turkmenistan	Total
Exports													
Value	64.2	8.4	2.9	1.1	1.4	0.4	0.6	0.3	0.1	0.5	0.1	0.2	80.1
Share (per cent)	80.2	10.5	3.6	1.4	1.7	0.5	0.7	0.4	0.1	0.6	0.1	0.2	100.0
Imports													
Value	44.7	11.6	3.4	2.3	2.9	2.6	1.4	1.0	1.0	0.8	1.4	0.7	73.8
Share (per cent)	60.6	15.7	4.6	3.1	3.9	3.5	1.9	1.4	1.4	1.0	1.9	1.0	100.0
Trade balance	19.5	-3.2	-0.5	-1.2	-1.5	-2.2	-0.8	-0.7	-0.9	-0.3	-1.3	-0.5	6.3

Source: USSR Goskomstat, *Ekonomika stran-chlenov SNG v 1991 godu,* Moscow, 1992, p.134.

[a] "Valuta" roubles, obtained from foreign currency values at the 1991 "commercial" exchange rate (ca. 1.75 roubles per dollar).

Newly published estimates of the Russian *balance of payments* in dollars are more detailed than data previously available, but they suffer from some serious methodological shortcomings (see table 4.4.7 and notes). The current account balance shown is quite plausibly more favourable than that for the USSR/CIS, but the capital account contains several problematic elements.

The fall in production was not accompanied by a commensurate decline in *employment*. Some 73.6 million persons − 1.2 million less than in 1990 − were officially estimated to be employed in the Russian national economy. This probably reflects a margin of under-reporting of employment as the independent sector expanded rapidly. *Employment in the state sector* fell by 5 million or 8 per cent. A new law on employment, which came into force on 1 July 1991, officially recognized the existence of *unemployment* and made provision for payment of unemployment benefits. 60,000 unemployed were registered in Russia by the state unemployment agencies on 1 January 1992. Of these, only 12,000 (20 per cent) received allowances.[318] Job offers appear actually to have exceeded the number of job seekers in 1991.[319]

For most of 1991, developments in *costs, prices* and the resulting *demand and supply imbalances* were de-

---

[318] However, the Russian Federation of Independent Trade Unions estimated that there were 1.5 million unemployed in the republic already in June 1991. (BBC, *Summary of World Broadcasts,* SU/1102, 19 June 1991). Another source put the number of unemployed in Russia in December at 2-2.5 million (*Trud,* 19 December 1991).

[319] The employment service registered 850-900,000 job offers as against 110,000 job seekers for the year (*Ekonomika i zhizn',* 1992, No.4, p.4).

TABLE 4.4.6
Russian Federation: Basic economic indicators, 1987-1991
(Percentage change over same period of preceding year)

	1987	1988	1989	1990	1991 QI	1991 QI-QII	1991 QI-QIII	1991 QI-QIV
GDP	..	..	..	-2.0	..	..	..	-9.0
NMP	0.7	4.5	1.9	-5.0	..	-9.0	-9.0	-11.0
Employment [a]	-0.3	-1.5	-1.7	-2.6	..	-1.2	-2.0	-1.1
Gross industrial production	3.5	3.8	1.4	-0.1	..	-3.5	-3.3	-8.0 [b]
Group "A"	3.5	3.2	0.5	-2.1	..	..	..	-2.2
Group "B"	3.6	5.8	5.3	6.1	..	..	..	-2.2
Gross agricultural production	-1.2	3.2	1.7	-3.6	..	..	..	-5.0
Gross investment	5.9	7.7	4.1	0.1	..	-7.0	-7.0	-11.0
Exports	..	..	..	-12.0	..	-23.0	-26.0	-29.4
Imports	..	..	..	-1.5	..	..	-47.0	-45.6
Money wages	4.0	8.0	9.0	15.0	13.9 [c]	35.0 [c]	60.0 [c]	80.0
Retail sales	2.9	5.8	6.0	10.1	..	-11.0	-11.0	-6.0
Retail prices [d]	1.0	2.3	2.0	5.6	..	58.0	77.1	89.1
Industrial wholesale prices	..	..	..	..	..	100.0	116.0	138.0
Agricultural procurement prices	..	..	..	..	56.0	56.0	..	80.0
Money incomes	4.2	8.7	13.0	18.5	..	39.8	72.0	100.0 [e]
Expenditures	3.6	8.2	11.5	16.2	..	34.8	53.1	80.0

Sources: Based on data in *Narodnoe khozyaistvo RSFSR v 1990 g.*, Moscow 1991, pp.11-15; *Ekonomika stran-chlenov SNG v 1991 godu*, Goskomstat, Moscow 1992; *Soyuznye respubliki: osnovnye ekonomicheskie i sotsial'nye pokazateli*, Goskomstat, Moscow, 1991; Russian Federation Goskomstat, *Ob itogakh funktsionirovaniya narodnogo khozyaistva Rossiiskoi Federatsii v 1991 godu*, Moscow, 1992.

[a] The available data for 1987-1990 are for state employment only (workers and employees). Data for 1991 are for all gainfully occupied persons, including collective farmers and private-sector employees. Growth rates for 1991 over 1990 are therefore not comparable with the earlier series.
[b] Calculated on the basis of comparable commodity groups. According to enterprise reports, with only partial adjustment for inflation, industrial output fell by 2.2 per cent.
[c] Resources directed towards average consumption per worker and employee per month.
[d] For 1987-1989, data relate to the USSR and cover retail prices in the state sector only. For 1990-1991 the series relates to the Russian Federation only and to consumer goods and services in all sectors. The growth rate in 1991 over 1990 is therefore not comparable with the earlier series.
[e] Excludes the "compensation" payments to personal savings made by the state to reduce the impact of State-decreed price rises in April 1991.

termined largely by factors common to the USSR as a whole. The administrative *price reforms* carried out by the Union authorities, as noted in section 4.1, had raised producer prices at the beginning of the year and consumer prices in April. While most prices were kept under state control, "contract prices" — which are, in effect, determined by market forces, albeit on a highly monopolized market and one from which many products were still excluded — were introduced for a much wider range of goods than in the past.

It had been anticipated by the Union government that the April 1991 retail price reform would contribute to the stabilization of *consumer supply and demand*. However, the low level of stocks, the fall in industrial production and imports, and above all the fact that prices were revised, not decontrolled, meant that imbalances in consumer markets continued to be severe. Shortages of cereals, meat, butter, cheese, tea — indeed of practically everything — persisted for the rest of the year.

In the last quarter of 1991, when it had become clear that the reform plans of the Russian government included far-reaching price liberalization, a surge of consumer stockpiling ahead of the anticipated price rises finally emptied the state stores, and consumer price inflation accelerated sharply — from 4 per cent (over the preceding month) in October to 9 per cent in November and 12 per cent in December. For 1991 as a whole, the price index for consumer goods and services in Russia was 89 per cent higher than in 1990 (and slightly above the 86 per cent registered as an all-CIS average), with particularly high increases for foodstuffs (some 150 per cent). But consumer prices in December 1991 were some 150 per cent (and producer prices some 220-240 per cent) above those a year earlier,[320] and it is from this base that they more than tripled after the Russian price liberalization in January 1992.[321]

In 1991, the aggregate *money incomes* of the population totalled R828 billion, an increase of 116 per cent as compared with 1990. Some 20 percentage points of this stemmed from an adjustment of savings balances granted to compensate citizens partially for the loss in the real value of their holdings due to the price increases of April 1991. The average *monthly wage* of workers and employees increased 78 per cent, from R297 in 1990 to R530 in 1991, also reflecting partial compensation for the price changes.[322] However, given the

---

[320] *Ekonomicheskii obzor*, No.12, 1992, p.16; Goskomstat RF, *Ob itogakh funktsionirovaniya narodnogo khozyaistva Rossiiskoi Federatsii v 1991 godu*, Moscow, 1992, p.3.

[321] The January 1992 average retail price index for goods and services sold in the Russian Federation was 339 relative to December 1990 and 873 relative to January 1990. *Ekonomika stran-chlenov Sodruzhestva Nezavisimykh Gosudarstv v yanvare 1992 goda*, p.5.

[322] The corresponding figures for collective farm members' earnings were R266 and R388, an increase of 46 per cent. Incomes from work in cooperatives and joint stock companies were 50 per cent higher than in state employment.

TABLE 4.4.7

Russian Federation: Balance of payments in 1990-1991
(Billion US dollars, annual totals)

	1990 Convertible currency [a]	1990 Other	1990 Total	1991 Convertible currency [a]	1991 Other	1991 Total
Exports	26.1	54.8	80.9	24.8	29.9	54.7
Imports	-24.1	-58.8	-82.9	-20.0	-25.6	-45.6
Trade balance	2.0	-4.0	-2.0	4.8	4.3	9.1
Other current account	-1.9	-0.4	-2.3	-1.4	-0.6	-2.0
of which:						
Interest (net)	-2.5	-	-2.5	-2.1	-	-2.1
Gold sales [b]	1.8	-	1.8	2.5	-	2.5
Other	-0.7	-	-0.7	-1.8	-0.6	-2.4
Current account	0.1	-4.4	-4.3	3.4	3.7	7.1
Capital account	-4.7	11.3	6.6	-0.8	-0.1	-0.9
of which:						
Net credits (long-term)	1.6	-	1.6	1.5	-1.6	-0.1
Net credits (short-term)	-6.3	10.2	3.9	-3.5	1.5	-2.0
Grant aid	-	-	-	1.2	-	1.2
Other capital	0.3	-0.4	-0.1	0.2	-0.1	0.1
Errors and omissions [c]	-0.3	1.5	1.2	-0.2	0.1	-0.1
Basic balance	-4.6	6.9	2.3	2.6	3.6	6.2
Financing, changes in: [d]						
reserves	5.0	-	5.0	1.6	-	1.6
arrears	2.8	-	2.8	-0.5	-	-0.5
Rescheduling	-	-	-	0.2	-	0.2
Transfers to other republics [e]	-3.2	-7.0	-10.2	-3.9	-3.6	-7.5

Source: Ekonomika i zhizn', 1992, No.6, p.11. Columns and rows do not always add up because of rounding. The attribution to Russia of specific quantities from recorded Soviet totals is in several instances highly stylized.

[a] Convertible currency transactions are transactions with Soviet trade partners that were neither members of CMEA nor had clearing agreements with the USSR. The latter two categories are grouped here as "other". See the discussion in 4.2 above of the corresponding data for the USSR.
[b] Excluding movements into swaps. The Russian total is derived as the Russian share of total "production", said to be 67 per cent. Whether gold that is extracted in Central Asia but processed (separated from other metals) in Russia is treated as Russian production, is not explained.
[c] Adjusted (secretariat estimates). As printed in the Russian source, the capital account rows and columns are inconsistent.
[d] Decrease (+), increase (-).
[e] The figures in this row are described in the source on showing Russian funding (not repayable) of the external trade deficits of other republics. Whether independent estimates of (a) the dollar value of the sum of other republics' excess of imports over exports and (b) the Russian basic balance and financing coincide, is not explained. Nor is the rationale for restricting this measurement to merchandise trade balances. If, as is likely, the two independent estimates do not coincide, there is no indication of what was adjusted, or how. There is no reason to think that there is any systematic relationship between inter-republic goods flows and this estimated resource transfer.

---

cost-of-living increase, the average *real wage* fell by 12 per cent by comparison to 1990.

As noted in section 4.1 above, the money supply for the USSR as a whole increased dramatically over the year (table 4.1.3). New rouble notes and coins continued to be issued in a routine fashion to finance wage claims. Towards the end of the year, capacity limitations of the plants printing money emerged as a constraint on the expansion of the basic money supply.[323] In reflection of the continuing passive response to the demand for money, the Russian monetary authorities were planning to ease the constraint imposed by the capacity of printing presses by issuing new, larger-denomination notes — of R200, R500, and R1,000.[324] Three factors in particular have contributed to softness in monetary policy: the absence of efficient regulation of commercial banks, the subordination of the Russian central bank to a parliament that is "softer" on financial policy than the government, and Russian policy makers' inability to control the budget deficit of the other successor states in the rouble monetary area. No effective mechanism for the coordination of budgetary and monetary policy among the CIS republics appears to be in sight (see section 4.2).

The *fiscal* situation of the Russian republic became increasingly precarious during the year as revenues did not keep pace with expenditures. The revenue of the republican budget and stabilization fund for 1991 were estimated at R161 billion, and expenditures at R221 billion. Taking account of an increase in the debt to the Central Bank of Russia equalling R48 billion, the *overall deficit* was over R108 billion (about 9 per cent of GDP).

Economic reforms 1991-1992

Between its election in March 1990 and the end of January 1992, the Russian Parliament adopted about 40 laws, many of them of considerable importance in preparing the transition to a market economy (see box 4.4.1). However, results, in terms of institutional and structural change actually implemented, were few. In part this was due to the continuing preponderance of the central USSR authorities in the economic sphere

---

[323] Delays in paying wages became chronic. In some regions of Russia, wages for November-December 1991 had still not been paid by the end of January 1992. By 25 January 1992, the shortfall in cash payments due to the population amounted to R14 billion. *Izvestiya*, 31 January 1992.

[324] *Rossiiskaya gazeta*, 28 January 1992.

and the many unresolved instances of split jurisdiction, and in part to a lack of resolve and clarity about the road to follow in the Russian parliament and government itself.

Some three months after the failure of the August *coup*, a new Russian government, headed by President Yeltsin and comprising a number of young economists, among whom Finance Minister and Deputy Premier Egor Gaidar plays the leading role, took in hand a determined reform programme and stabilization package.[325]

The main elements of the stabilization package include:

— The goal of reducing the combined budget deficits of Russia and the former USSR from several hundred billion roubles to zero in the first quarter of 1992.

— Large cuts in social programmes, military procurement and investment.

— The creation of a value-added tax, set at 28 per cent, and an increase in payroll taxes.

— Sharp cuts in the money supply and the volume of credit to be implemented by the Russian Central Bank.

In addition the package of decrees outlines steps to be taken towards a market economy. They initiate the legal establishment of an internally convertible currency, the abolition of import restrictions, the decontrol of prices and the launching of an ambitious privatization programme. The main measures in this package are listed in box 4.4.2. (The programme as a whole is assessed in section 4.3 above.)

The liberalization of prices was from the beginning a key element of the new Russian government's programme. Initial intentions appear to have been to introduce it very rapidly already in November or December, to avoid the dislocations associated with a long period of anticipation, but eventually a delay had to be granted to accommodate the other CIS republics. By a presidential decree and a government resolution,[326] the Russian government determined in December 1991 that "enterprises and organizations and other juridical persons located on Russian territory, irrespective of their subordination and forms of ownership, are from 2 January 1992 to apply free (market) prices and rates to all production and technical output, consumer goods, jobs and services" other than those included in a group of goods that remains regulated by government.

The long-feared price liberalization, ending decades of administrative price setting, freed the prices of non-food consumer goods and most food products. Certain key *consumer* items — bread, milk, matches, salt, vodka, electricity charges, housing rentals — remain under government price control, but prices are to be raised from three to five times from their previous levels. Prices and tariffs in the "regulated" group of *producer* goods were to increase by an average of 200 to 400 per cent.

The government resolution in fact reveals an odd notion of a "free market" economy. The document begins by ordering enterprises to free their prices, but includes a long list of goods whose prices are to be set by the state. An even more serious weakness is indicated in article 11 of the resolution, which says that "enterprises violating the rules of applying free prices" will have all the excess profits obtained thereby confiscated by the government. Press reports indicate that government guidelines were issued even with respect to the setting of the supposedly "free" prices.

The production of certain goods and services was to be subsidized by the government if price restrictions make the goods unprofitable.[327]

The January 1992 price reforms reportedly increased the availability of some products in state stores in some cities, but many staples remained hard to find. Privately run shops and farmers' markets still sell a variety of different products, but their prices are beyond the reach of most Russians.[328]

The achievement of *fiscal balance* is another key target of the Russian government's stabilization package. Given the wide range of uncertainty necessarily surrounding any estimation of revenue and expenditure parameters after the large change in price levels at the beginning of the year, it was decided to take budgetary decisions only on one quarter at a time.[329]

President Yeltsin submitted his budget proposals for the first quarter of 1992 to the Russian parliament on 17 January.[330] Revenues for the first quarter were

---

[325] The outlines of President Yeltsin's reform programme were presented to the RSFSR Congress of People's Deputies on 28 October 1991, together with a request for additional powers for the implementation of the reforms. Both requests were approved by the Congress on 1 November. The Congress also resolved to establish before 1 December 1992 procedures to give priority to the measures incorporated in the reform programme, to suspend earlier legislation that conflicted with it, and to ensure that draft presidential reform decrees would take effect automatically if not rejected by the parliament or its presidium within seven days of their submission. See RSFSR Congress of People's Deputies resolution "On legal support for the economic reform", *Rossiiskaya gazeta*, 5 November 1991. The new government, with a sharply reduced number of ministries (23 instead of 46), was presented to Parliament on 15 November and adopted a first package of Presidential decrees and Government resolutions on economic reforms the same day. See *Izvestiya*, 16 November 1991.

[326] Decree "On measures for the liberalization of prices" of 3 December 1991, *Rossiiskaya gazeta*, 4 December 1991, and "Resolution on price liberalization" of 19 December 1991, *Rossiiskaya gazeta*, 25 December 1991.

[327] For instance, there will be free prices for grain and restricted prices for bread. Bakeries, for example, were to be subsidized. The government was to earmark about R200 billion to make up for the difference between "free" and restricted prices across the board. *Kommersant*, December 1991, p.16.

[328] According to some estimates, the population of Russia bought 80 per cent less (in real terms) in January 1992 than in December 1991. *Rossiiskaya gazeta*, 3 February 1992.

[329] Russian Government Resolution, 24 December 1991, on the draft RSFSR budget system for the first quarter of 1992. *Rossiiskaya gazeta*, 31 December 1991. The new Russian budget system implies formation of a consolidated Russian Federation budget, which includes the republican and the territorial budgets, on the basis of new legislation that allows a further widening of local executive power to tax and spend.

[330] *Izvestiya*, 24, 25 and 27 January 1992.

BOX 4.4.1
Russian Federation: Selected enactments of economic institutional change, 1990-January 1992

1990

Declaration of State sovereignty *(12 June)*.
Law on property on the territory of the RSFSR *(14 July)*.
Law on the implementation of the USSR law on taxation of enterprises and organizations in the RSFSR *(1 December)*.
Law on banks and banking activity *(2 December)*.
Law on the RSFSR Central bank *(2 December)*.
Law on the Programme of revival of the Russian countryside *(3 December)*.
Law on property in the RSFSR *(24 December)*.
Law on enterprises and entrepreneurial activity *(25 December)*.
Law on peasant farms *(22 November, with amendments of 27 December)*.
Law on land reform *(23 November, with amendments of 27 December)*.

1991

Law on the RSFSR state tax service *(21 March)*.
Law on competition and limiting of monopoly behaviour on product markets *(22 March)*.
Law on social protection of working people *(19 April)*.
Law on public employment *(19 April)*.
The RSFSR land code *(25 April)*.
Law on privatization of State and municipal enterprises *(3 July)*.
Law on personal privatization accounts and deposits *(3 July)*.
Law on the privatization of the housing stock *(4 July)*.
Law on foreign investment *(4 July)*.
Law on budget arrangements and the budgetary process *(10 October)*.
Law on land fees *(11 October)*.
Law on indexation of incomes and savings *(25 October)*.
Law on securing the economic basis of RSFSR sovereignty *(14 November)*.
Law on amendments to the RSFSR criminal code *(5 December)*.
Law on value added tax *(6 December)*.
Law on excise duties *(6 December)*.
Law on taxation of individual incomes *(7 December)*.
Law on registration fee for individual entrepreneurs *(7 December)*.
Law on property of individuals *(9 December)*.
Law on a State levy *(9 December)*.
Law on taxing the profits of enterprises and organizations *(27 December)*.
Law on the fundamentals of the taxation system in the Russian Federation *(27 December)*.

1992

Law on the budget system *(24 January)*.

---

projected at R398 billion and expenditures R409 billion, with a deficit of R11.5 billion or 3 per cent of expenditures (1 per cent of GDP). State subsidies for products still under state price regulation were projected at R11.5 billion. After a prolonged and difficult debate, the Russian Parliament endorsed a law "On the budget system of the Russian Federation",[331] permitting Government spending of R420 billion for the first three months of 1992 on assumption of revenues of equal magnitude. While no deficit has thus been authorized, the fiscal deficit is likely in fact to be large, since both VAT yield and local revenue projections were projected at levels unlikely to be realized.

In implementation of the reform package's target of opening the Russian economy to the outside, President Yeltsin at the end of January 1992 suspended all import restrictions and declared Russia open to foreign investment. A government resolution suspended customs tariffs with effect from 15 January.[332] Until 1 April, the date of introduction of new customs rates, all imports will be admitted to Russian territory without customs duties or other levies.

Under presidential decrees issued still in November 1991, Russia is introducing radical changes in the foreign-exchange system, including a massive devaluation of the rouble and a freely floating inter-bank exchange rate for all non-government foreign-exchange transactions. The new exchange-rate system also includes a fixed commercial rate of R110 to the dollar for government trade transactions, compared with R1.75 per dollar in 1991.[333]

The Russian government aims to free the market for foreign exchange, making the rouble internally convertible for current transactions. To achieve this limited convertibility at a stable exchange rate, however, will

---

[331] *Rossiiskaya gazeta*, 25 February 1992, p.3.

[332] "On customs duties for imported goods", 15 January 1992. *Rossiiskaya gazeta*, 22 January 1992.

[333] See the two presidential decrees "On the liberalization of foreign economic activity", 15 November 1991, *Rossiiskaya gazeta*, 19 November 1991 and "On the formation of the republican currency reserve in 1992", 30 December 1991, *Rossiiskaya gazeta*, 7 January 1992.

> **BOX 4.4.2**
>
> **Russian Federation: Selected Presidential decrees and government resolutions on economic reform since November 1991**
>
> *1991*
>
> *Presidential decree on reorganization of the RSFSR government (6 November).*
> *Presidential decree on organization of the government work (6 November).*
> *Presidential decree on liberalization of foreign economic activity (15 November).*
> *Presidential decree on the extraction and utilization of precious metals (15 November).*
> *Presidential decree on 90 per cent increase in wages for employees in budget establishments (15 November).*
> *Presidential decree on abolition of wage limits (15 November).*
> *Resolution of RSFSR government on regulation of exports of oil and oil products (15 November).*
> *Resolution of RSFSR government on financing the economic reforms and protection of RSFSR financing system (15 November).*
> *Resolution of RSFSR government on abolition of USSR Ministries (15 November).*
> *Presidential decree on reorganization of the State management (28 November).*
> *Presidential decree on price liberalization (3 December).*
> *Presidential decree on compensations increase in 1991-1992 and indexation of incomes in 1992 (18 December).*
> *Resolution of RSFSR government on price liberalization (19 December).*
> *Resolution of RSFSR government on the draft RSFSR budget system for the first quarter of 1992 (24 December).*
> *Presidential decree on urgent measures on implementation of land reform (27 December).*
> *Presidential decree on the State regulation (licensing) of goods deliveries to other members of CIS (27 December).*
> *Resolution of RF Supreme Soviet on sharing out state property in Russia (27 December).*
> *Resolution of RF government on the procedure of reorganization of collective and state farms (29 December).*
> *Presidential decree on forming of the republican currency reserve in 1992 (30 December).*
> *Presidential decree on the acceleration of privatization of the State and municipal enterprises (30 December).*
> *Resolution of the RF government on excise duties on individual categories of goods (30 December).*
> *Resolution of the RF government on licensing and quotas for export and import of goods in the territory of Russia in 1992 (31 December).*
> *Presidential decree on the State taxation service (31 December).*
>
> *1992*
>
> *Presidential decree on the formation of state food stocks for the year 1992 (4 January).*
> *Resolution of the Supreme Soviet on urgent normalization of currency circulation (13 January).*
> *Resolution of the RF Supreme Soviet on the USSR Bank of foreign economic activity (13 January).*
> *Resolution of the RF government on the customs duties for imported goods (15 January).*

not be easy.[334] At present, the rouble is grossly undervalued in a purchasing-power parity sense. Domestic prices of traded goods in Russia today are, at the existing market exchange rate, only about one twentieth of world prices. A move to convertibility is thus likely to aggravate inflation. Tight money and a pegging of the exchange rate are the keys to raising the external value of the rouble. However, Russia has no international reserves for the latter purpose.[335]

During his press conference on 18 January, Deputy Prime Minister Egor Gaidar said that Russia had taken complete responsibility for the Soviet foreign debt and the shares of the other republics will be treated as debt to Russia.[336] It is apparently on this basis the agreement was reached with western countries to postpone repayment of $11 billion of debt during 1992.

By taking the lead over other CIS states in negotiation with the IMF and aid donor nations, and by offering to take responsibility for the repayment of the former Soviet Union's debt to the west, Russia has had some success in unblocking for itself at least some of the *western aid* commitment earlier announced for the USSR and then frozen because of uncertainty about the status and solvency of the potential recipients. On the other hand, actual disbursements of humanitarian aid during 1991 appear to have been very small.[337]

The position of the Russian government leadership regarding the *short-run outlook* is that reform can begin to work if Russia can "hold out for at least six months".[338] Provided destructive forces "do not rock the boat", the growth of prices in February-March could be limited to 150 per cent. If there are no social explosions, by April-May inflation could, in Gaidar's view, fall to 5-7 per cent per month. The critical requirement is that the money supply be brought under control. At the same time he expected that in the first

---

[334] See interviews with Egor Gaidar, *Izvestiya*, 2 January 1992 and *Financial Times*, 22 January 1992. See section 4.3 for further discussion of plans to move towards convertibility.

[335] Minister of Foreign Economic Relations Petr Aven stated that Russia needs a $4-5 billion stabilization fund to make the rouble convertible at a pegged exchange rate this year. *Rossiiskaya gazeta*, 1 January 1992. He referred to a target rate of between R15 and R35 to the dollar.

[336] *Izvestiya*, 20 January 1992.

[337] According to the Russian State Committee for Statistics, as of 1 January 1992, Russia had been provided in 1991 with humanitarian aid of 32,700 tons, of which 18,100 tons were foodstuffs, 1,000 tons medicines, 500 tons medical equipment, etc. *Ekonomika i zhizn'*, 1992, No.4 (January), p.5.

[338] Gaidar's interview in *Trud*, 28 January 1992.

quarter alone Russian GDP would fall by 19 per cent.[339]

According to a forecast submitted by the Russian government,[340] the decline in national income in 1992 as a whole will be about 11-12 per cent and that of industrial production 8 per cent. Agricultural output is officially projected to decline by a further 3.1 per cent, including a 9 per cent fall in meat output.

Total employment in the national economy could fall by 8 million. On the other hand, over one million emigrants are expected to leave. The number of unemployed in Russia could thus reach 7-8 million by October.[341] The gloomy employment forecast is based on the Polish reform experience which led, after some delay, to a sharp growth of unemployment. On this scenario it would stop increasing by the middle of 1993. The 8 million figure is roughly 5 per cent of the total labour force, and will first affect industrial areas and large cities. On the other hand, the Deputy Prime Minister responsible for social policy expects only some 2 million to be officially classed as unemployed by the end of the year.

(iii) Ukraine

Ukraine is economically the second strongest successor state of the former Soviet Union as well as the second biggest in terms of output and population (table 4.4.1, panel A). Almost 30 per cent of the nearly 52 million population consists of non-Ukrainians, mostly Russians (22 per cent) but also substantial numbers of Crimean Tartars and others. Two thirds of the population lives in urban areas.

Ukraine's shares in the all-Union GDP, NMP, industrial output, the capital stock and also of both imports and exports fall some way behind its 18 per cent share of the population. In per capita terms, Ukrainian GDP in fact falls some 20 per cent below that of Russia and 8 per cent below the all-Union average (table 4.4.1, panel B). This appears at first sight surprising, given the republic's high share in the output of key industrial commodities, its substantial chemical sector — responsible for 50 per cent of total Soviet chemical output — and its disproportionately high share of farm products in total and of most individual temperate zone commodities (see table 4.4.3). However, it may be precisely the structure of these contributions which account for the lag. In industrial products, machine tools apart, most of the commodities in which Ukraine accounts for a high share of output are products for further processing rather than high value-added goods. And the above-average contribution to Soviet agricultural production is a direct cause of low measured value added because of the artificially low procurement prices of agricultural products.[342] To that extent, the Ukraine's apparent lag is likely to be a figment due to the traditional pricing and accounting system.

Ukraine's greater orientation toward agriculture relative to Russia shows up not only in the high share of the labour force engaged in farming but also in the considerably greater intensity with which its agricultural land is used. This reflects the fact that its population density is 10 times higher than that of Russia (albeit about half the west European level), as well as its fertile soil types and long growing season.

Despite the importance of agriculture to the Ukraine, the republic is only slightly less industrialized than Russia; just under 40 per cent of the population is engaged in industry and construction and 20 per cent in agriculture.

Its productive apparatus in terms of capital stocks is rather smaller, relative to population, than in Russia. This is partially offset by its slightly higher capital productivity relative either to Russia or to the Soviet average.

However, a further problem faced by Ukraine is the obsolescence of a considerable proportion of its productive equipment. According to one estimate, approximately 11 per cent of installed machinery and equipment is over 20 years old.[343] In some sectors, over 50 per cent of the initial book value of capital equipment has been written off. While obsolescence is, for various reasons, a common heritage of all the centrally planned economies and the successor states to the Soviet Union, one reason for this is specific to Ukraine. Gross fixed investment per head allocated to the territories of the Russian republic was some 60 per cent higher than that placed in Ukraine during the whole of the 1980s. The disparity mainly reflects the strong emphasis of Soviet investment during the 1970s and 1980s on the fuel energy sector. While coal has traditionally been a main source of Ukrainian wealth, it is beginning to show signs of exhaustion. Higher returns to investment were obtainable from new oil wells in the eastern Soviet Union. It was, moreover, even more cost-effective (at least under centrally planned pricing) for Ukraine to import coal from Kazakhstan than to sink new shafts at home.[344]

The Ukrainian economy in 1991

Ukraine's respectable annual rate of economic growth of 3.5 per cent between 1986 and 1989 weakened in the latter year. In 1990, for the first time since the Second World War, the republic experienced a fall in NMP produced. The 1.5 per cent decline was not as big as for the Soviet Union as a whole (4 per cent)

---

339 Gaidar's budget report. BBC, *Summary of World Broadcasts*, SU/1288, 27 January 1992.

340 *Pravda*, 22 January 1992.

341 Fedor Prokopov, chairman of the Russian employment committee — see BBC, *Summary of World Broadcasts*, SU/WO215, 28 January 1992.

342 Part of the value added in agriculture is in the traditional NMP accounting system registered in the contribution of down-stream users, such as food and light industry, as well as the trade and procurement system. See, e.g., *Narodnoe khozyaistvo SSSR v 1990 g.*, 1991, p.11.

343 See D. Marples, Radio Liberty Research, *Report on the USSR*, Vol.3, No.40, 4 October, 1991, p.15.

344 N.A. Feduschak, "Ukraine set for success after Union", *Sunday Chicago Tribune*, 4 November 1991.

TABLE 4.4.8
Ukraine: Basic economic indicators, 1987-1991
(Percentage change over same period of preceding year)

	1987	1988	1989	1990	1991 QI	1991 QI-QII	1991 QI-QIII	1991 QI-QIV
GNP	..	..	..	..	..	..	..	-10.0
NMP	5.3	2.5	4.1	-1.5	..	-9.3	..	-11.0
Employment a	-0.1	-0.9	-1.3	-3.8	-1.9	..	..	-2.0
Gross industrial production	3.9	4.1	2.8	-0.1	..	-5.2	-4.6 b	-4.5
Group "A"	3.5	3.7	1.7	-2.2	..	..	..	..
Group "B"	5.0	5.1	5.5	5.0	..	-5.0 c	..	-5.0 b,c
Gross agricultural production	2.2	-1.6	5.1	-3.7	..	..	..	-12.0
Gross investment	2.5	4.0	3.7	-1.5	..	..	..	..
Exports	..	..	..	..	..	..	..	-46.3
Imports	..	..	..	..	..	..	..	-38.8
Money wages	3.4	8.0	9.0	13.6	9.5 d	..	..	..
Retail sales	0.7	6.8	8.0	11.5	..	..	-10.2 b	-10.1
Retail prices e	1.0	2.3	2.0	4.0	..	50.0	..	82.5
Industrial wholesale prices	..	..	..	..	..	95.0	107.0	122.0
Agricultural procurement prices	..	..	..	..	..	..	76.0	..
Money incomes	2.7	9.0	11.0	15.3	..	..	57.1	..
Expenditures	3.1	6.6	9.4	16.3	..	..	47.1	..

Source: Based on data in URSR Ministry of Statistics, *Narodne gospodarstvo Ukrainskoi RSR u 1990 rotsi*, Kiev, 1991; USSR Goskomstat, *Narodnoe khozyaistvo SSSR v 1990 g.*, Moscow 1991, pp.166, 173, 459, 553; USSR Goskomstat, *Ekonomika stran-chlenov SNG v 1991 godu*, Moscow 1992; USSR Goskomstat, *Soyuznye respubliki: osnovnye ekonomicheskie i sotsial'nye pokazateli*, Moscow, 1991;

a The available data for 1987-1990 are for state employment only (workers and employees). Data for 1991 are for all gainfully occupied persons, including collective farmers and private-sector employees. The growth rates for 1991 over 1990 are therefore not comparable with the earlier series.
b January-November.
c Consumer goods.
d Resources directed towards average consumption per worker and employee per month.
e For 1987-1989, data relate to the USSR and cover retail prices in the state sector only. For 1990-1991 the series relates to Ukraine only and to consumer goods and services in all sectors. The growth rate in 1991 over 1990 is therefore not comparable with the earlier series.

or Russia (5 per cent). In fact, Ukraine's NMP growth during the last and the current decades usually surpassed that of the former Soviet Union.[345]

In 1991, Ukraine participated fully in the accelerating decline in output registered by the Soviet economy. NMP produced fell by 11 per cent (table 4.4.8). The output falls reflected breakdowns in previous supply and distribution channels similar to those described for Russia and the other successor states in 1991 (see section 4.1). Ukraine is, like the other republics, enmeshed in a complex network of inter-republican supplies of production inputs. As well as being heavily reliant on imported fuel, Ukraine also buys 60-80 per cent of its ferrous metals and synthetic fibres, and approximately 40-50 per cent of its wood, paper, and pulp requirements from other former Soviet republics and mainly from Russia. Flows from the other Soviet successor states include wine, fruit and vegetables from Azerbaijan, lorries, cable, tea, tobacco, and ferrous metals from Georgia, machine tools, precision instruments, building materials, foodstuffs, paper and light industrial products from Lithuania, cotton fabrics and machinery products from Tajikistan, and cotton and woollen fabrics from Russia, Moldavia, Kazakhstan, Uzbekistan and the Transcaucasus.

However, many shortages were due to the severing of intra-Ukrainian rather than inter-republican delivery linkages. Within Ukraine, one in six enterprises failed to fulfil its contractual obligations in 1991, of which one in three was with enterprises in other successor states and one in eight with other Ukrainian firms.[346] To safeguard future supplies, Ukraine has signed economic agreements for 1992 with seven out of the other ten CIS states and also with all the Baltic republics.

Industrial gross output fell by nearly 5 per cent in 1991, with contraction in consumer and producer goods production by about the same amount. Inside the consumer goods category, production of non-food goods continued to rise but food output fell by as much as 11 per cent. This reflected poor *agricultural performance* — a contraction of over a quarter in grain harvested, nearly half in the case of potatoes and just under 10 per cent for the main livestock products. The overall decline in total gross agricultural production was nearly 12 per cent.

Declining output has been accompanied by substantial real cost increases. The employment fall which accompanied the 11 per cent drop in NMP produced was 500,000 workers or 2 per cent only. Wholesale prices went up by 122 per cent (slightly less than in Russia). As in the other republics, declining real labour

---

[345] See *Narodne gospodarstvo Ukrainskoi RSR u 1990 rotsi*, Kiev, 1991, pp.7-8; *Narodnoe khozyaistvo SSSR v 1990 godu*, Moscow, 1991, pp.7-8.

[346] *Pravda Ukrainy*, 2 August 1991.

> **BOX 4.4.3**
>
> **Ukraine: Selected list of main instruments of economic institutional change since July 1990**
>
> *1990*
>
> Law on Economic Independence of the Ukrainian State (drafted 28 June 1990).
> Declaration of State Sovereignty of the Ukraine (16 July 1990).
> Decree of the Presidium of the Soviet Supreme of the Ukraine on Responsibilities Incurred in Case of Violation of the Regulations on Removing Consumer Goods from the Territory of the Ukraine (3 August 1990).
> Resolution of the Ukrainian Supreme Soviet Establishment on Ukrainian Territory of Joint State Orders on Consumer Goods Production and the Carrying Out of Work and Services (15 October 1990).
> Resolution of the Ukrainian Supreme Soviet on Plans for the Design and Sequencing of the Ukrainian Transition to a Market Economy (1 November 1990).
> Resolution of the Ukrainian Supreme Soviet Ratification of the Treaty between the Ukrainian SSR and the RSFSR (22 November 1990).
> Resolution of the Ukrainian Supreme Soviet on Protecting Sovereignty Laws on Ukrainian Territory (29 November 1990).
> Law on the Budgetary System of the Ukraine (5 December 1990).
> Law on the Ukrainian Land Code (18 December 1990).
> Decree of the Presidium of the Ukrainian Supreme Soviet on ration cards or other documents for the purchase of consumer goods (26 December 1990).
>
> *1991*
>
> Resolution of the Council of Ministers of the Ukraine on the Creation of an Employment Agency (4 January 1991).
> Law on the Free Enterprise (7 February 1991).
> Law on Employment (1 March 1991).
> Resolution of the Ukrainian Supreme Soviet on the Elaboration of Acts Concerning the Right of Possession and Use of Land and Provisions for Regulating the Allocation and Withdrawal of Plots of Land (27 March 1991).
> Resolution of the Ukrainian Supreme Soviet on the Creation during 1991 of an Extra-Budgetary Republican Fund for the Stabilization of the Ukrainian Economy (27 March 1991).
> Resolution of the Ukrainian Council of Ministers on New Retail Prices for Consumer Goods and Tariffs for Services offered by the Population (28 March 1991).
> Decision of the Ukrainian Council of Ministers on Measures of Social Protection of the Population in Connection with the Reform of Retail Prices (28 March 1991).
> Decision of the Ukrainian Council of Ministers on Resources to Compensate Expenditures of the Population Linked with Retail Price Reforms (28 March 1991).
> Law on Banks and Banking Activities (24 March 1991).
> Resolution of the Ukrainian Supreme Soviet on Transfer of State Enterprises and Organizations under Soviet Subordination Located on the Territory of Ukraine to the Jurisdiction of the Ukrainian SSR (6 June 1991.
> Law of Ukrainian SSR on the Indexation of Money Incomes of the Population (3 July 1991).
> Resolution of the Ukrainian Supreme Soviet Banning the Communist Party (3 September 1991).
> Law on the Protection of Foreign Investment Activity (3 September 1991).
> Law on Investment Activity (18 September 1991).
> Resolution if the Ukrainian Supreme Soviet on the Inappropriateness of Ukraine's Participation in any Inter-Republican Structure which could lead to its Inclusion into Another State. (25 October 1991).
> Resolution of the Ukrainian Supreme Soviet on Secession from the Soviet Union (5 December 1991).
> Law On Commodity Exchanges (10 December 1991).
> Law on Foreign Investment (20 December 1991).
> Law On Peasant Farming (30 December 1991).
> Presidential Decree on the Protection of the Population under Conditions of Price Liberalization (27 December 1991).
> Resolution of the Ukrainian Cabinet of Ministers on the Social Protection of the Population and of the Internal Market of Ukraine (27 December 1991).
> Resolution of the Cabinet of Ministers of Ukraine on Additional Social Protection Measures Following the 2 January 1992 Price Liberalization (27 December 1991).
>
> *1992*
>
> Plan on Urgent Reforms (2-3 March 1992).

productivity has been accompanied by higher nominal as well as real unit labour costs.[347] Consumer prices in Ukraine went up by 83 per cent in 1991, suggesting that real income fell by some 10 per cent at least. However, the increasing share of transactions outside traditional channels (including the black market), which according to data for the Commonwealth are not included in the price deflators, leaves room for a much steeper decline in consumption.

The rise in money incomes of the population, in nominal enterprise profits, in bank deposits and in credits outstanding were all very large in Ukraine also. The corresponding increases for the Commonwealth as a whole were 90, 75, 74 and 73 per cent. No figure is available for money incomes, but the other three of the above monetary indicators in the Ukraine rose by 68, 72 and 73 per cent respectively. Weak control of the growth of both government and enterprise expenditures has resulted from fears of social unrest which could

---

[347] I. Lukinov, "Current tendencies and forecasts of economic developments of Ukraine in 1991-1992", a background report prepared for the United Nations Economic Commission for Europe, Kiev, 29 January 1992.

follow large-scale enterprise closures or income restraints in the face of big price increases. Growth in the money supply — during 1991 the volume of money in circulation doubled compared to 1990 — fed the rapid build-up of inflationary pressure already apparent at the beginning of 1991.[348]

Thus the inflationary tendencies which characterized the other republics were present in Ukraine in similar strength and monetary imbalances had the same underlying causes. Generous wage compensation for the rises in administered prices during 1991, as well as compensation for the erosion of savings due to inflation, were financed in part from higher wholesale and farm procurement prices. But they were also accompanied by a build-up of large budgetary deficits at the republican as well as the union level and a seemingly uncontrolled rise in bank credits. The Ukrainian budgetary deficit alone rose to some R48.5 billion (including advance by banks of R9 billion),[349] equivalent to 17 per cent of estimated Ukrainian GDP at current prices in 1991. No data are available on the detail of budgetary receipts and expenditures. But it is likely that continuing subsidies to loss-making firms supplemented failure to control the growth of credit and especially advances to enterprises.

It is already clear that transition to a market economy cannot be carried through without living standards being pulled down by falling output, inflation, and ultimately job losses as enterprises with no long-term prospects under market conditions are weeded out. The Ukrainian leadership has emphasized the need for a *social safety net* to contain the popular unrest which could ensue. But tax and other government revenues were already squeezed in 1991 and will remain sluggish until a recovery gets under way. Thus sizeable government budget deficits, which run counter to the policies which will ultimately achieve internal stabilization, have been incurred.

During 1991 there were several increases in state-regulated prices. On 1 January 1991 new wholesale prices were introduced. To soften the widespread and abrupt impact of the removal of consumer subsidies, the increases in administered price during 1991 were partially offset by *compensation payments* introduced by the central and Ukrainian governments. These were set on the basis of a minimum consumer basket and the minimum income which would be needed to purchase this.[350] On 2 April 1991, state regulated increases in retail prices were promulgated, ranging from 20 per cent for telecommunications to 240 per cent for salt. Other goods, notably fish, dairy products and meat, continued to be subsidized. The impact of these increases was softened by compensation payments of 65 and 70 roubles per month for wage earners and pensioners respectively. Persons with a monthly income below 165 roubles were to be tax exempt.[351] Moreover, following a decision of the Ukrainian Council of Ministers, the Ukrainian government allocated an additional R3.1 billion for compensation payments.

The eligibility and extent of indemnities to the population for the 2 April increase in retail prices was defined in a decree of the Ukrainian Council of Ministers.[352] It specified that these compensation payments would be financed from social protection funds to be administered by the Ukrainian Ministry of Finance, and financed from the proceeds of the retail price increases, the abolition of subsidies on certain products, and taxes levied on enterprises.[353]

Additional government measures consisted of approximately R30 billion in allocations from the government budget to compensate for the decline in purchasing power, which was to be paid in wage and pension supplements.[354]

Following the January 1992 price liberalization, the Ukrainian Cabinet of Ministers adopted a resolution on additional social welfare protection which raised the minimum wage to R400 per month and doubled student grants and pensions. The prices of some foodstuffs (sausages, milk and dairy products) were also reduced by administrative fiat, but this did little to ease the impact of the reform on living standards.[355]

Ukraine's population has witnessed an absolute decline in its *living standards*, which has considerably enlarged the already large share of the population which lived in reduced circumstances under central planning. Two recent studies concluded that approximately 40 per cent of the population could be considered as below the poverty line well before the dismantling of central planning began to accelerate.[356] This situation must have worsened considerably already in 1991 and again following the price liberalization of January 1992.

The structure of Ukrainian *employment* in 1991 showed very gradual progress away from the predominance of the state sector. Employment in the state and collectivized sectors together in that year declined from 93.2 to 87.5 per cent of total employment. The shift thus affected under 6 per cent, or 1.5 million workers, over half of whom were classified as engaged in *arenda* enterprises, a quarter as members of independent co-

---

[348] I. Lukinov, op.cit.

[349] BBC, *Summary of World Broadcasts*, SU/W0217, 20 February 1991, p.B/10.

[350] *Ibid.*

[351] Decree entitled "Measures for the social protection of the population linked to the reforms of retail prices", *Pravda Ukrainy*, 2 April 1991

[352] "Resources for the compensation of the expenses of the population linked to the reforms of retail prices", *Pravda Ukrainy*, 2 April 1991.

[353] *Pravda Ukrainy*, 2 April 1991.

[354] BBC, *Summary of World Broadcasts*, SU/1004, 23 February 1991 p.B/11.

[355] BBC, *Summary of World Broadcasts*, SU/1277, 14 January 1992, p.B/15.

[356] See O. Moskvin: "Analiz tendentsii zminy rivnya zhyttya naselennya URSR", *Ekonomika Radyans'koi Ukrainy*, No.2, 1990, pp.13-21; David Marples, "Poverty and hunger become widespread in Ukraine", RL/RFE, Munich, 14 May 1990.

operatives and the rest as small entrepreneurs and independent peasants. (Just over 7 per cent of the labour force shifted similarly into the non-state sector in Russia).[357]

It was estimated that *unemployment* in Ukraine due to the implementation of transition policies could reach up to 1.5 million during 1991. Even as early as 1990, the ILO estimated that the number of persons classified as temporarily unemployed was 300,000. To anticipate the requirements of higher unemployment, a State Employment Service was set up in January 1991 by the Ukrainian Ministry of Labour.[358] This was to centralize demands for employment, provide information on vacancies and arrange for the retraining of redundant workers.[359]

With regard to *foreign trade*, in 1991 Ukraine experienced a bigger drop in its exports (46 per cent) than any of the other states of the Commonwealth, and a smaller drop in imports (39 per cent) than any but Armenia and Turkmenistan.[360] This compares with contractions of 33 and 44 per cent for the exports and imports of the Commonwealth as a whole.

Ukraine's exports outside the territory of the former Soviet Union constituted approximately 7 per cent of its NMP during 1989. In 1991, Ukrainian imports from the world accounted for nearly 16 per cent of the Soviet Union's total purchases from abroad. This was about the same as the republic's share in the population of the Soviet Union. On the export side, however, Ukraine's share was only 10.5 per cent of the all-Union total in the same period (table 4.4.5). Ukraine's main (non-Soviet) trading partner was Germany.

Full year trade data for 1991 by commodity were not available at the time of writing. In the first 10 months of the year, Ukraine was responsible for 31 per cent of Soviet exports of coal, 42 per cent of finished rolled steel, 47 per cent of slates, 20 per cent of mineral fertilizers, and 9 per cent of cement. These items do not for the most part fall into high value-added commodity groups — a commodity pattern which reflects the output structures referred to earlier.

Since no balance-of-payments statistics have yet been published for Ukraine, an indication of the importance of flows of *foreign direct investment* can only be inferred from data on joint ventures set up on Ukrainian territory. Between May 1987 and December 1990, the growth of joint ventures in Ukraine exceeded the rate of growth of joint ventures in the Soviet Union as a whole. However, the share of Ukraine in joint ventures registered in the Soviet Union remained disproportionately small — some 7 per cent at the beginning of 1991, with a total of 209 joint venture registrations.[361]

Ukraine's path to IMF membership has not so far been a smooth one. Its programmes were reviewed by an IMF team in late 1991. Current policies of the republic reportedly were subjected to severe criticism, principally on the grounds that measures to stabilize the economy, including bringing the budget into balance, were inadequate.[362]

An important precondition for full participation in world trade and finance will be the conclusion of satisfactory arrangements for Ukraine's participation in the settlement of the Soviet foreign debt. Ukraine had agreed in December 1991 to participate with other CIS states in the joint servicing of the external debt of the former Soviet Union, but thereafter withdrew from that agreement in favour of independent arrangements for servicing its share of the debt. However, by mid-March 1992 the modalities for a joint approach, with shared control over the debt service department of Vneshekonombank, appeared to have been settled with the other CIS states.[363]

While it now seems that the international organizations concerned are receptive to Ukraine's application for membership in the World Bank and the IMF, acceptance is expected to be contingent on Ukraine's agreement on debt with the other successor states.[364]

The Ukrainian transition strategy

The sovereignty declaration adopted by Parliament in July 1990 already contained a number of provisions relating to the economy — including an assertion of Ukrainian rights to natural resources on its territory, clauses on environmental protection and the right of Ukraine to establish direct links, including economic, with other republics on the basis of treaties. The basic constitutional documents on which the new state is founded, i.e., those passed since the Declaration of Sovereignty of July 1990, include a law on economic independence, a resolution by the Ukrainian Supreme Soviet transferring state enterprises and organizations on Ukrainian territory from Union to republican jurisdiction and amendments to the Ukrainian Constitution claiming supremacy of republican over Union law on

---

[357] Goskomstat, *Ekonomicheskii obzor*, No.12, 1992, p.21.

[358] For details, see Decree of the Council of Ministers of Ukraine entitled "Creation of an Employment Agency", *Pravda Ukrainy*, 4 January 1991.

[359] In September 1991, 123,500 persons applied for a job with the state employment services. However, only 3,700 were recognized as unemployed and only 2,600 were deemed eligible for unemployment benefits. Furthermore, only 13.3 per cent of applicants were assigned a job. V. Myachin and M.J. Sagers, "The Ukraine: An Economic Profile Through The First Nine Months of 1991", *PlanEcon Report*, Vol. VII, No.42, 27 November 1991, p.17.

[360] Goskomstat, *Ekonomicheskii obzor*, No.12, 1992, p.31.

[361] United Nations Economic Commission for Europe, "Ukraine — Survey of Foreign Investments", *East-West Joint Ventures News*, No.10, December 1991, p.15.

[362] *The Times*, 24 December 1991.

[363] See section 4.1(vi) and footnote (225) above.

[364] Ukraine submitted an application for associate membership on 19 December 1991 and is likely to attain this status in April 1992.

Ukrainian territory, and measures to lay the foundations of Ukraine's financial autonomy.[365]

The plan for Ukraine's transition to the market was agreed in parliament, following heated debate on the speed and sequencing of the transition process, on 2 November 1990. "Shock therapy" was rejected on the grounds that the likely transition costs in terms of structural unemployment would be too high. The Council of Ministers had drawn up a law on the transition to a market economy on 1 November 1990 which stipulated that the transition process should be accompanied by the raising of living standards − an ambition that was so clearly unrealistic in the light of developments in eastern and central Europe as to cast doubts on how far the underlying issues had been understood. Measures adopted in 1990-1991 to provide for transition to a market economy seem to have reflected efforts to find some kind of "third way", including the retention of command-type elements (state orders, regulated prices) which could only hinder the transition to a market. However, these efforts were soon abandoned.

At the time of the Minsk Agreement of 8 December 1991 which created the Commonwealth of Independent States, it had been envisaged that the Commonwealth would provide some degree of stability for Ukraine's economic relations with other Soviet successor states. But there were early signs that such stability could be difficult to secure. More recently, Ukrainian dissatisfaction with the 2 January 1992 price liberalization in Russia, which Ukraine was forced to follow in order to protect its domestic consumer market, added to the instability of the newly-formed Commonwealth. The freeing of prices in Russia resulted in increases of 6-10 times for some products and removed any possibility for Ukraine to pursue a more gradual transition to the market. These events also underlined the fact that Ukraine is not free to pursue its own policies while it is tied to the rouble. These discords, which had parallels in the political sphere,[366] prompted President Kravchuk to emphasize the need for Ukraine to introduce its own currency, the *grivna*, as rapidly as possible − perhaps as early as March 1992.

The year 1991 witnessed a considerable volume of legislative acts designed to achieve the twin goals of economic independence and the transition to a market economy (see box 4.4.3).

Already at the time of its first declaration of sovereignty, Ukraine had voiced the intention of establishing an *independent banking system* and issuing its *own currency*. The first legislative steps to transform the banking system were endorsed by the Ukrainian parliament in March 1991.[367] The law provided for the early creation of a Ukrainian National Bank (Ukrbank), which began operations in November 1991, and for the establishment of a network of commercial banks. These were to open their doors on 1 April 1991. Ukrbank is now to be the main regulator of monetary and credit policy. As the central bank of the republic it has the right "to put money into circulation and to regulate the money supply", and "to open branch offices abroad". It declared its priorities as formulating a money and credit system capable of bringing inflation to a halt and assisting in the creation of the structures and conditions appropriate to a functioning market economy.

In addition, the dismantling of the former Soviet *Vneshekonombank*, the organ formally responsible for the foreign debt of the former Soviet Union, has resulted in the designation of the newly-established Export-Import Bank of Ukraine to take over the Ukrainian departments of *Vneshekonombank*.[368] In January 1992, Ukraine's first international bank opened in Donetsk.[369]

The stabilization programme was originally expected to be bolstered by the introduction of the *grivna* in March 1992. Problems caused by physical shortages of banknotes, as well as by a desire to lay the foundations for a Ukrainian currency and, in doing so, to prevent outsiders from purchasing more plentiful Ukrainian food, prompted the introduction of a scheme on 10 January 1992 to issue a limited quantity of reusable, rouble-denominated "coupons" as 25 per cent of pay packets. At the same time shops were instructed to require coupons in part-payment for food and some other consumer items.[370] Meanwhile it had been announced on 22 January 1992 that a comprehensive *monetary reform* would take place in mid-1992 and that this would coincide with the introduction of the *grivna*. Thus the introduction of the new currency has been put back from the original March deadline.[371] Correspondingly, at present a dual currency coexists in Ukraine; with the interim coupon being used in state

---

[365] "Law on the Economic Independence of Ukraine's Statehood", 28 June 1990, *Pravda Ukrainy*, 2 July 1990; "Resolution of the Ukrainian Supreme Soviet on the transfer of state enterprises located on Ukrainian territory from subordination to Union jurisdiction to Republican jurisdiction" of 6 June 1991, *Pravda Ukrainy*, 12 June 1991; "Law on the Economic Autonomy of the Soviet Socialist Republic of Ukraine" of 3 August 1990, *Pravda Ukrainy:ecit*, 8 August 1990: "*Law on Financial Autonomy of Ukraine*" of 3 August 1990, BBC, *Summary of World Broadcasts*, SU/0836, B/2, 7 August 1990.

[366] Most notably concerning arrangements for the control and eventual disposition of military assets as well as army and fleet units.

[367] "Law on banks and banking activities" of 26 March 1991.

[368] The Export-Import Bank was granted initial funding of 500 million "valuta" roubles belonging to Ukraine. It is envisaged that by April 1992 it will have separated all its operations from those of the former USSR Bank for Foreign Economic Activity. BBC, *Summary of World Broadcasts*, SU/W0214, 24 January 1992, p.A/3; *Russia Express*, No.69, 23 December 1991, p.19.

[369] This bank was established by a consortium of major enterprises in the Donbass and the Donetsk subsidiary of the Industrial Construction Bank, together with American and Dutch financiers. It is to provide services to factories and firms in the Donbass and other areas. BBC, *Summary of World Broadcasts*, SU/W0215, 31 January 1992, p.A/2.

[370] Initially the authorities set a price of 10 roubles per coupon for purchase of additional coupons. Soon, however, peasant markets in Kiev were accepting coupons at a rate of 2 roubles per coupon and street traders were accepting up to 5 roubles. The coupons were designed to create incentives for the privatization of certain services, to induce producers to augment their output of goods. Even internal commentators estimated that the coupon was overvalued at the rate of 10 coupons per dollar. In fact the National Bank of Ukraine revised its official exchange rate for the interim coupons to 14 coupons per dollar on 28 January 1992 and made corresponding adjustments for other currencies. BBC, *Summary of World Broadcasts*, SU/1291 30 January 1992, p.B/14.

[371] BBC, *Summary of World Broadcasts*, SU/W0215, 31 January 1992, p.A/9.

trade, while the rouble is being used for public catering, transport, and communal services. However, insufficient coupons were printed to cover pensions and wages. The reusable coupons facilitate Ukraine's transfer to its own currency, but provoke an additional obstacle to price liberalization.[372]

Ukraine's *privatization* measures are as yet only at the preparatory stage. The authorities have proceeded cautiously. In particular the decollectivization of land is apparently not yet foreseen, the outright sale of land having been rejected. According to a draft government programme which was not endorsed, large-scale privatization should already have begun during 1991. In fact only 2 per cent of state assets have as yet been transferred to private ownership.[373]

Several obstacles to Ukraine's privatization process exist. First, it is certain that the price liberalization on 2 January 1992 reduced already low levels of personal savings. The government's privatization concept has little to say on its practical implementation. Other obstacles stem from the dilapidated state in which central planning left the capital stock and the disparities between the actual structures of the productive base (capital stock, skills, input availabilities and costs) and demand at market prices.

An important segment of the new legislation covers *foreign investment*, the importance of which has apparently been fully recognized by the Ukrainian leadership. On 18 September 1991, the "Law on Investment Activity" was adopted. On 23 September 1991 the Ukrainian Council of Ministers formulated and endorsed a "Decree on the Protection of Foreign Investment" which guarantees foreign investors the right to repatriate profits, either in roubles or in foreign currency, or to reinvest them in Ukraine.

Foreign investors receive some privileges denied to indigenous companies. Joint ventures, for instance, are tax exempt for a period of two years, while indigenous firms face a 65 per cent profits tax. Furthermore, a joint venture in which the foreign partner controls more than 30 per cent of the company is exempt from customs duties even after the expiration of these two years.[374] Finally, on 20 December 1991, the Ukrainian parliament introduced a "Law on Foreign Investment" which, some expert opinion considers, conforms fully with international standards. The law stipulates that investors, who may be foreign citizens, legal entities or states, may make investments in various forms (money, special bank deposits, shares, stocks, and other securities) and can invest in all economic sectors. The regulations for foreign investment on Ukrainian territory guarantee that all investors possess equal rights, and regardless of ownership, have virtually unrestricted investment possibilities. The investor has the right to transfer his rights of ownership, management or administration to other individuals or legal entities, to solicit loans and to issue securities in order to undertake his investment activity.[375] Other elements in this legislation are more restrictive. Land and other forms of real estate cannot yet be bought but can be leased for up to 90 years.[376] Investors are obliged to declare the nature of their investment activity to the relevant financial authorities, submit appraisals of potential investment projects in terms of technological, sanitary and environmental effects, submit relevant information to government agencies, undertake to refrain from unfair competition and observe anti-monopoly legislation.

Economic restructuring

At the end of January 1992 President Kravchuk appealed to the Ukrainian parliament for more powers, proposing that the activities of local councils and their executive committees be suspended and their functions of local administration be transferred to presidential representatives in order to prevent them from blocking the implementation of economic reform.[377]

A survey carried out in February 1991 by the Ukrainian State Committee for Statistics found that only 25 per cent of state-owned firms made profits.[378] Ukraine's machine building industry is in a poor state. Loss-making branches of industry include sulphur and coal (the prices of these minerals were held below their extraction and transport costs). The coal industry in particular suffered from rising extraction costs due to resource depletion and obsolescent equipment.[379]

This points up an area of vulnerability common to all the successor states — the lack of products other than some fuels and primary products which can compete on western markets.[380]

The importance of *conversion of defence industries* to civilian production should be emphasized because of its size.[381] While there is no doubt that the potential

---

[372] " Roubles, coupons ... what next ?", *Izvestiya*, 21 January 1992.

[373] O.G. Belorus, "The privatization of state property in the Ukraine", background report to the United Nations Economic Ccommission for Europe, December 1991.

[374] Duncan Robinson, "Ukrainian exporters have high hopes", *Journal of Commerce*, 21 October 1991.

[375] *Ibid*, 20 December 1991.

[376] *Financial Times*, 28 February 1992.

[377] BBC, *Summary of World Broadcasts*, SU/1292, B/11, 31 January 1992.

[378] BBC, *Summary of World Broadcasts*, 1 March 1991.

[379] In the Yenakievo region, for example, a ton of coal sold for R100 roubles while its production cost was R700. John Morrison, "Ukraine's rust belt industries face uncertain future", *Reuter*, Donetsk, 11 December 1991.

[380] Even so, given the high share of oil alone in total Soviet exports, which considerably exceeds the share of coal in Ukrainian exports, Ukraine might even have a competitive edge in this respect *vis-à-vis* the rest of the former Soviet Union.

[381] However, even this is not firmly established. The minister in charge of the conversion process in Ukraine estimated in 1991 that the republic possessed over 700 defence plants employing over 1 million workers (BBC, *Summary of World Broadcasts*, SU/W0214, A/7, 24 January 1992, p.A/7). An official estimate

for conversion is large, the cost of re-equipment and the quality and price of its output will determine the size and scope of its contribution to the restructuring process.

Prospects

Many features of the old system remained in place during 1991. Though prices were liberalized at the beginning of 1992, the monopoly structure of output remains largely intact, as does the predominant form of state ownership. No coherent policy concerning the privatization or creation of a market in land has been adopted. Neither the new central bank nor the government have attempted to mitigate accelerating inflation by an appropriate tightening of monetary policy or by higher interest rates. In February 1992 there was still no budget set for 1992.

The creation of a competitive environment through privatization thus still needs to be underpinned by a number of institutional reforms. The resolution of land and property ownership questions and the implementation of small-scale privatization as an earnest of intent and as a test bed for such new market-oriented institutions as are now, or will shortly be, functioning, are overdue. Other facilities, including the creation of a rational tax system which removes disincentives to individual or corporate economic activity and which encourages the mobilization of voluntary savings also need urgent attention. Perhaps the most urgent requirement is the creation of the basic market institutions. Although some examples of market institutions are appearing (the creation of commodity markets is a case in point), basic instruments to exploit and regulate the banking system are not yet in place. Without tighter control of credit and the money supply it is difficult to see how the first steps to stabilize the economy can be taken.

Short-term policy is based on the expectation of further falls in output in 1992. Personal consumption is expected to decline further. The volume of state investments is to be further reduced by 25 per cent and state investment resources are to be channelled only into priority programmes and the development of a social infrastructure which had been greatly neglected under the former command-administered system.[382] Planned sharp cuts in defence expenditures should help to restrain the growth of the deficit.[383]

In the medium term the lack of a clear commitment to economic reform on the part of the Ukrainian leadership is an obstacle in its own right. The relatively restrictive nature of many would-be reform measures does not augur well for the future.

In the longer term, Ukraine's agricultural and mineral riches, combined with a relatively high level of industrialization, geographical compactness and relative proximity to western Europe would all seem to offer a favourable outlook for resumed growth. But it is unlikely that a sustainable increase in the presently tiny Ukrainian share of the world market will be feasible without considerable alteration of the existing output structure.

This could be held back by several factors. Perhaps most importantly, like most of the other former Soviet republics, Ukraine faces a large potential deterioration in its terms of trade with Russia and some other CIS republics as the structure of prices in inter-republican trade shifts towards world prices. This stems from the Ukraine's status as a net energy importer.[384] The decision to close the Chernobyl nuclear power plant will expand requirements for conventional fuels and the transition from the centrally set prices used in inter-republican trade towards the structure of world prices implies that Ukraine's fuel deficit with other successor states of the former Soviet Union could increase substantially. On the other hand, real food prices within the former USSR are now higher than they have ever been. They are also likely to remain high relative to world market price levels, and Ukraine, in common with the Baltic states, may find that this lends some support to its terms of trade with Russia.

(iv) Belarus

Belarus is the fifth biggest republic of the former USSR in terms of population (3.6 per cent or over 10 million inhabitants). Some 67 per cent of these are of Belarussian nationality. Over half of the rest are of Russian and almost all the others of Polish or Ukrainian origin. Its population density, 49 inhabitants per square kilometre, is somewhat lower than Ukraine but higher than in the European areas of Russia. Some 40 per cent of its labour force is occupied in industry and construction and about 20 per cent in agriculture. The similarity of basic population structures in Ukraine and in Belarus is also reflected in urbanization levels and in the high (over 30 per cent) share of residents of non-Belarus nationality.

In contrast with Russia and Ukraine, Belarus is not richly endowed with natural resources. Like Ukraine but in contrast with Russia, the republic holds a smaller share of the capital stock than its share in the total

---

for 1985 was that some 18.6 per cent of Ukraine's labour force (compared with 24 per cent in Russia), equal to about 500,000 people, were employed in the defence sector. In fact, consumer goods already account for some 60 per cent of total defence industry output in Ukraine, consisting of some 1,500 different products including passenger aircraft, ships, sprinklers, and equipment for both light industry and the medical sector (Viktor Antonov, Ukrainian Minister of State for Defence and Conversion, in BBC, *Summary of World Broadcasts*, SU/W0185, 7 June 1991). On the other hand, part of output in what was administratively classified as civilian industry (i.e., formerly coming under ministries not supervised by the Military-Industrial Commission) would have been supplied as material inputs to the military sector. This may be the case of some of the divergent estimate of "military" industry in Ukraine as elsewhere (*Le Monde*, 11 February 1992, pp.35, 38).

382 I. Lukinov, op.cit.

383 Ukraine will limit the size of its army to 220,000 men. BBC, *Summary of World Broadcasts*, SU/1288, 27 January 1992, p.A1/1.

384 By 1988 Ukraine had turned from a net fuel exporter into a net importer to the tune of 40 per cent of its requirements. Ukraine produces only 5 million tons of crude oil annually but consumes 60 million tons and also imports 78 per cent of its natural gas requirements. In 1988, approximately 11 per cent of the Ukraine's total imports from other former Soviet republics consisted of oil and gas alone. In spite of some offsetting fuel exports, Ukraine's deficit on trade in fuel was R3.6 billion (See John Tedstrom, "USSR – costs and benefits for Ukrainian independence", RL/RFE, Munich, 20 November 1990).

TABLE 4.4.9
Belarus: Basic economic indicators, 1987-1991
(Percentage change over same period of preceding year)

	1987	1988	1989	1990	1991 QI	QI-QII	QI-QIII	QI-QIV
GDP	..	..	..	..	..	..	..	-3.0
NMP	3.5	2.4	7.9	-1.4	..	-5.0	..	-3.0
Employment [a]	0.5	-0.1	-0.2	-1.4	..	..	..	-0.0
Gross industrial production	6.7	6.3	4.6	1.6	..	-4.3	..	-2.2 [b]
Group "A"	6.5	5.7	4.4	1.2	..	..	..	-0.2 [b,c]
Group "B"	6.9	7.6	5.1	2.6	..	-1.0 [c]	..	-0.2 [b,c]
Gross agricultural production	0.1	-7.3	8.9	-5.9	..	..	..	-3.0
Gross investment	19.7	-0.2	10.0	1.0	..	..	..	..
Exports	..	..	..	..	..	..	..	-41.8
Imports	..	..	..	..	..	..	..	-46.9
Money wages	5.3	9.3	9.7	15.9	13.9 [d]	..	..	..
Retail sales	4.6	6.4	9.0	15.4	..	..	-3.4 [b]	-2.7
Retail prices [e]	1.0	2.3	2.0	5.3	..	..	..	81.3
Industrial wholesale prices	..	..	..	..	..	125.0	134.0	151.0
Agricultural procurement prices	..	..	..	..	..	..	59.0	..
Money incomes	5.1	9.9	11.7	19.3	..	..	67.1	..
Expenditures	6.4	6.8	10.1	18.9	..	..	56.0	..

Source: Based on data in *Narodnoe khozyaistvo Belorusskor SSR v 1990g.*, Minsk, 1991 pp.3-6, 47; USSR Goskomstat, *Narodnoe khozyaistvo SSSR v 1990 g.*, Goskomstat, Moscow 1991, pp.166, 173, 459, 553; USSR Goskomstat, *Ekonomika stran-chlenov SNG v 1991 godu*, Moscow, 1992; USSR Goskomstat, *Soyuznye respubliki: osnovnye ekonomicheskie i sotsial'nye pokazateli*, Moscow, 1991;

[a] The available data for 1987-1990 are for state employment only (workers and employees). Data for 1991 are for all gainfully occupied persons, including collective farmers and private-sector employees. The growth rates for 1991 over 1990 are therefore not comparable with the earlier series.
[b] January - November.
[c] Consumer goods.
[d] Resources directed towards average consumption per worker and employee per month.
[e] For 1987-1990, data relate to the USSR and cover retail prices in the state sector only. For 1991 the series relates to Belarus only and to consumer goods and services in all sectors. The growth rate in 1991 over 1990 is therefore not comparable with the earlier series.

Soviet population. The opposite is true for the republic's share in total industrial and agricultural production (table 4.4.1, panel A). It produced 10 per cent or more of the more sophisticated industrial products shown in table 4.4.3 — machine tools, TV sets, refrigerators, footwear and woollen cloth as well as chemicals. It also produced 10 per cent or more of half the main agricultural products tabulated. Its GDP per head was just above the Soviet average — almost the same as in Russia and considerably above Ukraine (table 4.4.1, panel B). Its overall economic efficiency was also relatively high by Soviet standards — industrial labour productivity was above the Soviet average and in agriculture it was also higher than in any other non-Baltic republic in 1990. Its total capital stock was more productive than in Russia or in the former Soviet Union as a whole. These advantages may go some way to explain the republic's high (relative to population) 4 per cent share in the former Soviet Union's foreign trade (table 4.4.5).

The Belarussian economy in 1991

In 1991 the Belarussian economy showed the same symptoms of falling output, macroeconomic imbalance and the transformation of rapid price rises into hyperinflation as the other former Soviet republics. However, the registered falls in *production* were pronouncedly more moderate than those shown for most other CIS republics. NMP produced fell by 3 per cent, gross industrial output by just over 2 per cent, and agricultural production by 3 per cent (see table 4.4.9, and table 4.4.4 for a comparative perspective).[385] This rather contrasts with the fact that in foreign trade the republic fully shared in the general downturn (with a fall in export value of 42 per cent and a 47 per cent contraction of imports).

Nominal *production costs* were inflated by price rises. Wholesale prices grew by 150 per cent in industry and the republic's wage bill was affected by the same union-wide price compensation payments as in the other successor states.

Given the supply risks which have resulted from breakdowns in inter-republican relations, it is of interest that as early as 1990 the Byelorussian authorities concluded economic, scientific, technical, and cultural co-operation agreements with all of the then Soviet republics apart from the Baltic states. This policy was actively continued in 1991, when agreements were signed with seven of the other Commonwealth members.

---

[385] Attention has earlier been drawn to the discrepancy between all-CIS data on the 1991 contraction and the rates of decline reported by the republics (see footnote (203) above), with the suggestion that republican data may have been inadequately adjusted for inflation. However, in the case of Belarus the contrast is so large that it may indeed reflect a noticeably different performance in 1991.

Monetary imbalances have appeared, as in other republics, from excessive rises in budgetary expenditures at a time of falling tax and other revenues and failure to control the growth of credit to the personal and the enterprise sectors. The budget deficit for 1991 was originally planned at R3.5 billion, or 21 per cent of revenues (almost 10 per cent of estimated 1990 GDP).[386] An anti-crisis programme, announced in mid-year,[387] called for curbs on government spending and set concrete objectives for the transition to a market economy.

No figure is available for the rise in personal nominal incomes in Belarus during 1991, but it was probably similar to the Commonwealth average. Enterprise profits grew by R11 billion or over 70 per cent. Credits to non-government borrowers rose by over R11 billion and almost doubled. Personal savings deposits went up by about R12 billion or over 70 per cent indicating, as for the Commonwealth as a whole, a considerable imbalance between the rise in the money supply and in the stock of goods on which it could be spent.

Employment appears to have remained virtually unchanged between 1990 and 1991. There was however some shift out of the state sector. Some 250,000 workers out the 5.1 million strong labour force were affected, just under half beginning employment in semi-privatized enterprises, one third in various leasing activities and the rest as private peasants or artisans.

As in other successor states, *unemployment* resulting from the "transition crisis" appears to have been negligible so far. In order to cope with the expected redundancies, the Belarussian government has implemented a number of measures. Its job placement services have been reconstructed and an association of personnel departments to promote the conclusion of labour contracts between employers and employees was created in the republic. It is expected that of about 300,000 job seekers in 1992, approximately 60,000 would remain unemployed and draw benefits. Retraining courses would also be provided.

In 1989 (only scanty data are available for later years) Belarus, with Azerbaijan, were the only two republics to register a positive balance on *total external trade* (i.e. trade with other Soviet republics and with countries outside the Soviet Union). This reflected a large surplus on trade with the other Soviet republics (expressed in current domestic prices) and a much smaller deficit on trade with other countries. Since Belarus has no fuels and few primary products except farm commodities, this is perhaps an indication that relatively high levels of tradable manufactures are produced domestically. However, they are unlikely to be competitive enough to cover its imports from countries outside the territory of the former Soviet Union.

In trade with the rest of the world, the republic's deficit declined substantially (from R1.5 billion in 1990 to R0.4 billion in 1991), reflecting the faster fall of imports relative to exports.

In the December 1991 agreement on sharing the former Soviet Union's *foreign debt* liabilities, Belarus assumed a share of 4.1 per cent, slightly above its export share.[388]

Transition strategy and legislative provisions

The transformation in Belarus has scarcely begun. Macroeconomic stabilization cannot be undertaken independently of Russia as long as Belarus remains within a common rouble area. Price liberalization was forced on Belarus by Russia's decontrol of prices in January 1992. The processes of privatization and internationalization have not yet gone beyond their initial stages. Nevertheless there have been some developments in the direction of a market economy in legislation.

Belarus' plan of 14 November 1990 for the transition to the market led to the establishment of a *Committee for Management of State Property*. This committee was to deal with the major difficulties that would arise in attempting to initiate the process of destatization and privatization of the economy. An outline timetable was laid down for *privatization*,[389] according to which the privatization of 20 medium-sized and large enterprises was to be completed by the end of 1991. However, the process of transferring state control to a newly emerging private sector was hampered by the absence of a legal framework. (This was still incomplete at the beginning of 1992.)

The early measures adopted by the newly elected Byelorussian Supreme Soviet during 1990 were cautious or even restrictive. They represented in many respects a governmental reflex to take charge and manipulate the process of marketization rather than using the market for resource allocation. On 1 November 1990, for example, a law passed by the Byelorussian Supreme Soviet came into effect to protect the domestic consumer market.[390] It set out a number of priority measures. First, it banned the export of consumer goods, raw materials and foreign currency. Second, enterprises were forbidden to export any technology or technological know-how. Third, restrictions were placed on the import of certain foodstuffs and industrial goods by individuals. Fourth, the Byelorussian Supreme Soviet granted the government the right to identify monopoly sellers of certain goods and to take appropriate action. Fifth, measures to punish profiteering were announced and penalties for breaking the trade laws were tightened. Finally, the law provided for the establishment of checkpoints on the republic's borders, the appointment of inspectorates with wide-ranging powers and an in-

---

[386] The outturn was actually better, a deficit of R1.3 billion, largely because Belarus, like other republics, withheld transfers owed to the Union budget.

[387] BBC, *Summary of World Broadcasts*, SU/0180, 24 May 1991, p.A/2.

[388] See section 4.1(vi) and footnote (225) above.

[389] N. Petrachkova, "The model of privatization for the Republic of Belarus", report prepared for the United Nations Economic Commission for Europe, January 1992.

[390] Law "On temporary measures to protect the Republic's consumer market", cited in N. Petrachkova, op.cit.

crease in the staff in the republic's Ministry of Internal Affairs.[391]

Indeed, attitudes similar to those reflected in this law seem to persist up to the present. At the beginning of 1992 — as in the Soviet Union a year earlier — some government circles appear to remain ambivalent or even hostile towards the emerging business sector.[392] Restrictive attitudes can be discerned also with regard to privatization. In December 1991, a legislative basis for leasing productive plant and property was adopted.[393] But the leasing option is clearly considered by some simply as a less drastic alternative to full-blooded privatization.

Still in 1990, a *Law on the enterprise* was introduced to set up a new legal basis for the ownership status and functioning of enterprises.[394]

An important market-oriented departure was the *Law on bankruptcy* of 2 June 1991, which forbids the government to subsidize insolvent or bankrupt enterprises using state funds. This came into effect on 1 July 1991.[395] Unprofitable firms must ultimately be declared bankrupt and their property sold by auction. This law could affect numerous unprofitable state and collective farms which have only managed to survive with state subsidies and the write-off of debt. The consequences of good or bad economic performance are thus placed firmly with the entrepreneurs and managers concerned.[396] The liquidation and reorganization of enterprises with foreign funds remains subject to the separate Law on enterprises.

A *Law on entrepreneurship* affecting property rights was also adopted by the Byelorussian Supreme Soviet on 28 May 1991. The central aim of this law is the creation of economic incentives for enterprise activity, based on equality of all forms of ownership. The law states that an entrepreneur can be an individual, an entire working collective or a foreign citizen or stateless person. Entrepreneurs are allowed to establish any form of enterprise using capital or property whether of indigenous or foreign origin. The law establishes concrete guarantees for entrepreneurship and sets procedures for the winding-up of a business.[397]

At the end of 1991, a *Law on foreign investments* was adopted to regulate and encourage foreign investment in Belarus.[398] This law states that foreign investment may take the form of joint ventures or be undertaken by foreign enterprises or individuals acting independently. Investment activities permitted include the acquisition of existing enterprises and the purchase of property rights in certain natural resources (including long land leases).

Foreign investors are able to open "unlimited accounts" in any branch of a national or commercial bank, and are able to repatriate profits. Enterprises in which foreign capital is invested must comply with the standard provisions of the *Law on investment activity* in the Republic of Belarus. They are generally subject to the same laws as apply to indigenous enterprises, entrepreneurs, and investment activities, but are eligible for a period of exemption from profits taxes. The establishment of a joint venture with capital exceeding R30 million at current prices must also be approved by the Council of Ministers. Joint ventures must also be licensed by the state. The Finance Ministry and State Committee for Foreign Economic Relations of the republic are responsible for monitoring the activities of enterprises wholly or partially owned by foreign investors. The State Committee on Foreign Economic Relations registers enterprises with foreign investments.

A new initiative to promote foreign investment has been the designation of an area north of Brest as a *free economic zone*.[399] The government resolution establishing the zone grants preferential company taxation rates not exceeding 25 per cent and tax exemption on profits. Joint ventures in which the foreign partner owns no more than 30 per cent of the venture are granted tax-exemption for a five-year period. The zone is to be administered by a committee responsible to the Brest regional authority.

On 17 December 1990 Belarus adopted two *Laws* dealing with the republic's *banking system*.[400] These seem to have closely emulated the USSR banking laws passed at the same time, except that they emphasized the need for the republic to establish its own financial and credit system and secured the right to establish specialized banks on its territory. Their passage was thus one of the first steps towards implementing the declaration of state sovereignty.

These laws essentially laid the foundation for a two-tier banking system based on a clear distinction between the Byelorussian National Bank (acting as the central or reserve institution) and the commercial banking network. Under the banking law, commercial banks could be either private, cooperative, or state-

---

[391] BBC, *Summary of World Broadcasts*, SU/W0152, 2 November 1990, p.A/9.

[392] Business circles see this expressed in the introduction of a new 60 per cent profits tax on 28 January 1992. They consider that even a profits tax of 50 per cent would be a disincentive to entrepreneurial activities. BBC, *Summary of World Broadcasts*, SU/1291 B/15, 30 January 1992.

[393] "Law on leasing", cited in N. Petrachkova, op.cit.

[394] See "Law on enterprises", *Sovetskaya Belorussiya*, 27 December 1990.

[395] "Weniger Staatshilfe für weissrussische Firmen", *Neue Zürcher Zeitung*, 5 June 1991.

[396] BBC, *Summary of World Broadcasts*, SU/1087, 1 June 1991, B/11.

[397] BBC, *Summary of World Broadcasts*, SU/1087 B/11, 1 June 1991.

[398] "Law on foreign investments on the territory of the republic of Belarus" of 14 November 1991. See *Kommersant*, 23 December 1991, p.4.

[399] BBC, *Summary of World Broadcasts*, SU/W0215, 31 January 1992, p. A/10.

[400] Law "On the National Bank of the Byelorussian SSR", and Law "On banks and banking in the Byelorussian SSR". See BBC, *Summary of World Broadcasts*, SU/W0160, 4 January 1991, p. A/14.

owned; would possess the status of legal persons; and would operate on the principles of financial autonomy. It was envisaged that the Byelorussian National Bank would possess normal central bank powers — the exclusive right of monetary issue and withdrawal and hence of regulating monetary policy. It would also monitor the establishment of banks and their branches in the republic and would participate in global and inter-republican payments and credit systems.

On 24 November 1991, permission was granted by the Council of Ministers for the first commercial bank with foreign capital to open in Brest. Foreign firms are able to open their own accounts either in roubles or in hard currency in this bank or in certain others. Foreign partners of joint ventures can use them to finance the further development of joint ventures, or for asset purchase in the privatization process.[401]

On 25 November 1991 — considerably later than the comparable development in Russia or the Baltic states — Belarus' first *commercial currency exchange* opened in Minsk. At the time of writing there is discussion about the creation of exchanges in other locations. Regulations on the sale of currency are the same as those of the now defunct USSR Vneshekonombank and Gosbank. Individuals must have a passport with an exit visa and can purchase only a limited amount of hard currency.

As regards *privatization*, Belarus has fallen well behind other successor states. The main innovation regarding property rights was the introduction, following earlier USSR legislation, of *leasing*. This appears to have advanced fairly rapidly — with 56 industrial enterprises and 30 construction organizations having been leased to their workers by June 1991.[402] At the end of 1991, leasehold enterprises employed 6 per cent of Belarus' work force, and accounted for over 9 per cent of the republic's total value of construction output, 25 per cent of retail turnover, a third of domestic services and 40 per cent of agricultural output. These shares are high compared with other successor states.

Privatization in Belarus has otherwise barely begun, with the state still maintaining control of property. At the end of 1991, 81 per cent of basic productive capacities still belonged to the state, 18 per cent to cooperatives (including collective farms) and only 1.4 per cent to the private sector.[403]

It is envisaged that the privatization process will begin in earnest in 1992. Some R56 out of R84 billion of state enterprises' capital stock will ultimately be transferred to some form of private ownership. Some R800 million of this is to be sold in 1992.[404] The process will consist in its simplest form in the direct sale of an enterprise, the purchaser becoming sole proprietor. Legislation for more complex forms of privatization has not as yet been developed, but will involve the transformation of state-owned enterprises into joint-stock companies. Privatization of almost any enterprise will be allowed other than those deemed to be of strategic importance (defence and security), natural monopolies, or those which provide public goods. These exceptions apart, the state is henceforth forbidden to acquire — or retain — ownership; i.e., no less than 50 per cent of an enterprise has to be privatized.[405]

An important obstacle to privatization is the low level of personal savings, which amount to R3 billion. Though this may represent some 10 per cent of consumption, it is very small in relation to the R56 billion book value of the assets to be privatized. This valuation at book value, however, may turn out to be far too high.[406]

Belarus like some other successor states, notably Ukraine, has declared its intention of introducing a national *currency*. The new monetary unit, the *taler*, which is to become legal tender before April 1992. This will replace the coupons Belarus introduced on 1 January 1992 — comparable to the interim system adopted in the Ukraine.[407]

Prospects

Belarus' strength lies in its high degree of industrialization, its above-average labour force skills and its considerably diversified economy, though it is highly dependent on imported raw materials. Given also its favoured geographical location close to the most densely populated regions of Russia, the elements of complementarity between Russian and Belarussian production and its relatively productive economy, Belarus could experience a smaller decrease in its output over the next year than most other successor states of the former Soviet Union.

On 28 January 1992, Russia and Belarus signed an agreement on removing restrictions on mutual trade, emphasizing that their trade and economic relations would be conducted within a single economic space. Whether or not this is implemented, the signing of this agreement reflects Belarus' continuing close relationship with Russia. Its integration into the world economy,

---

[401] BBC, *Summary of World Broadcasts*, SU/W0208, 6 December 1991, p. B/16.

[402] BBC, *Summary of World Broadcasts*, SU/1100 B/16, 17 June 1991.

[403] N. Petrachkova, op.cit.

[404] N. Petrachkova, op.cit. In 1992 the government aims to obtain some R796 million in revenues from privatization, of which R423 million will be obtained from leasing, R302 million from transforming state enterprises into joint stock companies, R64 million from the establishment of collectively-owned enterprises, and a further R7 million from auction sales. Credits of R500 million are to be advanced by the state to help finance such arrangements. Thus the state budget's net proceeds will not exceed about R300 million.

[405] BBC, *Summary of World Broadcasts*, SU/W0208, 6 December 1991, p. B/16.

[406] N. Petrachkova, op.cit.

[407] BBC, *Summary of World Broadcasts*, SU/W0215, A/8, 31 January 1992. The backing for this proposal is less than total. President Shushkevich, for one, is against it. *Le Monde*, 22 February 1992.

on the other hand, is a more complex and long drawn out process. If it is to be speeded up, the leadership will need to show deeper and more wholehearted commitment to the marketization process than hitherto.

4.5. THE BALTIC STATES

(i) Introduction

In September 1991, Estonia, Latvia and Lithuania became independent states. Following the failure of the August *coup* attempt in Moscow, they renewed their independence declarations, and were soon officially recognized by many other nations, including the United States and the Russian Federation. On 17 September they became members of the United Nations. By the end of the year they were receiving, or had been pledged, some technical and other assistance from the European Community and the Scandinavian countries;[408] their membership of the European Bank for Reconstruction and Development (EBRD) had been approved,[409] official contacts with the European Community, the European Free Trade Area (EFTA) and the OECD had got under way, and the three states' applications for IMF/World Bank membership were being processed with membership by summer 1992 a possibility; and there had been some progress in the reclaiming of gold held abroad on behalf of the pre-war independent predecessor states.[410]

None of this, however, has stopped their economic descent. More closely bound than any east European state to the former Soviet economy, the three Baltic nations have experienced a mixture of rapid inflation, declining output and severe shortages that is not substantially different from what has been experienced across the former USSR as a whole. Moreover, their design and implementation of programmes of institutional transformation are closer to the embryonic stage exemplified by the Russian Federation than to the more developed stage exemplified by Poland and Hungary.

In restoring and transforming their economic performance, the Baltic states face two distinct sets of hurdles: those common to the transformation attempt across the entire ex-Soviet and east European region, and those that arise from their being intricately entangled in the workings of the former Soviet economy. In the latter respect, the difference in their position from that of other central and east European economies is partly a matter of the degree of trade-dependence — their exports to the other ex-Soviet republics have been equivalent to around 50 per cent of their GDP — and partly derives from the fact that they share the Russian or Soviet rouble currency with the other Soviet successor states. Neither of these circumstances can be changed overnight.[411]

Indicators of the relative size of the Baltic economies within the economy of the former Soviet Union are given in table 4.4.1. More detailed information on their characteristics in 1990 and performance indicators from 1985 through September 1991 have been assembled in tables 4.5.1 to 4.5.6. With a combined population that was less than 3 per cent of that of the ex-USSR, and a history of comparatively recent, and clearly forcible, incorporation into the Soviet Union, the Baltic states have been able lately to capitalize on the advantages both of being marginal and of having a clear historical basis for their independence.

It is also widely believed that they have a number of potential advantages so far as economic transformation is concerned: a population with higher average levels of education than that of other former Soviet republics;[412] a higher development level than other Soviet republics;[413] a geographical position favouring the development of east-west transit services and close links with the wealthy Nordic countries; and what is widely believed to be a relatively westernized and pro-business outlook amongst their peoples.

(ii) Developments during 1991

Output in each of the three states fell significantly between 1990 and 1991. Just how large the fall was is less clear. Tables 4.5.2, 4.5.4 and 4.5.6 show substantial differences in the estimates for the fall of real NMP, January-September 1991 over January-September 1990, amongst the three economies. These differences prob-

---

[408] Some technical assistance targeted specifically at the Baltic states, particularly from Scandinavia, had begun before they attained formal independence.

[409] An EBRD strategic programme for the Baltic states was adopted by the EBRD administrative council on 28 January. *Le Monde*, 30 January 1992, p.13. The EBRD Baltic strategy report gives no figures, but states EBRD investment priorities: raising energy efficiency, reducing water pollution and assisting the diversification of energy supplies. NCA from Munich, 29 January 1992.

[410] On 22 January 1992, agreement was reached on the return of Baltic states' gold previously held by the Bank of England (or repayment of the equivalent amount), with a current value of about $140 million. *Financial Times*, 23 January 1992.

[411] For a detailed analysis of the status and prospects of Baltic states' external economic relations, see United Nations Economic Commission for Europe, *Economic Bulletin for Europe*, Vol. 43, New York, 1991, pp.74-86.

[412] See Mats Karlsson and Brian Van Arkadie (eds.), *Economic Survey of the Baltic States*, London: Pinter, 1992.

[413] PlanEcon estimates of per capita real GNP (dollars per annum) in 1989, at 1989 prices, are: Estonia 6,240; Latvia 6,740, and Lithuania 5,880, against a Soviet average of about 5,000 (Keith Crane and Matthew J. Sagers, "Estonia, Latvia and Lithuania: Baltic States' Political Profile Overshadows Economic Clout", *PlanEcon Report*, vol.VII, No.47-48, 23 December 1991). A Russian estimate for 1990 of $8,200 (probably in 1989 dollars) and an Estonian estimate, also for 1990, of $6,000 are cited by Teet Rajasalu, "Estonian Economy from Macroeconomic Standpoint", Tallinn, mimeo, November 1991. All of these estimates are based on conversion to dollars on the basis of purchasing power parities. The rough correspondence, for Estonia, between the PlanEcon and the (independent) Estonian estimates is encouraging, but all currently available assessments of the development levels of Soviet successor states in comparison with western countries are problematic..

TABLE 4.5.1

Estonia: Basic economic data, 1990

(Millions of roubles, current prices, unless otherwise indicated)

Population (end-year, thousands)	1 582
Employment (average, thousands)	796
GDP	7 936
NMP produced	5 456
NMP utilized	6 009
of which:	
consumption	4 989
accumulation	1 020
NMP in the industrial sector [a]	2 755
NMP in the agricultural sector [a]	1 107
Gross fixed investment [b]	1 966
Average money wage per month [c]	343
Retail sales	4 293
State budget revenue	2 480
State budget expenditure	2 323
Exports (domestic prices) to USSR	2 469
Exports (domestic prices) to rest of world	154
Imports (domestic prices) from USSR	2 804
Imports (domestic prices) from rest of world	612
Primary fuel in thousand tons coal equivalent [d]	
production	30 000
usage and stock change	37 600
imports from USSR (net)	7 600
imports from elsewhere	-
Electricity (million kWh)	
produced	17 200
received from other republics	..
delivered to other republics (net)	7 200

Sources: Statistical Office for Estonia; Seppo Moisio, "Economic Survey of Estonia", mimeo, Helsinki, October 1991; loc.cit., "Recent developments in the economic situation and reforms in Estonia", mimeo, Helsinki, November 1991; *Narodnoe khozyaistvo SSSR v 1990 g.*, Moscow, 1991; Statistics Finland, *The Baltic States in Figures*, Helsinki, 1991; Teet Rajasalu "Estonian Economy from Macroeconomic Viewpoint", mimeo, November 1991.

[a] Some conflict of reported figures; data here are from Moisio, November 1991.
[b] As defined for the UN System of National Accounts.
[c] Weighted average of state and *kolkhoz* earnings.
[d] Excluding hydro and nuclear energy generation.

ably have more to do with measurement errors in the various crude estimates employed than with differences in experience between the three countries.

The official Latvian assessment for 1991 as a whole is an 8 per cent fall in real GDP from the level of 1990.[414] The official GDP figures for Estonia and Lithuania will probably give a broadly similar picture. Like similar estimates for other Soviet successor states, this measure is likely to be based on an underestimate of inflation but also some underestimating of the real growth of the new private sector. With worsening shortages concentrated around the end of the year, however, the perception of a worsening economic situation on the part of the Estonian, Latvian and Lithuanian populations is likely to be more acute than a reported fall of this order would suggest.

So far as prices are concerned, the differences in consumer price index changes between the three states are probably largely the result of differences in the timing of administrative price increases and price decontrol during 1991. The Estonian authorities raised some prices administratively early in the year, decontrolled farm wholesale prices at the beginning of July, along with a number of consumer prices, and were set to remove all food price controls at the end of the year. In Latvia retail food prices were decontrolled in early December. An attempt by then Prime Minister Kazimiera Prunskiene to introduce a large rise in administered retail food prices in January provoked a sharp reaction in the Lithuanian parliament, leading to her resignation. Subsequently, however, prices were raised and then decontrolled later in the year. By the end of the year the three Baltic states had decontrolled most consumer prices, leaving some controls in place. In slightly different steps at somewhat different times, they had arrived at substantial price liberalization a little ahead of the Russian Federation. The political cost has none the less been substantial, at least in Estonia. The government of Edgar Savisaar resigned on 23 January 1992.[415]

Output in both industry and agriculture was reduced by supply bottlenecks, particularly of fuel, raw materials and components normally supplied from Russia and other CIS states. These bottlenecks included reduced supplies of animal fodder to maintain livestock production — the latter being a major item of Baltic export to other Soviet successor states. The whole question of trade with CIS states is considered in section (iv) below.

The Baltic republics all reported state budget surpluses or balanced budgets during the first three quarters of 1991. They were also running merchandise trade surpluses with Russia. Both these outcomes were expected to obtain for the year as a whole.[416] Both were at first sight rather surprising.

The two developments are closely connected. It is true that part of the explanation of the budget outcomes must be that Baltic policy makers have been less timid in raising prices and cutting food price subsidies than the leaders in other Soviet successor states. But the major source of these countries' fiscal ease has probably been a shift in their favour in the terms of trade between themselves, on the one hand, and Russia and other Soviet successor states, on the other. With the Baltic states being net exporters of food and other consumer goods to the other republics (table 4.5.8), and with energy prices, still denominated and settled in roubles, not having been raised as much as many other prices, Baltic enterprises, though handicapped by reduced volumes of imported inputs, were able to raise the current value of their sales and profits substantially.

---

[414] Maris Gailis, Deputy Foreign Minister of the Republic of Latvia, "The Current Economic Situation and Investment Opportunities", talk given at the Conference on Reintegrating the Baltic States into the World Community, Royal Institute of International Affairs, London, 23-24 January, 1992.

[415] This was the indirect result of Savisaar's request for Parliament to give his government extraordinary powers to deal with the economic crisis (*Independent*, 24 January 1992, p.10). By the end of 1992, according to the Estonian Statistical Office, the consumer price index had quadrupled (*Izvestiya*, 16 January 1992, p.1; the source does not make it clear whether this is a year-on-year or end-year-on-end-year comparison). On 30 January a new government "of experts" was approved by parliament. It is headed by Tiit Vahi, and includes seven of the former government's ministers, amongst them the Minister of Finance but not the former Economics Minister, Jaak Leimann. Baltfax from Tallinn, 30 January 1992.

[416] Mimeo reports from Statistical Office for Estonia; State Committee for Statistics of the Republic of Latvia; Lithuanian Department of Statistics; Ministry of Finance of the Republic of Latvia; Seppo Moisio, "Recent developments in the economic situation and reforms in Estonia", mimeo, Helsinki, November 1991; Rajasalu, op.cit.

TABLE 4.5.2

Estonia: Year-on-year changes in the economy, 1985-1991
(Annual percentage change; constant prices unless otherwise indicated) [a]

	1985	1986	1987	1988	1989	1990	1991 projected
Population	0.8	0.9	0.8 [b]	0.8 [b]	0.6	0.1	..
Employment	0.5	1.1	-0.9	..	-0.7	-2.0	..
NMP	2	4.4	0.8	5.3	5.5	1.1	-13.1
NMP utilized	..	..	..	..	..	..	..
Gross industrial output	3	4	3	3.1	0.7	0.1	-6.9 [c]
Gross agricultural output	-5	6.0	0.3	-5	5.5	-13	-15.1 [c]
Investment	4.7	7.2	2.9	8.5	6.2	2.7	..
Average wage [d]	..	3.2	3.5	10.5	12.0	18.7	..
Total money incomes	3.5	4.0	4.3	9.7	15.8	27.3	..
Retail sales	3.9	2	2	6.9	6	7	..
Retail prices	1	0.7	0.7	-	4 [e]	18 [f]	319 [g]

Sources: As for table 4.5.1 and *Narodnoe khozyaistvo Estonskoi SSR v 1987 g.*, Tallinn, 1988; *Narodnoe khozyaistvo SSSR v 1984 g. ... 1990 g.*, Moscow, 1985-1991; secretariat calculations.

a Percentage changes are given to the nearest whole number where the calculation did not allow more precision.
b Some conflicting end-year population figures make year-on-year calculations for 1987 and 1988 less reliable than those for other years.
c Projected 1991/1990 change in net material product of the sector.
d Weighted average of state and *kolkhoz* earnings.
e The basis of calculation of the retail price index changed in 1989-1990 from a calculation of official changes in official price-lists to observation of prices of a sample of goods. The change was partial in 1989, and completed by the end of 1990. The retail price series is therefore not comparable between 1989 and either earlier or later years.
f Implicit price index change, derived from value and volume series.
g Change in the consumer price index, not the retail price index.

The increased profits helped to swell budget revenues. This situation is, however, precarious.

(iii) Institutional changes

Estonia was clearly in the lead in economic reform thinking and legislation amongst the Soviet republics in 1987-1990.[417] This was not entirely surprising. Estonian intellectual life had for some time been comparatively emancipated. And for a long time before *perestroika* Estonia had served as a laboratory for experiments in economic organizations within the USSR. Current reforms, however, originate more directly in the IME concept (the acronym in Estonian for "Self-Managed Estonia"; *Ime* in Estonian also means "miracle") proposed by a group of Estonian economists in 1987. This was the starting point for increasingly bold legislation from 1989 onward.

Thus, before independence, policy makers in Tallinn were the first in any Soviet republic to pass a company law and a linked "transformation law", approximately on Hungarian lines, as frameworks for the commercialization of state enterprises. Plans for price liberalization were more advanced at the start of 1991 than in any other republic. And the Estonians had moved early to amalgamate separate branch ministries into a single ministry for industry.

The whole reform process before September 1991, however, developed amidst expectations that formal political independence was a long way off. A great deal of the reformers' energy went into devising measures for increasing Estonian economic autonomy within the Soviet Union. Negotiations and confrontations about conflicts of Estonian and Soviet laws, control over tax revenues and the subordination of state enterprises to Moscow dominated the process of institutional transformation. This situation has now changed, but the continued incorporation of Estonia in a single rouble currency area, and the extremely close production linkages with other Soviet successor states still constrain the process of reform. Thus a separate Estonian macroeconomic stabilization remains beyond the present powers of the Estonian authorities, though some preparation for the introduction of the Estonian *kroon* can be carried out.

Jaak Leimann, the Minister of Economics in the Savisaar government of 1990-1992, approached economic policy after independence with the aim of achieving economic improvement in two to three years — in other words, with a more modest and realistic view of the possibilities than that adopted in Russia by president Yeltsin.

In 1991, the emphasis of policy makers was on price liberalization, the establishment of Estonian control over the budget, the customs service and state enterprises, and the drafting of more reform legislation. With respect to output controls, the government in late 1991 retained the right to acquire up to 20 per cent of any state firm's output by compulsory purchase. The purpose of this residual administrative control was to enable the government to exchange Estonian products on an ad hoc basis for supplies of oil, medicines and food items in inter-state deals with other governments.

---

[417] This section draws on country reports prepared by consultants for the United Nations Economic Commission for Europe, on meetings with Baltic officials, and on *The Baltic States: A Reference Book*, Tallinn Riga Vilnius, 1991; Gailis, op.cit.; P. Hanson, *The Baltic States: the economic and political implications of the secession of Estonia, Latvia and Lithuania from the USSR*, London: Economist Intelligence Unit Briefing Report No.2033, April 1990; Karlsson and Van Arkadie, op.cit.; Moisio, op.cit.; Rajasalu, op.cit.; *Selected Anthology of Institutional, Economic and Financial Legislation* of Lithuania, Vilnius, 1991; Swedish Ministry of Finance, *Lithuania: Development Towards a Market Economy*, Stockholm, mimeo, October 1991; and issues of the Estonian reform legislation publication, *Bulletin' IME*.

TABLE 4.5.3

Latvia: Basic economic data, 1990

(Millions of roubles, current prices, unless otherwise indicated)

Population (end-year, thousands)	2 680
Labour force in employment (average, thousands)	1 409
GDP (1989)	10 928
NMP produced	8 854
NMP utilised	9 120
Gross industrial output	12 639
Gross agricultural output	4 132
Gross fixed investment	1 880
Average monthly income from employment (roubles)	292
Household consumption (1989 prices)	6 370
Retail sales	6 636
State budget revenue	4 574
State budget expenditure	4 376
Exports (domestic prices) to USSR [a]	5 039
Exports (domestic prices) to rest of world [a]	374
Imports (domestic prices) from USSR [a]	4 520
Imports (domestic prices) from rest of world [a]	1 510
Primary fuel in thousand tons coal equivalent [b]	
production	557
usage	11 959
stock-change	306
imports from USSR	10 440
imports from elsewhere	656
Electricity (million kWh)	
produced	6 647
received from other republics	7 138
delivered to other republics	3 555

Sources: State Committee for Statistics of the Republic of Latvia, *Latvia Today*, Riga, 1991; op.cit., National Accounts, mimeo, 1991; secretariat calculations.

[a] 1989.
[b] Excluding hydro and nuclear energy generation.

The privatization process had extended, by November 1991, to the divestment by the state of 150 small firms, some 10-15 state farms and three large state enterprises. Sales of enterprises had been predominantly to workers and managers in them, and management-and-labour buy-outs are considered by many to be the most practical technique of divestment for state industrial enterprises. Two major obstacles to the privatization process can be identified in Estonia that are not common to all transition economies. The first is uncertainty about how to handle restitution claims of former owners. The second is fears of a re-establishment of Russian control, in the form of private ownership by Russian firms and individuals if assets were sold off to all comers for roubles.

Country-specific obstacles to the transformation process more broadly are also linked to nationality matters. For example, the restructuring of the industrial sector, when it really gets under way, will have a particularly large impact on the Russian population of the Baltic states. Ethnic Russians account for a large share of the industrial labour force — significantly more than their 30 per cent share in the general population. Moreover, job losses are likely to be concentrated in the heavy industry branches where Russians are particularly numerous. Therefore the risk of economically driven ethnic conflicts is present, despite the fact that current opinion surveys show most Russians preferring to remain in an independent Estonia.

In *Latvia* the state of the transformation process was very broadly similar to that in Estonia. As was mentioned in the introduction, retail prices, as in Estonia, were mostly decontrolled by the end of 1991. The Bank of Latvia had taken over the local branches of the old Soviet state bank and the related specialist state banks (parallel hand-overs have occurred in Estonia and Lithuania), but by January 1992 had not organizationally separated the embryonic central bank and state-owned commercial bank functions thus acquired. Thinking on future financial institutions, however, is relatively advanced. In January the central bank president, Einars Repse, was advocating a currency board basis for the Latvian currency, the *lat*, at present scheduled for introduction in the second half of 1992.[418]

As in the other Baltic states, the privatization process has gone rather further in the farm sector than in Russia, but is not noticeably more advanced outside agriculture. In 1989-1991 some 10,000 family farms were started up. The establishment of a further 35,000 is expected in 1992, and the government projects a total of 60,000 private farms, covering 70 per cent of Latvia's arable land, by 1996. In the economy as a whole, the government objective is to move quickly to the full privatization of 25-30 per cent of all state assets other than land. The priority at this stage is for petty privatization (variously defined as enterprises with less than 300 and with less than 500 employees) and, sectorally, with branches producing directly for the consumer.

Meanwhile, the most significant development on the property rights front has been one that has no direct connection with privatization: the transfer from Soviet to Latvian state ownership of some key assets such as ports and shipping. The hard currency earning potential of these assets is considerable.

In *Lithuania* price liberalization was concentrated in the last quarter of the year. In the last three months, the official figure for the percentage of state sector sales (retail and wholesale) involving free prices went from 40 to 80. If the existence of a substantial non-state sector, employing about 10 per cent of the workforce in late 1991, is taken into account, it would seem that the environment at the end of the year was one of generally decontrolled prices. Controls remained on bread, milk and butter prices, however, and also on the prices of natural gas, oil and timber.

In principle, such price liberalization should generate a once-for-all rise in prices. It is vital to limit any second round inflationary effects by tight monetary policies. In Lithuania, as in other Soviet successor states, this has not been possible because rouble cash emission and credit expansion from Moscow have been uncontrolled. In addition, in Lithuania, policy measures have hardly been helpful: the Bank of Lithuania has put a 25 per cent ceiling on nominal bank interest

---

[418] On currency boards, see section 4.3 above and Steve H. Hanke and Kurt Schuler, *Monetary Reform and the Development of the Yugoslav Market Economy*, London: Centre for Research into Communist Economies, 1991.

TABLE 4.5.4

Latvia: Selected economic indicators, 1985-1991
(Percentage annual change; constant prices unless otherwise indicated)

	1985	1986	1987	1988	1989	1990	1991 QI-QIII
Population	0.7	0.9	1.1	0.9	0.3	-0.2	-0.3 [a]
Employment	0.3	0.6	0.6	-	-0.4	0.1	-4.8 [b]
NMP produced	-0.2	4.6	1.5	6.2	7.4	-0.2	-3.0 [c]
NMP utilized	4.3	3.7	1.7	2.3	0.4	0.5	..
Consumption	3.3	1.1	1.8	4.8	2.4	5.8	..
Accumulation	7.6	12.0	0.9	-5.8	-6.6	-17.0	..
Gross industrial output	3.4	3.5	4.0	3.3	2.8	-0.2	2.8 [c]
Gross agricultural output	-3.2	5.5	-1.7	-1.5	3.9	-10.2	-11.1 [c]
Investment	10.4	9.5	-5.7	-0.2	4.2	-8.1	..
Average wage [d]	3.1	3.0	2.9	9.0	9.8	16.3	63.4
Money incomes	3.7	3.8	3.9	9.9	15.7	18.2	..
Retail sales	2.9	1.1	1.0	8.4	5.4	8.5	..
Retail prices	0.5	5.4	4.4	4.2	5.2	10.9	115

Sources: As for table 4.5.3 and communication of 19 November 1991 from the State Committee for Statistics.

[a] Projected for 1991; population figures are end-year throughout.
[b] Projected for 1991; employment figures are averages of monthly totals.
[c] Third quarter 1991 over third quarter 1990.
[d] Average monthly earnings in the state sector and collective farms.

---

rates, and indexation of a broad range of money incomes has been at 70 per cent of price increases.[419]

In most other areas of policy, the Lithuanian government seems to have moved towards liberalization to a lesser extent than the other two Baltic republics. In particular, administrative control over the activities of most state enterprises remains extensive. In the privatization process, however, Lithuanian policy, though still at an early stage, has been managed in quite a systematic way. Tricky issues such as restitution, the role of foreign buyers, the desired degree of diffusion of future ownership, the role of vouchers in divestment, the handling of the early stages of corporatization, the method of sale, questions of land ownership — all these have been directly addressed in legislation, particularly in 1991.

The legislative solutions seem coherent, though generally rather restrictive. Thus, the Law on the Initial Privatization of State Enterprises of February 1991 provides a framework for initial corporatization and commercialization in the form of partial sale of assets to the private sector, while further divestment comes under the Law on State Enterprises. Foreigners cannot participate in the privatization process but foreign investment is otherwise facilitated by the existing foreign investment laws. Restitution may be by the return of physical assets or by financial compensation. The role of vouchers and of preferential terms sales of stock to employees are to be modest. By the end of 1991, 990 enterprises (in all branches) were reported sold (22 in industry). The reported total sale value of 660 million roubles was equivalent to 2.7 per cent of the book value of material sphere assets in the republic at the end of 1990.[420]

The Lithuanian currency, the *litas*, is scheduled to be introduced during 1992. Indications are that the banking system is far from ready to manage the macroeconomic stabilization that will be needed to give credibility to the new currency and prepare for the move to convertibility.

(iv) Relations with Moscow and the CIS

The quantities and terms of trade incorporated in transactions between the Baltic states, on the one hand, and other Soviet successor states, on the other, are central to the economic prospects of the Baltic states over the next three years. What was known about these flows during the last years of *perestroika* suggested that the Baltic states faced a rude awakening when they distanced themselves from Moscow: an abrupt shift to world market prices would reduce domestic consumption and investment substantially. The reality is less threatening, however, than it seems at first sight; none the less there are sizeable adjustment costs involved.[421]

Available data on inter-republican trade flows (as they then were), in domestic prices, in 1989 or 1990, are shown in tables 4.5.1, 4.5.3. and 4.5.5. In table 4.5.7 the apparent effects of a switch to world market prices with the established real flows are illustrated.

The underlying data used for those tables were released by the former USSR State Statistics Committee

---

[419] It might be argued (a) that there has been a certain amount of monetary restraint imposed by the supply side (rouble printing capacity) and (b) that financial prudence for a state other than Russia within the present rouble area is counter productive. These matters are discussed in section 4.3 above.

[420] Sale price and book value are not strictly comparable. It appears that total sales value exceeded slightly to book value of the assets sold.

[421] The question is discussed in greater detail in section 2.4 of United Nations Economic Commission for Europe, *Economic Bulletin for Europe*, vol.43, New York, 1991. The treatment here, though more cursory, incorporates more recent information.

TABLE 4.5.5

Lithuania: Basic economic data, 1990

(Millions of roubles, current prices, unless otherwise indicated)

Population (end-year, thousands) [a]	3 752
Labour force in employment (average, thousands)	1 853
GDP	12 907
NMP produced	9 997
NMP utilized	10 061
Gross industrial output	13 554
Gross agricultural output	5 399
Gross fixed investment	2 809
Average monthly income from employment (roubles)	283
Household consumption [b]	7 516
Retail sales	7 553
State budget revenue	4 629
State budget expenditure	4 446
Exports (domestic prices) to USSR	5 386
Exports (domestic prices) to rest of world	386
Imports (domestic prices) from USSR	5 210
Imports (domestic prices) from rest of world	809
Primary fuel in thousands tons coal equivalent	
production	..
usage	..
stock-change	..
imports from USSR	21 500
imports from elsewhere	..
Electricity (million kWh)	
produced	28 400
received from other republics	..
delivered to other republics (net)	11 800

Sources: Lithuanian Department of Statistics; idem, *Statisticheskii ezhegodnik Litvy 1990*, Vilnius, 1991; Statistics Finland, *The Baltic States in Figures*, Helsinki, 1991; Michel Pagnier, "La République de Lituanie à l'aube de son indépendance", mimeo, September 1991; secretariat calculations.

[a] The USSR annual statistical handbook gives a slightly different figure: 3728.

[b] System of National Accounts basis; resident households only.

(USSR Goskomstat) during the period of sharply rising independence demands from several republics. They showed that, in trade with the outside world, the Russian Federation accounted for 70-80 per cent of all Soviet merchandise export earnings but took a substantially smaller share of imports; that the Baltic states, like most Soviet republics, received imports from abroad to a significantly greater value than their exports (whether valued in domestic or world prices); that the cross-border merchandise flows of the Baltic republics were 90-95 per cent with other republics rather than the outside world; and that conversion of their cross-border merchandise transactions to world market prices would leave them with trade deficits that were extremely large relatively to national income. If, further, settlement of these deficits were required to be in convertible currencies, there would be no way in which the Baltic states could cope, as they had next to no hard currency.

The conclusions to be reached from these data, however, needed to be modified by taking account of a number of other considerations.

First, the balance of payments consists of more than merchandise trade, and the transit and port services of the Baltic states, supporting large shares of Soviet grain imports and oil exports, provided actually or potentially a large offsetting net credit item. They also contributed (net), through the budget and through centralization of residual profits of enterprises on their territory, to expenditure elsewhere in the USSR.[422]

Second, adjustment for turnover tax and subsidy incidence in the inter-republic flows, and for cross-border shopping, made the Baltic states' balances with other republics more favourable.

Third, a substantial component of imports into the Baltic states was for the Soviet military stationed there and for other Moscow-directed activities not necessarily desired by the local population. More generally, there was no reason to expect that the composition of trade flows amongst separate successor states making a transition to the market would closely resemble that which obtained under the old order in 1989-1990. In particular, the Baltic states' salient role as net exporters of food and manufactured goods within the old USSR (table 4.5.8) would be likely to stand them in good stead as the terms of trade evolved in circumstances of acute shortage and declining administrative control over enterprises.

Finally, the Goskomstat calculation of values in world market prices was done with a rather small number of conversion rates for broad categories of goods. Serious negotiation over prices in trade amongst successor states might throw up new terms of trade that were less unfavourable to the Baltic states than these estimates suggested, even if they did tend towards world market relative prices.

At the same time, the substantial net energy dependence of the Baltic states on Russia, in the medium term, is clear (tables 4.5.1, 4.5.3, 4.5.5). So are the Baltic states' high ratio of "intra-Soviet" trade to GDP, their acute shortage of foreign currency, the relatively low level of intra-Baltic-state trade (less than 10 per cent of cross-border merchandise flows), and the weakness of their export potential in the medium term so far as the world at large is concerned. In the medium term, therefore, it is extremely important for them to reach amicable commercial arrangements with the non-Baltic successor states, and with Russia in particular.

On the whole, developments on this front in 1991 and early 1992 have illustrated the mitigating circumstances, listed above, that are favourable to the Baltic states.[423]

---

[422] Another bargaining chip available to the Baltic states in dealings with the Russian Federation is that the region of Kaliningrad, though part of the RSFSR, is physically cut off from Russia and partly dependent on shipment through Lithuania. It also relies heavily on electricity generated in Lithuania. In bargaining with Moscow over oil supplies in early 1992, the Lithuanian government threatened to cut off electricity supplies to Kaliningrad if Russia did not deliver the quantities of oil it had agreed to provide. *Financial Times*, 13 January 1992, p.2.

[423] A careful narrative and assessment of the three months' blockade by Moscow of Lithuania in 1990 shows that some of the hidden strengths of the Baltic states were in evidence then. Above all, the Soviet leadership was unable to ensure that individual Soviet enterprises and regions did not break ranks and do mutually beneficial deals with Lithuania. (Duncan Reid-Thomas, *The Economic Blockade of Lithuania, 1990*, MSocSc dissertation, Centre for Russian and East European Studies, University of Birmingham, 1991.)

TABLE 4.5.6

Lithuania: Selected economic indicators, 1985-1991
(Percentage annual change; constant prices unless otherwise specified)

	1985	1986	1987	1988	1989	1990	1991 QI-QIII
Population [a]	0.9	1.1	1.1	1.1	0.9	0.8	..
Employment	1.1	0.9	0.9	-0.7	0.2	-2.7	-
NMP	3.3	6.3	4.8	10.7	1.6	-14.0	(-21) [b]
Gross industrial output	4	5	5	5	4	-3.9	-1.3 [c]
Gross agricultural output	8.7	-1.7	4.6	-	2.4	1.5	-9.0
Investment	6.8	14.3	5.1	11.9	-4.8	-10.4	-40.2 [d]
Average nominal wage	..	3.2	4.6	9.3	10.3	16.3	..
Money incomes	..	..	..	..	..	..	111.3 [e]
Retail sales [f]	5	0.8	2	9.9	12.3	4	..
Retail prices	..	..	..	..	..	9.1	193.3 [g]

Sources: As for table 4.5.5 and USSR Goskomstat, *Narodnoe khozyaistvo SSSR v 1984...1990 godu*, Moscow, 1985-1991.

[a] The USSR and Lithuanian statistical handbooks give slightly different population figures for some years. The growth rates here are calculated on USSR figures for 1985, and otherwise on Lithuanian Department of Statistics data.
[b] Crude estimate: current-price NMP deflated by the consumer price index for October 1991 over December 1990.
[c] January-November.
[d] 1991 projected over 1990.
[e] 1991 QIII over 1990 QIV.
[f] Reported as "volume" changes, but containing some concealed inflation.
[g] Consumer price index; 1991 QIII over 1990 QIII.

As has already been noted, the evolution of prices so far has been to the Baltic states' advantage. Acute shortages of oil and gas in the Baltic states at the end of last year are the result primarily of a general fall in output and chaos in deliveries, rather than deliberate blockade or payments difficulties.

Negotiations with the Russian Federation over mutual trade in 1992 have not so far led either to a deliberate cut-off in fuel supplies or to insistence by Moscow on hard currency payments. Bartering for food deliveries is the interim solution reached in at least one case. The Lithuanian agreement with the Russian Federation on the framework for their trade in 1992 envisages bilateral balancing with "contract prices" and a rouble clearing arrangement.[424]

Meanwhile the Latvian authorities have had some initial success in negotiating for payment by Moscow of port charges in convertible currency.[425]

Furthermore, merchant ships and port facilities in the Baltic states have been assigned, apparently free, to the governments of the region.[426]

Apart from the overriding concern with the effects of being inside the rouble area, the most urgent item on the agenda in relations with Moscow is the maintenance of the quantities of products exchanged. Under present conditions this issue is partly independent of the terms of trade. In other words, with only limited marketization of either the Baltic economies or the Russian economy, administrative controls (export licences and quotas, the use of locally issued ration coupons, etc.), rather than prices, remain the main determinants of the gains from mutual trade. To this trade problem should perhaps be added the simple matter of production and supply breakdowns for reasons beyond the immediate control of policy makers.

Internal and external debts are another, less urgent, item on the agenda. The budgets of the three Baltic states became independent of the USSR budget in 1990/91, rather ahead of the more widespread and chaotic devolution of fiscal control generally to republic level. Household deposits in Baltic branches of the old state savings bank (Sberbank) were in part sequestrated by Moscow as the Baltic state banks moved to take over the local affiliates of the former USSR state banks. Negotiations over these funds continue, though leaving them in Moscow's hands might be a politically acceptable method by which Baltic policy makers could reduce the household monetary overhang — if the current inflation does not suffice.

Negotiations between the Baltic governments and Moscow over the apportionment of the external debt of the former USSR continue. Here, as in many other areas, the stances of the three Baltic governments differ. For example, the Estonian position has been that Estonia is prepared to take responsibility for 0.5 per cent of the Soviet gross external debt (perhaps $350 million), on condition that it also can claim a share of Soviet gold and diamonds and of debt to the USSR. Lithuania is prepared to accept responsibility only for the hard currency liabilities of Lithuanian business entities; its government puts these at $37 million. The Russian leadership has shown signs of a readiness sim-

---

[424] *Ekonomika i zhizn'*, 1992 No.1, p.2. There is a provision that if either party introduces its own currency during the year the clearing arrangements will be revised.

[425] Initially only at 0.1 per cent of the value of oil products throughput. The Latvian objective for the port of Ventspils is 7 per cent. There has been talk of Russia establishing a new oil terminal near St. Petersburg in order to avoid dependence on Ventspils. Logistics, climatic conditions and the current dearth of investment funds all suggest that this would be import substitution at its most inefficient. Reasonable negotiation over port charges remains the more sensible way forward.

[426] For Estonia: *Izvestiya*, 2 January 1992, p.2; for Latvia: private communication from Latvian officials.

TABLE 4.5.7

Baltic states' merchandise trade values, 1989 or 1990
(Million roubles or dollars)

	Estonia 1989	Latvia 1989	Lithuania 1990
Panel A1. Trade flows, million roubles at domestic prices			
With the USSR [a]			
exports	2 900	5 039	5 386
imports	3 230	4 520	5 210
balance	-370	519	176
With the rest of the world [b]			
exports	270	374	386
imports	590	1 510	829
balance	-370	-1 136	-423
Panel A2. Trade flows in million roubles at world prices [c]			
With the USSR [a]			
exports	1 943	3 560	4 120
imports	4 483	6 274	7 231
balance	-2 540	-2 714	-3 111
With the rest of the world [d]			
exports	181	264	295
imports	539	893	920
balance	-358	-629	-625
Panel B. Trade flows, million dollars at world prices [e]			
With all partners			
exports	3 369	6 065	7 551
imports	7 966	11 368	13 940
balance	-4 597	-5 302	-6 389

Sources: Derived from *Narodnoe khozyaistvo SSSR v 1989 g.*, Moscow, 1991; State Statistics Committee for the Republic of Latvia; Lithuanian Department of Statistics.

[a] Including trade with the other Baltic states.
[b] These are not the values of actual transactions with foreign partners.
[c] Estimated; see box 4.5.1.
[d] Estimated for Estonia and Lithuania.
[e] Converted at average official exchange rates: 1989: R0.6034 = $1; 1990: R0.5847 = $1.

ply to take on to Russia's account the Baltics' share (however it is reckoned) of the Soviet foreign debt; certainly the possible sums involved are much smaller than the gap between the Russian share of the debt burden agreed with a number of other republics in November and the Russian share of Soviet export earnings.

All these issues should be kept in perspective. The role of negotiations with Moscow in the management of Baltic economic relations with other successor states at present can easily be exaggerated. Despite the paucity of market institutions, many of the decisions that determine the transactions that occur are taken at the enterprise level. They are often barter deals rather than the kind of transactions that occur in a developed market environment, but they are none the less at least partly out of the direct control of governments. Moreover, if the Lithuanian trade statistics for the first nine months of 1991 are any guide, the role of Russia is currently less than would be expected: it is the source of less than a half of all Lithuanian imports from other successor states.

(v) Relations with the outside world

So long as the Baltic states continue to trade with other Soviet successor states on a barter and rouble basis, their trade with other partners remains a separate category for the purposes of policy, and requires separate analysis. They all aim to shift their transactions towards the west, and they share the common east European objective of eventual membership of the European Community. In building up these links, they start from an extremely weak position.

In 1989/90 the annual merchandise exports of the three republics outside the USSR, according to the Goskomstat data, ranged between $450 million and $660 million. A large part of those exports were to eastern Europe, and did not generate hard currency earnings. An early 1992 estimate of Estonia's hard currency earning capability in the short term puts it at about $300 million per annum.[427] This is tiny in relation to Estonia's ambitions, but still quite high in relation to reported exports in 1989. The fact that Lithuanian trade in 1991 exhibited a marked shift from eastern Europe to the west, however, suggests that such a shift in the partner composition of the small amounts of

---

[427] Rein Kaarepere, chairman of the Tartu Commerzbank, speaking at the RIIA/LCCI conference in London cited above, 24 January 1992. The estimate probably applies to merchandise exports only.

TABLE 4.5.8

The Baltic states: Net export values of consumer items, 1989
(Million roubles, inter-republic and foreign trade combined; valuation at domestic prices)

	Estonia	Latvia	Lithuania	RSFSR
Non-food items				
Exports	1 809	2 451	3 029	21 368
Imports	1 136	1 416	1 842	47 419
Balance [a]	674	1 035	1 187	-26 051
Food items				
Exports	589	672	879	3 124
Imports	242	183	308	17 277
Balance	348	489	571	-14 153

Source: *Narodnoe khozyaistvo SSSR v 1990 g.*, Moscow, 1991, p.637.

[a] Apparent discrepancy due to rounding.

non-Soviet Baltic trade may be proceeding quite quickly.[428]

The fact remains that so far the export earnings of these countries must be extremely small. They may be supplemented by net earnings from tourism, transport services, remittances from abroad (some 100,000 Estonians legally visited Finland in 1990, for example, and many of them worked there), but realizing the potentially large hard currency earnings from transit and port services depends on negotiations with other successor states, and is not likely to be achieved quickly.

The external financial position of the Baltic states is strengthened by their progress in re-establishing their claims to gold held abroad on behalf of the pre-war governments. This totals some $300 million at current prices.[429] It is small, however, in light of the Baltic states' ambitions to launch their own currencies and make them convertible. The Estonian government, for example, estimates the stabilization fund required to back the move to convertibility of a future Estonian *kroon* at $200-300 million, while its likely gold holdings at current prices are of the order of $130 million.[430] Moreover, estimates made outside the Baltic states of the appropriate shares of Soviet debt that they might take on are considerably higher than those put forward in Vilnius, Tallinn or Riga.[431]

The external position will not be transformed in the near term by inflows of foreign commercial investment. It is true that the numbers of joint ventures registered in the region rose substantially last year. In Lithuania 550 joint ventures were registered, in addition to the 98 recorded by the end of 1990, together with 106 fully-owned foreign companies; in Estonia in late 1991 there were reported to be 250 joint ventures (120 with Finnish partners) registered.[432] The cumulative totals of foreign capital invested, however, remain low. One estimate puts the figure for Lithuania at the end of 1991 at $110 million,[433] and that probably refers to the authorized capital rather than the inflow that had already occurred by that time. The position in Estonia and Latvia is probably healthier, and in Estonia (especially) there has been some subcontracting of production to Estonian firms, particularly by Finnish companies, in order to take advantage of the low cost of Estonian labour; this is not necessarily done within joint venture arrangements. But a take-off in foreign direct investment is not yet in evidence.

In this situation, progress in gaining access to western public sector assistance has been important. The development of Baltic states' links with OECD, IMF/IBRD, EBRD and the EC were noted in the introduction to this section. On 10 December 1991, the three Baltic states signed declarations paving the way to membership of EFTA, and technical assistance from the Nordic states and Switzerland is already flowing. The European Commission in December approved plans for EC food aid that included $58 million for the Baltic states.[434]

So far, however, flows of Western aid have been small, and have been chiefly confined to technical assistance.

---

[428] In January-September 1991, about one fifth of reported Lithuanian "non-Soviet" exports went to Belgium, some 13 per cent to Scandinavia, and little more than a fifth to former socialist countries. Much Latvian trade with Scandinavian partners is known to be on a barter or counter-trade basis, and this probably applies to all three Baltic states.

[429] For details see United Nations Economic Commission for Europe, *Economic Bulletin for Europe*, vol.43, New York, 1991, chapter 2.4.

[430] A stabilization fund need not be touched if the exchange rate chosen for the new currency and the supporting government and central bank policies create sufficient confidence. It is hard to envisage the successful introduction and transition to convertibility of Baltic currencies, however, in the absence of visible support of this sort.

[431] E.g., a 1991 Paribas estimate, based on export shares, of $880 million for Lithuania, $680 million for Latvia and $480 million for Estonia. *Le Monde*, 22 October 1991, p.23.

[432] *Financial Times*, 2 January 1992.

[433] Vitalija Gaucaite, "Privatization in the Republic of Lithuania", report commissioned for United Nations Economic Commission for Europe, Geneva, December 1991.

[434] Radio Free Europe Radio Liberty Research Institute, "This Week in the Baltic States", 20 December 1991. Earlier EC aid arrangements also included EC subsidies for food supplies to Russia *from* the Baltic states.

> **BOX 4.5.1**
>
> *Valuation of the Baltic states' trade at world prices*
>
> *Narodnoe khozyaistvo SSSR v 1990 g.* gives data for total trade, inter-republic trade and extra-USSR trade of each republic in 1989 in domestic prices. It also gives the total trade (only) of each republic in "world prices", also in roubles (*valuta roubles*). The method of calculation of the world-price figures has not been fully explained; it is thought to be defective in some respects, but useable. For Latvia, direct reporting of extra-USSR totals at their actual transaction prices is also available. From the two valuations, a conversion ratio between world and domestic prices can be derived as follows.
>
> *Foreign trade prices of the USSR states, 1989*
> *(Ratios of world to domestic prices.)*
>
> | | USSR | Estonia | Latvia total | Latvia foreign trade only | Lithuania |
> |---|---|---|---|---|---|
> | Exports | 1.388 | 0.670 | 0.817 | 0.706 | 0.765 |
> | Imports | 0.661 | 0.914 | 0.942 | 0.591 | 1.110 |
>
> In the calculations for inter-republic trade in table 4.5.7, Panel A1, the republic export conversion rate for total trade is used to convert the domestic-price value of republic exports to the USSR into a world-price valuation, and the USSR export conversion rate is used to convert each republic's imports from the USSR into world prices. The rationale for this is that the Baltic republics' imports from the rest of the USSR were dominated by the fuel and raw material items that also dominate USSR exports in general, while Baltic export-composition in trade with the USSR is assumed to approximate that of Baltic trade overall. In calculating Estonian and Lithuanian extra-USSR trade at world prices, the republics' ratios of world to domestic prices are used for both exports and imports. (In the case of Latvia, directly reported data on extra-USSR trade in world prices, in the sense of the actual transaction prices, are available.)

(vi) Prospects

The Baltic states have coped with the first stage of independence, sustaining less damage from deteriorating terms of trade with Russia than had been predicted. Their main immediate problem has proved to be the side effects of Soviet/Russian inflation and declining real output. Cut-offs in supply seem primarily to have been the product of the chaotic situation in the former USSR. There have been no ready alternative sources of material input supplies that could mitigate the impact of these rapidly narrowing bottlenecks on Baltic production. The absence of these alternatives reflects the absence of Baltic earning power in the wider world.[435] This in turn is unlikely to be quickly expanded by increased Baltic exports, or by sharply increased foreign direct investment or aid.

The vulnerability of the Baltic states to Russian inflation, on the other hand, could in principle be ended in 1992 by the introduction of independent currencies. All three Baltic states, in fact, plan to introduce their currencies this year. The general case for a move to separate currencies in the Soviet successor states has been set out in section 4.3 above. The difficulties of carrying this through successfully, however, are as formidable for the Baltic states as for any other Soviet successor state. Above all, the institutions and skills required in the banking system to control the money supply must be in place. Technical assistance to the banks in the Baltic states is already helping, but it is questionable whether the necessary determination and clarity of purpose on the part of policy makers and the leaders of the new banking systems are yet available. There are some indications that in Latvia they may be, but the step will be a risky one in all three countries.

There is an alternative: staying within the rouble area and trusting to the success of Russia's macroeconomic stabilization efforts. It would be unwise to take such success for granted, however, in the near term; and nationalist sentiment in any case limits the options of Baltic politicians.

In 1992, regardless of the steps taken on the currency front, output is likely to decline in line with the overall decline in activity amongst the Soviet successor states as a group. The Baltic governments intend to continue with liberalization and the process of privatization, even while they remain unable to embark on independent efforts at macroeconomic stabilization.

In this situation, the opening of trading arrangements with all the neighbouring states becomes exceptionally important. The present mixture of inter-state barter, inter-enterprise barter and numerous export restrictions makes the marketization of such highly trade dependent states extremely difficult. The customs union declared between the three Baltic states themselves is something.[436] But policy makers in the region are aware that it is a minor matter, since trade flows amongst the Baltic states are very small and will not greatly increase in the near term.

---

[435] Even if the Baltic states had abundant hard currency, there would be some supply bottlenecks that could not be quickly widened, for logistical reasons. For example, the oil terminal at Ventspils has an exporting but not at present an importing capability.

[436] *Ekonomika i zhizn'*, 1991, No.41, p.2.

For all policy makers in transition economies, co-ordination and cooperation with their counterparts in other transition economies is difficult, and tends in practice to be given a low priority. This is because the pressure of coping with radical change in the domestic system preoccupies the small number of competent reform politicians and advisors, leaving them little capacity for the further chores of policy coordination. Nevertheless, for the Baltic states, negotiations to maintain trade links with other Soviet successor states should continue to be a matter of priority. Even so, it is unlikely that relatively sophisticated schemes such as a payments union can be put in place in 1992. With governments of all the successor states lacking power to ensure the fulfilment of agreements, there is likely to be constant renegotiation of barter arrangements on an ad hoc basis.

The total aid flows that might plausibly be available to the Baltic states in the near term are hard to assess. They are likely to be well below what might be needed to facilitate the transition without further sharp falls in consumption. If the EC provided aid for a few years at the rate currently applicable to its assistance to its own poor regions (about $120 per head of the target population per year), that would mean an annual flow of $960 million. That is the upper limit of likely EC assistance. One year of it would be roughly equivalent to the (once-for-all) requirements for currency stabilization funds for three Baltic currencies.[437] Assistance from Scandinavia and elsewhere will also be available. IMF finance could perhaps begin to be available from autumn 1992, providing reform programmes are acceptable.

All in all, it is clear that technical assistance, and the domestic development of market institutions and sustainable transition programmes, will be critical.

---

[437] In addition to the $200-300 million figure already mentioned for Estonia, the Lithuanians have in mind a stabilization fund of $200 million for the litas. *Financial Times*, 13 January, 1992, p.2.

4.6 PROSPECTS FOR 1992 AND BEYOND

For the time being, the prospects of the 15 Soviet successor states are closely bound to the fortunes of Russia. This close linkage will weaken in future if the more outward looking successor states manage to re-orient their economies away from the present Russian core.

The establishment of some separate currencies may, even before that, provide a degree of independence in macroeconomic policies. Several of the former Soviet republics plan to introduce currencies of their own before the end of 1992, so it is possible that some divergence in economic fortunes may be witnessed before the year is out. For the reasons discussed above, however, there is considerable doubt about the chances of success of these new currencies in the near term. It therefore makes sense to consider the prospects of the successor states in 1992 as still bound up with those of Russia. Further ahead, some divergence is likely.

At the Moscow LINK meeting of economic forecasters in September 1991, output (GDP) in what was then still the USSR was projected to fall 5.8 per cent between 1991 and 1992. At that same meeting, the 1991 outturn was projected at 12 per cent below that of 1990, or 5 per cent better than has now been reported. No known method of short-term forecasting can cope with the uncertainties of the current successor-state economy. Has the ex-Soviet economy reached a point where mechanical extrapolation of recent past rates of change will prove too optimistic or too pessimistic? With so much of the economic and political framework in doubt, it is impossible to say.

If, in 1992 as a whole, total output falls to 12 per cent below the 1991 level, the level of economic activity (as officially recorded) would be 28 per cent below that of 1989. Comparison with experience in central and eastern Europe suggests that this is quite plausible. The former Soviet Union has lagged about a year behind most of its former European allies, so far as the decline of aggregate output is concerned. If its trajectory were to follow theirs, a three-year decline of roughly this order of magnitude would be about par for this dismal course.

The most urgent policy priority is *macroeconomic stabilization*. If monetary growth is not controlled quickly, the current resort to barter and autarky will be extended still further. That will tend to pull output down still further and distort even more grossly than at present the functioning of the embryonic non-state sector. The inflationary problem is closely linked with that of inter-republic relations, for reasons set out above, and it is this nexus that makes the successor states' problems especially intractable.

It appears that the most likely route to macro-economic stabilization now passes through the establishment of several *separate currencies,* bringing fiscal and monetary policy making together at the level of successor states, and thereby strengthening incentives to budgetary prudence.[438] However, the main difficulties ahead are, with that proviso, much the same in principle whether they are tackled in one centre or several. It is now clear that all require substantial western assistance if they are to be resolved without politically dangerous losses of real income.

To reduce budget deficits and halt the growth of the money supply, the various governments — and primarily that of Russia — have to do three things that require western assistance: *contain public spending,* maintain or *increase tax revenue* and establish *control over currency emission and the volume of credit.*

The greatest pressure to raise government *expenditure* now comes from a political requirement: the need to preserve the minimum necessary support for economic transformation by maintaining real wage and social benefit levels that are tolerable. Existing "compensation", indexation and other social-safety-net arrangements can easily replace state subsidies, state investment funding and defence spending as built-in destabilizers of budgets. Western assistance, particularly in the form of large, grant-based deliveries of food, medicine and medical equipment, can in this way play more than a purely emergency role.[439]

So far as the raising of *tax revenue* is concerned, the need is for a different kind of western assistance: primarily technical assistance to design, establish and operate an effective tax collection system. The doctrine behind some western nations' technical assistance schemes, of targeting the emerging private sector, is inimical to this.[440] Yet the extreme feebleness of tax-collection is a substantial impediment to macroeconomic stabilization. Advice on the design of tax systems is already being provided to several of the successor states by the IMF, but effective implementation is needed, as well as appropriate design. The absence over much of the territory of the former Soviet

---

[438] See the discussion in section 4.3 above. Devolution of monetary policy to 15 separate authorities is less likely than devolution to a mixture of separate republics and clusters of republics. At least some leaders of successor states are explicitly opposed to the introduction of a separate currency in their own state. See the interview with President Stanislav Shushkevich of Belarus in *Le Monde,* 22 February 1992, p.6.

[439] The European Community scheme in which food delivered as food aid is sold at somewhat less than "market" prices, and the profits used to finance high priority social benefits, illustrates one mechanism. Basically, any arrangement that underpins the lowest real incomes without adding immediately to state expenditure is helpful to stabilization.

[440] The other problem is that the target is very small and partly camouflaged.

Union of a minimally efficient state administration is one of the less obvious legacies of the old system.

Western assistance now seems to be required in bringing the *money supply* under control, as well. Part of the assistance required is technical, and entails the provision of expertise in both central and commercial banking so as to create quickly institutions that could implement effective control of the money supply, as well as introducing such basic arrangements as functioning inter-bank payment systems. As with tax collection, the assistance necessary to introduce real changes soon goes beyond what can be achieved by a handful of advisors. Unfortunately, this is not all.

Until late in 1991, it was generally believed that the Soviet or Russian authorities had at their disposal some 2-3,000 tons of gold. It was therefore possible to argue that the provision of a stabilization fund to back the movement to *convertibility* for the rouble, or (in some schemes) the placing of the rouble on a gold standard,[441] was something that the country was capable of financing for itself. Technical assistance might be appropriate, but the provision of the stabilization fund or reserve was not needed. It is now reasonably clear that the successor states can neither service their external debt nor provide from their own resources any sort of backing that could create confidence in the internal value of the rouble and facilitate a move to internal convertibility at a rate that could then be held.

In Russia, the present Yeltsin-Gaidar government has apparently accepted that substantial financial assistance is not imminent. They have therefore developed plans for an autonomous stabilization attempt. This depends critically on their ability to mobilize tax revenue, to control the money supply and to build up rapidly a reserve of convertible currency by improved incentives to exporters to surrender hard currency to the Russian monetary authorities. It is doubtful whether these capabilities are sufficient, without more western help, to effect the stabilization in the course of 1992. There must be considerable doubt whether, in the absence of effective stabilization this year, the bold but rather desperate bid for rapid liberalization and privatization can be sustained.

The stabilization problem in early 1992 is therefore urgent. Its urgency calls into question the reliance of western policy makers on IMF membership as the key that will unlock all these problems. Even if Russia is admitted to the IMF before the summer, the autumn of 1992 would be the earliest time at which substantial flows of assistance could be expected from the Bretton Woods institutions. It may well be, however, that such assistance will not come before 1993,[442] and there are questions about the ability of the IMF to provide sufficient funding within present operating rules and conventions.[443]

The strong doubts about the capability of the Russian government to implement its reforms extend to a much more general question of government capability. In addition to the weakness of existing economic skills and institutions, there is a larger problem of *confidence* on the part of the population in general. There is little confidence that the present government will stay in office; there is also little confidence that, even if it does, policies and legislation will not be constantly changed; there is little trust in the legal and customary constraints on the behaviour of politicians and officials; and there is little trust between most of the governments of the various successor states. This larger weakness in the social and political environment for economic transformation is a phenomenon that can also be discerned in Hungary, Poland and Czechoslovakia, but it seems to be substantially more serious an obstacle to change in Russia and the other non-Baltic successor states.

The immediate consequence of this pervasive scepticism is that the signals sent by economic policies are either not received or, if received, are not believed. It may well be that only a reform programme that has the imprimatur of an international grouping or organization of standing, such as the IMF or the G-7, will be capable of systematically influencing expectations in the Soviet successor states, and thus giving the transformation process a chance of proceeding.

An imprimatur in the sense simply of publicly expressed approval would be helpful. But probably only *approval backed by substantial funding* would be effective. Whether the funding in support of stabilization was channelled into a successor states payments union, into the reserves for one or more currency boards, or into currency stabilization funds,[444] is perhaps less important than that some such backing for a well designed stabilization programme should be seen soon to be available.

One possibility is that the extensive analyses and discussions being conducted in successor state capitals by IMF teams at the time of writing may be leading to programmes for which financial support could be forthcoming immediately upon admission to the IMF, rather than with some delay thereafter. If that is the case, however, no stabilizing effect on expectations inside or outside the former Soviet Union can occur until it is publicly known to be the case. In the meantime, a continuation of rapid output decline and accelerating inflation is the most plausible scenario for 1992.

In the longer run, if stabilization is achieved, the development of market institutions and the subsequent revival of economic activity and eventual growth could be envisaged. In this medium-term perspective, the one clear advantage that the former Soviet Union has over central and eastern Europe is that it has two large sec-

---

[441] Advocated in the recent past by US Federal Reserve Governor Wayne Angell and by the American consultant Jude Wanniski. See the interview with Wanniski in Keith Bush (interviewer and editor), *From the Command Economy to the Market. A Collection of Interviews*, Aldershot, Dartmouth Publishing Co. for RFE RL Research Institute, 1991, pp.181-190.

[442] See David C. Roche and Richard Davidson, "Eastern European and Soviet Outlook", in Morgan Stanley Research, *Greater Europe 1992 – The Year of Living Dangerously*, Eurostrategy No.14, January 1992.

[443] This issue is summarized by Peter Torday in *The Independent*, 30 January 1992.

[444] See section 4.3 above.

tors that are already internationally competitive. These are the *natural resource extraction* sector and, more problematically, the *arms industry*. Despite very low labour costs,[445] the working of the traditional economic system seems to have precluded international competitiveness in every other part of the economy: agriculture, services and civilian manufacturing alike. In armaments and natural resource extraction, however, there is a potential for an early resumption of export growth and for the attraction of foreign investment at an early stage. The bulk of both sectors is located in Russia. At present, however, the resumption of export growth and a significant inflow of foreign direct investment seem a long way off.

---

[445] In the traditional system, exports could be priced in foreign currencies at whatever level was judged necessary to raise the revenues sought, regardless of domestic costs. None the less, the Soviet market share in OECD imports of manufactures was very small, and declined from the 1960s onwards. In the present circumstances, if foreign firms could invest and purchase inputs at the R20 per dollar rate suggested by some Russian officials for the near future, labour costs would be very low indeed. If wages average R1,500 a month, and employers' social insurance and wage-bill taxes add a further 30 per cent, hourly labour costs at an exchange rate of R20 to the dollar would be around 70 cents, compared with $1.85 in Mexico, $2.75 in Poland and $3.20 in Hong Kong (the latter figures are DRI McGraw-Hill estimates).

Chapter 5

INTERNATIONAL SUPPORT FOR EASTERN TRANSFORMATION

In the wake of the political and economic changes in the east, international assistance for transition has been progressively extended to all east European countries and the successor states of the Soviet Union. In section 5.1 the approach to assistance adopted by the international community is discussed. Financial commitments and disbursements to the east are analysed in section 5.2. Trade policy measures giving the eastern countries greater access to western markets are presented in section 5.3. Some of the policy issues stemming from this discussion are treated in chapter 1.

5.1 APPROACHES TO ASSISTANCE AND COORDINATION

When the leaders of the seven largest industrialized countries (G-7) took the decision in July 1989 to entrust the European Community with the coordination of western assistance for economic transformation in the east, only Hungary and Poland qualified for foreign support. During the next year, in the wake of the political changes throughout eastern Europe, assistance from the Group of 24 countries (G-24) was formally extended to Bulgaria, Czechoslovakia, Romania, Yugoslavia, and Albania; and after the declaration of their independence, to Estonia, Latvia and Lithuania (in October 1991). All of these countries have joined, or applied for membership of the international financial institutions.

With the breakup of the Soviet Union and the emergence of the 11 republics of the Commonwealth of Independent States (CIS) as separate policy-making entities, the number of countries embarking on the transformation of their economic systems and requiring external assistance has doubled again. In terms of the populations, and perhaps the problems to be solved, the increase in demand for support is considerably larger.

These developments pose unprecedented challenges (and opportunities), first of all for eastern countries themselves, but also for the international community — for the latter, in terms of marshalling resources for assistance, organization and vision. The following sections discuss, first of all, the approach to assistance adopted by the international community (section 5.1). Initiatives taken in favour of eastern Europe and the ex-Soviet Union are treated separately since the approaches adopted by the west have differed. Financial assistance is analysed in 5.2, and western trade policy changes designed to improve market access for the east are treated in section 5.3.

(i) Support for eastern Europe

From the very inception of the international initiative in support of the reforming east European countries, there has been broad agreement on the ultimate objectives. Assistance is to be used to promote the establishment of democratic political systems, the creation of market-based economies, and the reintegration of these countries into the world economy. Humanitarian aid may be the first necessary step to get the process of transition under way.

The achievement of these economic goals is an unprecedented task requiring, among other things, the recreation of legal and institutional frameworks essential for the efficient functioning of markets, economic stabilization and a very broadly conceived structural change.[446] The private sector has been assigned a key role by the newly elected eastern authorities and western donors, as is reflected in the focus of the G-24 programmes and the philosophy of the newly created European Bank for Economic Reconstruction and Development (EBRD).

In the light of the difficult financial situation faced by the eastern countries during the early stages of tran-

---

[446] The conditions for economic transition have been discussed in detail in United Nations Economic Commission for Europe, *Economic Survey of Europe in 1990-1991*, New York, 1991, chapter 4.

sition, external support has been indispensable.[447] It has been advanced in the form of improved access to western markets, wide-ranging technical assistance, and various types of financial support provided by the G-24, the international financial institutions[448] and, in some cases, the foreign private sector.

This assistance is intended to secure the essential reforms, help stabilize the economies, set economic restructuring in motion and thereby establish the underlying conditions for sustained economic growth. In the longer term, however, economic growth is to derive chiefly from these countries' own resources and foreign private capital, although in the area of public infrastructure development, a continuing role is seen for the development banks.[449]

Foreign capital is seen as instrumental for loosening balance of payments constraints and bringing in managerial and marketing skills and new technology. To this end, the transition economies have enacted legislation permitting foreign investment, launched privatization programmes, and negotiated a network of investment protection and double taxation agreements with the rest of the world. Many western governments have granted investment guarantees to cover the operations of their enterprises in the transition countries and have given the east greater market access with a view to increasing the attractiveness of the east European countries as domiciles for private capital. The operations of the EBRD and the International Finance Corporation (IFC) are intended to catalyse foreign private investments.

As the number of recipient countries has grown, the effective coordination of official assistance programmes, all drawing upon very limited resources, has become an increasingly challenging and pressing issue. Efficient allocation of this assistance is desirable not only in its own right, but also because it raises the chances for a successful transition to stable democratic and market systems and reduces the large social costs and the long period of the transition.

The coordination role entrusted to the EC at the G-7 Summit in July 1989, now involves the original 24 donor countries (G-24), the international financial institutions (EBRD, IMF, and the IBRD group),[450] the European Investment Bank (EIB) and the European Coal and Steel Community (ECSC) and, as regards the countries of operation, seven central and east European countries and the three Baltic states.

G-24 assistance has been organized primarily on bilateral lines. Individual G-24 (donor) countries have developed programmes in cooperation with the countries in transition (although not all G-24 members are involved in all central and east European countries). In addition to the individual efforts of the EC member states, the EC has organized and funded its own programme entitled PHARE. In its role as coordinator, a key responsibility of the EC Commission is to ensure that the offers of assistance made by the individual donor countries are complementary and also that there is no overlap with PHARE projects. This requires the oversight of numerous, often small and very narrowly defined project proposals,[451] and matching these up with the specific requirements of the recipient countries. Efforts are made to identify "gaps" in assistance.

To facilitate this coordination process, the EC makes available, among other information, an inventory of PHARE projects[452] and acts as a clearing-house for the information provided by the G-24 countries on their programmes. The process of coordination is both helped and complicated by direct contacts between the donor and recipient countries. On the one hand, this assists the recipient countries to screen out duplicate offers and allows them some choice between similar proposals. On the other hand, such aid is agreed within the framework of bilateral arrangements, the negotiation of which can severely test the limited resources of the recipient countries.[453] EC aid coordinators are now installed in all eastern countries of operation to facilitate on the spot coordination.

The *donor countries*, too, may find it challenging to achieve effective internal coordination, interact with the EC Commission and the recipient country, and assess the progress of their aid programmes. The coordinating ministry's responsibility may extend over numerous national governmental bodies, each often pursuing its own agenda.[454] Typically, these bodies deal directly with their counterparts or other interlocutors in the recipient

---

[447] See "Economic Reform in the East: a Framework for Western Support", in United Nations Economic Commission for Europe, *Economic Survey of Europe in 1989-1990*, New York, 1990, pp.5-26.

[448] Hungary, Poland, Romania and Yugoslavia were already members of the IMF and IBRD when they started to benefit from G-24 programmes, although Poland had not accessed the financial resources of these institutions. Romania had not actively participated in the institutions since the early 1980s. Bulgaria and Czechoslovakia joined the Bretton Woods institutions in 1990 and Albania in 1991.

[449] In general, western governments and to some extent also the international financial institutions have tended to view their financial contributions as exceptional and temporary.

[450] The IBRD group also includes the International Finance Corporation (IFC) and the Multilateral Investment Guarantee Agency (MIGA).

[451] See, for example, EC, *Rapport sur l'état d'avancement de l'assistance coordonnée des 24 à l'Europe Centrale et Orientale (addendum)*, 30 October 1990. Many of the G-24 projects are small, involving only tens or hundreds of thousands of dollars.

[452] See Commission of the European Communities, *Operation PHARE, Project Summaries*, first series 1990 (revision foreseen for January 1992), Brussels. This compendium provides key information on PHARE projects, by country of operation (title of programme, sector, EC monetary contribution, description, etc.).

[453] Certain authorities responsible for the coordination of aid in the recipient countries have noted that they have had to undertake simultaneous negotiations with several donor countries on the specific contents of individual aid packages. Recipients have had to define their priorities and match them with specific offers of assistance. However, achieving the desired mix of aid projects has been complicated by the tendency of donors to offer very similar types of aid (e.g., advice on privatization, business school training, etc.), often to the exclusion of other urgently needed assistance.

[454] In many G-24 countries, new administrative structures have been created to deal with assistance to the east which are separate from those administering long-running aid programmes for the developing countries. The rationale for this decision was both political and economic. On the one hand, donor countries tried to avoid charges that the new programmes were being created at the expense of the existing ones and, on the other hand, it was felt that the needs of the countries in transition were somewhat different.

countries. In some donor countries, aid programmes have been initiated at both the federal and regional levels (e.g., the German *Länder* have set up their own aid programmes for certain eastern countries).

Within the *recipient countries*, existing ministries have been assigned or new agencies formed to evaluate requirements for assistance and coordinate the incoming flows.[455] Implementation of these functions has often proved difficult because recipients lack experience in the practices of donor countries and development banks as well as in the more general activity of managing aid programmes. Not surprisingly, internal coordination has sometimes proved inadequate and new solutions have had to be tried.[456] In certain eastern countries too, the responsibility for coordinating assistance may be split between the federal and republican governments.

The EBRD, EIB, and IBRD have started up operations in all of the east European countries. Current activities involve economic infrastructure projects, the restructuring of industrial sectors and tackling environmental problems. In general, their strategies are focused on telecommunications, energy, transport, agriculture and the agro-industrial sectors. In a number of cases, these institutions have coordinated their efforts through the cofinancing of projects.[457]

Equity investments by the EBRD and IFC in east European enterprises have been picking up. Their participation is welcomed by foreign investors at a time of high uncertainty. So far their equity investments appear to be concentrated in Czechoslovakia and Hungary.

The EBRD and EIB have used *global loans* as a means to provide long-term finance for small-scale projects. Under these schemes, the development banks make available finance through an intermediary financial institution, operating on a national or regional basis, which on-lends the funds in a number of sub-loans for selected small and medium-sized projects agreed by the Banks. EIB sub-loans under its global loan facility are intended to promote investment projects with a total cost not exceeding ECU 15-20 million.[458]

In the area of restructuring of the east European economies, the EC Commission has coordinated PHARE activities (a large share of the EC aid budget is focused on economic restructuring) with the programmes of the international financial institutions. In 1990, when the programmes for Hungary and Poland were just getting under way, the EC cofinanced preparatory studies for sectoral projects (with the World Bank and the European Investment Bank) and several technical assistance programmes (with the International Finance Corporation and the World Bank).[459] Subsequently, the EC has funded numerous preparatory studies of infrastructure projects throughout eastern Europe. Project finance for these is to be provided by the development banks.

"Triangular" operations in food and medical products aim at specifically involving certain east European countries in regional solutions to problems of emergency assistance. The deals now planned are intended to help the east European countries maintain their traditional trading patterns with the former USSR and/or the successor states through the provision of external finance by the EC.[460] In earlier triangular operations, Hungary exported food to Poland and Albania. The possibility of meeting Romania's recent request for food through triangular operations has been raised by EC ministers.[461]

Provision and coordination of *macroeconomic financing* for the east European countries have been the responsibility of the EC, the G-24 and the international financial institutions. In this process, the IMF has worked with the recipient countries to design programmes for stabilization and comprehensive economic reform. Together the two define the domestic policy environment so important for the proper functioning of the various internationally backed projects and programmes. Disbursement of macroeconomic financing

---

[455] It has been frequently observed that while the reform process fundamentally aims at the decentralization of economic activity, the process of managing the transition and foreign assistance has unavoidably required the formation of new bureaucratic structures, strengthening some of the organs of central control.

[456] For example, it has been reported that the Czechoslovak government's dissatisfaction with interdepartmental coordination led it to replace the former Commission for Coordination on Non-investment Aid with a new body, the Council for Foreign Aid and Cooperation. *East European Markets*, 10 January 1992, p.4.

[457] For example, the World Bank and the EBRD are both providing loans for a district heating project in Poland. These two banks and the EIB appear to have cofinanced a telecommunications project in Hungary. It might be noted that the banks' statutes allow them to cofinance with other international institutions and governments. The EIB is a complementary source of funds. Within the framework of an appropriate financing plan, it is able to provide loans which cannot exceed 50 per cent of the cost of a project. The statutory global limitation on the EBRD's financing of the state sector may constrain its financial contributions to individual projects and encourage cofinancing activities (not more than 40 per cent of the amount of the EBRD's total committed loans, guarantees and equity investment shall be provided to the state sector).

The EIB has subscribed 3 per cent of the EBRD's capital and is represented on the Boards of Governors and Directors. The EIB played a role in the establishment of EBRD by providing appropriate assistance during its start-up phase. EIB, *Financing in Central and East European countries: Bulgaria, CSFR, Hungary, Poland and Romania*, Luxembourg, April 1991 (mimeo).

[458] EIB, op.cit.

[459] For example, in 1990 the EC financed studies evaluating Polish state enterprises to prepare them for restructuring (with the World Bank) and funded technical assistance and training for the financial sector in Hungary and Yugoslavia. See EC, *First Annual Report on the Implementation of Economic Aid to CEEC (PHARE)*, October 1991.

[460] With hard currency settlements the ex-Soviet states can no longer pay for agricultural goods traditionally purchased from eastern Europe while the east European countries cannot afford to extend convertible currency credits. The alternative, the provision of food to the ex-Soviet Union from western stocks, would only reinforce the exclusion of eastern Europe from this market. Of the ECU 500 million credit granted by the EC to the ex-Soviet Union (subsequently the loan was earmarked exclusively for Russia), ECU 125 million is to be allocated to triangular operations. The remaining ECU 375 million are to finance food shipments from EC supplies. *Agence Europe*, 16 January 1992.

[461] At the November 1991 G-24 meeting, ministers decided that Romania's request for food deliveries will be examined and any response could include financial support from the G-24 for triangular operations involving supplies from the other east European countries. EC, "Declaration of Ministers of the Group of 24 countries on coordinated economic assistance to the countries of central and eastern Europe (the CEEC)", *Press Release*, IP (91) 994.

contributed by the G-24 is conditional upon the recipient country meeting performance criteria agreed with the IMF.

By the end of 1991, two types of operations had been undertaken to provide macroeconomic support for the countries in transition. At the end of 1989, the G-24 put together the $1 billion requested by Poland for its currency stabilization fund (see section 5.2). A larger, more complex, initiative involved financing to provide support for new stabilization programmes, reform of trade and payments regimes (including the introduction of unified exchange rates and internal convertibility), and large prospective payments imbalances. In late 1990, the economic prospects for these countries appeared dismal. Among other things, the outlook was for an intensification of existing (and new) external shocks (see section 3.3) and an *ex ante* financing gap in 1991 estimated at $4 billion. Funding from the IMF (standby and oil facilities),[462] the World Bank (structural adjustment loans, project and sector financing) and the G-24 (exceptional complementary funding)[463] was arranged to meet the anticipated requirements.

This operation met with mixed success. Pledges for the full amounts requested by Czechoslovakia ($1 billion) and Hungary ($500 million) were obtained without difficulty. However, the pledges required to cover the entire financing gaps of Bulgaria and Romania ($800 million and $1 billion, respectively) could not be secured, the shortfall in each case amounting to $200-300 million.[464] Indirectly, the failure to meet the initial targets contributed to subsequent delays in disbursing committed funds.[465]

These delays were not critical for Hungary and Czechoslovakia. Both enjoyed a boom in imports from the west and still posted better than expected results on current account (see section 3.3). Only the build-up of reserves was slower than foreseen. However, shortfalls of financing had serious repercussions in Bulgaria and Romania. Since exports were falling, imports were squeezed, which exacerbated the decline in domestic output. In other words, the financial constraint resulted in sharper external adjustment than had been planned with the IMF and, presumably, unnecessary losses in economic and social welfare. The experience of Albania appears to be similar. In 1991, the country was engaged in the preparation of an IMF-approved stabilization programme. Hence, only emergency aid and limited bilateral loans were available from the G-24. These outcomes suggest that the present system of cooperation cannot always be relied upon to make funds available on a timely basis.

Aside from the question of coordination, problems typically associated with "donor driven" assistance in other areas of the world have been reported in the east European context as well. For example, donors often focus on, indeed compete for, highly visible projects. While these may be indispensable for a successful transition, less prestigious, but equally essential, projects tend to be overlooked. Offers of tied aid have been sufficiently prevalent for G-24 ministers to make recommendations on the matter.[466] Such issues are always difficult for decision makers in the recipient countries to deal with. In the east, however, the problem is exacerbated by lack of experience in managing foreign assistance.

Given the broad scope and complexity of the overall assistance effort, it is not surprising that some aspects of coordination have been found wanting and recommendations made for its improvement. For example, at the November 1991 ministerial meeting of the G-24, among others, it was stated:

"Ministers noted that the transition has reached a critical stage and that more effective international support is required to assist countries in carrying through their reforms. This will require more rapid disbursement of resources by the G-24 and the international financial institutions, increased information sharing among donors to avoid duplication of effort, closer cooperation between the international financial institutions

---

[462] A list of programmes for eastern Europe approved by the IMF during 1991 is presented in United Nations Economic Commission for Europe, *Economic Bulletin for Europe*, vol.43, New York, 1991, table 3.4.1.

[463] In addition to multilateral financing, the determination of the level of G-24 complementary financing takes account of any bilateral official grants and credits, including export credits, debt restructuring agreements with both official and private creditors, and expected flows from the private sector. The evaluation of requests for G-24 balance-of-payments assistance takes place at the level of the Brussels Network and is coordinated with the appropriate multilateral institutions. Implementation of the G-24 assistance is coordinated by a monitoring group of Financial Counsellors. Commission of the European Communities, *Common Guidelines for Coordinated G-24 Exceptional Balance-of-payments Assistance to Central and East European Countries*, Brussels, 14 June 1991.

[464] In both cases "there was broad agreement among members of the G-24 that the basic prerequisites for the granting of assistance (i.e., IMF-backed programmes, substantial financing gaps) had been met, although for Romania some participants to the initiative had reservations on the commitment of the country's authorities to far-reaching economic and political reform". EC, *Progress Report on the G-24 Balance-of-payments Assistance Initiative for Central and East European Countries*, June 1991.

[465] Under conditions initially set by the European parliament, the release of EC funds (50 per cent of each of the country loans) was to be authorized only when other G-24 countries pledged the full remaining portion. However, the EC subsequently relaxed its position when it became clear that the targets for Bulgaria and Romania would not be met and that their programmes were threatened by the delays in obtaining agreed finance. Even when donor governments had pledged funds, there were cases when the process of signing contracts and appropriating funds proved slow.

In two cases the Bank for International Settlement played an important role in providing bridging loans to the National Bank of Romania. In March 1991, the BIS extended a $300 million loan in anticipation of the disbursement by the IMF of the first tranche of a stand-by credit to Romania. In September, it granted another $180 million bridging loan, guaranteed by EC members' central banks, to provide liquidity until disbursement of the macroeconomic loan agreed by the G-24. Banque des Règlements Internationaux, *Assistance Financière et Technique Fournie par la BRI aux Banques Centrales des Pays d'Europe Centrale et Orientale* (mimeo), 6 November 1991.

The BIS has been entrusted with the coordination of technical assistance extended by the central banks of the G-10 and Austria to the central and east European countries. This has involved cooperation with the international financial institutions, in particular with the IMF.

[466] At the November 1991 G-24 meeting, ministers drew attention to the "desirability of untying assistance flows, in accordance with the rules recognized by the OECD, in order to provide enhanced opportunities for the economic reform process". EC, *Press Release*, IP (91) 994, op.cit.

and the G-24, and the taking of further steps to increase trade in accordance with the GATT".[467]

Closer coordination of assistance may be difficult to achieve. For various reasons, some G-24 governments and international institutions prefer to run their programmes independently, though this may result in parallel, perhaps competing, efforts. This may partly explain the paucity of information on certain programmes. Moreover, the overall level of resources allocated to the cooperation function may be inadequate.[468]

(ii) Support for the ex-Soviet Union

The organization of foreign assistance for the Soviet Union and its successor states has evolved somewhat differently from that set up for central and eastern Europe. International assistance has been extended chiefly on a bilateral basis, without a coordinating structure comparable to the EC/G-24 arrangements. The areas of assistance for the ex-Soviet Union comprise credits facilities, humanitarian and technical assistance, development of relations with the international financial organizations, and the resolution of certain financial issues through the involvement of the G-7.

In the year after the ex-Soviet Union showed the first signs of financial difficulties (in early 1990),[469] the international community pledged loan guarantees and trade credits worth over $20 billion.[470] The loans, generally restricted for specific purposes, have been arranged bilaterally. In contrast to the conditionality attached to financing for eastern Europe, that to the ex-Soviet Union was not formally linked to fundamental economic reform. However, donors did strongly encourage the Soviet authorities to put a credible reform programme in place.

A large share of the financial assistance contributed to the former Soviet Union and its successor states has been designated for the purchase of food. Responding to growing Soviet needs, the EC and the United States allocated some $2 billion in food credits and grants in late 1990. In October 1991, a package amounting to some $7.5 billion was assembled under the auspices of the G-7,[471] with the EC, Japan and the United States contributing equally. Separately, Germany has launched major relief initiatives which have included significant private participation. In the emergency efforts undertaken during the winter of 1991-1992, some donor countries have provided transportation to the CIS states and have distributed the food locally to selected groups. The EC programme involves selling donated food, chiefly in Moscow and St. Petersburg, which have been hit particularly hard by the breakdown of the centralized distribution system. This policy aims at bringing prices down without discouraging the entrance of new suppliers into the market. Revenues raised through sales (counterpart funds) have been used to support the needy.

The Soviet Union has received increasing amounts of technical assistance from bilateral and multilateral sources.[472] The immediate aim of much of it is to help the country mobilize its own resources to overcome pressing internal problems in the areas of public and private management, financial services, energy, transport and foodstuffs distribution. However, longer-term structural issues are also being addressed.

Against the background of a worsening domestic supply situation and the multiplication of western aid initiatives, the United States called an international conference to improve coordination and plan new initiatives.[473] Five working groups were set up by the conference (technical assistance, energy, medical assistance, shelter, and food assistance). Each group identified the key problems in its area, established working plans for future action, including consultations with CIS authorities and setting priorities. A common thread running through the plans is the use of market solutions to deal with the problems and the use of external assistance to strengthen emerging markets. The EC will host a follow-up conference in Lisbon in May,[474] which is to examine the progress of the work groups. Currently the conference constitutes the only formal structure for coordinating bilateral assistance to the CIS.

Acting on behalf of official creditors, the G-7 has undertaken to resolve certain questions stemming from the ex-Soviet Union's financial crisis (see section 4.1(vi)). In October 1991, the group was instrumental in getting most of the republics to accept responsibility for collectively servicing the ex-Soviet Union's debt (although the agreement appears to have broken down). This agreement was significant for two other reasons. First, G-7 governments made new credit guarantees to individual republics conditional upon

---

[467] EC, *Press Release*, IP (91) 994, ibid.

[468] For example, see EC, *First Annual Report on the Implementation of Economic Aid to CEEC (PHARE)*, October 1991. Referring to the PHARE programme and the G-24's overall assistance, the report notes that "Constraints on staffing levels will continue to be a major preoccupation for the Commission over the years ahead ...".

[469] The emergence of the Soviet Union's financial difficulties is discussed in United Nations Economic Commission for Europe, *Economic Survey of Europe in 1990-1991*, New York, 1991, chapter 3.

[470] Financial assistance granted during the past two years is discussed in section 5.2.

[471] This package included some funds committed already in the previous year.

[472] The EC, for example, allocated ECU 400 million for technical assistance to the ex-Soviet Union in 1991 and a further ECU 500 million was made available for 1992. The EBRD, of which the ex-Soviet Union was a founding member, established a programme of technical assistance for the ex-Soviet Union, which has now been extended to the successor states. The World Bank set aside $30 million to fund technical assistance projects in the ex-Soviet Union after the country had gained associate membership (see below).

[473] The International Conference on Humanitarian Assistance to the former USSR (Washington conference) was held on 22 and 23 January 1992. Forty-seven countries and international organizations participated, including those countries comprising the G-24.

[474] Japan may offer to host the third conference.

their adherence to the accord. Second, it set the stage for the formal rescheduling of the ex-Soviet Union's outstanding official (Paris Club) and commercial (London Club) bank obligations in January 1992.

It should be noted that a number of issues related to the CIS states' servicing of ex-Soviet and future debt have led western authorities to hold back the disbursement of some assistance pledged during the past two years. In the wake of the political upheavals and the absence of credible interlocutors, several western countries suspended credit facilities (some originally arranged in 1990), which have only recently been reactivated. Second, the Ukraine's decision to service its share of ex-Soviet obligations (16.37 per cent) independently has disqualified it from new loans. A third problem encountered by western donors (or their banks) has been the reluctance of the Russian financial authorities to guarantee new loans. For example, this stance is reported to have delayed agreement with the EC on an ECU 1.25 billion ($1.6 billion) credit intended for purchases of food and medicine.

Unlike the other eastern countries, the Soviet Union has not been a member of the Bretton Woods organizations and thus has not been entitled to draw upon their considerable resources. Until recently, the relations of the ex-Soviet Union with these institutions had grown slowly. In 1990, the Soviet authorities cooperated with international organizations to prepare a study on the Soviet economy.[475] A special association status in the IMF was granted in October 1991, entitling the Soviet Union to technical assistance, but not access to the credit facilities. However, since then the IMF has been very active in collecting the information required to design economic reforms and stabilization packages for the successor states of the Soviet Union.

Given the deteriorating economic conditions in the CIS states, their membership in the IMF has taken on urgency.[476] Their membership is now fully backed by the largest industrialized market economies, which also see the Bretton Woods institutions as the main source of large-scale financial assistance. The decision of the successor states to seek membership independently should facilitate the process.[477] However, the size of the CIS states' quotas is a key issue requiring resolution before their admission is approved. It has been reported that the G-7 have proposed a quota of 2-2.5 per cent of the IMF's capital for Russia, equivalent to SDR 3.6-4.5 billion.[478] This would entitle it to drawings of around $20 billion over a period of four years. The combined quota of the 15 republics would amount to 4.5 per cent of the Fund's capital. Individual quotas would be determined applying a formula similar to that used by eight of the republics to share out the former Soviet Union's assets and liabilities. Russia, however, is reported to be seeking a quota of 4-4.2 per cent for itself.[479]

Prospects for the creation of a *rouble stabilization fund* for Russia appear to have improved. However, it is not clear whether the other CIS countries would be eligible to access the fund or whether separate funds would eventually be created for them.[480]

As the CIS states embark on economic reform and begin to implement stabilization policies, they will require substantial additional financial support from the international community. One option for them is to introduce a common stabilization programme based upon the maintenance of a single currency (the rouble). An IMF stand-by credit and other macroeconomic support, perhaps including a currency stabilization fund – would be envisaged in the event of balance-of-payments disequilibria and to strengthen foreign exchange reserves.

However, a number of the republics intend to introduce their own currencies.[481] In this situation, the republics may have to adopt individual stabilization programmes, supported by separate stabilization funds and adequate national reserves. Other payments arrangements might be workable – a system of currency boards or a payments union among the republics – and perhaps useful to help avoid the entrenchment of bilateral trading in the area. However, these options too, would require external funding. It has been estimated, for example, that some $50 billion would be required to form a currency board reserve for all of the successor states of the former Soviet Union (these options are discussed in section 4.3(vii)).

Estimates of the macroeconomic financing requirements of the CIS countries vary considerably. Russia has requested $12 billion for balance-of-payments support and $5 billion for a stabilization fund.[482] Presumably the combined needs of the other CIS countries would be smaller. Separately, stabilization funds estimated at some $200-300 million and $200 million will

---

[475] The study was undertaken at the behest of the G-7, meeting in Houston in July 1990. See International Monetary Fund, International Bank for Reconstruction and Development, Organization for Economic Cooperation and Development, and European Bank for Reconstruction and Development, *The Economy of the USSR: Summary and Recommendations*, December 1990. Soviet participation in the study was one of the preconditions for the possible extension of large-scale financial assistance.

[476] Membership in the IBRD is obtained automatically with membership in the IMF.

[477] Estonia, Latvia and Lithuania applied for IMF membership in 1991 and Ukraine in late December 1991; the Republics of Armenia, Azerbaijan, Kazakhstan, Kyrgyzstan, Moldava and the Russian Federation in January 1992.

[478] *Financial Times*, 22 February and 3 March 1992. The quotas in SDRs are calculated on the basis of a total capital of SDR 180 billion, which assumes that the planned 50 per cent increase in quota is ratified.

[479] Ibid.

[480] *International Herald Tribune*, 17 February 1992.

[481] Aside from their stated intension to introduce national currencies, it is probable that a CIS-wide stabilization programme would not succeed. If the republics fail to restrict national budget deficits, the target for the central budget is likely to be missed as well. A system of individual currencies, with each republic assuming full responsibility for its own budget, may be a more workable arrangement for gaining control over inflation. On these points see section 4.3(vii).

[482] These figures were mentioned by Russian President B. Yeltsin on the occasion of his trip to Washington, D.C.

be required to back the planned Estonian *kroon* and the Lithuanian *litas*, respectively.[483]

In the absence of reliable statistics, the potential contribution of the CIS to these efforts is uncertain. The most recent BIS data on deposits of the ex-Soviet Union (generally used as estimates for foreign currency reserves) show a position of $7.6 billion at the end of September 1991. This represents scarcely two months' import requirements in convertible currencies. However, it is unclear how much of this remains since Russian officials have claimed recently that reserves had essentially run out by the end of the year. Gold holdings of some 240 tons (worth some $2.5 billion) were reported toward the end of 1991,[484] but more recently it has been claimed that, with the demise of the Soviet Union, all gold was gone.[485] The authorities of the ex-Soviet Union had on various occasions reported financial claims on the developing countries amounting to over $100 billion, but debt service to the Soviet Union was said to be very low. Proposals have been made within the G-7 to help the successor states tap this potential source of funds. However, even if this is feasible, it is unlikely to help the CIS states with their immediate needs for cash. By some estimates, considerable amounts of capital have left the country (see section 4.1(iii)). However, the chances are small that it will be repatriated before a stabilization programme is in place and confidence develops. A forthcoming IMF and IBRD report, scheduled for presentation at the Lisbon Conference in May 1992, is expected to clear up uncertainties about the CIS states' financial positions.

---

[483] *Financial Times*, 13 January 1992. These currencies may be introduced in late 1992, but no precise date has been announced.

[484] For a review of reports on the level of Soviet gold holdings in 1991, production and internal use, United Nations Economic Commission for Europe, *Economic Bulletin for Europe*, vol.43, New York, 1991, chapter 3.

[485] According to Mr. Matukhin, Chairman of the Central Bank of Russia. The gold holdings of Estonia, Latvia and Lithuania are discussed in section 4.5.

5.2 FINANCIAL ASSISTANCE

The objectives of this section are to establish the magnitude, type, and availability of financial assistance committed to eastern Europe and the successor states of the Soviet Union; to measure the actual flows of assistance in 1990 and 1991; and to examine the outlook for the flow of assistance in 1992.

(i) Eastern Europe

Commitments

As coordinator of the G-24 programme, the EC has been entrusted with the collection of information on the financial commitments of G-24 member countries to central and eastern Europe. Between January 1990 and the end of June 1991, these commitments cumulated to nearly $32 billion (ECU 26 billion; see table 5.2.1).[486]

Poland and Hungary, the first countries to commence the transition process and request assistance, have received the greatest share of specified commitments (30 per cent and 18 per cent respectively). Yugoslavia (15 per cent), CSFR (7 per cent), and Bulgaria and Romania (5 per cent) trail further behind; and funds for regional programmes[487] account for the remaining 20 per cent (table 5.2.1). Of the donors, the European Community (73 per cent), Japan (9 per cent), and the USA (8 per cent) have made the highest nominal contributions.

Trade credits (including guaranteed bank credits) and investment guarantees comprise the largest type of G-24 assistance (36 per cent). Poland is the largest beneficiary.

The bulk of *macroeconomic assistance* consists of exceptional untied balance-of-payments financing which was intended to complement IMF lending during 1991. Disbursal of these funds to the countries involved is conditional on their achievement of criteria agreed with the IMF. The total commitment to Hungary includes an ECU 870 million ($1 billion) structural adjustment loan agreed by the EC in 1990 which also helped Hungary to meet its high debt-servicing obligations. It might be noted that the initial targets for support for Bulgaria and Romania amounted to $800 million and $1 billion, respectively. They were later reduced to $600 million and $700 million, respectively, because several potential donors did not contribute as expected.

Also included in this category is the $1 billion *currency stabilization fund* established for Poland for possible use in 1990, which was subsequently extended through 1991.[488] It differs from other types of macroeconomic assistance in that the funds could only be drawn if the exchange value of the zloty were threatened (which it never was during that period). The fund was never considered part of the country's foreign exchange reserves. None the less the fund's existence was undoubtedly an important source of support for Poland's newly-established exchange rate in 1990.

The value of *debt reorganization* is put at $2.8 billion (table 5.2.1). However, this figure appears incomplete, since it is lower than the combined operations in favour of Bulgaria and Poland. Also the ex-German Democratic Republic's claims on former CMEA trade partners (originally in roubles), taken over by Germany at reunification, are absent (but these are recorded in the flow data below).

The *economic restructuring* category comprises technical assistance and funds for specific projects, a considerable part of which is accounted for by EIB and ECSC loan commitments. The EIB has been authorized by the EC to lend a total of ECU 1 billion to Hungary and Poland and ECU 700 million to Bulgaria, Czechoslovakia and Romania.[489]

In addition to the assistance provided by the G-24, substantial funds have been made available by the *multilateral financial institutions* (table 5.2.2). IMF facilities totalled some $8 billion, of which $3 billion was disbursed in 1991, while the World Bank approved loans of some $5 billion during its 1990 and 1991 fiscal years (around $2 billion was disbursed in 1991).[490]

Since donor countries attach various terms and conditions to assistance, recipients' access is not automatic and any disbursements may considerably lag the

---

[486] The EC compiles the data on commitments on a rolling 18-month basis. The previous period used extended from July 1989 (when the G-24 effort was launched) to end-1990. The data were presented in the United Nations Economic Commission for Europe, *Economic Bulletin for Europe*, vol.43, New York, 1991.

[487] This category includes commitments for unspecified purposes.

[488] The $1 billion stabilization fund for Poland was assembled by the G-24 in late 1989 and has been administered through the Federal Reserve Bank in New York. The funds were intended to support the new exchange rate of the zloty when internal convertibility was introduced in early 1990. The funds were not required in 1990 or 1991. However, they may eventually be available for the promotion of foreign investment in Poland.

[489] EIB and ECSC lending to Yugoslavia takes place under an earlier protocol.

[490] For a list of World Bank projects approved for central and eastern Europe since 1989, see *Economic Bulletin for Europe*, vol.43 New York, 1991, table 3.4.2. The European Bank for Reconstruction and Development decided on loans and investments of $500 million through the end of 1991 (lending having started in September 1991), which are not reflected in table 5.2.2.

TABLE 5.2.1

Assistance committed by the G-24 to eastern Europe
(Cumulative January 1990-June 1991, billion US dollars)

Recipients	Total Assistance	of which:[a] Economic restructuring	Trade credits & investment guarantees	Debt reorganization	Emergency aid	Macro-economic assistance	of which: related to IMF lending
Bulgaria	1.6	0.2	0.7	-	0.1	0.6	0.6
Czechoslovakia	2.2	0.3	1.0	-	-	1.0	1.0
Hungary	5.9	0.6	1.9	-	-	3.4	0.5
Poland	9.7	1.2	3.8	2.8	0.5	1.4	-
Romania	1.7	0.4	0.3	-	0.3	0.7	0.7
Yugoslavia	4.7	0.4	2.8	-	-	-	-
Regional/Unallocated	6.2	2.3	1.0	-	0.1	0.2	-
Total	31.9	5.8	11.5	2.8	1.0	7.1	2.9

Source: Commission of the European Communities, *Scoreboard of G-24 assistance, US$ Tables*, Brussels, 30 October 1991 and *G-24 Assistance to central and eastern Europe, Summary Tables*, Brussels, 11 November 1991. For a discussion of the individual categories, see text.

a Selected types of assistance are presented here, hence these columns do not necessarily add to the reported total (column 1).

TABLE 5.2.2

Global assistance committed to eastern Europe
(Cumulative January 1990-June 1991, billion US dollars)

Recipients	Total	of which: G-24	International financial institutions	Of which: IMF	IBRD
Bulgaria	2.2	1.6	0.5	0.5	-
Czechoslovakia	4.0	2.2	1.9	1.5	0.4
Hungary	9.1	5.9	3.2	2.2	1.0
Poland	14.6	9.7	4.9	2.8	2.1
Romania	2.8	1.7	1.1	1.0	0.2
Yugoslavia	5.9	4.7	1.2	0.1	1.1
Regional/Unallocated	6.2	6.2	-	-	-
Total	44.8	31.9	12.8	8.1	4.7

Source: Commission of the European Communities, *Scoreboard of G-24 assistance, US$ Tables*, Brussels, 30 October 1991 and *G-24 Assistance to Central and eastern Europe, Summary Tables*, Brussels, 11 November 1991.

actual commitment. Practices restraining use of committed funds include:

— the tying of credits to the purchase of specific goods and services;

— the need to obtain commercial banks' acceptance of the conditions attached to an official guarantee prior to the opening of a line of credit;[491]

— the access to loans is spread over a number of years;

— the acceptance of an IMF-approved stabilization programme set as a precondition for disbursal of the first tranches; disbursal of subsequent tranches is conditional upon achievement of programme targets.

— the need for legislative approval in the donor country or lengthy bilateral negotiations over specific conditions;

— the G-24's reported commitments include their capital subscriptions to the EBRD (at least part of which is recorded as grants); however this money will become available to the east only through eventual EBRD loans and investments.

It should also be borne in mind that some types of commitment listed in table 5.2.1, while considerably easing recipient countries' balance-of-payments constraint or promoting capital inflows, may not provide a good measure of the size of direct flows of new credits which might result. These includes debt restructuring and forgiveness, stabilization funds of the type set up for Poland and investment guarantees, the latter intended to foster flows of private investment. Taken together, such support accounts for an important share of G-24 commitments.

The EC has estimated grants at $6.5 billion, or somewhat over 20 per cent of total commitments to eastern Europe. However, the EC has been unable to estimate the full *aid element* of these commitments, as defined in box 5.1, since it lacks sufficient information from donor countries to calculate the value of bilateral loans given on concessionary terms (all multilateral credits appear to be non-concessional).

---

[491] As the perceived creditworthiness of most eastern countries deteriorated in 1990, private banks were no longer willing to accept normal conditions on guarantees (e.g., principal repayments guaranteed only up to 98 per cent).

> **BOX 5.1**
>
> *Framework for measuring external financial resource flows*
>
> 1. Aid; *of which:*
>   Grants
>   Aid loans, including reschedulings
>
> 2. Other official loans (OOF)
>   Official export credits
>   Official sector equity and portfolio investment
>   Reschedulings and loans to refinance repayments
>
> 3. Private sector flows
>   Direct investment
>   Portfolio investment
>   Export credits (unguaranteed bank loans)
>
> 4. Total resource flows (total receipts)
>
> *Definitions:*
>
> Aid: Comprises those grants and loans to recipient countries provided by official agencies, each transaction of which meets the following tests; (i) it is administered with the promotion of the economic development and welfare of the recipient countries as its main objective; (ii) it is concessional in character and contains a grant element (the degree of concessionality of a loan) of at least 25 per cent.
>
> Grants: Includes transfers, in money or in kind, for which no payment is required. It includes grants for technical cooperation and grant-like flows (e.g., loans repayable in recipients currencies).
>
> Aid loans: Comprises loans with maturities of over 1 year and meeting the criteria set out for aid (above) extended by governments or official agencies. This category includes reschedulings and loans made by a government or an official agency to refinance indebtedness due to the private or official sector when they are reported as aid.
>
> Other official flows: Transactions by the official sector whose main objective is other than development-motivated, or, if development-motivated, whose grant element is below the 25 per cent threshold. The category includes debt reorganization undertaken by official sector at non-concessional terms (irrespective of the nature of the original creditor).
>
> *Source:* OECD, *Geographical Distribution of Financial Flows to Developing Countries, 1986/1989*, Paris 1991.

Disbursements: 1990-1992

During the past year, the OECD secretariat has begun to collect data on financial flows into eastern Europe from its member countries and multilateral agencies. In table 5.2.3 these data, so far available only for 1990, have been arranged according to the standard framework developed for recording flows of financial resources to the developing countries.[492] Since this is the first time that such data have become available for the east European countries, the financial framework and relevant definitions are presented in box 5.1.

Gross resource flows into eastern Europe amounted in 1990 to $9.7 billion.[493] Of this Poland accounts for over 40 per cent, Hungary for one quarter and the other countries about equally for the remainder. This distribution in part reflects the fact that Hungary and Poland were the first countries to benefit from G-24 programmes and qualified for assistance from the beginning of 1990. The eligibility of the other east European countries was formalized only in the latter part of that year, with few actions being initiated. Indeed, aside from the restructuring of debt, financial inflows into these countries were marginal, the largest being humanitarian assistance for Romania.

The bulk of the reported assistance in 1990, nearly $6 billion, was *exceptional financing* (rescheduled official and private debt), of which $4.5 billion represents Germany's refinancing of transferable rouble deficits of

---

[492] These data are compiled by the OECD from questionnaires to member countries and will be available annually. The figures for 1990 are incomplete (particularly regarding "Other official flows", including "refinancing", "direct investment" and "Other private flows" and thus are subject to revision (table 5.2.3). Data on flows to Albania and Yugoslavia are not included in this compilation. Both have been classified as developing countries by the Development Assistance Committee (DAC) and thus are covered in the annual publication, *Geographical Distribution of Financial Flows to Developing Countries*. At this time only figures for 1989 are available.

[493] Information on *repayments* to OECD countries is particularly incomplete, which vitiates estimates of *net flows*. However, it is probable that a full accounting of rescheduled debt and the large outflows of bank credits in 1990 (both representing repayments) would show a negative flow of financing for eastern Europe in 1990 (as the data below indicate).

TABLE 5.2.3
G-24 disbursements and other financial flows to eastern Europe in 1990

Type of assistance	Bulgaria	CSFR	Hungary	Poland	Romania	Total
Official aid	12	21	64	1 295	240	1 710
of which:						
Grants	12	21	64	845	221	1 241
Loans	..	..	..	450	19	469
Other official flows	770	1 021	1 579	2 744	741	6 865
of which:						
Export and other credits	26	37	776	263	-	1 101
Rescheduled debt to west	..	..	..	1 231	..	1 231
Rescheduled debt to ex-GDR	744	984	803	1 250	741	4 522
Multilateral (IBRD)	-	-	113	54	..	167
Total official flows	781	1 042	1 755	4 093	981	8 742
FDI and other private flows	45	26	428	37	..	925 [a]
Total resource flows (gross)	827	1 068	2 184	4 129	981	9 667 [a]

Source: OECD, *Flows to Central and Eastern Europe in 1990*, Paris, October 1991.

Note: Estimates of Germany's contributions are based on budgetary appropriations since no figures on gross disbursements and repayments are presently available. The data may not reflect the full extent of support provided, in particular as regards debt rescheduling.

[a] Total private flows as reported in the OECD source. All components are not available, therefore total resource flows for individual countries do not add to the reported total ($9.7 billion).

the east European countries in their trade with the former German Democratic Republic in 1990.[494]

Disbursed *official aid* totalled $1.7 billion, most of which is *grants* ($1.2 billion) and the remainder *loans at concessional terms*. This latter category includes reported commitments of $546 million to Poland's $1 billion stabilization fund.[495]

The EC has estimated the value of G-24 (including EC) gross official resource flows to the five east European countries in 1990 at some $4 billion.[496] This represents a *disbursal rate* of about 20 per cent in 1990 (calculated relative to G-24 commitments adjusted on a 12-month pro rata basis).[497] If the restructured debt to the west ($1.2 billion) and the approximately $600 designated for Poland's stabilization fund are excluded, the flows amount to some $2.3 billion (reducing the disbursal rate to some 12 per cent). The lower figure may give a better picture of the flow of *new* official funds to the east European countries in 1990. It should be stressed that both figures exclude private finance, which is not covered by the EC's statistics and for which the OECD data are incomplete (only $925 million were reported).

TABLE 5.2.4
Eastern Europe: Gross financial resource flows, 1990, and outlook for 1991 and 1992

	1990	1991 [a]	1992 [b]
Private capital [c]	2.0	3.8	4.8
of which:			
Foreign direct investment	0.6	1.6	1.9
Official capital	2.2	8.6	5.0
Development banks [d]	0.2	1.6	3.0
G-24/EC	1.5	3.0	0.6
IMF	0.5	4.0	1.4 [e]
Total new capital	4.2	12.4	9.8
Rescheduled obligations	5.8	7.4	4.7
Total resources	10.0	19.8	14.5

Sources: For 1990, ECE estimates based on table 5.2.3 (excluding grants). Private capital reflects only publicized credits (table 3.3.8) and FDI (table 3.3.11). For 1991 and 1992, same as table 3.3.14.

[a] Revised outlook.
[b] Preliminary.
[c] Includes officially supported export credits.
[d] IBRD and EBRD.
[e] Reflects only programmes arranged in 1991 (see section 3.3).

---

[494] "Exceptional financing" consists of rescheduled principal and interest coming due and debt forgiveness. The incomplete data presented here are believed to understate the importance of assistance extended through the refinancing of debt in 1990. Revisions to the data are foreseen. It should be noted that the rescheduling of debt (recorded as a *gross* flows) represents a zero *net* flow of resources since the refinancing of debt (in effect a loan to the recipient country) simply covers the repayment coming due (but which the debtor is unable to settle from his own resources).

[495] The $546 million committed to the stabilization fund includes a grant of $110 million made by the United Kingdom. Poland earns interest on at least a part of the funds comprising the stabilization facility.

[496] This comparison involves adjusting the OECD data in table 5.2.3 to achieve rough comparability to the stock of G-24 commitments in table 5.2.1. This requires excluding private flows (including direct investment), the contributions of the international financial institutions, and the (rescheduled) rouble trade balances. See Commission of the European Communities, *Scoreboard of G-24 Assistance: Commentary*, Brussels, 30 October 1991.

[497] As regards the rate of disbursement, the EC has noted that it was only toward the end of 1990 and the beginning of 1991 that the process of implementation of assistance programmes could get into full swing. As most of the programmes, including PHARE, consist of or have important initial elements of technical assistance, the amounts of disbursement is expected to be small in relation to commitments over the first 2 to 3 years. EC, *First Annual Report*, op.cit.

Although data on disbursements are not yet available for 1991, a rough idea of the magnitudes can be obtained from preliminary estimates in table 5.2.4. Bearing in mind that the data for 1990 and 1991 are not fully comparable,[498] gross financial resource flows into eastern Europe are estimated to have nearly doubled to $20 billion in 1991 while new capital (i.e., excluding debt restructuring) tripled to $12 billion. All official creditors boosted disbursements rapidly.

Preliminary forecasts for 1992 indicate that total new capital may fall to less than $10 billion (table 5.2.4). IMF and G-24 lending are slated to fall, a decline which will be only partially offset by higher disbursements from the development banks. Private capital (including guaranteed export credits) is to rise, in part because of a further increase in direct investment.[499]

Net transfer of financial resources

A net inflow of financial resources[500] during the critical stages of economic reform would have been desirable, but in fact most east European countries, including the pacesetters, Hungary and Poland, experienced a net outflow in 1990 (table 5.2.5). In general, this was due to the withdrawal of funds by commercial banks (see section 3.3). This outflow more than offset new lending by the international financial institutions and G-24 countries. The heavy interest obligations of Poland and Hungary (and Hungary's large repayments of medium- and long-term debt) were also a factor in this regard.

In 1991 the situation improved, the combined transfer of resources into Czechoslovakia, Hungary, Poland and Romania amounting to $4.4 billion. Only Poland continued to experience an outflow. Hungary and, to a lesser extent, Czechoslovakia benefited from operations in the international capital markets, greater foreign direct investment and EC/G-24 credits. Excluding IMF lending — the $3 billion drawn from the IMF was primarily intended to bolster foreign currency reserves[501] — financial transfers into these four countries amounted to $1 billion. Or put differently, only $1 billion in foreign funds entered their domestic economies.

The financial outlook for 1992 (table 5.2.4) suggests that total new capital available to eastern Europe will decline, which in turn would tend to reduce the positive transfer of resources enjoyed in 1991. However, the actual flow will also depend on, among other things, repayments coming due and the commercial banks' policies on new credits.

Concluding comments

G-24 *commitments* of assistance made to eastern Europe are quite large (some $32 billion), all of it with the potential for reducing balance-of-payments constraints and giving impetus to economic development. Since the figure includes very different types of assistance, it needs to be interpreted with caution. In particular it should be borne in mind that rescheduled debt is included and that the various conditions attached to the resources are likely to preclude automatic disbursal.

The bulk of the assistance to the east has been extended on a non-concessionary basis, and thus is debt-creating. The amount of aid (grants and concessional loans) appears to be relatively small. Since the terms "aid" and "assistance" tend to be used interchangeably, the large commitments of assistance have led to misunderstandings about the magnitude of western aid to the east and concern about the diversion of aid from the developing world.

Virtually all bilateral and multilateral loans — for example those extended so far by the G-24 and EC for macroeconomic support — have been offered at market conditions (i.e., at cost to the creditor country or institution plus fees). None the less, for the transition countries these loans contain an implicit subsidy and are an important source of external support. Most eastern countries lack access to the private credit markets and those which do have access pay a large premium (CSFR and Hungary have paid some two to three percentage points over the benchmark rates for ECU and DM bonds — see section 3.3).

Further efforts are required to harmonize methodologies to improve the comparability of data on commitments and disbursements and to fill in missing data, especially as regards rescheduled debt obligations and forgiveness.

From the viewpoint of policy and coordination, more information is needed on undisbursed bilateral loans, terms and conditions. This information would also allow determination of the degree of concessionality of loan commitments and thus the value of aid.

(ii) Commonwealth of Independent States

The most comprehensive source currently available on international assistance to the ex-Soviet Union and/or Commonwealth of Independent States is a compilation circulated by the EC at the Washington conference in January 1992, which has been reproduced as table 5.2.6. According to these estimates, between

---

[498] The estimates for 1991 are based upon the IMF revised balance of payments outlook for eastern Europe presented to the meeting of the G-24 in October 1991 (see table 3.3.14). These estimates reflect the disbursement plans of official creditors and estimates of private capital inflows. To facilitate comparisons of disbursements in 1990 and 1991 (table 5.2.4), the ECE secretariat has restructured OECD data in table 5.2.3 and added estimates of private capital flows. Both years exclude grants (in principle, recorded as transfers), estimates for which were not available for 1991. Also, the lack of complete information on debt rescheduled in 1990 should be kept in mind.

[499] These figures are based upon IMF estimates made in the second half of 1991. They may be too pessimistic as regards direct investment.

[500] The net transfer of financial resources measure used here reflects net interest payments and net borrowing from the IMF and is based on the balance-of-payments statistics reported by the east European countries. In all of these respects, it differs from the data on financial flows reported in table 5.2.3.

[501] For Bulgaria and Romania, IMF resources constituted a crucial part of their balance-of-payments financing. Their reserves remained very low (see section 3.3).

TABLE 5.2.5

Eastern Europe and the Soviet Union: Net transfers of financial resources: 1990-1991
(Million US dollars)

	Bulgaria 1990	Bulgaria 1991	Czechoslovakia[a] 1990	Czechoslovakia[a] 1991	Hungary 1990	Hungary 1991	Poland[a] 1990	Poland[a] 1991	Romania 1990	Romania 1991	Yugoslavia 1990	Yugoslavia 1991	Soviet Union[b] 1990	Soviet Union[b] 1991
Interest payments	-750	-600 *	-316	-321	-1 438	-1 363	-3 329	-2 343	137	-25	-822	-632 [c]	-4.0	-3.7
Capital flows	-3 395	..	326	1 485	-689	2 453	-6 678	-3 993	47	488	3 607	..	-6.9	0.4 [d]
IMF lending	-	320	-	1 004	-145	793	509	322	-	772	-266	-110	-	-
Exceptional financing	3 576	..	-	-	-	-	7 803	5 148	-	-	-	..	4.5	-0.5
Total	-569	..	10	2 168	-2 272	1 883	-1 695	-866	184	1 235	2 519	..	-6.4	-3.8
Memorandum item:														
Reserves (net) [e]	862	..	1 110	-1 990	562	-2 740	-2 153	819	1 664	789	-1 590	..	8.4	2.5

Source: As for table 3.3.7.

Note: All flows are net, in convertible currencies only. Official transfers are not included.

a January-November 1991.
b Billion US dollars.
c January-October.
d Includes $1.9 billion in grants.
e Changes, a negative sign indicates an increase in reserves.

September 1990 and January 1992, financial *commitments* extended to the CIS states amounted to ECU 63 billion (nearly $79 billion). Of this, the European Community and its member states represent 76 per cent. Germany is the leading provider, accounting for 57 per cent of the total (50 per cent if the assistance to pay for the withdrawal of Soviet troops is excluded).

The notes accompanying the EC compilation indicate that these commitments may cover several years and that the figures do not include debt rescheduling[502] or grants from private sources.[503]

The purposes and conditions attached to these loans at the time of their original announcement include:[504]

— export credits tied to the purchase of national goods, including a high component of guaranteed credits for food purchases;

— credits extended specifically for the purpose of settling arrears owed to domestic companies in the donor countries;

— credits and grants to be made available over a period of several years, including some DM 12 billion from Germany to the ex-Soviet Union for disbursal through 1994 in conjunction with the repatriation of Soviet troops from the former GDR.[505]

As regards actual *disbursements* of assistance, information available from the creditors is incomplete. Presumably, disbursals of these funds have been affected by some of the same factors as have been discussed with respect to G-24 assistance to eastern Europe above. Recent press reports indicate that some of the pledges made in 1990 have not yet been released. Several creditor countries suspended the facilities during the political upheavals in the Soviet Union in 1991 and have only recently recommitted the loans. In consequence, only a fraction of commitments are likely to have been released during the past two years.

An idea of the magnitude of credits actually drawn may be obtained from the recently published balance-of-payments statistics of the former Soviet Union. According to these data, the Soviet Union received medium- and long-term credits (in convertible currencies) of $10.9 billion and $12 billion in 1990 and 1991, respectively,[506] and $1.9 billion in total grants, of which $1.7 billion went to Russia. (These reflect inflows from all sources, and not only from the creditors registered in table 5.2.6). Very roughly, the inflows reported by the ex-Soviet Union for 1990-1991 constitute some one quarter to one third of the $79 billion in commitments.[507] Repayments of $16.4 billion are reported for the same period, implying a net inflow of medium- and long-term capital of some $6.5 billion. However, this was not enough to compensate for the net outflow of nearly $16 billion in short-term credits (see table 3.3.7 and section 4.1(iii). In other words, of-

---

[502] The notes to the data do not specify whether the claims of the former German Democratic Republic on the ex-Soviet Union, taken over by Germany, are included. Germany had acquired similar claims, originally denominated in roubles, on the GDR's former east European trade partners and reported these to the OECD as assistance (table 5.2.3). It is also uncertain whether western countries have included the arrears owed on their exports to the Soviet Union (some $4.5 billion in 1990). The Paris Club agreed to reschedule $3.3 billion in Soviet debt falling due in December 1991 and an unknown amount was restructured by commercial banks (see section 4.1(iii)). The treatment of these reschedulings in also uncertain.

[503] The private grants cited are DM 400 million and $20 million from private German and United States sources, respectively. Commission of the European Communities, *Fact Sheet*, Brussels, 31 January 1992.

[504] For a detailed compilation of pledges announced during 1990 and early 1991, see United Nations Economic Commission for Europe, *Economic Survey of Europe in 1990-1991*, New York, 1991, table 3.3.16.

[505] According to the EC fact sheet, nearly ECU 4 billion is earmarked for housing for Soviet soldiers leaving the ex-German Democratic Republic.

[506] Also see tables 3.3.7, 4.1.7 and section 4.1(iii). The source reports medium- and long-term loans received by the ex-Soviet Union, but these are not shown separately in these tables. The wording used in the source ("credits") suggests that this includes only drawings on loans received, but this is not certain. The figures may also include the inflow of repayments outstanding on Soviet loans, in which case the figures would overstate the assistance received from international community. It should be borne in mind that these data are probably preliminary and are subject to certain reservations.

[507] This calculation may also overestimate the disbursement rate since it incorporates credits received by the Soviet Union during all of 1990, while the figures on commitments of assistance are said to be cumulated only as of September 1990.

TABLE 5.2.6

International assistance to the CIS states [a]

A Food and medical aid (grants)   B Balance of payments support   C Export credits and/or guarantees
D Other credits   E Strategic assistance: withdrawal of Soviet troops and destruction of nuclear warheads
F Technical assistance   G Other or not available

(Million ECU)

	A	B	C	D	E	F	G	Total
EEC	453	-	1 750	-	-	885	-	3 088
Member states	1 249	5 942	18 849	8 402	8 353	312	1 671	44 777
of which:								
Germany	1 189	4 521	11 522	8 402	8 353	197	1 671	35 855
Italy	-	1 421	3 241	-	-	-	-	4 662
Spain	-	-	1 118	-	-	-	-	1 118
France	22	-	1 675	-	-	30	-	1 726
United Kingdom	31	-	391	-	-	80	-	503
EFTA countries	38	-	734	-	-	87	28	887
of which:								
Finland	6	-	80	-	-	26	-	111
Norway	4	-	94	-	-	39	4	140
Sweden	12	-	-	-	-	18	-	29
Other countries	288	746	9 066	373	298	196	3 366	14 332
of which:								
USA	224	-	2 982	-	298	168	384	4 057
Japan	22	-	1 938	-	-	1	-	1 961
South Korea	-	746	1 118	373	-	-	-	2 237
Total	2 028	6 687	30 398	8 776	8 651	1 480	5 065	63 084

Source: Commission of the European Communities, *Fact Sheet*, Brussels, 31 January 1992.

a Cumulative, September 1990-January 1992.
b In some case components may not add to the reported totals.

ficial assistance could not compensate for the action of private banks reducing their exposure *vis-à-vis* the ex-Soviet Union.

These outflows of short-term credits are a major explanation for the significant negative transfer (outflow) of financial resources experienced by the ex-Soviet Union in both 1990 and 1991 (table 5.2.5).

As noted above, the failure of certain ex-Soviet republics to adhere to the agreement on the joint servicing of Soviet debt concluded last year has held up the release of loans in early 1992.

5.3 WESTERN TRADE POLICIES AND IMPROVEMENT OF MARKET ACCESS

(i) Measures implemented in 1990-1991

Within the framework of the G-24 initiative to support structural reform in eastern Europe, western governments took a range of measures during 1990-1991 to give additional market access to east European products. Further progress has been made with a series of new agreements and measures which already have or will enter into force in 1992. Improving market access is considered one of the most effective means of supporting transition in the eastern countries. It is expected to facilitate the development of a new pattern of trade, reflecting comparative advantage, based upon new relative prices.

Since the European Community is the largest western market for eastern goods, the liberalization measures it has implemented are the most important for east European trade. By the beginning of 1991, the European Community had eliminated quantitative restrictions on exports of most manufactures from all east European countries and extended GSP privileges to all of them.[508] In 1990, the EC had permanently lifted "specific" quantitative restrictions[509] and later suspended all remaining quantitative restrictions on these east European exports.[510] This suspension, granted initially through 31 December 1991, was extended for another year. Agricultural, textile and steel products were excluded from these actions and were addressed separately.

Bilateral agreements governing trade in *textiles* between the EC and east European countries (except Albania) and the Soviet Union were signed in 1990 and 1991. The new arrangements, which were within the Multi-Fibre Agreement (MFA), included an increase in market access for re-imports into the EC, but left most textile products subject to quantitative restrictions.[511]

In the *steel* sector, some 90 per cent of metals and common metal products were entitled to benefit from GSP as a result of the liberalization measures undertaken during 1990 and 1991.[512] Furthermore, in July 1991, EC imports of steel and pig iron originating from Bulgaria, Czechoslovakia, Hungary, Poland, Romania and the ex-Soviet Union were liberalized.[513]

As these market-opening measures were being implemented, other measures — especially some new anti-dumping actions — tended to restrict market access.

Other industrial countries have also increased market access for east European products during the past two years. The EFTA countries have granted concessions which vary from one country to another. Austria has granted GSP treatment to Hungary and Poland, while Finland, Norway, Sweden and Switzerland have granted GSP treatment to Bulgaria and Romania. Canada has granted GSP to Poland, Hungary, Bulgaria and Albania and is in the process of doing the same for Czechoslovakia.

In 1990, the United States instituted or improved GSP benefits for Poland, Hungary, Czechoslovakia and Yugoslavia. The privilege for the latter country was suspended at the end of 1991. Prior to 1990, only Hungary, Poland, and Yugoslavia had enjoyed MFN status. Czechoslovakia was granted MFN in 1990 and Bulgaria in 1991, qualifying them for GSP treatment as well.

As of the end of 1991, all OECD countries have granted MFN status to Hungary, Poland, the Czech and Slovak Republic and Bulgaria. All OECD countries except the United States extend MFN treatment to Romania.

(ii) Measures to be implemented in 1992

Association agreements

In December 1991, the European Communities concluded bilateral association agreements with Hungary, Poland and the Czech and Slovak Republic.[514] A

---

[508] Under the GSP schemes, certain shares of eastern exports have been freed of all tariffs (i.e., duty free quotas) and another part of exports may benefit from preferential rates. Any exports above these levels incur Most-Favoured-Nation tariffs. The Soviet Union continued to be considered as a state-trading country and therefore was not granted access to the GSP.

[509] "Specific" here refers to quotas which were applied only to the exports of certain eastern exporters.

[510] The Portuguese and Spanish markets were excluded from the latter action. The date at which these measures came into effect are summarized in United Nations Economic Commission for Europe, *Economic Bulletin for Europe*, vol.43, New York, 1991, table 1.4.4. Certain non-specific quantitative restriction remain in place for the Soviet Union.

[511] The agreements introduce some flexibility, allowing, for example, transfers of a product from one category to another. Up to certain limits, non-utilized allocations can be carried over from one year to the next.

[512] Council Decision 89/645/ECSC. Romania was excluded from the benefits.

[513] Quantitative restrictions on steel were suppressed entirely in several EC countries, but remained in Germany, Italy and the Benelux, although there were some market-access gains in these markets (Council Decision 91/463 ECSC).

[514] EC, *Europe Agreement*, EC/CSFR; EC, *Europe Agreement*, EC Hungary; EC, *Europe Agreement*, EC/Poland, mimeos, January 1992. Title III, Free Movement of Goods, and Protocols and Annexes of the Agreements cover changes in market access. While there are some differences between the three agree-

free trade area between the two groups of countries is to be phased in over a period of 10 years, in accordance with Article XXIV of the General Agreement on Tariffs and Trade. This 10-year transition period is divided into two five-year stages, after the first of which there shall be an evaluation of the association process.

The EC, as the more developed of the two contracting parties, offers to accomplish tariff reductions and their consequent suppression, as well as quota dismantlement, at a faster pace than the three east European economies.[515] Import duties on four groups of *industrial products* (except for "sensitive goods") are to be eliminated according to separate timetables. For products in a first category, tariffs were eliminated on 1 March 1992, when the trade measures covered entered into force.[516] For goods included in a second schedule, customs duties shall be reduced by 50 per cent on the date of entry into force of the agreements and eliminated one year thereafter. For goods in a third category, tariffs will be progressively reduced by 20 per cent annually, and completely eliminated by the fourth year after the agreement enters into force. As regards the fourth category of goods, tariffs will be suspended on a share of EC imports, determined by fixed tariff quotas and/or progressively increasing ceilings (specified in the annexes). The remainder of the goods in this category will be subject to tariffs which will be progressively reduced and eliminated not later than five years after the agreements enter into force. The basic duty considered for the reductions is the rate prevailing before the agreements for each product. However, if, as a result of the Uruguay Round, lower rates are established, these shall replace the rates originally envisaged as basic. Quantitative restrictions are to be eliminated from the date the agreements enter into force.

Separate provisions apply to trade in the "sensitive" areas of textiles, agriculture and steel. As regards *textiles*, the EC agreed to eliminate all tariffs and quotas for direct imports from the three east European countries over a period of six years. The initial tariff reduction — to five sevenths of the basic duty — shall take place upon the entry into effect of the association agreements. Thereafter, a reduction of one seventh of the basic duty shall take place annually between the third and the sixth years. Duties applied to reimports of textile products from the three countries into the EC shall be abolished on entry into effect of the agreements. Quantitative restrictions will remain in place during 1992. A new Protocol regarding quantitative restrictions and other non-tariff measures on textiles is to be negotiated as soon as a new agreement on textile trade emerges from the Uruguay Round.[517] It appears, however, that the EC will offer to dismantle all quantitative restrictions on textiles only after a transitional period of not less than five years.

In *agriculture*, duties on certain base products are to be reduced, subject to quantitative limits, above which normal MFN duties are to apply.

In the *steel sector*, the EC offered to phase out the voluntary export restrictions to which products of the three countries are subject in 1992. The Community will maintain strict surveillance on steel imports, however, which might be restricted in case of market disruption. As regards customs duties, they shall be reduced to 80 per cent of the basic duty on the date of entry into effect of the association agreements. Further annual reductions to 60, 40, 20, 10 and zero per cent shall take place between the second and sixth years. Quantitative restrictions on steel products will be eliminated on the date of entry into force of the agreements.

Anti-dumping duties may be applied when injury within the Article VI of the GATT is proven. Similarly, in case of market disruption or economic and balance-of-payments difficulties, restrictions may be applied.

The agreements include also an elimination of import charges which have an effect similar to customs duties. In the case of the EC, the elimination takes place after the agreement enters into force.

It is thus clear that the association agreements will grant an important increase in market access to Czechoslovakia, Hungary and Poland, although the impact will be felt only gradually. Market access will be very limited in the agricultural sector, and in this sense, Hungary and Poland will benefit less on the whole than the Czech and Slovak Republic (see section 3.3). In textiles, gains in market access will proceed slowly, but will eventually lead to a complete liberalization of access to the EC market. Since this sector appears as the most dynamic of the three sensitive areas, the three countries have much to gain from its liberalization. The liberalization of the steel sector might prove less beneficial: once existing subsidies are abolished in the three countries, comparative advantage criteria may reduce exports, despite the gain in market access.

Negotiations on association agreements are currently under way between the EC and Bulgaria and Romania. Talks on cooperation agreements between the EC and Estonia, Latvia and Lithuania were finalized in early 1992. Similar cooperation accords, committing the signatories to improved mutual market access, had previously been concluded with the other east European countries (until superseded by the association agreements). As a result of separate actions taken by the EC last year, from the beginning of 1992 Albania and the Baltic Republics benefit from the

---

ments, they do not effect the discussion below. The exceptions are coal, for which there are some differences in the timetables for the reduction of customs duties, and agricultural goods.

515 Only EC policy measures benefiting the exports of the three eastern countries are reviewed here. At the same time, the three eastern signatories undertook contractual obligations to lower obstacles facing EC goods and services.

516 Under interim agreements between the EC and Czechoslovakia, Hungary and Poland, the trade measures of the associations agreements entered into force on 1 March 1992. Entry into force of the whole agreements is pending parliamentary ratification by the 12 member states of the EC and the three east European countries, which is expected to take place at the beginning of 1993. *Agence Europe*, 24 February 1992.

517 Currently the Multi-Fibre Agreement is the governing regime, but it will expire in December 1992. A transitional period of ten years for the liberalization of textiles is expected to emerge from the Uruguay Round. The EC is offering the signatories of the association agreements a transitional period of only half the length agreed upon in the Uruguay Round, but not shorter than five years, starting 1 January 1993.

elimination of quantitative restrictions for goods other than those considered sensitive.[518] These benefits were recently withdrawn for Yugoslavia, but granted to the republics of Bosnia-Hercegovina, Croatia, Macedonia and Slovenia.

Free trade agreements

In early 1992, EFTA signed a free trade agreement with Czechoslovakia. Negotiations with Hungary and Poland continued. Once the agreements are ratified, tariffs on most exports of manufactured goods from these countries will be lifted.[519] Those EFTA countries which currently apply customs duties to steel imports will reduce them according to the same timetable as adopted in the EC association agreements (see above). Reductions in tariffs on textile and apparel imports will be subject to special timetables extending over several years. Access to the EFTA agricultural sector is being negotiated bilaterally.

EFTA envisages negotiating trade and cooperation agreements with the Baltic countries. Finland has recently initialled a free trade protocol with Estonia.

Trade enhancement initiative

Under its Trade Enhancement Initiative (TEI) for Central and Eastern Europe, the United States has taken steps to further liberalize access to its market. All quotas for east European steel exports to the United States will expire on 31 March 1992. With respect to current voluntary restraint agreements (VRAs) concerning steel, the overall ceiling for east European steel exports is to remain constant, but the United States has agreed to allow any transfers of tonnage between product categories that are requested by the east European countries.[520] Memoranda of understanding were signed in 1991 extending existing bilateral textile agreements (negotiated under the MFA) for CSFR for one year, Hungary and Poland for two years. Many of the restraints were rescinded, and most of the remaining quotas were increased by 30 to 100 per cent.[521] The east European countries will obtain increased access for quota-covered cheeses at the same time when the results of the Uruguay Round negotiations on agriculture are implemented.[522]

Further measures to improve eastern access to western markets are under consideration. At their November 1991 meeting, G-24 ministers reconfirmed their governments' willingness to consider such steps to help the eastern countries' better exploit market opportunities.

(iii) The Uruguay Round and eastern Europe

The results of the Uruguay Round of trade negotiations in GATT, started in 1986, are still uncertain. The Round – the eighth attempt to liberalize world trade within GATT – is an ambitious attempt to extend multilateral rules to most trading areas, including agriculture, services, intellectual property rights and investment related measures. It is also an attempt to reduce tariffs and consolidate them at lower levels, binding mostly for developed countries (developing countries may make use of special provisions).

The failure of the contracting parties to reach an agreement in 1991 led the GATT's Director-General to propose a text for the Uruguay Round which would lead – among other things – to the creation of a General Agreement for Trade in Services (GATS) and possibly to a Multilateral Trade Organization. The GATS would lead to the implementation of a Most Favoured Nation treatment in services for its signatories. In agriculture, the main disputed area threatening the success of the Uruguay Round, the Proposal envisages a 20 per cent reduction of trade-distorting aid before 1999; the conversion of all kinds of farm protectionist measures into tariffs (which would be curtailed by 36 per cent by 1999); the reduction in the volume of each country's subsidized exports by 24 per cent; and a 36 per cent cut in export subsidy payments.

It is hoped that the negotiations will come to an end in the spring of 1992. A successful conclusion to the Uruguay Round would promote trade and growth in the 1990s. If it fails, the result could be a resurgence of protectionism, managed trade and bilateral trade negotiations.

A successful Uruguay Round would represent a reduction in trade restrictions for eastern Europe. The eastern countries would benefit greatly from global tariff reductions, especially in the industrial countries, which are their main markets. This would provide an impulse for their exports, since MFN tariffs – which most of their exports actually face – would be lower, and less recourse to GSP treatment would be necessary. An agreement in agriculture would benefit net exporters of food, not only because their market share could increase, but also because the initial effect of liberalization will be higher prices. Countries like Hungary, Poland and the Ukraine, would particularly benefit. In the two other sensitive areas, textiles and steel, potential gains for exporters will be more modest. The Multi-Fibre Agreement is expected to remain in place for some ten years, and the dismantlement of "voluntary" export restraints in the steel sector will be, at best, gradual.

In the light of the recently-signed association agreements between the EC, and the Czech and Slovak Re-

---

[518] Council Regulation (EEC) No.3859/91 of 23 December 1991.

[519] Finland had previously eliminated most tariffs under its existing free trade agreement with these countries.

[520] In practice east European exports of steel are not close to that ceiling. In 1991 only one product category under the VRAs was filled by the east European countries (oil country tubular goods from CSFR). (Direct communication from the Office of the US Trade Representative.)

[521] No restraints currently affect Bulgarian textile exports to the United States. The country will receive equivalent treatment to CSFR, Hungary and Poland if the need for restraints is perceived (ibid.).

[522] Cheese quotas are the only US non-tariff barrier significantly affecting east European agricultural exports (ibid.).

public, Hungary and Poland, a global tariff reduction would mean that lower rates would replace the basic rates originally agreed, which would contribute to accelerate market access gains.

Chapter 6

ON PROPERTY RIGHTS AND PRIVATIZATION IN THE TRANSITION ECONOMIES

6.1 PROPERTY RIGHTS CONCEPTS

(i) Introduction

Many momentous changes have taken place in the eastern part of Europe since late 1989. The demise of communism as a doctrine left few policy issues more cumbersome than how to proceed with the dismantlement of the overbearing role of the state in these countries.

Moving toward a "civil society", in the view of those spearheading the revolution, since then embraced as *Leitmotiv* by those in charge of managing the transition, involved two basic goals. One was the installation of a pluralistic society and quick advance toward implanting democracy as the core principle of socio-political organization. The other was the elimination of centralized planning, or rather the administrative variant of the ministerial system into which planning had degenerated by the late 1980s. In its stead, a "private market economy" was envisaged as the counterpart in the economic domain of democracy in the political arena. Such an order for the economy entails not only decentralization in the sphere of economic decision-making, but also the full recognition, in law and in fact, of private property rights and the withdrawal of the state from heavy involvement in the allocation of scarce resources.

This chapter is devoted to property rights and the process whereby state-owned assets in the former centrally planned economies of Europe as well as Yugoslavia (and its successor republics) will become private property.[523] Together these countries are here referred to as "east", a designation chosen purely as a convenient shorthand label. Property rights reform and the privatization process of course constitute only one aspect of the economic transformations that have been unfolding in these countries and of the process whereby eventually market-type economies will take root in the eastern part of Europe.

The chapter is organized into two distinct parts. The *first*, comprising the first two sections, deals essentially with the more conceptual aspects of privatization and the experience with such campaigns in market economies. Both topics are explored here solely, and, therefore, somewhat cursorily, as a backdrop to the far more convoluted corresponding issues in the east's transitions. The *second* part provides a conceptual overview as well as concrete factual details on the purposes, obstacles, and means of as well as the experience to date with and the expectations regarding the privatization processes in the near term in the various eastern countries. It comprises the last five sections and the appendix of this chapter.

In the present section, a summary of the concepts and salient points made in the chapter in section (ii) is followed by a brief identification of where property rights reform and privatization belong in the transition *problématique* in section (iii).[524] Next, basic characteristics of the recent experience with privatization in market economies are summarized in section (iv), with a view mainly to identifying their relevance to the ambitions that are currently widely shared by policy makers in the east.

Section 6.2 then argues the case for anchoring clear property rights as a necessary prelude to the establishment of a market economy and to embarking on privatization. That is to say, clear property rights are seen as a necessary ingredient for developing market-based economic systems; but they generally do not constitute a sufficient condition for such a socio-economic order to emerge. What precisely could be understood under the term privatization and the concept that will be used throughout this chapter are explained in section 6.3.

---

[523] For the preparation of the factual details of this chapter, country notes commissioned by the ECE secretariat from outside authors, in addition to data and analyses prepared within the secretariat, were available. Among the former country studies, papers were obtained for Belarus, Bulgaria, Lithuania, Romania, the Russian Federation, the ex-Soviet Union, Ukraine, and Yugoslavia (prior to the recognition of the independence of Croatia and Slovenia, and so this paper had also some details on the situation of the two republics as well as Serbia). The annex is based on the running inventory of the Trade Division of the ECE secretariat.

[524] For a broader overview of the transition and the precise place of property rights and privatization therein, see United Nations Economic Commission for Europe, *Economic Survey of Europe in 1990-1991*, New York, 1991, pp.124-183.

Sections 6.4-6.6 survey the motivations for and the goals pursued with privatization, the obstacles encountered in the process, and the various alternative privatization mechanisms that can be mobilized. Then section 6.7 analyses the salient features of the experience with privatization in individual countries and closes the chapter with a brief account of the agenda for the near term.

(ii) Key concepts and the thrust of the chapter

The pervasive involvement of the "state" in economic decision-making and its apparent inability to ensure efficiency either statically and, even less, in an adaptive perspective has been one of the paramount problems of poor economic performance in the former planned economies, in particular since the early 1970s. This derived in part from the fact that a basic tenet of socialism as practised in these countries was state ownership of the means of production.

It is now widely felt that taking the state out of the decision-making on the allocation of assets that it nominally owns is one of the most urgent and difficult tasks confronting those managing the transition. There is virtual unanimity in the leaderships of the transition economies that the share of the private sector will eventually have to approach proportions typical of west European market economies. That implies that the state sector will have to shrink from its presently very high level (perhaps 70 to 95 per cent)[525] to between 20 and 50 per cent. But that part of the ownership transformation cannot be accomplished rapidly. Yet taking the state out of the economy should be initiated as quickly as administrative and legal rules permit.

The process stretching from when these countries first embark upon the transition to the market economy until there is widespread private ownership of presently existing state assets is the subject dealt with below. As will be explained more fully in section 6.3, it comprises a number of distinct phases, which are here captured under the notions of corporatization, commercialization, usufruct divestment, and full divestment through sale or free distribution to the population at large and former owners.

Admittedly, this concept of privatization differs from that widely current in the case of market economies. It does so precisely because market economies that decided to shrink their public sector never faced the daunting complexity of making a market economy out of a mismanaged planned economy. And the great number and diversity of obstacles to privatization confronting the east (as discussed in section 6.5) should not be used as an excuse for not moving forward to take the state out of the micromanagement of the economy at the earliest possible opportunity. That is why the process of privatization is here conceived in such a broad framework tailored to the transition to the market economy in the eastern economies.[526]

When the privatization process in the east since 1989 is looked at in this format, several useful messages emerge. These can be grouped in five parts, which are expanded below: the thrust of privatization has been misguided by focusing too much on divesting the large state firms; too much attention is being given to the valuation issues, while other aspects of restructuring enterprise operations are being ignored; many of the real ownership obstacles to moving to the market economy have not yet been sufficiently tackled, let alone resolved; the dynamics of moving to the market economy with large private property depends critically on a vibrant small and medium-sized sector which, given the uncertainty and institutional obstacles in the transition economies, needs to be fostered; and it is a serious mistake to approach privatization solely as a technical issue, for it is an issue of political economy *par excellence*.

First, the recent discussions around privatization have been focused disproportionately on the question of the ownership transfer and valuation for this purpose of the state-owned enterprises in industrial sectors. Certainly, these issues are at the fore also in market economies that resort to privatization. But in those countries divestment can take place in an environment that is broadly market-oriented and based on private property, and the process of divestment, although being hobbled, can generally proceed in an orderly fashion. In the transition countries, however, some other issues are ultimately of at least equal importance for the enhancement of the efficiency of the work of these firms. Among them is the generation of competition from domestic sources as well as from abroad, a recognition of the importance of interesting the workforce as a whole in large firms through positive monitoring, a new regulatory environment, and ensuring better monitoring of management by the owners of assets (whether private or public).

Second, assessing values of these companies is a hazardous undertaking under the best of circumstances. This is even true when the object of the assessment is being narrowed down chiefly to plant and equipment, in the process ignoring many of the other assets, such as goodwill, land, human capital, and market position. Aside from generating much work for accounting firms at great expense either to deliverers of assistance from the western community and international organizations, or, in the end, to the taxpayer in the countries in transition, such cumbersome, costly evaluations are in any case rather meaningless in the disorderly, highly inflationary environment of the countries going through this historic transition. At the same time, the erosion of the value of these companies is likely to continue along with the deep depression that is currently holding these countries in its grip and the emergence of a vibrant, if still small, private sector.

The third broad conclusion that can be drawn is that much of the debate about privatization really deals with establishing clear property rights as the means enabling owners to ensure that their assets are used to best

---

[525] In some countries, notably Poland and Yugoslavia, agriculture was on the whole privately organized, and this explains the different size of the state sector. In industry, however, virtually the entire sector used to be state-owned.

[526] A more rounded justification of the concepts used here is provided in section 6.3.

purpose. This is an extremely important matter that has not yet received its full due. Certainly, this is an issue also with regard to the big industrial enterprises mentioned earlier. It would seem much more important, however, for the establishment of transparent and unambiguous property rights to other assets, notably land (in particular for arable and real-estate purposes).

Fourth, a viable, vibrant market economy in the east will emerge only through a thorough restructuring of the entire production process. Excepting the territories formerly known as the German Democratic Republic, that restructuring will have to be brought about by domestic entrepreneurs and largely through domestic savings. Foreign direct investment may be a boon, but it will move from the present trickle to a sizeable stream only once basic economic, political, and social stability has been attained in the east. A sizeable sector of small and medium-sized enterprises will be instrumental in solidifying this stability. But that cannot come about as long as the present institutional and other obstacles to bolstering that sector are at work.

Finally, it would help if all involved in the east's transition were to realize that privatization is an issue of political economy *par excellence*. Neat economic arguments have their value. But they tend to be impossible to implement in practice when matters concerning transition in general and privatization in particular have to be thrashed out in the highly volatile environment of fledgling democracies with at best rudimentary provisions for effective decision-making. This makes it important that measures to gain technical control over the large firms that were released from the grip of the political centres should be embraced as early as possible. Significant progress can be made by turning state firms into corporations and forcing management to respect market-based conditions through incentives and constraints imposed by supervisory bodies. Initially, these will be far from perfect. But not taking early action cannot but send perverse signals to those that, in the end, will have to carry out the transition in general and divestment in particular.

(iii) Property rights and privatization on the transition agenda

In a stylized approach, the transition in the eastern economies can be sketched as consisting of four distinct phases, which are, however, not necessarily widely separated in time or may even run parallel to each other.

The first involves a *redistribution of basic political powers*, in line with a better-balanced representation of the popular will. This, in fact, entails the removal of the Communist Party and its appendages from the centre of societal life in these countries. In and of itself, this political revolution should in due course lead to the formation of a government on the strength of freely organized, pluralistic elections[527] and a redrafting of the constitution. On its foundations, the basic markers of political democracy should in time be solidified. But there is no guarantee that this part of the transition will be altogether smooth. Without it, political uncertainty is likely to be so great and society's consensus on other basic ingredients of the transition so elusive, that the transformation may essentially linger in *statu nascendi* for quite some time. This may occur even though the transformation is neither aborted nor efforts to move it forward are abandoned.

The second phase of the transformation of these societies consists of *regaining broad macroeconomic stability*. As a rule, this involves adopting some programme that envisages economic stabilization through stringent monetary and fiscal policies. Its aim is to compress domestic absorption and remove any "monetary overhang", possibly through inflation or monetary reform. By definition, the horizon of economic stabilization in the stock sense is short term. Because this part of the transformation process entails at least the relaxation of pervasive government administration of the economy, in the first instance by abandoning central control over price-setting for most goods and services,[528] it can be accomplished relatively quickly once broad sociopolitical agreement has been reached. Success depends not only on the design of the programme, but also on maintaining societal consensus on the the adjustment cost, the speed at which it will be absorbed, and its distribution over the various layers of these countries.

The third and fourth phases encompass focusing the attention of policy makers on the *creation of the basic "institutions" of the market economy* — where this is the objective — and on *structural change in the economy's production potential*. The latter in the end will require some kind of "industrial policy", however much distance the "state" may wish to take from the economy and market interference.

The creation of basic institutions can be envisaged as consisting of two separate agendas. One comprises tasks that can be accomplished relatively quickly, either because they are not costly or because they can be imported from abroad lock, stock, and barrel, perhaps with minor modifications to suit local needs. Other tasks, such as maintaining economic stability in the flow sense, are largely a matter of proper policy formulation. Assistance from abroad can play a major role in focusing on the rapid realization of these aspects of the new institution-building in the transition economies.

The institution of clear property rights appears on the surface to be a target that could be realized relatively quickly. But whether any given solution resolves the existing uncertainty around who in the end will own what in the transition economies depends on how it deals with the past. If it encompasses a *tabula rasa* approach, that is, if society mandates forgoing restitution claims or limiting to compensation the claims

---

[527] In a sense, the Polish experience deviated slightly from this model, until full parliamentary elections were held in October 1991. Full multi-party parliamentary elections have to date still not been accomplished in the successor Soviet republics, including the Baltic states, and in at least some of the Yugoslav republics. In several other countries, including Albania, the outcomes have been tenuous, and new elections are scheduled for the near future.

[528] Excluded are notably wages, housing rents, pharmaceuticals, basic fuels, some food staples, and a few other products and services for which a more gradual adjustment to market-clearing level is as a rule envisaged.

of economic agents whose property had earlier been expropriated, swift progress should be a distinct possibility.[529] In the contrary case, in fact, the only unambiguous property rights that can be assigned without too much effort are those deriving from investment in newly-produced or imported goods. In particular, any acquisition of land and fixed structures might turn out to be subject to restitution or compensation claims, with an impact on how the new owner can exercise his property rights that constrains effective management for productive purposes.

Clarifying basic property rights can, in fact, be accomplished through renationalizing all non-private assets with a view to then quickly entrusting user rights to agents in charge of privatization (in the sense in which this concept is defined in section 6.3). Needless to say, even in the few societies where at the outset of the transition there was such a consensus, efforts to reestablish property rights have quickly become mired in the politicization of the transformation processes. Hence, essential components of property rights reform, in fact, also belong to the fourth phase.

All other institutions to be reconstructed or created, in particular those that are bound to exert a major effect on the structure of supply in these economies can, by necessity, emerge only over time. Together with the basic transformation of production, the creation of the other institutions of the market economy comprises the fourth phase of the transition. There are many items that belong in this category. Among them, one — privatization — is the subject of this chapter. Related to this, as noted, are those claims to property rights that cannot be quickly resolved, including restitution and compensation claims. In this category also belongs the resolution of property rights that are held presumptively, for example, by workers and management. These may derive from the prior assignment of authority over assets under workers' councils, enterprise councils, or self-management arrangements. Policy makers also must come to grips in this phase with attempts to capture property rights that, in fact, belong to society, by vested-interest groups, including the old *nomenklatura*.

At the height of the political revolution in the economies in transition, many of the new policy makers and their advisers assumed that the establishment of clear property rights and the privatization of state-owned assets could be accomplished very quickly, chiefly in a technocratic fashion. This view was also held by the majority of foreign advisers, including those from regional and international organizations. Actually, the response within the transition economies to the formulation of the transition agenda owed a good deal to the encouragement received from outside advisers. But the expectation of engineering quick changes in property rights and ownership were frustrated in a matter of months.

Now, barely two years after the initiation of the momentous economic, political, and social mutations, it has become clear to nearly everyone that the fourth phase of the transition is bound to be very lengthy, bumpy, and arduous. Furthermore, it is beset by conflictual political claims which generate pervasive uncertainty over the medium run. These observations apply in particular to the twin issues of central concern here: the creation of unambiguous property rights that can be enforced in law and the privatization of state-owned assets.

(iv) Privatization in market economies — lessons for the east?

The experience gathered by several developing and developed market economies, chiefly during the 1980s, will be briefly highlighted here. Clarity on the purposes of privatization pursued in the west, the methods embraced, the obstacles encountered, and the results obtained can help isolate the aspects of the experience that are relevant to the privatization campaigns in the east.

Since the early 1980s, there has been a wholesale wave of divestment of state assets in market economies. Especially pertinent may be the experiences of France, Italy, and the United Kingdom, but the campaigns pursued in other countries are also relevant to the present analysis.[530]

In this connection, two questions can usefully be posed with a view to deriving inferences for the policy options that eastern policy makers face: first, what were the motivations and the goals envisaged for these privatizations? and, second, how successful have these policies been in terms of the goals set? The answer to the first question can shed light on whether the goals now envisaged in the east overlap with those of market economies. The investigation of the second question

---

[529] True, there are objects that were nationalized upon the establishment of the communist societies that could be duly returned to expropriated owners without encountering many complications. Items that spring readily to mind include paintings in museums or book manuscripts in national libraries. But such selectivity may run counter to the spirit, if perhaps not the letter, of the new constitutional provisions; it may even lead to resentment, as discussed in section 6.2. Matters are quite different with assets that are used for the production of goods and services, however.

[530] For some useful references to these experiences, see Wladimir Andreff, "Techniques et expériences de privatisation: la 'success story' des privatisations en France et les besoins actuels des pays d'Europe de l'Est", Paris: ROSES, September 1990, mimeo; Olivier Bouin and Charles-Albert Michalet, *Rebalancing the public and private sectors: developing country experience*, Paris: Development Centre of the Organization for Economic Co-operation and Development, 1991; Paul Cook and Colin Kirkpatrick, (eds.), *Privatization in less developed countries*, New York and London: Harvester Wheatsheaf, 1988; Richard Hemming and Ali M. Mansoor, *Privatization and public enterprises*, Washington, D.C.: International Monetary Fund, Occasional Paper No.56, 1988; Calvin A. Kent, (ed.), *Entrepreneurship and the privatizing of government*, New York-Westport, CT: Quorum Books, 1987; Tony Killick, *A reaction too far — economic theory and the role of the state in developing countries*, London: Overseas Development Institute, 1990; Paul W. MacAvoy, W.T. Stanbury, George Yarrow, and Richard J. Zeckhauser, (eds.), *Privatization and state-owned enterprises — lessons from the United States, Great Britain and Canada*, Boston-Dordrecht-London: Kluwer Academic Publishers, 1989; V.V. Ramanadham, (ed.), *Privatization in the UK*, London-New York: Routledge, 1988; Ben Ross Schneider, "La politica de privatización en Brasil y México: variaciones sobre un tema estatista", *Foro Internacional*, 1990:1, pp.5-37; Ezra N. Suleiman and John Waterbury, (eds.), *The political economy of public sector reform and privatization*, Boulder, CO: Westview Press, 1990; Dennis Swann, *The retreat of the state — deregulation and privatization in the UK and US*, Ann Arbor, MI: The University of Michigan Press, 1988; Pál Valentiny, "Valuation of enterprises to be privatized", Magyar Tudományos Akadémiai Közgazdaságtudományi Intézet, 1991; Cento Veljanovski, (ed.), *Privatization & competition — a market prospectus*, London: The Institute of Economic Affairs, 1989; Raymond Vernon, (ed.), *The promise of privatization: a challenge for American foreign policy*, New York: The Council on Foreign Relations, 1988; John Vickers and George Yarrow, *Privatization: an economic analysis*, Cambridge, MA: The MIT Press, 1988.

TABLE 6.1
Distribution of firms by type, as of end-1991
(Non-agricultural sectors)

	Number of state firms around 1989/90 (1)	as of end 1991 (2)	Shareholding companies (old + new) (3) = (4) + (5)	Joint stock companies (4)	Limited liability companies (5)	Cooperatives (6)	Leased enterprises (7)
Albania	..	..	..	..	..	..	..
Belarus	1 467 [a, b]	..	..	115	5 200 [c]	5 300 [c]	2 980 [c]
Bulgaria	2 201 [a, b]	2 3000 [d]	14	..	..	..	..
Czechoslovakia	4 864	4 338 [e]	15 874 [e]	2 528 [e]	13 346 [e]	5 658 [e]	..
Estonia	4 282	4 535	8 736	228	8 508	3 793	224
Hungary	2 400	2 267 [f]	37 425 [f]	1 005 [f]	36 420 [f]	6 331 [f]	..
Latvia	406 [a, g]	349 [a, h]	..	..	..	..	..
Lithuania	629 [a]	3 357	5 383	137	5 246	497 [i]	..
Poland	8 453	8 419	48 989 [e, j]	..	..	2 531 [a]	..
Romania	2 102	693 [k]	92 204 [l]	7 466	75 917 [m]	2 437	6 000
Russian Federation	41 394 [a]	..	73 900 [f]	8 900	65 000	100 000 [f]	2 700 [c]
Ukraine	7 851 [a, b]	5 533	..	..	..	50 000	569
USSR	46 700 [a]	..	..	..	..	255 500	3 700
Yugoslavia	21 000	18 000	3 000	..	..	..	..
Memorandum item:							
Ex-GDR	8 000 [n]	6 200 [n, p]	10 300 [n, p]	..	..	..	..
Croatia	5 000	4 200	800	..	..	..	..
Slovenia	3 500	3 500	..	..	..	..	..

[a] Industry only.
[b] 1988.
[c] October 1991.
[d] In 1990 and 1991 129 state firms have been decentralized into 754 new ones.
[e] September 1991.
[f] November 1991.
[g] 1986.
[h] By November 1991, the state had divested itself of 150 small firms, 10-15 state firms, and 3 large state enterprises.
[i] At the end of 1990, cooperatives were organized into partnership companies.
[j] Total economy.
[k] These are state owned autonomous units to replace the former enterprises and economic centrals.
[l] Includes 8,377 joint ventures.
[m] All private.
[n] Autumn 1991.
[p] Companies still owned by *Treuhandanstalt*.

can suggest useful lessons for the east's privatization campaigns.

Divestment in market economies has proceeded in an *environment* characterized by a comparatively small state sector, established property rights, functioning capital markets, sufficient wealth to acquire state property at some "fair price" (on which more in section 6.5), in principle properly conceived monitoring mechanisms of corporate governance,[531] a choice for appointing alternative managerial teams, the limited duration of the confiscation of private property, and the fact that managerial incentive schemes can be readily enacted. None of these features can presently be found in any of the transition economies. The sheer magnitude of the number of economic organizations to be privatized in the economies in transition if they are to reach a "normal" west European-type of market economy, can be gleaned from table 6.1, which shows data on the distribution of firms in selected transition economies; table 6.2 does likewise for land. And given that the share of the private sector is expected to reach about 50 to 80 per cent of economic activity in these countries in a few years, there are potentially significant pitfalls in transplanting privatization policies appropriate for market economies into an environment lacking the basic institutions of the market economy, notably those pertaining to the smooth operation of credit and financial markets.[532]

Among the many *motives* for privatization in market economies the following are crucial: improving the use of scarce resources; plugging budget deficits and seeking budgetary relief by curtailment of the role of the state; ideological precepts claiming that freedom and liberty necessitate private ownership, and for those reasons the role of the state has to be compressed to the bare essentials; and breaking up entrenched trade-union (or similar group) privileges that inhibited resource reallocation.[533]

Although privatization in the eastern countries involves redistributing property rights in an environment that differs in many respects from that of the market

---

[531] They are of course far from perfect also in the market economies, as argued, for example, by Joseph E. Stiglitz. See *Government, financial markets, and economic development*, Cambridge, MA: National Bureau of Economic Research, Working Paper No.3669, April 1991; and "Capital markets and economic fluctuations in capitalist economies" (paper presented to the Sixth Annual Congress of the European Economic Association, Cambridge, 30 August-2 September 1991).

[532] A matter to be carefully pondered is whether this underscores the benefits of an early development of domestic credit and financial markets, as well as the desirability of finding ways to "clean" the balance sheets of enterprises and banks by expunging bad debts, as argued by Guillermo Calvo and Jacob Frenkel in *Obstacles to transforming centrally-planned economies: the role of capital markets*, Washington, D.C.: International Monetary Fund, IMF Working Paper No.WP/91/66, 1991; and "From centrally planned to market economy: the road from CPE to PCPE", *IMF Staff Papers*, 1991:2, pp.268-299.

[533] See David Heald, "The United Kingdom: privatization and its political context", *West European Politics*, 1988:4, pp.31-48; and "The relevance of UK privatization for LDCs", in *Privatization in less developed countries*, edited by Paul Cook and Colin Kirkpatrick, op.cit., pp.68-90; Dennis Swann, op.cit.

TABLE 6.2
Privatization of agricultural land

	The share of agricultural land owned by state farms and cooperatives		Restitution of land to original owners	Sale or free distribution to domestic nationals	Role of foreign capital
	as of 1989/90	as of end-1991			
	(Percentages)				
Albania	95.7	..	Yes	Yes	Prohibited
Belarus	..	..	No	Planned	Planned
Bulgaria	96.4 [a]	..	Yes [b]	No decision	Prohibited
Czechoslovakia	30-40 [c]	..	Yes	Sale	Prohibited
Estonia	_ [d, e]	..	Yes	Yes [f]	Prohibited
Hungary	50 [g]	No change yet	Partially [f]	Both planned [h]	Prohibited
Latvia	..	..	Yes	..	Prohibited [i]
Lithuania	_ [d]	-	Yes	Free distribution	Under discussion [j]
Poland	22.3 [a]	..	Yes	Sale	Negligible [i]
Romania	92.0	20.1	Yes	Yes	Prohibited
Russian Federation	_ [d]	0.7 [k]	No	Yes	Negligible
Ukraine	_ [d, l]	..	No	Partially	Prohibited
Yugoslavia	18 [a]	17.8	Partially [l]	Yes	Prohibited [i]
Memorandum item:					
Ex-GDR	99.6	..	Yes [m]	Sale	No restrictions
Croatia	22.0 [a]	22.0	No	Yes	Prohibited
Slovenia	11.9 [a]	11.9	No	Yes	Prohibited

a December 1990.
b It is expected that 2 million restitution claims will be filed in and some 40 per cent of the land will be given back to original owners.
c 95 per cent of land was used by cooperatives and state farms.
d Land was legally owned by the state.
e 86 per cent of land was used by cooperatives and state farms.
f Compensation certificates can be used to re-purchase confiscated land.
g 88 per cent of land was used by cooperatives and state farms.
h For registered members of the cooperatives only.
i Leasing for 99 years is possible.
j Proposal before Parliament in January 1992 to allow 99-year leasing or outright purchase.
k September 1991.
l 97 per cent of land was used by cooperatives and state farms.
m Not for 1945-1949 expropriations.

economies, useful lessons can none the less be profitably derived. This is notably the case when privatization was pursued with explicit economic and wealth intentions. When it envisaged realization of the political philosophy on ownership, constraining the role of trade unions in the post-industrial society, disentangling the ineluctable mingling of goals for public enterprises as compared to the presumed singular function of profit maximization for private enterprise, and reached a social contract on this policy, privatization was by definition a success. As regards economic tasks, however, divestment of state-owned assets in market economies has not unambiguously led to lower product prices, improved allocative efficiency, ameliorated internal efficiency in privatized enterprises, brought about people's capitalism, or generated better service or quality of delivery. Moreover, public enterprises were often divested well below their "market value" thus generating sizeable short-term capital gains at the expense of the state — ultimately the taxpayer at large.[534]

Above all, the experience of market economies has underlined that the superiority of private enterprise depends critically on the degree of competition prevailing in the market,[535] the incentive structures in alternative organizational forms of production, and the coherence of regulatory policies designed to correct market failures, rather than on ownership *per se*.[536] Prevailing market structures are, therefore, critical in designing the privatization programme.

Public ownership under conditions of monopoly suffers from a lack of product-market competition. Hence, it yields productive inefficiency, just like a private monopoly. Unlike a private monopoly, however, a public monopoly as a rule is not threatened by bankruptcy, as government is likely to bail out troubled firms. This occurs as "political expediency" eventually blurs the original separation between ownership and management of the public firm, thus sacrificing cost minimization.

State firms operating under conditions of competition could reach productive efficiency. But this market form does not impose the threat of take-over or bank-

---

[534] See John Vickers and Vincent Wright, "The politics of industrial privatization in Western Europe: an overview", *West European Politics*, 1988:4, pp.1-30; John Vickers and George Yarrow, op.cit. and "Economic perspectives on privatization", *Journal of Economic Perspectives*, 1991:2, pp.111-132; George Yarrow, "Privatization in theory and practice", *Economic Policy*, No.2 (1986), pp.324-377.

[535] In fact, the less rigorous literature on privatization is at times quite confusing on these issues, thus imparting many different meanings to it (see section 6.3). In recognition of this, Norman Macrae ("A future history of privatization, 1992-2022", *The Economist*, 21 December 1991, pp.17-20), has coined the notion "recompetitioning". This may be awkward English, but it none the less accurately conveys the message: the accent of privatization must be placed on competition rather than ownership *per se*. Where competition cannot be achieved at all, such as in the case of natural monopoly, or not quickly, privatization has to be accompanied by regulatory reforms.

[536] See Dieter Helm and George Yarrow, "The assessment: the regulation of utilities", *Oxford Review of Economic Policy*, 1988:2, pp.i-xxxi; George Yarrow, op.cit. and "Does ownership matter?" in *Privatization & competition* ..., op.cit., pp.52-69.

ruptcy;[537] at best it can do so through the political process. Neither does it eliminate the inhibiting effect of various kinds of political interference in the operational affairs of public firms. The latter's supply schedules will, therefore, continue to be distorted, making the firm less profitable than its private competitor.

A private monopoly, unlike a public monopoly, is potentially under threat of take-over. This should impart incentives to managers to care about productive efficiency, provided the capital market functions properly. However, the evidence of the disciplining role of potential take-overs in practice is not very strong and it tends to decline with the size of the firm; and capital markets function with a number of failures in any case. A private monopoly, however, tends to exploit its market power, leading to higher prices for smaller supplies and allocative inefficiency for lack of product competition. This suggests that a private monopoly in and of itself might not be superior to a public monopoly.

Finally, with private ownership and competition, productive efficiency should improve since product-market competition is reinforced by the market for corporate control. Moreover, the firm faces the threat of bankruptcy and is not inhibited by government interference. Competitive conditions will also tend to align prices with costs, hence generate allocative efficiency.

This suggests that the "environment" for enterprises is crucial, with competition as a norm yielding the most desirable outcome. Enterprises may be of different size and be variously organized. The critical factor, though, is that they operate in a general market environment, where capital markets and mechanisms for contesting corporate control are extant; all of these features of the environment will have to be established nearly *ab ovo* in the economies in transition. Once incipient forces of competition, corporate control, and capital markets are crystallizing, the key factor determining the efficiency of an enterprise is not whether it is publicly or privately owned, but how it is managed. In theory, it is possible to create the kind of incentives that will maximize efficiency under any type of ownership, provided the other building blocks of the market economy are at least being poured.

But there is a great difference between what is theoretically feasible and what typically materializes. Whereas there can thus be a presumption that private enterprise tends to be more efficient than public enterprise, there is no guarantee that the discounted additional gains over the firm's lifetime, in terms of either appreciating net-asset values or generating additional fiscal revenues in the future, will offset the initial loss in selling assets below market value. Although there is some support for the superiority of private enterprise, most studies on the diverse experience of market economies illustrate that such divestments are rarely conducted simply on the basis of economic motives, say within a bold pro-competitive approach. Results must, therefore, perforce be assessed against the broader backdrop of what originally motivated privatization.

This suggests that the desirability of privatization depends not only on the alternative forms of resource allocation that can be imagined, but also on the purposes policy makers wish to pursue and the weights attached to the, possibly mutually incompatible, goals sought. In other words, for each form of privatization, one needs to specify an objective function with many different arguments tailored, in this case, to the particularities of the specific economy in transition. The optimization of such a function depends importantly on market structures. In that respect, those advocating outright sale of state assets have often overly simplified the issues, especially regarding the distinction between the market as an instrument for coordinating decisions and capitalist ownership. Also, it is easy to advocate the sale of a public firm. But it is much more difficult to specify how the sale should be conducted, how quickly it should be organized, to whom the rights should ideally be transferred, in what state the assets should be sold, how the assets should be sold or else reorganized, and how best to allocate the proceeds. These matters are elaborated upon in section 6.5.

---

[537] But this is a potent weapon only when the constraint is being faced, that is, when firms are in trouble; it does not much affect decisions of successful firms. For details, see Barry W. Ickes, "Obstacles to economic reform of socialism: an institutional-choice approach", *Annals of the American Academy of Political and Social Sciences*, 1990:1, pp.53-64; Joseph E. Stiglitz, "Government, financial markets, ...", loc.cit.

6.2 ON ESTABLISHING PROPERTY RIGHTS

Property rights reform and *privatization* are two core components of transformation policies in the east. They are usually lumped together. But that is not the best approach, for they have quite distinct features in addition to shared characteristics. Property rights reform has several dimensions. One includes questions revolving around the assignment of property rights associated with existing assets. This exhibits obvious links to privatization as the subject matter of this chapter. Another aspect is the assignment and guarantee of property rights to assets created from public and private savings. This is not the preoccupation here, however.

Property rights reform is an integral component of the measures to sensitize the eastern societies to market incentives. Not coincidentally, this many-faceted debate has taken on, with a vengeance, the obverse character of the role played by nationalization at the beginning of the socialization processes in the east, mostly after the Second World War. But the focus in this chapter is on the economic dimensions of property rights reform, especially as they pertain to privatization as defined (see section 6.3). Against this backdrop, the present section first looks into the more general aspects of the importance of property rights and the need for incisive reforms in the east. It then spells out two important constraints on the conceptualization of this reform, namely those stemming from attempts to embrace restitution of property, in particular that now commercially utilized, even in the form of compensation, and those stemming from ignoring property rights presumptively inherited from the old structures.

(i) The role of property rights in resource allocation

Why do property rights matter? A market economy principally consists of individual economic agents, whether physical or legal persons, pursuing their own interests, possibly heavily weighed in favour of profit maximization, within an arena for such operations set by macroeconomic policy makers and the "institutions" of the market. Tradability of goods and services as well as production factors, that is, handing over property rights from one party to another usually at some positive price, is among the essential traits of a market economy. The indirect coordination of diffused, decentralized economic decisions can function well only if economic agents have secure, alienable property rights. That implies the possibility to trade physical and other assets, possibly in unbundled form, at mutually agreed prices in reliable contracts. The latter must be negotiable and enforceable at a fairly low transaction cost.

Property rights are important in explaining the uses of resources in terms of both allocative efficiency[538] and internal (or productive) efficiency of firms.[539] Without a doubt, alternative property rights exert different effects on the allocation of resources. Because the owner of property rights should be entitled to the residual benefits of that ownership, property rights affect the objectives of the "owners" of the firm and the way in which resources are utilized, either by owners or their agents. Public and private ownership differ in both respects.[540] As a result, changes in property rights from public to private sectors necessarily modify the relationship between those responsible for the firm's decisions and the beneficiaries of its profits, thereby materially affecting the incentive structure of management, hence managerial behaviour and company performance.

The allocative and productive efficiency implications of property assignments depend very much on the competitive and regulatory environment in which economic agents operate, as discussed earlier (see section 6.1(iv) above). This environment typically has substantially greater effects on performance than ownership *per se*.[541] But ownership, competition (hence the monitoring system) and regulation are essentially three shorthand expressions for complex sets of mutually interlocking influences. The efficiency implications of a change in one of these elements will, as a rule, be contingent upon what happens to the other two. Effects of privatization, therefore, cannot properly be assessed in isolation from these additional influences on incentives.

---

[538] The property rights school usually stresses adaptive efficiency separately. However, because adaptive efficiency is essentially efficient allocation of material and other resources over time, it is here subsumed under allocative efficiency.

[539] For details, see John Vickers and George Yarrow, *Privatization: an economic analysis*, op.cit.; and "Economic perspectives on privatization", loc.cit.

[540] For a succinct statement of the key differences, see D. Mario Nuti, "Privatization of socialist economies: general issues and the Polish case", in *Transformation of planned economies: property rights reform and macroeconomic stability*, edited by Hans Blommestein and Michael Marrese, Paris: Organisation for Economic Co-operation and Development, 1991, pp.51-68.

[541] In contrast to many other treatments of the subject (for example, see Hans Blommestein and Michael Marrese, "Creating conditions for the development of competitive markets in economies in transition" (1991 revised draft of the paper prepared for the conference on "The Transition to a Market Economy in Central and Eastern Europe", organized by the OECD's Centre for Co-operation with the European Economies in Transition and the World Bank, Paris, 29-30 November 1990), it is here argued that these multiple determinants of a firm's performance also apply to the transition economies. Of course, by virtue of the nature of state-owned assets in most market economies, the various weights of regulation, competition, and ownership assume different values. But all three are relevant to the transformation of the east.

Establishment of clear property rights[542] and an environment conducive to enforcing them[543] are, therefore, essential ingredients of moving toward market-based economic systems. And both are of vital importance in imparting credibility to a privatization policy. The latter by definition hinges on the transfer of some property rights. This can occur more or less smoothly only when property rights are clearly defined, preferably at the earliest opportunity during the transition.

This is not the place to elaborate on the nature of efficient property rights systems.[544] Suffice it simply to assert that unambiguously demarcated property rights must be vested as much as possible in the hands of actors with purely economic responsibilities; they must be enforceable by a neutral party through an effective juridical system that can adjudicate according to modern civil and commercial codes; and policy-making authority, including the ability to prescribe what kinds of activities the bearer of property rights can engage in, must be entrusted to institutions that themselves neither exercise property rights nor enforce them — a role that normally belongs to the legislative branch of government.

Regarding the effect of property rights on economic decisions, two observations are important. One is that there are transaction costs to economic behaviour that, in addition to intrinsic resource scarcity, determine outcomes. The magnitude of these costs can generally be verified only in the process of enforcing property rights.[545] Because property rights thus embody an element of uncertainty, those willing to take the risk must be able to anticipate a reasonable return in the case of success and a substantial penalty in the case of failure. Also, property rights cannot always be unambiguously defined *ex ante*. There must, therefore, be an environment, including legal institutions, for orderly adjudication of conflicting claims. What does such a system of ownership imply for the transformation of the eastern societies?

As analysed in greater depth in the preceding issue of this *Survey*,[546] property rights must be delineated urgently because of two uncertainties. One is the blurred nature of property rights for some assets in some countries, as examined in sections 6.2(ii)-(iii). The other one is that under planning legal ownership of most assets was restricted to state, societal, or social property, hence non-private property. In consequence, it is clear that without an explicit reinstitution of private property and its unambiguous recognition and protection in law, the impulse for economic restructuring, and eventually attaining a path of self-sustainable growth expected from private capital and initiative will not materialize. This is true even if the privatization campaign does not involve commitments to restitution or to more general compensation of former owners.

The uncertainties stemming from the blurring of property rights in the course of their evolution under communism and the transition can be sketched in five phases shown in chart 6.1. The public property rights established on the basis of confiscated (nationalized) private property rights during the first phase of the communist regime became gradually less firm. This occurred first because of a slackening of monitoring even under central planning. It was later exacerbated by the economic decentralization pursued. This effect is captured under the label "neglected" rights. These and part of the public rights were further dissipated early on during the transition in a confusing web of "denied" property rights (those gradually recognized under restitution or compensation claims), and "vested", "accrued" and "implicit" property rights which reflected the evolution during the end-phase of the communist system. This is discussed in detail in section 6.2(iii) below.

The crux of the matter is that the aim of the transformation is to revert by and large to the property structure of the first phase, which requires a redistribution of these rights. Matters are clear when it comes to the "denied" rights, which will be transformed directly through restitution or indirectly through compensation. Whereas the "vested" rights may be recognized, at least in part, "implicit" and "accrued" rights will be distributed over the limited public and the unlimited private rights, but in proportions which are as yet indeterminate.[547]

The chart does not reflect that each set of rights can be unbundled. It is important to be aware of this. Property rights reform in the east cannot be confined to full divestment of state and related government assets to other entities that can take possession of property.[548] This is too narrow a perspective. Some non-physical assets (e.g., broadcasting rights) cannot be fully transferred. Others, such as patents and licences, can, but the transfer need not be in full. The implications of including also these assets in the privatization process are set forth in section 6.3 and beyond. But the transfer of property rights in the privatization process need not be restricted to cases of outright divestment. Indeed, ownership may simply be divorced from the exercise

---

[542] For a useful historical backdrop, see Douglas C. North, *Institutions, institutional change and economic performance*, Cambridge and New York: Cambridge University Press, 1990; and "Institutions", *Journal of Economic Perspectives*, 1991:1, pp.97-112.

[543] For a rounded picture of the legal aspects of property, see Stephen R. Munzer, *A theory of property* (Cambridge and New York: Cambridge University Press, 1990).

[544] For details, see Ellen Comisso, "Property rights in focus", *Acta Oeconomica*, 1989:4, pp.210-216; and "Property rights, liberalism, and the transition from 'actually existing' socialism", *East European Politics and Societies*, 1991:1, pp.162-188; and Stephen R. Munzer, op.cit.

[545] For a useful economic perspective, see Yoram Barzel, *Economic analysis of property rights*, Cambridge: Cambridge University Press, 1989.

[546] See United Nations Economic Commission for Europe, *Economic Survey of Europe in 1990-1991*, New York, 1991, p.123.

[547] The presumption is that the proportion of "implicit" rights flowing back to the public domain, at least in the short run, will be larger than in the case of "accrued" rights.

[548] For an argument to the contrary, see Branko Milanovic, "Privatization in post-communist societies", *Communist Economies and Economic Transformation*, 1991:1, pp.5-39.

of most other ownership rights,[549] on which more in the next section.

(ii) Denied property rights and restitution

A sociopolitical consensus on *restituting* property that was earlier confiscated, as one important wrong to be righted, first emerged in Czechoslovakia after the "velvet revolution". But it was also an integral component of the negotiations that merged the territories of the German Democratic Republic into the institutional framework of the Federal Republic of Germany. As indicated in table 6.3, restitution is now on the policy and privatization agendas in a number of countries, at least for some classes of assets. But the bewildering tangles that result have been far from unravelled in any of these countries. This certainly is the case for those countries where the debate on restitution or compensation as principles is still being waged (e.g., in Bulgaria, where a minimum consensus was only reached in late January 1992),[550] It may be noted that the issue is less acute for most state-owned assets of the successor republics of the former Soviet Union, given that confiscation took place about seven decades ago and it would, hence, be quite difficult to identify former owners or their rightful heirs. But restitution is on the agenda in the Baltic republics.

Especially problematic in this context has been the question of land ownership. Yet rapid progress is urgent, for without it not only will there be no stimulus to increase output generation from the farm sector, but even current levels of production may not be maintainable in some countries. It should be noted that in many eastern countries land was not outrightly confiscated or nationalized. Very frequently, the land in the hands of individuals remained individual property, but the state arrogated to itself the usufruct to those assets. The basic mechanism was the forced "contribution" of privately held land to the agricultural cooperatives. In addition to private contributions, agricultural cooperatives have acquired land also from the state and through other transactions. How it will be carved up among the membership of the cooperatives or whether the state will reassert its rights to part of the land has remained an unresolved issue in most eastern countries.

Similar issues arise in connection with non-agricultural land and housing. In the case of housing, not all housing stock was appropriated; for smaller houses, especially in the rural areas, ownership as such remained with the individual. To the degree that proper cadastres have been kept, the transfer to original owners in the remaining cases should be relatively uncomplicated. However, even that transfer may be possible

TABLE 6.3

Restitution measures approved or planned in main sectors of the economy

	Industry [a]	Retail trade and catering [b]	Agricultural land [c]
Albania	Yes	..	Yes
Belarus	No	No	No
Bulgaria	Yes	Yes	Yes
Czechoslovakia	Yes	Yes	Yes
Estonia	Yes	Yes	Yes
Hungary	No	No	Partially
Latvia	Yes	Yes	Yes
Lithuania	Yes	Yes	Yes
Poland	Occasionally	Yes	Yes
Romania	No	No	Yes
Russian Federation	No	No	No
Ukraine	No	No	No
USSR	..	..	..
Yugoslavia	No	No	Partially
Memorandum item:			
Ex-GDR	Yes	Yes	Yes
Croatia	..	No	No
Slovenia	No decision	No	No

  a For footnotes see first column of table 6.11.
  b For footnotes see third column of table 6.13.
  c For footnotes see third column of table 6.2.

only once the more general questions of restitution and compensation have been tackled.

The new commitment or recommitment to democratic values and respect for the rule of law in the eastern countries argues in favour of *restitution* for moral or ethical reasons. Yet, any such promise is bound to complicate the transformation of these societies into market entities in general and the privatization process in particular.

The basic problems that arise in this connection can be summarized as follows. Even if the former owners can be clearly identified, it is by no means self-evident where justice lies if restitution requires that the usufruct which has since been entrusted to, or the property rights which have since been acquired by others, be revoked.[551] Of course, matters become far more complex in the case of factories whose structure has been substantially modified in one way or another during the period of central planning than, say, in the case of land on which no structures were erected. But deciding for restitution in one case and not the other may be unfair, or even unconstitutional as in Hungary.[552] When the essence of the confiscated property rights can no longer be separated from presently existing property rights, however inadequately they may have been defined and monitored under administrative planning, resort to restitution generates enormous difficulties.

---

[549] For details, see Calvin A. Kent, op.cit.; Lester M. Salamon, (ed.), *Beyond privatization – the tools of government action*, Washington, D.C.: The Urban Institute Press, 1989; Ezra N. Suleiman and John Waterbury, op.cit.

[550] See *Neue Zürcher Zeitung*, 31 January 1992, p.38.

[551] In the case of Bulgaria, for example, many of the smaller commercial establishments were leased to private citizens in 1990-1991. A restitution law was only passed on 11 December 1991, but it says nothing about how the property rights can be restored to former owners and revoked for the lessees.

[552] The question there was launched in the political arena because one of the coalition partners in the Government had made it a central plank to restore land ownership as it existed in 1947, even though a decision had been made earlier not to resort to restitution. Reluctantly the Government agreed to restitution of agricultural land. However, the Constitutional Court declared this law invalid on the ground that it entailed unlawful discrimination against citizens. The ruling is reproduced in *Népszabadság*, 3 October 1990.

The greatest problem facing any but the narrowest form of restitution (for example, the return of a confiscated painting) is that the legal infrastructure of the eastern economies, already inadequate at the inception of the transformation, is likely to get hopelessly entangled in claims and liens for years to come.[553] Forging ahead with divestment in the absence of clear titles may embroil the divestment agency with crippling claims from either the former owner or its contract partner if the property is eventually returned to its former owner. It has been this potential problem that has been slowing down the process of privatization notably in Germany, even though radical policy measures were put in place in early 1991.[554] These sought to replace the right to restitution by a right to compensation, guaranteed by the German Government, in cases where the contested property could be put to productive use by the potential buyer making a commitment to investment in the object of contention. This may be an issue of disproportionately large weight in Germany because of the constitutional obligation to restore rights. But it weighs heavily in other countries too. If only for that reason, a commitment to compensate those whose assets were earlier confiscated is less troublesome.

Of course, *compensation* too presents some complications. It could put pressure on current or future government budgets. And ascertaining the propriety of claims would still have to be tackled. Any attempt to ask the new governments to compensate former owners out of *general state revenues* must be considered dangerous, given the already exceedingly weak fiscal base of the eastern economies.[555]

Perhaps a commitment in principle to compensate former owners from the proceeds of the sale of capital assets (including the transfer of shares in state firms to be privatized, if so desired) would go a long way to see justice done without disrupting the transition process.

The restitution intentions in the various eastern countries at this stage are summarized in table 6.3. The measures embraced are anything but uniform. They range from awarding some claim on state property when selected state firm will be privatized for restitution claims that exceed a comparatively small amount of money, as in the case of Czechoslovakia, where the limit is about $1,000, to full restitution for physical and legal persons who had their property on the territory of the former German Democratic Republic expropriated under Nazi rule or communism (excepting actions by the Soviet Military Government between 1945 and 1949).[556] In Bulgaria, a minimum consensus was only reached in late January 1992,[557] after a bruising political battle over ownership, privatization, and moving toward the market economy that has now been evolving for nearly two years. Though a restitution-cum-compensation law was passed, the lack of resolution of the issue of land claims may seriously complicate the enforcement of the law.

A potentially worrisome development is cross-border claims. As the data in table 6.3 reveal, thus far only Germany recognizes old property rights, either through restitution or through compensation, of all former owners regardless of nationality and residence. Elsewhere, claims of those who voluntarily or under compulsion had left their country, and the claims of foreigners who were expropriated mainly after the Second World War, were largely ignored or excluded. Whereas initially these issues were thought best avoided, and virtually all countries tried to do so, the thorny issue of foreign claims has slowly been surfacing, most recently regarding those of the Sudeten Germans expelled from Czechoslovakia after the Second World War.[558] A quick and fair resolution of these vexatious issues would seem important, but may encounter considerable political difficulties.

(iii) Implicit, vested, and accrued property rights: phenomena of late communism

Although the means of production in the planned economy legally belonged to "society", in most countries legal ownership became severely blurred for four reasons. One was the incompleteness of plan instructions to firm management and the gradual easing of the intensity of monitoring state-owned assets. These gave rise to *implicit* property rights on the part of those entrusted with the poorly monitored assets, as noted in chart 6.1. At least in some countries, another was the weakening of property rights which stemmed from an investment of management or workers with some authority over the usufruct of assets. This gave rise to *vested* property rights. At the same time, the erosion of effective monitoring by the state (or other nominally legal authority) further expanded implicit property rights. At least in federally organized states (but also in countries that sought to decentralize administration of society), disputes have arisen over the respective rights of different levels of state authority.[559] Finally, communist ideology emphasized the societal

---

[553] As an example, there are reported to be over 2 million restitution claim cases pending in Germany. To date only 67,000 claims have been closed. See *Financial Times*, 25-26 January 1992, p.2.

[554] For the legal reference, see "Gesetz zur Beseitigung von Hemmnissen bei der Privatisierung von Unternehmen und zur Förderung von Investitionen vom 22. März 1991", *Bundesgesetzblatt*, 1991:I/20, pp.766 ff.

[555] Many economists would like to entrust the state with all kinds of liabilities that may be hard to discharge under weak market arrangements, including taking over the bad assets of banks and state firms, compensating former owners, minimizing fiscal distortions, cleaning up the environment, and funding a broad social safety net. For an example, see Stanley Fischer, *Privatization in East European transformation*, Cambridge, MA: National Bureau of Economic Research, Working Paper No.3703, May 1991. Entrusting all these liabilities to the government would free the private sector to engage in "ostensibly clean" operations. But its financial burden would all but paralyze and debilitate the government at a time when it needs to muster all resources to manage the transition.

[556] See "Gesetz zur Regelung offener Vermögensfragen vom 23. September 1990", *Bundesgesetzblatt*, 1990:II, pp.885 ff.

[557] *Neue Zürcher Zeitung*, 31 January 1992, p.38.

[558] See *Financial Times*, 30 January 1992, p.2.

[559] In the case of the states which were part of the former Soviet Union, for example, there are conflicting claims to property at least on the levels of the city ward,

nature of property and the right of workers to the firm's assets. Even when no rights were explicitly vested in them, management or workers more generally may lay claim to *accrued* rights, for example, because their "firm" performed reasonably well over time.

Vested rights emerge as an issue especially in countries, such as Hungary, Poland, and Yugoslavia, where the political authorities, realizing the limits to improving factor productivity through central administrative planning, simply turned over enterprise assets to enterprise councils (Hungary), self-management councils (Yugoslavia), or workers' councils (Poland).[560] Though property remained in essence the state's, as in Hungary and Poland, or was considered commonly owned, as in Yugoslavia, the inadequate monitoring by central or communal authorities ensured that those entrusted with the usufruct of capital in fact built up a strong case for adding to their accrued and implicit property rights by expanding their vested rights to mean ownership as well.

These became even more vested as a result of two factors. One was the emergence of new legal statutes on the enterprise and their incorporation as legal persons. Another was the fact that the political leadership began to encourage enterprise managers to take initiatives to help restructure their units and make them profitable. As a result, those entrusted with the usufruct began to engage in "spontaneous privatization from below". Although there are several variants of spontaneous privatization, as analysed in section 6.6, the one that has been found most objectionable takes the form of some layer of society, usually the old *nomenklatura*, capturing some rights for its own purposes.[561] But implicit property rights had been built up much earlier than the above cases might suggest. Inadequate monitoring of state-owned assets under central planning, in particular after the first measures of economic decentralization were implemented in the 1960s, conferred such rights already then to those entrusted with decision-making power over the usufruct of these assets, usually management of state-owned firms.

The circumstances summarized above afforded economic agents an incentive for the capture by insiders of basic property rights, including those *not* explicitly transferred to them. This capture devolved from three circumstances that should have different implications for the privatization process. One is the "rights" built up by management, enterprise councils, self-management bodies, or workers' councils in the use of resources and to the benefits of improving resources for which less than full capture of residual benefits was possible under the *ancien régime*. These are called *accrued* rights. Another is that the mere fact of entrusting these enterprise organs with usufruct rights, without clearly defining them in detail and with haphazard monitoring in any case, bestows upon those organs some claim to the future benefits of those resources. These are *vested* rights. Finally, because of bad monitoring by the state, some of the these organs, depending on the degree of de facto or formal decentralization, were also enticed to capture rights over assets that the state had not really intended to be transferred, certainly not in the peculiar form of spontaneous privatization from below. These are called *implicit* rights.

In other words, there were agents other than the state that had property rights that were not clearly defined as private property rights. Such claims cannot all be swept aside. Honouring such rights, however, must be different from allowing insider information to remove property rights that legitimately belong to others, possibly society at large.

Pre-emptive renationalization of these assets, as discussed earlier, would remove the uncertainty also over these assets. But doing so without resolving the claims of accrued, implicit, or vested property rights might be unfair, as well as counter-productive in view of the aim of rapidly anchoring market-based economic systems and decision-making as this process can be carried out only if there is broad cooperation on the part of enterprise management and workers.

It can be argued that management under central planning, however appointed, has earned some of the property rights to which it is now laying claim. Taking these rights away altogether may well destroy the assets themselves, as in the case of proprietary knowledge about a particular firm. This might even be unfair as adjudicated by the new democratic values. Györgyi Matolcsy, a former high official of the Ministry of Finance concerned with Hungary's privatization, made a strong case for this recognition of management's claims.[562] His principal argument was that management in place in Hungary had built up property rights by virtue of their having rescued technically bankrupt state enterprises.[563]

The *nomenklatura* has, of course, other property rights, some of which it arrogated to itself in ways that, under the new constellation of sociopolitical precepts, are no longer acceptable. Some undoubtedly were deviously acquired even under the old rules. But seeking to redress them is bound to be at least as contentious as doing nothing about the situation.

---

the city, the region, the republic, and the successors to the former federal government. In Yugoslavia, the republics were implicitly identified as owners of the "social" means of production (except for those managed directly by the Federal authorities) in the constitution of 1974.

560 For useful analyses, see Ellen Comisso, "Property rights in focus", loc.cit. and "Property rights, liberalism ...", loc.cit.; András Nagy, "'Social choice' in Eastern Europe", *Journal of Comparative Economics*, 1991:2, pp.266-283; and Erzsébet Szalai, "Integration of special interests in the Hungarian economy: the struggle between large companies and the Party and state bureaucracy", *Journal of Comparative Economics*, 1991:2, pp.284-303.

561 In that sense, "spontaneous privatization" is a polite term for grand larceny in these societies.

562 See "Defending the cause of the spontaneous reform of ownership", *Acta Oeconomica*, 1990:1/2, pp.1-22.

563 Jadwiga Staniszkis gingerly endorses this interpretation for Poland too, provided the "the more blatant forms of speculation with (political) power are limited." (see her "'Political capitalism' in Poland", *East European Politics and Societies*, 1991:1, pp.127-141; (quote from p.141)). A similar defence has been made for the Soviet Union (see Leonid Grigoriev, "Ulterior property rights and privatization: even God cannot change the past", Stockholm: Östekonomiska Institutet, *Working Paper No.32*, 1991). But his argument goes well beyond the property rights claims that Matolcsy or Staniszkis would be prepared to legitimate. Grigoriev indeed is willing to recognize also the implicit rents of each level of the government bureaucracy, which he refers to as "ulterior property rights".

CHART 6.1

Transformations of property rights

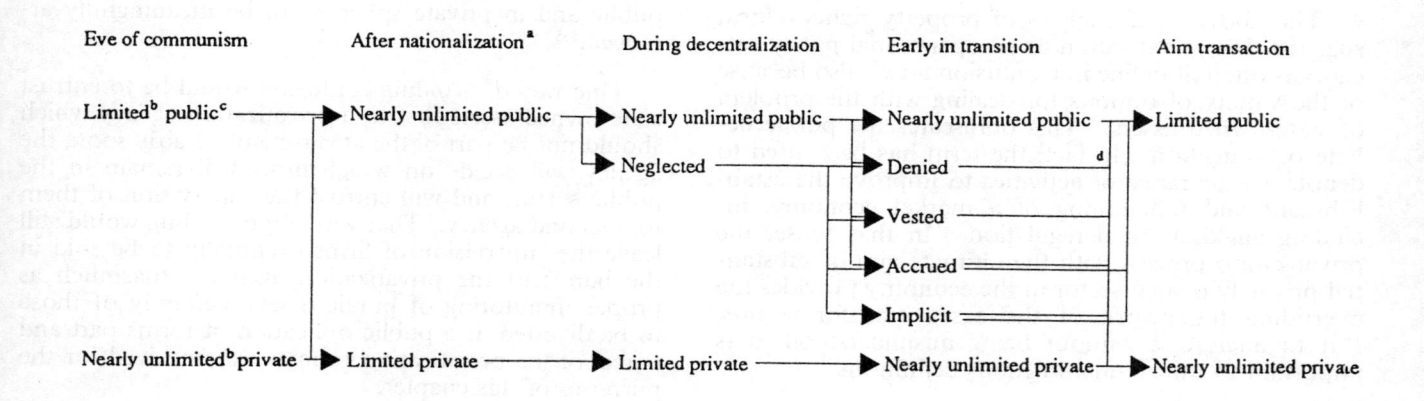

Eve of communism	After nationalization[a]	During decentralization	Early in transition	Aim transaction
Limited[b] public[c] →	Nearly unlimited public →	Nearly unlimited public →	Nearly unlimited public →	Limited public
		↘ Neglected →	Denied [d]	
			Vested	
			Accrued	
			Implicit	
Nearly unlimited[b] private →	Limited private →	Limited private →	Nearly unlimited private →	Nearly unlimited private

[a] There may be several rounds of nationalizations during which the balance between private and public rights shifts, and there may be some vested, implicit, and accrued property rights.
[b] The precise content of limited and unlimited may change during each phase.
[c] Public rights are also known as state, society, common, or communal rights.
[d] Through restitution or compensation (but possibly limited); the rest is through sale or give-away.

Although this capture of rights may in fact improve the process of resource allocation and thus shorten the adversity of the transition, this alienation of state-owned assets may well fail to be condoned by society at large. Considerable resentment has built up over the more egregious ways in which part of society's wealth in several eastern economies has been transformed into private property over the past four years or so.

The question now is precisely how and to what degree these claimed rights will be recognized in the privatization process. It would be useful to settle these issues as early as possible in the privatization campaign in order to stave off potentially disruptive sociopolitical debates and to be able to forge ahead with enterprise restructuring and divestment.

6.3 PRIVATIZATION AS AN ITEM OF TRANSITION POLICY

The above brief analysis of property rights reform suggests that privatization as an operational policy category is often ill-defined. Confusion arises also because of the variety of options for dealing with the problem of state-owned assets. This obfuscates the public debate on transition. In fact, the term has been used to denote a wide range of activities to improve the establishment and functioning of a market economy, including all kinds of deregulation. In that sense, the privatization process with the ultimate aim of substantial privately owned sector in the economy provides the overriding framework of the east's transformations. But to analyse it without being misunderstood, it is important to utilize unambiguous definitions.

(i) Basic definitions

"Privatization" is here used as defined in the preceding issue of this *Survey*;[564] the same applies to the terms *"corporatization"*, *"commercialization"*, and *"divestment"* introduced later. That is, privatization is essentially defined as all those actions which take the "state" (that is, the political process and its subordinated bureaucratic institutions and power centres) out of the decision-making about *at least* the allocation of the usufruct of state-owned assets as quickly as possible. Whenever this can be done at little cost and organizational disruptions, the transfer should extend to all property rights. But outright *divestment* of the large portion of the capital stock at issue in the transition countries is a long and slow undertaking under the best of circumstances. A rapid assignment of the usufruct of assets to non-state agents according to clear-cut criteria that cannot be distorted out of political or administrative expediency could constitute a useful prelude to full divestment.

This does, of course, raise semantic questions regarding the treatment of firms that eventually will be kept in the public domain and the public character of other firms for as long as they cannot be divested outright. Although these firms will as soon as possible have to be made more self-sufficient than has been the case during planning, managing public firms that are there to stay or public firms that are being queued for privatization cannot be equated with the transfer of full property rights. After all, public enterprises for better or worse cannot have identical incentive criteria as their private "counterparts", making due allowance for the fact that in most economies there are few firms for which a direct comparison between performance in public and in private spheres can be meaningfully arranged.[565]

One way of avoiding confusion would be to entrust state-owned assets first to a privatization agency which should not be part of the government. Fairly soon, the agency will decide on which firms will remain in the public sector, and will entrust the supervision of them to a second agency. That way of proceeding would still leave the supervision of firms eventually to be sold in the hands of the privatization agency. Inasmuch as proper monitoring of public assets, certainly of those to be divested, is a public obligation, it forms part and parcel of the privatization process as conceived for the purposes of this chapter.

When talking about assets, it should be borne in mind that they encompass a great variety, including land, plant and equipment, housing, infrastructure, financial institutions, public utilities, and others. And there are, of course, non-physical assets, including patents and licences. (Some issues arising from the wide variety of assets that should be of concern to policy makers are discussed in box 6.1.)

Even though all are capital assets capable of yielding some stream of services to consumption or the production process, it will be useful to keep such distinctions in mind as a number of countries proceed differently with the privatization of, say, industrial assets as compared to land. This choice is sometimes dictated by political circumstances. But it also stems from the different approaches to rapid divestment that can realistically be adopted for each such class of assets. Thus, it is intrinsically easier to sell a truck than to sell an entire factory. Likewise it is much easier to end the previous policy of patents and licences belonging not to the inventor but to the state or its agent than to sell off an automobile plant.

Recalling the exposition on property rights in section 6.2, the privatization process as defined here can usefully be divided into several stages. But these need not invariably be rigidly structured in the sense of one following another, nor do all stages apply to resolving the question of how best to handle the various categories of assets enumerated above (see also section 6.6). But the full range could profitably be considered as options for taking the state machinery out of the decision-making concerning in particular the large industrial enterprises.

A *first* step is to undertake enterprise reforms that alter the legal status of the enterprise from being a state

---

[564] United Nations Economic Commission for Europe, *Economic Survey of Europe in 1990-1991*, New York, 1991, pp.131-132.

[565] For details on this question, see, among others, Pierre Pestieau, "Measuring the performance of public enterprises – a must in times of privatization", *Annals of Public and Cooperative Economics*, 1989:3, pp.293-305; and J.A. Chandler, "Public administration and private management. Is there a difference?" *Public Administration*, 1991:3, pp.385-392.

> **BOX 6.1**
>
> **On the meaning of assets**
>
> Most of the discussion about privatization in the post-communism transition economies has been focused on taking the state out of the decision-making about the allocation of fixed assets and inventories of industrial enterprises. Undoubtedly, these constitute the core of the state-owned enterprises in these countries. But there are other assets over which the state has had, at least in principle, full control. To the extent that they meet the criterion used in this chapter, namely that the comparative cost of coordinating and maximizing the service streams potentially emanating from these assets in the public sector exceeds that of some private arrangement, there is no **a priori** reason why other assets should be excluded from the privatization policy. This is certainly true for land and farm operations. The same applies to various financial institutions, however primitively organized they may have been under central planning. The same applies for housing and public utilities. Of course, there may remain a significant role for the state in organizing financial institutions and public utilities. But a good proportion of these tasks can be taken care of, again according to the above-mentioned criterion, through appropriate regulatory policies.
>
> To appreciate the need for broad privatization of those sectors too, it may be best to envisage the production process as consisting of procedures that combine various types of primary and intermediate inputs from which a profit accrues to the owners and possibly their agents. All production factors (land, labour, natural resources, and capital) can be looked upon as potentially yielding a sequence of service streams that need to be allocated in the most effective way to economic activities with a view to maximizing profit during the life of the asset. This necessitates that the decision maker scrutinizes the intensity with which production factors may yield this stream of services over time. Uncertainty may be substantial. But expectations must be formed for otherwise the investment process would grind to a halt and capital assets would simply be made idle.
>
> In this process, it has been claimed, ownership and property rights, once clearly defined, no longer play a major role. Certainly, ownership does matter, but that "is an extremely weak conclusion" [1] Of much greater significance is how ownership affects incentives and what are the magnitudes of the resulting effects. The structure of markets and the conduct of regulatory policies affect the answer to both questions. And indeed the outcome entirely depends on having clear property rights. Until they are clearly delineated, they are certainly critical to the economic outcomes that can realistically be entertained. And clear property rights are, of course, of paramount importance in eliciting proper monitoring of management when ownership of and control over assets are separated because that is more efficient than owner-operator or public-sector arrangements.
>
> Capital is one of the most confusing and least clearly defined concepts in economics. Perhaps some headway can be made by first clarifying the concept of the "wealth" of a nation. This consists of natural resources, the stock of goods, and net foreign claims. The stock of goods includes structures, durable equipment that yields usable services to consumers and producers, and inventories of finished goods, raw materials, and semi-finished goods. There are also many intangible forms of wealth, notably the skill, knowledge, and character of individuals as well as the "institutions", namely the framework of laws, conventions, and social interactions that sustains a viable division of labour in society.
>
> In addition to these real assets, personal wealth may include assets evidencing claims of various kinds against other individuals, legal entities, and public institutions and various levels of government. Note that in an accounting framework, individual claims will be offset to a large extent by individual liabilities, so that in the end the sum of net claims of all individuals in a society will be equal to a nation's wealth as defined earlier.
>
> Wealth can be looked upon as a store of goods and services that will meet future needs of those possessing that wealth. Tangible assets do so in a variety of ways. Sometimes they do so by yielding directly consumable goods and services. But more often the value of assets is marketable because it enhances the power of human effort and intelligence in producing consumable goods and services.
>
> The foregoing suggests that the value of wealth depends on the goods and services that will eventually be produced to satisfy human needs. In other words, efficient resource allocation can take place only when the trade-off between present and future consumption is properly accommodated through market relations. For that flexible capital markets, including for land and real estate, is indispensable.
>
> But what precisely is capital? Because production is a process that evolves over time, during which inputs are followed by outputs, capital is an expression of sequential production and, therefore, must have a time structure. This means that capital must belong to the **stream** of inputs, giving rise to a **stream** of outputs. It is then the pricing of making available the particular elements of that stream of inputs that leads to a stream of outputs which is at the heart of capital and its proper evaluation according to scarcity criteria.
>
> ---
> [1] See George Yarrow, "Does ownership matter?" loc.cit., pp.52-69.

agent subject to ad hoc bureaucratic interferences to some form of joint-stock or limited-liability company. This switch is here denoted as *"corporatization."* The state legally remains the ultimate owner of the firm and its assets. But their usufruct falls within the competence of management, which may have to be changed. And, it is hoped that the latter will be the subject of adequate monitoring by some asset-management agency. Its operations, in turn, however wide an authority it may be delegated, should be subject to tight supervision by the emerging democratic process (parliament or one of its watch-dog committees).

Second, when the above corporations are also subjected to a "hard budget" constraint, that is, have to be profitable or otherwise be sold or dissolved, the term *"commercialization"* is used. In addition to adequate monitoring, commercialization involves largely the fine-tuning of managerial incentive schemes by boards of directors (acting on behalf of the asset-management agencies) with a view to induce management to improve net asset values, ultimately on behalf of the state until divestment can realistically be undertaken. These incentive mechanisms should parallel as closely as possible those as a rule assigned to a private corporation, including notably the necessity of arranging financing through the commercial banks. This is considered an important first, pragmatic step in delinking state and economy, including for firms that will remain in the public sector. Ideally, management should be contestable so that the boards of directors and the asset-management agencies acting on behalf of the ultimate owner can appoint the team that best serves the owner's interests. This is difficult to arrange for public enterprises, but there are ways in which the interests of various groups may lead to partly contestable management during the first phases of the transition.

A *third* stage consists of establishing *modalities to contract out assets*. This encompasses various arrangements (such as leases, management contracts, franchising, subcontracting, and so on) whereby management obtains the usufruct of assets under conditions that are set out in a contractual arrangement usually at a positive price to the ultimate owner. This differs from commercialization in that the contracted management will have considerable autonomy. The asset-management agencies will monitor only to ensure that the contractual terms are observed, including that assets are not stripped for private gain.

Finally, the term *"divestment"* denotes the full transfer of all property rights from the state to another agent. Such transactions include outright sales through a variety of channels as well as programmes for the free distribution of the assets, often referred to as "give-aways".

The above categorization was chosen because of the phasing of the transition discussed in section 6.1(iii). In other words, the argument here is for the recognition of full property rights for all agents at the earliest moment of the transition, a quick resolution of restitution or compensation claims, a firm stance on whether to recognize various kinds of claimed property rights and in what form, and rapid corporatization and commercialization of state-owned firms. Further, the encouragement of private capital formation, land reform, and the movement toward divestment of state-owned assets through sale or free-distribution schemes if such is mandated by economic rationality or the sociopolitical consensus, or possibly both. The latter should proceed much faster for some assets than for others, in particular the large firms for which intermediate privatization modes can be explored on the way to full divestment.

The privatization process in the east is generally separated into so-called "small" (or "petty") and "big" (or "real" or "mass") privatization. This distinction has since gained wide acceptance for two reasons. One is the goal of improving the efficiency of asset use, buttressing private ownership as a key ingredient for strengthening democracy, and permitting the population at large to acquire in some form, possibly through free-distribution schemes, assets that it was formerly denied access to for ideological, political, or administrative reasons. The other is that it is now widely recognized that divestment, especially in the case of core industry ("real privatization"), can proceed only over a fairly protracted period of time even if policy makers are bent on divesting assets without having to worry too much about proceeds and wealth distribution implications.

The dividing line between small and big privatization is not set hard and fast, however. The first is essentially concerned with the sale to the public-at-large (possibly residents, nationals, expatriates, and other foreign private and legal persons) of assets that the state should never have arrogated to itself in the first place. These are essentially capital goods (including possibly arable land and housing, but certainly service shops, retail outlets, catering establishments, small workshops, and similar productive units) where private (essentially operator) ownership is the least-cost solution for the process of coordinating the service streams potentially released by these assets in production and consumption. The range of what constitutes "petty" assets varies widely from country to country. Thus, Hungary defines petty privatization as encompassing firms with at most 10 employees (15 in the case of public catering and hotels). But Czechoslovakia defines it negatively, by taking "large privatization" to refer basically to firms with at least 500 employees.

However defined, petty assets should be sold quickly through fair allocation mechanisms, such as public auctions in most cases (but land reform may be organized differently), even though this is not a patent recipe for speed. The goal is to establish quickly a core of private agent-owners who constitute the nucleus of an emerging middle class and can help strengthen democracy, the efficient production of new goods and services, and job creation for those made idle by the transformation of the old economic structures.

On the other hand, big privatization refers in particular to the divestment through the sale or free distribution of shares in public firms that tend to be large, organized in conglomerates, and highly monopolistic. The conglomerates may first have to be broken up into meaningful units, as suggested later. The objectives of such divestment as well as the ways in which it could be achieved are, therefore, considerably more complex than is the case for assets that form the subject of small privatization.

(ii) The dispute about the meaning of privatization

The definition of privatization as a process with various stages embraced here is often rejected because it is too broad and, hence, encompasses activities that do not unambiguously place all property rights in the hands of private agents or their representatives.[566] Other analysts and commentators prefer to define it with ref-

---

566 See, for example, Hans Blommestein, Michael Marrese, and Salvatore Zecchini, "Centrally planned economies in transition: an introductory overview of selected issues and strategies", in *Transformation of Planned Economies* ..., op.cit., pp.11-28; Olivier Bouin and Charles-Albert Michalet, op.cit.

erence to the dismantling of the state sector, and would thus include deregulation, the delivery of some public and many quasi-public goods by the private sector, tax abatement, and trade liberalization.[567] At the other extreme are those who prefer to confine the notion of privatization to outright divestment alone, through sale or free distribution of state-owned assets. An intermediate position is advocated in this chapter.

Definitions should, of course, in the end reflect the type of remit that facilitates a comprehensive analysis of the topic selected for in-depth investigation in all its aspects. Thus, whereas the notion of privatization might be utilized to refer narrowly only to the emergence of private institutions, this is not quite the issue faced by policy makers in the economies in transition. Certainly, private institutions and their legal foundations will have to be established and anchored. But this leaves aside many issues relating to the core question of what to do with the stock of state-owned assets.

The same applies to, say, deregulation and trade liberalization. These and related measures are part and parcel of the transition agenda. That constitutes a vast area of inquiry in its own right, which was partly reviewed in a previous issue of this *Survey*.[568] Unless the notion of privatization is set so broadly that it becomes less and less useful as an operational category for policy making, deregulation[569] and other ways of liberalizing the economic mechanism are not quite components of the privatization process. Deregulation and trade liberalization are agendas in their own right.

It is felt here that terms should be defined for their usefulness in tackling the main issues at hand. Here this is seen to be the rapid enhancement of efficiency in the use of *existing* capital assets by taking the state out of the decision-making about the allocation of the service streams obtainable from these assets. This is such an urgent and daunting task that a whole panoply of remedies to state involvement must be examined — and acted upon — immediately, for doing nothing until state-owned assets can be sold or given away is a sure recipe for unsettling economic affairs at the micro level.[570]

There are of course different ways in which the state can be so relieved. Divestment is one such way. But there are others. Some of these approaches will be best suited because outright divestment is either simply not yet possible or not the best way of changing the decision-making arena for the allocation of capital services. In this context, due attention must be paid to the time element, given the path-dependency of the transition.[571] That implies, for example, that although divestment may be possible in the long run, certainly in the case of sale but also when free distribution is being contemplated, in the interim the focus is best placed on taking the political bodies out of the microeconomic spheres.

Also, as noted in connection with the transferability of property rights, privatization cannot really be confined to divestment for three reasons. One is that some non-physical assets (such as the right to airwaves or port management) in modern societies cannot be sold. But the exploitation of their usufruct can be ensured by private agents, who will pay at least a fee to the state. The second reason is that complex market economies do not solely have owner-operators; otherwise the modern corporation and much of the institutions performing financial intermediation would not exist. Finally, when viewed as bundles, property rights can be divided into several components that are not necessarily best exploited by the owner-operator. In that case, privatization may simply divorce ownership *per se* from the exercise of most ownership rights.

Privatization, as a result, can be taken to encompass a wide variety of changes in the control over assets; some are concerned with alternative approaches to the supply and indeed financing of local and central government services. As such, "privatization" can be described as an umbrella term for a variety of different actions that are linked by the fact of their contribution to strengthening the market at the expense of the state.[572]

As stressed earlier, the primordial purpose of privatization in the former planned economies is to rectify the rather disheartening economic performance or the low efficiency with which resources were used there, in particular since the early 1970s. It was indeed at that time, after fairly solid economic gains obtained during some three decades, that secular economic performance began its inexorable downward trend.

Clearly, economic performance depends on a number of factors, including primary inputs and management-cum-organization or X-efficiency. What is at stake in raising the economic performance of the former planned economies is twofold. One is to eliminate the most intrusive vestiges of central planning and replace it with market-based decision-making, preferably under competitive conditions. The other is that all property forms should be recognized as potentially useful, as argued in section 6.2. The "usefulness" is then a matter of determining the way in which coordinating the service stream potentially emanating from assets can be ensured at least cost over time. In many cases, this will be done largely through the owner-operator. In others, it will be the state that is best

---

[567] For an extreme example, see Gunnar Eliasson, "The micro frustrations of privatizing Eastern Europe" (paper prepared for the conference "Privatization in Eastern Europe", organized by the International Center for Monetary and Banking Studies, Geneva, Switzerland, 20-21 September 1991).

[568] United Nations Economic Commission for Europe, *Economic Survey of Europe in 1990-1991*, New York, 1991, pp.124-185, advocates one agenda for the transition and applies it in some detail to the various experiences of the countries of eastern Europe and the then Soviet Union.

[569] Deregulation is essentially concerned with the total abolition, the reduction in scope and intensity, and the modification of the regulatory control system.

[570] Indeed, management and workers in place have a common interest in safeguarding their position through mechanisms that are essentially inimical to the aims of the transition (see section 6.5).

[571] See David M. Newbery, "Sequencing the transition", London: Centre for Economic Policy Research, Discussion Paper Series No.575, August 1991.

[572] See John Vickers and Vincent Wright, loc.cit.

TABLE 6.4
Share of the socialized sector in 1987

	NMP produced	Gross industrial output	Gross agricultural output	Retail trade (including catering)
Albania	..	..	90.7	..
Belarus	100.0	100.0	100.0	100.0
Bulgaria	100.0	99.9	99.9	100.0
Czechoslovakia	99.3	100.0	78.3	100.0
Estonia	100.0	100.0	100.0	100.0
Hungary	92.7	98.4	99.3	97.7
Latvia	100.0	100.0	100.0	100.0
Lithuania	100.0	100.0	100.0	100.0
Poland	82.9	96.6	21.6	97.6
Romania	95.5 [a]	99.5 [b]	85.6 [a]	100.0
Russian Federation	100.0	100.0	100.0	100.0
Ukraine	100.0	100.0	100.0	100.0
USSR	100.0	100.0	100.0	100.0
Yugoslavia	93.3	100.0	30.1 [c]	99.8 [d]
Memorandum item:				
Ex-GDR	96.5	98.3	94.9	88.8

Source: National statistics and CMEA statistical yearbooks (various years).

Note: These officially reported data are biased upwards, since most governments were interested to show the highest possible degree of "socialization". The distortion is particularly large in agriculture, where the output of auxiliary farms was always grouped together with the output of the cooperatives. The justification of this practice was that, in most cases the owners of these plots were members of the cooperatives.

[a] 1980.
[b] From national accounts (GMP) statistics.
[c] Includes fishing.

suited to produce the goods and services. In between these poles, there exists a whole range of ownership forms that divorce either public or private ownership from control. Inasmuch as in most economies in transition the vast bulk of assets were owned by the state, society, or in common without a clear attribution (see table 6.4), there is a strong presumption that this is not the best way in which the optimal service stream embedded in the existing assets can be arranged. Hence, the overriding call for taking the state out of the decision-making over economic resources, including the allocation of capital assets.

Unlike what can be expected for the private sector, on which more in section 6.3(iii), improvements in the allocation of resources presently in the form of sizeable state firms or undertakings that cannot, at any rate not yet, be handed over to private initiative presents a real challenge for policy makers. This includes a vast amount of assets the property rights are which are in the hands of the state or subject to ill-defined surrogates, such as enterprise or workers' councils. This is an area of concern that the transition *per se* has to come to grips with in order to prop up genuine economic transformation and structural change. The central problem for improving the efficient use of these resources is that rapid divestment itself is unlikely to suffice. Rather, measures are needed to ensure that existing capital assets are utilized better than under central or administrative planning as quickly as feasible and in whatever form circumstances allow to be utilized.

(iii) The private sector and its role in the transition

Once the transition economy has clear property rights and adequate basic market institutions, the role of the private sector in charting the onward course of transformation will be very important indeed. Private capital formation becomes particularly important for the rapid growth of a layer of small and medium-sized firms. Fostering the formation of such firms, whether through a structural policy of the state or simply through the market, should rank high among the priorities on the agenda of the transition.

Although private capital formation and the role of small and medium-sized firms are not the subject proper of the type of privatizations discussed here, two remarks are in order. One is that some forms of divestment will involve new capital formation, including from private sources. The other is that a vibrant private sector may so erode the intrinsic value of the public sector that the issue of how best to privatize those assets loses some of the urgency and acuity with which it has recently been viewed. This has a lot to do with the notion of the value of capital assets, as explained later (see section 6.5).

(a) Privatization and new firms

The multiple issues of bringing about modifications in saving behaviour and ensuring effective financial intermediation cannot be addressed here. But one of the most important institutions to emerge during the transition to market-based economic systems in the east will be a solid sector of small and medium-sized enterprises, in marked contrast to the gigantomania that characterized the microeconomic organization of the planned economy under communism. Indeed, virtually all eastern countries had their economy organized around large firms. These were either monopolies or conglomerates that dominated large tracts of the economy, particularly in industry but also in wholesale and retail trade.

The scale of the effort involved in moving decisively forward with privatization can be placed in relief by comparing the tasks faced by Germany upon the establishment of economic and monetary union and, even more, upon full merger on 3 October 1990. Table 6.5 illustrates the extreme concentration in the eastern *Länder* of Germany, where the entire production sphere was divided into some 220 *Kombinate*. The industrial sector, by far the largest in the economy, encompassed only 126 such conglomerates with an average workforce of 20,000 in 1989.[573]

TABLE 6.5

Germany: Size distribution of firms in mining and manufacturing in 1989

Number of employees	Number of firms (Percentage) West	East	Employees (Percentage) West	East
Less than 100	72.1	17.4	18.2	1.0
101-1-1,000	25.7	57.7	43.2	23.2
Over 1,000	2.2	24.9	38.6	75.8
Total	100.0	100.0	100.0	100.0

Source: Based on Statistisches Amt der DDR, *Statistisches Jahrbuch der Deutschen Demokratischen Republik, 1990*, p.161 and Statistisches Bundesamt, *Statistisches Jahrbuch, 1991*, pp.204-205.

Some of those giants can be disaggregated into self-contained smaller units through deconcentration. Multi-product or multi-plant conglomerates that have few links can be quickly split up, normally at a small cost. Likewise with monopolies, which in some cases can be disaggregated into smaller, competing units. However, the economies of scale and sunk costs of existing state-owned enterprises are such that they place stringent limits on the degree of deconcentration and demonopolization that can be pushed through at an acceptable cost. If, for example, owner-operators are endowed with scaled-down operations of the erstwhile conglomerate, but no provision is made for ensuring adequately smooth input supply and output disposal, the deconcentration may turn out to be very disruptive indeed.

Advocacy of the critical role of small and medium-sized firms does not, however, form a simple counterpoint to the erstwhile preference for creating gigantic monopolies. Rather, it emanates from the key features of the structural transformation that is being envisaged in the light of the real domestic and foreign possibilities of these countries. It does so in at least five respects: markets, property rights, technical change, entrepreneurship, and efficient managerial operations.[574]

Perhaps most important, the volume of private capital that can be mustered for investment purposes in these countries will, on the whole, remain constrained for years to come. In the absence of a shareholder culture, direct ownership and control through new small and medium-sized firms will probably be more attractive to most savers in these countries.

Moreover, small enterprises can be seen as embodying the spirit of independence from government that has been a yearning for the more entrepreneurial layers of the eastern societies for quite some time. Of course, that entrepreneurial spirit is by no means limited to industrial operations. And a solid middle class in these countries is likely to emerge from entrepreneurship in many other activities for which owner-operator property relations are most suitable in effectively coordinating the service streams.

Also, because of immediate and firm ownership control, small enterprises in particular are likely to provide a faster response to the urgent needs of improving consumer services and distribution in these countries. The same applies with even greater poignancy to the revival of entrepreneurship that central or administrative planning had stifled for so many decades.

Finally, small and medium-sized firms can stimulate regional economies and create local jobs especially in areas where unemployment is rapidly taking its toll on the sociopolitical support for the transition (see chapters 3 and 4). Such room for initiative will need to be accommodated at the macroeconomic policy level. This includes seeking out potential trading opportunities abroad, in partner countries of the now defunct Council for Mutual Economic Assistance (CMEA) as well as elsewhere. Rapid privatization of existing state-owned assets through outright sale may, however, place a damper on the ability of new savings to be channelled into the most promising areas of economic activity, for the reasons briefly outlined above.

One of the main impediments to the rapid progress in those sectors and firms where owner-management is a practical proposition is the insecurity of property rights discussed in section 6.2. Unless this issue is rapidly resolved, small-scale privatization will be unnecessarily delayed. The cost in terms of deferring economic revival will be higher than need be, given the tasks of industrial restructuring. Without an environment of small and medium-sized firms, reflecting the ability of new firms to enter existing markets, there will be no competitive pressure on large firms, and the soft-budget syndrome will continue, though now exacerbated by weaker fiscal control.[575]

(b) Value and relative price changes

If the private sector becomes a buoyant actor in the economy in transition, and early signs of this are on the horizon, particularly in countries that have embraced transformations with a modicum of sociopolitical consensus, it is bound to ease the urgency of moving toward divestment of the large firms. This conclusion

---

[573] See Doris Cornelsen, "Privatization in the former GDR: lessons for the Central and East European economies" (paper prepared for the conference "Impediments to the Transition: the East European Countries and the Policies of the European Community", organized by the European Policy Unit, European University Institute, 24-25 January 1992).

[574] It is also important for the emergence of a solid middle class. This would help buttress democracy and render the transformation process irreversible, if only because of the costs of renationalization.

[575] For lucid clarifications of these and related issues, see David M. Newbery, "Reform in Hungary – sequencing and privatization", *European Economic Review*, 1991:3, pp.571-580; and "Sequencing the transition", loc.cit.

derives in part from the shift in the relative prices of assets as a result of the severe economic depression and inflation in countries that have sought rapid movement toward market-based decision-making or that have been drifting in a policy vacuum. Even in this inauspicious climate, the private sector has thrived, both on the basis of the few assets held over from the planning regime as well as those acquired from petty privatization and through new investment. This must have sharply appreciated the relative value of assets held in non-state hands for which clear property rights exist.

As a result, an updated approximation of the market value of assets, on which more in section 6.5, would probably show a much smaller share of the total capital stock owned by the state than is generally believed. As long as the core production sectors of these economies remain depressed, that shift is bound to continue in favour of raising productive wealth in the private sector. Of course, this shift does not solve the issue of what should be done about state-owned assets. But it does suggest that a vibrant private sector renders the problem of divesting large state firms less acute than seems to be the case at first glance. The corollary is that there is now greater urgency in making those assets perform, to the extent they are still worth something. The suggested policy of commercializing these firms and moving forward with alternatives to outright divestment thus gains further urgency.

(c) Privatization through private capital formation

In addition to improving the utilization of existing state assets once clear property rights are set, privatization is likely to involve the infusion of funds from domestic or foreign savings. Thus, one way in which a state-owned enterprise can be taken private is by having a private investor acquire a minority interest, which can be expanded with the infusion of new capital, while remaining shares are held by financial institutions that will not be involved in direct management but will, of course, be engaged in monitoring activities. The very act of transfer of state ownership to the minority shareholder and financial institutions is considered part and parcel of privatization here. The policy pursued by the new management, possibly the minority shareholder, however, is not. The reason is simply that monitoring of these privatized companies will no longer be in the remit of the state or its asset-management agencies, but will be entrusted to private agents, be they individuals or corporations, even when the latter are in part owned by the government. As argued in section 6.6, this is very important for the Hungarian strategy of fostering cross-ownership among the large firms and banks.

6.4 THE MOTIVES FOR AND OBJECTIVES OF PRIVATIZATION

Privatization measures are justified on a number of very different grounds, among which economic reasons constitute only one component. This is quite distinct from the rationale undergirding the advocacy of public-sector reform, which is as a rule economic and involves engineering a fundamental transformation of state economic activity.[576] Likewise with respect to the consequences of privatization: they are rarely limited to economic effects. Indeed, the driving force behind privatization in the west, however defined, is nearly always explicitly political (such as reducing trade-union power or enhancing sociopolitical stability), although this motivation is not always overtly avowed. It is also clear that privatization measures vary from country to country, and nowhere is the policy driven by one overriding objective.

Matters are no different in the east. In the context of the convoluted transitions there, it is hard to imagine how privatization could have been kept unpoliticized. Any hope of being able to treat privatization as a purely technical issue is bound to be frustrated very soon. Perhaps the paramount reason is a negative one. The initial policy formulation on privatization in one country after another has been largely a reaction to the denial of private property rights under communism and, in turn, the desire to rectify the all-embracing power, including that over the state-owned capital assets, assumed by the entrenched bureaucracy. Related motives are to enhance freedom and hence the democratic process. For that, some critical minimum of property rights reform and outright divestment may have to be undertaken quickly, for a democracy without a solid market economy is unthinkable.[577]

Of course, while all eastern countries share most of these motives and goals, their relative intensity and weight in the privatization process differ between countries in many respects. But determining the national priorities in this respect, let alone establishing tentative measurements, is very difficult.[578] None the less, one can hazard a guess that in countries where the role of communist rule and centralized economic planning were watered down in the course of decentralization, political relaxation, or in reaction to the financial crises in 1981-1982, more emphasis tends to be placed on economic aims. Elsewhere, political ambitions and convictions must probably be given the greater weight.

Even where economic concerns are uppermost, there is a good deal of differentiation between countries.

Thus, the campaign in Hungary, at least until late 1991, was dominated by concern about maintaining fiscal revenues and thus the imperative to move forward gradually. By contrast, both Czechoslovakia and Poland have been more concerned with getting private economic agents established. Until mid-1991, Poland aimed at doing so by preparing enterprises for divestment and then moving rapidly forward with some form of sale. Czechoslovakia has been more optimistic about the market economy taking root quickly and almost automatically once private economic agents are at work. It has, therefore, stressed the imperative of mass privatization through free distribution of shares in state-owned firms and selling off rapidly a large volume of smaller assets.

It is difficult to identify the most important motives for and aims of privatization without first looking at the variety that can be pursued during any such campaign. Their wide range is schematically depicted in table 6.6. These are not necessarily ends in themselves. Thus, reaching effective competition is certainly a means to ensuring improved allocative efficiency, which in turn will help to improve prosperity in the economy in transition. Thus seen, the most important motives for and goals of privatization can be brought under five labels, as in table 6.6, although some elements could be allotted to more than one category.

(i) Economic motives

These include questions of economic efficiency in particular as related to the role of the state as producer, the presence of a shareholder culture, the generation of budget revenues and compression of budget outlays, eliciting savings for development, buttressing economic stabilization, and promoting competition and the profit drive at the firm level.

(a) Economic efficiency

Too large a public sector leads to intolerable inefficiency in production, resource allocation, and/or adaption to structural change. To reverse this, assets need to be entrusted to private owners or privately motivated managers. Note that whereas a priori one would expect private owners to do a better job in terms of economic efficiency, this need not be the case. Market structures and regulatory environments, as detailed in section 6.1(iv), are critical too.

---

[576] See Ezra N. Suleiman and John Waterbury, "Introduction", in *The political economy of public ...*, op.cit., pp.1-21.

[577] Yet there continues to be a considerable degree of egalitarian thinking and a strong public sentiment for economic equality in the eastern countries. But economic differentiation is bound to occur in the process of establishing market-based economies.

[578] An attempt was made to elicit such an ordering of priorities from the authors of the country notes mentioned at the beginning of the chapter. Either the issue was side-stepped altogether or the priorities assigned remained too vague to afford useful conclusions.

TABLE 6.6

The main motivations for and goals of privatization

Economic	Political	Social	Trade union	Wealth distribution
Efficiency	De-etatization	Integrate	Less wage pressure	People's property
Profit maximization	Strengthen democracy	Social peace	Reform consensus	Portfolio diversification
Shareholding	Social stability			
Budget easing	Remove *nomenklatura*			
Finance growth				
Foster competition				
Enhance stabilization				

(b) The government as producer

The government is not a good manager of economic resources or a good monitor of the assets it entrusts to others. Indeed, its motive is not really — and cannot truly be — profit maximization. To divest assets to economic agents having only that goal will raise economic efficiency in at least one of the senses defined earlier (adaptive, allocative, and productive), and often in all. However, there are areas in which the government can deliver at lesser cost than the private sector. And reorienting the focus of public-sector firms to profit maximization is bound to be accompanied by a worsening of the performance with respect to the other functions assigned to them (such as housing, social welfare, employment, vacation, rest and recreation, and medical care).

(c) Shareholding culture

Divesting assets will familiarize the population at large with holding shares as part of their wealth portfolio and will raise the degree of monitoring of management. This may bolster private wealth, hence perhaps lower expectations with respect to the contribution of the state as a guarantor of social security and stability. Neither need be true, of course. The population at large may be so risk-averse with regard to its wealth portfolio that the acquired shares will be sold quickly. Nor is there certainty that private monitoring will improve over public monitoring, actually or potentially.

(d) Budget revenues and expenditures

Sale of assets generates revenue for the state and reduces outlays on public enterprises that are technically bankrupt or cannot otherwise finance themselves. It should be noted that from a flow-of-funds point of view a sale of assets obviously raises money that accrues to the budget. That it can provide supplementary income for state spending while modifying the portfolios of private owners and the state is also clear. As such, the sale of assets could help close the budget gap that tends to widen in the early phases of the transition. But it certainly cannot generate additional wealth in the nation as a whole, and in fact may well destroy some in the process of divestment. And in an inflationary environment, the proceeds from the sale may have to be sterilized in order to absorb a monetary overhang. In the same vein, divestment may lead to a sharp cutback in tax revenues if effective fiscal reform cannot be formulated and implemented quickly, and hence the tax base is changed, or if privatization as part of the transition leads to a worsening economic environment.

(e) Financing of development

Divestment contributes to the development of financial markets. As such, it can provide the necessary impetus to financing new and growing enterprises in the "modern" sector, in both industry and services. Privatized firms will be better managed and better financed through capital markets than through the state budget, provided at least rudimentary capital markets are in place or can be quickly brought about.[579]

(f) Promote competition

A market economy without competition cannot function well. Liberalizing the foreign sectors and stimulating new investments from private and public savings may help improve competition. But more will be required, including measures aimed at deconcentration, demonopolization, and divestment of state-owned assets, especially in economic activities for which the state cannot claim any comparative advantage.

Privatization may also generate pressures to reduce competition. Thus, agents operating in the former second economy were earning rents from the state controlling the public sector. Upon privatization and the transition, they stand to lose much of those rents and will seek protection (this phenomenon came to the fore rather early during the transition in Poland). Privatizing without opening up product markets may also raise domestic political pressures for protection against external competition,[580] a phenomenon often observed in the political debate on transition (as in the case of the successor Soviet republics). And privatization with the participation of foreign investors may have to contend with claims for monopolistic positions, tax holidays and related privileges (as has already happened in the case of some transnational corporations in

---

[579] On the role of the banking sector in an incipient capital market, see United Nations Economic Commission for Europe *Economic Survey of Europe in 1990-1991*, New York, 1991, pp.128 ff.

[580] See Philip Hanson, "Property rights in the new phase of reforms", *Soviet Economy*, 1990:2, pp.95-124.

Czechoslovakia,[581] Hungary,[582] and Poland.[583] In other words, even opening up the economy is no guarantee that pressures for solutions that undermine the emergence of competition can altogether be avoided. Any such development is, of course, contrary to the aim of monetizing part of the monopoly rents, hence fetching higher revenue for the budget, and thereby retard the process of bolstering competition and allocative efficiency.[584]

(g) Enhance economic stabilization

Because it promises radically to change the prevailing patterns of microeconomic behaviour of firms that exert an inflationary bias, privatization can help with stabilizing the economy in a flow sense. By soaking up money in circulation, provided sale revenues are sterilized, it can also facilitate stabilization in the stock sense. Note that the latter requires sale, but the former could be obtained by commercializing state firms.

(ii) Political motives

Among the many issues that could be examined, it is useful to pick up the role of the state in the economy and economic development, the need to strengthen democracy and shore up social stability, and to replace or retrain the politically appointed managers.

(a) Role of the state

Libertarians emphasize that true liberty requires private ownership with the role of government in economic affairs restricted as much as possible to the enforcement of property rights. Among the goods and services to be delivered, a sharp distinction should be made between private and public items. Public goods should be provided by the state only when it has a comparative advantage; that is usually the case when there are market failures but not government failures. But even then it is not always necessary for the government itself to engage in direct production.

(b) Strengthen democracy and social stability

As argued earlier, a democracy without private property rights is hard to envisage. Establishing a democracy in a society without a middle class may require the quick divestment of at least a substantial part of state assets to make the political revolution irreversible and to provide a buttress for market-oriented economic transformations. Furthermore, by promoting broad-based shareholding in society, privatization may lead to the constitution of a strong bulwark against social dis-

order. Democratic institutions and decision-making should also help maintain social stability as people now feel to have a voice in the way in which their society is being run.

(c) Eradicate the nomenklatura and old-style management

Taking the political and government bureaucracy out of the decision-making over the allocation of capital assets and removing the politically appointed enterprise management, which, for the sake of simplicity, is considered here part of the *nomenklatura*, should help focus the behaviour of economic agents more sharply on economic matters. However, managers of public firms as well as enterprise or workers' councils in a number of economies have implicitly or explicitly accumulated certain property rights that cannot be easily taken away through an internal reform of the public sector (see section 6.2). Privatization provides an opportunity for new owners to monitor management and hire labour according to market-based criteria.

(iii) Social framework

Items tabled here include abandoning the class struggle in an effort to reach a better-integrated society and coming to terms with co-determination claims and maintaining coherence at the firm level.

(a) Class struggle and social integration

The eastern societies in part adhered to the doctrine of the class struggle, leading to the polarization of societies (such as intelligentsia versus workers, workers versus peasants, and those in the *nomenklatura* versus the vast majority of people). Societies that have a coherent framework on sharing and how to navigate around sharp points tend to be more productive and stable than others in which the class struggle, even if under a different name, continues to affect interhuman relations in a pronounced way. Removing the repercussions of this approach throughout society must rank very high on the ultimate agenda of the democratization and stabilization of the transition economies.

(b) Co-determination

Even though the issue of the class struggle may have become remote in the transition economies, that of what to do with property rights claimed by workers and management remains to be addressed in a comprehensive fashion and it is urgent. Privatization will not ob-

---

[581] The current negotiations with Mercedes over the take-over of the Czechoslovak manufacturers of light and heavy trucks appear to have stalled because of requests from the investor side for long-term tax exemption (10 years) and a 40 per cent customs duty as protection against import competition. For details, see *Financial Times*, 15 January 1992, p.3.

[582] For the first half of 1992, the import quota for passenger cars was fixed at 60,000 as compared to a quota for 1991 of 300,000, allegedly in response to requests from General Motors and Suzuki for protection in order to start up their car assembly and later production facilities. This has caused dismay on the part of other automobile exporters who have established substantial representations in Hungary. See *Heti Világgazdaság*, 1992:4 (25 January 1992), p.16.

[583] Thus, FIAT was reported in 1990 to have negotiated for an exclusive licence with considerable foreign-sector protection.

[584] This has come to the fore in a few instances, especially with regard to undertakings with large sunk costs (such as the automobile sector). The experience of the *Treuhandanstalt* in the eastern territories of Germany has on the whole been the reverse, however. That agency has found it easier to divest itself of firms by breaking up the large monopolistic conglomerates.

literate the expectations of workers of having some say in their enterprise.

It is especially critical to ensure that labour will not be the only stratum that bears the burden of adjustment. Co-determination rights, for example, exist and cannot be taken away without arousing resistance.[585] This will be inimical to the process of transition toward an effective market economy. Some substitute for them needs to be found, such as privileged share allotments, in order to maintain a semblance of stability.[586] To embark on widespread privatization, such as in the transition economies, without soliciting the active co-operation of managers and workers is likely to lead to serious frictions that will be counter-productive and interfere with the aims of the campaign.[587]

(iv) Reducing the role of labour intransigence

Placing economic activity on an economic last requires a remoulding of labour rewards according to performance and, at the same time, protecting labour from the potential abuses of capital.

(a) Wage demands

By breaking down the structures that support high wage demands on the part of civil servants, the government not only eases its own fiscal position but sets a signal for wage demands throughout the economy. If the public sector can hold the line on wages, perhaps as part of stabilization policies, the private sector will benefit both on the degree of profitability that can be generated and in attracting talented individuals willing to change their behaviour and thinking about economic matters.

In countries where previously there was a tenuous relationship, if that, between work effort and reward, a restructuring of the remuneration system will need to be elaborated out quickly to encourage private enterprise.

(b) The social contract

By undermining, or at least seriously weakening, trade unions of the traditional mould or by eliminating the lifetime job-security system so pervasive in some economies, notably the ones now in transition, the state may help rearrange the social contract. In turn, this may lead to a more corporatist approach to reaching social consensus, notably on questions of income distribution and wages.

(v) Wealth distribution

Motivations here include the distribution of society's wealth on an equitable basis and providing new instruments for economic agents to diversify and enlarge their wealth portfolios.

(a) Social property is people's property

Since the assets entrusted to the state, it is argued, in fact, belong to society at large, in emerging pluralistic societies that property should be distributed to the entire population on as egalitarian a basis as feasible.

(b) Portfolio diversification

Private wealth accumulation in forms that were previously denied to all but the state would help reduce the demand placed on government transfers for funding of various social programmes. Individuals would more and more take care of their own intertemporal income redistribution by varying the size and composition of their portfolios. Moreover, it might contribute to changing their time preference, thereby generating additional savings for development purposes.

(vi) On prioritizing the aims of privatization

Inasmuch as the outcome of privatization policies depends critically on the tasks set, as argued earlier, it is important to isolate the key motivations for and goals of the privatization process that the various transition economies have been pursuing. This might help identify the best mechanisms to be implemented.

In many market economies, the prime motivations for privatization have been improving the productive, adaptive, and allocative efficiency of the use of assets; raising government revenues while at the same time seeking budget relief by curtailing the role of the state; breaking the back of entrenched interest groups in government-owned property, notably the political rents deriving therefrom and the deeply entrenched vested interests, rights, and privileges of labour unions that inhibited resource reallocation; and living up to the libertarian ideology that posits that democracy and freedom can best be served by private ownership and a small state.

Though some of these considerations apply also in the east, aside from the commitment to improving efficiency, the order of priorities and the range of motivations for privatization are noticeably different. Six are especially important.

---

[585] See, for example, Barbara Blaszczyk, "Dylematy prywatyzacji w Polsce", *Gospodarka narodowa*, 1991:7/8, pp.14-20; Igor V. Filatotchev, "Privatisation in the USSR: economic and social problems", *Communist Economies and Economic Transformation*, 1991:4, pp.481-498; Lena Kolarska-Bobinska, "Privatization in Poland – evolution of opinions and interests (1988-90)" (paper prepared for the colloquium on "Privatization in Central and Eastern Europe – what are the first lessons?", organized by Maison des Sciences de l'Homme, Paris, 25-26 November 1991).

[586] This is one of the few, but important, positive lessons that can be learned from the privatization campaigns in mature market economies, especially the United Kingdom (see Trevor Buck, Steve Thompson and Mike Wright, "Post-communist privatisation and the British experience", *Public Enterprise*, 1991:2/3, pp.185-200).

[587] For a deeper analysis of the situation in Poland, see Janusz M. Dabrowski, Michal Federowicz, and Anthony Levitas, "Polish state enterprises and the properties of performance: stabilization, marketization, privatization", Gdansk: Gdansk Institute of Economics, 1991.

First, as already mentioned, one of the principal motivations for privatization has been the general belief that all the institutions of the communist past were fundamentally wrong and corrupt, and therefore need to be excised as quickly and as soon as possible. This is essentially *political in nature,* namely getting even for the long years during which private ownership was denied and the state arrogated to itself the entire capital-formation and allocation process. This exclusiveness was neither necessary nor is it desirable from any point of view. Its rationale in the end rested on political arrogance.

Second, management and economic organization need to be reconceived. This is not just a matter of recent history but a reality of the transition. Under central planning, management was often entrusted to the Party faithful and their protégés rather than to individuals with demonstrated abilities to operate capital assets in the state's (or society's) best interests, on the basis of positive incentive schemes. Obliterating the influence of Party politics on economic affairs and the hold of government bureaucracy and its appointed enterprise officials and organizations over a highly monopolized enterprise sphere provides one of the most cogent arguments for privatization in the eastern economies.

Breaking up political and ministerial control over public enterprises was the single most important argument in favour of privatizing capital formation, maintenance and allocation at the time when the process of casting off the grip of the Communist Party over society got under way. Casting off the legacies of central planning and abuses of power under communist rule by breaking this power structure through outright divestment can be crucial when the political process of moving in the direction of democracy has not yet been completed or is still rather weak. Once the new political structures are firmly in place, however, the abuses of the *nomenklatura* in operating state-owned assets as their own fiefdom should be curtailed or altogether excised through that political process. It would not necessarily require outright divestment. In fact, an outright "confiscation" of the property rights vested de facto with the *nomenklatura* might be counterproductive from the point of view of improving efficiency in the short run, as observed in section 6.2.

Once this rupture with the past is accomplished, however, as would now seem to be the case in several eastern countries, economic arguments should receive a more technical reading. State-owned assets in essence represent societal savings enforced through socialist precepts. The custodians of society, who spearheaded the political revolution or who may have gained a popular mandate at the ballot box, must, therefore, ensure that these resources are utilized as efficiently as possible, given the new environment for allocating them, until more effective ways of resource allocation can be instituted. This raises a number of technical issues about how best to conduct the privatization process. These are the subject of the following sections.

Third, certainly an important general determinant has been the aspiration to *build a "normal society",* without there being a very explicit role model to be emulated either at the present time or when seen in an evolutionary perspective. Many of the new policy makers of the east hold visions of an economic, political, and social order that is both freer and more prosperous. In some cases, these attitudes survived persecution under communism or emerged from some form of "positive alienation".[588] Among the positive motivations are endeavours to enhance freedom and hence the democratic process. This requires a change in the traditional egalitarian attitude toward income levelling and in the profound culture of envy as regards economic inequality. All this has implications for both the political process as well as the economic system in evolution.

Fourth, privatization is seen as a buttress for *democracy,* not just ownership diversification as in most market economies. The process of firmly rooting democracy in most eastern countries has some way to go. To strengthen it and render it irreversible some critical minimum of property rights reform and divestment may have to be undertaken quickly, as already argued. Inasmuch as the ability to raise savings in these countries commensurate with the vast capital required for economic reconstruction is limited, it may be desirable to divest quickly some portion of the existing capital stock through imaginative schemes other than outright sales and to foster private-property formation from new savings as rapidly as possible.

Fifth, some transition economies in particular have been concerned about obtaining *revenue for the budget,* contributing to economic stabilization,[589] and reducing budgetary allocations (as for subsidies), including the administrative burden involved in the government's running or monitoring of state-owned assets. This parallels the goal in some market economies. But it is probably less well founded in the case of the eastern countries because of the enormous cost of divestment and the consequent erosion of the fiscal base.

Finally, to move effectively toward a market economy care has to be taken to make *firms raise their capital in commercial markets.* But this can only occur by widening and deepening the capital market. High priority must be given to cleaning up the balance sheets of financial institutions and to create new institutions to enhance competition in basic financial services (on which more in section 6.5), while other parts can be built up as the transition progresses.

Some forms of divestment may help capitalize in particular those institutions that form the rudiments of emerging capital markets to a level where they can take an active part in the privatization campaign. If properly designed, divestment programmes can also help to en-

---

[588] See Elemér Hankiss, *East European alternatives,* Oxford: Clarendon Press, 1990, pp.7 ff.

[589] The literature on this aspect has been confusing. Thus, if a government seeks to contain inflationary pressures by selling assets it can do so only if it freezes the revenue from privatization. There would then be no spendable income for the budget. A similar confusion about wealth exists. Privatization will simply exchange assets for current revenue that should be earmarked to amortize some state liabilities, unless the country's wealth vastly outweighs its liabilities or existing liabilities will henceforth be financed out of prospective fiscal revenues.

courage savings, in the form of workers' shareholding or incentives to accumulate stocks, perhaps through formal employee share ownership programmes (ESOPs).

The privatization motives that decision makers pursue determine to a large degree the methods of divestment to be explored. Thus, if budget revenues must be maximized, assets must be priced at the highest value that can be obtained from those possessing wealth. But if the prime motive is to buttress democracy or serve libertarian values anchored to private property, divestment through outright sale or by giving away assets should be carried out as rapidly as possible. If those who can reasonably be anticipated to have an interest in exercising property rights for maximum economic benefit can be reached, so much the better. Whether that should be done by giving each citizen an equal share in social property or through the creation of the institutions of the emerging capital market (including pension funds, insurance companies, holding companies, and investment or mutual funds) is something to be carefully pondered. This issue will be examined in section 6.6.

6.5 OBSTACLES TO PRIVATIZATION

At the outset of the east's revolutions, the complexity of managing divestment programmes was vastly underestimated by virtually all observers — most notably the new political leaderships as well as the phalanx of foreign advisers who have since gathered in the transition economies. The hurdles to be jumped have been many indeed. The obstacles can be divided into those that beset virtually any privatization programme and items that are specific, yet of special importance, to the east.

Indeed, privatization has thus far been a very cumbersome process throughout the east for reasons that derive from the nature of the transition, including the multiple legacies of communist-style planning. Some of these difficulties were already invoked at one point or another. But others should be recognized too for the range of issues that inhibit swiftly moving forward with privatization in most countries is extremely wide. Some are mostly technical in nature. Others ensue from the social and political characteristics of these economies.

In view of recent experience, it would have been highly useful to construct a succinct overview of the major obstacles to the process of privatization as conceived or as regards its implementation by early 1992. Most of the obstacles that can be listed are shared by the eastern countries. Just as in the case of the motives for and goals of privatization, however, the intensity and weight of the various obstacles encountered differ in many respects. But identifying those that are most acute, let alone assigning them and others some tentative measurements, is an arduous and, perhaps, inevitably subjective exercise.[590]

None the less, countries that pursued some form of economic decentralization, notably Hungary and Poland, are likely to face fewer economic, managerial, and attitudinal obstacles, and the political aversion to moving ahead with privatization is probably less problematic. The long, slow forward movement of reforms in Hungary succeeded in putting in place a number of legal and other institutions that have come in handy in its transition. Also Poland had experience with these elements of the "market", albeit with much more social discord than in Hungary. The situation is, of course, far more difficult in those countries that undertook very limited experimentation. This is now hampering the transition, notably in the successor republics of the Soviet Union.

However, even allowing for those head start advantages, the shared obstacles and even the acuity of a number of them remain overwhelming, except arguably in the former German Democratic Republic. It may be useful, then, to take a broader look at these hindrances to outright divestment.

The obstacles to privatization that hold centre stage in this discourse can be variously divided. Here they are organized under five headings: salient, technical, economic, managerial, and attitudinal problems. The most important entries under each label, including some that have specific features that divert from the more general problems touched upon earlier, will be discussed in this section. They are schematically presented in table 6.7.

(i) Salient problems

These are critical policy decisions that must be resolved before any headway with privatization can realistically be made. In looking at the mechanics of privatization policies, the key issues to be tackled are:

(1) the speed of privatization, the types of firms to be privatized, and the extent of restructuring to be undertaken prior to privatization;

(2) whether to proceed primarily with sales or free distribution, and which method should be preferred for each class of assets;

(3) to whom privatization should in the first instance be addressed, including the respective roles of former owners and of foreigners; the desirability of spreading ownership; and the possibility of concentrating ownership by allowing those with financial resources to acquire real assets without questions asked about the provenance of their resources;

(4) whether the implicit property rights of managers, and in the case of the east those of the *nomenklatura* more generally, and the accrued and vested property rights of managers and workers deriving from self-management councils and enterprise, or workers' councils, or co-determination schemes should be recognized and validated fully or only in part;

(5) the role of financial institutions (such as banks, insurance companies, pension funds, mutual and investment funds, as well as holding companies) in intermediating between corporations and households;

---

[590] As with motives and aims, also for obstacles an attempt was made to elicit a reaction from the authors of the country notes, mentioned at the beginning of the chapter. Either the issue was side-stepped altogether or the order in which the obstacles were viewed remained too vague to derive useful conclusions.

TABLE 6.7

The main obstacles to privatization

Salient	Technical	Economic	Managerial	Attitudinal
Speed (how fast)	Market structures	Savings	Principal-agent	Time preference and risk-taking
Priorities (why?)	Absence of capital markets	Distributive aspects	Information	Role foreign capital
Foster competition				
Enhance stabilization				
Restructuring (in what state?)	Information and regulation	Organization of auctions	Efficiency of new management	Entrepreneurship
Selection of mechanisms (how?)	Valuation	Protecting assets	Corporate governance (implicit, vested, denied)	Claimed property rights
New owners (for whom?)	Starting conditions	Macroeconomic environment	Sequencing	Conflicts of interest

(6) the degree to which it is desirable for government to hold back shares for later sale and how these shares should be administered;

(7) the role, if any, that policy makers may wish to assign to a stable core of investors; and

(8) the desirability of pursuing a rather eclectic approach to the privatization process as an alternative to a course motivated largely by ideological or purely technical considerations. From among the many items in this list, five main ones will be discussed: speed, objects to be privatized, restructuring, type of new owners, and forms of privatization.

(a) Speed

The speed of privatization is one of the central problems that have bedevilled the debate on the economic transition, and even wider issues, because it may affect — and will be influenced by — how other paramount aspects of sociopolitical stability can be anchored. It also is a function of the chosen sequence of the transition and its management. And indeed the whole range of issues concerning the degree to which the new state institutions should try to micromanage the privatization process need to be addressed as soon as possible.

This leads to a central paradox: if it is deemed desirable to move very quickly with privatization, chiefly in the form of outright divestment, there would be little point in hammering out a strategy on privatization *per se*. But precisely such a "plan" will be required to ensure that the transferred resources are used to maximum economic, social, and political effect. Certainly, rapid progress with the institution of property rights will be a must, but there are severe constraints faced here, as discussed in section 6.2.

Rapid movement with privatization by its nature is bound to be relative. A clear strategy, therefore, needs to be devised as a matter of priority. At the same time, it is necessary to put in place machinery that not only fine-tunes the privatization process as it unfolds, but that can also act swiftly so as to come to grips with various crises that are bound to emerge, especially during the initial phases. This applies in particular to those events whose scope, intensity, and specific features at the outset can at best partly be guessed.

(b) Priorities

In establishing some order of priority in remoulding ownership and control over various state-owned assets, it must be recognized that rapid progress with implementing the privatization process, including divestment of some assets, is possible and indeed desirable. In fact, there is little choice but to move ahead first with "small" privatization.[591] It is by no means obvious that the "best" policy is to pursue this through actual payments, and hence by siphoning off savings that could otherwise be earmarked for establishing new small and medium-sized enterprises. Similarly, even in some of the categories of small privatization and for all instances of large privatization, cognizance must be taken of the fact that there are various alternatives, each of which has its peculiar characteristics — advantages as well as drawbacks — of which transition managers should at least be aware. The implications for and the best choices of what type of privatization can be pursued at each stage of the transition is bound to be ordered differently for housing, land, small businesses, large public industrial firms, financial institutions, and public utilities, to mention only this six-tiered grouping.

(c) Restructuring

This is especially important for medium-sized and large industrial enterprises[592] and financial institutions. Some are quite large and must hence first be disaggregated into separately manageable components. Improvement of land, including state farms, and housing can best be left to individuals. On the other hand, re-

---

591 Even on that topic there is some controversy, as some observers feel that the heart of the problem in the east is the large public enterprises (see, for example, Rudiger Dornbusch, "Strategies and priorities for reform", in *The transition to a market economy – the broad issues*, vol.I, edited by Paul Marer and Salvatore Zecchini, Paris: Organisation for Economic Co-operation and Development, 1991, pp.169-183; Olivier Blanchard, Rudiger Dornbusch, Paul Krugman, Richard Layard, and Lawrence Summers, *Reform in eastern Europe*, Cambridge, MA and London: The MIT Press, 1991), chapter 3.

592 Large enterprises are as a rule those with at least 500 workers. But in the case of the former German Democratic Republic, large firms assigned to the central privatization agency have at least 1,500 workers. Very often, as in Czechoslovakia and Poland, the cut-off of 500 workers is used to earmark enterprises for special divestment (see section 6.6).

organizing public utilities and instituting clear operating criteria with incentives for management must, at least for now, remain a task for government, though this does not necessarily imply that government should produce the targeted goods and services. But when it comes to small undertakings, financial institutions, and other large firms, the question of restructuring is not so easy to answer.

In the case of small undertakings, it is probably best to leave the restructuring up to those individuals interested in operating those assets. It would seem advisable to transfer those assets, through sales, leases, or free distribution, as unencumbered and expeditiously as possible. Thus, a resolution for the existing debt of these undertakings is a priority item. This is even more the case for the financial institutions and also the core industrial firms. The balance sheets of these institutions must be cleaned up relatively quickly. Of critical importance is making financial institutions into viable entities, given the assigned role for banks in intermediating between savers and investors and indeed in fostering the coordination process of microeconomic agents more generally. There is little point in saddling the so-called commercial banks of a two-tier system with nonperforming assets or to expect banks to do their job, namely seek a profit from lending money that belongs to others, by monitoring indebted enterprises or evaluating credit requests on any other criteria than financial probity.

No less important are the issues of dividing the existing large firms into various groups. There are perhaps four such groups that can usefully be separately treated. Aside from identifying firms to be sold off relatively quickly and others that will be left in state hands, firms need to be allocated to a group to be wound down or to another for firms in need of some restructuring prior to being privatized. In choosing these groups, it will obviously be of importance to recognize the limitations of existing institutions to ensure that commercial transactions can take place smoothly. It is especially important to restructure enterprise debts, which are really the counterpart of the problem faced by existing financial institutions (see section 6.5(ii)(b)).

(d) Forms of privatization

The choice is essentially between outright divestment, either through sale or free distribution, and other forms of taking the state out of operational decision-making about assets. And given the speed at which privatization can realistically be pursued, the priority of turning state ventures into corporations and holding them to commercial criteria needs to be carefully examined. These matters are so involved that section 6.6 in its entirety will deal with them.

(e) New owners

To avoid needless confusion, it is useful to resolve as soon as possible whether national property can be acquired by foreigners at any stage of the privatization campaign or whether such transactions should be deferred for the present. Also important is the recognition of property rights of former owners (through restitution or compensation), the treatment of accrued and vested rights of management and workers (perhaps through preferential access to shares or properties), and the implicit rights of the *nomenklatura* at large. These issues were explored at length in section 6.2.

Whereas these questions have been debated to some degree, implementation of the measures agreed upon has become quite messy for two reasons. One is the question of restitution. Some of the countries that favour restitution (perhaps only in the form of compensation) in the east have distinguished between resident nationals and others. The latter are usually excluded. But in the case of Poland, for example, former Polish citizens are being invited to reacquire their original citizenship and thus participate in the privatization. Although residency as a criterion may foster social harmony to some degree, its role in allocating resources is less clear cut.

Precisely because of the modest inflow of foreign direct investment to date, some countries are now advocating that foreigners participate in some fashion in the privatization effort, usually with quite some strings attached. One of the most important is that non-resident individuals as a rule are excluded from participating in privatization. Legal persons are usually accommodated through discreet sales or similar arrangements.

Once these basic subjects of the privatization campaign are resolved, policy makers need to decide what role to accord to financial institutions in the implementation of the campaign, either on the demand or the supply side, or perhaps even both. Areas of potential conflicts of interest need to be addressed as soon as feasible with a view to mitigating to the extent possible both their scope and occurrence.

Finally, there is an entire array of issues pertaining to whether the government should hold back shares for later sale, and in that case what its position in monitoring management should be, and whether it should strive to attain a stable core of investors, possibly of foreign origin, soon or later, once the economic situation is stabilized.

(ii) Technical obstacles

These are here brought together under five headings: market structures, capital markets, information and regulation in the broad sense, valuation, and other legacies of planning.

(a) Market structures

Market structures cannot be ignored in formulating informed decisions about divestment. This is particularly the case when the campaign aims at improving economic results.[593] Substituting private for state monopolies properly defined will not necessarily enhance efficiency or increase the net worth of the firm as com-

---

[593] On these questions, see Chaim Fershtman, "The interdependence between ownership and market structure: the case of privatization", *Economica*, 1990:3,

petitive bidding is virtually precluded in the process.[594] Unless effective competition and regulation are introduced, divestment of firms with market power brings about private ownership in precisely the circumstances where it has least to offer.[595]

Most observers assume all too facilely that the eastern countries will soon be able to reach fair market competition through privatization, deconcentration, new capital formation, and trade liberalization. But there is no guarantee that this goal can be reached quickly. True, most multi-product or multi-plant conglomerates can be broken up into separate units, if perhaps at some overhead costs and initial disarray as established links are being severed and new ones have yet to be knit. But the experience of most eastern countries (with perhaps the exception of Czechoslovakia), especially the former German Democratic Republic and Poland, has demonstrated that deconcentration is not all that easy; in any case, disregarding the special case of the former German Democratic Republic,[596] it has not been pursued with the attention it deserves.

New private capital formation from domestic and foreign sources can help to strengthen competition too. But the experience of Czechoslovakia, Hungary, and Poland in particular have shown that new private capital formation is likely to be subdued and largely confined to the service sector. This may be partly because of the climate of uncertainty that prevails in these countries. But also the vested interests of the management and bureaucracy, as argued later, have obstructed the breaking up of the large state-owned enterprises.

(b) Absence of capital markets

At the inception of the transition process, the former centrally planned economies found themselves literally without capital markets for two reasons. One was the limited ability of individuals to acquire and hold financial wealth under communism, coupled with the considerable degree of social protection (in terms of jobs, wages, pensions, medical care, and other aspects) enjoyed under administrative planning. The other derived from the arrangements for central or administrative allocation of resources. At best, a start had been made towards the development of a financial sector through the breaking up of the state bank into a genuine central bank with some measure of autonomy and the commercialization of the departments of the old state bank that dealt with enterprise lending. Apart from Yugoslavia, which has had "commercial" banks (with rather limited commercial autonomy) since the 1960s, Hungary had begun that process in 1987; its initiatives were followed to some degree by Bulgaria and later Poland. But in the other eastern countries not even that limited financial sector structure was in place.

Unfortunately, the experience with this two-tier banking system should not be overrated. Indeed when it was set up, the new banks were burdened with non-performing assets inherited from the administrative planning past that can no longer be supported under a regime seeking to base economic decisions on market criteria. This sector needs to be quickly recapitalized and the old debts removed through some injection of public money.

Much has been written, for the benefit of the economies in transition, about capital markets and their role in market economies. Some of this advise has been useful, if only to acquaint those managing the transitions with the kind of obstacles that they have to face. But when attention was focused on the more exotic aspects of stock markets operations in London or New York as one part of fully fledged capital markets, this did not serve much purpose. Countries cannot forgo a certain measure of order in moving from their present situation to a new one. (The key issues are discussed in box 6.2.)

(c) Information and regulation

Information is an important input into reaching responsible decisions about the acquisition and allocation of capital assets. Unfortunately, this is an area in which there is a great dearth in all transition economies. Part of the problem derives from the legacies of planning in these countries, where firms had a very different role from the one they are expected to play in a market environment. Their books are accordingly not structured in such a way as to afford a comprehensive picture of their worth.[597] Much of the available information is now, of course, patently inapplicable, even where it had been accurate in the first place.[598] A substantial part of the available data was compiled to deceive the planning authorities (e.g., to regulate the ratchet phenomenon,[599] or to justify the introduction of a "new" product at a higher price). Inadequate monitoring by the planning authorities often made this a desirable option for enterprise managers to pursue.

---

pp.319-328; David Newbery, "Reform in Hungary ...", loc.cit. and "Sequencing the transition", loc.cit.; John S. Vickers and George Yarrow, *Privatization: an economic analysis*, op.cit.

[594] The theory of contestable markets says essentially that this is a problem of a lesser order of magnitude if sunk costs are small. But that is precisely the problem with most monopolies, including those in the east.

[595] See John A. Kay and John S. Vickers, "Regulatory reform in Britain", *Economic Policy*, No.7 (1988), pp.288-351; Irwin Stelzer, "Privatisation and regulation: oft-necessary", in *Privatisation & Competition* ..., op.cit., pp.70-77; John S. Vickers, "Government regulatory policy", *Oxford Review of Economic Policy*, 1991:3, pp.13-30.

[596] Because with economic and monetary union, the authorities of the Federal Republic of Germany decided to commercialize all firms and to break up the mammoth organizations known as *Kombinate*. But even there the process could not be completed as swiftly as it had been anticipated. In late 1991, 50 out of the original 220 *Kombinate* were still reported as extant (see Doris Cornelsen, loc.cit., p.2).

[597] But this has been an extremely difficult problem in privatization in the west as well (see Pál Valentiny, loc.cit.).

[598] For a detailed examination in the case of Poland, see Maureen Berry, "The privatization process in Poland and its accounting implications", Urbana, IL: University of Illinois, 1991, mimeo.

[599] This came about because planners set targets for, say, the current year (or a longer plan cycle) on the basis of achievements reported for the previous year (or plan cycle). Bonuses could be protected only by not overstating achievements, so that "soft" new targets would be obtained. Of course, the reverse prevailed also with respect to bad performance. The penalty-reward system was indeed asymmetric because wages were generally downwardly rigid.

> **BOX 6.2**
>
> **On the emergence of capital markets**
>
> *Capital as defined in box 6.1 need not be valued solely for its actual production potential of goods and services as perceived by the present owner of the asset embodying capital. Indeed, some of the components of tangible as well as some intangible (such as patents and copyright) wealth enumerated in box 6.1 can be appropriated. They can be owned by individuals, other private legal entities, or various levels of government. In a market economy, most wealth is owned by the private sector; in a planned economy, by the state or society at large. Private properties are generally transferable from one agent to another at a positive price in some form of capital market. But this need not be conceptualized as a "market" in the heuristic sense of an institution accommodating highly-organized auctions. Under planning, transfer of state-owned property occurred too, but rarely at a positive price; if priced, as under administrative planning, that value was really determined discretely or by administrative fiat. It rarely approximated a magnitude that would have cleared the "market".*
>
> *Transactions in capital as defined should facilitate exit and entry for new privately-held capital assets, including newly-divested assets, at relatively low transaction costs; appropriate monitor agents acting on behalf of private owners; and ensure that capital assets nominally publicly owned are utilized effectively and not abused through forms of "asset stripping". These tasks cannot be accommodated without there being some markets in which assets can be traded.*
>
> *But capital is far from homogeneous and, as argued in box 6.1, there are many assets other than industrial enterprises. It may be useful to distinguish at least among land, housing, non-residential infrastructure, financial institutions, other service institutions, and small and large production assets. Because the services that these assets provide and the nature of the assets themselves are quite different, as a rule, in mature market economies both the assets and their services are traded in alternative markets, which are not necessarily highly interlinked, however. Historically, most of these tasks were first handled through a rudimentary banking infrastructure and, in the case of land, the notary public, within some rules and regulations on proper behaviour that may or may not have been spelled out in a clear legal framework. In this, ensuring tradability as such was far more critical to the emergence of viable capital markets than having the entire panoply of ostensibly efficient intermediating institutions all at once. This consideration should weigh heavily in designing the transition strategy. It also has an important bearing on how best to proceed with privatization.*
>
> *One way in which the capital market could be given a jump-start is by transforming existing financial institutions into capital-market actors or to create new financial institutions whose job would be to fuel one class of transactions of "the capital market". The former could be accomplished by divesting the state of assets in return for taking over some of its liabilities. Thus, if a number of intermediating institutions now held as state-owned enterprises were to be spun off into independent organizations whose capital would offset a portfolio of liabilities, the capital market could be given a critical mass, on the basis of which it could then more or less steadily expand on its own strength. Candidates would be various types of insurance companies, social-security agencies, pension funds, and similar existing state organizations. The other alternative is to create special mutual funds, holding companies, investment funds, or divestment funds, and to entrust them with monitoring, as core investors, some category of companies whose shares could also be contested by other fund managers. The ultimate owners of most such funds would be the population at large through free distribution of shares in these funds.*

This is unfortunate, for accurate data could permit a close analysis and classification of firms to identify, even if only crudely, candidates for divestment, firms that can be sold immediately with success (perhaps because they had significant exports to western markets at competitive prices), those that need rehabilitation prior to divestment (for example, because their ex-CMEA markets have collapsed), those that must be retained (owing to their strategic or social importance), and others that must be liquidated (perhaps because their eastern markets depended critically on the existence of the now defunct transferable rouble regime).

Radical changes in enterprise accounting will take time. Yet, it will be important to realize them together with corporatization and certainly when it is decided to introduce commercial criteria for firms that are not being divested right away. This is certainly the case for most firms falling under the "large" privatization, but also for many being privatized otherwise (see section 6.6).[600]

(d) Valuation

Perhaps the knottiest problem with privatization, once the political hurdles have been taken, is the determination of a proper value of assets. This applies not only to outright divestment, in particular privatization sales, but also to other forms of trading the usufruct of assets. Thus, leasing or contracting out operations to private managers or entrepreneurs requires a "proper" rent accruing to the state, and this price too will have to be established in an environment that lacks stable markets. As noted in section 6.6, such alternatives can provide a much greater degree of freedom for the ultimate disposal of state assets.

Whereas valuation has been a very serious problem in market economies, it has proved to be a critical one in the case of the transition economies. Reformers are legitimately expected to avoid a sell-out of existing firms at prices that deviate substantially from their "intrinsic" value, however approximately this must be gauged. A political backlash against perceived under-

---

[600] This is an area in which western assistance could be of great value (see United Nations Economic Commission for Europe, *Economic Survey of Europe in 1989-1990*, New York, 1910, pp.13 ff.) and has already been widely explored.

> **BOX 6.3**
>
> **Is there a fair price for assets?**
>
> *Upon considered deliberation, the answer to this question must be negative: there is no such thing as "**the** scarcity value" of assets. It must be based directly or indirectly on some estimate of the discounted value of the service stream potentially emanating from the asset. But there is simply no single discounted value of expected returns. Indeed, the future residual profit streams depend on how the assets are managed under alternative conditions. Bidders for assets in well-functioning markets will generally have different ideas about what they can accomplish with them, given their managerial skills and anticipations about the best purposes for which the assets can be mobilized. Hence the stream of expected returns depends critically on how the assets are managed, and any serious bidder for assets will have different estimates of how well he can expect to manage them. This multiplicity of evaluations holds a fortiori when assets have to be priced outside a competitive, orderly market environment, and even more when there is pervasive uncertainty.*
>
> *So what is a "fair" price of the assets now held by the state in the economies in transition? However complex asset valuation may be in general, it is a daunting assignment in the East, given the lack of transparency that is inherent in these economies. This is a major stumbling block in designing and implementing orderly transformations even when those negotiating various forms of divestment have the best intention of doing it "right". Involving foreign experts, possibly through foreign assistance, but usually at considerable expense to the country in transition, may help clear up some points. But it cannot circumvent the pervasive uncertainty. Indeed, many foreign experts involved in the valuation process come to the East with only the most elementary knowledge of how the public sector functions, of the legacies of communist planning for individual companies, or, for that matter, of the macroeconomic and legal settings of the Eastern countries.*
>
> *There are inherent impediments to deriving the value of assets that have never been priced in a competitive environment. Adequate pricing must, in the first instance, be based on the discounted value of the expected residual returns to capital over the lifetime of the assets as viewed by prospective buyers. Unfortunately, in the East such an income stream cannot be even approximately anticipated until stable markets emerge and lead to at least "moderately predictable" product prices. Market valuation, hence setting a fair price, can only begin once a certain volume of shares or assets has been distributed. This suggests the following proposition: determining asset values outside a competitive market environment is hazardous under the best of circumstances.*

pricing of assets has already occurred in several eastern countries, including Hungary and Poland.

The impediments to and doubts surrounding the validity of any valuation of assets in the volatile situation of the countries in transition must be very vividly impressed on decision makers and the public at large. Although there may be a veneer of great rectitude obtainable from having asset values ascertained by reputable western accounting firms or consultants, this procedure is necessarily slow and costly (either for the privatizing country or for the provider of assistance). And in the end it is not clear that resources thus used are well spent.[601] Any suggestion that there is a "right price" that is ascertainable at a low cost — and frequently there is none that can be assessed at any cost — should be avoided. This is certainly the case in economies experiencing rapid inflation. Any estimated value, no matter how accurately it has been computed, is likely to be well out of line with present values when actual sale occurs.[602] A broader discussion in the public media of the difficulties of pricing assets in these countries would be desirable.

External assistance in many cases would do more good for the process of transformation if it refrained from counselling costly asset-valuation procedures. More resources could usefully be appropriated, however, to generating greater transparency and competition in transactions, and monitoring sales or leases to ensure that privileged deals for insiders are avoided.

This poses the broader question of proper pricing which is closely related to the issue of what is capital (discussed in box 6.2). The most important considerations regarding a "fair" price in the east are set forth in box 6.3.

In market economies, one or more components of the capital markets as a rule price a firm in terms of the discounted stream of the expected residual returns to capital over the lifetime of the assets. This may be done indirectly, by looking at prospective price-equity ratios for assets that are publicly traded. Otherwise a direct estimate of expected net returns for the foreseeable future, the length depending upon the discount rate adopted, must be prepared.

Whereas one can arrive at asset value estimates, these magnitudes must be looked at with two important caveats. Because of their high costs, such assessments can be justified only on behalf of owners or potential owners. Furthermore, such assessments can be anything but accurate.[603] They do intrinsically depend on

---

[601] In Poland, the cost of preparing the five companies whose shares were floated in late 1990 amounted to 22.3 per cent of the value of the issued shares and 13.4 per cent of the total value of these companies (see Grazina Garlinska, "Patologia", *Zycie gospodarcze*, 1991, No.42, p.7).

[602] It is simply unhelpful to stress the "classical" methods of valuation and illustrate how they could be applied in the transition economies. For one such approach, see M.S. Klapkiv, "Metody otsenki imushchestva privatiziruemykh predpriyatiy v Pol'she", *Finansy SSSR*, 1991:11, pp.61-66.

[603] Indeed, financial markets in mature market economies function less than optimally (see Jenny Corbett and Colin P. Mayer, "Financial reform in Eastern Europe: progress with the wrong model", London: Centre for Economic Policy Research, *Discussion Paper Series No.603*, September 1991; Ajit Singh, "The stock market in a socialist economy", in *Economic reform in post-Mao China*, edited by Peter Nolan and Dong Furen, Cambridge: Polity Press, 1990) pp.161-178; Joseph E. Stiglitz, "Government, financial markets, and economic development", Cambridge, MA: National Bureau of Economic Research, *Working Paper No.3669*, April 1991 and "Capital markets and economic fluctuations in capitalist economies" (paper presented to the Sixth Annual Congress of the European Economic Association, Cambridge, 30 August-2 September 1991).

the nature of the monitor, his assessment of the production process in place and how best it could be restructured.[604] It is the view on restructuring that is of critical importance in the eastern countries; hence the paramount role of information emphasized earlier.

Pricing assets correctly is by no means easy, given the problems of establishing a market value for assets that have never been, and cannot quickly be, priced in a competitive environment. Market valuation, hence selection of a fair price, can only begin once a certain volume of shares has been distributed to market participants, perhaps to the population at large. This gives rise to many questions concerning the starting conditions of the east's transformation and the potential abuses by those involved in the campaign as overseer or regulator.

Although free distribution of shares may seem to circumvent the valuation issue, this can hold only at the time of divestment and even then only under highly restrictive circumstances. Granted an electorate with a longer memory, the backlash from an asset give-away that generates considerable inequalities is likely to be explosive.

Some commentators have suggested that, for all practical purposes, the assets in the east, in particular those deployed in industrial activities, are worthless and one should, therefore, not worry too much about divesting the big firms. Instead, they should be closed as fast as administrative rules permit.[605] This would seem wrong unless it could be established that the goods and services still being produced — and consumed — in the east can be manufactured without the use of capital, that the populations are living under a wealth illusion, and that western offer prices reflect other considerations than the merit of the assets being acquired.

(e) The starting conditions of privatization

The legacies of more than four decades of central planning in most of the east include the lack of competent — and honest — privatizers as well as the presence of groups with a vested interest in underpricing assets or capturing them before a price can be set, on which more in section 6.6. The process had led to numerous complaints, particularly in Hungary and Poland. It is still evident in the confused circumstances of the transition in many other countries, notably in the Soviet successor republics.

The broader legacies of administrative planning and the communist ideology, and what they entail for the design of the transition strategy, including privatization, were discussed at length in an earlier issue of the *Survey*.[606]

(iii) Economic obstacles to privatization

As far as economics is concerned, the privatization process should aim at improving the allocation of existing capital assets while protecting their value. It is important to recall the critical role of secure property rights and full recognition of all property forms to enhance the efficiency of resource allocation in general and not just of existing state-owned assets. The discussion below therefore broadens to address the role of savings in transformation through sales, the distributive aspects of divestment, the organization of auctions, how best to protect the integrity of assets in the interim, and the macroeconomics of the transition.

(a) Availability of savings

To begin with, there is simply no capitalist class in the east. This lacuna gives rise to several problems: inadequate indigenous savings, reluctance to earmark savings for the purchase of state-owned assets,[607] absence of financial institutions, and others.[608] One way around this would be if the state were to take an active stance financing the purchases of those willing to buy up state property, i.e., were to turn itself into a *rentier* by making available credit for this purpose. Although several eastern countries have debated this issue, credit is not now widely available, except to mainly those who had nursed links with banks in the pre-transition economy.

Are savings a constraint on the transition? Certainly, as already demonstrated in countries that have chosen to move rapidly through "shock therapy" (such as Czechoslovakia, Poland, and Yugoslavia in 1990), there is room for mobilizing private savings. There is also ample opportunity to ensure that these savings are used most effectively for investment purposes in small and medium-sized firms, for which the necessary institutions need to be put in place. But even if all this could be accomplished rapidly, available savings are not likely to be adequate to finance *both* the purchase of state-owned assets and the new private firms that will be so vital to the successful transition to market-based economic systems. These include, of course, investment in private firms that are privatized through auctions of petty assets. If the transition economy does not suffer hyperinflation with massive structural dislocations, the funds obtained from sale could be rechannelled through the emerging financial infrastructure for bolstering the small and medium-sized enterprise sector.

---

[604] The rowdy experience with divestment in Germany under the *Treuhandanstalt* and the rough-shod take-overs in many market economies during the 1980s offer vivid illustrations of the wide range of values that different individuals may propose for given capital assets.

[605] For two such recommendations by prominent economists, see Olivier Blanchard, Rudiger Dornbusch, Paul Krugman, Richard Layard, and Lawrence Summers, op.cit.; and Rudiger Dornbusch, "Comments and discussion", *Brookings Papers on Economic Activity*, 1991:1, pp.88-92.

[606] United Nations Economic Commission for Europe, *Economic Survey of Europe in 1990-1991*, New York, 1991, pp.119-183.

[607] This also reflects the volatile socio-economic and political situation in most countries. Potential investors are probably also awaiting resolutions as regards the direction of institutional transformation, including macroeconomic stabilization, a more market-supportive fiscal system, demonopolization, and genuine wholesale trading; there are, of course, numerous legal and sociopolitical issues that need to be settled to impart confidence.

[608] Those having funds carry the social onus of being thought remnants of the *nomenklatura* or underground wheeler-dealers.

There is one aspect of the use of savings for privatization which will be mentioned here, although it could also be discussed under the role of foreign capital (in 6.5(v)(c)). This concerns the former Soviet and Yugoslav republics that currently desire to soak up the rouble and dinar holdings, respectively, to replace them in time with their own currency. Fear of "foreign" acquisitions, largely by Russian firms and individuals, if assets were sold off to all comers for roubles, has been a serious constraint on moving forward with privatization in Estonia and Lithuania, for example. A makeshift solution was adopted in the Lithuania, which prescribed citizenship as qualification for participation in the privatization, while in Estonia the question appears to be still open. Similar issues are probably important in many other post-USSR and post-Yugoslav republics bent on jettisoning the "old" currency and adopting their own.

(b) Distributive aspects of divestment

Whether part of the state assets should be distributed without compensation to the population at large or some group, such as workers, needs to be carefully weighed. The state's assets were built up by denying most private agents the right to accumulate wealth in most forms and by limiting monetary incomes. An argument can, therefore, be made in favour of an egalitarian distribution, but this cannot be pushed too far.

The confiscatory approach to forced savings did not affect all citizens, or workers for that matter, equally, even though the principle applied to all but the highly privileged few. It certainly did not apply equally to those presently alive. Even if legitimate heirs can be identified, equal distribution to the present population is rather suspect on strict egalitarian grounds. There would, then, seem to be a case for *un*equal distribution of assets. But this has not been given much attention, except in the context of recognizing accrued, implicit, and vested property rights.

Free distribution of shares poses several technical problems, on which more in section 6.6(ii). A wide distribution of assets would avoid future resentment about give-aways to a favoured class, a danger in selling firms to their managers or others at firesale prices. It would also garner support for the temporarily painful measures to restructure those undertakings. Above all, it would shore up democracy by greatly reducing the economic influence of the *nomenklatura*, strengthening the economic power of the electorate, and making the move toward market-based systems irreversible.

(c) Organization of auctions

If revenue must be raised and concerns about improving resource allocation, property administration, and principal-agent problems loom large, perhaps the organization of auction markets that are as transparent as circumstances permit offers the most advisable strategy. This transparency can be measurably enhanced by rationalizing the state-owned firm, at least to improve bookkeeping so that accounts can be audited according to standard criteria of probity. In the absence of widespread experience with this method of divestment, however, careful experimentation appears to be warranted both in the methodology of organizing markets and in phasing in the sale of assets.

Although initially auctions are likely to be rather disorderly, some information can be imparted that will prove useful in guiding individuals' expectations. Thus, the state can provide some guidance to auctions by offering assets at a cost that reflects its own expected rate of return and value of assets.[609] This may create ample opportunity for capital gains, which is not necessarily bad, provided those managing the transition take broader views of what is at stake. One could look at the organization of auctions as a risky investment in laying the foundations of a capital market or a market economy more generally.

(d) Protecting the integrity of assets

Whenever assets are entrusted to those who are not the ultimate owner, questions arise as to how best to ensure through transparent incentive mechanisms that the agent is properly monitored so that net asset value is maximized over time. This, of course, includes the protection of the integrity of existing assets through legal redress mechanisms, for which the infrastructure is, at best, rather backwards. It also refers to the minimization of the principal-agent problems, on which more in section 6.5(iv)(a). Even rudimentary institutions of hedging against risk, such as insurance companies, have still to be established for all but elementary risks (such as automobile accidents).

(e) The macroeconomic environment

Privatization has been hailed as a cure-all for many macro- and microeconomic problems, as well as a device whereby basic sociopolitical problems in the new societies can begin to be resolved. This is a highly simplistic approach. At the very least, the question should be turned around: to what extent can macro- and microeconomic problems be solved through the privatization process? Further, one may well ask what are the micro- and macroeconomic requirements for successful privatization in general or divestment in particular. Without progress in the sphere of monetary and fiscal institutions, policies, and policy instruments, the advance towards privatization is likely to remain slow. The arena within which private agents can pursue their own interest without constantly running counter to the social interest is still being built.[610]

On the monetary side, the sale of assets from the state to private agents is deflationary if revenues from

---

[609] In the case of Czechoslovakia and Lithuania, for example, the initial offer price of most assets was the book value. Because this was based on historical cost, which has little, if any, relation to current or anticipated prices, the scope for capital gains is likely to be considerable for most such undertakings (even if, as in Lithuania, some effort has been made to adjust book value for the impact of inflation on rouble prices). Of course, some assets will be offered well above any economically warranted valuation, and prices will have to be reduced. Thus, of the assets privatized in Lithuania by 1 December 1991, the total return obtained remained well below book value, except in commerce and catering, where auction prices reached nearly three times the appraised value, and, to a lesser extent, in small service enterprises.

[610] For details, see United Nations Economic Commission for Europe, *Economic Survey of Europe in 1990-1991*, New York, 1991, pp.122-136.

divestment are sterilized. This may be desirable when there is an inflationary overhang. But otherwise it may curtail the buoyancy of the economy at a time that most resources should be marshalled to shore up viable economic activity. In fact, monetary policy is being remoulded when the institutions are not yet present; notably lacking is even a functioning banking system. This includes an autonomous central bank with operational instruments to influence money supply. The concrete circumstances within which the privatization campaign must perforce be pursued make it very difficult to avoid a severe recession that may turn into a protracted depression.

On the fiscal side, there are issues connected with stocks and flows. By its very nature divestment changes the stock of assets owned by the state. Without a shift in fiscal regime, it is also bound to change the nature and size of the flows, that is, current taxes and subsidies. Asset sales improve the government's financial position only in a flow sense. But this may undermine the stability of the budget in the longer run, unless the proceeds are utilized to retire some liabilities. Without this, existing liabilities will have to be financed from prospective tax revenues. This raises the question of whether present and future generations should be held liable for the stock of government liabilities.

(iv) Managerial problems of privatization

From among the many items that could be discussed here, this section focuses on five: information, principal-agent problems, managerial capabilities, corporate governance, and the place in the sequencing of the transformation.

(a) Principal-agent problems

Management that holds a monopoly on information, because of widely dispersed shareholders or of a market monopoly, leads to principal-agent problems that can be potentially quite deleterious. If managers are not owners, and the intensity with which management is monitored is low, those in charge have discretion to pursue their own objectives rather than those of owners. It does not matter much whether present managers are in place because of the favours they obtained under the *ancien régime* or those of the new constellation of forces. The danger of management abuses in the absence of effective supervision should not be ignored.

Many aspects of the problems of managerial abilities and behaviour, fostering the rapid emergence of a competitive environment, and putting in place sufficiently comprehensive, yet not stultifying, regulatory mechanisms could usefully be considered here. Those designed to induce enterprise management to behave like one acting on behalf of private owners remain acute, regardless of ownership. This is true even in cases where the state retains control and enjoins enterprise management, for example, through management contracts, to behave as its counterpart in privately-owned corporations. It is, therefore, important to monitor management and put in place transparent incentive schemes that are likely to induce management to serve according to the instructions of owners, regardless of whether they are private or public.

(b) Information

As already noted, it is critical to ensure that the firms' monopoly of information is broken through the establishment regulatory standards on accounting and publication. This is the case in publicly-owned corporations in market economies. It is even more important in the process of privatization so that the regulator has independent access to detailed information bearing on, for example, the potential for cost reduction and the relative costs of services supplied by a multi-product firm.

(c) Efficiency of new management

It is possible that the inefficiency of state-owned enterprises under central planning stemmed, at least in part, from incompetence on the part of those running the firms. One reason for this was that management was frequently entrusted to political appointees or their minions. But it would be wrong to extend this verdict to all managers. Neither would it be appropriate to rate all of the *nomenklatura*-appointed managers as being intrinsically incompetent. For one thing, under administrative planning managers had a multiple objective function. Some certainly maximized this function and did quite well, given the set tasks. They may have done poorly in terms of maximizing profit, however this could be measured under the circumstances. But that was not their main job.

It is often assumed that new owners or managers of newly-privatized state assets will by definition allocate the services of the capital assets that they own or are entrusted with more efficiently than erstwhile state-appointed officials. Yet, as long as competition with flexible markets cannot be assured there is no guarantee that owners or managers will automatically begin to maximize the net worth of assets, even in a market economy environment. Such expectations are also quite unrealistic insofar as few individuals in the eastern countries have had experience with proper enterprise management because planners did not encourage the acquisition of an economic or managerial culture. Such a culture cannot be quickly assimilated. Hence for years to come, for better or worse, the transition will mainly have to rely on those who formed the backbone of the old managerial technocracy.

Surely, once new transparent incentives and behavioural guidelines for management are be in place, there is no reason to believe that former managers will necessarily fail to adapt themselves to market-based criteria. After all, under central planning and, even more, under administrative planning, some managers were quite ingenious in fulfilling plan targets and maximizing their own objectives.[611] But not all of them can be expected to adjust their behaviour successfully in

---

[611] It could be argued *a contrario*, using the notion of the "bureaucratic entrepreneur" (see Albert Breton and Ronald Wintrobe, "The bureaucracy of murder re-

accordance with the new environment for management. Yet few are likely to yield their entrenched position of economic power voluntarily.

Regardless of what kind of ownership may soon emerge in the east, market relations for assets are likely to be quite chaotic. Stabilization of asset values can emerge only with the institution of basic regulatory mechanisms, effective bankruptcy proceedings, rules on disclosure, basic bank supervision, and other elements that can be instituted only gradually.

(d) Corporate governance

If perhaps the scarcest "production factor" during the transition, in particular during its crucial first stages, will be a corps of managers to take better charge of resources than their predecessors and to take initiative and display some imagination, which does not necessarily make them into entrepreneurs,[612] the same applies to enterprise monitors with a track record. To some degree there is, of course, an overlap between management and monitors or, for that matter, managers and genuine entrepreneurs (see below). But there are also considerable differences. This may be seen by looking at the requirements for good corporate governance, something that is nearly as important for the market to function properly as governance of the polity is for political stability under democracy.

Corporate governance encompasses all those mechanisms and behavioural rules that ensure that managers of enterprises which are the property of absentee owners act as much as is feasible in the latter's interest rather than overwhelmingly in their own. This requires effective monitoring. It also calls for obligating management to pursue its tasks in as transparent a manner as the law calls for, especially with regard to disclosure, reporting, and adherence to standards. Accounting and accountability through disclosure obligations should be especially clear and standard, and indeed made public. It also calls for effective penalization in case of failure on the part of management.

There is presently in the east very little by way of prescription or experience that would provide a solid start for corporate governance institutions. And as briefly touched upon in section 6.5(v) below, there are serious attitudinal obstacles to putting in place even its rudiments.

Although difficult to realize and spread, corporate governance must be built up quickly, regardless of divestment commitments. Gaining a solid form of corporate governance will be even more important if divestment is eschewed or delayed. In that case, not having managers or monitors who risk their own money is a feature peculiar to the east's transition. But it would be most unwise not to explore ways in which it could be put in place.

(e) Privatization and the sequencing of the transition

There is also a large array of questions connected with the order in which privatization, chiefly large privatization, should be pursued to minimize transitional difficulties and hold delays in getting the economy going again and obtaining more efficient utilization of available capital assets to a reasonable minimum. Order matters if privatization is to enhance efficiency and raise revenue. A strategy on how best to proceed with the process is, then, called for.

Some countries emphasize properly preparing the agents to be privatized. This requires at least deconcentration prior to the restructuring of the firm; to enhance efficiency and revenue, it also calls for demonopolization through competition. Ensuring that privatization will unfold in as competitive an environment as can be secured, given the circumstances, is deemed critical. But some commentators prefer to leave even these tasks up to the private sector.[613]

Because of the critical importance of small and medium-sized firms for economic revival, "petty" privatization should proceed as quickly as possible. In particular, the owner-operator will ensure greater efficiency in many activities than can be obtained by the state, provided a minimum of "market institutions" are quickly realized. But expectations that all private efforts will succeed are unjustified. In the absence of smoothly functioning financial markets, for example, the state may implement special incentives, such as generous credit to those willing and expected to be able to run the risks involved. But the "market" for such assets should be as transparent as possible. Open auctions are probably to be preferred here. But other mechanisms are being used (see section 6.6).

When it comes to the core state-owned firms, however, the options are somewhat wider than for petty assets. Whether first to turn these firms into corporations and then commercialize them prior to divestment is an issue to be carefully contemplated. If they cannot be divested quickly, it would be useful to place them within a different legal framework that grants the firm autonomy and enables the nomination of corporate boards, who, for now, will act on behalf of the state as real owner without necessarily becoming pawns of the political power play. Regulatory statutes and parliamentary supervision should ward off the worst such tendencies. Once the legal infrastructure is in place, corporatization can be accomplished as speedily as the available administrative structures afford. However, as explained in section 6.6, the various eastern countries have to date not made the kind of progress with corporatization that would seem to have been feasible and warranted.

The key obstacle here is the membership of the boards and control over these firms. Can those managing the transition prevent the reproduction of old-style management under a different guise? There can simply be no certainty about this. And the best safe-

---

visited", *Journal of Political Economy*, 1986:5, pp.905-926), that managers of state enterprises have had to fight in an "entrepreneurial" manner for status and rewards, and thus are "entrepreneur-managers", some of whom will make it during the transition.

612 For a broader discussion of entrepreneurship in the east's transitions, see *World Economic Survey 1992*, New York, 1992, forthcoming.

613 See, for example, Rudiger Dornbusch, "Strategies and priorities for reform", loc.cit.; Olivier Blanchard et al., op.cit., chapter 3.

guards that can be expected to emerge in the short run will be the contingent control that the political process in place can exert through its direct or indirect monitoring of these organs.

Most attention in privatization has been focused on bringing manufacturing and service enterprises into the private sector, the latter being part of petty privatization. But that is a limited perspective, even if, as some do, financial institutions are included in the discourse (see section 6.6(v)). Indeed, there are parallel questions to be dealt with for agriculture, housing, and land. These should be considered separately for each such form of privatization has a different bearing on the various purposes to be served in improving the efficiency of resource allocation. They also can best be explored at different states of the transition.[614]

(v) Attitudinal problems associated with privatization

Some of the most important legacies of the long years of administrative planning are implanted in the behaviour and expectations of economic agents. This concerns savings behaviour and risk-taking, attitudes toward foreign ownership, entrepreneurship, the recognition of claimed property rights, and comportment in managing state assets.

(a) Intertemporal consumer preferences

A counterpart to the absence of a capitalist segment in the transition societies is the predisposition of savers to be risk-averse. The population of these countries used to enjoy a great deal of certainty over jobs, labour incomes and related perquisites, as well as social transfers. Many individuals, although perhaps now espousing the ideals of a market economy, may find it difficult in the short run to reconcile themselves to the consequences of, say, bankruptcy on their wealth and jobs.[615]

This has an obvious bearing on whether individuals will be interested in holding part of their wealth in the form of enterprise shares (directly, or indirectly through, say, mutual funds) and will decide to exercise their ownership rights by monitoring management. High expectations in this regard are hardly realistic. Individuals of these countries are scarcely likely to become very different from their counterparts in market economies. The average consumer does not keep a substantial share of his wealth in shares, either directly or indirectly.

Giving each individual a stake, perhaps on an equitable basis, by distributing public assets free of charge certainly may help create such a shareholding culture. But it would take time and ultimately is not likely to be very broadly based. And setbacks are bound to occur in part because of unavoidable errors. Two consequences are likely to emerge. Given that only a minority of the population normally holds wealth in enterprise shares, it can be expected that most recipients will soon dispose of their papers. If that process is not handled carefully, adverse signals to the already weak stock market, where it exists (see table 6.8), and inflationary pressures are bound to come to the fore. Yet outright injunctions against share trading for some time to come is bound to undermine the purposes of the privatization process, namely giving a quick impetus to raising efficiency.

Moreover, not all of those who keep their shares are likely to become active monitors, because of apathy and high transaction costs. Furthermore, monitoring through intermediaries, such as mutual fund managers, is not quite the same as that done by a core owner. With a worsening economic situation in most countries, these drawbacks to free share allocations are more likely to become aggravated than not.

(b) Role of foreign capital in privatization

In addition to the mobilization of national savings, private foreign capital will eventually be the key to the economic health of the eastern economies. But the expected role of foreign capital is far from clear and deserves somewhat more attention than it has recently been receiving. Especially important in this connection is whether the role of foreign investment should be controlled by Government or given free rein? Should foreigners be advantaged as compared to domestic investors? Should the market for capital in general and cross-border capital in particular be liberalized?

Regarding the privatization process, an answer has to be found to the question of whether foreign direct investment should be encouraged by admission to the divestment process. The eastern countries, where they have formulated an answer, have taken very different stances on this issue. Rules on the participation of foreigners in divestment certainly diverge widely, reflecting concerns about selling off the national patrimony or perceptions that prices obtained are somehow "unfair".[616] At the same time, uncertainty regarding property rights continues to discourage foreign investors.

Where the balance lies between the advantages of foreign direct investment and the potential for an erosion of economic sovereignty which it entails, so soon after most of these countries managed to regain their political and economic sovereignty, is something that still needs to be worked out. The issue is particularly intricate in precariously established states, such as the Baltics, Croatia, and Slovenia, and several of the post-

---

[614] One such proposal on the order to be pursued in the sequencing of the entire transition was presented in United Nations Economic Commission for Europe, *Economic Survey of Europe in 1990-1991*, New York, 1991, pp.135-136.

[615] There is some sociological evidence of an emerging wide, and worsening, gap between attitudes of most individuals, workers in particular, to transformation of the economy as a whole and the restructuring of their "own" firm. For a useful report concerning Poland, see Lena Kolarska-Bobinska, loc.cit.; for Russia and the ex-USSR, see Igor V. Filatotchev, loc.cit. and Aleksandr D. Radygin and Helen G. Zhuravskaya, "Problems of privatization in the USSR", Moscow: mimeo, 1991.

[616] Virtually no country allows land to be sold to foreigners (see table 6.2). Participation in real estate other than land is highly limited and the potential role in the financial sector is generally restricted to new establishments, as reported in section 6.6. Also in retail trade and catering, foreign capital generally cannot enter without limitations, which are quite severe in some cases.

TABLE 6.8
The role of the stock exchange in privatization [a]

	Date of inception	Number of quoted shares	Daily turnover (million dollars)
Albania	No plan yet	..	..
Belarus	Planned in 1992 [b]	..	..
Bulgaria	December 1991	..	..
Czechoslovakia	Planned in 1992	..	..
Estonia	Not a priority	..	..
Hungary	June 1990	19	0.5
Latvia		..	..
Lithuania		..	..
Poland	April 1991	9	70
Romania	Planned in April 1992	..	..
Russian Federation	November 1990 [c]	21	1 [d]
Ukraine	October 1992 [e]	..	..
Yugoslavia	December 1989	4 + 60 [f]	0.6
Memorandum item:			
Ex-GDR	Not involved	..	..
Croatia	April 1991	-	-
Slovenia	December 1989	2 + 30 [f]	..

a Many stock exchanges are open only on a limited basis.
b Declared in October 1991, but not functioning yet.
c As of end 1991, shares were traded on 12 stock exchanges.
d 100 million roubles.
e Located in Odessa.
f Firm shares and other securities.

Soviet republics engaged in establishing national independence (see section 6.5(iii)(a)).

(c) Entrepreneurship and market entry and exit

Competition must apply also to the acquisition and disposal of private assets, if only because without it proper monitoring and supervision would be impossible. For that, it is necessary to have in place adequate capital markets with a proper regulatory environment. This "institution" of the market economy can emerge only over time and will probably have to start with a much-strengthened commercial banking sector.[617]

A well-functioning banking sector is critical as an intermediator between savers and investors, ensuring expeditious settlement of reciprocal claims, and indeed to facilitate initially the transfers of title and payments for parts of publicly-quoted enterprises. If German or Japanese-style banking sectors were to emerge, the banks themselves would take active positions in key firms. Together with industrial cross-ownership, this would force the banking sector to initiate effective monitoring.

(d) Claimed property rights

Aside from the issues of restitution and compensation, the question of how best to resolve the accrued, implicit, and vested property rights of managers and workers is far from resolved. There is considerable, and in a number of countries growing,[618] opposition to the former political, bureaucratic, and enterprise cadres staking out claims for property rights in the assets of their establishments.[619] Yet, as in the case of enterprise managers and workers, their cooperation is required for successful privatization of these firms. Under the circumstances, it would be desirable to transfer legal title to state-owned assets to some national trustee charged with divestment, as argued in section 6.3.

Such an agency should enjoy considerable independence, be staffed by professionals and technicians (such as lawyers, economists, accountants, and engineers), be responsible to parliament rather than the government, and be closely monitored itself by parliament. As the experience with *Treuhandanstalt* (the agency entrusted with privatizing the state assets of the eastern *Länder* in Germany) shows, politics and setbacks cannot be precluded, regardless of the resources available. It has also shown that privatization becomes even more messy when the trustee is given multiple tasks (such as industrial policy, social objectives, and employment targets) that have nothing to do with asset management, and when the managing boards of such agencies are themselves partly staffed by politicians.

The integrity of the privatization agency merits much attention, given that it will necessarily be entrusted with wide powers. Similar issues arise in connection with the agency that will supervise the selected firms that will remain public. There is a real danger that these agencies may transform themselves into powerful bureaucratic decision-makers – a sort of *ersatz* planning boards.

While this danger should not be minimized, it also need not be blown up beyond reasonable proportions. And how best to move forward should be formulated in the context of existing choices on what to do with state-owned assets in the short run. These are essentially either continued political control or severance of such ties and the setting up of supervised enterprise autonomy under such agencies. Provided parliamentary scrutiny is possible, the pragmatic choice would be for establishing this type of arrangement for all assets that cannot be divested quickly.

In the short term, as already argued, divestment is not necessarily the best strategy, for it takes time and little can be gained by abrogating workers' and management rights. Instead, those managing the transition will need to explore new ways of the state monitoring reasonable "contracts". Only through such positive monitoring can workers and managers be enticed into improving net asset values. That may require some participation in ownership, for example, through ESOP

---

[617] On this question, see John A. Bohn, Jr. and David H. Levey, "Models of capital market development", in *The emerging Russian bear – integrating the Soviet Union into the world economy*, edited by Josef C. Brada and Michael P. Claudon (New York and London: New York University Press, 1991), pp.87-113; Lawrence Brainard, "Strategies for economic transformation in Central and Eastern Europe: role of financial market reform", in *Transformation of planned economies ...*, op.cit., pp.95-108.; Jenny Corbett and Colin P. Mayer, loc.cit.; and Ajit Singh, loc.cit.

[618] This would not seem to be the case, for example, in Hungary. Perhaps the promises of reversing the decline in economic fortunes experienced during the past decade or so, if at the cost of what is known as privatization through "cross-ownership" (on which more in section 6.6) appears to have reconciled broader layers of the population with the country's path to new ownership relations.

[619] Jadwiga Staniszkis has aptly termed this "political capitalism". (see her "'Political capitalism' in Poland", loc.cit.).

schemes.[620] Especially in countries where experiments with decentralization were never pursued beyond the mere formalities of the *khozraschet* system, many problems will be incurred by moving against the interests of the workforce.[621]

Virtually all eastern countries now have a privatization agency in one form or another. But, as noted in section 6.6, the experiences have not all been positive. There are many reasons for this state of affairs, but they cannot be explored in detail here. A key issue would seem to be the question of investing the agency with a clear mandate (namely the privatization process leading up to outright divestment) under the direct authority of the parliament, making available sufficient human capital and other resources for the agency to proceed with its mandate, and finding the properly trained personnel.

(e) Conflicts of interest

Conflicts of interest in the privatization campaign are bound to come to the fore, even if all those who compromised themselves for one reason or another under the *ancien régime*[622] could be replaced. That is often impossible for lack of adequate elementary skills. But as the privatization in the eastern *Länder* in Germany has amply demonstrated, having the skills and the institutions is no panacea for successful and speedy privatization.

Conflicts of interest have been especially conspicuous in the privatization campaign, with managers or bureaucrats privatizing themselves, politicians involved with privatization also being on company boards, and banks entrusted with the implementation and supervision of some aspects of the privatization campaign being funnels for the acquisition of property. Arguably the worst instance of potential abuse occurs when heads of privatization agencies are directly guiding the emerging stock exchange and/or steering management of commercial banks whose portfolio consists of tied debts owed by firms that will soon be privatized.

The potential for gross abuse is alarming and will lead to further recriminations and social tensions that may engender a political backlash. The first salvos were fired in Hungary and the former German Democratic Republic but they have since spread to several other countries, including Belarus, Bulgaria, the Russian Federation, and Ukraine. Very few of the allegations have been legally settled. This is not a useful way of inspiring confidence and infusing the economic environment with greater certainty for economic transactions.

---

[620] For an illuminating discussion, see Janusz M. Dabrowski, Michal Federowicz, and Anthony Levitas, loc.cit.

[621] For two interesting inquiries into managerial attitudes toward privatization in the former USSR, see Nadezhda Vasil'eva, "Razgosudarstvlenie: vozmozhnye varianty", *Sotsialisticheskiy trud*, 1992:12, pp.20-24; and Abel Aganbegyan, "Tsel' – stabilizatsiya", ibid., pp.15-19.

[622] What precisely that means is, of course, a paramount issue in establishing the *Rechtsstaat* in the east, "Der Ruf nach Sühne – Osteuropas Dilemma", *Neue Zürcher Zeitung*, 11-12 January 1992, p.1.

6.6 MECHANISM OF PRIVATIZATION

The privatization process can be carried forward "from below", "from above", or "from abroad". At each level, a wide array of possibilities can be envisioned. But the choice is largest for privatization from below. As argued, the options cannot be limited to divestment through sales or otherwise. They include all ways of placing managerial control over the use of state-owned assets into the hands of those who can credibly promise to maximize net asset values; that requires effective monitoring and adequate incentive mechanisms, positive as well as negative ones. The key issue is how quickly and in what form assets can be taken out of the immediate control of the state or its political power centres.

Yet, it is important to remember that privatization mechanisms cannot be devised in technocratic isolation, since property allocation is political economy *par excellence*. In given conditions, some options are unquestionably superior to others, judged in terms of the motivations for and goals of privatization. At the same time, the prevailing environment for privatization during the transition may be very unstable, as it undoubtedly is, albeit to varying degrees, in most of the East. Under those circumstances, even though there is a fairly clear mandate for policy makers to proceed with one or another form of privatization, that endorsement to proceed is likely to be short-lived. Some measure of pragmatism and arbitrariness during the already prevailing uncertainty in the privatization campaign will be needed to maintain a workable consensus. That, moreover, forms an integral component of the politics of transition. Rather than being able to work with a clearly defined blueprint, according to one Czechoslovak author:

> Each reform step is the result of the compromise achieved in very complicated and protracted manners by various groups holding different views; such steps are not necessarily optimal solutions when one regards both their character and the time factor, and moreover, it is difficult to define who should assume concrete political responsibility for the consequences of such steps.[623]

Minimizing this uncertainty and arbitrariness with a view to improve the utilization of capital assets should be one priority among the tasks of transition policymaking in the East.

The state and its political power centres can be taken out of the decision-making about resource allocation through a wide panoply of alternatives. It may be recalled that the phases of privatization considered here consist of corporatization, commercialization, and divestment. The latter in particular has numerous variants. In what follows, the focus is on the forms of divestment that have been implemented or are now seriously being considered in the East. Even so, not all forms can be dealt with here, if only because some variants that were on the agenda of the policy debate at some point during the past three years or so appear to have been abandoned by now.[624] Those that are included here are schematically presented in table 6.9.

For the discussion below, the divestment mechanism is reviewed in terms of four generic categories: spontaneous privatization, the free transfer of title, contracting out, and outright sale. The "free transfer" option merits special attention, if only because of the many alternatives that have been proposed and are currently being entertained.

From commitments made by those in charge of managing the transition, it is clear that some sectors (such as defence and security-related activities, public utilities, many transportation ventures such as railroads and airlines, and possibly certain key industries) are to remain in public hands. Though not the subject of eventual divestment, such public-sector firms can, and certainly should, be corporatized and commercialized. That this process has started in the East is indicated in table 6.10: it is evident that all countries except perhaps Estonia have made some progress with the corporatization of major public utilities. But the transformation of enterprises still has a long way to go, as can be gleaned from table 6.1. Though the data shown there are far from comparable, the very large number of still unincorporated state firms suggests that the privatization of state enterprises in most countries has only

---

[623] Karel Kopp, "Privatization in Czechoslovakia", *Czechoslovak Economic Digest*, 1991:2, pp.2-7 (quoted from p.2).

[624] For the range of proposals recently under discussion see, among others, Eduardo Borensztein and Manmohan S. Kumar, "Proposals for privatization in Eastern Europe", *IMF Staff Papers*, 1991:2, pp.300-326; Guillermo de la Dehesa, *Privatization in Eastern and Central Europe*, Washington, D.C.: Group of Thirty, 1991; Farid Dhanji and Branko Milanovic, "Privatisation", in *The transition to a market economy – special issues*, vol.II, edited by Paul Marer and Salvatore Zecchini, Paris: Organisation for Economic Co-operation and Development, 1991, pp.13-43; Roman Frydman and Andrzej Rapaczynski, "Markets and institutions in large-scale privatization: an approach to economic and social transformation in Eastern Europe", in *Reforming Central and Eastern European economies – initial results and challenges*, edited by Vittorio Corbo, Fabrizio Coricelli, and Jan Bossak, Washington, D.C.: The World Bank, 1991, pp.253-274; Irena Grosfeld, "Privatization of state enterprises in Eastern Europe: the search for a market environment", *East European Politics and Societies*, 1991:1, pp.142-161; Helen B. Nankani, *Techniques of privatization of state-owned enterprises*, volume II: *Selected country case studies*, Washington, D.C.: World Bank, 1988; L. Rapp, *Techniques de privatisation des entreprises publiques*, Paris: Librairies Techniques, 1986; Lester M. Salamon, (ed.), *Beyond privatization – the tools of government action*, Washington, D.C.: The Urban Institute Press, 1989; John S. Vickers and George Yarrow, *Privatization: an economic analysis*, op.cit.; Charles Vuylsteke, *Techniques of privatization of state-owned enterprises*, volume I: *Methods and implementation* Washington, D.C.: World Bank, 1988.

TABLE 6.9

The main mechanisms of privatization

Spontaneous	Free distribution	Usufruct divestment	Sales of assets
From below	To workers' councils	Franchises	Stock flotations
Wild privatization	To workers	Management contracts	Auctions
Insider privatization	Mass distribution	Leases	Negotiated
Workers' self-management	Shares	Sub-contracting	Management buy-outs
From above	Investment funds		Workers' buy-outs
Ministry	Mutual funds		Unsubscribed capital expansion
Local authority	Decentralized government agencies		Debt-equity swap
From abroad	Financial institutions		
Offer to buy (see sales of assets)	Holding companies		

just got underway, excepting the eastern parts of Germany.[625]

This stands in some contrast to the evidently soaring rate at which new private firms have been established. As table 6.1 suggests, progress appears to have been very rapid indeed in those countries that embarked upon the privatization process the earliest (notably Czechoslovakia, Hungary and Poland). Many new firms have also been created elsewhere, but often the reported numbers refer to registered companies. Just as in the case of many ventures with foreign partners, many registered corporations have by and large remained empty shells up to now.

Although in principle any of the four forms of divestment could be entertained for any assets presently owned by the state, in practice matters are unlikely to be so indeterminate. Petty privatization is generally confined to contracting out or outright sale, except in the case of housing for which free distribution can be entertained. Likewise in the case of land, where the alternatives are essentially free distribution, long-term leasing, or outright sale in some form.

Large privatization, however, can be the subject of any of the four modes specified earlier, and thus will now be discussed in some detail.

(i) Spontaneous privatization

Many economies in transition have had some experience with this form of divestment. It essentially means that those entrusted with state assets take possession of them in one way or another or initiate arrangements for their disposal to private agents.

The basis for spontaneous privatization was created when the still communist political leadership of several countries of eastern Europe, particularly Hungary and Poland, sought to distance itself from the day-to-day operations of the bulk of microeconomic activities. Thus, in Hungary in 1984-1985 and in Poland mainly in 1987-1988, enterprises were turned over to enterprise and workers' councils, respectively, as part of the administrative reforms;[626] in Yugoslavia, the provisions on self-management were made even more explicit, rendering the legal status of these enterprises more than ever indeterminate.[627] By allowing management in place or self-management councils, enterprise or workers councils to turn existing firms into corporations, these "autonomous" firms were to become fully responsible for their own financial health. To make this possible, they were entitled to seek out new partners, usually from abroad.

Thus, spontaneous privatization arose out of the enterprise-reform acts.[628] As part of the new thinking about administrative decentralization, governments sought to cut the financial burden of state firms. Also, decision makers in some countries did not wish — or dare — to renationalize assets, even after the initial hurdles of the political transitions had been taken.[629]

There are various forms that are at times labelled "spontaneous privatization". It will be useful to keep them apart as much as possible, if only because of the negative aura attached to the earlier forms of "wild" spontaneous privatization, a more or less sophisticated theft from the state or society as a whole. One favoured variant involved turning a firm into some form of a joint-stock company, whose shares can subsequently be sold to private agents, including foreigners, a process

---

[625] A law adopted by the GDR parliament on 17 June 1990, in the approach to economic and monetary union, required that by 1 July 1990 all firms in the German Democratic Republic be registered as corporations (see "Gesetz zur Privatisierung und Reorganisation des volkseigenen Vermögens *(Treuhandgesetz)* vom 17. Juni 1990", *Gesetzblatt der Deutschen Demokratischen Republik*, 1990:I/33.

[626] Workers councils were created in Poland in the aftermath of the labour strife led by *Solidarnosc* in 1980-1981. However, the process did not get very far when martial law imposed in December 1981 neutralized the workers' councils where they had already been established and impeded their emergence elsewhere. When this regime was lifted in 1983, the councils returned but did not gain wide currency, owing to the rivalry between the government-installed unions and *Solidarnosc*, which was then one of the illegal ones. With the start of the second phase of the Polish economic reform of the 1980s, especially in 1987-1988, greater rein was given to the workers' councils, and indeed it was hoped that that institution would facilitate reaching greater efficiency. For details, see D. Mario Nuti, "Privatisation of socialist economies ...", loc.cit.; and Lajos Bokros, "Privatization in Hungary" (paper presented to the meeting on "Privatization in Eastern Europe", organized by the IMF Institute, Washington, D.C., 9-19 July 1990).

[627] For details, see Ellen Comisso, "Property rights, liberalism, ...", loc.cit.; Saul Estrin, "Some reflections on self-management, social choice, and reform in Eastern Europe", *Journal of Comparative Economics*, 1991:2, pp.349-366 and "Privatisation, self-management and social ownership", *Communist Economies and Economic Transformation*, 1991:3, pp.355-365; D. Mario Nuti, "Privatisation of socialist economies ...", loc.cit.

[628] Their evolution can be gleaned from United Nations Economic Commission for Europe, *Economic Survey of Europe in 1989-1990*, New York, 1990, pp.233-269; and *Economic Survey of Europe in 1990-1991*, New York, 1991, pp.137-183.

[629] It is of some interest to note that with the disintegration of the Soviet Union, the large corporations, which were mostly all-union firms, have been "renationalized" by the republican leaderships on the principle of territorial privilege.

TABLE 6.10
Privatization of public utilities and housing

	Public utilities			Housing and other types of real estate	
	Corporatization of major networks	Decentralization	Role of foreign capital	Number of state-owned dwellings recently sold	Role of foreign capital
Albania	..	..	..	Planned in 1992	..
Belarus	In process	Planned	Limited	46 000	Limited
Bulgaria	..	..	..	..	..
Czechoslovakia	In process	Started	Limited	In process	..
Estonia	Not started	..	..	2 500 [a]	..
Hungary	In process	Started	Limited	100 000 [b]	Strictly limited
Latvia	In process	..	..	15 000	Strictly limited
Lithuania	In process	No	Strictly limited	In process	Limited [c]
Poland	In process	In process	Limited	120 000 [d]	Land ownership prohibited
Romania	In process	Started	Limited	65 000 [e]	Limited
Russian Federation	In process	Just started	Negligible	In process [f]	Very limited
Ukraine	In process	Just started	Negligible	1000 000	Very limited
Yugoslavia	Started	No	Limited		
Memorandum item:					
Ex-GDR	Completed	Completed	Limited	In process [g]	..
Croatia	Started	No	Limited	..	Very limited
Slovenia	Started	No	Limited	..	Very limited

[a] January 1990-July 1991.
[b] 1987-1990.
[c] Land can be purchased with permission of the Ministry of Interior, but no restriction on house ownership.
[d] As of July 1991.
[e] January-August 1991. Almost 5,000 was given gratis to tenants.
[f] De-statization and privatization of housing are planned through free acquisition of state housing fund by citizens, with additional help of coupons. Up to a "normative" comfort level flats are to be sold at differentiated prices.
[g] Ownership transferred to communal housing companies and private housing cooperatives. Part of communal housing stock is subject to restitution claims; privatization of the remainder communal dwellings difficult because of low quality of housing and high renovation costs.

which management in place can utilize to obtain some privileges (such as a guaranteed job). In other variants, management signed over property rights (but not necessarily all) to private ventures that it wholly owned.

Other forms of privatization initiated by enterprise institutions are quite legitimate. Without active participation of management in place, and indeed the workers, it would be all but impossible to proceed with the privatization process. After all, they have the knowledge and skills required to "assess" their own firm and so make it easier for new owners to emerge.

Spontaneous privatization has ushered into the transition debate an array of highly contentious issues. In some countries, "wild" privatization was halted when the new governments put in place appropriate legislation and oversight agencies. But though the crassest forms of "wild" privatization may no longer occur, all spontaneous privatization, even if regulated, appears to entail the transfer of assets at less than fair value (box 6.3). It probably cannot be otherwise, given the lack of clarity about some property rights. When these rights have become better defined, spontaneous privatization has become more orderly and indeed, as in Hungary (box 6.4), an appreciated way of divesting state assets and have decision-making proceed with minimal political interference.[630]

Because of the problems encountered with this form, policy makers in a number of countries have either eschewed the modality or placed it under strict rules and regulations supervised by some privatization agency. But this does not mean that spontaneous privatization is over. Instead of the more rapacious forms of the past, spontaneous privatization has become regulated and supervised, as in Hungary, where it can now be proposed by existing enterprise councils, by the governmental authority (such as central government or municipality), and by foreign offers. The process is, however, still evolving in economies where the debate on the ends and means of the transition is still in its infancy. This is perhaps most conspicuous in the Soviet Union's successor republics, where the basic contours of the transition are only now being intensively debated. But "wild" spontaneous privatization is far from over also in some of the Balkan states and the Baltic republics.

(ii) Free distribution of state assets

Apart from the forms entailed in the recognition of restitution and compensation claims, several other modalities of free distribution have been entertained, as indicated in table 6.9: recognition of management and workers' rights in the form of "self-management", recognition of workers' rights, mass distribution in various forms, capitalization of financial institutions, and endowing lower-level government agencies.

(a) Self-management

This form is essentially confined to Yugoslavia, where it has constituted the core of the organization of society for several decades. It has been entertained as a means of accelerating privatization elsewhere as well.

---

[630] In Hungary, the State Property Agency itself acknowledged that 99 per cent of ongoing privatization actions were launched at the initiative of the enterprise to be privatized and 90 per cent of privatization revenue came from such spontaneous privatization (*Heti Világgazdaság*, 28 September 1991).

> **BOX 6.4**
>
> **Hungary's unique "big privatization" strategy**
>
> Although initially Hungarian policymakers were bent on obtaining as much revenue from privatization as possible, largely to finance the foreign debt service, which has worked to some degree, [1] and to retire domestic debt, which has not worked well, gradually a unique, almost moneyless, approach to privatization has come to the fore.
>
> The privatization of large companies involves the establishment of corporations and the co-opting of new owners, in some cases by trading in bank or inter-enterprise debt, and to some degree also debt forgiveness on the part of the Treasury or the social security fund. As a result, the former state firms' finances are largely restructured. Also the company structure is changing. For one thing, large conglomerates are being broken up into separate entities and the former hierarchical links of the state firms with the state administration are severed. In the new companies, the stock of fixed assets is partly replaced and upgraded, while redundant workers are laid off.
>
> This restructuring involves a shift toward cross-ownership which has been going on spontaneously since 1987. Enterprise autonomy at a time of economic recession and monetary stringency has forced management to come to grips with liquidity problems by exploring additional sources of finance, among which is the establishment of ownership links with banks and other partners.
>
> The deconcentration of the large conglomerates led to the creation of subsidiaries or the partial divestment of production units, thus forging further cross-ownership relationships. This process was strengthened through legislation enacted since 1989, as a result of which a certain proportion (usually 25 to 30 per cent) of the shares of a newly-incorporated firms accrues to local governments which own the buildings of the enterprise or the land beneath it.
>
> Foreign capital has often functioned as a catalyst in these transformations, although its significance should not be overstated. In fact, the share of foreign capital in the total value of restructured companies is about 9 per cent, in contrast to some 40 per cent in the case of joint ventures involving state firms. In any case, each transformation involving a certain book value limit (ranging from Ft 20 million to Ft 50 million − some $300,000 to $700,000 − depending on the circumstances) must be approved by the State Property Agency. And this process is not merely a formality. For example, during the first year of its existence, the Agency blocked 9 transformation cases, 7 proposals for joint ventures, 3 merger plans and 14 other divestment proposals. [2] None the less, in 1990-1991, over 200 applications with a value of incorporation of Ft 460 billion were approved − about one quarter of the aggregate book value of some 2,200 state-owned firms extant at the end of 1989. [3]
>
> The process of transformation has advanced further in some sectors (in particular trade and construction) than in others, notably in industry and transport. It remains quite limited in the financial sector. Because the state owns a substantial portion of the shares of financial institutions (direct ownership varies between 30 and 40 per cent), [4] the Ministry of Finance has a guaranteed influence.
>
> The key questions outstanding are whether this cross-ownership of medium-sized and large firms will lead to "strong" owners, who will exert a beneficial influence on management through direct monitoring, and what this may entail for the competitive environment and Hungary's road to a "normal" market economy. An unequivocal answer to these questions is almost impossible, given that the privatization process is unfolding at a time of broader changes in the economy's organizational make-up, including the proliferation of joint ventures, the effects of domestic stabilization measures, the loss of the Soviet market, and the competition resulting from import liberalization.
>
> It is now government policy to emphasize speedier measures, and the cross-ownership model may help in realizing this goal. This will also be facilitated through the fact that a growing part of the Hungarian economy has already freed itself from state tutelage and has been exposed to some market discipline, owing to regulatory actions on the part of the parliament, both domestic and foreign competition, and some financial supervision on the part of the banks.
>
> However, the Hungarian Government remains committed to a gradual pace in the dismantling of its state sector. There are various reasons for its stance. One is social pressures. Another is inability to restructure its fiscal-revenue base and collection system, in particular as regards the booming private sector. For example, existing public firms guarantee a steady flow of social security contributions, in contrast to the private sector. As a result of various arrangements, mostly legal, the contributions from this sector relative to income are much smaller. Strong owners are apparently bent on obtaining tax exemptions, like many foreign-owned ventures, or on circumventing fiscal regulations, like the private sector. In addition, the artificially low amortization allowances compel state firms to record a mostly fictitious profit, and thus to transfer taxes to the government.
>
> ---
>
> [1] Thus, of the revenue obtained in 1991 (Ft 40 billion according to the Agency's accounting), 85 per cent was from abroad (as reported in *Világgazdaság*, 14 January 1992, p.5).
>
> [2] *SPA Annual Report 1990*, pp.20, 24, 26, 29.
>
> [3] Correction for inflation since end-1989 would raise that book value, but this has been offset by the erosion of public-sector asset values since then owing to the recession.
>
> [4] About one third on average. The rest is held by enterprises and cooperatives (some 35 per cent), other financial institutions (some 15 per cent) and foreign owners (some 11 per cent).

To some degree the economic decentralization pursued in Hungary in the mid-1980s and in Poland at several points in the 1980s conferred fairly wide authority to enterprise and workers' councils, respectively. But the experience in none of these countries has been very positive.

Self-management entrusted with full property rights would differ substantially from the mode of enterprise organization instituted in Yugoslavia. That tended to encourage maximization of income per worker and borrowing from banks – and ultimately the public purse – rather than foster the long-run profitability of the firm, in part because of unclear property rights. There are other problems with self-management, however, including a bias to protect labour in place and defer technological innovation and competition.

It can be argued that self-management in its pure form has never been realized.[631] Indeed, the labour-income bias under self-management is exacerbated when there is no capital market where workers can voluntarily sell their rights to participate in future profits at a market valuation based on the expected earnings of the enterprise. That is to say, workers' self-management is insufficient to ensure adaptive, allocative, and productive efficiency; ownership and a market in which such property can be traded are also required.

Many observers[632] contend that the rules of the labour-managed firms could be sufficiently adapted to encourage greater productivity and maximization of asset value. The key addition would have to be tradability of shares in the labour-managed firm. This requires that individuals with no connections with to the firm may in principle purchase or otherwise acquire shares (such as through gift, legacy, or inheritance); in other words, capital ownership must, in principle, be condoned. Certainly, trading in shares owned by workers might lead to the minorization of labour-management in the end. But also this outcome is not predestined. Workers' self-management could be considered a form of more general, not necessarily odious, spontaneous privatization.

In addition to being saddled with the particular problems of self-management as practised in Yugoslavia, the broader experience with this and other forms of spontaneous privatization has on the whole not been satisfactory for financial, economic, political, and organizational reasons.[633] Financially, spontaneous privatization allows former management and possibly workers to become owners without paying a fair price, thus depriving government of revenue. Economically, there is no reason to believe that turning over assets to those who earlier ran these facilities poorly will improve resource allocation, although the new incentives associated with private property rights are likely to induce "owners" to change their habits and behaviour. And there are wealth effects to be taken into account. Also, worker ownership will make it more difficult for individuals to spread their risks or to restructure their portfolio in accordance with their individual time preferences. Politically, the vast majority of people in the transition economies do not think it is right that management in place, in particular the notorious *nomenklatura*, possibly in conjunction with only some class of workers, captures state assets for its own pocket. Finally, there is an organizational problem in that either workers may want to replace the management in place or the latter may wish to lay off a substantial fraction of the existing workforce. In either case, potentially valuable inside information – a form of human capital – may get lost.

(b) Free distribution to workers

This essentially implies the recognition of accrued, implicit, or vested property rights, particularly those of workers, for reasons dealt with in section 6.2. Although there may be good social and political reasons for so doing, from a strictly economic point of view the only rationale for recognition of some of these rights is to obtain a cooperative labour force in the privatization process, essentially to capitalize on insider information and to avoid social conflicts.

In virtually all Eastern countries, workers receive some privileges, but not necessarily a monetary concession, as a result of privatization processes currently under way. Insofar as the divestment of industrial assets is concerned, the treatments meted out in the various Eastern countries are schematically presented in table 6.11.

The key economic assumption of such transfers is that making the workforce property owners will automatically improve the allocation process and render the firm profitable. This is fallacious; it is also inequitable. For one thing, the value of capital per worker in state firms varies a great deal for reasons that have nothing to do with the relative merits of the present labour force. Furthermore, free distribution of assets fails to provide funding for the government to sink some liabilities, and it would tend to favour reinvestment in existing activities over restructuring.

Instead of constituting labour-managed firms, be they of the Yugoslav or a new variety, some variant of employee share ownership programme (ESOP) is worth considering, especially if it can be coupled with promises to limit demands for monetary compensation, to foster productivity, to change work rules, and to accept other measures that would give workers a material stake in their enterprise.[634] Note that this can be done without divesting the firm completely. Few countries, however, have any ESOP scheme in place. As far as industrial assets are concerned, only Croatia and

---

631 For useful elaborations, see Ellen Comisso, "Property rights, liberalism, ...", loc.cit.; Saul Estrin, "Some reflections ...", loc.cit. and "Privatisation, self-management ...", loc.cit.; D. Mario Nuti, "Competitive valuation and efficiency of capital investment in the socialist economy", *European Economic Review*, 1988:1, pp.2-6 and "Feasible financial innovation under market socialism", in *Financial reform in socialist economies*, edited by Christine Kessides, Timothy King, Mario Nuti, and Catherine Sokil, Washington, D.C.: The World Bank, 1989, pp.85-105.

632 See, among others, Marek Dabrowski, "The economic effectiveness of the self-managed enterprise – a review of the theoretical literature", *Acta Oeconomica*, 1989:1/2, pp.39-54; Saul Estrin, "Some reflections ...", loc.cit. and "Privatisation, self-management ...", loc.cit.; Janez Prasnikar and Jan Svejnar, "Workers' participation in management vs. social ownership and government policies: Yugoslav lessons for transforming socialist economies" (paper presented for the conference "Perspectives on Market Socialism", Berkeley, CA, 16-19 May 1991).

633 For a detailed discussion, see Barbara Lee and John Nellis, "Enterprise reform and privatization in market economies", Washington, D.C.: The World Bank, April 1990, mimeo.

634 See Janusz M. Dabrowski, Michal Federowicz, and Anthony Levitas, loc.cit.

TABLE 6.11

Distribution schemes for industrial assets

	Restitution to previous owners	Financial compensation to previous owners	Gratis transfer of property — Management and/or workers	Gratis transfer of property — Population at large	Gratis transfer of property — Decentralized state bodies and/or funds	ESOP-type arrangements
Albania	..	..	Partially	Vouchers	..	No
Belarus	No	No	Yes	Yes	Yes	No
Bulgaria	Yes	No decision	No decision	No decision	No decision	No
Czechoslovakia	Yes [a]	Partial	No	Vouchers	Yes	No
Estonia	Yes [b]	Yes [c]	Yes	Yes	Yes	No
Hungary	No [d]	Yes [c]	No	No	No	Planned
Latvia	Yes [b]	Partially	Yes [e]	..	..	..
Lithuania	Yes [b]	Partial	No [f]	Vouchers	No	Planned
Poland	Occasionally	No	Yes [g]	Coupons	Yes	No
Romania	No	No	Yes [h]	Coupons	Yes	..
Russian Federation	No	No	Partially	Partially	Yes	No
Ukraine	No	No	Yes	Partially	Yes	No
Yugoslavia	No	No	Yes [i]	No	Yes [j]	Yes
Memorandum item:						
Ex-GDR	Yes [k]	Yes [l]	No	No	No	..
Croatia	..	No	Yes [m]	No	Yes	Yes
Slovenia	No decision	No decision	No decision	No decision	No decision [n]	No decision

a Restitution of expropriated property, occurred from February 1948 onwards.
b In cases of expropriation in 1940 and following the annexation to the USSR.
c Through compensation certificates.
d Only in exceptional cases (e.g., churches).
e Face value reduced according to seniority and sold on term plan (25 per cent down payment; rest done in 1 year).
f But first call on shares.
g Legally workers or retired workers with at least two years of work experience in the firm can obtain 20 per cent of the shares at a 50 per cent discount. In fact, however, they are being given 10 per cent free of charge.
h Workers and employees of the firm can buy up to 10 per cent at 10 per cent discount.
i Workers and retired workers with at least two years work experience have first claims on shares at a discount of at least 30 per cent, increasing with seniority to 70 per cent.
j No federal regulation, but occurring in Serbia.
k Full restitution or compensation for all having had their property confiscated, except under Soviet military occupation between 1945-1949.
l In case restitution is not possible.
m Federal law set aside by republican law, which allows smaller privileges to workers in place or retired workers with at least two years work experience in the firm. They can get a discount of at least 20 per cent, increasing with seniority to 50 per cent.
n Third draft law foresees provisions similar to those of Croatia.

Yugoslavia have it (table 6.11). Lithuania appears to be the only country that has some such scheme in its financial institutions (see table 6.12). The few schemes in operation usually involve giving or selling existing shares to workers, their future revenue basically remaining wage earnings.

(c) Mass distribution of shares

This involves giving away to the population at large (or adults) a share of the state assets to be privatized. The basic philosophy on the free distribution is that, once restitution and perhaps other claims are settled, remaining state assets are common property and should, therefore, be distributed free of charge. It is also advocated in view of the inadequacies of capital markets and the shortage of domestic capital in the countries,[635] both of which can in this way be bypassed.

The merits of various forms of free distribution have been debated at great length as a matter of state policy first in Czechoslovakia and more recently in Poland.[636]

Czechoslovakia initially envisaged sharing out virtually all state assets coming under large privatization through such a scheme. But the scale of the project that is now in the process of being introduced there, as well as in Poland, is much less ambitious. This form of divestment has since been explored in other countries too. The first elements of a voucher scheme are, for example, in place in Lithuania (where vouchers have already been distributed) and Romania (where the legal infrastructure is in place). Such a scheme is also being actively debated in Albania, Belarus, Estonia, Russia, Slovenia, and Ukraine (table 6.11).

Free distribution can take a number of forms of which the following three cover most alternatives: distribution of society's wealth (or a sizeable part thereof) directly to the population at large; creation of financial intermediaries (such as investment, mutual, or privatization funds) and distribution of shares in these to the population at large; and the establishment of holdings to manage groups of state-owned enterprises according to commercial criteria and subsequently sell them off in an orderly mode.

---

[635] See, for example, Roman Frydman and Andrzej Rapaczynski, "Markets and institutions in large-scale privatization: an approach to economic and social transformation in Eastern Europe", in *Reforming Central and Eastern European economies ...*, op.cit., pp.253-274; Manuel Hinds, "Issues in the introduction of market forces in Eastern European socialist economies − Annex I − enterprise reform issues", Washington, D.C.: The World Bank, March 1990, mimeo, and "Issues in the introduction of market forces in Eastern European socialist economies", in *Managing inflation in socialist economies in transition*, edited by Simon Commander, Washington, D.C.: The World Bank, 1991a, pp.121-153; David Lipton and Jeffrey D. Sachs, "Privatization in Eastern Europe: the case of Poland", *Brookings Papers on Economic Activity*, 1990:2, pp.293-341; and Jeffrey D. Sachs, "Accelerating privatization in Eastern Europe" (paper prepared for "World Bank Annual Conference on Development Economics 1991", organized by The World Bank, Washington, D.C., 25-26 April 1991).

[636] This solution to the property problem was first introduced in the Polish literature in the second half of the 1980s, notably by the previous Minister in charge of ownership transformation, J. Lewandowski. (See, for instance, J. Lewandowski and J. Szomburg, "Property reform as a basis for social and economic reform", *Communist Economies*, 1989, No.3). But the scheme currently tabled in Poland is not quite his original proposal.

The fast movers (Czechoslovakia and Poland)

The two countries are actively pursuing free distribution of claims to a number of large state-owned firms. But the path chosen differs in a number of respects.

Poland initially opted largely for sale of assets. The decision to redirect the emphasis to "mass" (and also "sectoral") privatization, after a disappointing first year of divestment (see section 6.6(iv)(a)), was based on two basic postulates. One was that public wealth is owned by the entire society, because it was produced by its toil. The other was that an economy which belongs to all in practice belongs to no one, and that the creation of owners was critical to progressing toward an effective market economy.

The objective of the effort is to entrust a substantial part (30 per cent) of shares in selected large firms — of which there are about 500 — to "National Investment Funds",[637] whose shares in turn will be distributed free of charge to every Polish citizen of 18 years or older,[638] to keep another portion (30 per cent) of shares in the firms with the Treasury with a view to selling those later, once the stock market is functioning, and to hand over 10 per cent respectively to workers[639] and state-owned banks, and 20 per cent to the Social Security Fund (ZUS).

Initially (in mid-1991) it was planned to set up about 20 investment funds in which adult citizens were to own shares that, after some time, could be openly traded. Both national and foreign experts from western investment management firms were to be invited to manage these funds. Though the leadership will be mixed Polish and foreign, effective day-to-day operations will initially be in the hands of western managers,[640] who will receive substantial compensation, in part according to the performance of the companies in their assigned portfolio. Overseen by a supervisory council appointed by the Ministry of Ownership Transformation, the outside managers are selected by the ministry with the aid of S.C. Warburg, the British merchant bank.[641] Their main task is to generate a profit while the firms entrusted to them as majority owner are being privatized.

Shares in the companies included in the mass privatization were to be distributed over the various funds according to the core principle: one third of a company was to be allocated to one fund, as a way of ensuring adequate monitoring of the firm, and the remainder was be divided over the other 19 funds. Initially it was decided to favour some sectoral specialization by endowing each fund with a cluster of firms in the same sector. This now seems to have been abandoned, since firms will be allocated according to an auction system. Each investment fund will receive an identical number of points that can be bid against the packages of one-third shares in the firms earmarked for this type of privatization. The highest bid will receive core ownership of the firm.[642] Once established, the funds are expected to change their portfolios through trade among themselves.

In the first effort of "mass" privatization, as it is called in Poland, 400 large firms were selected, accounting for a quarter of industrial sales and perhaps 12 per cent of industrial employment. But getting this process under way proved to be too ambitious because of various practical, social, and political problems concerning the implementation of the programme. As a result, the scale of the operation was lowered to some 204 firms, accounting for 8 per cent of industrial sales and perhaps 4 per cent of industrial employment.[643] The number of closed-end investment funds, which are yet to be established, may have been reduced to about ten.[644] They are expected to be formed in February or March 1992 and to function broadly according to the above-cited principles.

All Polish citizens over 18 years residing in Poland will receive gratis (or perhaps against a nominal fee)[645] one share in each of the investment funds to ensure equity in the distribution of public wealth. To avoid premature and disorderly speculation in these scrips, trading will not be possible until the late spring of 1993, once the first year's financial results of the funds will have been published and widely disseminated. In the meantime, all shares will be held in the form of computerized accounts from which owners can later withdraw shares to be traded.

The Polish mass privatization approach places enormous faith in being able to attract western-trained managers against a fee and an incentive scheme that will sufficiently awaken their abilities to restructure the firms entrusted to their fund on a competitive basis. Some observers have also questioned whether western investment-fund managers are capable of getting in-

---

[637] Although no official terminology has been adopted, the term currently used is *Narodowe fundusze inwestycyjne*, but they are also referred to as "National Assets Boards" (see *Rzeczpospolita*, 18 July 1991, p.VII).

[638] This means those born before 1 January 1974, who number roughly 27 million.

[639] Although in principle (on the basis of Poland's privatization law of July 1990) entitled to up to 20 per cent of the shares at half price, the present aim is to give the workforce 10 per cent free. Financially this has, of course, the same result, but in terms of ownership control it does not.

[640] See *Financial Times*, 3 December 1991.

[641] Note that the initial fee of the merchant bank was covered by the United Kingdom Government's know-how fund for Poland.

[642] *Rzeczpospolita*, 17 September 1991. At least as reported there, the scheme does not seem to have been well thought out for, unless points are available on demand, there is bound to be an incongruity between the numbers bid and the number of firms available for privatization.

[643] *Rzeczpospolita*, 11 December 1991.

[644] This was reported in late November by Olivier Bouin and Jaroslav Horak ("The free distribution of shares in Czechoslovakia and Poland", paper prepared for the colloquium "Privatization in Central and Eastern Europe – what are the first lessons?", organized by Maison des Sciences de l'Homme, Paris, 25-26 November 1991). But another authoritative source still affirms that 20 funds are envisaged (see interview with Jerzy Thieme, director of the mass privatization project, in *Financial Times*, 3 December 1991, p.2).

[645] This appears to be under consideration (see *Financial Times*, 3 December 1991, p.2).

volved in the day-to-day management of the enterprises they monitor and indeed furnish useful information on how best to restructure these companies. Lack of acquaintance with Polish-type socio-economic conditions may well lead to decisions that are ultimately not in the interest of Polish society.

In *Czechoslovakia,* vouchers for the acquisition of nearly all large assets to be privatized were initially slated to be distributed free of charge to all adult Czechoslovak citizens. That ambition has since been modified. Policy makers now envisage that of about 4,000 medium-sized and large firms, about one quarter will remain in state hands, another quarter will be divested through standard methods (meaning essentially sales through public offerings or discretionary arrangements), and the remainder will be divested quickly through non-conventional methods — the so-called voucher privatization.[646] Vouchers for the "first round" of privatization were made available at a positive price (there are expected to be several more rounds in the future; a second is already scheduled for later in 1992). Every adult citizen (18 years or over) resident in Czechoslovakia[647] is entitled to obtain a voucher book for a nominal fee of Kcs 35; to validate it, a "registration stamp" must be purchased for Kcs 1,000 (roughly a quarter of the average monthly salary).[648] Registration of the voucher books is to be completed by the end of February 1992.[649] Once the first round of "large" privatization gets under way in early 1992, the voucher "points" can be used to place bids for shares of enterprises.

Initially it was intended that individuals were to do so directly by bidding on shares with voucher points in country-wide computerized auctions. Voucher points were not be transferable and shares would not be tradeable for some time, until a stock market could be put in place. On the basis of the denominations contained in the booklets, each individual could bid on up to 10 different enterprises. To permit individuals to spread their risk more widely, and also to facilitate the participation of those without the knowledge or interest to manage vouchers and shares, it was eventually decided to admit the formation of "Privatization Investment Funds".[650] These mutual funds pool the voucher points of registered holders, who can either deposit them for management by the fund (under instructions or according to the latter's investment strategy) or exchange them against certificates of ownership (shares) in the fund. In the wake of this decision, privatization funds mushroomed, their number reaching well over 400 by late January,[651] and heated competition for the deposit of vouchers developed. Other problems also arose, including the embarrassing disappearance of 5 million voucher books, for which the funds were blamed.[652]

Enterprises to be divested in this manner are selected by their respective "founding" ministries in two rounds. The first was to have been completed by the end of 1991, but it was postponed until March 1992, ostensibly for lack of adequate preparation time. A second list will be drawn up sometime in 1992 and be the subject of voucher bidding later that year.

Shares in the companies to be privatized will be offered at set prices. If the market clears, the sale takes place. If demand exceeds supply, no sale occurs, but another auction will be organized at a higher starting price. If supply exceeds demand, the remaining shares will be offered again in a subsequent auction at a lower price. The current estimate is that in some cases five rounds may be required to ensure disposal of the shares by bidding voucher points in a competitive fashion.

Opinions on the intrinsic merit of the voucher scheme and the way in which Czechoslovakia has pursued the idea straddle a wide range. Some estimate that the voucher campaign has thus far been quite successful, but recent allegations of widespread fraud, especially now that the campaign for the parliamentary elections in June 1992 is getting under way, may change this impression. Others have reservations about either the intrinsic merit of divestment through vouchers or the way in which Czechoslovakia has pursued the strategy.

Initially the demand for vouchers and the registration stamp was anaemic. By late 1991, after the books had been on sale for nearly 3 months, only some 700,000 had been registered.[653] But under the impact of the aggressive marketing by the privatization funds, expectations of substantial returns on the investment were raised. Advertisements indeed promised ten- to twentyfold increases in the value of the vouchers in one year, and the funds signed up voucher book registrants

---

[646] Interview with Dusan Trâska, the spiritual father of the voucher scheme in *Hospodárské noviny,* 22 October 1991, p.12.

[647] All those born prior to 1 January 1974, about 11.5 million citizens. For vouchers to be made available in 1992, the cut-off date for entitlement will be 1 January 1975.

[648] This stamp-fee was imposed to ensure that the administrative cost of voucher privatization would be self-liquidating. To cover the estimated costs of voucher privatization of about Kcs 1.5 billion, the sale of 1.5 million registration stamps was needed. In the event, actual sales far exceeded this requirement.

[649] *Lidové noviny,* 24 January 1992, p.1. In fact, the deadline for the registration of voucher booklets was extended several times. The registration stamps for the voucher books were on sale until 31 January 1992, but because of the brisk demand the registration of the voucher books (a separate act) will continue in the bigger cities until the end of February.

[650] *Investicne privatizacni fondy* (IPF). See Federal Ministry of Finance, *Kuponova privatizace — informacni prirucka,* Prague, 1991, p.9. In the absence of specialized legislation, these funds are registered as joint-stock companies under the business code, which in effect means that they are practically unregulated (*Financial Times* 13 February 1991, p.3; *Neue Zürcher Zeitung,* 3 February 1992, p.9).

[651] Finance Minister V. Klaus stated that on 28 January there were 484 privatization funds in existence (*Rzeczpospolita,* 1-2 February 1992). A supplement with the addresses and investment codes of 437 registered funds was published in *Lidové noviny,* 18 February 1992.

[652] Interview with Tomás Jezek, Minister in Charge of Privatization for the Czech Republic (*Lidové noviny,* 24 January 1992). In mid-January, when the demand for vouchers suddenly rose, officials discovered that some 5 million coupon books, out of a total of 8 million printed, could not be located (see *Financial Times,* 21 January 1992, p.3). As an emergency solution, claimants were issued temporary registration cards (see *New York Times,* 21 January 1992, p.A9).

[653] *Financial Times,* 29 January 1992, p.2.

at a rapid rate.[654] Hence, in the first weeks of 1992, the earlier apathy on the part of the population dissipated and a veritable investment frenzy seemed to take hold of the country. Whereas in mid-January 1992 only some 3 million out of 11.5 million eligible people had registered voucher books, by the end of January that number had soared to over 8 million and it was expected that all in all up to 9 million voucher books would be registered.[655]

Whereas the Czechoslovak undertaking is unique in its conception and scope, there are obviously several dangers of proceeding in this way. One is the potential for massive fraud by the investment funds, if only because there are no legal regulations in place. There is indeed simply no way in which the promises of capital gains made to entice voucher purchasers to deposit their stake with the funds can be guaranteed. And if there were to be a stampede of cashing in the promised gains, a very severe shock through the fragile financial system is bound to be unleashed. According to some information, one fund with western backing has amassed about a third of the voucher books and is expected to corner about half of them by the time the first privatization auctions will be held. That would place that one fund in charge of so many firms that its own ability to coordinate the activities of these firms would seem in doubt for the same reason that the erstwhile central planning office exhibited severe defects in its ability to coordinate such widely diverging decisions. To counter these tendencies, a government decree was issued, in time for the registration deadline, providing that any fund's share in a given company cannot exceed 20 per cent of its total capital, that each fund must distribute its vouchers over at least 10 firms, and that multiple funds owned by an individual founder are jointly restricted to holding no more than 40 per cent of the issued capital of a given enterprise.[656]

The followers (Bulgaria, Lithuania, and Romania)

Although the issues of coupon-type privatization have been debated at some length in *Bulgaria*, there is as yet no law on privatization, and it is, therefore, uncertain whether in the end the authorities will implement any such scheme. Matters are clearer in Lithuania and Romania, however.

In *Lithuania*, vouchers have already been distributed to all citizens. They will eventually be utilized for distributing ownership of about one fifth of public property free of charge. This is estimated to be approximately equivalent of two thirds of the asset value[657] of industrial firms earmarked for privatization.[658] Unlike in other countries, however, vouchers can be used only in conjunction with money (for the time being roubles, but it is expected that the lita, the Lithuanian currency unit, will be introduced sometime in 1992). Any property earmarked for voucher privatization (which can be any real asset except farmland), as determined by the privatization agency, can be divided into sale (at least one third) and voucher-type divestment (up to two thirds). Furthermore, vouchers must be supplemented with at least 5 per cent in currency.

Other distinguishing marks of the Lithuanian approach are that vouchers have been unequally distributed. Thus, starting from 1,000 roubles' worth for those under 18 years of age allocations range up to 5,000 roubles for those over age 35.[659] The vouchers themselves are not transferable, except among members of the same family in case of pooling resources with a view to establishing an enterprise. Furthermore, their validity is limited, but the date of expiry has not yet been determined.

Romania's law on privatization embodies a voucher-type scheme with unique features. Free distribution of so-called property certificates will encompass all adults. It is estimated that about 17 million individuals will be eligible for this free distribution. The shares of big firms selected for voucher privatization will be divided between the certificate pool (30 per cent) and the government (70 per cent). The government holdings will subsequently be sold over a period of seven years, and in the process the firm's labour force will have the opportunity to acquire up to 10 per cent of the firm's total shares at a 10 per cent discount. The government's stake will be managed by a newly-established State Property Fund. This is an independent entity created by the privatization law, which will also be charged with administering the enterprises to be retained in the public sector.[660] Though a public institution, it is expected to function along commercial principles; but it will be partly exempt from income tax.

The firms selected for full privatization and the 30 per cent share of their stocks to be distributed to the population will be divided among five Private Property Funds. These will, in fact, administer the enterprises assigned to them until full divestment, with the state's share remaining in principle a silent partner. But so are the certificate holders, for they cannot exercise their vote the first five years.

---

[654] Legally the voucher remains the property of the person who registered it until trading is allowed. Some of the funds therefore promised to purchase the clients' 1,000 voucher points for Kcs 10,000 to Kcs 20,000 at that later date.

[655] The numbers rose very rapidly indeed as the stampede to the registration and mutual-fund offices got under way. On 24 January, *Rudé právo* reported a total of 5 million that was expected to climb to 7 million by the end of the registration period; on 28 January, the total exceeded 6.9 million (*Rudé právo*, 31 January 1992, p.3). An early estimate of end-January registrants put the total at 8.2 million (*Neue Zürcher Zeitung*, 3 February 1992, p.9).

[656] See *Hospodarske noviny*, 31 January 1992, p.1; *Rudé právo*, 31 January 1992, p.3.

[657] Estimated book value of the capital stock, which may or may not reflect real value at a given moment of time. In any case, the value of capital is, of course, in flux for a variety of reasons, including the rapid depreciation of the rouble and the problems of setting asset values (see box 6.3).

[658] Lithuania is also considering issuing vouchers for the privatization of agriculture, but the discussions on the details of this issue are still preliminary.

[659] Because of the rapid rouble inflation, these nominal values were recently doubled.

[660] Of the total state firms subject to enterprise restructuring (some 6,000 enterprises), about 53 per cent will be privatized while the rest will remain in the state sector as autonomous firms, much like the French parastatals.

The Private Property Funds (PPFs) are to issue certificates, and each eligible person will receive one certificate in each of the five funds. These can subsequently be utilized to acquire shares in enterprises when the firms are privatized. After five years, when not exercised to acquire shares, the certificates will automatically become shares in the PPFs, which would then be mutual funds managing the remaining firms not yet privatized. Once the latter privatize, it would be the Funds that are direct shareholders, while their own shareholders acquire only indirect ownership. Shares in privatized firms or, later on, in the PPFs can eventually be traded in a stock exchange, which is yet to be established. In principle, owners of certificates can form mutual fund associations that could exert some influence over the PPFs, but the latter's constitution protects management of these funds exceedingly well.

Whereas certificates can be owned solely by Romanian citizens (presumably resident citizens), anyone can acquire shares. Provided the state indeed puts its 70 per cent stake on the market, foreign investors should thus be able to acquire a majority stake in any of the enterprises being privatized. The "worth" of the certificates in terms of shares can be known only at a later date. This follows logically from the fact that there is simply no way to assign a value to the 17 million shares in any one PPF as long as the value of the companies assigned to the fund is not known. But the latter remains unknown until actual privatization gets under way.[661]

However, the real danger of the Romanian scheme is that the erstwhile ministerial system will be recreated in the Private Property Funds. Although there is no real need to privatize privatization, as it is so often called for, in the case of Romania there are at least strong concerns that the voucher-type privatization could perpetuate old structures.

The deliberators (Albania, Belarus, Estonia, Russia, Slovenia, and Ukraine)

In *Albania*, given the poverty of the country and the urgency of starting market-type relations, the authorities have been considering a rapid and massive transfer of title to citizens, including distribution free of charge. So far, however, privatization in Albania has been limited to *nomenklatura* privatization[662] and a few special deals with foreign companies. This stems no doubt from the fact that the draft law was only readied in August 1991 and has apparently not yet been ratified.

In spite of the chaotic conditions in Albania, the Government reported in early 1992 that very rapid progress had been made with privatization in retail trade, handicraft, and communal services. However, claims that nearly all of retail trade has already been privatized seem to be contradicted by other data, and it would seem that much of the petty privatization has been taking place not through regular channels.[663]

On present expectations, the Government is considering moving ahead very quickly in the course of 1992 with the privatization of large industrial enterprises that are viable through free distribution via financial intermediaries (possibly mutual funds along the Polish model). All adult resident citizens will be issued coupons free of charge, with perhaps some asymmetry to recognize workers' rights.

In *Slovenia,* the second draft law on privatization embodied a Polish-type voucher scheme. But this law was rejected. A third draft is currently under discussion and it may lead to a watered-down version of the voucher scheme.[664]

The *Russian Federation* and *Ukraine* are presently considering moving forward with rapid privatization through a coupon-like scheme, but its modalities remain to be determined. *Belarus* has already decided to do so, but implementation has apparently not yet started. Similar conditions appear to prevail in *Estonia*.

Toward a more generalized format?

Initially, the main stress on voucher-type privatization remained a Czechoslovak preserve. It has since been extended, with modifications, to several Eastern countries. In this connection the question has been raised whether this form of massive distribution of shares directly or indirectly, although it is administratively complex and experience is lacking, would not be the preferred way after all to lead the Eastern countries to a well-anchored market economy.

The answer to that question must necessarily focus on the critical issue of control, given the substantial potential for principal-agent problems. In the East, this concern should not only extend to the relationship between ultimate owner and his agent. It should also focus on the links between the agents and the political process. It is in this connection that the concerns are aroused whether voucher-type privatization with such large authority left in the hands of a few fund managers might not lead to a re-creation of institutions akin to the ministerial system so typical of administrative planning.

A concern that is common with any kind of mass privatization is how to ensure control. Principal-agent problems of course arise in other contexts also (see

---

[661] Some 30 firms were originally earmarked in late 1991 for experimental privatization. But actual sale does not yet seem to have taken place. It has now apparently been decided to experiment with 12 projects which the government selected from some 111 projects presented by the privatization agency. Share distribution of these firms is now scheduled for January 1992 (*Rynki zagraniczne*, 17 December 1991, p.1).

[662] Even though attempts were instituted by political bodies to bring it under political control, asset-stripping for all kinds of purposes appears to be continuing.

[663] Achievement of full trade privatization was claimed by V. Mubaraj, director of the privatization agency, on 6 January 1992 (BBC, *Summary of World Broadcasts,* EE/1273, p.B/1). However a few days earlier the Albanian news agency reported that "57 per cent of retail shops had been evaluated, the business of almost 100 per cent of them had become private and 14 per cent of the units have become mainly private". The latter presumably refers to regular transfer of full title. The same source put crafts and public services as 93 per cent evaluated, 80 per cent private, and 15 per cent completely private (BBC, *Summary of World Broadcasts,* EE/W0212, p.A/4).

[664] The main thrust of the third draft appears to be "internal shares", i.e., shares earmarked primarily for sale to workers and retired workers, at increasing discounts depending on seniority, up to the equivalent of six years' worth of wage bills. Only if the firm's capital value exceeds six annual wage bills can the issue of external shares be contemplated.

section 6.5(iv) above). But dispersed ownership of large companies is likely to leave management in place or new management with too many degrees of freedom in selecting enterprise goals that differ from those that maximize net asset values. It is precisely for that reason that various schemes have been proposed whereby the financial intermediaries typical of market economies will be simulated, at least during the initial phases of the transition. There are basically three variants: investment funds, mutual funds, and divestment funds. They all have in common that a small number of institutions, holding both a large interest in firms and a large portfolio of firms, are assumed to become effective monitors of the firms' managers.

Divestment holdings are firms created for the specific purpose of selling state-owned enterprises. What is involved essentially is that the fund managers will be placed in charge of enterprise restructuring and privatization. *Mutual funds* are conceived largely as their counterparts in market economies. That is to say, they distance themselves from individual companies and engage mainly in monitoring assets. Individuals hold shares in the mutual funds and are expected to monitor the mutual fund managers. Finally, *investment funds*, as their name suggests, are more directly involved in reconstructing the enterprises entrusted to them or that they acquire. Shares in those funds too are widely owned and individuals are assumed to monitor investment fund managers.

Holding companies are created by governments and endowed with full control over a portfolio of individual firms. Each holding company is headed by a manager, appointed by government, who is assisted by a team composed of domestic and foreign experts. Shares in the holding companies are distributed equally to all and traded on the stock market, perhaps after some phase-in period. Each holding company receives a firm deadline for divesting the firms entrusted to it. If that is not achieved at the terminal date, the remaining firms will be liquidated or sold through auctions or the stock market. Proceeds from the sale of firms are distributed to shareholders through dividends, and holding companies are prevented from either borrowing or issuing additional equity. Subject to these constraints and the confines of the law, including on antitrust, the holding companies are allowed to strike any deal they see fit.

There are a number of advantages and drawbacks of promoting free distribution. The advantages are mainly the egalitarian and transparent nature and speed with which the privatization process can be carried forward under some semblance of government supervision. But there are many drawbacks and dangers. First of all, there are bound to be losers as well as beneficiaries, as valuation problems will crop up even in the most egalitarian-designed scheme. Furthermore, free distribution yields no revenue to the government and may erode future fiscal revenues for as long as the fiscal base cannot be radically revamped. Moreover, any large-scale distribution would introduce the principal-agent problem. Unquestionably the most serious shortcoming of this approach would be that privatization through near-universal free distribution can exert at best a weak influence on managerial behaviour.

Obtaining proprietor capitalism, rather than "punter" capitalism, should normally be the principal aim of divestment for economic motives (see section 6.4). The effect of "punter" capitalism on managerial behaviour essentially emanates through share-trading according to fluctuating market assessments. These transactions would, at best, exert a weak control on management, and the effect might often be distorted because short-term share-price fluctuations are often out of line with the "fundamentals". The population at large is unlikely soon to become an effective monitor, be it of companies or investment or mutual funds, and thus the amplitude of fluctuations without core monitoring will tend to be larger than otherwise. Even mutual fund managers will not have the knowledge or incentive to assess managerial performance and promote take-overs when needed.

(d) Decentralized government agencies

At least for some state-owned assets, it has been argued that it would be useful to endow decentralized government agencies with some stake from which they would be able to finance themselves. It has been suggested that the vast bulk of firms be entrusted with various kinds of local-level administrative organs (such as municipalities), welfare organizations (such as hospitals), educational foundations (to foster training and scientific research), and basic financial organizations (such as insurance companies, pension funds, and social-security institutions). The spiritual father of this proposal, which was first made in 1972, has since disavowed the modus as too etatist.[665] His idea was to establish a small number of profit-maximizing financial institutions, organized as holdings, as decentralized monitors of state ownership.

Even though the original proposal has been overtaken by political developments, Hungary has made legal provisions that upon transformation into share companies, a certain share of equity (25 to 30 per cent) must be allotted to the local authorities in those cases when they own the buildings of the enterprise or the land, which occurs rather frequently. Similar sharing, but usually at a much smaller scale, is being enacted in several other countries.

Some countries, including Czechoslovakia (especially in small privatization), Hungary, and Poland (the latter two in both small and large privatization), have indeed endowed lower-level public organs with state assets that were either in their care, and hence for which property rights were unclear, or were directly under central control.

(e) Recapitalizing the financial sector

As noted, capital markets in the Eastern countries are all but nonexistent, the banking sector is very underdeveloped, and all kinds of microeconomic institutions, including banks and many state-owned firms,

---

[665] See Márton Tardos, "A gazdasági verseny problémai hazánkban" (The problems of competition in our country), *Kozgazdasagi Szemle*, 1972. Nos.7-8, and more recently his "Property Ownership", *Eastern European Economics*, Spring 1990, pp.4-29.

are heavily indebted, including *vis-à-vis* each other (box 6.2). Without clearing up these portfolios and getting the banks to function as effective intermediaries between savers and investors, as centres for the swift clearing of transactions, and as units that actively mobilize savings through their own role in financing and capitalizing enterprises, the transition is likely to evolve very slowly at best.

To remedy this situation, the state could allocate its assets in part or entirely for the recapitalization of these financial institutions and indeed for capitalizing institutions (such as insurance companies and pension funds) still lacking. Thus, the Polish mass privatization explicitly allocates part of the new shares to financial institutions and the social-security fund. In the Hungarian privatization modes too some share is transferred to various municipal and related organs, and of course the financial institutions obtain part of their recapitalization through cross-ownership (box 6.4). In some cases such a initiative would be coupled with swapping liabilities, as in the case of insurance companies and pension funds.

A variant of this approach is the proposal to create holding companies, whose shares would be traded on the stock market and who would have a mandate to restructure and/or divest themselves of firms in their portfolio over some period of time; but they would not be owned by the people at large. This option has received considerable attention in the western advisory literature. There are two variants. One has as its distinguishing feature that these companies would essentially be divestment agencies, as already discussed.[666] The other aims at endowing holding companies with the presently existing state firms as a more permanent form of divestment.[667] These organs are not expected to divest themselves according to a set schedule, but may eventually be taken over through stock-market transactions by private agents.

(iii) Distribution of user rights

The principal purpose of separating user rights from ultimate ownership through subcontracting, franchising, leasing, and management contracts is to increase the role of non-state decision makers in the allocation of the usufruct of state-owned assets. It is important to recall that such usufruct divestment goes well beyond the stages of corporatization and commercialization discussed earlier. For one thing, private investors and managers take over the day-to-day affairs of the assets for which the contract is signed, hopefully with a view to maximizing residual benefits after defraying operating and amortization costs, as well as the contract fee. But there will not be a transfer of the ultimate ownership of the economic activities, or enterprises, concerned. This form of usufruct transfer, in addition to auctions, is very important notably in the privatization of catering and retail establishments (see table 6.13).

In principle, this way of proceeding with privatization offers greater flexibility and should enable potential subcontractors, franchisees, lessees, and managers to compete during the tendering stage. But there are serious problems associated with spelling out clearly the contracts for managers and, even more, with enforcing them. Likewise there are problems in negotiating a proper lease or franchise fee and ensuring that the assets are utilized for best purposes.[668] But it would give the state more time to settle the more intricate divestment issues, yet yield some revenue from those to whom the user rights are assigned and, in the case of subcontracting, franchising, or leasing, remove it from responsibility for financing these firms. But the contract must stipulate the details of such an arrangement. Hence, these forms cannot be the proper means of divesting user rights for complex enterprises. But they may work in the case of comparatively small production and service undertakings, such as those that are objects of "petty" privatization (see table 6.13). This approach is particularly apt in the case of the liquidation of firms with buildings and rolling stock which can be leased out. Poland demonstrated the usefulness of the leasing of trucks and related rolling stock from state firms. This led to a substantially "privatized" road transportation sector already in 1990.

(iv) Sale of state-owned assets

As indicated, the final form of privatization involves the outright sale of state assets. This can occur in many different ways, but virtually all can be reduced to six variants: public offering with resort to the stock market, public offering through various kinds of auctions, the negotiated sale of shares or assets, worker and/or management buy-outs, a non-subscribed increase of capital, and debt-equity swaps.

(a) Public offering through capital-market operations

Although this form of divestiture is not completely unknown in the East — it has been most widely experimented with in Hungary and also in Poland — it cannot play a major role during the initial phases of the transition because there is no functioning domestic capital market, and the costs of organizing stock offerings on foreign capital markets, as tried by Hungary, is a difficult and expensive undertaking. And effective demand for shares has been disappointing. Thus, Poland readied seven companies for public offering in 1990 and actually brought five to market. But for four out of five, demand remained well below expectations, and hasty measures had to be taken to "interest" potential shareholders.

---

[666] See Olivier Blanchard et al., op.cit., pp.32 ff.

[667] The most elaborate proposal along those lines is in Frydman and Rapaczynski, loc.cit.

[668] For a lengthy discussion of the problems with leases and management contracts, see Olivier Bouin and Charles-Albert Michalet, loc.cit., pp.126-140.

Poland now has nine shares that were sold to the general public,[669] and these are now traded in the Warsaw Stock Exchange, which is currently open twice a week. Though transactions per trading session average some $70 million (as compared to less than $1 million in Hungary), trading has remained shallow and most stocks are being quoted well below their emission price, which in a number of cases was set too high. There are other reasons for the depressed prices of shares, including the economic recession, the pervasive uncertainty, and rates of return on bank deposits which are are rather high and riskless.

Because of the problem with floating shares, Hungary launched only one issue abroad (in Austria) and has not brought another issue to the domestic market since. Poland's experience with the first flotations in late 1990, as discussed, forced those in charge of privatization to look for alternatives. In addition to the coupon scheme, they have now opted for the so-called "sectoral" privatization. This encompasses readying an entire sector for divestment, chiefly through foreign direct investment. The government has selected 34 industrial sectors at the sub-branch level, for which sectoral restructuring and privatization studies have been commissioned from a variety of mostly foreign consulting firms. The purpose is to obtain some gauge on the long-term economic viability of any one sector under the new domestic and international market conditions. This procedure has given rise to two concerns. One is the rather high cost (apparently varying between $100,000 and $700,000) of each of these studies and the fact that it is being left up to "foreigners" to decide the future of entire sub-branches of the Polish economy. Another is that this advisory service may simply become a disguised form of centralized state intervention in the determination of the potential viability of any economic sector.

Some of the successor republics of the Soviet Union (including the Russian Federation), as did Czechoslovakia in the beginning, are hoping to float shares in both Budapest and Vienna. But if the experience of the more advanced east European countries is any indication, this road is bound to be rocky.

The realization of Hungarian policy makers, that the value of large companies would in any case remain far below earlier expectations, and indeed well below "carefully prepared estimates" by foreign advisers,[670] and that many firms previously heavily dependent on the Soviet market will not be able to survive as such, prompted a reassessment of the earlier strategy of a slow pace of privatization aimed at maximizing values through public subscriptions or stock flotations, including on foreign exchanges.

To the surprise of many managers of the transition, there has been widespread apathy among western investors, as well as attempts to carve up the Eastern markets (as occurred in the case of domestic chemicals) and to obtain favourable treatment. And the erosion of the economic strength of the big companies as a result of the depression throughout the East at the same time that the small private sector has been developing vigorously has markedly depreciated the realizable value of the big firms.

Of course, if the stock-market option is feasible, it should be used as widely as possible. A public offering underlines the state's stance on divesting its assets to a potentially wide circle of shareholders at a price set on a competitive basis in markets that are equally transparent (or obscure) for the vast majority of participants. However, the widespread existence of privileged information and the far-from-perfect functioning of the stock market in any case, even in mature market economies, poses problems that must be reckoned with. Also, the introduction of shares has to be managed over time, not only in order to prepare the companies for privatization but also to avoid imparting adverse effects on share prices.

(b) Auctions

Auctions offer the next best opportunity for selling assets, especially those that will have to be transferred as a unit, for it gives virtually everyone a chance to acquire the assets, albeit in some cases on different terms. Particularly those agents familiar with the undertaking will possess asymmetric information, and will be able to modify their offer price accordingly.

None the less, open auctions that are as transparent as possible offer the most appropriate way to divest an entire range of assets presently owned by the state, most notably petty assets (see table 6.13), whose disposal can hardly be negotiated in a stock market. The goals of petty privatization can be pursued more easily through straightforward auctions. Czechoslovakia chose to enact a "Dutch" version[671] since early 1991. But there are other variants that can be explored.

There are valuation, technical, and administrative problems with all kinds of auctions, even for petty privatization. But they are more pronounced with large privatization. To proceed, however, clear property rights must exist. This has proved difficult to ascertain, owing to the problems discussed in section 6.2.

(c) Private transfers

This is a discretionary form of divestment that may be initiated by any party. Rather than sell shares, the private transfer as a rule involves the sale of the assets as an entity, just like in an auction. But the price would be negotiated differently. In some cases, such a transfer may be organized as a way of swapping debt. Especially Czechoslovakia has utilized such private deals to attract foreign direct investment, and presumably Poland's "sectoral privatization" will follow suit once it gets fully underway.

---

[669] Two more are to be accepted on the Exchange in the near future. But there are no plans to have the Exchange grow substantially in the near future.

[670] Thus, to avoid any suggestion of impropriety, the Hungarian privatization agency, after had been placed under parliamentary control, decided to have every offer carefully audited by outside consulting firms, frequently foreign-based.

[671] As opposed to a straight auction, a "Dutch" auction starts from an upper-limit price set by the seller or the auctioneer which is then lowered according to a pre-set gradation schedule until either a buyer is found or the floor reservation price is reached, in which case no sale occurs.

TABLE 6.12

Privatization in the financial sector

	Breaking up monopolies (Number of banks)	Sales or transfers of financial institutions to domestic nationals	Role of foreign capital
Albania	..	..	..
Belarus	25 [a, b]	No	In new banks only
Bulgaria	75 [c]	Partially	Strictly limited
Czechoslovakia	37 [a]	Partially	Limited
Estonia	24	Yes	In new banks only
Hungary	36 [a]	Only exceptionally	In new banks only
Latvia	..	..	..
Lithuania	20	Only exceptionally [d]	In new banks only
Poland	90 [e]	No	In new banks only [f]
Romania	15	No	In new banks only
Russian Federation	1 300 [g]	No	In new banks only
Ukraine	51	No	Very limited
USSR	1 500 [h]	..	..
Yugoslavia	180	No limitations	
Memorandum item:			
Ex-GDR	593 [i]	Sales	No limitations [j]
Croatia	38	No	No limitations
Slovenia	31	No	No limitations

[a] September 1991.
[b] With 320 affiliates registered.
[c] August 1991.
[d] ESOP-scheme in the national savings bank.
[e] December 1991.
[f] Sales of 20 per cent of shares in selected banks to foreign banks planned for 1992.
[g] November 1991.
[h] June 1991.
[i] Number of banking institutions in September 1991. Includes new subsidiaries set up by foreign banks.
[j] Little actual involvement.

(d) Worker and management buy-outs

Because of the peculiar situation with property rights and the inability of most Eastern countries to displace management in place, it may be useful to focus under some circumstances on monetizing the property rights vested in those employed in a given firm. Worker and management rights have been recognized in all countries, at least to some degree (see tables 6.11 and 6.13). There have been many worker/management buy-outs notably in Estonia, the eastern parts of Germany, Poland, and Yugoslavia (prior to the civil war and political disintegration).

(e) Unsubscribed expansion of capital

This is like a partial transfer of assets because it dilutes the state's holdings. It might be useful given that many would-be purchasers lack the capital to pay immediately for a full acquisition. By acquiring stock rights, the private financier may raise the value of capital and thus finance his involvement. This has been resorted to mostly in order to attract foreign direct investment.

(f) Debt-equity swaps

Although most Eastern countries have by and large decided that there is great urgency to clean up the books of state-owned firms and banks directly or indirectly, Hungary is one of the few that adheres to the notion that much of the problem will resolve itself. The government has recently encouraged the "privatization" of state-owned companies by swapping them for bank or enterprise debt (see box 6.4).

There is nothing seriously wrong with this way of proceeding, provided the books are cleaned up in the end. That is not now the case. Instead, banks, which are largely state-owned, become the "owners" of the erstwhile autonomous enterprise. Potentially this may yield "phony" privatization, for if the bank or the acquiring enterprise remains under state control nothing much will have changed.

In some cases, however, Hungary has also encouraged the acquisition of firms by other firms with some offsetting for inter-enterprise debt, but also real money being put into the acquisition. This has led to considerable cross-ownership. While this may ensure control, it is, in fact, a more sophisticated variant of spontaneous privatization.

(g) Advantages and drawbacks

Perhaps the greatest advantage of widespread sale is that it widens effective ownership. As such it would strengthen democracy, prevent renationalization, and forestall any criticism of the state encouraging the very rich or foreigners or insiders to acquire real wealth at anything but a competitively determined price. Second, popular capitalism may instill a shareholder culture in the population at large and abate the strong risk aversion that is still pervasive in most Eastern countries. It may thus be an integral component of the attitudinal changes mentioned in section 6.5(v). Third, it would provide a strengthening of the capital and securities' markets by those having built up a financial interest from their own resources.

Among the drawbacks of large privatization, as already intimated in the individual sections, are the problems of ensuring effective monitoring − hence

TABLE 6.13

Privatization of retail trade and catering

	Corporatization	Leasing	Restitution	Free distribution	Auctions	Direct sale	Role of foreign capital
Albania	..	Yes	..	..	Yes	Yes	..
Belarus	Yes	Yes	No	No	Yes	Yes	Limited [a]
Bulgaria	Yes	Yes	Yes	No	Yes	Yes	..
Czechoslovakia	No	Yes	Yes	No	Yes	Yes	Limited [b]
Estonia	Yes	Yes	Not regulated	No	Yes [c]	Yes [c]	Not regulated
Hungary	Yes	Yes	No [d]	No	Yes	Exceptionally	Prohibited [a]
Latvia	Yes	Yes	Yes	No	Yes	Yes	..
Lithuania	Yes	No	Yes	No	Yes	No	Limited
Poland	No	Yes	Yes	No	Yes	Yes	No limitations
Romania	No	Yes	No	No	Yes	Yes	No limitations
Russian Federation	Yes	Yes	No	No	Yes	Yes	Negligible
Ukraine	Yes	Yes	No	Possibly	Possibly	Possibly	Possibly
Yugoslavia	No	Yes	No	No	Yes	Yes	No limits
Memorandum item:							
Ex-GDR	No	Yes [e]	Yes	No	No	Yes	No restrictions
Croatia	No	Yes	No	No	Yes	Yes	No limits
Slovenia	No	Yes	No	No	Yes	Yes	No limits

a But foreigners are allowed to buy chains directly from the state or individual shops from private owners.
b But foreigners are allowed to participate in the second round of auctions or to buy shops from private owners, or from the state in big privatization.
c Only for adults, with more than 10 years of residence in Estonia. Employees of the enterprise, local inhabitants and/or current leaseholders have priority.
d Partial compensation is possible through "compensation certificates".
e Shop space only.

proper management — of these privatized firms. There will also be considerable income inequality. Financial markets being fragile, if present at all, are vulnerable to "normal" shocks, but also to manipulation and outright fraud. In the process of readying firms for privatization, including the petty auctions, widespread disruptions in the retail and wholesale distribution networks have been observed. And firms to be privatized are plunged into considerable uncertainty for the duration of the privatization campaign and until effective monitors are in place, something that is unlikely to be realized immediately upon the sale of shares. Finally, there appears to be considerable resentment about the alleged profiteering and speculation, including through "laundered" money from the domestic underground economy as well as foreign sources.

(v) The privatization of financial institutions

As indicated in table 6.12, several countries have formulated visions of what will eventually be done with the existing financial institutions, essentially the "commercial" banks. The preferred method for those that envisage privatization of existing banks is to sell off blocks of shares to foreign investors, as an alternative to having foreign investors set up new institutions altogether. Czechoslovakia has recently signed several such agreements with German financial institutions.[672] The present Government aims at transferring some 50 to 60 per cent of the shares in financial institutions to private agents, the rest being subject to voucher privatization during the first two rounds.[673] The recent transactions with foreign financial institutions are undertaken from the share that still belongs to the state. A commitment was made to hold the share of foreign capital in Czechoslovak financial institutions to 25 per cent, with any one foreign bank's position not to exceed 10 per cent of total capital.[674]

Several countries prohibit the sale of the existing financial institutions, probably because there are so few of them and all suffer from the legacies of planning discussed earlier. Diversification of the financial sector and the emergence of new financial markets, including stock exchanges, is being left to new investment, and hence is not the subject of this chapter.

(vi) The question of land

Excepting notably Poland and Yugoslavia,[675] where land was largely in the hands of private farmers, arguably the most troublesome question in the privatization process was everywhere what to do with land. As table 6.2 indicates for agricultural land, progress has been

---

[672] For example, *Zivnostenská Banka*'s augmented capital will be taken over for 40 per cent by the *Berliner Handels- und Frankfurter Bank*. The remainder will be split into 12 per cent for the International Finance Corporation and 48 per cent for mass privatization purposes. For details, see *Neue Zürcher Zeitung*, 11-12 January 1992, p.33.

[673] For instance, the *Komercni Banka* is earmarked for voucher privatization. About 53 per cent of its capital will be distributed in the first round, 3 per cent will be set aside for restitution, and the remainder will be kept by the state, at least for the present. For details, see *Neue Zürcher Zeitung*, 20 January 1992.

[674] See *Hospodárské noviny*, 20 September 1991. The cited transactions with German financial institutions would seem to be in violation of this intention, however.

[675] The share of arable land in the hands of the state came to less than one fifth in the case of Poland. Because of the dominance of private land ownership, land privatization was not an issue that drew much attention in the privatization debate. Some state farms are being offered for sale on commercial terms. Some cooperatives (less than 4 per cent of arable land) are being dissolved with distribution of the assets to members. Little information is available on the modalities of the process.

spotty, except in Albania,[676] Estonia, and Latvia, and, of course, the eastern parts of Germany. Elsewhere the land question has been subject to conflicting property claims (some aspects were discussed in section 6.3).

Particularly problematic has been the question of what to do with agricultural collectives — especially the cooperatives (variants of the Soviet *kolkhozy*), whose property rights are highly uncertain. In some countries, the state had arrogated to itself only the usufruct to land usage, leaving ownership formally with the individual farmers who "volunteered" their land and sundry means of production to the collective. In addition, some collectives acquired their own land either from endowments of the state or through outright purchases. Similar questions arise with the state farms, whose property rights ostensibly belong to the state.

Although several countries have succeeded in adopting a law on land, this has not meant the end of the problem. Czechoslovakia, for example, finally placed a land law on the books in May 1991. The law envisaged the restitution of usufruct rights over land (but not unambiguous ownership) to former owners or their legal heirs, provided they are resident citizens and they stake out a claim by the end of 1992. A special provision enjoins agricultural cooperatives from engaging in capital transactions in order to protect the rights of restitution claimants. Other assets of cooperatives will be dealt with through the transformation law for cooperatives, which was adopted in the beginning of 1992. State farms are being taken care of in the context of "large" privatization. Because the law was adopted only after a bruising, highly controversial, political battle, its practical implications are still unclear. Perhaps more worrisome is the apparent lack of interest on the part of former owners in having their property restituted in this fashion.[677]

Even in the former German Democratic Republic, the land question has continued to be a controversial issue, in spite of the importation of a clear legal framework and the fact that nearly 85 per cent of arable land had formally remained in private hands. The cooperatives, which are not under the supervision of the *Treuhandanstalt*, were to have been restructured by the end of 1991. But the process has been very complicated, owing largely to the difficulty of determining who actually owns what share in each cooperative and how claims can be settled when members decide to leave. The *Treuhandanstalt* was, however, entrusted with the agricultural land (about 2.1 million hectares) and forests (about 1.9 million hectares) in the hands of the state.

The latter were largely transferred to local authorities in the course of 1991. In some cases, such land was also transferred to former private owners, but progress here has been much slower. At the end of October 1991, about 2 per cent of the agency's land had been sold or leased to private investors. This slow pace stems in part from a deliberate policy to avoid a rapid erosion of land prices, notably relative to those in the western *Länder*.[678] About half of agricultural land and a fifth of forest land remains with the agency at this stage and is currently been exploited through lease contracts. From mid-1992, when existing leases expire, the agency intends to sell off these areas to private investors, notably farmers, who will benefit from various subsidy schemes. Former owners expropriated under Soviet military occupation and members of the cooperatives will be favoured.[679]

The restitution question in the transformation of land ownership has been highly contested in the political and constitutional arena also in Hungary (see section 6.2). After at least two years of controversy about the legal framework and the necessary institutional infra-structure, there is presently a good chance that the machinery is in place to begin issuing compensation certificates to former owners of arable land and to begin the process of auctioning off arable land.[680] Former owners permanently residing in rural areas can stake out a claim to their land and use their certificates to "buy back" their holdings from the local cooperatives or state farms.

The search for a resolution of the intricate land question through some workable compromise has been nowhere more complex than in the former Soviet Union and now the successor republics. It was only in January 1992 that the Russian Federation resolved in principle (but only by presidential decree) to accelerate land reform, including "the transformation of collective and state farms into new forms of management".[681] In the same statement, it was made clear apparently for the first time that "the transfer of land into ownership, into normal, real ownership, private ownership — with the right to use this land as collateral in banks in order to receive credits, with the right to sell this land if necessary — must be the main form of allotting land". But the legislation in place does not yet permit such transactions because the parliament remains deeply divided over the issue. The first step will probably be an organizational overhaul of the state and cooperative farms, whose councils are requested to decide by the end of February 1992 whether to transform themselves into a joint-stock company or an association of peasant

---

[676] In early 1992, Minister of Agriculture Zydi Pepa declared that about 60 per cent of the Albanian land area had been distributed: BBC, *Summary of World Broadcasts*, EE/1271, p.B/1 of 7 January 1992.

[677] In the Czech Republic, for example, a poll conducted among village inhabitants found that less than 10 per cent of the respondents were ready to set up a private farm (*Zemedelská ekonomika*, 1991:7, p.440).

[678] See "Die Lage der Weltwirtschaft und der deutschen Wirtschaft im Herbst 1991", DIW, *Wochenbericht*, 1991:42/43, p.596.

[679] See "Privatisierung der ostdeutschen Landwirtschaft", *Neue Zürcher Zeitung*, 19 December 1991.

[680] The first compensation law went into effect in August 1991 and the second is planned for early 1992. Because both give generous deadlines for people to present their claims, actual privatization transactions cannot begin until late 1992 at the earliest. To complicate matters further, in January 1992 a law was passed by which the collectively owned land of cooperatives will have to be distributed to the membership at large (with only partial sale through auctions).

[681] Comment by Viktor N. Khlystun, Minister of Agriculture of the Russian Federation, made on 14 January 1992, as reported in BBC, *Summary of World Broadcasts*, SU/1279 C1/2, 16 January 1992, p.2. See also *Financial Times*, 23 January 1992, p.3 and *Neue Zürcher Zeitung*, 15 January 1992, p.31.

holdings.[682] The Presidential decree sets 1 January 1993 as the deadline for the reorganization of state and co-operative farms.[683]

Similar problems have been observed with non-agricultural land. Absence of a clear-cut stance on property rights associated with urban land has been inhibiting the establishment of new small and medium-sized firms. It has also led to a series of practical problems in the petty privatization, hindering notably the injection of new capital into those undertakings for lack of certainty about title and the future basis of the firm.

---

[682] Interview with Viktor N. Khlystun as reported in BBC, *Summary of World Broadcasts*, SU/1268, p.C3/5 of 3 January 1992.

[683] See "O poryadke reorganizatsii kolkhozov i sovkhozov", *Ekonomika i zhizn'*, 1992:3, p.19.

6.7 EXPERIENCE AND AGENDA

(i) Lessons from the experience with privatization to date

Although the debate on privatization in general, and divestment of state-owned assets in particular, has been at the centre of the economic and sociopolitical discussion in the East, the progress made by early 1992 remained rather modest throughout the group (excepting, of course, the eastern *Länder* of Germany, as shown in table 6.14). Certainly, a few spectacular sales, mostly to foreigners, have occurred and more or less rounded laws on privatization and property rights have been put in place in nearly all Eastern countries. Otherwise, most action has been in the form of petty privatization, with which rapid progress has been made notably in Czechoslovakia and Poland.[684]

TABLE 6.14

The privatization process in east Germany
(As of end-September 1991)

	Treuhand companies [a]	Privatized firms	Management buy-outs
Agriculture	567	13	3
Energy, water, mining	188	48	-
Manufacturing	5 445	1 918	224
Construction	941	402	165
Commerce	1 208	261	62
Transport	310	123	9
Financial institutions	9	9	-

Source: H.J. Overstolz, "Zentrales Beteilligungscontrolling – Das Frühwarnsytem der Treuhand", *Die Wirtschaft*, special issue, Autumn 1991, p.34 and *Treuhandanstalt*, "Privatisierung, Stand 30. September 1991", Berlin, pp.1.8, 1.20, 1.21.

[a] Including firms already privatized by the agency.

Thus, in Czechoslovakia, by late October 1991, about half of the proposed 22,000 petty assets in the Czech republic had been sold, chiefly through auctions (over 90 per cent). But the total number of such petty assets for the country as a whole exceeds 100,000. Although the Czechoslovak Government had originally hoped to be able to privatize these assets in a matter of two years, current estimates are that it will take at least five to accomplish the task set.[685] The process has been vastly complicated by restitution claims. About 90 per cent of the petty auctions involve some kind of restitution claim which necessitates that the new "owner" can at best lease the building and land until the claim has been legally resolved. This inhibits the renovation and expansion of such undertakings.

Whereas on its assumption of power in May 1990 the Hungarian Government had hoped to divest itself at auction of almost the entire retail trade and service sector under the so-called "pre-privatization" law then under preparation,[686] by the end of 1991 only some 1,700 units had been sold, and the proceeds from these sales remained well below expectations.[687] There were various reasons for this result. One important one was the overestimation of the number of "petty" undertakings that would fall under the jurisdiction of the law. In the event, four fifths of the more than 50,000 shops registered (table 6.15) will be privatized outside the law by their "owners", largely state enterprises, who thus effectively undercut the Government's original commitment to transparency, competition, and protection of the public interest.

TABLE 6.15

The petty privatization process in Hungary

Shops in retail trade and catering as of 1989	53 502
Units falling under the jurisdiction of the petty privatization law	10 193
Not saleable	2 977
Ready for privatization [a]	4 983
Auctions held (first round) [b]	2648
Auctions held (second round) [b]	563
Units sold through auctions	1 729
With full ownership	458
With lease	1 271
Units disposed of otherwise	391

Source: *Statisztikai Évkönyv 1989* (Budapest, 1990), p.174, State Property Agency: *Annual Report 1990* (Budapest: SPA, 1991), *Magyar Hirlap*, 13 February 1992.

[a] As of 15 August 1991.
[b] As of 31 December 1991.

In Poland, which was the first to embark upon comprehensive transformation policies, including a wide-ranging privatization debate, by the end of 1990 very little had changed if the assessment is based on a number of key macroeconomic aggregates classified by ownership. Only the indicators for fixed assets and investment in the public sector registered a decline (see

---

[684] It was estimated that by the end of 1990 in Poland of the 100,000 or so small enterprises about four fifths had been turned over to private owners through sales or, in most cases, to managers through lease arrangements (see Christoph G. Bandyk, "Privatisation in Poland – program, achievements and foreign investment policy" (paper prepared for the conference "Privatization in Eastern Europe", organized by International Center for Monetary and Banking Studies, Geneva, Switzerland, 20-21 September 1991).

[685] For details, see Martin Kupka, "Transformation of ownership in Czechoslovakia" (paper prepared for the conference "Privatization in Eastern Europe", organized by International Center for Monetary and Banking Studies, Geneva, Switzerland, 20-21 September 1991).

[686] This law was adopted by Parliament in September 1990 (see *The Hungarian Economy*, 1990:3/4).

[687] Recommended values have tended to be too high to attract buyers, and the privatization agency has had to reduce values on average by 25 per cent in the past year and a half. In fact, when political pressure was exerted to speed up the process, valuation had to be further reduced (see interview with Mr. E. Rácz, one of the agency's directors, in *Magyar Nemzet*, 25 September 1991).

TABLE 6.16

Macroeconomic indicators by ownership structure in Poland
(Percentages)

	Public			Private		
	1989	1990	1991	1989	1990	1991
NMP produced	69.9	67.8	..	30.1	32.2	..
Employment	55.7	54.2	48 [a]	44.3	45.8	52 [a]
Fixed capital	71.0	64.9	..	29.0	35.1	..
Investment	64.7	58.7	..	35.3	41.3	..
Industrial output	83.8	82.6	75.8	16.2	17.4	24.2

Source: *Rocznik Statystyczny 1991* (Warsaw: G US, 1991) and *Rzecapospolita*, 6 February 1992.

Note: Economically active units belonging to social and political organizations have now been classified as belonging to the "private" sector, whereas in earlier editions of the yearbook they were including in the "public" sector.

[a] Preliminary estimates.

---

table 6.16). Although similar data for 1991 are not yet available, this observation would seem to apply also to that year. Even when cognizance is taken of the number of enterprises taken out of the state sector, the results to date are rather modest (table 6.17).[688]

But elsewhere, apart from spontaneous privatization that may or may not be recognized once the commotions attending transition subside, achievements are small. In some cases, no progress at all has thus far been booked, aside from the worst emanations of spontaneous privatization.

This suggests that it is far too early to draw any firm inferences from the experiences with privatization. All one can try to compile at this stage is a set of tentative indicators of the positive and negative sides of the course of privatization to date. Though far from conclusive at this stage, the observations that can be drawn could be viewed as warning signals which the countries that have not yet moved forward with privatization and others that still have leeway in designing the nuts and bolts of their privatization policies may wish to take into account in determining their approach or streamlining their privatization processes.

From the many lessons that can be learned, it may be useful to retain the following. *First* of all, *neither privatization nor divestment can be pursued solely for economic reasons*. It must be part and parcel of the political economy of the transition. The process is bound to be protracted and very costly indeed, even when there remains a broad sociopolitical consensus for the transition and privatization. Without it, the transformation process in general and the privatization campaign in particular are bound to be utilized as vehicles in supporting the power base of the coalescing political parties. The rediscovery of "political rents", while not surprising, is not an encouraging omen for economic efficiency in these economies. One can only hope to minimize the degree of political interference and to avoid building up a new *nomenklatura*, even if more broadly based than under communism.[689] But it is unrealistic to hope to proceed without it altogether.

What is then needed is not only a sociopolitical consensus on how best to proceed (see the salient questions of section 6.5(i) above). Also a sufficiently robust machinery must be in place to tackle unexpected setbacks or new problems that come to the fore only once privatization gets well under way. A strong government with technically competent and a well-motivated privatization agency would seem to be required. That should facilitate making rapid progress with corporatization and commercialization.

Second, the internal management of the privatization agency is a critical ingredient to steering clear of a number of pitfalls. It would be useful to have a transparent agenda — a coherent strategy — for the trustee set by parliament. It should not be endowed with the obligation to come to grips with the socio-economic problems of labour displacement or redeployment, for example. Similarly in the case of subsidies or government-guaranteed credits to those willing to take over state firms: those should be arranged by other government agencies. Likewise for those firms that will remain public. They should be placed under the control of a different agency.

Third, the trustee agencies, while highly independent, are best placed under strict parliamentary oversight,[690] and as transparent a mandate and agenda for change as circumstances permit need to be issued to this organ, to avoid embroiling the trustee agencies in political bickering. To avert conflicts of interest, the officials of these agencies need to be held to the strictest norms of personal conduct. Political and economic vested-interest groups, both unavoidable, should be kept at a distance to the extent possible. Economic

---

[688] The table reflects the situation on 1 October 1991. For 1991 as a whole, 932 firms were "liquidated", 406 through the law on privatization and 526 through bankruptcy proceedings under the enterprise law: see *Rzeczpospolita*, 8 January 1992.

[689] As an example, shortly after the first free parliamentary elections in Hungary, the Antall Government insisted that the chief executive officers of the self-governing state enterprises be appointed through new elections. Over 90 per cent of the incumbents were re-elected, to the surprise of many observers. But this outcome could have been anticipated, as argued, for example, by Éva Voszka, "Tulajdonreform vagy privatizáció? (Ownership reform or privatization?)", *Közgazdasági Szemle*, 1991:2, pp.117-133; and "Homályból homályba — a tulajdonosi szerkezet átalakulása a nagyiparban (From mist to mist — the change of ownership structure in industry)", *Társadalmi Szemle*, 1991:5, pp.3-12.

[690] In Hungary, for example, the privatization agency was first placed under parliamentary supervision. With the formation of the Antall Government, it was temporarily (for 15 months) placed under government supervision. Because the issue of who should supervise the agency was not resolved by the time the Guidelines for its activities expired at the end of September 1991, the agency and the entire privatization process has been outside the law since then.

TABLE 6.17

Number of transformation of economically active firms in Poland
(As of 1 October 1991)

State sector	
State firms in material production	8 419
Municipal enterprises	673
Corporations (joint-stock and limited)	1 251
Private sector	
Companies (joint stock and limited)	47 734
Joint ventures	3 512
Cooperatives	17 381
Foundation enterprises	175
Others	825
Transformed firms	
Shareholding companies	227
Joint stock companies	175
Limited liability companies	52
Effectively sold	38
Through public offerings	9
Through discretionary sales	18
Partly workers's buy-outs, sales and auctions	11
Liquidation	875
Through bankruptcy	502
Through law on privatization	373
Workers' buy-outs or leases	324
Incorporated in other companies	49

Source: National statistics.

criminality arising from industrialists colluding with the former *nomenklatura*, in particular enterprise management, must be guarded against. To prevent trustees from simply rubberstamping deals worked out behind their back, it is necessary to foster transparency and enjoin the agency to adhere to a fairly uniform policy, for example by organizing auctions for individual firms or for groups of enterprises. For this, effective parliamentary oversight is a prime requirement. But it would be useful to keep the broader political process as much as possible out of the daily operations of the agency or agencies entrusted with the mechanics of privatization. And these agencies should have sufficient staffing to deal adequately with the tasks at hand. They should be able to rely upon outside expert advice if and when desired. Delegation of authority should then be restricted as much as possible to the technical details.

Fourth, the revenues obtained from privatization invariably remain well below estimates made at the outset of the transition, regardless of how these values were derived. It is sometimes said that the simultaneous privatization programmes of about 70 countries at this stage cannot but exert a downward bias on values that the transition economies can realistically hope to attain. This may be the case in the short run. But viable projects in an economic, political, and social environment which is not hostile will elicit proper financing. And it is in this field that inauspicious features of the Eastern countries could usefully be singled out for action. Of course, downward pressure on value obtained through sales has also emanated from the adverse economic conjuncture within which privatization in the East has been unfolding. Moreover, this may well become a low-level equilibrium trap from which it may be very difficult to emerge.

Fifth, restitution and compensation claims gravely impede headway with privatization and clog the legal system, which in most countries is rather rudimentary and already overburdened. Unresolved restitution issues also tend to choke the political process. An early resolution to confine them to self-financed compensation transactions would be the better alternative. The same claim can be made with respect to the accrued, implicit, and vested property rights. And settlement of the land issue is fundamental to making solid progress with privatization and indeed in nursing along new capital formation.

Sixth, even with successful divestment, the new owners of privatized assets may engage in strategic behaviour, waiting with exercising their rights until the *sociopolitical situation* becomes less unstable and opaque. Such reactions may be economically warranted, given the potential benefits of waiting under uncertainty. This suggests that governments may want to stimulate private initiative by tackling also the cost and risk of capital formation. If funds can be earmarked to encourage the establishment or growth of new small and medium-sized firms, possibly from the divestment proceeds of state enterprises, this may be a useful inducement. But the fiscal burden of reviving the economy may soon become unsupportable. Hence, ways and means have to be found to blend every unit of public money with as much private capital as possible, including investment from abroad.

Seventh, distribution of most of the nation's wealth directly to the population at large is not a promising road to achieve the aims of privatization. Above all, by itself it leaves unsolved the question of how to ensure monitoring of enterprise management. In any case, free distribution does not obviate the need to come to terms with key obstacles to privatization. Thorough preparation is required to identify and reach the beneficiaries, to select the mode of distribution, and to elicit an active role from the beneficiaries in the governance of the privatized companies. Even valuation cannot be side-stepped altogether, if only to come to grips with the need for restructuring. Any attempt to give different portfolios of shares to different people raises serious questions about equity, since there is no way to ensure that one portfolio is worth as much as another.

Eighth, early commitments to one form of privatization as the preferred method do not appear helpful. Both in Czechoslovakia and Poland, where this was the case, especially the mass or large privatization campaigns have been inadequately prepared. A diverse, pragmatic strategy with as little ideological commitment or politicization as possible seems the best way of muddling through the complexities of privatization.

Ninth, inadequate *information on firms,* and even economic affairs more generally, is a major handicap impeding rapid success of policies aimed at encouraging individuals to take an interest as owner in "their" companies. This gets compounded by inadequate preparation of the auctions and the way in which the acquired property, particularly in small privatization, can be utilized. As a result, auction markets in the beginning tend to be chaotic at best, with prices stabilizing

TABLE 6.18

Legislative acts relevant to privatization [a]

	Restitution Passed by Parliament	Restitution Entered into force	Small privatization Passed by Parliament	Small privatization Entered into force	Large privatization Passed by parliament	Large privatization Entered into force	Agricultural land	Foreign investment law
Albania	..	..	Mar-91 [b]	..	Mar-91	..	..	Jul-90
Belarus	..	..	..	..	Oct-91	..	Dec-90	Nov-91
Bulgaria	Jan-92	..	Mar-91 [c]	..	..	..	Feb-91	May-91
Czechoslovakia	Oct-90, Feb-91	..	Oct-91	Jan-91	Feb-91	Apr-91	Mar-91, Jun-91	Mar-90
Estonia	Jun-91	Jun-91	Dec-90	Jan-91	Jun-91	Jun-91	Oct-91	Sep-91
Hungary [d]	Exceptionally 1991	1991	Sep-90	Sep-90	Oct-88 [d]	Jan-89	1991	Jan-89
Latvia	Jun-91	Aug-91	1991?	1991?	Pending		Jul-91	Nov-91
Lithuania	..	..	Mar-89	May-89	May-89	May-89	..	Dec-90
Poland	Feb-91	Mar-91	Feb-90, Nov-90	Mar-90, Dec-90	Jul-90	Jul-90	Feb-91	Jun-91
Romania	..	..	Jul-91	Jul-91	Aug-91	Aug-91	Nov-90	Mar-90, Apr-91
Russian Fed.	None	..	Jan-92 [f]	Jan-92 [f]	Dec-91	Jan-92 [e]	Jan-92 [f]	Jul-91
Ukraine	None [g]	..	Dec-89 [h]	Dec-89 [h]	Jan-92 [f]	Not a priority issue	Dec-89 [i]	Sep-91, Dec-91
Yugoslavia	..	..			Dec-89	Not a priority issue		
Memorandum item:								
Ex-GDR	Sep-90	Sep-90	Jun-90 [j]	Jul-90	Jun-90 [j]	Jul-90	Jun-90	..
Croatia	..	None	Apr-91 [k]	Apr-91	Apr-91 [k]	Apr-91	..	..
Slovenia	..	None	..	..	..	..	..	..

[a] There are several acts concerning large privatization, beginning with the Company Act of 1988, the Transformation Act of 1989, and the Act on the stock exchange of 1990.
[b] *Treuhandanstalt* passed by the GDR Parliament.
[c] Regulated by various laws such as on churches and cooperatives.
[d] Only in Serbia in March 1991.
[e] Regulated by a single act.
[f] Latest revision.
[g] Ministerial edict on auctions.
[h] Put into effect by Presidential decree on 29 December 1991, but Parliament will discuss it again in February 1992.
[i] Law on "The free enterprise".
[j] Law entitles "The concept of de-centralization and privatization of enterprises, land and the housing fund".
[k] Government decree.

only after some considerable lapse of time. Expectations during these periods are extremely volatile.

Tenth, efforts to restrict access to the assets under privatization to resident nationals (and possibly in later rounds to citizens, regardless of where they reside) are bound to founder, as proxies can always be found, albeit at a cost. A similar observation applies with respect to attempts to keep the patrimonium in domestic hands by interdicting new owners from quickly selling their shares. Even though an early admission of trading may inject volatility into the incipient capital markets, more harm to the stability of markets may come from an injunction against trading as many transactions will have to be made "on the sly".

Eleventh, because the process of mass privatization is only in its initial phases, *problems of control* have not yet openly come to the fore. But it might be just as well to be concerned early how the monitoring of management on behalf of the population at large will be undertaken. This issue arises also in other forms of divestment on the basis of shares, whether they go to financial intermediaries, to a core investor, or to mutual or investment funds. The experience in market economies underlines that the process of privatization is far more complex than a mere change in ownership. Rather, it involves a comprehensive social and economic transformation aimed at changing the way every firm is run and every business decision is made.

Finally, although the countries that are most advanced with privatization have paid some attention to organizing the rudiments of capital markets, *market monitoring and regulation* appears to have received rather short shrift so far. It is therefore worth noting that skimpy regulation of markets, including for newly-privatized firms, is an open invitation to trouble. At the least, there is the danger of unfair use of insider information (such as details regarding firms that will have their debts written off and others that will be supported by the government) and other shady deals. Charges of collusion of interests have been levied notably in the case of petty privatization. This of course endangers the transition process at large in that it generates scepticism about the benefits of the revolution and apathy in the population.

(ii) The agenda for the near term

Whereas progress with privatization has to date remained confined, the ambitions for the near term harboured by virtually all transition countries are considerable. Some are promising, if only because of decisions now in place. These include the creation of legal frameworks and institutions to enact various forms of privatization. Table 6.18 shows where the various countries stand with the legal infrastructure. In some countries which set up a complement of laws and institutions, rapid progress can be expected on the strength of policy measures introduced in 1991. It is to

TABLE 6.19

Tentative proportion of assets to be sold and auctioned off in the Russian Federation during 1992-1994
(Per cent)

	Share sale	Auctions
Light and food-processing	50	50
Construction, building materials, road transport	50	50
Retail trade, catering, household services	10	90
Wholesale trade	90	10
Other sectors	80	20

Source: Rossiyskaya gazeta, 15 January 1992, p.2.

TABLE 6.20

Normative revenues and asset shares to be privatized in the Russian Federation during 1992

	Revenue *(Billion roubles)*	Share *(Percentages)*
Light industry	10.6	70
Food-processing industry	23.8	60
Construction industry	13.2	70
Building materials industry	6.8	50
Agro-industrial enterprises	1.3	60
Road transport and servicing	5.5	70
Retail trade outlets	10.0	60
Wholesale trade firms	2.6	50
Catering	5.5	20
Household services	5.7	60
Incomplete construction projects	7.0	20
Total above	92.0	..

Source: Rossiyskaya gazeta, 10 January 1992, pp.3-4 and 15 January 1992, p.2.

be hoped that the others will move rapidly to complete their own institutions. Without a legal infrastructure, as the recent experience has proved, it is very difficult to make orderly progress.

In the near-term agenda, the aims recently reset by the *Treuhandanstalt* for the eastern *Länder* of Germany are very ambitious. It has decided to adjust its marketing strategy with a view to selling off by the end of 1992, if possible, all remaining enterprises under its control (presently some 6,000) or to close those that are beyond salvation (about one third).[691]

The outlook for rapid progress in 1992 and beyond is favourable for Czechoslovakia and Poland, whose voucher-type privatization programmes should give privatization a major impulse in the course of the year. In Poland, the new Government of Prime Minister Jan Olszewski has furthermore expressed its determination to accelerate the process by radically tackling the ownership issue.[692] It hopes to complete the so-called "reprivatization" even if firms have to be made available to domestic investors for a nominal price of 1 zloty. For that purpose, two new agencies were set up which will supervise the privatization process instead of the

---

[691] *Financial Times*, 8 January 1992, p.2 and 21 January 1992, p.2.

[692] See interviews with Minister of Ownership Transformation Tomasz Gruszecki, in *International Herald Tribune*, 7 January 1992, p.13 and *Financial Times*, 7 January 1992, p.2. Also his statement in *Rzeczpospolita*, 30 December 1991 is illuminating on the issue.

> **BOX 6.5**
>
> **The privatization programme of the Russian Federation**
>
> *Although initially privatization was not to be undertaken very rapidly, the shock therapy of the price liberalization introduced on 2 January 1992 (see chapter 4) has made action on the transformation of state-owned enterprises a very urgent task. Aside from "wild" privatization, which has accompanied the decline in central authority, very little by way of divestment or less final forms of placing state assets under the control of non-state agents was accomplished by late 1991. The "basic provisions" of a governmental programme of privatization in 1992 were published on 10 January 1992, but concrete laws and annexes to the basic provisions are yet to appear.* [1]
>
> *The "basic provisions" allocate existing economic organizations belonging to state and municipal authorities to four groups: facilities subject to compulsory privatization, facilities subject to privatization but on a voluntary basis, facilities subject to restrictions (meaning the transformation must first be approved by the Government or the relevant state or municipal authorities), and facilities whose privatization is prohibited.* **Compulsory privatization** *in principle extends to firms in wholesale and retail trade, public catering, and household services; construction firms and producers of building materials; state agricultural firms other than state farms and firms carrying out primary processing of agricultural output as well as firms servicing agricultural production and those producing technical inputs for its activities; firms in food and light industry; loss-making enterprises in various sectors of the economy; mothballed facilities and incomplete construction projects whose normative construction time has been exceeded; and catering enterprises.*
>
> *The privatization of firms in the obligatory group is intended to be carried out in two stages. The bulk should take place during the first three quarters of 1992. The privatization of the remainder (including road transport, independent vehicle repair, construction firms, building materials industry, and all other small enterprises (up to 200 workers) in food and light industry) will begin in the second half of 1992. The aim is to divest the state and municipal authorities of roughly one fifth to one quarter of their property in the course of 1992, and it is expected that the first beneficial effects will be felt beginning with the third quarter of the year.* [2]
>
> *All other economic activities are subject to various kinds of restrictions or prohibitions on privatization in 1992.* [3] *Land reform will have to await the introduction of special regulations, existing agricultural units being under orders to restructure themselves in the course of 1992. Most public utilities and state banks remain in state hands.*
>
> *The presumptive rights of workers in companies that will become corporatized will be recognized through the issue of "privileged" shares amounting to one quarter of the capital (up to 20 times the guaranteed minimum monthly earnings per worker). Further shares, called "ordinary" shares can be acquired by workers and pensioners through purchase at a 3 per cent discount. The money required to purchase shares in this way will be made available on an instalment plan yet to be worked out. All these shares can apparently be transferred without any restrictions at all.*
>
> *As to the mechanisms of privatization, the initiative can be taken by the workers in place, the administration of the enterprise, or other individuals. Apparently anyone can lodge an application for privatization of an enterprise with the local territorial property committee, which are to exist in every* **oblast'** *and even in many* **rayony**. *The committees have the obligation to respond to any such application within one month by setting up a privatization commission, which must draw up a plan for privatization within six months. The commission's tasks include valuation according to procedures issued by the State Property Committee and determination of the procedure for and form of sale (joint-stock company shares or open auctions). Sale will be the principal method of privatization, with direct sales and auctions taking the proportions shown in table 6.19.*
>
> *Attracting foreign capital is one of the objectives envisaged. Because of the rapid erosion of rouble prices and the precipitate decline of the rouble's exchange rate (now approaching 200 roubles per dollar) these past few months, the central bank has determined that foreign capital must be converted into roubles at a special exchange rate for capital transactions of between 8 and 10 roubles per dollar.*
>
> *One notable aim is to obtain budget revenues, which will be used for social protection of the population, the implementation of ecological remedies, and the development of the engineering infrastructure of towns and territories. Revenues are to be distributed to various local and state authorities for the above purposes according to a predetermined distribution modus.*
>
> *... continued*
>
> ---
>
> [1] "Osnovnye polozheniya programmy privatizatsii gosudarstvennykh i munitsipal'nykh predpriyatii v Rossiiskoi Federatsii na 1992 god", **Rossiiskaya gazeta**, 10 January 1992, pp.3-4; and "Tselevye pokazateli i zadaniya po privatizatsii", **Rossiiskaya gazeta**, 15 January 1992, p.2. The first annexes were published in **Ekonomika i zhizn'**, 1992:3, p.17.
>
> [2] Interview with A. Chubays, Chairman of the State Committee for the Management of State Property, as reported in BBC, **Summary of World Broadcasts**, SU/1268, p.C3/4, 3 January 1992.
>
> [3] This has already led one commentator to observe that the privatization programme gives too much power to bureaucrats (see M. Sergeev in **Izvestiya**, 13 January 1992).

Ministry (an Agency for the Development of Industry and an Agency for State-owned Agricultural Property). Actual privatization will be left to commercial firms and not state officials. And any revenue will be primarily appropriated for financing changes in industry and vo-

> **BOX 6.5 (continued)**
> **The privatization programme of the Russian Federation**
>
> *The privatization targets to be accomplished in 1992 have been laid down in great detail for each of the 20 republics of the Federation and each of the 57 administrative districts for ten economic sectors in an ukaz (No.341) of 29 December 1991.* [4] *Table 6.20 summarizes the privatization goals for 1992 by sector in terms of expected revenues and the proportions of assets due to be sold off. Abstracting from whether the revenue targets can realistically be met, it is evident that transferring such a large fraction of several sectors from public to private hands in an economy where rouble assets are being eroded at an alarming rate is an exceedingly ambitious agenda indeed.*
>
> [4] *Rossiiskaya gazeta*, 15 January 1992, p.2.

cational training, as part and parcel of a fully-fledged industrial policy yet to be formulated.[693]

Also Hungary has introduced measures, including financial incentives, that will accelerate privatization of assets, either through cross-ownership in the case of large firms or through petty privatization. Rather than expect revenues to accrue chiefly to finance domestic and external debt service, the Government recently decided to plough back proceeds into three funds designed to remove much of the political and business risk involved in take-overs.[694] Moreover, a number of firms will be removed from the privatization agency's remit in favour of having outside consulting firms come up with proposals for their privatization. The aim is to build upon the progress made in 1991 so that the original tasks set for privatization by the end of 1993 can be reached. These tasks called for changing the ownership structure in such a way that by late 1992 private owner-operator firms would account for 30 to 35 per cent, corporate owners and non-profit organizations for about 20 to 30 per cent, and the state for 35 to 50 per cent of the total.[695]

In the Baltic republics, notably Lithuania, the legal framework for all but land privatization is in place. But there are some remaining conflicts in the legal provisions that will have to be ironed out. In Estonia and Latvia, progress will be more limited by virtue of the fact that it has been declared policy to proceed slowly with divestment of large assets. But corporatization and commercialization of firms is expected to advance swiftly.

Elsewhere, particularly in the republics that constitute the Commonwealth of Independent States (CIS), an acceleration of privatization is certainly a policy intention. In the Russian Federation an ambitious programme has been drafted that, if it can be implemented, will transform the structure of ownership in a very radical manner during 1992-1994, with a substantial proportion (perhaps one quarter) to be accomplished already in 1992.[696] Box 6.5 summarizes the Russian policy agenda. Though there have been precedents for such far-reaching and rapid transformation "plans", none of the eastern transition economies has thus far succeeded in implementing an equally ambitious — or even a much more moderate — agenda for drastic change. If only for that reason, it would seem doubtful that the Russian Federation in its turn can succeed at the pace suggested.

Yet, whereas there may be some setbacks and delays, the negative experience with spontaneous privatization and the bandwagon effect that the experience of the east European countries exerts are such that, barring serious sociopolitical conflict or complete economic chaos, some of the policy intentions will undoubtedly be carried out. The more ambitious agendas will probably have to be revised, even those that envision a more modest effort than the Russian Federation. But if the CIS republics that have not yet moved ahead with privatization at all succeed in getting the process under way, that in itself would signal real progress after the past delays and failures.

APPENDIX

Legislation on privatization in the economies in transition[697]

Albania

Law on the Land from Article 16 of Law No.7491 on the Main Dispositions of the Constitution, 29 April 1991.

---

[693] Interview with Minister Gruszecki on 6 January 1992 as reported in BBC, *Summary of World Broadcasts*, EE/1272, p.B-10 of 8 January 1992. See also Barbara Blaszczyk, "Co dalej w prywatyzacja", *Rzeczpospolita*, 16 January 1992.

[694] See interview with Lajos Csepi, Managing Director of the privatization agency, in *Financial Times*, 14 January 1992, p.2.

[695] See *A nemzeti megojhodás programja – a köztársaság elsö három éve* (The programme of national revival – the first three years of the Republic), Budapest, 1990, p.38.

[696] See "Osnovnye polozheniya programmy privatizatsii gosudarstvennykh i munitsipal'nykh predpriyatiy v Rossiyskoy Federatsii na 1992 god" (Basic guidelines for the programme of privatization of state and municipal enterprises in the Russian Federation in 1992), *Rossiyskaya gazeta*, 10 January 1992, pp.3-4; and "Tselevye pokazateli i zadaniya po privatizatsii" (Target indicators and tasks for privatization), *Rossiyskaya gazeta*, 15 January 1992, p.2. The first addenda were published in *Ekonomika i zhizn'*, 1992:3, p.17.

[697] This listing covers only laws dealing directly with privatization, as opposed to those that are indirectly related, such as laws passed to establish and regulate joint stock companies, stock exchanges, and the trading of securities. Laws marked with an asterisk (*) are reproduced in English in the Annex to United Nations Economic Commission for Europe, *Guide on Legal Aspects of Privatization*, New York 1992.

Law No.255 on the criteria of distributing agricultural land, 2 August 1991.

Law No.7512 on sanctioning and protection of private property, free enterprise, independent private activities and privatization, 15 August 1991.

Decision No.307 on duties and rights of the National Agency of Privatization and the Preparatory Commission of the Privatization Process, 29 August 1991.

Instruction No.3 on organization of work and realization of the transition of state ownership to private ownership through auction, 30 August 1991.

Belarus

Law on privatization in the Belorussian Soviet Socialist Republic, June 1991.

Law on foreign investments, 14 November 1991.

Bulgaria

Government decree No.56 on economic activity, 13 January 1989 (amended on 28 February 1991).

Government decree No.16 on the establishment of the Privatization Agency, 8 February 1991.

Law of ownership and usage of agrarian lands, 22 February 1991 (amended on 10 September 1991).

Government decree No.42 on auctioning state owned and municipal assets, 14 March 1991.

Government decree No.54 on decentralization and demonopolization of state owned and municipal enterprises, 3 April 1991.

Law on foreign investments, 17 May 1991 (amended in January 1992).

Law on the transformation of state owned enterprises into single person commercial partnerships, July 1991.

Law on restitution of shops and similar business units, 11 December 1991.

Czech and Slovak Federal Republic

Law on transfers of state property to other legal or physical persons ("small" privatization), 25 October 1990.

Law on relieving the consequences of some property injuries ("small" restitution), 1 November 1990.

Law on the transfer of state property to other persons act ("big" privatization), 26 February 1991.(*)

Law on out-of-court rehabilitation ("large" restitution), 1 April 1991.

Law on agricultural land, May 1991.

Estonia

Law on peasant farming, 6 December 1989 (amended by the law on land reform on 17 October 1991).

Law on property, 13 June 1990.

Law on small privatization, 13 December 1990.

Law on the bases of property reform, 20 June 1991.

Law on foreign investment, 17 September 1991.

Hungary

Act XXIV of 1988 on foreign investment in Hungary, December 1988.

Act XIII of 1991 on the transformation of economic organizations and economic associations, 30 May 1989.

Act V of 1990 on individual entrepreneurship, 26 January 1990.

Act VII of 1990 on the State Property Agency, 26 January 1990 (*) (amended on 18 July 1990).

Act VIII of 1990 on management and utilization of state assets, 26 January 1990.

Resolution 20/190 of Parliament on the Provisional Property Policy Guidelines for 1990, 28 February 1990.

Act LXXIV of 1990 on the privatization (disposal, utilization) of assets of the state-owned companies engaged in retailing, catering and consumer services, 18 September 1990.

Act XXV of 1991 on partial compensation of unjust losses caused by the state pertaining to assets owned by citizens with a view to a definite settlement of property rights, 26 June 1991.

Act XXXII of 1991 on the settlement of property rights concerning real estate previously owned by the churches, 10 July 1991.

Act XXXIII of 1991 on transferring certain state-owned assets into municipal ownership, 12 July 1991.

Latvia

Law on denationalizing housing, 1991.

Law on the return of housing to legal owners, 1991.

Law on foreign investment, 5 November 1991.

Lithuania

Law on initial privatization of state property, 28 February 1991 (amended on 14 March 1991).

Law on restitution of property of pre-1940 owners, 18 June 1991.

Government decree on sale of agricultural land, September 1991.

Poland

Law on privatization of state owned enterprises, 13 July 1990 (amended on 9 November 1990).

Law on the creation of the Office of Minister of Ownership Transformation, 13 July 1990.(*)

Law on revising the law land management and real estate expropriation, 28 September 1990.

Romania

Decree-Law No.42/1990 on the future of agricultural cooperatives, auxiliary farms and agricultural mechanization stations, 30 January 1990.

Decree-Law No.54/1990 on free initiative and small private establishments, 5 February 1990.

Decree-Law No.96/1990 of foreign investment, 20 March 1990 (superseded by Law No.35/1991).

Law No.15/1990 on restructuring of state-owned economic units and the creation of the National Agency for Privatization, 7 August 1990 (superseded by law No.58/1991).

Government decision No.945/1990 on the requirement to transfer 30 per cent of equity to the National Agency for Privatization, 15 August 1990.

Government decision No.1228/1990 on concessioning, renting and location of business management methodology, 12 December 1990.

Law No.35 on foreign investment, 3 April 1991.

Law on the Privatization of Commercial Companies, 14 August 1991.(*)

Government decision No.140/1991 on renting some enterprises by direct auction.

Law No.18 on land, 20 February 1991.

Russian Federation

Law on property on the RSFSR's territory, 14 July 1990.

Law on peasant farms, 22 November 1990 (amended on 27 December 1990).

Law on the land reform, 23 November 1990 (amended on 27 December 1990).

Law on property in the RSFSR, 24 December 1990.

The RSFSR land **code**, 25 April 1991.

Law on privatization of state and municipal enterprises in the RSFSR, 3 July 1991.

Law on personal privatization accounts and deposits, 3 July 1991.

Law on privatization of the housing stock, 4 July 1991.

Government decree on the statute of the State Property Fund, 3 July 1991.

Law on foreign investments, 4 July 1991.

Presidential decree on liberalization of foreign economic activity, 15 November 1991.

Law on registration fee for individual entrepreneurs, 7 December 1991.

Law on personal property, 9 December 1991.

Presidential decree on urgent measures on implementation of land reform, 27 December 1991.

Presidential decree on speeding up privatization of the state and municipal enterprises, 29 December 1991.

Ukraine

Law on privatization of state enterprises, 29-30 January 1992.

Law on small state enterprises, 29-30 January 1992.

Law on land, 29-30 January 1992.

Yugoslavia (federal laws)

Law on enterprises, December 1989.

Law on social capital, December 1989 (amended in August 1990).

Croatia (republican laws)

Law on transformation of social enterprises, 23 April 1991.

Slovenia (republican laws)

No approved law yet.

USSR

Law on cooperatives, 26 May 1988 (amended on 16 October 1989 and 6 June 1990).

Basic legislation on leasing (*arenda*), 23 November 1989.

Basic legislation on land, 28 February 1990 (amended on 16 March 1991).

Law on property, 6 March 1990.

Law on enterprises, 4 June 1990.

Presidential decree on the first priority measures to implement land reform, 5 January 1991.

Law on the general principles of entrepreneurship, 2 April 1991.

Resolution of the USSR Supreme Soviet on the legal basis of land legislation in the USSR and in the Union Republics, 27 May 1991.

Law on basic principles of de-statization and privatization of enterprises, 1 July 1991.

Basic legislation on foreign investment in the USSR, 5 July 1991.

Law on the limitation of monopoly activity in the USSR, 10 July 1991.

Presidential decree confirming the regulations governing the USSR State Property Fund, 10 August 1991.

Memorandum item: ex-GDR

Decision on the creation of a trust agency (*Treuhandanstalt*) to administrate state-owned assets, 1 March 1990.

Decree on the transformation of state-owned combines *(Kombinate)* and enterprises into joint stock companies, 1 March 1990.

Law on the privatization and reorganization of state-owned assets (*Treuhandgesetz*), 17 June 1990.

Treaty on the establishment of German unity (*Einigungsvertrag*), 31 August 1990.

Law on the settlement of open property issues, 23 September 1990 (amended on 29 March 1991).

Law on removing obstacles to privatization of companies and on the promotion of investment, 22 March 1991.

Law on the breaking up of companies held by the trust agency (*Treuhandanstalt*), 5 April 1991.

Chapter 7

MIGRATION FROM EAST TO WEST: A FRAMEWORK FOR ANALYSIS

This chapter provides an initial assessment of the prospects for east-west labour migration in the light of the experience of post-war migration from southern Europe. Section 7.1 introduces the subject and describes the recent patterns of east-west migration while section 7.2 summarizes the main features of labour migration from southern Europe in the 1960s. The third section, 7.3, assesses the possible impacts of demographic and economic developments on the potential for east-west migration. The final section, 7.4, discusses the policy choices facing west European governments.

7.1 INTRODUCTION AND HISTORICAL BACKGROUND

(i) Introduction

The collapse of the "iron curtain" has dramatically increased the freedom of movement of the peoples of the ex-communist countries of central and east Europe. Opportunities for foreign travel which were previously kept under strict political control are now available to any citizen with the resources to pay for their trip.

West European countries find themselves placed in a potentially embarrassing situation by these changes. They welcome the increased respect for human rights — which they had been urging on the eastern countries for many years — but are now worried that substantial numbers of east Europeans will move to the western countries, so increasing social tensions and exacerbating existing problems of high unemployment. Recent attempts by thousands of Albanians to enter Italy by crossing the Adriatic were seen by many as one instance of a new phase of substantial east-west population movements.

However, the worries are not solely on the western side. Some eastern countries fear that the most educated members of their labour forces will move to foreign countries so that they will lose a substantial part of their ability to compete in international markets before they have even had a chance to establish themselves in the world trading system. Others are concerned that they too will become the unwilling recipients of migrants from elsewhere in the region.

This chapter makes an initial attempt to assess the likelihood of large migration flows from eastern Europe and the former Soviet Union to western Europe using a combination of economic reasoning and generalizations based on recent experience of international labour migration in western Europe since the 1960s.[698]

The structure of the chapter is as follows. First of all, this section outlines the nature and extent of recent east-west migration flows. Then the process of postwar labour migration is described in section 7.2 — concentrating on the movements of labour from southern Europe (Spain, Portugal, Italy, Greece, Turkey and Yugoslavia) to the west and north European countries from the late 1950s. This section discusses the reasons why labour migration appeared beneficial at the time to both sending and receiving countries and then looks at how the actual consequences of labour migration often diverged from the expected outcomes.

The present and projected future economic situation of the eastern countries is assessed in section 7.3, with particular stress being laid on the similarities and differences between eastern Europe now and southern Europe at the end of the 1950s. Taking into account projected labour market developments in western Europe, this comparison is used to draw some tentative conclusions on the likely nature of migration flows from eastern Europe and the former Soviet Union.

Finally, the chapter concludes with a look at the policy options which are available to governments. As 1960s style official migration programmes appear neither politically feasible in the present climate nor especially economically beneficial, the paper concludes that policy measures, if they are to be effective, will have to

---

[698] For brevity and to avoid confusion, the term *eastern Europe* is used in this chapter to denote Albania, Bulgaria, the Czech and Slovakia Federal Republic, Hungary, Poland, Romania and Yugoslavia. The term *former Soviet Union* is used to describe all of the republics of the former Soviet Union, including the Baltic states and Georgia. East-west migration should be understood to mean migration from eastern Europe and the former Soviet Union to western Europe.

be directed to eliminating the root causes of labour migration — the economic disparities between eastern and western Europe. The chapter's focus is on international labour migration and therefore only treats the issue of future flows of refugees and asylum seekers in passing. Possible large-scale population movements as the result of political instability, for example following the outbreak of civil war in Yugoslavia, are therefore outside the scope of this study. However, it should be borne in mind that uncontrolled ethnic conflicts could lead to far larger flows of people than those provoked by purely economic pressures.

(ii) East-west migration: the cold war and recent developments

Since the start of the cold war — and especially from the construction of the Berlin Wall — and until very recently, population movements between eastern and western Europe have been extremely limited. What flows did take place were mainly driven by political, rather than economic, factors.

For most of the post-war period, governments in the socialist bloc (with the exception of Yugoslavia from the mid-1960s) kept very tight control of individuals' movements to western Europe. This attitude is most strikingly exemplified by the East German authorities' construction of the Berlin Wall and their attempts to prevent any more of the population of the German Democratic Republic moving to the Federal Republic in 1961.[699] Migration to the west was therefore limited and consisted mainly of movements for family reunification, migration of pensioners (who were implicitly regarded as a burden on their country of origin and therefore allowed to migrate) and limited emigration of ethnic minorities (for example, Soviet Jews moving to Israel and ethnic Turks leaving Bulgaria for Turkey).

However, periodic political upheavals in the east led to streams of ideological migrants or refugees leaving their country either because they found political conditions there intolerable or because they themselves were deemed unacceptable and expelled by their own governments. Thus we find large increases in migration flows from Hungary in 1956 and from Czechoslovakia after 1968, when periods of relative openness and tolerance were brought to a sudden end. While economic motives may have played a role in the choice to leave the home country, it seems unlikely that these were significant in comparison with the political pressures.

Recent Polish experience appears to be an exception to this trend. Western experts estimate that there was a (mostly illegal) flow of about 100,000 people a year leaving the country in the 1980s, driven by a mixture of political motives and the deteriorating economic situation. In contrast, migration from the other countries of eastern Europe during the decade was very low.[700]

This situation has changed only recently with the collapse of communist governments throughout eastern Europe, and has since been transformed further with the disintegration of the former Soviet Union. In fact, population movements themselves played a large role in the fall of the regime in the ex-GDR, as GDR citizens streamed through Hungary, Czechoslovakia and Poland to take advantage of their right to west German citizenship.

As a result of these political changes, the right to a passport and the opportunity to travel abroad are now available to all those who can afford it. These changes have altered the "rules of the game" of east-west migration so completely that past experience of population movements from the countries of eastern Europe may well be a poor guide to future trends.

Unfortunately, official migration statistics, giving only a limited picture of actual population flows, are usually not comparable between different countries and suffer from long delays in their publication. This means that no reasonably comprehensive information is yet available on migration flows in 1991 and very little is available for flows in 1990.[701] There is thus little reliable information on the nature of international migration flows since the revolutionary changes of 1989.

Figures on long-term migration for several European countries, which have been collated by the ECE for the years up to 1989 (see ECE (1991)), suggest that the vast majority of recorded east-west movements were then due to movements of people to Germany. Thus, if the differences between countries in the coverage of their statistics on migration are neglected, the ECE figures suggest that some 490,000 people moved to Germany from eastern Europe and the former Soviet Union in 1989. In contrast, less than 30,000 long-term migrants from eastern Europe and the former Soviet Union were recorded as entering Denmark, France, Iceland, the Netherlands, Sweden, Switzerland and the United Kingdom together.

In turn, the German figures suggest that a large proportion of the recorded immigration into Germany from eastern Europe is accounted for by movements of ethnic Germans (*Aussiedler*) taking advantage of their constitutional right to settle in Germany. Total immigration of *Aussiedler* increased from under 80,000 in 1987 to nearly 400,000 in 1990 but then fell back to some 220,000 in 1991. In the five years between 1987 and 1991 a total of almost 1.3 million *Aussiedler* moved back to Germany. Ethnic Germans returning from Poland accounted for most of this type of immigration in 1988 and 1989 but flows from Poland have since fallen and are now much lower than the flows from the former Soviet Union.

---

[699] Between 1950 and 1961, the GDR lost over 2.5 million people (the population of the GDR in 1960 was some 17 million) through migration to the Federal Republic. This flood of emigration was slowed to a trickle by the construction of the Berlin wall. See "Aussiedler und Übersiedler: Zahlmässige Entwicklung und Struktur", *Wirtschaft und Statistik*, No.9, 1991, pp.581-589.

[700] See Chesnais (1991a), Okolski (1991) and Ghosh (1991) for more detailed discussions of recent trends in east-west migration. The Yugoslav situation is described in section 7.3 as it was already a country of labour migration in the 1960s.

[701] ECE figures (ECE (1991)) currently run to 1989, though statistics for 1990 should be available in May 1992; the most recent issue of SOPEMI (the OECD continuous reporting system on migration) also only contains data for 1989.

TABLE 7.1

Net emigration from eastern Europe, 1987-1989, and the former Soviet Union to western Germany, 1987-1991
(In thousands)

	Poland	Romania	Yugoslavia	Other eastern Europe	Total eastern Europe	Former USSR	Total
Panel A: Official German figures on long-term migration							
1987	86.7	17.1	9.8	7.6	121.2	14.8	136.0
1988	212.4	16.8	30.0	10.7	269.9	48.9	318.8
1989	309.2	25.9	26.9	15.0	376.9	110.5	487.5
Panel B: Official German figures on Aussiedler returning to Germany							
1987	48.4	14.0	0.2	1.5	64.0	14.5	78.5
1988	140.2	12.9	0.2	1.8	155.1	47.6	202.7
1989	250.3	23.4	1.5	3.7	278.9	98.1	377.1
1990	113.2	107.2	0.5	2.4	223.3	147.5	397.1
1991	40.1	32.2	..	2.3	74.7	147.3	222.0

Source: ECE Statistics on long-term migration (ECE (1991)); Statistisches Bundesamt, *Statistisches Jahrbuch Deutschlands*, Stuttgart (1991), p.94; Bundesausgleichsamt; *Wall Street Journal*, 2 January 1992.

Note: Figures for 1990 and 1991 cover the whole of the unified Germany (including the former GDR); figures for earlier years only include those returning to the western *Länder*. The figures for 1990 do not sum to the overall total in panel (b) as areas of origin appear only to be recorded for those returning to the western *Länder*.

Similar increases in ethnically based emigration can be seen in the movements of Soviet Jews to Israel.[702] The number of Soviet citizens given permission to emigrate to Israel increased dramatically from a level of about 140 a year in the mid-1980s to about 8,000 in 1987, 74,000 in 1989 and 197,000 in 1990. However, worries about the employment situation in Israel now appear to be slowing the flow of Jewish migrants from the former Soviet Union.[703]

While these flows of ethnic minorities are still determined to a considerable extent by economic conditions in both sending and receiving countries, the resulting shifts of population are likely to be relatively permanent. They will also have the secondary effect of strengthening existing or of establishing new east European communities abroad (particularly in Germany) and future short-term labour migration may well be directed towards these communities, as moving to an existing immigrant community is far easier than moving to completely unknown territory.

Another indicator often used to measure population movements is the number of applicants for political asylum. Figures for the number of registered asylum seekers in Germany are shown in table 7.2.[704] Despite the introduction of more liberal political systems in eastern Europe, the flow of those from the region seeking political asylum in Germany increased in 1990 and almost doubled in 1991. However, the regional pattern has changed significantly since 1988. The number of asylum seekers from countries where pluralist political systems were set up quickly and seem relatively secure has fallen sharply. Much of the increase in the number of asylum seekers in 1990 was due to a large increase in the flow from Romania and in 1991 there was a large jump in asylum seekers from Yugoslavia following the outbreak of the civil war. Other sources of information on applications for asylum show the same trends. Thus, applications for political asylum in Austria from Romanians increased sharply between 1988 and 1990 but those from Poles and from nationals of the other countries of eastern Europe fell.[705] All west European countries have seen a sharp increase in political asylum seekers from Yugoslavia in 1991.[706]

Recent discussion of the general increase in applications for political asylum in western Europe has often stressed the increasing use of asylum applications as a means of evading western governments' strict controls on labour migration.[707] The number of asylum applications then becomes a measure, albeit imperfect, of the pressures for labour migration and perhaps of illegal immigration as well. This interpretation of recent increases in requests for asylum seems more relevant to questions of south-north migration than to movements from eastern Europe. In particular, the increases in the number of asylum seekers from Yugoslavia and, perhaps to a lesser extent, Romania seem to have been mainly caused by political rather than economic factors. Recent trends in the number of asylum seekers from eastern Europe do not therefore seem to be a good measure of the pressures for east-west labour migration.

---

[702] See Chesnais (1991b) for a more detailed discussion of recent and likely future ethnically-based migration from the former Soviet Union.

[703] For example, see *Financial Times*, 28-29 December 1991.

[704] Germany accounts for a large proportion of the total number of asylum seekers in Europe. According to the latest issue of SOPEMI, in 1989 there were twice as many asylum seekers (from all countries) in Germany (over 120,000) as there were in France; all the other countries had much lower numbers of requests for asylum. The total number of asylum seekers for the 13 European countries included in the report came to 318,000 in 1989.

[705] See *Statistisches Handbuch für die Republik Österreich*, Österreiches Statistischen Zentralamt, Wien (1991), p.52.

[706] Direct communication to ECE secretariat from the secretariat of the Inter-Governmental Consultations on Asylum, Migration and Refugee Policies in Europe, North America and Australia.

[707] See for example Tapinos (1991), p.37.

TABLE 7.2

Asylum seekers from eastern Europe in Germany, 1987-1991
(In thousands)

	Poland	Romania	Yugoslavia	Other eastern Europe	Former USSR	Total
1987	15.2	2.0	4.7	-	3.3	25.2
1988	29.0	2.6	20.8	-	4.1	56.5
1989	26.1	3.1	19.4	4.4	0.3	53.4
1990	9.2	35.3	22.1	28.6	2.3	79.5
1991	..	40.5	74.9	21.8	5.7	142.9

Sources: Statistisches Jahrbuch Deutschlands (1991), p.73; Neue Zürcher Zeitung, 6 January 1992.

Note: Figures for 1990 and 1991 cover the whole of the unified Germany (including the former GDR); figures for earlier years only include those returning to the western Länder.

With little information which reflects the completely new international political and economic environment currently available, the only feasible approach to assessing future trends in east-west labour migration would seem to be to argue by analogy with (what appears to be) similar situations from the past, take account of any a priori theoretical insights (which one hopes are relevant and will still be valid in the new situation) and view any conclusions with a great deal of caution. In this spirit, the next section looks at the general experience of labour migration in western Europe since the 1960s to see if this holds any lessons for the eastern countries now.

Four of the south European countries of emigration in the 1960s are now members of the EC and so are almost free from controls on labour migration.[708] They thus offer concrete evidence on the relationship between trade and migration, which may be applicable in the longer term to the countries of eastern Europe. On the other hand, the Yugoslav experience of a sharp increase in emigration after the adoption of more market-based and decentralized economic policies may prove to be the more relevant parallel in the short term, particularly if the transition process runs into problems.

---

[708] There is a seven-year transition period after joining the EC during which restrictions on the freedom of movement of labour are gradually removed. The movement of labour from Spain and Portugal (who joined in 1986) is thus not yet free of all restrictions.

7.2 EUROPEAN EXPERIENCE OF INTERNATIONAL LABOUR MIGRATION IN THE 1960s

(i) The extent and nature of labour migration from southern Europe in the 1960s

Labour migration in western Europe between the mid-1950s and 1973/74 (when labour migration was effectively halted by the receiving countries) was dominated by flows from the relatively less developed countries of southern Europe (Italy, Spain, Portugal, Greece and, also Yugoslavia and Turkey) to the rapidly growing northern countries (mainly Germany and Switzerland but also France, Belgium and the Netherlands).[709]

Table 7.3 shows the population change due to net migration (or proxy measures of migration flows) for each of the six countries. The flow information for Greece, Italy, Spain and Portugal covers all migrants (not solely labour migration) to and from all countries. Figures for net migration flows are not available for Turkey and Yugoslavia and therefore proxy measures have had to be used. For Yugoslavia, these figures are OECD estimates (up to 1966) and then figures supplied by the Yugoslav Federal Bureau of Employment. These figures are therefore likely to exclude those who found work abroad without using the official labour offices[710] but they also include Yugoslavs working outside western Europe, for example in North Africa and the Middle East. For the case of Turkey, German figures on the number of Turks registered as employed for social insurance purposes have been used. Again, these figures are likely to be an underestimate as they exclude those working in Germany who were not registered for social insurance and all those working in other countries. However, the statistics presented should give a fairly accurate picture of broad trends over time even if they underestimate flows at a given moment.

Table 7.3 should therefore be viewed as showing how migration flows evolved over time, with net flows from the initial wave of sending countries (Italy and Spain) falling by the end of the 1960s at the same time as flows from Portugal, Turkey and Yugoslavia were increasing rapidly. Since 1973, net emigration flows have been small and there has been a general trend towards the gradual reversal of the movements seen in the 1960s. Greece and Italy, followed by Spain, Portugal and Yugoslavia, have all seen their populations increase as a result of net migration between the mid-1970s and the end of the 1980s. Only Turkey appears to be an exception to this trend, with a small overall increase in the number of Turkish workers in Germany since 1973.

Table 7.4 shows two snapshots of the stock of migrant workers in the main receiving countries in 1974 and 1989. For all the sending countries except Turkey, the number of migrant workers has fallen and, with the exception of Portugal, these falls have been relatively large. The tables also show that Portugal and Yugoslavia were exceptional in the number of their nationals moving abroad to work — the equivalent of one sixth of the Portuguese domestic labour force and nearly a tenth of the Yugoslav labour force were working abroad in 1974.

The institutional arrangements which governed these flows varied between the countries. As Italy was one of the original members of the EC, Italians had, in theory at least, more opportunities to work in other Community countries than nationals from non-member states. From 1968, when the clauses of the Treaty of Rome on free movement of labour within the Community came into full effect (after a transitional period of liberalization beginning in 1961), Italians had the right to work anywhere in the Community. Indeed, the clauses in the Treaty of Rome relating to the free movement of labour were a major factor behind Italian support for the setting up of the original Common Market. Italy expected to gain from exporting its labour to the other countries of the Community while the northern countries expected to benefit from increasing their exports of manufactured goods. In practice, most of the economic benefits from the Common Market for both Italy and other member countries seem to have arisen from gains from the movement of goods rather than people, and net emigration from Italy fell off rapidly in the 1960s.[711]

The other countries of emigration were not members of the EC and thus their workers did not enjoy preferential rights of freedom of movement and employment in the northern economies which were members of the EC. However, in practice this institutional difference was less of a constraint than might have been expected and flows from the non-EC sending countries in the 1960s tended to be proportionately larger than those from Italy.

Overall labour flows were agreed by the sending and receiving governments in a series of labour recruitment agreements.[712] Workers were only allowed to stay in the

---

[709] See Kindleberger (1967), Böhning (1984) and Straubhaar (1988) for more detailed discussions of the whole process of post-war European migration and OECD (1979), OECD (1985) for a discussion of the reasons for, and the effects of, the abrupt halt in migration.

[710] OECD estimates have been used for the years up to 1966 as for these years the official Yugoslav figures were considerably lower than the number of Yugoslavs working in Germany alone.

[711] See section 7.4. Straubhaar (1991) discusses recent studies on this question.

[712] For example, Germany signed agreements with Spain and Greece in 1960, with Turkey in 1961, Portugal in 1964 and Yugoslavia in 1968 (Werner (1986)).

TABLE 7.3

Annual population change due to net migration from southern Europe, 1960-1989
(Average annual flows, in thousands)

	Greece	Italy	Portugal	Spain	Turkey [a]	Yugoslavia [b]
1960-1963	-43	-114	-57 [c]	-82	-8	-17
1964-1967	-16	-140	-112	-66	-27	-56
1968-1972	-42	-44	-116	-24	-72	-145
1973-1976	13	-3	102 [d]	-2	-8	38
1977-1980	55	4	-42	20	-6	25
1981-1984	8	79	26	20	23	-3
1985-1989	17	68	14	-14 [d]	-12	1 [e]

Source: OECD, *Labour Force Statistics* unless otherwise specified.

Note: For Italy, Portugal and Spain, the figures incorporate the statistical adjustment required to balance the figures for migration and overall population change with those for births and deaths.

[a] Proxy measure. The figures shown are the changes in the number of Turkish workers registered for social insurance in the Federal Republic of Germany, taken from various issues of *Amtliche Nachrichten der Bundesanstalt für Arbeit*.
[b] Proxy measure. The figures shown are OECD estimates (to 1966) and then official Yugoslav figures of changes in the number of Yugoslavs working abroad taken from various issues of OECD, *Economic Survey of Yugoslavia*.
[c] First available figure is for 1962.
[d] This increase was mainly caused by the return of Portugese colonists following the independence of Angola and Mozambique.
[e] Last observation in 1988.

receiving country for a limited period of time and were not allowed to be joined by other members of their families. Moreover, the level of the agreed flow varied with the economic situation in the receiving country, so that flows of migrants were reduced administratively during periods of recession (the fall in the number of migrant workers admitted to Germany during the 1967-1968 recession is the most striking example of this. Labour migration returned to its previous levels after the end of the recession).

How restrictive these agreements were in practice is difficult to assess: as far as the countries of emigration were concerned, and especially for Turkey and Yugoslavia, it appears that substantial numbers of workers were recruited outside the framework of the agreements. Moreover, attempts by governments in the sending countries to determine the skill composition of flows of workers (sending governments generally wished to send unskilled workers abroad so that the national investment in skilled workers would not be used abroad) seem to have been generally ineffective.[713] Indeed in the Yugoslav case, the government appears to have been taken by surprise by the wave of emigration, whose immediate cause seems to have been the removal of restrictions on travel to western countries, and the government found it difficult to regain control of the process.

The economic slow-down provoked by the first oil shock led to rising unemployment and political pressure on governments in the receiving countries to keep jobs for nationals. In addition, labour migration was posing increasing social problems. Receiving country governments therefore unilaterally blocked further flows of labour migrants during 1973 and 1974. Although existing migrants were not usually sent home, they were sometimes given financial and other inducements to return home. For the most part, these incentives for return migration proved to be ineffective. After 1974, labour migration into Germany and the other receiving countries effectively ceased, though there was a continuing flow of immigration for the purposes of family unification. This latter immigration flow can be taken as indicating tacit acceptance by the governments of the former receiving countries that many of the remaining stock of migrant workers were not going to return to their home countries in the short term and that they therefore needed to be more closely integrated into the host societies.

(ii) The expected benefits and unexpected disadvantages of labour migration in the 1960s

The southern countries shared two general features in common during the 1960s which tended to make emigration attractive. Firstly, all the countries had large agricultural sectors which were becoming steadily less labour-intensive and thus freeing substantial amounts of unskilled labour (see table 7.5). This flow of labour into the non-agricultural labour market was expected to lead to higher unemployment, especially in countries where the labour force was also growing rapidly. Secondly, all the countries required increased inflows of foreign exchange to finance their industrial development. Migration appeared to provide a solution to both these problems.

Yugoslavia and Turkey had additional problems which also tended to encourage emigration. In Yugoslavia, economic reforms designed to decentralize economic decision-making and improve productivity were leading to high youth unemployment as existing, often worker-controlled, enterprises reduced their recruitment of new workers and did not replace those who left. Employment creation elsewhere in the economy did not occur quickly enough to reduce this unemployment and this labour market slack increased the incentives for emigration. In Turkey, particularly rapid population growth had led to large annual increases in the labour force which were proving difficult to absorb on the domestic labour market.

Table 7.6 shows the actual growth of population and the labour force between 1960 and 1974 for each

---

[713] See contemporary issues of the OECD *Economic Surveys* of the two countries, for example, for discussion of this.

TABLE 7.4

Stocks of southern European workers in other European countries in 1974 and 1989
(In thousands)

Emigration countries	Immigration countries					Total migrant workers as per cent of domestic labour force
	Germany	France	Switzerland	Other countries	Total migrant workers	
1974						
Greece	223	5	5	16	249	7.6
Italy	405	230	306	96	1037	5.1
Portugal	81	475	3	28	587	15.6
Spain	160	265	75	74	574	4.4
Turkey	585	25	14	74	698	4.5
Yugoslavia	495	50	23	202 [a]	770	9.5 [b]
1989						
Greece	116.4	..	..	13.1	129.5	3.3
Italy	206.6	103.8	232.7	106.0	649.1	2.7
Portugal	42.5	413.3	45.3	27.5	528.6	11.5
Spain	67.3	101.5	74.1	46.4	289.3	2.0
Turkey	651.6	65.0	30.8	120.2	867.6	4.6
Yugoslavia	329.3	30.7	112.2	123.8 [c]	596.0	5.8

Sources: Figures for number of foreign workers: 1974 figures taken directly from OECD (1979) — original source SOPEMI; 1989 figures taken from SOPEMI (1990); domestic labour force figures taken from OECD, *Labour Force Statistics*, and for Yugoslavia, from various issues of OECD, *Economic Survey of Yugoslavia*.

Note: "Other countries" comprises Belgium (latest available figures 1987), Netherlands, Luxembourg (latest available figures 1984), Austria, Sweden and the UK (1974 only).

[a] Of which 166,000 in Austria.
[b] If official Yugoslav figures for numbers of workers temporarily working abroad are used instead of SOPEMI estimates, this figures rises to 12.7 per cent.
[c] Of which 90,800 in Austria.

of the six emigration countries, as well as crude estimates of these growth rates in the absence of migration. Assessing the counterfactual situation of what the growth in the labour force would have been had there been no labour migration is difficult. Population figures, assuming no migration, are estimated by adding back net population migration figures, when these are available. The labour force and population of working age figures in the table are estimated on the assumption that the stock of migrant workers abroad in 1960 was zero and that the SOPEMI figures used in table 7.4 are an accurate representation of the stock of migrant workers in 1974.[714] This latter figure is simply added to the 1974 labour force figures to obtain an imputed figure for the labour force assuming no migration.

The labour force growth rates thus obtained will tend to be an overestimate for two reasons: firstly, there will have been some migrant workers (particularly from Italy) already abroad in 1960 so that the 1974 stock is greater than net emigration between 1960 and 1974; secondly, some of the domestic labour force growth will have been induced by improved conditions on the domestic labour market resulting from the process of labour migration ("encouraged workers"). On the other hand, any unrecorded labour migration would lead to underestimation of the imputed growth rates. The estimates for growth in the population of working age are even less reliable as they also assume that there was no net emigration of non-working individuals of working age.

Even with these crude estimates, it is clear that Turkey was exceptional in the rate of its population growth, with all the other countries showing rates of population increase which were near or below the overall average rate for the European OECD countries. Even after allowing for the effects of migration, Greece and Italy appear to have had slower than average labour force growth and only in Turkey, Portugal and, to a lesser extent, Spain did labour force growth appear to be particularly rapid.

Although the above estimates are likely to give an overestimate of the effects of migration, net migration in the 1960s and early 1970s does appear to have substantially reduced domestic population and labour force growth, especially for Portugal and Yugoslavia. Whether this had more than a short-term effect on unemployment is not clear; imperfections in the labour market may mean that small increases in the labour force result in higher unemployment in the short term but, in general, one would expect that the long-run rate of unemployment in a well functioning economy is not effected by an overall reduction in the labour force.[715]

The flow of remittances from migrants back to their home countries provided a valuable source of foreign exchange which weakened the balance-of-payments constraint on economic growth. Many observers have concluded that this was the most significant benefit of international migration for the sending countries but that the unpredictability of the flow of remittances

---

[714] For Yugoslavia the national estimates of the number of Yugoslavs temporarily working abroad are used. As an additional complication, contemporary Yugoslav statistics included Yugoslavs temporarily working abroad. Therefore, the figures for domestic labour force growth in the presence of migration have had to be derived by subtracting the numbers working abroad.

[715] This is less likely to be true in a less developed economy, such as Turkey, which is experiencing rapid population growth and where the non-agricultural sector is relatively small.

TABLE 7.5

Structure of civilian employment in southern Europe in 1960 and 1970
(Percentage share of total civilian employment)

Country	Year	Agriculture Self-employed	Agriculture Total	Industry	Services
Greece	1960	52.4	57.1	19.1	23.8
	1970	38.8	40.8	25.0	34.2
Italy	1960	24.0	32.6	33.9	33.5
	1970	13.7	20.2	39.5	40.3
Portugal	1960	17.2	43.9	31.3	24.8
	1970	14.7	30.0	32.9	37.1
Spain	1960	23.2	38.7	30.3	31.0
	1970	21.4	27.1	35.5	37.4
Turkey	1960	70.6	75.9	10.7	13.4
	1970	63.6	67.6	14.5	17.9
Yugoslavia	1961	53.5	58.3	22.5	19.1
	1971	45.1	48.5	29.4	22.0
OECD Europe	1960	..	25.9	37.5	36.6
	1970	..	18.1	39.0	42.9

Source: OECD, *Labour Force Statistics*; ILO, *Yearbook of Labour Statistics* (special issue on population censuses).

Note: The division between self-employed (including unpaid family workers) in 1960 is derived on the basis of the figures in the nearest census (1960 for Italy and Greece; 1961 for Spain and Portugal). These proportions are then applied to the OECD figure for total civilian employment in agriculture.

---

made it an unreliable means of financing long-term development.[716]

The receiving countries saw international migration as a means of easing the pressure on their own overheated labour markets. Rapid economic growth was demanding increasing supplies of labour. As the reserves of labour embodied in an inefficient agricultural sector began to dry up, domestic workers, confident of secure employment, became increasingly choosy about which jobs they would take on and filling low status and repetitive jobs in industry became more and more difficult.

In principle, adjustments to this type of imbalance on the labour market could take place purely internally. For this to happen, the wage structure would have to alter so that low status jobs received relatively higher pay and wages would have to increase relative to profits, so that overall labour demand was brought into line with labour supply. While valid in theory, and perhaps in practice over the long term, such adjustments in most existing labour markets only take place very slowly. In particular, a radical change in the structure of relative wages would disrupt existing social structures and erode the social positions of those in higher paid occupations. In addition, some industries in the northern countries which were already experiencing a secular decline in their competitive position (for example, textiles) would find their existence threatened if wage levels increased further.

In these circumstances, it was not surprising that some sectors of industry pressed for, and some governments chose, the option of allowing the increased use of migrant workers. These workers were not expected to stay in the receiving country for long periods of time, so that problems of social integration in the host country were thought to be minor, and they would provide a welcome boost to the host country's labour supply. As migrant workers filled vacancies in low status jobs which domestic workers were becoming reluctant to take, the two groups of workers were, initially at least, not seen to be in competition with each other. In most cases, domestic labour was therefore not opposed to the use of migrant workers.

Moreover, the higher savings propensities of unmarried migrant workers and their low use of collectively provided social infrastructure, such as schools and hospitals, meant that the immigration-induced increase in the demand for goods would be lower than the increase in supply which they represented. In the short term at least, this helped to reduce inflationary pressures as well as to improve the host country's public finances.

Further labour market benefits were expected for the receiving countries as a result of accepting migrant workers. As migrants' period of stay was expected to be short (and this was often a legal requirement), the process of continual immigration and re-emigration back to the home country would lead to an increase in labour turnover in the host country. When combined with the willingness of migrant labour to take low status jobs, the introduction of migrant labour was expected to increase the flexibility of the host country's labour market and thus provide another supply-side boost to the host country's economy.

While the economic consequences of the oil shock were the immediate cause of the effective cessation of

---

[716] In particular, the abrupt slow-down in the growth of remittances after 1974 led to considerable balance-of-payments problems for several countries. See for example OECD (1979).

TABLE 7.6

Population and labour force growth between 1960 and 1974 in southern Europe: actual figures and estimates assuming no labour migration
(Average annual percentage growth rates)

	Population [a] Actual	Population [a] Excluding migration	Population (15-64) [b] Actual	Population (15-64) [b] Excluding migration	Labour force [c] Actual	Labour force [c] Excluding migration
Greece	0.5	0.9	0.3	0.6	-0.7	-0.2
Italy	0.7	0.8	0.6	0.8	-0.3	0.0
Portugal	0.1	1.2	0.0	0.7	0.8	1.9
Spain	1.0	1.2	0.8	1.0	0.8	1.1
Turkey	2.5	..	2.4	2.6	1.3	1.6
Yugoslavia [c]	..	1.0	0.8	1.4	-0.2	0.7
OECD Europe	0.9	..	0.7	..	0.5	..

Sources: For all countries except Yugoslavia, domestic figures are taken from OECD, *Labour Force Statistics*, information on number of migrant workers in 1974 as in table 7.5; for Yugoslavia: ILO, *Yearbook of Labour Statistics* (special issue on population censuses) for 1961 figures, UN, *Yearbook of Demographic Statistics 1976* for 1974 population figures and OECD, *Economic Survey of Yugoslavia 1984* for figures on the 1974 labour force and number of workers temporarily abroad.

Notes: The table presents two sets of figures: the domestic population or labour force growth that actually took place ("actual" columns) and an estimate of population and labour force growth if no migration had taken place ("excluding migration" columns).

[a] The figures for population growth assuming no migration add the figures for population change from net migration in OECD, *Labour Force Statistics* to the actual population change. For Italy, Portugal and Spain these figures include the statistical adjustment required to balance the actual, natural and migration induced changes in population.
[b] For all countries except Yugoslavia, the estimates for growth in the population of working age and the civilian labour force excluding migration use the SOPEMI figures from table 7.5 on the stock of migrant workers in 1974. Under the assumption that this stock was zero in 1960, the number of migrant workers in 1974 have been added to the actual figures to arrive at the "no migration" estimates.
[c] Yugoslav figures refer to the period between 1961 and 1974. As Yugoslav population and labour force statistics during this period included those temporarily working abroad, official estimates of the number of Yugoslavs temporarily employed abroad have been deducted from the original population and labour force statistics to arrive at the estimate of actual population growth.

labour migration from 1973 onwards, unexpected problems with labour migration also played a large role in the decision of the receiving countries to bring the process to a halt.[717] Initially, the process of labour migration followed its expected course as outlined in the paragraphs above. However, as time progressed, migrants' periods of stay in the receiving country became longer and longer. Migrants moved from regarding their stay abroad as being temporary to seeing it as something longer term (though not usually permanent).

As stays became longer, migrants became more integrated in the receiving countries' labour markets and the range of occupations filled by migrant workers steadily increased. From being complementary to less-skilled indigenous labour (taking jobs which nationals were not prepared to fill in normal times and thus allowing nationals to take higher paid jobs), migrants moved to a situation where the two groups were increasingly competing for the same type of jobs (thus acting as a depressing influence on nationals' wages).

Longer staying migrants tended to save less and their consumption behaviour moved more towards that of natives. For married migrants, longer periods of work abroad increased the incentive for bringing the rest of the family out to the foreign country. Family unification was increasing even before 1973 and became almost the sole form of immigration after 1973, undermining many of the advantages which the receiving countries obtained from migration. Once wives and children were installed in the receiving country, migrants became more intensive users of education and health services (putting more pressure on host country public finances) and their housing requirements increased, which often led to tension with local communities. In addition, once reunited with their families, migrant workers' labour market mobility and flexibility tended to fall.

In short, as migrants' stays abroad became longer, the economic advantages of continued labour migration (which depended on the differences between migrants and indigenous workers in their labour market and consumption behaviour) tended to fall and social tensions (often provoked by the presence of "alien cultures" in otherwise largely homogenous societies) tended to increase. These considerations all played a role in the decision of receiving countries to halt labour immigration in 1973-1974 and have dominated European discussion of migration issues ever since.

For the sending countries too, additional problems with labour migration and the integration of returning migrants also caused questions to be raised about the benefits of the process. Returning migrants' acquired skills tended not to be well suited to the needs of the local economy and they often found it difficult to reintegrate into the domestic labour market. Savings accumulated during stays abroad were often invested in small private businesses with poor prospects for growth, in property or in imported consumption goods and were thus unavailable for investment in the industrial sector.

While section 7.4 studies the likely similarities and differences between southern Europe in the 1960s and eastern Europe in the near future as far as the various factors (labour market pressures, income differentials, etc.) which tend to encourage emigration are concerned, the above general analysis of the often unexpected results of labour migration in the 1960s and early 1970s also seems to contain some lessons for the present sit-

---

[717] It should be emphasized that the decision to stop labour migration was taken unilaterally by governments in the receiving countries. This illustrates the asymmetric nature of migration policies: citizens have the right to leave their own country (though this has only recently become true for the countries of eastern Europe), independent of the wishes of their government, but they may only enter another country legally with the agreement of the receiving country's authorities.

uation, especially in explaining the generally negative attitudes of western governments to future labour migration from eastern Europe.

Firstly, with hindsight, temporary labour migration does not appear to have been a durable solution to the problems of overheating in particular sectors of the labour market. Indeed, access to short-term migrant labour may well have delayed necessary structural change in declining industries and made the eventual adjustments more difficult. In the light of this experience, possible future labour shortages in western Europe are unlikely to be met through inflows of foreign labour.

Secondly, labour migration, once under way, proved to be difficult to control. Governments in sending countries had very little effective control over the magnitude or nature of migration flows. Governments in receiving countries, although they could limit the numbers of new migrants legally entering the country, found they had far less effective control (once the constraints imposed by liberal political systems are taken into account) over migrant workers already inside the country.[718] The unexpectedly high degree of persistence of the stock of migrant labour is another factor making it unlikely that west European governments will allow large-scale flows of migrant labour from eastern Europe in the future.

---

[718] For example, there was no direct attempt to send back guest workers from Germany after 1974, though indirect means such as financial payments were attempted.

7.3 IMPACT OF ECONOMIC CONDITIONS IN TRANSITION COUNTRIES ON MIGRATION

This section looks at the likely evolution of the labour force in eastern Europe and then at the overall economic situation and the disparities in standards of living between east and west to see where possible sources of migration may occur. The prospects facing different industries and occupational groups in the countries of eastern Europe are then discussed in order to discover some idea of which groups are most likely to become future sources of migration pressure. Where it seems appropriate, analogies are drawn with the migration experience of southern Europe in the 1960s or with the reactions of west European labour markets to structural change in the 1970s and 1980s. It should be stressed that this entire section is highly speculative but, in the absence of any directly comparable experience, this type of speculation seems to be the only feasible approach.

(i) Projections of labour force growth for eastern Europe and the former Soviet Union

Table 7.7 presents some projections of population and labour force growth for the countries of eastern Europe and the former Soviet Union to the year 2000. In each case, the projections are based on the most recent (1990) round of UN population projections by sex and age group. Projections of age- and sex-specific activity rates produced by the ILO in 1986 are combined with the UN population projections to produce the labour force estimates. For comparison, crude estimates of growth in the European Community labour force, assuming age- and sex-specific participation rates remain at 1989 levels, are also presented.[719]

The ILO activity rate projections were prepared well before the political changes of 1989 and it is likely that the structure of participation in the labour force will change considerably in response to the current, radically different economic situation. Change is most likely amongst women, whose activity rates are currently much higher in eastern Europe than in western Europe. One might therefore expect to see some decrease in female participation rates over the next few years in eastern Europe, thus causing labour force growth to be lower than presented here.

However, the scope for such a fall in female participation should not be exaggerated. While both male and female participation in the labour force was a social and legal obligation which restricted the individual's choice between work and leisure, the former system did give women greater opportunities to work outside the home which many women will have appreciated. Already, women in the former GDR seem reluctant to adopt the lower levels of female participation seen in the western *Länder* of the Federal Republic. In addition, the extremely difficult economic situation is likely to make continuing large-scale female participation a necessity for most households in the near future. Female activity rates in eastern Europe are therefore likely to remain relatively high compared with the average in western Europe.

Evidence on participation which has been gathered since 1989 is difficult to interpret as the emergence of open unemployment has invalidated the former practice of equating the economically active population with the employed population. Until results from household-based labour force surveys are available, it will not be possible to assess to what extent the falls in employment rates (and especially female employment rates) indicated in recent census results from Poland (1990) and Czechoslovakia (1991) have their counterpart in female withdrawal from the labour force or in unrecorded unemployment.[720]

Even if, in the light of the above discussion, the projections in table 7.7 are viewed as probable overestimates of future labour force growth, it is clear that Albania has by far the highest forecast increase in labour supply over the next ten years. In most of the other countries of eastern Europe, labour force growth is likely to be somewhat below 0.8 per cent a year, and it is set to be lower still in the ex-Soviet republics. With the exception of Albania, the growth rates of population and, to a slightly lesser extent, the labour force, are set to be generally lower than was the case in the south European countries of migration in the 1960s, though they will still be higher than projected rates for the European Community.

Moreover, the growth in the young male labour force (on previous experience the group most likely to emigrate) is generally slower than for the labour force as a whole (the exceptions are Romania and, to a less important extent, Bulgaria) and is in fact negative for the ex-Soviet republics. Direct pressures for migration from rapid population and labour force growth would therefore appear to be limited for the region as a whole but may prove to be significant for individual countries, especially Albania and Romania.

---

[719] These estimates use only Community-wide figures and therefore ignore variations between member states.

[720] Estimates of the total labour force, obtained by adding together total employment and recorded unemployment, show distinct falls in apparent labour force participation. However, recorded unemployment may not be a good measure of unemployment according to the standard (ILO) definition.

TABLE 7.7

Eastern Europe and the former Soviet Union: projected population and labour force growth between 1990 and 2000
(Average annual percentage change)

	Population	Population 15-64	Labour force	Labour force aged 15-34 Total	Male	Female
Albania	1.6	2.1	2.1	1.0	0.8	1.3
Bulgaria	0.1	-0.1	-0.1	0.3	0.3	0.3
Czechoslovakia	0.3	0.7	0.8	0.7	0.7	0.8
Hungary	-	0.1	0.4	0.6	0.4	0.8
Poland	0.5	0.8	0.8	0.2	0.0	0.5
Romania	0.5	0.4	0.7	1.1	1.0	1.3
Yugoslavia	0.4	0.4	0.7	0.2	-0.1	0.7
Eastern Europe	0.4	0.5	0.7	0.5	0.3	0.8
Former Soviet Union	0.7	0.6	0.6	-0.5	-0.5	-0.5
Eastern Europe and former Soviet Union	0.6	0.6	0.6	-0.2	-0.2	-0.1
European Community	0.3	0.2	0.4	-0.4	-0.1	-0.7

Note: For eastern Europe and the former Soviet Union, ILO projections of age and sex specific activity rates in ILO, *Estimates and projections of the economically active population 1950-2025* were applied to the latest set of UN population projections by age and sex (UN (1991)). For the European Community countries, 1989 EC-wide participation rates by age and sex taken from the 1989 *EC Labour Force Survey* were applied to Eurostat population projections contained in *EC Demographic Statistics 1990*. No attempt to forecast changes in EC activity rates has been made.

(ii) General economic pressures for migration arising from the transition

Even before the process of transition to a market economy began, there was a large gap between the living standards in eastern and western Europe and this gap has since widened further as production in eastern Europe has fallen dramatically in the last two years.

Tables 7.8 and 7.9 show estimates of the levels of GDP per capita for southern Europe from 1960 and for eastern Europe in 1987, both relative to contemporary figures for the Federal Republic of Germany. It should be stressed that many of these figures are merely educated guesses and that estimates of GDP per capita for the countries of eastern Europe vary widely between different sources. They should therefore be regarded as indicating approximate orders of magnitude rather than precise differences between countries.[721] As an illustration of the uncertainty of these measures, the first GDP per capita figures for the ex-GDR prepared according to western methods (which cover the second half of 1990) are also given. These figures show a much lower level of GDP per capita in the ex-GDR than had previously been expected, suggesting that income levels in the other countries may also have been overestimated in the past.[722]

Bearing these caveats in mind, it appears that Albania and Romania have the lowest standards of living and, in addition, that the differences in income levels between these two countries and western Europe were larger even in 1987 than the relative disparity between Portugal, Greece and Turkey and the more developed European economies in the 1960s and 1970s.

The prospects for a rapid reduction of the gap between east and west appear slight in the short term. No general economic recovery is now expected before 1993 and growth after that is expected to be slow, so that it will take several years for these economies to recover to even their 1989 levels of production. There would therefore appear to be considerable economic incentives for migration, especially from the Balkan countries (Albania, Romania and Bulgaria and, for different reasons linked to the effects of the civil war, probably now Yugoslavia as well). Even under the former system, the Balkan countries were less developed than the other eastern countries and they have since been hit particularly hard by the collapse of the system of central planning (see the rest of this *Survey* for detailed discussion of the economic situation in eastern Europe and the former Soviet Union).

In addition, the overall labour market situation in all the countries has deteriorated sharply. Unemployment has risen rapidly while real wages for those still in employment have fallen. Currently, registered unemployment seems to be disproportionately concentrated on women, which should reduce the tendency for a given level of joblessness to induce migration. On the other hand, youth unemployment (which may not be registered officially) is set to rise sharply as established patterns of entry into employment break down[723] and the size of the armed forces is reduced. High youth unemployment would appear to be particularly likely to lead to emigration as the costs of emigration are

---

[721] Note the differing estimates of Yugoslav GDP per capita in tables 7.8 and 7.9. See also Begg et al. (1990), p.33, for a presentation of widely varying estimates of GDP per capita in eastern Europe.

[722] The 1990 figures for GDP per capita may slightly understate living standards in the ex-GDR as prices there, particularly for non-traded and still subsidized goods, will tend to be lower than in the former Federal Republic.

[723] When relatively small reductions in employment are required, "natural wastage" (i.e., not replacing workers who leave) is usually an easier option for enterprise managers than imposing redundancies on existing workers. The resulting unemployment tends to disproportionately affect new entrants to the labour market. Only at a later stage, when large scale job losses are required, are existing workers made redundant. Current evidence (including the continuing fall in labour productivity in industry, the low level of enterprise bankruptcies and, in Poland, the low proportion of redundant workers amongst the unemployed) suggests that this second stage has not yet been reached in eastern Europe.

TABLE 7.8

Estimates of GDP per capita in southern Europe adjusted for purchasing power differences, 1960-1989
(Western Germany = 100)

	Greece	Italy	Portugal	Spain	Turkey	Yugoslavia [a]	Western Germany
1960	32	73	33	51	35	34	100
1970	45	84	43	65	28	39	100
1980	51	90	49	65	28	48	100
1988	49	93	48	68	31	..	100
1989	49	93	49	69	30	..	100

Source: OECD, *National Accounts* unless otherwise specified.

Note: From 1970 onwards, figures are OECD estimates of GDP per capita using current purchasing power parities (PPPs). The 1960 figures are less reliable estimates based on real GDP growth rates between 1960 and 1970 and are derived on the assumption that the relationship between PPPs and actual exchange rates did not alter between 1960 and 1970.

[a] Yugoslav figures are estimates taken from Summers and Heston (1988) and expressed relative to their estimates of west German GDP per capita.

generally lower for young people. If pressures for emigration are not to increase, it is very important that new enterprises emerge to provide job opportunities for the young unemployed. The results of economic reforms in Yugoslavia in the 1960s illustrate the possible dangers of a partially successful reform programme. The Yugoslav reforms did succeed in improving the efficiency of existing enterprises and this led to a rise in unemployment, which was concentrated on the young and new entrants to the labour force. However, the growth of employment elsewhere in the economy was insufficient to absorb this pool of unemployed labour. High unemployment among the young seems to have been one of the main factors behind the wave of emigration from Yugoslavia from 1967.

However, current differences in the levels of national income and high rates of unemployment may be misleading guides to future migration trends if these factors are expected to improve in the future. There has been no large increase in migration from Greece, Spain or Portugal after they joined the EC, despite significant, though decreasing, disparities in the levels of GDP per capita between them and the rest of the Community. What seems to matter in migration decisions is not the current levels of standards of living but individuals' assessments of their future prospects. If people in eastern Europe believe that the process of reform will lead to real economic benefits in the relatively near future, then they will be less likely to move abroad. Maintaining the population's belief in the future success of the transition process will therefore be important if pressures for large scale migration are not to build up. This task will have been made more difficult by the repeated postponement of the expected start of the economic recovery and by the initial, misleadingly optimistic estimates of the speed and costs of the whole transition process.

While the process of transition seems set to involve a steep (and much larger than expected) fall in production followed by a gradual (and much slower than expected) recovery on average, its impact will vary considerably over different occupations and sectors of the economy and it is this variation, rather than the average picture, which is likely to play the greatest role in determining future migration pressures. The next section therefore discuss some likely sectoral and occupational effects of the current reform programmes in an initial attempt to discover which sectors of the population are most likely to be potential migrants.

(iii) Possible sectoral and occupational effects on the potential for migration

In all the countries of eastern Europe, except Czechoslovakia and, to a lesser extent, Hungary, *agriculture* absorbs a larger proportion of the labour force (see table below) than is the case in the European countries of the OECD. Albania is a particularly extreme example of this with over 50 per cent of employment in agriculture. Much of this labour is already likely to be underemployed and this underemployment is likely to increase as more efficient methods of farming are introduced under the pressures of market competition. However the rate at which labour is displaced from agriculture will depend on the country's particular institutional arrangements.

Firstly, the *economic policies* adopted will influence the rate at which labour is displaced from agriculture. A country adopting a policy of agricultural support, following the example of the European Community's Common Agricultural Policy, would expect to see a slower exodus from agriculture (as well as higher prices and the associated economic waste of resources) than one which followed less interventionist policies. While this type of policy undoubtedly runs counter to the generally non-interventionist approach adopted so far, governments will come under increasing pressure to introduce support policies if foreign markets remain closed to east European exports. Indeed, Poland has already increased the protection of its mainly private agricultural sector as a result of the sharp fall in agricultural incomes in 1990.

Secondly, the *organizational structure* of agriculture is likely to be important and this varies considerably across the different countries. Where agriculture had been collectivized under communist rule and is now being returned to individual private farmers, the process of labour displacement can be expected to take place comparatively slowly. Newly restored peasant farmers are likely to place a higher value on the independence of self-employment than on the higher monetary returns available on their capital and labour in other occupations, thus slowing the outflow of labour out of agriculture. This situation would appear to apply particularly to Romania, Bulgaria and perhaps the former

TABLE 7.9

Typical estimates of GDP per capita in eastern Europe and the former Soviet Union in 1987, adjusted for purchasing power differences
(Western Germany = 100)

	GDP per capita
Albania	13
Bulgaria	32
Czechoslovakia	52
ex-GDR	54 [a]
Hungary	31
Poland	27
Romania	20
Yugoslavia	33
Former Soviet Union	40
Western Germany	100

Sources: UNDP, *Human Development Report.*

[a] The first national accounts prepared on western principles for the former GDR show GDP per capita in the former GDR in the second half of 1990 as being 31 per cent of the level in the western Länder (see *Statistisches Jahrbuch Deutschlands* (1991)).

Soviet republics as well. Countries where private farming remained intact under communist rule (for example, Poland and Yugoslavia) are likely to show a more rapid exodus from agriculture. Private food markets will become more competitive with the shift to a market economy and this will put heavy pressure on the incomes of private farmers. However, the most rapid falls in agricultural employment are to be expected where the eventual ownership structure of land is more concentrated, farms are run as commercial enterprises and most agricultural workers are employees.

The *age structure* of employment in agriculture may also be an important factor in determining the likelihood of migration. Migration will be less likely in those countries where agriculture is already an activity dominated by older workers than in areas where entering the agricultural sector is still a normal route into employment for young people. In the latter case, reductions in agricultural employment are likely to come about through natural wastage (not replacing workers who retire or leave) and the workers affected will be predominantly young and therefore more likely to move elsewhere to find alternative employment.

The displacement of workers from agriculture provided much of the driving force behind post-war migration and economic growth in southern Europe (see Kindleberger (1967)) for a detailed discussion).[724] While the differences between the levels of employment in agriculture in eastern Europe and western Europe now are lower than those between southern Europe and northern Europe in the 1960s, there would still appear to be a substantial degree of underemployment in east European agriculture. Moreover, given that finding a new job outside agriculture almost inevitably involves a move to an unfamiliar location, the additional costs of moving abroad will be lower for displaced agricultural (and other rural) workers than for those coming from industries in the large towns.

In comparison with western Europe, eastern Europe and the former Soviet Union have a higher proportion of employment in industry and a lower proportion in services (table 7.10). Within *industry*, the heavy industries of energy, steel and heavy engineering have historically enjoyed a privileged position, employing a substantial part of the industrial workforce and paying the highest salaries.

These heavy industries would appear to be the most vulnerable to the restructuring involved in the transition to a market economy. Their capital stock is old and highly energy-intensive and the relatively low level of labour costs in eastern Europe is unlikely to be sufficient to compensate for this in competition against more efficient foreign firms. As a result, the share of heavy industry in production and employment is likely to fall substantially, especially when large scale privatization gets under way.[725]

In contrast, prospects for light industries such as textiles and food processing with their lower capital requirements and more labour-intensive means of production would appear to be brighter, provided that trade restrictions do not impede these industries' abilities to export goods in which they have a comparative advantage. While there are still likely to be falls in employment in these industries as overstaffing is reduced, job losses should be less severe and future prospects brighter than in heavy industry or agriculture.

Modernization of infrastructure and improvement of the housing stock will both be required on a substantial scale if the transition to a western-style economy is to be successful. The construction industry would therefore appear to have the potential to generate considerable extra employment, once the present phase of stabilization is over and economic recovery eventually begins. Although there is currently substantial excess capacity in the sector, demand for extra building workers should provide one means of reducing domestic unemployment and thus lowering pressures for emigration.

Western experience of the (more or less) continuous decline of heavy industry since 1973 suggests that it will be difficult to carry out industrial restructuring without substantial unemployment. In western Europe (in contrast to the situation in the US) workers made redundant from declining industries (who are usually older than average) have often found it difficult to obtain jobs in the growing sectors of the economy, resulting in high concentrations of often long-term unemployment in areas of declining industry. However, many of the underlying causes of such unemployment (for example, a reluctance to move away from close-knit communities, difficulties in finding affordable accommodation in a new location and problems in learning new skills more relevant to the current needs of the job market) tend also to make individuals

---

[724] Although migrants generally came from the most industrialized areas of the country and often from industry, the displacement of labour from agriculture seems to have played a considerable role in encouraging migration by increasing the pressure in the non-agricultural labour market.

[725] In the short term, heavy industry (even if privately owned) may be able to delay restructuring through its preferential access to the emerging banking system. As the banking system becomes more independent of its clients, this market power of heavy industry in the credit market will fall.

TABLE 7.10

Sectoral structure of employment in eastern Europe and the former Soviet Union in 1989
(Percentage share of total employment)

Country	Agriculture Self-employed	Agriculture Total	Industry	Services
Albania	..	50.5	31.0	18.5
Bulgaria [a]	..	20.7	45.0	34.3
Czechoslovakia [a]	0.1	11.2	45.1	43.6
Hungary [a,b]	1.9	19.3	36.5	44.3
Poland [a]	20.5	25.7	37.5	36.8
Romania	..	27.9	45.1	27.0
Yugoslavia	22.1	25.4	35.5	39.1
Eastern Europe	..	23.3	40.1	36.6
Former Soviet Union [a]	3.1	19.9	35.0	45.1
Eastern Europe and former USSR	..	20.9	36.5	42.6
OECD Europe	..	11.3	31.2	57.6

Sources: Chernyshev (1991); national statistical yearbooks; OECD, *Labour Force Statistics*; OECD, *Economic Survey of Yugoslavia 1989-1990*.

[a] Sectoral breakdowns for these countries are taken from the ILO-consistent series contained in Chernyshev (1990). Figures for Albania and Romania are taken from national statistical yearbooks and those for Yugoslavia are taken from the statistical yearbook and supplemented by information contained in OECD, *Economic Survey of Yugoslavia 1989-1990*. Figures for self-employed farmers are taken from national statistical yearbooks and, for Yugoslavia, from the OECD survey.
[b] The figure for the percentage of self-employed farmers in Hungary refers to beginning of 1989. The figure for the percentage of self-employed farmers in the former Soviet Union refers to 1990.

affected by this type of joblessness less likely to migrate within their own country and even less likely to move abroad.[726]

Though the situation in eastern Europe differs in many respects from the situation in western Europe (for example, the tradition of industrial employment is generally not as well established as in the west, as many of the industries were only established in the 1950s), it seems unlikely that workers displaced by the decline of heavy industry will be particularly likely to emigrate.

Firstly, enterprises which are forced to make redundancies, will tend to make older workers redundant first as older workers are generally less adaptable to new techniques.[727] National governments may also contribute to this tendency through schemes to encourage early retirement. As older workers are generally less likely to migrate than the young, this will reduce the overall propensity of the unemployed to migrate. In addition, all the countries of the region have introduced systems of unemployment compensation in which benefits are related to earnings in the previous employment. This will tend to discourage those made redundant from heavy industry from moving, at least for a period.[728] Finally, the general shortage of housing will, as in western Europe, act as a disincentive to mobility.

The *service sector* was relatively underdeveloped in eastern Europe and the former Soviet Union under central planning[729] and this would appear to be the main likely source of future job growth. In particular, services to businesses and privately provided services to households should grow rapidly, once the foundations of a market economy have been established. These sectors often require little capital to enter and have proved to be substantial net creators of jobs in western Europe over the last 10 or 15 years.

Highly qualified workers in these areas would appear to be the ones who would have most to gain immediately from working abroad (this is the category of workers expected to be in the highest demand in western Europe in the next few years) but at the same time, they are the ones with the most to gain over the medium and longer term from staying in their home country. If they stay, their absolute and relative standard of living will be expected to improve substantially as the market economy becomes more established and demand for their skills increases.

The migration decision for such individuals is therefore finely balanced and the following discussion should be regarded as being even more speculative than the rest of this section. The highly qualified worker's migration decision would seem to hinge on the trade-off between the immediate benefits of moving and the possible advantages of establishing a position now in what may be fast-growing economies (and rapidly

---

[726] For example, see successive issues of the *OECD Employment Outlook* for discussion of the problems of long-term unemployment and of the differences in mobility between European and US labour markets.

[727] The tendency to make older workers redundant may be weaker in enterprises which are subject to some degree of control by the workforce. Such enterprises are more likely to make younger workers redundant as they will be less well integrated into the structures of the firm.

[728] Minimum benefits are usually related to the minimum wage. Although these systems of unemployment benefit generally have a time limit on the benefits payable, it is likely that there will be considerable pressure to extend these limits as unemployment increases.

[729] For example, see United Nations Economic Commission for Europe, *Economic Survey of Europe in 1984-1985*, New York, 1985, pp.154-163. However, existing statistics probably exaggerate the weight of the industrial sector at the expense of the service sector. Industrial enterprises often contained substantial numbers of employees engaged in service sector activities (catering, distribution etc.) who were counted in official statistics as working in industry. Note that this phenomenon is not entirely limited to eastern Europe, as the increased sub-contracting of subsidiary activities by western enterprises may well have led to some purely statistical increases in service sector employment in the 1980s.

evolving occupational labour markets) in a few years time. In arriving at a decision, the prospects for the supply of future highly qualified workers would seem to be particularly important. If such workers are expected to continue to be in short supply at home, re-entering the domestic labour market after a period abroad will not be too difficult and the incentives for migration will be higher. On the other hand, if the supply of qualified workers with qualifications relevant to market needs is expected to increase significantly, competition from non-migrants who have established positions for themselves and from newly trained entrants may make it difficult to return to the domestic labour market.

On this reasoning, if belief in the progress of reforms can be maintained (so that permanent migration is not the preferred option), it seems unlikely that there will be a substantial long-term loss of highly qualified workers from east to west. Rather, there will probably be a continuous stream of such workers to western Europe, who stay abroad for relatively short periods to increase their earnings and improve their qualifications and experience and then return to avoid losing their positions in their domestic labour market. Indeed, there would seem to be scope for substantial west-east migration in this area as western experts are brought in to pass on their expertise (the human capital equivalent of direct investment). Of course, if prospects in the home country show no sign of improving then this group will be amongst the most likely to seek opportunities abroad.[730]

Workers in the conventional public sector activities (health, education, etc.) are likely to face a far less favourable outlook. Public sector finances are likely to be under severe pressure for the foreseeable future, initially as budget deficits are cut as part of macro-economic stabilization programmes and then later as the public sector shrinks to provide room for a growing private sector. Within limited public budgets, resources are likely to be concentrated on improving infrastructure (for example, transport and telecommunications) rather than in areas where public sector provision was already relatively high, such as education, health and social welfare.

Individuals working in these areas are therefore likely to be initially left behind in improvements in standards of living after any eventual economic recovery, reinforcing the already existing unfavourable pattern of wage differentials.[731] In so far as their qualifications are accepted in other countries, there would seem to be clear incentives for workers in these occupations to move abroad. Even though these occupations are filled disproportionately by women who, up to now, have been less likely to move than men, there may well be some migration of young women from eastern Europe to public sector jobs in the west which are difficult to fill with domestic labour (trained nurses would seem to be an obvious example here).

(iv) Prospects for emigration in individual countries

This section attempts to draw together the various aspects presented above and to assess their importance for individual countries.

In *Poland*, recent experience of migration suggests that if economic conditions are bad enough at home, considerable numbers of people are prepared to consider moving abroad. The disappearance of the black market for hard currencies, following the introduction of the internal convertibility of the zloty at an (almost) fixed exchange rate at the end of 1989, may have temporarily reduced the attractions of working abroad. However, the inexorable rise in unemployment (the unemployment rate was over 11 per cent at the end of November 1991) suggests that unless the economy begins to recover soon, pressures for emigration may begin to rise again. Indeed, anecdotal reports of Poles working illegally in Germany during their holidays ("labour tourism") as well as the Polish domination of German government schemes for east European workers[732] suggest that emigration is already becoming more attractive. In the longer term and assuming the reform programme succeeds, Poland's economic prospects are relatively good. Providing that the labour displaced by the likely decline of agricultural employment can be absorbed outside agriculture, medium-term pressures for emigration appear to be limited.

For *Hungary* and *Czechoslovakia*, the absence of any recent experience of migration and both countries' generally good medium-term economic prospects suggest that pressures for emigration in the medium term will be low. Despite sharp falls in production and employment, both countries appear to be coping fairly well with the problems of stabilization (at least relative to the other countries of eastern Europe) and economic recovery is likely to begin earlier in Hungary and Czechoslovakia than in the other countries. The potential for short-term migration therefore also appears to be relatively low.

The *Balkan countries* appear to be the likeliest sources of emigration. These countries were less economically developed than the three more northern countries and they have been hit harder by the current economic slump. Even in the medium term, their economic prospects would seem to be less favourable. In *Albania* and, to a slightly lesser extent, *Romania* the combination of high population growth, economic backwardness and poor economic prospects all suggest there will be considerable incentives for emigration for the foreseeable future. The attempts by large numbers

---

[730] However, highly educated scientists in areas with little commercial demand for their skills at home may well emigrate to countries with better facilities and higher material rewards. To this extent, there may be a "brain drain" from eastern Europe and the former Soviet Union. The problems of Soviet nuclear scientists are an obvious example here. See *Financial Times*, 13 January 1992.

[731] Under the system of central planning, which was strongly influenced by the doctrinal distinction between the "productive" (material) and "non-productive" (non-material) sectors, workers in health, education and social welfare generally received lower salaries than workers in the material sector. See United Nations Economic Commission for Europe, *Economic Survey of Europe 1984-1985*, New York, 1985. See also Cazes and Le Cacheux (1991) for a more recent study on income differentials in the USSR.

[732] See Heyden (1991).

of Albanians to cross the Adriatic to Italy and the sharp increase in emigration from Romania in 1990[733] indicate that the possibility of large scale emigration from both countries is real.[734] *Bulgaria's* relative isolation from western Europe and slow population growth may reduce the likelihood of widespread emigration but, according to a recent survey, 5 per cent of Bulgarians of working age would go to any lengths to leave the country.[735] Finally, any meaningful discussion of future labour migration from *Yugoslavia* is impossible until the civil war has been brought to an end and the political situation stabilized.

In the *former Soviet Union*, economic conditions are still deteriorating and are likely to worsen further in the short term. Slow growth in the labour force (and a likely fall in the young labour force, especially in the European republics) and a traditional reluctance to move abroad are likely to keep labour emigration (except of ethnic minorities such as Germans and Jews) from the Russian republic to western Europe low.[736] The populations of the other European republics, including the Baltic states, appear to be more mobile and could be a possible source of emigration to neighbouring countries. Minorities (for example, Poles in Lithuania and Belarus) may also be tempted to move if conditions appear to be better in their areas of ethnic origin. As mentioned earlier, highly-educated specialists, and particularly scientists, may also try to move abroad. However, at this stage, population movements between the ex-Soviet republics caused by political instability appear to be more likely than does widespread labour emigration.

(v) Influences from western Europe

The above discussion has all been in terms of migration pressure from eastern Europe (or "push factors"). This section attempts to assess briefly the impact of developments in western Europe on the incentives to migrate, paying particular attention to the prospects for any change in immigration policy.

Future developments in the economic situation in western Europe as a whole are difficult to predict, but the projections of widespread labour shortages in western Europe (most of which were prepared in the climate of "Euro-optimism" generated by the peak of the 1980s boom and the EC's 1992 programme) seem increasingly questionable, given the unexpected depth of the recent recession, the weakness of the likely recovery from it and still high levels of unemployment. Currently, the prospects seem to be that there will be some areas of labour shortage in the 1990s, particularly in occupations formerly dominated by young workers, but no general problem of a lack of labour supply. The shortage areas are projected to be either occupations requiring high levels of education (finance, medicine and science based occupations, especially information technology) or difficult to fill low status jobs in services such as catering and hotels.[737]

The demographic problems of an ageing population, on the other hand, are increasingly apparent. Some countries may encourage a limited degree of short-term labour immigration in order to reduce such problems and to increase the flexibility of their labour markets. However, a recent OECD study[738] concluded that there is little chance of reversing, or even significantly slowing, the trend towards an ageing population through immigration, as the flows required would be far in excess of any seen in the past and so would be extremely unlikely to be politically acceptable.

Any general liberalization of immigration policy appears even more unlikely when the political climate is taken into account. West European public opinion is almost uniformly hostile to any relaxation of immigration controls. Popular sentiments against further migration were gaining ground even before the latest recession and have since grown further, with right-wing nationalist movements gaining ground in Austria, Belgium, France, Germany and Switzerland. Given this public pressure, the increased slack in domestic labour markets and the problems with previous waves of labour migration, the likelihood of western governments reducing the legal barriers to general labour migration from eastern Europe would appear to be very low.

What seems more probable is that some restricted liberalization may take place in particular areas where vacancies are particularly hard to fill with domestic labour. Nursing would appear to be a prime example of a skilled occupation where such developments are likely. There is also likely to be some relaxation of regulations governing the movement of highly qualified workers. If the arguments of section 7.4(iii) are valid and the reform process proceeds along the hoped for lines, then this type of exchange of labour will mainly consist of large numbers of short spells abroad, without much prolonged labour migration. Some liberalization of rules governing cross-border commuting (for example, workers resident in Czechoslovakia working in Germany or Austria) is also to be expected as well as some training schemes for east European workers.[739]

---

[733] See Chesnais (1991a), p.11.

[734] In order to reduce the likelihood of mass emigration from Albania to Italy, the Italian government has sent soldiers to Albania to distribute food aid.

[735] See BBC, *Summary of World Broadcasts*, Third series, EE/1227, 12 November 1991.

[736] Migration from the central Asian ex-Soviet republics is very unlikely.

[737] See Coleman (1991) for references and a discussion of how future demographic trends may affect the desirability of immigration in western Europe.

[738] OECD (1991).

[739] The German government has already introduced some schemes along these lines though these are on a relatively small scale. The German government has also allowed the short-term employment (for up to three months) of nationals from Poland, Hungary, Czechoslovakia and Romania provided priority is given to German workers. See Heyden (1991).

7.4 EAST-WEST MIGRATION: PROSPECTS AND POLICY CHOICES

Many of the conditions which led to migration in the recent past from southern Europe will be present, to a varying extent, in the countries of eastern Europe and the former Soviet Union in the next few years. Given the huge uncertainties of the present situation, the question of whether significant migration flows will actually take place is impossible to answer. However, it is clear that the pressures which can lead to migration will not be felt uniformly across the populations of eastern Europe and the former Soviet Union but will affect some groups and nationalities more than others. Poland, in the short term, and the Balkan countries, for the foreseeable future, would appear to be the countries where the potential for emigration is highest.

Western governments have a policy choice to make in these circumstances. They can attempt to prevent the pressure for immigration turning into flows of people by implementing increasingly strict border controls, tightening up work permit regimes and increasing the penalties for employing foreign labour illegally ("turning off the tap" while ignoring the underlying build-up of migratory pressures). Such policies are already in place for discouraging south-north immigration, especially immigration from the countries of the Maghreb (Algeria, Morocco and Tunisia) to southern Europe.

However, while these policies have been relatively successful in curbing observed, legal immigration, they have been much less successful in stopping illegal (and, almost by definition, unobserved) immigration. Illegal immigrants are then forced into working in the underground economy, leading to economic distortions and exploitation and increasing social tensions.[740] It therefore seems unlikely that tighter border controls will be the long-term solution to problems of unwanted migration either for south-north and east-west flows.[741]

The small moves towards liberalization which can be expected will not affect the majority of those who are likely to consider becoming illegal immigrants (relatively unskilled agricultural and industrial workers). Instead, action is needed to deal directly with the underlying economic disparities which lead to the pressure for migration in the first place. The post-war experience of the former sending countries of southern Europe provides some room for encouragement in this respect: once economic development (and political stability and freedoms) was seen to be secure, outward migration flows fell and were then outweighed by return migration first for Greece and Italy, and then for Spain and Portugal, even when the post-1973 barriers to migration did not exist (Italy) or were being gradually removed (Greece, Spain and Portugal).

In this respect, membership of the European Community appears to have played a considerable role in reducing the need for migration. Pursuit of a policy of joining the EC provides an external discipline on national governments and is evidence of an internal commitment to a high degree of political stability. Incentives for migration due to the uncertainty of the domestic situation are therefore reduced.

Economically, the liberalization of trade following membership of a free trade area such as the EC appears to have played a far larger role in improving standards of living than do the freedom of movement provisions of the Treaty of Rome. In line with the predictions of trade theory, and contrary to the expectations of the founders of the original Community (especially Italy), the free movement of goods (and of capital) has drastically reduced both the need for and the incentives for large scale movements of labour.[742]

The case of Italy illustrates the point. Net migration from Italy slowed and was then reversed as economic development there was stimulated by the liberalization of trade and flows of investment encouraged by the generally lower level of labour costs in Italy. Similarly, there has not been an explosion of migration following Greece's membership of the EC in 1981 or from the Iberian peninsula since Spain and Portugal joined the EC in 1986. Instead, the reduction in trade barriers has led to a flood of inward investment and an acceleration of economic growth, reducing the incentives for migration.

Free trade, together with the free movement of capital therefore seems to be able to reduce the incentives for large scale international movements of labour within Europe. For eastern Europe, the lesson would seem to be clear. Access to west European markets for east European goods (and access to eastern labour markets for western capital) will encourage economic

---

[740] It could be argued that illegal immigration can only take place with the tacit acquiescence of the receiving country's authorities. However, such an argument appears unrealistic when applied to the current situation in western Europe.

[741] If the only means of labour migration to western Europe were to be via illegal immigration, migrants from eastern Europe would appear to be at a disadvantage with respect to illegal migrants from the Maghreb in the competition for underground employment, as one would expect immigrants from the poorer countries of the Maghreb to have a lower reservation wage. Tighter controls on the employment of foreigners may therefore reduce east-west migration more than they do south-north migration.

[742] Modern trade theory predicts that free trade removes the need for both capital and labour movements: countries specialize in production according to their static comparative advantage which is determined by their initial endowments of capital, labour and land. When there are different types of labour, non-traded goods or in a dynamic setting, where endowments of physical and human capital evolve over time, thus altering the pattern of comparative advantage, theoretical predictions are not so clear cut. However, in the development of the EC, trade flows have played a larger role in economic convergence than have movements of labour (see Straubhaar (1991) for a discussion of recent studies).

development there and, over time, reduce the incentives for migration.

If the present process of economic transformation succeeds, closer economic integration and a reduction in economic disparities between east and west can be expected to reduce the pressure for east-west labour migration in the medium and long term. However, during the transition process, substantial pressures for migration could develop if the populations of eastern Europe lose faith in the ability of the current process of economic transformation to deliver benefits relatively quickly. The current economic collapse in eastern Europe, and especially in the Balkans, can only increase the chances of such a loss of faith. Western countries would therefore appear to have an additional motive for supporting the path of reform in eastern Europe as illegal migration could transmit the costs of setbacks in eastern Europe to the west as well. Such indirect linkages should be taken into account when decisions on the nature and extent of western support are taken.

References

D. Begg et al., *Monitoring European Integration: the impact of eastern Europe*, CEPR: London (1990).

W. Böhning, *Studies in international labour migration*, St. Martin's Press: New York (1984).

S. Cazes and J. Le Cacheux, "Inégalités de revenu, pauvreté et protection sociale en Union Soviétique", *Observations et Diagnostiques Economiques* (1991), No.38, pp.143-205.

I. Chernyshev and S. Lawrence, "ILO comparable annual employment and unemployment estimates: updated results and methodology", ILO, *Bulletin of Labour Statistics* (1991), 1991-4, pp.IX-XLVII.

J-C. Chesnais, "Migration from eastern to western Europe, past (1946-1989) and future (1900-2000)", paper presented to the Council of Europe conference of ministers on the movement of persons coming from central and eastern Europe, Vienna, 24-25 January 1991 (1991a).

J-C. Chesnais, "The USSR migration: past, present and future", paper presented to joint OECD-Italian government conference, Rome, 13-15 January 1991 (1991b).

D.A. Coleman, "Demographic projections: is there a need for immigration?", paper presented at joint International Migration Review – Giovanni Agnelli Foundation conference, Turin, 26 November 1991 (1991).

ECE, "International migration flows among ECE countries 1987, 1988 and 1989 (CES/710)", note prepared by the ECE secretariat for the 1992 Conference of European Statisticians (1991).

B. Ghosh, "East-west migration: the European perspective, current trends and prospects beyond 1992", paper presented to IOM-Greek government regional seminar on prospects of migration in Europe beyond 1992, Athens, 1-3 October 1991 (1991).

H. Heyden, "Ost-west Wanderung: neue sozialpolitische Herausforderung", (1991) *Bundesarbeitsblatt*, 9/1991.

C. Kindleberger, *Europe's post-war growth: the role of labour supply*, Harvard University Press, Cambridge: Mass. (1967).

OECD, *Migration, growth and development*, (also known as the Kindleberger report), Paris (1979).

OECD, "The effects of international migration on the labour markets of certain member states", Chapter 3 of the *1985 OECD Employment Outlook*, Paris (1985).

OECD, *Migration: the demographic aspects*, Paris (1991)

M. Okolski, "Migratory movements from countries of central and eastern Europe", paper presented to the Council of Europe conference of ministers on the movement of persons coming from central and eastern Europe, Vienna, 24-25 January 1991 (1991).

SOPEMI, *Continuous reporting system on migration*, OECD, Paris (various issues).

T. Straubhaar, *On the economics of international labour migration*, Haupt: Bern (1988).

T. Straubhaar, "How does economic structural change affect immigration policies and migration flows?", paper presented to the joint OECD-Italian government conference, Rome, 13-15 January 1991 (1991).

R. Summers and A. Heston, "A new set of international comparisons of real product and price levels", *Review of Income and Wealth*, (1988) March, pp.1-25.

G. Tapinos, "Les migrations européennes de main d'oeuvre", *Revue Economique et Sociale*, (1991) vol.49 No.1, pp.34-43.

UN, *The sex and age distribution of population: the 1990 revision*, UN Population Studies No.122, New York (1991).

H. Werner, "Post-war labour migration in western Europe: an overview", *International Migration*, (1986), Vol.24, No.3, pp.543-557.

STATISTICAL APPENDICES

INTRODUCTORY NOTE

For the user's convenience, as well as to lighten the text, the *Economic Survey of Europe* includes a set of appendix tables showing annual changes in main economic indicators over a longer period. The data are presented in three sections, following the structure of the text: *Appendix A* provides macroeconomic indicators for the market economies of western Europe and North America for 1970-1991, *Appendix B* does the same for the east European countries and the Soviet Union prior to the period of transition (1970-1990), and *Appendix C* collates time series on world trade and the development of foreign trade of the ECE economies between 1970 and 1990.

Except where otherwise stated, time series reflect levels or changes in *real* terms, i.e., at constant prices in case of series measured in value terms.

Data were compiled from international (United Nations, OECD, CMEA) or national statistical sources, as indicated in the notes to individual tables.

Regional aggregations are ECE secretariat calculations, based on 1985 US dollar weights in the case of the market economies and on CMEA estimates of relative per capita levels in the case of the CMEA economies.

All figures for 1990 are preliminary estimates, based on data available in the first weeks of March 1991.

Appendix A. Western Europe and North America

Data for this section were compiled from national and international [743] statistical sources, as indicated in the notes to individual tables. Volume figures underlying the data in tables A.1-A.6 reflect data at constant prices of the following years: Greece (1970), Yugoslavia (1972), Denmark, France, Netherlands, Switzerland (1980); Turkey (1982); Austria (1983), Belgium, Finland, Germany, Ireland, Italy, Portugal, Sweden, United Kingdom (1985); Spain, Canada (1986); United States (1987). Regional data in tables A.1-A.6, A.8 were aggregated from index series at 1985 US dollar exchange rates. Country data in tables A.9-A.10 reflect percentage changes expressed in national currencies.

---

[743] UN, OECD, EUROSTAT, IMF.

APPENDIX TABLE A.1
Gross domestic product
(Annual percentage change)

	1970	1971	1972	1973	1974	1975	1976	1977	1978	1979	1980	1981	1982	1983	1984	1985	1986	1987	1988	1989	1990	1991
France	5.7	4.8	4.4	5.4	3.1	-0.3	4.2	3.2	3.4	3.2	1.6	1.2	2.5	0.7	1.3	1.9	2.5	2.3	4.2	3.9	2.8	1.0
Germany	5.1	3.0	4.3	4.9	0.3	-1.4	5.3	2.8	3.0	4.1	1.1	0.2	-0.9	1.6	2.8	1.9	2.2	1.4	3.7	3.2	4.7	3.4
Italy	5.3	1.6	2.7	7.1	5.4	-2.7	6.6	3.4	3.7	6.0	5.0	0.6	0.2	1.0	2.7	2.6	2.9	3.1	4.1	3.0	2.0	1.0
United Kingdom	2.2	3.0	1.9	8.3	-1.0	-0.7	3.7	1.1	3.7	2.2	-1.9	-0.4	1.3	3.8	1.6	3.7	3.9	4.8	4.3	2.3	1.0	-2.2
Total 4 countries	4.6	3.2	3.4	6.3	1.6	-1.2	4.9	2.6	3.4	3.8	1.3	0.4	0.7	1.7	2.1	2.4	2.8	2.8	4.0	3.2	2.7	1.0
Austria	7.1	5.1	6.2	4.9	3.9	-0.4	4.6	4.5	0.1	4.7	2.9	-0.3	1.1	2.0	1.4	2.5	1.2	1.7	4.0	3.7	4.9	2.7
Belgium	6.4	3.7	5.3	5.9	4.1	-1.5	5.6	0.5	2.7	2.1	4.3	-0.9	1.5	0.4	2.0	0.8	1.6	2.3	4.9	3.8	3.7	1.5
Denmark	2.0	2.7	5.3	3.6	-0.9	-0.7	6.5	1.6	1.5	3.5	-0.4	-0.9	3.0	2.5	4.4	4.3	3.6	0.3	1.2	0.8	1.7	2.2
Finland	7.5	2.1	7.6	6.7	3.0	1.2	0.3	0.1	2.2	7.3	5.3	1.6	3.6	3.0	3.1	3.3	2.1	4.4	5.4	5.4	0.4	-6.2
Ireland	3.5	3.4	6.4	4.7	4.3	3.7	1.4	8.2	7.2	3.1	3.1	3.3	2.3	-0.2	4.4	2.5	-0.4	4.4	3.9	5.9	6.0	2.0
Netherlands	5.7	4.2	3.3	4.7	4.0	-0.1	5.1	2.3	2.5	2.4	0.9	-0.7	-1.4	1.4	3.1	2.7	2.0	0.8	2.7	4.0	3.9	2.0
Norway	2.0	4.6	5.2	4.1	5.2	4.2	6.8	3.6	4.5	5.1	4.2	0.9	0.3	4.6	5.7	5.3	4.2	2.0	-0.5	0.4	1.8	1.5
Sweden	6.5	0.9	2.3	4.0	3.2	2.6	1.1	-1.6	1.8	3.8	1.7	-	1.1	1.8	4.0	2.2	2.2	2.8	2.3	2.4	0.6	-0.7
Switzerland	6.4	4.1	3.2	3.0	1.5	-7.3	-1.4	2.4	0.4	2.5	4.6	1.5	-0.9	1.0	1.8	3.7	2.9	2.0	2.3	3.9	2.2	-0.5
Total 9 countries	5.6	3.4	4.3	4.5	3.0	-0.6	3.3	1.7	2.0	3.5	2.7	0.1	0.7	1.8	3.1	2.9	2.3	2.0	2.9	3.3	2.6	0.5
Total western Europe	4.8	3.2	3.6	5.8	2.0	-1.0	4.5	2.4	3.1	3.7	1.7	0.3	0.7	1.7	2.4	2.6	2.7	2.6	3.8	3.2	2.7	0.9
Greece	8.0	7.1	8.9	7.3	-3.6	6.1	6.4	3.4	6.7	3.7	1.8	0.1	0.4	0.4	2.8	3.1	1.4	-0.5	4.1	3.5	-0.1	1.0
Portugal	9.1	6.6	8.0	11.2	1.1	-4.3	6.9	5.6	2.8	5.6	4.6	1.6	2.1	-0.2	-1.9	2.8	4.1	5.3	4.0	5.4	4.2	2.7
Spain	4.1	4.6	8.0	7.7	5.3	0.5	3.3	3.0	1.4	-0.1	1.2	-0.2	1.8	1.8	1.8	2.3	3.2	5.6	5.2	4.8	3.7	2.5
Turkey	4.9	9.1	6.4	4.4	8.5	7.5	8.7	4.3	2.8	-0.9	-0.7	4.4	5.0	3.7	5.7	5.1	8.3	7.4	3.6	1.9	9.2	1.5
Total southern Europe	5.0	5.7	7.9	7.4	4.4	1.9	4.8	3.5	2.4	0.6	1.2	0.7	1.8	1.8	2.3	3.0	4.0	5.2	4.7	4.1	4.4	2.1
Total Europe	4.9	3.4	4.0	6.0	2.2	-0.8	4.5	2.5	3.0	3.5	1.6	0.4	0.8	1.7	2.4	2.6	2.8	2.8	3.8	3.3	2.9	1.0
United States	-	3.1	4.8	5.2	-0.6	-0.8	4.9	4.5	4.8	2.5	-0.5	1.8	-2.2	3.9	6.2	3.2	2.9	3.1	3.9	2.5	1.0	-0.7
Canada	2.6	5.8	5.7	7.7	4.4	2.6	6.2	3.6	4.6	3.9	1.5	3.7	-3.2	3.2	6.3	4.8	3.3	4.2	4.7	2.5	0.5	-1.5
North America	0.1	3.3	4.9	5.4	-0.3	-0.6	5.0	4.4	4.8	2.6	-0.4	1.9	-2.2	3.8	6.2	3.3	2.9	3.2	4.0	2.5	0.9	-0.8
Total above	2.0	3.3	4.5	5.6	0.7	-0.7	4.8	3.6	4.1	3.0	0.4	1.3	-1.0	3.0	4.6	3.0	2.9	3.0	3.9	2.8	1.7	-
Addendum: Yugoslavia [a]	5.6	8.1	4.2	5.0	8.5	3.6	3.9	8.0	6.9	7.0	2.3	1.4	0.5	-1.0	2.0	0.5	3.6	-1.1	-1.7	0.6	-8.5	-15.0

Sources: National statistics.

[a] Gross material product.

APPENDIX TABLE A.2

Private consumption
(Annual percentage change)

	1970	1971	1972	1973	1974	1975	1976	1977	1978	1979	1980	1981	1982	1983	1984	1985	1986	1987	1988	1989	1990	1991
France	4.3	4.9	4.9	5.3	1.2	2.8	4.9	2.7	3.7	3.0	1.2	2.1	3.5	0.9	1.1	2.4	3.9	2.9	3.4	3.2	3.1	1.5
Germany	7.6	5.6	4.6	3.0	0.5	3.1	3.9	4.5	3.6	3.3	1.2	-0.8	-1.5	1.3	1.6	1.5	3.4	3.3	2.7	1.7	4.7	2.4
Italy	8.4	3.5	3.7	6.9	3.7	0.3	5.2	4.1	3.4	7.3	5.6	1.5	1.2	0.7	2.0	3.0	3.7	4.2	4.2	3.6	2.7	2.4
United Kingdom	2.8	3.1	6.1	5.1	-1.5	-0.5	0.3	-0.5	5.6	4.2	-	1.1	1.0	4.5	1.6	3.5	6.2	5.2	7.4	3.5	1.0	-1.7
Total 4 countries	5.7	4.4	4.9	4.9	0.8	1.6	3.6	2.8	4.0	4.2	1.9	0.9	0.9	1.8	1.5	2.5	4.3	3.8	4.3	3.0	2.9	1.2
Austria	4.2	6.7	6.1	5.4	3.0	3.2	4.5	5.4	-1.5	4.4	1.5	0.3	1.2	5.0	-0.1	2.4	1.8	3.1	3.3	2.8	3.6	3.0
Belgium	4.4	4.7	6.0	7.8	2.6	0.6	4.8	2.4	2.3	4.8	2.0	-0.9	1.4	-1.6	1.1	2.0	2.6	3.2	3.1	3.4	2.6	1.6
Denmark	3.5	-0.8	1.7	4.8	-2.9	3.7	7.9	1.1	0.7	1.4	-3.7	-2.3	1.4	2.6	3.4	5.0	5.7	-1.5	-1.0	-0.4	0.4	1.2
Finland	7.6	1.7	8.4	5.9	1.8	3.1	0.9	-1.2	2.5	5.5	2.0	1.2	4.7	2.6	2.7	3.2	4.1	5.7	5.0	4.2	0.4	-4.3
Ireland	2.9	3.2	5.1	7.2	1.6	-2.7	2.8	6.8	9.1	4.4	0.4	1.7	-7.1	0.9	2.0	3.5	2.0	2.2	2.4	5.2	2.7	0.7
Netherlands	7.4	3.3	3.5	4.0	3.7	3.3	5.3	4.6	4.3	3.0	-	-2.5	-1.2	0.9	0.9	2.5	2.7	3.5	0.9	2.4	3.8	2.7
Norway	-	4.6	3.0	2.9	3.9	5.1	6.1	6.9	-1.6	3.2	2.3	1.1	1.8	1.5	2.7	9.9	5.6	-1.0	-2.8	-2.6	2.6	2.7
Sweden	3.5	0.1	3.4	2.6	3.4	2.8	4.2	-1.0	-0.7	2.4	-0.8	-0.5	0.7	-2.2	1.7	2.8	5.2	4.6	2.5	1.4	-0.2	-0.1
Switzerland	5.4	4.8	5.4	2.8	-0.5	-2.9	1.1	3.0	2.2	1.3	2.6	0.4	-	1.7	1.6	1.4	2.8	2.1	2.1	2.2	1.5	1.0
Total 9 countries	4.8	3.1	4.6	4.5	2.0	1.8	4.2	2.7	1.7	3.1	0.7	-0.6	0.5	0.9	1.5	3.1	3.5	2.7	1.8	2.1	2.0	1.0
Total western Europe	5.4	4.1	4.8	4.8	1.1	1.6	3.7	2.8	3.5	4.0	1.6	0.5	0.8	1.6	1.5	2.6	4.1	3.6	3.7	2.7	2.7	1.3
Greece	8.8	5.6	7.0	7.6	0.7	5.5	5.3	4.6	5.7	2.6	0.2	2.0	3.9	0.3	1.7	3.9	0.7	0.8	3.4	4.3	2.0	0.3
Portugal	2.6	12.7	4.0	12.0	9.7	-0.9	3.5	0.6	-2.0	-	3.7	2.9	2.4	-1.4	-2.9	0.7	5.6	5.4	6.8	3.3	4.9	5.6
Spain	4.2	5.1	8.3	7.8	5.1	1.8	5.6	1.5	0.9	1.3	0.6	-0.6	0.2	0.3	-0.4	2.4	4.1	5.8	4.7	5.5	3.7	2.9
Turkey	2.2	13.5	6.4	0.2	9.0	7.7	10.1	6.7	-3.9	-3.1	-5.2	0.6	4.2	5.0	6.8	1.3	11.5	6.5	2.6	3.9	10.6	4.1
Total southern Europe	4.2	7.3	7.4	6.6	5.7	3.1	6.3	2.8	0.2	0.4	-0.4	0.2	1.6	1.1	1.1	2.2	5.4	5.4	4.3	4.9	5.1	3.1
Total Europe	5.3	4.4	5.1	5.0	1.6	1.8	4.0	2.8	3.1	3.6	1.4	0.5	0.9	1.5	1.5	2.6	4.2	3.7	3.8	3.0	3.0	1.4
United States	2.4	3.3	5.6	4.5	-0.6	2.1	5.2	4.0	4.1	2.4	-0.1	1.2	1.1	4.6	4.8	4.4	3.6	2.8	3.6	1.9	1.2	-0.1
Canada	2.0	5.9	7.5	7.5	5.8	4.7	6.5	3.2	3.4	2.9	2.2	2.3	-2.6	3.4	4.6	5.2	4.4	4.4	4.1	3.2	1.3	-1.1
North America	2.4	3.5	5.7	4.7	-0.2	2.3	5.3	4.0	4.1	2.4	0.1	1.3	0.8	4.5	4.8	4.4	3.7	2.9	3.6	2.0	1.2	-0.2
Total above	3.5	3.8	5.4	4.8	0.5	2.1	4.8	3.5	3.7	2.9	0.6	1.0	0.8	3.3	3.5	3.7	3.9	3.2	3.7	2.4	1.9	0.5
Addendum: Yugoslavia	14.6	8.3	4.6	2.7	7.3	3.4	4.4	7.0	7.0	5.6	0.7	-1.0	-0.1	-1.7	-0.9	-0.1	4.5	0.3	-1.3	1.0	6.0	..

Sources: National statistics.

APPENDIX TABLE A.3
Public consumption
(Annual percentage change)

	1970	1971	1972	1973	1974	1975	1976	1977	1978	1979	1980	1981	1982	1983	1984	1985	1986	1987	1988	1989	1990	1991
France	4.2	3.9	3.5	3.4	1.2	4.4	4.2	2.4	5.2	3.0	2.5	3.1	3.8	2.1	1.2	2.3	1.7	2.8	2.8	0.1	3.1	0.8
Germany	4.3	5.1	4.1	5.0	4.0	3.9	1.6	1.4	3.9	3.4	2.6	1.8	-0.9	0.2	2.5	2.1	2.5	1.5	2.2	-1.7	2.1	1.2
Italy	4.4	5.2	5.1	2.6	2.5	2.5	2.3	2.8	3.5	3.0	2.6	2.3	2.6	3.4	2.3	3.4	2.6	3.4	2.8	0.9	1.0	1.5
United Kingdom	1.7	2.9	4.2	4.3	1.9	5.6	1.2	-1.7	2.3	2.2	1.6	0.1	0.8	2.0	1.0	-	1.8	1.2	0.6	0.9	3.1	2.4
Total 4 countries	3.6	4.3	4.2	4.0	2.5	4.2	2.2	1.0	3.7	2.9	2.3	1.8	1.3	1.7	1.7	1.8	2.1	2.1	2.1	-0.1	2.4	1.4
Austria	3.3	3.3	4.1	3.0	5.7	4.0	4.3	3.3	3.3	3.0	2.7	2.2	2.3	2.2	0.2	1.9	1.7	0.4	0.3	0.8	1.5	2.5
Belgium	3.1	5.5	5.9	5.3	3.4	4.5	3.7	2.3	6.0	2.5	1.5	0.3	-1.6	-	0.1	2.4	1.9	0.4	-0.3	-0.4	1.0	1.1
Denmark	6.9	5.5	5.7	4.0	3.5	2.0	4.5	2.4	6.2	5.9	4.3	2.6	3.1	-	-0.4	2.5	0.5	2.5	0.9	-0.3	-1.0	1.2
Finland	5.4	5.8	7.8	5.6	4.5	6.9	5.7	4.2	4.1	3.8	4.2	4.3	3.5	3.7	2.8	5.2	3.1	4.5	2.4	2.6	4.5	2.3
Ireland	7.5	8.7	7.5	6.7	7.6	6.5	2.6	2.1	7.9	4.6	7.1	0.3	3.2	-0.4	-0.7	1.8	2.5	-4.9	-4.2	-3.5	1.0	1.7
Netherlands	.0	4.4	0.8	0.8	2.2	4.1	4.1	3.4	5.3	2.8	0.6	2.0	0.7	1.2	-0.7	1.4	2.0	2.4	0.1	0.3	1.0	1.0
Norway	6.3	6.0	4.5	5.5	4.0	6.4	7.4	4.9	3.9	3.5	5.4	6.1	3.9	4.6	2.4	3.3	2.2	4.0	0.5	2.3	2.3	3.3
Sweden	8.1	2.2	2.4	2.6	3.1	4.7	3.5	3.0	3.3	4.7	2.2	2.3	1.0	0.8	2.3	2.4	1.4	1.0	0.6	1.9	2.1	1.1
Switzerland	4.8	5.8	2.9	2.4	1.6	0.7	2.7	0.5	2.0	1.1	0.9	2.5	1.1	3.9	1.2	3.3	3.7	1.8	4.3	4.1	3.2	2.2
Total 9 countries	5.8	4.5	3.7	3.3	3.4	4.1	4.1	2.9	4.3	3.6	2.5	2.4	1.5	1.6	0.9	2.6	1.9	1.8	0.8	1.2	1.6	1.1
Total western Europe	4.1	4.3	4.1	3.8	2.7	4.2	2.7	1.5	3.8	3.1	2.4	1.9	1.4	1.7	1.5	2.0	2.1	2.0	1.8	0.2	2.2	1.3
Greece	5.9	4.9	5.7	6.8	12.1	11.9	5.1	6.5	3.5	5.8	0.2	6.8	2.3	2.7	3.0	3.2	-0.8	1.3	6.6	4.2	0.6	0.7
Portugal	7.0	6.4	8.6	7.8	17.3	6.6	7.0	11.8	3.3	6.5	7.9	5.2	3.6	3.7	0.1	0.1	7.2	4.9	7.3	1.5	3.7	3.0
Spain	5.2	4.3	5.2	6.4	9.3	5.2	6.9	3.9	5.4	4.2	4.2	1.9	4.9	3.9	2.9	4.6	5.8	8.9	4.0	7.6	4.4	4.1
Turkey	3.6	6.1	7.3	10.3	9.9	13.4	10.8	3.2	9.9	1.7	8.8	0.9	2.0	1.7	2.1	3.1	6.5	5.0	3.0	4.4	15.3	6.0
Total southern Europe	5.3	4.8	5.7	7.0	10.4	7.3	7.0	4.9	5.4	4.4	4.3	2.9	3.9	3.4	2.6	3.8	4.8	6.8	4.6	6.2	4.9	3.5
Total Europe	4.2	4.3	4.2	4.0	3.1	4.4	2.9	1.7	3.9	3.1	2.5	2.0	1.5	1.8	1.6	2.2	2.3	2.4	2.0	0.7	2.4	1.5
United States	-2.7	-1.8	-0.4	-1.3	1.7	1.2	-0.6	0.7	1.9	1.8	2.2	1.3	1.5	2.8	3.1	6.1	5.2	3.1	0.6	1.5	3.2	0.9
Canada	9.4	4.4	2.7	5.8	5.6	6.5	2.0	4.6	1.7	0.6	2.8	2.5	2.4	1.4	1.2	3.2	1.6	1.7	4.0	2.9	3.1	2.7
North America	-2.0	-1.4	-0.2	-0.8	2.0	1.6	-0.4	1.1	1.9	1.7	2.2	1.4	1.5	2.7	2.9	5.8	4.9	2.9	0.9	1.6	3.2	1.0
Total above	0.1	0.6	1.4	1.0	2.4	2.7	0.9	1.3	2.7	2.3	2.3	1.6	1.5	2.3	2.4	4.3	3.8	2.7	1.3	1.3	2.9	1.2
Addendum: Yugoslavia	9.3	-0.1	5.1	4.1	7.3	9.3	9.5	7.4	6.5	4.5	-1.0	-4.8	-0.7	-5.1	-0.2	-0.2	6.8	-1.5	0.1	-1.8	-2.0	..

Sources: National statistics.

APPENDIX TABLE A.4

Gross domestic fixed capital formation
(Annual percentage change)

	1970	1971	1972	1973	1974	1975	1976	1977	1978	1979	1980	1981	1982	1983	1984	1985	1986	1987	1988	1989	1990	1991
France	4.6	7.3	6.0	8.5	1.3	-6.4	3.3	-1.8	2.1	3.1	2.6	-1.9	-1.4	-3.6	-2.6	3.2	4.5	4.8	8.6	7.5	3.9	-1.5
Germany	9.2	6.0	2.6	-0.3	-9.7	-5.2	3.7	3.8	4.3	6.9	2.3	-4.9	-5.3	3.3	0.3	-	3.6	2.1	4.6	7.0	8.8	6.9
Italy	3.0	0.2	1.3	8.8	2.0	-7.3	-	1.8	0.6	5.7	9.1	-3.1	-4.7	-0.6	3.6	0.6	2.2	5.0	6.9	4.6	3.0	-1.0
United Kingdom	2.5	1.8	-0.2	6.5	-2.4	-2.0	1.7	-1.8	3.0	2.8	-5.4	-9.6	5.4	5.0	8.5	4.0	2.4	9.6	13.1	6.8	-2.2	-10.3
Total 4 countries	5.3	4.2	2.7	5.2	-2.8	-5.4	2.4	0.7	2.6	4.8	2.4	-4.5	-2.3	0.8	1.8	1.8	3.3	5.0	8.0	6.5	3.8	-0.6
Austria	9.8	13.8	12.1	0.3	4.0	-5.0	3.8	5.1	-4.1	3.5	3.0	-1.4	-8.2	-0.6	2.1	5.0	3.7	3.1	6.0	5.4	4.7	6.2
Belgium	8.4	-1.9	3.4	7.0	6.9	-1.9	4.0	-	2.8	-2.7	4.6	-15.9	-2.0	-4.5	1.8	0.7	4.5	5.6	15.1	14.3	8.3	1.7
Denmark	2.2	1.9	9.3	3.5	-8.9	-12.4	17.1	-2.4	1.1	-0.4	-12.6	-19.2	7.1	1.9	12.9	12.6	17.1	-3.8	-6.6	-0.6	-0.5	-1.1
Finland	12.5	3.8	6.5	8.5	3.5	5.9	-8.8	-3.5	-6.9	3.0	10.4	2.2	4.4	4.1	-2.1	2.9	-	5.4	10.5	14.1	-4.9	-16.5
Ireland	0.3	8.8	7.4	16.2	-11.6	-2.6	13.6	4.1	18.9	13.6	-3.2	7.3	-3.3	-9.0	-2.7	-7.4	-1.3	-3.7	2.6	12.0	7.5	-4.7
Netherlands	7.5	1.5	-2.3	4.2	-4.0	-4.4	-2.2	9.7	2.5	-1.7	-0.9	-10.4	-4.1	2.1	5.2	7.0	7.4	1.1	8.1	4.6	4.2	1.3
Norway	14.9	18.7	-4.1	13.6	5.1	11.9	10.1	3.6	-11.2	-5.0	-1.5	17.9	-11.0	5.8	10.9	-13.9	23.9	-2.1	1.6	-4.8	28.5	0.2
Sweden	3.3	-0.6	4.2	2.7	-3.0	3.1	1.9	-2.9	-6.8	4.5	3.5	-5.8	-0.3	1.9	6.0	7.3	0.7	7.6	5.8	11.8	-0.9	-6.9
Switzerland	8.9	9.9	5.0	2.9	-4.3	-13.6	-10.5	1.6	6.1	5.1	9.9	2.4	-2.5	4.1	4.1	5.3	7.9	7.4	6.9	5.8	2.2	-2.8
Total 9 countries	7.6	5.0	3.7	4.9	-1.1	-2.8	1.1	2.1	-1.1	1.1	2.0	-3.8	-2.9	1.5	4.6	3.1	7.3	3.1	6.2	6.6	-0.5	-2.2
Total western Europe	5.9	4.4	2.9	5.1	-2.4	-4.8	2.0	1.1	1.7	3.9	2.3	-4.3	-2.4	1.0	2.5	2.1	4.3	4.5	7.5	6.6	2.7	-1.1
Greece	-1.4	14.0	15.4	7.7	-25.6	0.2	6.8	7.8	6.0	8.8	-6.5	-7.5	-1.9	-1.3	-5.7	5.2	-6.2	-8.7	8.8	10.0	4.8	1.0
Portugal	11.5	9.8	13.5	9.5	-7.0	-11.3	0.8	12.0	6.2	-1.3	8.5	5.5	2.3	-7.1	-17.4	-3.5	10.9	15.1	15.2	8.3	7.3	4.5
Spain	3.0	-3.0	14.2	13.0	6.2	-4.5	-0.8	-0.9	-2.7	-4.4	0.7	3.3	0.5	-2.5	-5.8	4.1	10.1	14.0	14.0	13.7	6.8	2.0
Turkey	13.5	-4.9	14.8	13.2	10.7	24.7	17.7	3.9	-10.0	-3.6	-10.0	1.7	3.5	3.0	0.5	16.7	11.0	5.6	-1.2	-1.0	14.1	-1.0
Total southern Europe	4.3	0.2	14.4	11.9	0.9	-0.8	3.2	2.0	-2.3	-2.3	-1.4	-2.1	0.9	-2.0	-5.9	5.9	8.3	9.9	10.5	10.2	7.9	1.6
Total Europe	5.8	4.0	3.9	5.7	-2.1	-4.4	2.1	1.1	1.2	3.3	2.0	-4.1	-2.1	0.7	1.7	2.4	4.7	5.0	7.8	6.9	3.2	-0.7
United States	-2.9	8.7	10.6	8.7	-7.6	-11.8	9.7	14.3	10.8	4.6	-8.1	0.6	-8.0	6.6	15.9	5.0	0.4	-0.5	4.2	0.4	-1.6	-7.6
Canada	0.3	7.9	4.3	9.9	6.6	5.8	4.6	2.1	3.1	8.5	10.1	11.8	-11.0	-0.7	2.1	9.5	6.2	10.8	10.4	5.6	-3.3	-5.7
North America	-2.7	8.6	10.1	8.8	-6.5	-10.3	9.2	13.2	10.2	4.9	-6.6	1.7	-8.3	5.9	14.5	5.4	0.9	0.6	4.9	1.0	-1.8	-7.4
Total above	1.6	6.2	6.9	7.2	-4.3	-7.3	5.5	7.1	5.9	4.1	-2.7	-1.1	-5.5	3.4	8.5	4.1	2.5	2.5	6.2	3.7	0.6	-4.2
Addendum: Yugoslavia	12.8	4.6	1.8	4.2	9.1	9.7	8.1	9.5	10.5	6.4	-5.9	-9.8	-5.5	-9.7	-9.6	-3.7	3.5	-5.1	-5.9	0.8	18.0	..

Sources: National statistics.

APPENDIX TABLE A.5
Volume of exports of goods and services
(Annual percentage change)

	1970	1971	1972	1973	1974	1975	1976	1977	1978	1979	1980	1981	1982	1983	1984	1985	1986	1987	1988	1989	1990	1991
France	16.1	9.2	12.0	10.8	8.8	-1.7	8.2	7.4	5.9	7.5	2.7	3.7	-1.7	3.7	7.0	1.9	-1.4	3.1	8.1	10.3	5.2	4.0
Germany	5.5	4.6	6.8	10.7	12.3	-6.4	9.6	3.9	2.9	4.3	5.2	7.2	3.7	-0.7	8.2	7.6	-0.6	0.4	5.5	10.1	10.3	12.1
Italy	-2.5	6.8	9.3	4.1	7.0	1.6	10.5	9.9	9.0	8.5	-8.1	7.9	-2.4	2.3	8.5	3.2	2.5	4.4	5.7	10.0	7.5	1.2
United Kingdom	5.2	7.0	1.1	11.9	7.3	-2.8	9.1	6.9	1.9	3.8	0.2	-1.0	0.8	2.0	6.6	5.9	4.7	5.6	-	4.2	5.0	0.7
Total 4 countries	6.1	6.6	6.7	10.0	9.4	-3.2	9.3	6.4	4.3	5.6	1.0	4.4	0.7	1.5	7.6	5.1	1.0	3.0	4.7	8.7	7.4	5.9
Austria	16.4	5.9	9.2	2.2	10.7	-2.4	11.1	4.2	7.3	11.7	5.2	4.9	2.7	3.2	6.1	6.9	-2.7	2.4	8.9	10.2	9.7	7.1
Belgium	10.2	4.5	11.1	14.2	3.8	-8.2	12.9	2.2	2.3	7.0	2.5	3.1	2.1	3.2	5.7	1.3	5.3	7.3	9.3	7.9	5.0	3.6
Denmark	5.6	5.6	5.6	7.8	3.5	-1.8	4.1	4.1	1.2	8.4	5.2	8.2	2.5	4.9	3.5	5.0	-	5.1	7.8	5.0	8.0	6.5
Finland	8.7	-1.3	14.5	7.3	-0.6	-14.0	12.8	15.7	8.9	8.8	8.4	4.9	-1.1	2.5	5.4	1.2	1.3	2.6	3.7	1.6	1.6	-6.5
Ireland	4.4	4.1	3.6	10.9	0.7	7.2	8.1	14.0	12.3	-6.5	6.4	2.0	5.5	10.5	16.6	6.6	2.9	13.4	8.7	10.1	6.2	5.7
Netherlands	11.9	10.7	10.0	12.1	2.6	-3.1	9.9	-1.8	3.3	7.4	1.5	1.4	-	3.5	7.3	5.5	1.6	3.5	7.8	6.3	4.9	3.8
Norway	0.1	1.1	14.1	8.3	0.7	3.1	11.3	3.6	8.4	2.6	2.1	2.0	-0.1	7.6	8.2	6.9	1.6	1.2	5.5	10.6	7.8	5.0
Sweden	8.6	4.8	5.9	13.7	5.3	-9.3	4.3	1.5	7.8	6.1	-0.6	2.0	5.7	9.9	6.9	1.4	3.2	3.9	3.0	3.0	2.0	-2.6
Switzerland	6.8	3.9	6.4	7.9	1.0	-6.6	9.3	9.7	3.7	2.5	5.1	4.6	-2.9	1.1	6.3	8.3	0.4	1.7	5.8	5.0	3.0	-0.8
Total 9 countries	9.0	5.7	9.2	10.6	3.2	-5.0	9.6	3.1	4.8	6.6	3.0	3.2	1.2	4.4	6.7	4.5	2.2	4.2	7.0	6.6	5.2	2.8
Total western Europe	7.1	6.2	7.7	10.2	7.0	-3.8	9.4	5.2	4.5	6.0	1.7	3.9	0.9	2.5	7.3	4.9	1.4	3.4	5.6	7.9	6.5	4.8
Greece	12.4	11.9	22.9	23.4	0.1	10.6	16.4	1.8	16.4	6.7	6.9	-5.9	-7.2	8.0	16.9	1.3	14.0	16.0	9.0	1.4	0.8	8.6
Portugal	-1.6	9.9	18.5	4.2	-15.7	-15.6	-	5.9	9.1	33.0	2.2	-4.4	4.7	13.6	11.6	6.7	6.8	8.6	7.2	16.8	11.1	1.5
Spain	17.5	14.2	13.4	10.0	-1.0	-0.4	5.0	12.1	10.7	5.6	2.3	8.4	4.8	10.1	11.7	2.7	1.6	6.1	5.2	2.9	4.2	6.5
Turkey	14.3	15.5	14.6	26.2	-11.0	-1.1	37.5	-21.8	12.9	-12.3	7.4	62.2	36.9	14.6	20.4	11.3	-0.6	26.0	16.5	11.3	7.9	3.5
Total southern Europe	12.8	13.3	15.3	11.9	-4.4	-1.4	9.2	5.6	11.5	7.2	3.3	8.8	7.0	11.0	13.7	4.5	3.2	11.0	8.1	6.2	5.5	5.4
Total Europe	7.4	6.6	8.0	10.3	6.4	-3.7	9.4	5.3	4.8	6.0	1.8	4.2	1.2	3.1	7.7	4.9	1.6	4.0	5.7	7.8	6.5	4.8
United States	9.1	0.4	7.3	21.1	11.5	-0.6	4.5	1.4	9.4	8.6	9.2	1.7	-9.0	-3.6	6.9	1.1	6.6	10.4	15.8	11.3	7.8	6.6
Canada	8.7	5.2	7.8	10.6	-2.0	-6.8	10.6	8.9	13.6	5.0	2.7	4.4	-2.2	6.4	17.7	6.0	4.5	3.5	9.2	0.6	3.8	-0.6
North America	9.0	1.4	7.4	18.7	8.7	-1.8	5.6	2.8	10.3	7.9	7.9	2.2	-7.7	-1.6	9.3	2.3	6.1	8.8	14.3	8.9	7.0	5.1
Total above	7.9	5.0	7.9	12.8	7.1	-3.1	8.2	4.5	6.5	6.6	3.8	3.5	-1.8	1.6	8.2	4.1	2.9	5.5	8.5	8.2	6.6	4.9
Addendum: Yugoslavia	3.3	3.7	17.6	6.8	1.0	-1.3	9.3	-3.1	-2.4	14.9	10.8	4.7	-9.3	-	6.4	7.9	-2.2	-0.6	-2.4	4.7	2.2	-20.7

Sources: National statistics.

APPENDIX TABLE A.6
Volume of imports of goods and services
(Annual percentage change)

	1970	1971	1972	1973	1974	1975	1976	1977	1978	1979	1980	1981	1982	1983	1984	1985	1986	1987	1988	1989	1990	1991
France	6.3	6.3	13.2	14.2	1.9	-9.7	17.4	0.1	3.0	10.1	2.5	-2.1	2.6	-2.7	2.7	4.5	7.1	7.7	8.7	8.2	6.4	3.2
Germany	15.9	8.7	5.9	4.5	0.4	1.2	10.8	3.4	5.6	9.3	3.7	-3.3	-0.9	1.6	5.4	4.7	2.8	4.2	5.1	8.4	10.2	11.0
Italy	12.4	2.7	9.8	9.3	2.2	-12.6	14.1	1.7	4.8	11.7	-0.8	-1.2	-0.3	-1.4	12.3	3.9	2.9	8.9	7.0	9.0	6.7	3.5
United Kingdom	4.9	5.3	9.8	12.0	0.9	-7.0	4.7	1.5	3.9	9.7	-3.4	-3.3	4.9	6.5	9.9	2.6	6.9	7.8	12.3	7.4	1.0	-2.9
Total 4 countries	10.1	6.2	9.2	9.6	1.2	-6.2	11.4	1.8	4.4	10.0	0.9	-2.6	1.3	1.1	7.0	4.0	4.8	6.8	8.1	8.2	6.3	4.3
Austria	16.9	5.8	11.1	6.2	6.9	-4.6	17.4	6.2	0.1	11.7	6.2	-0.8	-3.3	5.5	9.9	6.2	-1.2	4.7	9.4	8.6	9.7	7.2
Belgium	7.6	3.6	9.6	18.5	4.4	-9.0	12.2	4.8	2.6	9.0	-0.4	-2.7	0.9	-1.1	6.0	1.0	7.4	9.6	8.7	9.3	4.6	3.6
Denmark	9.3	-0.7	1.5	12.8	-3.8	-4.8	15.6	-	0.1	5.0	-6.8	-1.7	3.8	1.8	5.5	8.1	6.8	-2.0	1.5	4.4	2.1	3.1
Finland	20.3	-0.6	4.2	13.0	6.7	0.6	-2.0	-1.5	-3.7	18.4	8.3	-4.7	2.5	3.0	1.0	6.8	3.1	9.0	11.1	8.8	-0.9	-13.2
Ireland	2.3	4.7	5.1	19.0	-2.3	-10.2	14.7	13.3	15.7	13.9	-4.5	1.7	-3.1	4.7	9.9	3.2	5.6	5.0	3.9	10.9	6.0	2.2
Netherlands	14.7	6.1	4.8	11.0	-0.8	-4.1	10.1	2.9	6.3	6.0	-0.4	-5.9	1.1	3.9	5.0	6.5	3.6	5.0	6.6	6.4	4.5	3.6
Norway	13.6	6.4	-1.0	14.4	4.7	7.0	12.3	3.4	-13.5	-0.7	3.3	1.5	3.7	-	9.5	5.9	9.9	-7.3	-1.7	1.0	2.6	0.5
Sweden	10.4	-3.3	4.0	6.9	9.0	-3.5	9.0	-3.8	-5.5	11.6	0.4	-5.8	3.4	0.8	5.4	7.8	4.7	7.2	4.7	7.1	1.2	-6.5
Switzerland	13.9	6.2	7.3	6.5	-1.0	-15.4	13.1	9.3	10.9	6.9	7.2	-1.3	-2.6	4.4	7.1	5.1	7.1	5.5	5.3	5.4	3.0	-1.4
Total 9 countries	12.1	3.4	5.6	11.8	2.6	-5.4	11.3	3.2	1.7	8.1	1.1	-3.1	0.8	2.2	6.2	5.3	5.2	4.9	6.1	7.0	3.9	1.0
Total western Europe	10.8	5.2	7.9	10.4	1.7	-5.9	11.4	2.3	3.4	9.3	1.0	-2.8	1.1	1.5	6.7	4.5	4.9	6.1	7.4	7.8	5.4	3.3
Greece	6.2	7.6	15.4	32.2	-16.3	6.3	6.1	8.0	7.2	7.2	-8.0	3.6	7.0	6.6	0.2	12.8	3.8	16.6	8.0	10.8	11.8	3.6
Portugal	0.9	14.5	12.0	12.7	4.8	-25.2	3.4	12.0	-0.2	12.6	6.9	2.3	3.9	-6.1	-4.4	1.4	16.9	20.0	18.1	11.0	12.9	5.4
Spain	7.0	0.7	24.3	16.7	8.0	-0.9	9.8	-5.5	-1.0	11.4	3.3	-4.2	3.9	-0.6	-1.0	6.2	14.8	20.2	14.3	17.0	8.1	7.8
Turkey	22.0	9.7	17.4	0.6	18.3	26.1	32.1	-3.4	-31.8	-14.1	-0.4	12.5	13.0	18.6	14.9	6.9	14.5	15.6	3.5	13.7	25.5	1.8
Total southern Europe	7.7	5.3	19.7	15.8	4.9	-0.2	12.5	-1.3	-6.2	7.0	1.6	-0.1	5.6	2.4	1.3	6.7	13.2	18.7	11.9	14.7	12.3	5.7
Total Europe	10.6	5.2	8.7	10.7	2.0	-5.5	11.5	2.0	2.7	9.1	1.1	-2.6	1.5	1.6	6.3	4.6	5.6	7.1	7.8	8.4	6.1	3.5
United States	3.8	5.8	10.8	6.2	-2.5	-12.0	19.0	10.0	9.2	1.3	-4.7	4.9	-	12.5	25.0	6.3	6.6	4.6	3.7	3.7	2.2	0.3
Canada	-1.7	7.2	13.8	14.7	11.1	-3.3	8.6	1.7	7.4	11.4	4.9	8.5	-15.2	9.0	17.1	8.7	7.6	7.0	12.7	5.2	0.6	-0.3
North America	2.9	6.0	11.3	7.6	-0.1	-10.3	16.8	8.4	8.9	3.1	-2.8	5.7	-3.3	11.8	23.6	6.7	6.8	5.0	5.3	3.9	1.9	0.2
Total above	8.2	5.4	9.4	9.8	1.3	-6.9	13.0	3.9	4.6	7.2	-0.1	-0.1	-	4.7	11.9	5.4	6.0	6.3	6.9	6.8	4.6	2.4
Addendum: Yugoslavia	27.8	9.2	-6.5	16.4	14.4	-5.6	-3.2	12.5	4.5	18.7	-10.1	-12.7	-14.1	-7.3	2.5	2.6	7.8	-6.7	-8.7	13.1	21.9	-27.4

Sources: National statistics.

APPENDIX TABLE A.7
Current account balances
(Billion US dollars)

	1970	1972	1973	1974	1975	1976	1977	1978	1979	1980	1981	1982	1983	1984	1985	1986	1987	1988	1989	1990	1991
France	-0.2	-0.1	1.4	-3.9	2.7	-3.4	-0.4	7.1	5.1	-4.2	-4.8	-12.1	-5.2	-0.9	-	2.4	-4.4	-3.5	-4.6	-8.4	-5.1
Germany	0.8	1.1	5.0	10.5	4.2	3.5	3.8	8.9	-5.9	-14.4	-3.6	4.9	5.3	9.5	16.9	39.8	45.9	50.2	57.2	47.9	-20.6
Italy	0.8	2.1	-2.5	-8.0	-0.5	-2.8	2.5	6.3	5.5	-9.8	-9.6	-6.3	1.5	-2.4	-3.4	3.1	-1.3	-6.2	-10.6	-14.5	-18.9
United Kingdom	2.0	0.5	-2.4	-7.4	-3.5	-1.4	0.1	2.2	-0.8	6.9	14.1	8.0	5.7	2.3	4.1	0.2	-7.0	-27.6	-33.4	-26.9	-10.5
Total 4 countries	3.4	3.6	1.6	-8.8	3.0	-4.1	6.0	24.3	3.9	-21.6	-3.9	-5.5	7.3	8.5	17.6	45.6	33.3	12.9	8.6	-1.9	-55.1
Austria	-0.1	-0.2	-0.3	-0.2	-0.2	-1.1	-2.2	-0.7	-1.1	-1.7	-1.5	0.6	0.2	-0.3	-0.3	0.1	-0.4	-0.5	0.1	1.0	-0.5
Belgium	0.7	1.3	1.4	0.8	0.2	0.4	-0.6	-0.8	-3.1	-4.9	-4.2	-2.6	-0.5	-0.1	0.7	3.1	2.8	3.6	3.6	3.6	4.1
Denmark	-0.5	-0.1	-0.5	-1.0	-0.5	-1.9	-1.7	-1.5	-3.0	-2.5	-1.9	-2.3	-1.2	-1.6	-2.8	-4.5	-3.0	-1.3	-0.9	1.5	2.2
Finland	-0.2	-0.1	-0.4	-1.2	-2.1	-1.1	-0.1	0.7	-0.2	-1.4	-0.5	-0.9	-1.1	-1.0	-0.8	-0.7	-1.7	-2.7	-5.8	-6.7	-5.8
Ireland	-0.2	-0.1	-0.3	-0.7	-0.1	-0.4	-0.5	-0.8	-2.1	-2.1	-2.6	-1.9	-1.2	-1.0	-0.7	-0.7	0.4	0.6	0.5	1.4	2.0
Netherlands	-0.5	1.4	2.4	3.0	2.4	3.5	1.2	-1.2	0.1	-1.2	3.6	4.7	4.9	6.3	4.2	4.0	3.8	6.9	9.6	10.3	10.5
Norway	-0.2	-0.1	-0.4	-1.1	-2.5	-3.7	-5.0	-2.1	-1.0	1.1	2.2	0.7	2.0	2.9	3.1	-4.5	-4.1	-3.9	0.2	3.8	5.4
Sweden	-0.3	0.6	1.4	-0.6	-0.3	-1.6	-2.2	-0.3	-2.4	-4.4	-2.8	-3.4	-0.8	0.6	-1.2	0.6	-0.1	-0.7	-3.3	-5.8	-4.3
Switzerland	0.2	0.5	-0.9	-2.8	0.8	2.3	1.9	2.1	-0.2	-0.2	3.4	2.5	1.2	6.1	6.0	4.7	6.3	8.8	7.0	8.6	8.9
Total 9 countries	-1.2	3.2	2.6	-3.6	-2.5	-3.7	-9.2	-4.7	-13.0	-17.3	-4.3	-2.5	3.5	12.9	8.2	2.0	4.0	10.9	11.0	17.7	22.5
Total western Europe	2.2	6.8	4.3	-12.5	0.5	-7.8	-3.2	19.6	-9.1	-38.9	-8.1	-8.0	10.8	21.4	25.7	47.6	37.2	23.8	19.6	15.8	-32.6
Greece	-0.4	-0.4	-1.2	-1.1	-0.9	-0.9	-1.1	-1.0	-1.9	-2.2	-2.4	-1.9	-1.9	-2.1	-3.3	-1.7	-1.2	-1.0	-2.6	-3.5	-1.7
Portugal	0.1	0.4	0.3	-0.8	-0.8	-1.3	-1.0	-0.5	-0.1	-1.1	-2.6	-3.3	-1.0	-0.5	0.4	1.1	0.4	-1.1	0.2	-0.2	-0.6
Spain	0.1	0.6	0.6	-3.2	-3.5	-4.3	-2.1	1.6	1.1	-5.2	-5.0	-4.2	-2.7	2.0	2.9	4.0	-0.2	-3.8	-10.9	-16.8	-16.0
Turkey	-	0.2	0.7	-0.6	-1.6	-2.0	-3.1	-1.3	-1.4	-3.4	-1.9	-1.0	-1.9	-1.4	-1.0	-1.5	-0.8	1.6	1.0	-2.6	0.5
Total southern Europe	-0.3	0.7	0.4	-5.8	-6.8	-8.5	-7.3	-1.0	-2.2	-11.9	-11.9	-10.3	-7.6	-2.0	-1.0	2.0	-1.8	-4.2	-12.4	-23.2	-17.8
Total Europe	1.9	7.6	4.7	-18.3	-6.3	-16.4	-10.5	18.6	-11.3	-50.7	-20.1	-18.4	3.3	19.4	24.7	49.6	35.4	19.6	7.3	-7.4	-50.4
United States	2.3	-5.8	7.1	1.9	18.1	4.2	-14.5	-15.4	0.2	1.2	7.3	-5.9	-40.2	-99.0	-122.3	-145.4	-160.2	-126.4	-106.4	-92.2	-23.4
Canada	1.0	-0.3	0.3	-1.3	-4.6	-4.2	-4.1	-4.3	-4.1	-1.5	-5.7	1.6	1.7	1.2	-2.3	-8.2	-8.8	-11.2	-17.5	-18.8	-4.0
North America	3.3	-6.1	7.4	0.6	13.5	-	-18.6	-19.7	-3.9	-0.3	1.5	-4.3	-38.5	-97.8	-124.5	-153.6	-169.0	-137.6	-123.8	-111.0	-27.4
Total above	5.3	1.5	12.0	-17.6	7.2	-16.3	-29.1	-1.1	-15.2	-51.1	-18.6	-22.6	-35.2	-78.4	-99.8	-104.1	-133.5	-118.0	-116.6	-118.3	-77.8
Japan	2.0	6.6	-0.1	-4.7	-0.7	3.7	10.9	16.5	-8.7	-10.8	4.8	6.8	20.8	35.0	49.2	85.8	87.0	79.6	57.0	35.9	72.6
Total above	7.2	8.2	11.9	-22.4	6.5	-12.6	-18.2	15.4	-24.0	-61.8	-13.8	-15.8	-14.4	-43.4	-50.6	-18.2	-46.5	-38.4	-59.6	-82.5	-5.2
Addendum: Yugoslavia	-0.4	0.4	0.5	-1.0	-0.6	0.2	-1.3	-1.3	-3.7	-2.3	-1.0	-0.5	0.3	0.5	0.8	1.1	1.2	2.5	2.4	2.4	..

Sources: IMF, *International Financial Statistics*, February 1992; OECD, *Economic Outlook*, No.50, December 1991. National statistics.

APPENDIX TABLE A.8
Industrial production
(Annual percentage change)

	1970	1973	1974	1975	1976	1977	1978	1979	1980	1981	1982	1983	1984	1985	1986	1987	1988	1989	1990	1991 [a]
France	4.4	6.7	2.6	-7.2	8.8	1.4	2.4	4.5	2.2	-1.0	-0.8	-0.6	0.3	0.2	0.9	1.9	4.7	4.1	1.4	0.5
Germany	5.9	6.3	-1.7	-6.2	6.9	2.6	1.9	5.1	-	-1.9	-3.2	0.7	3.0	4.5	2.1	0.4	3.6	5.0	5.1	3.0
Italy	6.6	9.8	3.9	-8.8	11.6	-	2.0	6.6	5.2	-2.2	-3.1	-2.4	3.4	1.3	4.1	2.6	6.9	3.9	-0.7	-2.0
United Kingdom	0.4	9.0	-2.0	-5.4	3.4	5.1	2.9	3.9	-6.7	-3.2	1.7	4.1	0.1	5.5	2.4	3.2	3.6	0.4	-0.5	-3.0
Total 4 countries	4.3	7.8	0.3	-6.8	7.5	2.3	2.2	5.0	0.1	-2.1	-1.6	0.4	1.8	3.1	2.4	1.9	4.6	3.5	1.7	-
Austria	8.6	3.7	5.5	-6.3	6.6	3.8	2.1	7.7	2.7	-1.6	-0.8	1.0	5.3	4.5	1.1	1.0	4.4	5.9	7.4	1.5
Belgium	2.9	6.0	4.1	-9.9	7.7	0.6	2.4	4.5	-1.3	-2.7	-	1.9	2.5	2.5	0.8	2.2	6.5	3.4	4.4	-5.0
Denmark																				
Finland	12.4	7.2	4.6	-3.8	0.9	0.6	5.1	10.7	7.8	2.6	0.9	3.3	4.6	4.1	0.8	4.2	5.8	2.4	0.1	-9.0
Ireland	3.4	10.6	1.6	-4.0	8.8	8.0	7.8	7.8	-4.6	5.4	-0.6	7.8	9.9	3.3	2.1	9.1	10.6	11.6	4.7	3.0
Netherlands	9.4	7.2	5.1	-4.8	8.0	-	0.9	3.6	-0.8	-2.0	-3.8	1.9	5.0	4.8	0.2	1.0	0.1	5.1	2.3	4.0
Norway	4.1	5.4	4.9	5.0	6.1	-0.6	10.2	7.3	5.8	-1.0	-	9.1	6.5	5.5	3.5	7.5	5.1	16.3	3.7	4.5
Sweden [b]	5.6	7.2	4.5	-1.7	-2.4	-5.5	-1.3	6.7	-0.4	-1.8	-1.7	4.0	7.2	3.0	0.4	2.6	1.3	3.6	-2.7	-8.5
Switzerland	8.7	5.5	1.0	-12.4	-	5.9	-	2.2	5.4	-1.0	-3.1	-1.1	3.3	5.3	4.0	1.0	7.6	1.8	2.6	-
Total 9 countries [c]	7.1	6.3	4.2	-5.8	4.6	0.7	2.0	5.3	1.4	-1.3	-1.7	2.6	4.9	4.2	1.4	2.5	4.1	5.5	2.8	-0.7
Total western Europe [d]	4.8	7.5	1.0	-6.6	6.9	2.0	2.2	5.1	0.3	-1.9	-1.6	0.8	2.4	3.3	2.2	2.0	4.5	3.9	1.9	-0.1
Greece	10.3	15.3	-1.6	4.4	10.5	2.0	7.6	6.0	1.0	0.9	0.9	-0.3	2.3	4.2	-1.0	-1.5	5.1	1.9	-2.4	-0.5
Portugal	6.4	11.8	2.8	-4.9	3.3	13.2	6.8	7.2	5.5	2.4	7.7	3.5	2.5	0.7	7.3	4.4	3.7	6.8	8.9	2.0
Spain	10.5	15.1	9.3	-8.8	5.1	5.3	2.3	0.7	1.3	-1.0	-1.1	2.7	0.9	1.9	3.1	4.6	3.1	4.5	0.1	-0.5
Turkey [d]	1.6	12.8	7.1	8.6	8.9	6.5	3.1	-6.1	-3.1	9.7	8.6	9.8	11.4	4.2	11.0	10.7	1.0	2.2	9.5	3.0
Total southern Europe	8.7	14.4	7.6	-5.1	6.0	6.0	3.2	0.6	1.0	1.1	1.6	3.9	3.2	2.4	4.9	5.5	2.8	4.1	3.1	-0.6
Total Europe [c]	5.2	8.2	1.8	-6.5	6.8	2.5	2.3	4.5	-3.4	-1.6	-1.2	1.2	2.5	3.2	2.5	2.5	4.3	3.9	2.1	0.0
United States	-3.4	8.2	-1.5	-8.7	9.1	8.0	5.7	3.8	-1.9	1.9	-4.5	3.7	9.3	1.7	0.9	5.0	5.5	2.5	1.0	-2.0
Canada	-1.6	11.8	2.0	-7.3	6.7	3.4	3.4	4.8	-3.4	2.1	-9.9	6.6	12.1	5.6	-0.7	4.8	5.5	-0.2	-4.3	-4.0
North America	-3.3	8.5	-1.2	-8.6	8.9	7.5	5.5	3.9	-2.0	1.9	-5.0	3.9	9.6	2.1	0.8	4.9	5.5	2.3	0.6	-2.2
Total above [c]	1.0	8.3	0.3	-7.5	7.8	4.9	3.9	4.2	0.8	0.1	-3.1	2.5	6.0	2.6	1.6	3.7	4.9	3.1	1.3	-1.1
Addendum: Yugoslavia	7.5	5.9	11.1	5.0	3.2	10.8	8.3	9.0	3.5	3.4	-	1.1	5.4	3.1	3.9	0.8	-0.7	1.0	-10.8	-20.5

Sources: OECD, *Main Economic Indicators*, Paris (monthly), and national statistics.

Note: National data are aggregated by means of weights derived from GDP originating in industry, expressed in 1985 US dollar purchasing parities.

[a] Country data rounded to the nearest 0.5 percentage point.
[b] Refers to mining and manufacturing only.
[c] Excluding Denmark.
[d] Refers to manufacturing.

APPENDIX TABLE A.9

Consumer prices [a]
(Annual percentage change)

	1970	1971	1972	1973	1974	1975	1976	1977	1978	1979	1980	1981	1982	1983	1984	1985	1986	1987	1988	1989	1990	1991
France	5.2	5.5	6.2	7.3	13.7	11.8	9.6	9.4	9.1	10.8	13.6	13.4	11.8	9.6	7.4	5.8	2.5	3.3	2.8	3.6	3.3	3.1
Germany	3.3	5.4	5.5	7.0	7.0	5.9	4.3	3.7	2.7	4.1	5.5	6.3	5.2	3.3	2.4	2.0	-0.1	0.2	1.3	2.8	2.7	3.5
Italy	4.9	4.8	5.8	10.8	19.1	17.0	16.8	17.0	12.1	14.8	21.2	17.8	16.5	14.6	10.8	9.2	5.9	4.7	5.0	6.3	6.3	6.5
United Kingdom	6.4	9.4	7.1	9.1	16.0	24.2	16.5	15.8	8.3	13.4	18.0	11.9	8.6	4.6	5.0	6.1	3.4	4.1	4.9	7.8	9.5	5.9
Total 4 countries	4.8	6.2	6.1	8.4	13.5	14.0	11.2	10.8	7.7	10.3	13.9	11.9	10.2	7.7	6.1	5.5	2.7	2.9	3.3	4.9	5.2	4.6
Austria	4.4	4.7	6.3	7.6	9.5	8.4	7.3	5.5	3.6	3.7	6.3	6.8	5.4	3.3	5.7	3.2	1.7	1.4	2.0	2.5	3.2	3.4
Belgium	3.9	4.3	5.4	6.9	12.7	12.8	9.2	7.1	4.5	4.5	6.6	8.2	8.2	7.7	6.3	4.9	1.3	1.6	1.1	3.2	3.4	3.2
Denmark	6.5	5.8	6.6	9.3	15.2	9.6	9.0	11.1	10.1	9.6	12.3	6.8	5.4	3.3	5.6	3.2	1.7	4.0	4.6	4.8	2.7	2.4
Finland	2.7	6.1	7.4	11.4	17.8	17.4	14.4	12.5	7.7	7.1	11.7	12.2	9.6	8.3	7.1	5.9	2.9	4.1	5.1	6.6	6.2	4.1
Ireland	8.2	9.0	8.6	11.4	17.0	20.9	18.0	13.6	7.6	13.2	18.2	20.4	17.1	10.5	8.6	5.4	3.8	3.2	2.1	4.0	3.4	3.1
Netherlands	3.6	7.5	7.8	8.0	9.6	10.2	8.8	6.7	4.1	4.2	6.5	6.7	5.7	2.8	3.2	2.3	0.3	-0.2	0.7	1.1	2.4	4.0
Norway	10.7	6.0	7.2	7.6	9.4	11.6	9.2	9.0	8.2	4.8	10.9	13.6	11.3	8.4	6.3	5.7	7.2	8.7	6.7	4.6	4.1	3.4
Sweden	7.0	7.4	6.0	6.8	9.9	9.8	10.3	11.4	10.0	7.2	13.7	12.1	8.6	9.0	8.0	7.4	4.2	4.2	5.8	6.4	10.5	9.3
Switzerland	3.6	6.6	6.7	8.7	9.8	6.7	1.7	1.3	1.0	3.6	4.1	6.5	5.6	3.0	3.0	3.4	0.7	1.5	1.8	3.2	5.4	5.8
Total 9 countries	5.0	6.3	6.7	8.2	11.4	10.7	8.6	7.7	5.6	5.5	8.7	9.0	7.4	5.5	5.4	4.3	2.1	2.5	2.9	3.7	4.7	4.6
Total western Europe	4.9	6.2	6.2	8.3	13.0	13.3	10.6	10.1	7.2	9.2	12.6	11.2	9.5	7.2	6.0	5.2	2.5	2.8	3.2	4.6	5.1	4.6
Greece	2.9	3.0	4.3	15.5	26.9	13.4	13.3	12.1	12.6	19.0	24.9	24.5	21.0	20.2	18.5	19.3	23.0	16.4	13.5	13.7	20.5	18.9
Portugal [b,c]	6.4	11.9	10.7	12.9	25.1	15.3	21.0	27.4	22.0	24.2	16.6	20.0	22.4	25.5	29.3	19.2	11.8	10.2	9.6	12.7	13.5	11.3
Spain	5.6	8.3	8.3	11.4	15.7	16.9	14.9	24.5	19.8	15.7	15.5	14.5	14.4	12.2	11.3	8.8	8.7	5.3	4.8	6.8	6.7	6.0
Turkey [d]	8.1	16.3	12.9	16.6	18.7	20.1	15.3	28.4	49.5	56.5	116.6	35.9	27.1	31.4	48.4	44.9	34.6	38.9	73.7	63.3	60.3	66.0
Total southern Europe	5.8	9.7	9.0	13.1	18.4	17.1	15.3	24.1	25.4	25.4	38.3	20.7	18.5	18.3	21.5	18.6	16.2	14.2	20.9	20.1	20.3	20.8
Total Europe	5.0	6.6	6.5	8.8	13.5	13.6	11.0	11.5	9.1	10.8	15.3	12.2	10.4	8.3	7.5	6.6	3.9	4.0	5.0	6.2	6.6	6.3
United States [e]	5.9	4.3	3.3	6.2	11.0	9.1	5.8	6.4	7.6	11.3	13.5	10.3	6.2	3.2	4.3	3.6	1.9	3.7	4.1	4.8	5.4	4.2
Canada	3.3	2.9	4.7	7.8	10.8	10.8	7.5	8.0	9.0	9.1	10.2	12.3	10.9	5.7	4.4	3.9	4.2	4.4	4.0	5.0	4.8	5.6
North America	5.7	4.2	3.4	6.3	11.0	9.3	5.9	6.6	7.7	11.2	13.3	10.5	6.5	3.4	4.3	3.6	2.0	3.7	4.1	4.8	5.4	4.3
Total above	5.4	5.1	4.6	7.3	11.9	10.9	7.9	8.5	8.2	11.0	14.1	11.1	8.0	5.3	5.6	4.8	2.8	3.8	4.5	5.4	5.8	5.1
Addendum: Yugoslavia	10.6	15.6	16.6	19.7	21.1	24.3	11.7	14.9	14.3	20.6	30.2	40.9	32.3	42.9	50.0	60.0	87.5	126.7	194.1	1252.0	580.0	..

Source: National statistics.

Note: Regional aggregates were obtained from time series in annual percentage change form, with weights taken from OECD, *National Accounts* (various issues). (Private final consumption expenditure in US dollars for 1985 at current prices and exchange rates.)

[a] Cost-of-living index for the Federal Republic of Germany and Yugoslavia, retail price index for the United Kingdom.
[b] 1970-1976, Lisbon.
[c] Break in series after 1975.
[d] Urban areas.
[e] 1970-1978, urban wage earners and clerical workers; 1979 and thereafter, all urban consumers.

Appendix A. Western Europe and North America

APPENDIX TABLE A.10
Average hourly earnings in manufacturing
(Annual percentage change)

	1970	1971	1972	1973	1974	1975	1976	1977	1978	1979	1980	1981	1982	1983	1984	1985	1986	1987	1988	1989	1990
France [a]	10.8	11.2	11.1	14.5	19.6	17.3	14.0	12.7	12.9	13.0	15.1	14.5	15.2	11.2	7.7	5.8	4.3	2.8	3.1	3.8	4.5
Germany	13.8	10.8	8.9	10.7	10.6	8.0	6.4	7.6	5.0	5.5	6.3	5.3	4.9	3.4	2.3	4.5	3.5	4.2	4.3	4.2	4.9
Italy [a]	22.4	13.4	10.2	24.4	22.4	26.6	20.8	27.9	16.2	19.0	18.5	23.1	17.1	19.6	11.4	10.9	4.8	6.5	6.1	6.1	7.2
United Kingdom [b]	13.1	10.9	12.9	13.0	16.8	26.3	16.6	10.3	14.4	15.7	17.4	13.4	11.2	8.9	8.8	9.1	7.7	8.0	8.5	8.7	9.4
Total 4 countries	13.8	11.0	10.0	12.7	14.0	14.4	11.0	11.2	9.7	10.7	12.0	11.5	10.3	9.1	6.7	7.1	4.9	5.3	5.5	5.7	6.5
Austria [c]	9.4	13.7	11.6	12.7	15.9	13.3	9.1	8.5	5.7	5.8	7.9	6.2	6.1	4.5	5.0	6.1	4.5	3.1	3.8	4.4	7.1
Belgium [d]	15.0	13.0	11.5	17.2	20.6	19.5	12.2	9.1	6.7	7.8	8.7	10.7	6.0	4.5	5.4	3.1	2.5	1.9	0.9	5.5	4.4
Denmark [e]	12.4	14.1	12.3	14.1	19.6	22.4	11.5	9.1	10.8	11.1	11.1	9.0	10.1	6.7	5.0	4.9	4.8	9.3	6.6	4.7	4.8
Finland	11.1	15.6	14.1	16.6	22.4	21.3	14.8	8.8	7.5	11.4	12.8	12.8	10.5	9.6	10.3	7.6	6.1	6.8	8.7	8.8	10.4
Ireland	11.1	20.0	16.7	14.3	25.0	25.0	16.0	20.7	14.3	15.0	21.7	16.1	15.1	11.5	10.4	8.6	6.9	5.7	5.3	4.8	5.4
Netherlands [a]	8.3	10.3	14.0	14.3	17.9	12.1	9.5	7.4	5.7	4.3	4.2	3.0	6.8	2.7	0.9	5.3	1.7	1.5	1.3	1.3	2.9
Norway [f]	10.0	13.6	8.0	11.1	16.7	20.0	14.3	12.5	7.4	3.4	8.3	10.8	9.7	8.9	8.1	7.5	10.0	16.4	5.5	5.2	5.6
Sweden [e]	15.6	5.3	15.6	8.8	10.2	14.9	19.3	6.8	7.7	8.2	8.7	11.1	7.1	8.4	9.3	7.5	7.4	6.4	8.0	10.0	9.4
Switzerland [g]	6.2	9.7	9.0	9.2	13.9	7.4	1.6	1.7	3.4	2.1	5.2	5.1	6.2	6.8	1.8	3.6	3.5	2.4	3.0	3.7	5.0
Total 9 countries	10.2	11.1	12.1	12.5	16.4	14.4	10.4	7.4	6.5	6.4	7.9	8.0	7.5	6.2	5.3	5.6	4.7	4.9	4.5	5.5	6.3
Total western Europe	12.9	11.1	10.5	12.7	14.7	14.4	10.9	10.2	8.9	9.7	11.1	10.7	9.7	8.5	6.4	6.8	4.9	5.2	5.3	5.6	6.5
Greece	6.1	8.7	9.3	16.0	26.8	24.4	27.3	21.4	23.5	23.8	26.9	24.2	34.1	20.0	25.8	20.5	13.0	9.7	17.7	20.5	19.3
Portugal [h]	29.4	13.6	18.0	16.9	50.7	51.0	22.9	19.2	15.2	21.1	26.2	20.0	20.6	18.6	18.8	21.1	16.8	14.0	11.3	14.8	14.4
Spain [i]	13.2	15.0	15.9	20.0	27.1	31.1	30.0	29.3	27.5	23.9	15.3	24.7	15.9	15.0	11.7	10.0	10.9	7.6	6.5	7.3	8.7
Turkey [j]	..	..	..	..	..	..	..	..	..	..	..	..	..	..	..	..	..	..	..	..	..
Total southern Europe [j]	14.8	13.8	15.4	18.8	31.7	34.7	27.9	25.9	24.2	23.3	18.9	23.6	19.2	16.5	15.3	14.2	12.7	9.5	9.6	11.7	12.3
Total Europe [j]	12.9	11.1	10.7	12.9	15.3	15.2	11.7	11.1	9.8	10.7	11.7	11.8	10.6	9.3	7.3	7.6	5.8	5.8	5.9	6.5	7.3
United States	5.1	6.6	7.0	7.3	7.9	9.3	8.1	8.8	8.7	8.5	8.5	10.0	6.2	4.0	4.0	3.8	2.0	1.9	2.8	3.0	3.3
Canada	9.2	8.0	7.4	9.2	12.7	17.2	12.8	11.4	7.8	8.3	9.8	12.1	11.5	4.0	4.7	4.4	3.1	2.4	4.9	5.4	5.7
North America	5.3	6.7	7.0	7.4	8.2	9.8	8.5	9.0	8.7	8.5	8.6	10.1	6.6	4.0	4.1	3.9	2.1	1.9	3.0	3.2	3.5
Total above [j]	8.8	8.8	8.8	10.1	11.8	12.6	10.2	10.1	9.3	9.7	10.3	11.1	8.8	7.0	5.9	6.1	4.3	4.2	4.7	5.2	5.9
Addendum: Yugoslavia	16.3	22.3	16.1	19.3	27.8	22.4	14.2	17.9	19.1	20.7	24.2	37.0	27.7	27.5	45.3	76.9	105.4	105.0	171.2	1580.6	406.3

Sources: National Statistics; OECD, *Economic Outlook – Historical Statistics, 1960-1989*; Paris; OECD, *Main Economic Indicators*, No.2, 1992, Paris.

Notes: National data are aggregated by means of weights derived from manufacturing employment in 1985.

[a] Wage rates.
[b] Weekly earnings of all employees in Great Britain.
[c] Monthly earnings in mining and manufacturing.
[d] Including transport.
[e] Including mining.
[f] Males only.
[g] Data refers to workers who had accidents during the relevant period.
[h] Daily earnings; for 1970-1973, wage bill for all activities.
[i] Refers to all activities.
[j] Excluding Turkey.

APPENDIX TABLE A.11
Total employment
(Annual percentage change)

	1970	1971	1972	1973	1974	1975	1976	1977	1978	1979	1980	1981	1982	1983	1984	1985	1986	1987	1988	1989	1990	1991
France	0.9	0.4	0.6	1.4	0.9	-0.9	0.8	0.8	0.4	0.1	0.1	-0.6	0.2	-0.4	-0.9	-0.3	0.1	0.3	0.7	1.1	1.2	0.3
Germany	1.3	0.4	0.4	1.1	-1.2	-2.7	-0.5	0.1	0.8	1.7	1.6	-0.1	-1.2	-1.4	0.2	0.7	1.4	0.7	0.8	1.4	2.9	2.8
Italy [a]	0.2	-0.1	-0.6	2.2	2.0	0.1	1.5	1.0	0.5	1.5	1.9	-	0.6	0.6	0.4	0.9	0.8	0.4	0.9	0.2	1.0	0.7
United Kingdom [b]	-0.4	-0.9	-0.1	2.3	0.3	-0.4	-0.8	0.1	0.6	1.5	-0.3	-3.9	-1.8	-1.2	2.6	1.9	0.1	2.1	3.4	3.0	0.7	-2.6
Total 4 countries	0.5	-	0.1	1.7	0.4	-1.0	0.1	0.5	0.6	1.2	0.8	-1.2	-0.6	-0.6	0.6	0.7	0.6	0.9	1.5	1.5	1.5	0.3
Austria	0.4	1.1	0.7	1.7	0.9	-0.4	0.5	0.9	0.2	0.7	0.4	0.1	-1.2	-0.8	0.1	0.2	0.4	-	0.6	1.4	1.9	1.9
Belgium [b]	1.8	1.0	-0.1	1.3	1.4	-1.4	-0.7	-0.2	0.1	1.2	-0.1	-1.9	-1.3	-1.0	-0.2	0.6	0.6	0.5	1.5	1.6	0.9	0.1
Denmark	0.7	0.6	2.1	1.2	-0.3	-1.3	1.8	0.8	1.0	1.2	-0.4	-1.3	0.5	0.3	1.7	2.5	2.6	0.8	-0.6	-0.7	-0.5	-0.9
Finland	2.1	-0.6	1.0	2.0	0.4	-0.4	-1.3	-2.5	-1.1	2.2	2.9	1.0	0.7	0.4	0.3	-0.2	-0.5	0.2	0.2	0.5	-1.2	-5.0
Ireland [c]	-1.2	-0.4	0.3	1.4	1.4	-0.8	-0.8	1.8	2.5	3.2	1.0	-0.9	-	-1.9	-1.9	-2.2	0.2	-0.1	1.1	-0.2	3.3	-0.4
Netherlands [d]	1.1	0.5	-0.9	0.1	0.2	-0.7	-	0.2	0.7	1.3	0.7	-1.5	-2.5	-1.9	-0.1	1.5	2.0	1.4	1.4	1.7	2.1	1.0
Norway	1.5	0.9	1.1	0.7	1.3	1.9	3.3	2.6	1.8	1.5	2.3	1.0	0.1	-0.3	0.6	2.7	3.0	2.1	-0.8	-2.6	-0.6	-0.9
Sweden	2.0	-0.2	0.3	0.4	2.0	2.0	0.4	0.2	0.4	1.5	1.1	0.2	-0.2	-0.3	0.8	1.0	0.6	0.8	1.4	1.5	0.9	-1.6
Switzerland	1.5	1.8	1.4	1.0	-0.1	-4.8	-3.0	0.4	1.0	1.1	2.3	1.3	-0.7	-1.3	4.4	1.9	1.4	1.2	1.2	1.1	1.3	-0.3
Total 9 countries	1.3	0.6	0.5	1.0	0.8	-0.7	-0.1	0.3	0.6	1.4	1.0	-0.3	-0.8	-0.7	0.8	1.1	1.2	0.8	0.8	0.8	1.0	-0.4
Total western Europe	0.7	0.1	0.2	1.5	0.4	-1.0	0.1	0.4	0.6	1.3	0.9	-1.0	-0.7	-0.7	0.6	0.8	0.7	0.9	1.3	1.3	1.4	0.2
Greece	-0.1	0.3	0.5	1.0	0.1	0.1	1.2	0.8	0.4	1.1	1.4	5.2	-0.8	1.1	0.4	1.0	0.4	-0.1	1.6	0.4	0.4	-0.7
Portugal	-0.7	-0.3	-0.6	-0.8	-0.8	-1.4	0.2	-0.1	-0.3	-0.5	2.2	0.5	-0.1	4.0	-0.1	-0.4	0.2	2.6	2.6	2.2	2.2	3.0
Spain	1.0	0.9	0.3	2.5	0.5	-1.8	-1.1	-0.8	-2.7	-0.4	-3.0	-3.0	-1.3	-1.1	-1.8	-0.9	2.2	3.1	2.9	4.1	2.5	0.6
Turkey [e]	-0.3	2.1	2.3	1.7	1.6	1.7	2.3	1.9	1.0	0.1	-0.1	0.9	2.0	1.8	2.5	2.3	3.1	3.0	1.4	1.1	1.1	0.7
Total southern Europe	0.2	1.1	1.0	1.6	0.7	-0.2	0.7	0.5	-0.6	-0.1	-0.7	-0.1	0.3	1.0	0.5	0.8	2.2	2.6	2.1	2.1	1.6	0.8
Total Europe	0.6	0.3	0.4	1.6	0.5	-0.8	0.2	0.5	0.3	1.0	0.5	-0.8	-0.4	-0.3	0.6	0.8	1.1	1.3	1.5	1.5	1.4	0.3
United States [a]	-0.8	-0.4	2.5	4.3	1.6	-2.1	2.8	3.5	5.0	3.2	0.2	0.9	-1.6	1.0	4.9	2.4	1.7	2.9	2.8	2.3	0.5	-0.8
Canada	1.0	2.3	2.9	4.9	4.1	1.7	2.0	1.8	3.5	4.0	3.0	2.7	-3.4	0.5	2.4	2.6	2.7	2.9	3.2	2.0	0.7	-1.8
North America	-0.6	-0.2	2.5	4.4	1.8	-1.7	2.7	3.3	4.9	3.3	0.5	1.1	-1.8	1.0	4.6	2.4	1.8	2.9	2.9	2.3	0.5	-0.2
Total above	0.1	0.1	1.1	2.6	1.0	-1.2	1.2	1.5	2.1	1.9	0.5	-	-1.0	0.2	2.2	1.5	1.4	2.0	2.1	1.8	1.0	-0.4
Addendum: Yugoslavia [f]	3.9	4.8	4.3	2.4	5.0	5.5	3.6	4.5	4.5	4.3	3.2	2.9	2.3	2.0	2.1	2.5	2.9	2.1	0.2	-0.3	-3.8	-10.0

Sources: National statistics; OECD, *National Accounts*, detailed tables, vol.ii., 1977-1989, Paris; OECD, *Labour Force Statistics 1969-1989; Quarterly Labour Force Statistics*, No.4, Paris, 1991; ECE secretariat estimates.

Note: National data are aggregated by adding the annual data on the persons engaged taken from the national accounts statistics, where available. Otherwise the data refer to annual labour force surveys.

a Refers to full-time equivalent data.
b June of each year.
c April of each year.
d Man-years.
e Civilian employment.
f Socialist sector.

Appendix A. Western Europe and North America

APPENDIX TABLE A.12
Annual unemployment rates [a]
(Percentage of total labour force)

	1970	1971	1972	1973	1974	1975	1976	1977	1978	1979	1980	1981	1982	1983	1984	1985	1986	1987	1988	1989	1990	1991
France	2.5	2.7	2.8	2.7	2.8	4.0	4.4	4.9	5.2	5.9	6.3	7.4	8.1	8.3	9.7	10.2	10.4	10.5	10.0	9.4	9.0	9.4
Germany	0.8	0.9	0.8	0.8	1.6	3.6	3.7	3.6	3.5	3.2	2.9	4.2	5.9	7.7	7.1	7.2	6.4	6.2	6.2	5.6	5.1	4.5
Italy	5.3	5.3	6.3	6.2	5.3	5.8	6.6	7.0	7.1	7.6	7.5	7.8	8.4	8.8	9.4	9.6	10.5	10.9	11.0	10.9	10.3	9.9
United Kingdom	3.0	3.6	4.0	3.0	2.9	4.3	5.6	6.0	5.9	5.0	6.4	9.8	11.3	12.4	11.7	11.2	11.2	10.3	8.5	7.1	6.9	9.4
Total 4 countries	2.8	3.0	3.4	3.1	3.1	4.4	5.0	5.3	5.4	5.3	5.7	7.3	8.4	9.4	9.5	9.5	9.6	9.4	8.8	8.1	7.7	8.2
Austria	1.1	1.0	1.0	0.9	1.1	1.5	1.5	1.4	1.7	1.7	1.5	2.1	3.1	3.7	3.8	3.6	3.1	3.8	3.6	3.1	3.3	3.6
Belgium	2.1	2.1	2.7	2.7	3.0	5.0	6.4	7.4	7.9	8.2	8.8	10.8	12.6	12.1	12.1	11.3	11.2	11.0	9.7	8.0	7.3	7.7
Denmark	1.3	1.6	1.6	2.0	2.3	5.3	5.3	6.4	7.3	6.2	7.0	9.2	9.8	10.4	10.1	9.0	7.8	7.8	8.5	9.2	9.5	10.4
Finland	1.9	2.2	2.5	2.3	1.7	2.2	3.8	5.8	7.2	5.9	4.6	4.8	5.3	5.4	5.2	5.0	5.3	5.0	4.5	3.4	3.4	7.5
Ireland	5.8	5.5	6.2	5.7	5.3	8.3	9.2	9.0	8.2	7.3	8.1	10.0	12.1	13.7	15.4	16.8	17.4	17.7	16.7	15.6	13.7	15.8
Netherlands	1.0	1.3	2.2	2.2	2.7	5.2	5.5	5.3	5.3	5.4	6.0	8.5	11.4	12.0	11.8	10.6	9.9	9.6	9.2	8.3	7.5	6.9
Norway	1.6	1.5	1.6	1.5	1.5	2.3	1.7	1.4	1.8	2.0	1.6	2.0	2.6	3.4	3.1	2.6	2.0	2.1	3.2	4.9	5.2	5.5
Sweden	1.2	2.1	2.2	2.0	1.6	1.3	1.3	1.4	1.8	1.7	2.0	2.1	2.6	2.9	2.6	2.4	2.2	1.9	1.6	1.4	1.5	2.7
Switzerland	-	-	-	-	-	0.3	0.7	0.4	0.3	0.4	0.2	0.2	0.4	0.9	1.1	1.0	0.8	0.8	0.7	0.6	0.6	1.3
Total 9 countries	1.4	1.7	2.0	1.8	2.0	3.3	3.7	4.1	4.4	4.2	4.3	5.6	6.8	7.2	7.2	6.7	6.3	6.3	6.0	5.5	5.3	6.0
Total western Europe	2.5	2.7	3.1	2.8	2.8	4.1	4.7	5.0	5.1	5.1	5.4	6.9	8.1	8.9	9.0	8.9	8.8	8.7	8.2	7.5	7.1	7.7
Greece	4.2	3.1	2.1	2.0	2.1	2.3	1.9	1.7	1.8	1.9	2.8	4.0	5.8	7.8	8.1	7.8	7.4	7.4	7.7	7.5	7.2	8.6
Portugal	2.2	2.1	2.1	2.2	1.8	3.5	5.8	7.1	7.9	8.2	8.0	7.7	7.5	7.9	8.4	8.5	8.5	7.0	5.7	5.0	4.6	4.1
Spain	0.9	1.2	3.1	2.5	2.6	3.6	4.5	5.1	6.8	8.4	11.1	13.8	15.6	17.0	19.7	21.1	20.8	20.1	19.1	16.9	15.9	16.1
Turkey	7.8	7.8	7.6	7.9	8.4	8.7	7.9	7.5	7.8	9.7	11.6	11.6	12.3	12.1	11.8	11.3	10.5	9.5	9.8	10.2	10.4	11.5
Total southern Europe	4.4	4.4	4.9	4.8	5.0	5.7	5.9	6.1	6.9	8.3	10.2	11.2	12.3	12.9	13.8	14.0	13.5	12.7	12.4	11.7	11.3	12.0
Total Europe	3.0	3.1	3.5	3.3	3.3	4.5	5.0	5.3	5.6	5.8	6.5	7.9	9.0	9.8	10.1	10.1	9.9	9.6	9.1	8.5	8.1	8.7
United States	4.8	5.8	5.5	4.8	5.5	8.3	7.6	6.9	6.0	5.8	7.0	7.5	9.5	9.5	7.4	7.1	6.9	6.1	5.4	5.2	5.4	6.6
Canada	5.6	6.1	6.2	5.5	5.3	6.9	7.1	8.0	8.3	7.4	7.4	7.5	10.9	11.8	11.2	10.4	9.5	8.8	7.7	7.5	8.1	10.2
North America	9.8	11.7	11.1	9.7	11.0	16.3	15.1	14.0	12.4	11.9	14.1	15.0	19.3	19.4	15.5	14.8	14.3	12.7	11.2	10.8	11.3	13.9
Total above	3.8	4.3	4.4	4.0	4.3	6.1	6.1	6.0	5.8	5.9	6.7	7.7	9.3	9.8	9.1	8.9	8.7	8.2	7.6	7.2	7.1	8.0
Addendum: Yugoslavia	4.0	3.7	4.0	4.8	5.5	6.5	7.5	8.1	8.4	8.6	8.7	8.9	9.4	9.7	10.3	10.7	11.1	10.9	11.2	11.8	12.8	15.6

Sources: OECD, *Quarterly Labour Force Statistics*, No.4, 1991; *Main Economic Indicators*, No.2, Paris, 1992; *Yugoslavia: ILO Yearbook of Labour Statistics*, OECD, *Survey of Yugoslavia*, (various issues); ECE secretariat estimates.

Notes: National data are aggregated from annual figures on the number of unemployed and total labour force, and the rates have been calculated as percentages of the total labour force. Comparisons with previous years are limited due to changes in methodology in Germany (1984), United Kingdom (1984), Italy (1983), Belgium (1983), Ireland (1983), Portugal (1983), Netherlands (1983 and 1988), Finland (1982), Norway (1980) and Sweden (1987).

[a] Adjusted for comparability between countries, except for Denmark, Switzerland, Greece, Turkey and Yugoslavia.

Appendix B. Eastern Europe and the Soviet Union

Data for this section were compiled from national and international[44] statistical sources, as indicated in the notes to individual tables. Volume figures underlying the data in tables B.1-B.2, B.8-B.9, B.11 and B.14 reflect data at constant prices of the following years: Bulgaria, 1982; Czechoslovakia, 1984; German Democratic Republic, 1985; Hungary, 1981; Poland, 1982; Romania, 1977; Soviet Union, 1973.

---

[44] CMEA, UN, IMF.

Appendix B. Eastern Europe and the Soviet Union

APPENDIX TABLE B.1
Net material product
(Annual percentage change)

	1970	1971	1972	1973	1974	1975	1976	1977	1978	1979	1980	1981	1982	1983	1984	1985	1986	1987	1988	1989	1990
Bulgaria	7.1	6.9	7.7	8.1	7.6	8.8	6.5	6.3	5.6	6.6	5.4	5.0	4.2	3.0	4.6	1.8	5.3	4.7	2.4	-0.3	-11.5
Czechoslovakia	5.7	5.5	5.7	5.2	5.9	6.2	4.1	4.2	4.1	3.1	2.9	-0.1	0.2	2.3	3.5	3.0	2.6	2.1	2.3	0.7	-1.1
German Dem. Rep.	5.6	4.4	5.7	5.6	6.5	4.9	3.5	5.1	3.7	4.0	4.4	4.8	2.6	4.6	5.5	5.2	4.3	3.3	2.8	2.1	-13.4
Hungary	4.9	5.9	6.2	7.0	5.9	6.1	3.0	7.1	4.0	1.2	-0.9	2.5	2.7	0.3	2.5	-1.4	0.9	4.1	-0.5	-1.1	-5.5*
Poland	5.2	8.1	10.6	10.8	10.5	9.0	6.8	5.0	3.0	-2.3	-6.0	-12.0	-5.5	6.0	5.6	3.4	4.9	1.9	4.9	-0.2	-14.9
Romania	6.8	13.4	9.8	10.8	12.3	9.8	11.3	8.7	7.2	6.5	4.2	-0.4	4.0	6.0	6.5	-1.1	3.0	0.8	-2.0	-8.0	-9.9
Eastern Europe	5.7	7.3	8.0	8.3	8.6	7.6	6.1	5.8	4.2	2.0	0.3	-2.3	0.3	4.3	5.1	2.3	3.7	2.4	2.1	-1.0	-10.5
Soviet Union	9.0	5.6	3.9	8.9	5.5	4.4	5.9	4.5	5.1	2.2	3.9	3.3	3.9	4.2	2.9	1.6	2.3	1.6	4.4	2.5	-4.0
Eastern Europe and the Soviet Union	8.0	6.1	5.1	8.7	6.5	5.4	5.9	4.9	4.9	2.1	2.8	1.6	2.8	4.2	3.5	1.8	2.7	1.8	3.7	1.5	-5.9

Sources: ECE secretariat Common Data Base, derived from national or CMEA statistics.

Note: National data are aggregated by means of 1981 weights based on CMEA investigations.

APPENDIX TABLE B.2

Net material product used for domestic consumption and accumulation
(Annual percentage change)

	1970	1971	1972	1973	1974	1975	1976	1977	1978	1979	1980	1981	1982	1983	1984	1985	1986	1987	1988	1989	1990
Bulgaria [a]																					
Total	3.7	1.6	9.8	9.0	11.8	11.1	0.3	5.2	0.2	3.5	5.1	7.6	1.9	1.2	5.2	1.2	8.4	0.4	3.7	2.0	-9.2
Consumption	5.6	7.4	6.3	6.6	7.1	7.7	6.0	4.0	3.6	3.0	3.6	5.3	3.7	2.9	4.9	1.8	3.6	4.6	2.2	2.9	-4.9
Accumulation	-0.6	-11.5	21.0	16.0	24.2	18.7	-11.5	8.9	-9.3	5.0	9.5	14.8	-3.3	-3.6	6.2	-0.8	23.8	-10.7	8.3	-0.6	-22.6
Czechoslovakia																					
Total	5.0	4.9	5.7	7.3	8.1	4.5	3.1	1.6	2.7	1.1	2.7	-3.4	-1.6	0.6	1.2	3.2	4.9	2.8	2.0	3.2	4.7
Consumption	1.9	6.6	5.2	5.8	6.1	3.0	3.3	3.7	3.7	0.9	1.0	2.6	-1.1	2.8	3.0	2.8	3.4	3.6	4.5	3.6	3.4
Accumulation	16.7	-0.6	7.7	12.2	14.3	9.2	2.5	-4.5	-0.5	1.8	8.2	-21.7	-3.6	-8.0	-6.6	5.4	12.2	-1.1	-10.2	0.9	12.0
German Dem. Rep.																					
Total [b]	8.4	3.4	5.8	6.3	6.5	2.6	6.3	5.1	0.8	1.1	5.1	1.1	-3.4	-	3.4	4.8	4.2	4.5	5.1	1.6	..
Consumption [c]	4.4	5.0	6.1	5.1	6.7	5.4	5.1	4.6	3.2	3.3	3.0	2.2	1.4	0.1	3.8	4.5	4.3	4.0	3.7	2.8	..
Accumulation [c]	17.3	-2.0	2.5	10.3	5.3	-1.9	9.5	6.2	-5.3	-5.0	11.3	-2.2	-17.6	-0.5	2.0	5.8	3.7	6.2	10.2	-2.7	..
Hungary																					
Total	11.8	11.3	-3.7	2.0	12.7	6.4	1.2	6.0	9.2	-5.8	-1.7	0.7	-1.1	-2.8	-0.6	-0.6	3.9	3.0	-4.3	-1.3	-7.5*
Consumption	8.4	5.4	3.1	3.7	6.9	4.7	2.1	5.0	4.3	3.3	0.3	2.9	1.4	0.5	0.9	1.2	2.0	3.1	-2.9	-0.5	..
Accumulation	22.0	30.4	-21.4	-3.8	34.2	11.5	-1.4	9.3	24.0	-29.0	-8.9	-8.3	-12.4	-20.4	-11.3	-15.0	21.4	2.7	-15.0	-8.5	..
Poland																					
Total	5.0	9.8	12.5	14.3	12.0	9.5	6.5	2.2	0.5	-3.7	-6.0	-10.5	-10.5	5.6	5.0	3.8	5.0	1.8	4.7	0.1	-19.8
Consumption	4.1	7.7	9.1	8.1	7.4	11.1	8.8	6.8	1.7	3.1	2.1	-4.6	-11.5	5.8	4.4	2.9	4.8	2.8	2.9	-1.7	-13.0
Accumulation	7.4	15.2	20.9	27.8	20.5	7.0	2.4	-6.5	-2.0	-19.2	-29.6	-27.6	-6.6	4.9	7.3	7.2	5.4	-2.4	12.8	7.1	-45.0
Romania																					
Total	..	..	..	..	..	..	12.3	6.8	9.6	5.5	0.8	-6.5	-1.5	2.2	2.8	4.8	4.3	-1.3	-2.6	-4.1	11.3
Consumption	..	..	..	..	..	..	8.8	7.8	9.4	6.3	3.4	3.0	-1.3	0.7	5.9	7.4	1.1	3.4	2.4	0.8	12.0
Accumulation	..	..	..	..	..	..	18.9	5.1	10.1	3.9	-3.7	-24.5	-2.0	6.0	-4.7	-0.2	11.5	-13.9	-18.6	-23.8	7.2
Eastern Europe																					
Total	6.5 [d]	6.7 [d]	7.3 [d]	9.2 [d]	10.0 [d]	6.8 [d]	6.0	3.9	3.2	-0.2	-0.3	-4.2	-4.2	1.9	3.2	3.5	4.9	1.9 [d]	2.2 [d]	0.2	..
Consumption	4.3	6.5	6.7	6.3	6.9	-2.3	6.4	5.7	3.8	3.3	2.3	0.4	-3.4	2.6	4.0	3.7	3.5	3.4	2.7	1.0	..
Accumulation	13.5	6.8	5.8	15.0	17.1	6.8	5.7	1.1	2.8	-7.8	-4.8	-15.7	-7.8	-1.3	-1.2	2.1	10.6	-4.3	-2.0	-4.9	..
Soviet Union																					
Total	11.2 [e]	5.1 [e]	3.5 [e]	7.7 [e]	4.1 [d]	4.2 [d]	5.0	3.5	4.5	2.0	3.9	3.2	3.5	3.6	2.0	1.8	1.6	0.7	4.6	3.4	-1.8
Consumption	7.5	5.8	5.8	5.1	4.8	5.5	4.3	4.0	4.6	4.5	6.0	4.0	1.2	3.2	..	..	1.2	2.3	4.2	5.4	..
Accumulation	21.3	3.4	-2.1	14.4	0.5	-1.4	6.6	3.3	5.2	-2.9	-0.6	0.9	11.0	5.0	..	..	3.2	-4.4	5.6	-3.1	..
Eastern Europe and the Soviet Union																					
Total	9.9 [d]	5.6 [d]	4.6 [d]	8.1 [d]	5.8 [d]	5.0 [d]	5.3	3.6	4.0	1.3	2.5	0.8	1.2	3.1	2.3	2.3	2.6	1.0 [d]	3.9 [d]	2.4	..
Consumption	6.6	6.0	6.1	5.5	5.4	-2.2	5.0	4.5	4.3	4.1	4.7	2.8	-0.3	3.0	..	..	1.9	2.7	3.7	4.0	..
Accumulation	19.5	4.2	-0.3	14.6	4.6	0.8	6.3	2.6	4.4	-4.5	-1.9	-4.3	5.9	3.5	..	..	5.0	-4.4	3.7	-3.5	..

Sources: ECE secretariat Common Data Base, derived from national or CMEA statistics.

Note: National data are aggregated by means of 1981 weights based on CMEA investigations.

[a] Calculated from absolute volume figures at 1962 prices.
[b] Calculated from rounded index numbers (1950 = 100).
[c] Calculated from rounded index numbers (1970 = 100).
[d] Excluding Romania.
[e] Nominal.

APPENDIX TABLE B.3

Monthly nominal wages [a]
(In national currencies)

	1970	1971	1972	1973	1974	1975	1976	1977	1978	1979	1980	1981	1982	1983	1984	1985	1986	1987	1988	1989	1990
Bulgaria [b]	124	127	131	139	142	146	148	151	157	165	182	192	197	199	207	214	225	234	252	274	361
Czechoslovakia	1937	2009	2091	2161	2232	2304	2369	2444	2517	2579	2637	2677	2738	2789	2837	2883	2927	2985	3054	3123	3239
German Dem. Rep. [c]	750	779	808	835	860	889	920	947	977	1006	1021	1046	1066	1080	1102	1130	1170	1233	1269	1300	...
Hungary [d]	2139	2239	2342	2512	2682	2881	3042	3288	3567	3785	4014	4267	4542	4761	5342	5866	6291	6808	8817	10018	12664
Poland [e]	2235	2358	2509	2798	3185	3913	4281	4596	4887	5327	6040	7689f	11631f	14475f	16838f	20005f	24095f	29184f	53090	206758	1029637
Romania [g]	1289	1308	1332	1389	1478	1595	1712	1818	2011	2108	2238	2340	2525	2601	2773	2827	2855	2872	2946	3063	3384
Soviet Union [b]	122	126	130	135	141	146	151	155	160	163	169	173	177	181	185	190	196	203	220	240	275

Source: National statistics.

[a] Gross remuneration of full-time workers and employees in the socialist sector (excluding cooperative farmers).
[b] Before deductions for taxation.
[c] In six sectors of the material sphere.
[d] State sector only; excluding bonuses and compensation for price rises. 1988-1990: gross wages.
[e] Excluding bonuses. [f] Including compensations for price rises.
[g] Total economy; net remuneration, including bonuses.

APPENDIX TABLE B.4

Money incomes of population and volume of retail trade [a]
(Annual percentage change)

	1970	1971	1972	1973	1974	1975	1976	1977	1978	1979	1980	1981	1982	1983	1984	1985	1986	1987	1988	1989	1990
Bulgaria																					
Money incomes (nominal)	..	7.6	2.4	14.2	3.8	11.2	4.7	1.4	4.3	7.6	15.1	6.2	5.5	5.1	3.1	11.1	-1.8	6.8	6.1	6.4	16.5
Retail trade turnover (real) [b]	7.8	6.6	6.5	8.8	9.1	7.9	7.2	3.1	3.1	2.4	2.9	4.6	4.6	2.4	2.8	3.2	4.3	1.4	0.8	3.7	-8.8
Czechoslovakia																					
Money incomes (nominal)	4.6	5.5	6.0	6.4	4.6	3.7	4.9	4.5	3.5	3.6	4.0	2.6	4.3	3.1	2.6	3.2	3.2	3.3	4.3	3.2	6.6
Retail trade turnover (real)	1.3	5.5	5.2	5.9	6.8	2.6	2.7	2.2	3.7	-0.3	-0.7	1.4	-1.7	2.2	2.1	2.3	1.9	2.8	4.9	1.9	1.1
German Dem. Rep.																					
Money incomes (nominal)	3.1	3.4	6.2	6.3	5.1	3.8	3.7	5.5	3.6	3.0	2.5	3.1	2.8	2.3	3.9	4.0	5.6	4.7	3.9	3.0	..
Retail trade turnover (real) [c]	4.2	3.5	6.6	6.6	6.5	3.5	4.6	4.6	3.4	3.2	4.0	2.3	1.0	0.7	4.2	4.0	4.1	3.6	3.9	1.4	..
Hungary																					
Money incomes (nominal)	10.2	7.8	7.2	9.6	10.1	9.7	6.1	9.8	7.9	8.6	9.2	8.1	7.3	8.5	9.2	9.2	8.1	8.4	12.9	20.0	25.6
Retail trade turnover (real)	12.3	7.4	3.2	5.8	9.7	5.2	1.4	6.2	3.9	1.8	0.1	3.5	1.2	0.3	0.2	2.0	4.5	5.9	-5.3	-0.3	-7.6
Poland																					
Money incomes (nominal)	..	10.4	13.6	14.2	14.8	13.5	12.1	12.3	8.9	9.9	12.1	31.1	64.9	23.0	18.3	23.3	19.2	26.0	83.9	280.4	445.2
Retail trade turnover (real)	3.7	9.3	13.1	8.9	8.8	11.8	8.6	8.4	0.2	1.6	-0.4	-4.4	-15.0	7.3	5.0	3.1	6.2	4.3	5.3	-6.7	-12.7
Romania																					
Money incomes (nominal)	..	8.9	6.1	7.1	9.4	8.4	5.6	6.2	10.1	5.0	4.5	2.8	-3.8	-1.9	3.8	..	3.2	0.1	3.9	3.9	27.4
Retail trade turnover (real)	8.9	8.9	6.1	7.1	9.4	8.4	5.6	6.2	10.1	5.0	4.5	2.8	-3.8	-1.9	3.8	1.4	2.0	2.3	-1.2	0.7	14.7
Soviet Union																					
Money incomes (nominal)	7.6	7.0	6.8	5.6	7.4	7.4	4.9	5.0	5.1	4.6	5.2	4.3	4.2	4.8	3.8	3.7	3.5	3.9	9.2	13.1	16.9
Retail trade turnover (real) [b]	7.5	6.7	6.5	5.2	5.9	7.0	4.6	4.8	3.9	3.8	5.8	4.3	-0.1	2.8	4.7	1.8	0.4	1.8	6.3	8.3	10.6

Sources: National statistics and ECE secretariat estimates.

[a] Calculated from sales turnover figures (including public catering) by means of deflation with official retail price indices.
[b] State and cooperative sector only.
[c] Excluding sales in canteens of enterprises and institutions.

APPENDIX TABLE B.5

Real wages and per capita real incomes
(Annual percentage change)

	1970	1971	1972	1973	1974	1975	1976	1977	1978	1979	1980	1981	1982	1983	1984	1985	1986	1987	1988	1989	1990
Bulgaria																					
Real wages	6.1	2.2	3.5	6.1	1.5	2.8	0.9	1.8	2.3	0.4	-3.2	4.8	2.5	-0.1	3.2	1.4	2.4	1.5	5.0	2.5	6.9
Real incomes	4.9	4.3	7.0	8.7	3.3	5.3	4.5	0.7	1.2	2.8	3.5	5.8	4.2	2.6	3.0	2.9	2.8	4.0	3.4	-4.8	..
Czechoslovakia																					
Real wages	1.3	4.1	4.5	3.2	2.9	2.6	1.9	1.8	1.4	-0.5	-1.1	0.6	-2.3	0.7	0.8	0.3	1.1	1.9	2.8	0.1	-5.6
Real incomes	..	6.2	6.8	5.1	3.2	2.6	3.9	2.1	0.5	-0.3	0.1	1.6	0.2	1.5	2.5	2.3	2.6	3.6	4.0	2.4	-2.6 [a]
German Dem. Rep.																					
Real wages	4.7	3.6	4.2	3.9	3.4	3.4	3.5	3.0	3.3	2.7	1.1	2.2	1.9	1.3	2.0	-4.1	3.7	4.9	0.7	0.2	..
Real incomes	..	..	..	..	..	..	..	..	..	..	..	..	..	..	..	..	..	..	..	..	..
Hungary																					
Real wages	4.9	2.6	1.7	3.8	4.8	3.5	0.6	4.0	3.7	-2.5	-2.8	1.7	-0.4	-2.3	3.6	2.6	1.9	-0.4 ‖	12.1 [b]	-4.3	-1.9
Real incomes	7.0	4.2	3.4	4.6	6.2	4.3	0.9	4.8	2.9	-0.1	0.4	2.9	0.9	1.1	1.0	1.9	2.4	0.7	-1.3	2.4	1.6
Poland																					
Real wages	1.6	5.7	6.4	8.7	6.6	19.3	4.5	2.4	-2.2	2.2	3.9	2.4	-24.9	1.2	0.5	3.8	2.7	-3.5	14.4	8.3	-24.4
Real incomes	4.0	8.7	11.8	9.7	5.0	9.0	5.6	6.2	-0.5	2.5	0.8	3.3	-18.0	0.3	1.8	6.0	1.7	0.8	13.2	6.2	-14.9
Romania																					
Real wages	7.5	0.9	1.6	3.2	4.6	8.3	6.8	5.6	8.4	2.9	4.6	2.4	-7.8	-2.1	5.4	2.4	-1.2	-0.5	-0.2	3.2	6.0
Real incomes	3.4	11.8	5.8	4.8	6.1	5.8	8.5	3.5	8.0	2.9	2.8	1.5	-4.8	-2.4	4.3	2.0	3.0	-2.4	9.0	2.3	6.3
Soviet Union																					
Real wages	4.4	3.2	3.4	3.6	4.6	3.3	3.8	2.5	2.3	0.7	2.7	0.7	-0.6	1.1	3.8	2.1	0.9	2.7	7.3	7.3	9.1
Real incomes [c]	5.6	4.5	3.8	5.1	4.0	4.4	3.7	3.5	3.0	2.9	3.7	3.3	0.1	2.0	2.7	1.1	0.1	0.9	3.2	4.6	..

Sources: Appendix tables B.3 and B.6 (real wages); national statistics (per capita real incomes).

Note: Substantial discontinuities in the value series are indicated by ‖.

[a] Real money incomes.
[b] Not comparable with previous years, due to changes in personal incomes taxation.
[c] Material consumption of the population.

APPENDIX TABLE B.6
Consumer prices
(Annual percentage change)

	1970	1971	1972	1973	1974	1975	1976	1977	1978	1979	1980	1981	1982	1983	1984	1985	1986	1987	1988	1989	1990
Bulgaria [a]	-0.4	-0.1	-	0.2	0.5	0.3	0.3	0.4	1.5	4.5	14.0	0.4	0.3	1.4	0.7	1.7	2.7	2.7	2.4	6.2	19.3
Czechoslovakia [b]	1.7	-0.4	-0.4	0.2	0.4	0.6	0.9	1.4	1.5	3.0	3.4	0.9	4.7	1.1	0.9	1.3	0.4	0.1	-0.4	2.2	9.9
German Dem. Rep. [c]	-0.1	0.4	-0.5	-0.6	-0.4	-	-	-0.1	-0.1	0.3	0.4	0.2	-	-	-	6.9	-0.2	0.5	2.2	2.3	..
Hungary	1.3	2.0	2.8	3.3	1.8	3.8	5.0	3.9	4.6	8.9	9.1	4.6	6.9	7.3	8.3	7.0	5.3	8.6	15.5	18.8	28.9
Poland [d]	1.2	-0.2	-	2.6	6.8	3.0	4.7	4.9	8.7	6.7	9.1	24.4	101.5	23.0	15.8	14.4	17.3	25.5	59.0	259.5	558.4
Romania [a]	0.1	0.6	-	0.7	1.1	0.2	0.6	0.6	1.6	2.0	3.0	1.9	16.9	5.3	1.1	0.4	0.3	0.4	1.7	0.9	5.7
Soviet Union [a,e]								-	0.7	1.4	0.7	1.4	3.4	0.7	-1.3	0.8	2.0	1.0	1.0	1.9	4.7

Sources: National statistics; IMF, *International Financial Statistics* (various years) for Romania.

[a] Retail prices in the state sector.
[b] Cost-of-living index for workers and employees.
[c] Including fees and charges of various kinds (1985 weights).
[d] Cost-of-living index for workers and employees in the socialist sector.
[e] Including public catering; based on rounded index numbers; 1970-1987: approved "list price" changes only.

APPENDIX TABLE B.7
Dwellings constructed
(Thousands)

	1970	1971	1972	1973	1974	1975	1976	1977	1978	1979	1980	1981	1982	1983	1984	1985	1986	1987	1988	1989	1990
Bulgaria	45.7	48.9	46.5	54.2	44.1	57.2	67.6	75.9	67.8	66.2	74.3	71.4	68.2	69.7	68.9	64.9	56.0	63.6	62.8	40.5	26.2
Czechoslovakia	112.1	107.4	115.6	118.6	129.0	144.7	132.5	134.8	129.3	122.7	128.9	95.4	101.8	95.7	91.9	104.5	78.7	79.6	82.9	88.5	69.3
German Dem. Rep.	65.8	65.0	69.6	80.7	88.3	95.1	99.6	103.3	104.6	101.2	102.2	110.9	110.8	107.3	103.7	99.1	101.0	91.9	93.5	83.4	57.0*
Hungary	80.3	75.3	90.2	85.2	87.8	99.6	93.9	93.4	88.2	88.2	89.1	77.0	75.6	74.2	70.4	72.5	69.4	57.2	50.6	51.5	43.8
Poland	194.2	190.6	205.5	227.1	249.8	248.1	263.5	266.1	283.6	278.0	217.1	187.0	186.1	195.8	195.9	189.6	185.0	191.4	189.6	150.2	134.2
Romania	159.2	147.0	136.0	149.1	154.3	165.4	139.4	145.0	166.8	191.6	197.8	161.4	161.2	146.6	131.9	105.6	108.1	110.4	103.3	60.4	48.6
Eastern Europe	657.2	634.2	663.3	715.0	753.4	810.9	796.5	818.5	840.3	847.9	809.4	703.1	703.7	689.3	662.7	636.3	597.3	594.2	582.6	474.5	379.0
Soviet Union	2266.0	2256.0	2233.0	2276.0	2231.0	2228.0	2113.0	2111.0	2080.0	1932.0	2004.0	1997.0	2002.0	2030.0	2008.0	1991.0	2100.0	2264.0	2230.0	2120.0	1891.0
Eastern Europe and the Soviet Union	2923.2	2890.2	2896.3	2991.0	2984.4	3038.1	2909.5	2929.5	2920.3	2779.9	2813.4	2700.1	2705.7	2719.3	2670.7	2627.3	2696.3	2858.2	2812.6	2594.5	2270.0

Sources: National statistics.

Appendix B. Eastern Europe and the Soviet Union

APPENDIX TABLE B.8

Total gross investment
(Annual percentage change)

	1970	1971	1972	1973	1974	1975	1976	1977	1978	1979	1980	1981	1982	1983	1984	1985	1986	1987	1988	1989	1990
Bulgaria [a]																					
Total	10.6	1.7	10.0	6.9	7.8	17.3	0.6	14.2	0.6	-2.2	10.8	5.5	3.7	-	1.7	6.2	13.7	0.3	4.5	-10.1	-12.0
Material sphere	7.0	0.4	8.7	6.7	7.8	19.8	-1.3	16.0	0.4	-1.6	5.4	12.2	2.8	-0.9	2.0	10.6	5.6	11.3	3.3	4.1	..
Non-material sphere	24.0	6.7	13.2	7.2	7.8	10.2	6.6	8.9	1.3	-4.0	14.3	5.3	6.1	5.3	-3.7	3.8	13.6	-2.5	-1.4	-5.2	..
Czechoslovakia																					
Total	5.8	5.7	8.9	9.0	9.1	8.3	4.4	5.7	4.1	1.8	1.4	-4.6	-2.3	0.6	-4.2	5.4	1.4	4.4	4.1	1.6	7.7
Material sphere	-	4.9	6.2	14.4	9.0	7.7	5.8	6.7	4.8	3.8	2.5	-2.1	-2.1	0.6	-3.9	6.0	2.2	5.7	4.2	0.4	..
Non-material sphere	20.0	7.0	13.2	0.9	9.2	9.2	2.1	3.9	2.9	-2.0	-0.5	-9.5	-2.6	0.4	-5.0	4.1	-0.2	1.5	3.8	4.4	..
German Democratic Republic																					
Total	6.8	1.7	5.0	8.4	5.4	4.6	7.3	5.3	2.8	1.2	0.1	2.4	-5.1	-0.3	-4.9	3.4	5.3	8.0	7.3	0.9	-5.7
Material sphere	9.0	0.5	3.6	8.1	4.7	4.4	7.8	4.4	1.7	1.3	0.7	1.9	-5.1	0.1	-5.8	3.3	6.9	9.3	8.4	1.6	..
Non-material sphere	-1.0	6.8	11.1	9.6	8.1	5.4	5.5	8.8	6.8	0.9	-1.8	4.3	-5.1	-1.8	-1.7	3.5	0.1	3.3	2.9	-2.0	..
Hungary																					
Total	16.9	10.6	-1.1	3.2	10.9	11.5	-	12.2	4.8	0.8	-5.5	-4.7	-1.6	-3.4	-3.7	-3.0	6.5	9.8	-9.1	5.1	-8.7
Material sphere	15.0	8.6	-3.6	1.6	9.0	15.3	1.1	14.1	6.4	-	-7.8	-5.1	-2.6	-5.4	-4.9	-2.4	0.6	10.2	-7.6	5.8	..
Non-material sphere	29.0	16.4	6.9	10.1	8.6	8.0	-2.1	9.1	0.9	3.9	-0.3	-5.4	-1.1	2.7	1.5	-2.3	5.8	2.2	-8.0	2.1	..
Poland																					
Total	4.0	7.4	23.0	25.4	22.3	10.7	1.0	3.1	2.1	-7.9	-12.3	-22.3	-12.1	9.4	11.4	6.0	5.1	4.2	5.4	-2.4	-10.1
Material sphere	3.0	9.6	26.0	26.5	23.3	16.1	0.2	1.6	-0.1	-11.2	-12.8	-23.5	-15.3	8.2	13.8	6.7	5.8	4.2	5.6	-1.8	..
Non-material sphere	8.0	1.4	16.0	19.9	19.8	7.4	4.1	8.6	9.7	2.3	-11.0	-19.9	-5.7	11.4	7.2	4.6	3.7	4.3	5.1	-3.6	..
Romania																					
Total	11.6	10.5	10.4	8.2	13.4	15.1	8.5	11.7	16.0	4.1	3.0	-7.1	-3.1	2.4	6.0	1.6	1.1	-1.4	-2.2	-1.5	-38.3
Material sphere	10.0	12.2	10.4	8.2	12.0	13.8	9.3	13.4	17.0	3.9	3.4	-6.6	-3.2	4.8	7.5	1.7	0.3	-4.0	-2.1	-5.1	..
Non-material sphere	20.0	2.1	9.3	8.1	19.3	21.2	5.2	4.4	11.0	5.2	1.1	-9.4	-2.6	-8.6	-2.3	1.4	5.9	12.9	-2.4	14.8	..
Eastern Europe																					
Total	8.0	6.4	11.1	12.5	13.4	10.8	3.9	7.3	5.7	-1.0	-1.9	-7.6	-4.4	2.2	2.4	3.6	4.5	3.2	2.4	-1.8	-13.6
Material sphere	7.0	6.5	10.4	13.3	13.0	12.6	4.0	7.5	5.4	-1.6	-2.0	-6.6	-4.9	2.4	2.9	4.4	3.3	4.1	2.6	-0.4	..
Non-material sphere	13.0	5.1	12.4	10.7	14.1	10.2	4.0	7.1	7.1	1.7	-2.8	-8.9	-2.9	1.7	0.4	3.1	4.3	4.4	1.3	1.6	..
Soviet Union [b]																					
Total	11.4	7.2	7.0	4.6	7.0	8.6	4.3	3.5	5.8	0.7	2.2	3.7	3.5	5.6	1.9	3.0	8.3	5.7	6.2	4.7	0.6
Material sphere	13.0	8.5	8.6	6.5	7.8	9.3	5.0	3.5	7.1	0.7	2.5	3.5	3.3	5.3	1.3	2.6	7.5	4.0	6.2	4.6	..
Non-material sphere	8.0	4.4	3.7	0.1	5.4	6.7	3.0	4.1	3.1	1.0	1.8	4.6	4.6	6.9	3.6	4.0	10.6	9.5	6.3	4.8	..
Eastern Europe and the Soviet Union																					
Total	10.4	6.9	8.2	6.9	8.9	9.3	4.2	4.7	5.7	0.1	0.9	0.1	1.2	4.7	2.1	3.2	7.3	5.0	5.2	3.2	-2.8
Material sphere	11.0	7.9	9.1	8.5	9.4	10.3	4.7	4.8	6.5	-0.1	1.0	0.4	0.9	4.5	1.7	3.1	6.4	4.0	5.3	3.3	..
Non-material sphere	10.0	4.6	5.9	3.1	8.0	7.8	3.3	5.1	4.5	1.2	0.2	0.1	2.4	5.4	2.7	3.8	8.9	8.2	5.0	4.1	..

Sources: ECE secretariat Common Data Base, derived from national or CMEA statistics; *Statisticheskii ezhegodnik stran-chlenov SEV 1972* (CMEA statistical yearbook 1972), p.137; and plan fulfilment reports.

Note: National data are aggregated by means of 1975 weights based on CMEA investigations.

[a] At current prices in 1984-1990.
[b] Calculated from absolute volume figures at 1984 prices.

APPENDIX TABLE B.9

Total gross fixed assets [a]
(Annual percentage change)

	1970	1971	1972	1973	1974	1975	1976	1977	1978	1979	1980	1981	1982	1983	1984	1985	1986	1987	1988	1989
Bulgaria [b]																				
Total	8.6	7.3	7.6	7.4	8.7	8.6	7.8	20.8	7.2	6.9	7.1	5.4	7.9	7.4	5.4	6.4	5.4	7.4	5.6	4.6
Material sphere	10.5	8.3	8.2	7.8	11.0	9.4	7.6	8.5	7.6	7.3	8.2	7.3	8.3	7.2	5.2	6.2	5.2	7.8	5.5	5.6
Non-material sphere	5.8	5.5	6.5	6.6	4.1	6.9	8.0	8.1	6.3	6.0	5.8	7.4	6.9	8.0	5.9	6.9	5.9	6.5	4.9	3.6
Czechoslovakia																				
Total	5.2	4.9	4.9	5.5	5.6	6.1	6.2	5.4	5.6	5.3	5.4	5.6	4.7	4.5	4.7	4.7	4.4	3.7	3.8	3.4
Material sphere	4.7	5.4	5.2	6.0	5.8	6.6	6.7	6.1	6.1	6.0	5.9	6.5	5.0	4.7	5.2	5.5	4.7	4.2	4.3	4.0
Non-material sphere	3.9	4.4	4.5	4.9	5.5	5.5	5.5	4.4	5.1	4.5	4.6	4.4	4.3	4.1	4.1	3.6	4.0	3.0	3.3	3.4
German Democratic Republic [c]																				
Total	4.7	5.1	4.8	5.2	5.4	6.5	5.3	4.9	4.9	4.7	5.0	4.5	4.8	4.6	4.1	4.3	4.0	3.5	3.6	3.6
Material sphere	5.6	5.8	5.2	5.5	5.5	6.8	5.2	4.9	5.0	4.8	5.3	4.5	4.8	4.3	3.9	4.4	4.2	3.8	4.0	4.1
Non-material sphere	1.7	3.5	3.8	4.6	5.1	5.7	5.6	4.7	4.7	4.3	4.2	4.6	4.8	5.2	4.4	3.9	3.4	2.7	2.8	2.5
Hungary																				
Total	5.9	5.8	6.0	5.7	5.5	6.6	6.0	5.3	5.5	5.5	5.1	3.8	4.3	4.3	3.2	3.3	3.8	3.3	3.4	..
Material sphere	5.0	6.9	6.7	6.6	6.1	7.3	6.4	5.6	6.0	5.9	5.1	3.8	4.2	4.3	2.7	3.0	3.7	3.1	3.0	..
Non-material sphere	3.7	4.0	4.8	4.2	4.7	5.3	7.1	4.7	4.6	4.9	5.2	3.9	4.4	4.4	3.6	4.0	4.0	3.6	4.1	..
Poland																				
Total	5.0	2.9	5.2	5.8	7.8	7.6	7.3	7.5	6.7	6.2	4.4	3.3	1.9	2.5	2.4	2.7	2.5	3.8	2.5	3.7
Material sphere	6.9	4.5	7.2	7.9	10.6	9.7	9.8	9.8	8.6	6.4	5.1	3.5	1.8	2.6	2.8	3.0	2.1	3.2	2.6	2.8
Non-material sphere	3.1	0.9	2.5	2.9	3.6	4.3	3.5	4.2	4.2	4.4	3.1	3.1	2.1	2.4	2.0	2.3	1.6	4.7	2.4	4.8
Romania [b]																				
Total	9.1	9.2	8.2	8.8	10.4	11.7	10.1	9.7	8.7	8.7	8.5	8.3	8.6	8.5	9.0	7.0	7.0	6.4	..	..
Material sphere	10.9	12.0	9.8	10.6	12.5	14.4	12.0	10.7	10.1	9.2	9.2	8.8	9.4	9.1	10.1	7.7	7.7	7.0	6.0	5.3
Non-material sphere	5.2	4.0	4.8	4.6	5.3	5.8	5.5	6.7	5.6	6.6	6.2	6.4	6.6	6.2	6.3	4.7	4.8	4.2	3.9	3.9
Soviet Union																				
Total	8.2	7.9	8.1	8.0	7.8	7.6	7.1	6.8	7.0	6.5	6.4	6.3	6.3	6.2	5.8	5.5	5.2	4.9	4.7	5.2
Material sphere	8.8	8.7	8.0	8.3	9.8	8.6	7.8	7.4	7.7	7.0	7.1	6.9	6.8	6.6	6.1	5.6	5.2	4.8	4.5	4.1
Non-material sphere	6.7	7.9	7.0	7.1	4.2	6.4	5.8	5.9	5.5	5.6	5.2	5.1	5.3	5.5	5.2	5.1	5.5	5.1	5.2	5.1

Sources: ECE secretariat Common Data Base, derived from national and CMEA statistics.

[a] On replacement values in constant prices; end-year basis.
[b] On prices at time of installation.
[c] On an annual averages basis.

Appendix B. Eastern Europe and the Soviet Union

APPENDIX TABLE B.10
Employment [a]
(Annual percentage change)

	1970	1971	1972	1973	1974	1975	1976	1977	1978	1979	1980	1981	1982	1983	1984	1985	1986	1987	1988	1989	1990
Bulgaria																					
Total*	0.9	0.9	1.3	-	1.0	0.4	0.2	-0.6	0.2	0.9	0.7	1.3	0.7	0.1	-	0.1	0.3	0.3	-0.4	-2.3	..
Material sphere	0.3	0.9	0.7	-0.7	0.4	-0.5	-0.5	-0.6	0.1	0.8	0.1	1.2	0.6	0.1	-0.5	-0.2	0.1	0.1	-0.9	-3.0	..
Non-material sphere	5.4	0.9	5.1	4.3	4.5	5.3	3.8	-0.4	1.1	1.4	3.3	2.1	1.3	0.1	2.3	1.3	1.1	1.1	1.6	0.8	..
Czechoslovakia																					
Total	1.1	0.3	0.1	0.5	1.0	0.8	0.5	0.8	0.9	1.0	1.0	0.7	0.4	0.4	0.9	1.0	1.3	1.5	0.6	0.3	-0.4 [b]
Material sphere	1.1	0.4	-0.4	0.4	0.7	0.4	-	0.3	0.6	0.6	0.4	0.3	0.1	0.4	0.6	0.5	1.0	1.5	0.1	-0.2	-1.4
Non-material sphere	1.0	-	1.9	1.0	2.2	1.9	2.0	2.4	2.1	2.4	3.1	1.7	1.3	0.5	1.7	2.3	2.1	1.7	2.2	2.0	2.6
German Dem. Rep. [c,d,e]																					
Total	0.2	0.5	0.1	0.5	0.6	0.5	1.0	0.8	0.8	0.7	0.4	0.5	0.6	0.7	0.5	0.2	-	0.2	0.3	-1.0	..
Material sphere	-0.1	0.1	-0.3	0.1	0.3	0.3	0.8	0.6	0.6	0.4	0.2	0.2	0.2	0.4	0.3	0.1	-0.2	-0.1	0.2	-1.3	..
Non-material sphere	1.7	2.6	1.6	2.4	1.8	1.6	1.8	1.7	1.7	2.1	1.2	1.7	2.0	1.9	1.3	0.9	0.8	1.2	0.7	-0.1	..
Hungary [c,f]																					
Total	1.2	0.6	0.5	0.3	0.2	0.2	-	-0.2	-	-	-0.7	-0.7	-0.4	-0.6	-0.6	-0.5	-0.3	-0.5	-0.6	..	..
Material sphere	1.1	0.3	0.2	-0.1	-0.3	-0.3	-0.6	-0.7	-0.3	-0.5	-1.2	-1.1	-0.8	-0.4	-0.5	-1.2	-1.3	1.3	-1.6	..	..
Non-material sphere	2.3	2.3	2.4	2.7	3.0	2.9	2.8	1.8	1.4	2.5	1.9	1.1	0.9	-1.4	-0.1	2.7	4.0	2.8	2.8	..	..
Poland																					
Total	1.2	2.0	2.6	2.3	2.0	1.7	0.3	1.3	0.4	0.8	0.3	0.8	-2.9	-0.3	0.3	1.0	0.6	0.2	-0.6	-0.9	-7.8
Material sphere	2.0	1.4	2.3	1.9	1.7	1.9	-	1.2	0.1	0.5	-0.1	0.2	-3.1	-0.8	-0.3	0.5	0.3	-	-1.1	..	..
Non-material sphere	-3.1	5.7	4.5	4.5	3.4	0.4	1.9	2.0	2.0	2.5	2.3	4.0	-2.1	2.4	3.0	3.0	1.7	1.1	1.4	..	..
Romania																					
Total	-0.4	0.3	-	-0.1	0.4	0.8	0.4	0.2	0.6	0.4	0.1	-0.3	0.7	0.6	0.1	0.7	0.8	0.6	0.4	1.6	0.8
Material sphere	-0.4	-0.1	-0.4	-0.2	-	0.4	-0.2	0.2	0.3	-0.2	0.3	-0.6	0.5	0.7	-	0.5	-0.2	0.4	0.5	1.2	1.5
Non-material sphere	-0.9	2.9	3.0	0.1	3.1	3.6	5.0	0.7	2.5	3.8	-1.3	2.0	1.7	-0.2	0.8	1.6	7.2	1.5	-0.5	3.7	-3.2
EE6																					
Total	0.7	1.0	1.0	0.9	1.1	1.0	0.4	0.6	0.5	0.7	0.3	0.5	-0.7	0.1	0.3	0.6	0.5	0.4	-0.1	..	..
Material sphere	0.8	0.6	0.6	0.6	0.7	0.8	-	0.5	0.2	0.3	-	-	-0.9	-0.1	-0.1	0.2	-	0.2	-0.4	..	..
Non-material sphere	-	2.9	3.1	2.7	2.9	2.0	2.6	1.6	1.9	2.5	1.8	2.5	0.3	1.0	1.7	2.1	2.6	1.5	1.3	..	..
Soviet Union [g]																					
Total	1.7	2.0	2.0	1.9	1.9	1.6	1.4	1.5	1.6	1.3	1.2	0.9	0.9	0.6	0.6	0.6	0.5	-0.2	-1.6	-1.5	-2.0
Material sphere	1.3	1.6	1.5	1.5	1.6	1.2	1.5	1.2	1.3	0.8	0.8	0.7	0.7	0.5	0.4	0.3	0.5	-0.3	-2.7	-2.2	-2.8
Non-material sphere	3.4	3.5	3.5	3.4	3.0	3.0	1.1	2.5	2.7	2.9	2.6	1.8	1.3	1.1	1.3	1.5	0.5	0.2	2.0	0.8	0.4
Eastern Europe and the Soviet Union																					
Total	1.4	1.7	1.7	1.6	1.6	1.4	1.1	1.2	1.3	1.1	0.9	0.8	0.4	0.5	0.5	0.6	0.5	-	-1.1	..	..
Material sphere	1.1	1.3	1.2	1.2	1.3	1.1	1.0	1.0	0.9	0.6	0.6	0.5	0.2	0.3	0.2	0.3	0.3	-0.2	-2.0	..	..
Non-material sphere	2.5	3.4	3.4	3.2	3.0	2.7	1.5	2.3	2.5	2.8	2.4	2.0	1.0	1.1	1.4	1.7	1.0	0.5	1.8	..	..

Sources: ECE secretariat Common Data Base, derived from national statistics.

[a] Annual averages.
[b] State and cooperative sector only.
[c] Economically active population.
[d] 30 September of each year.
[e] Including apprentices.
[f] Mid-year estimates.
[g] 1970-1990: Workers and *kolkhoz* members engaged in the collective sector.

APPENDIX TABLE B.11

Gross industrial production
(Annual percentage change)

	1970	1971	1972	1973	1974	1975	1976	1977	1978	1979	1980	1981	1982	1983	1984	1985	1986	1987	1988	1989	1990
Bulgaria [a]	9.6	9.1	9.1	9.0	8.1	9.6	6.8	6.8	6.9	5.4	4.2	5.4	4.6	4.3	4.2	3.2	4.7	6.0	3.2	-0.3	-12.6
Czechoslovakia	8.5	6.9	6.6	6.8	6.2	7.0	5.5	5.6	5.0	3.7	3.5	2.1	1.1	2.8	3.9	3.5	3.2	2.5	2.1	0.8	-3.5
German Dem. Rep.	6.6	5.8	6.0	6.8	7.2	6.4	5.9	4.8	4.8	4.7	4.6	4.7	3.2	4.2	4.2	4.4	3.7	3.1	3.2	2.3	-28.1
Hungary	7.9	6.7	5.2	7.0	8.4	4.7	4.5	5.7	5.4	3.1	-1.7	2.4	2.5	1.2	3.2	0.7	1.9	3.5	-0.3	-2.5	-4.5*
Poland	8.1	7.9	10.7	11.2	11.4	10.9	9.3	6.9	4.9	2.7	-	-10.8	-2.1	6.4	5.2	4.5	4.7	3.4	5.3	-0.5	-24.2
Romania	12.1	12.0	11.6	14.4	14.7	12.2	11.4	12.2	9.1	8.0	6.6	2.8	1.0	4.7	6.7	3.9	7.3	2.4	3.1	-2.1	-19.0
Eastern Europe	8.4	7.7	8.3	9.3	9.5	8.8	7.7	7.0	5.8	4.5	3.1	-0.5	1.1	4.4	4.9	3.9	4.6	3.2	3.3	-0.1	-18.9
Soviet Union [b]	8.5	7.7	6.5	7.5	8.0	7.6	4.8	5.7	4.8	3.4	3.6	3.4	2.9	4.2	4.1	3.4	4.4	3.8	3.9	1.7	-1.2
Eastern Europe and the Soviet Union	8.5	7.7	7.0	8.0	8.4	7.9	5.6	6.1	5.1	3.7	3.4	2.3	2.4	4.3	4.3	3.5	4.5	3.6	3.7	-1.2	-6.2

Sources: ECE secretariat Common Data Base, derived from national or CMEA statistics.

Note: National data are aggregated by means of 1965 weights based on CMEA investigations.

[a] Based on rounded index numbers (1956 = 100).
[b] Based on rounded index numbers (1940 = 100).

Appendix B. Eastern Europe and the Soviet Union

APPENDIX TABLE B.12
Industry: Gross investments, gross fixed assets and employment [a]
(Annual percentage change)

	1970	1971	1972	1973	1974	1975	1976	1977	1978	1979	1980	1981	1982	1983	1984	1985	1986	1987	1988	1989
Bulgaria																				
Investment [a]	5.0	-0.9	2.7	7.8	1.1	18.5	1.7	17.8	1.2	-0.2	9.0	10.6	10.1	-2.8	4.3	12.2	11.7	8.6	4.0	1.2
Gross fixed assets	..	6.8	9.3	9.2	12.9	8.9	6.7	9.7	8.6	8.2	10.2	8.1	9.8	7.5	5.7	7.1	6.1	10.4	6.5	5.7
Employment	1.1	3.8	2.6	1.8	2.9	2.3	1.3	0.6	1.4	1.8	1.5	2.8	2.4	1.4	0.8	0.5	1.2	1.5	-0.5	-3.1
Czechoslovakia																				
Investment	5.0	4.7	3.2	15.5	7.8	5.0	8.4	7.3	3.2	6.6	3.6	-1.4	-4.4	-3.0	-4.8	6.5	1.6	10.1	6.7	1.4
Gross fixed assets	..	5.3	5.0	5.7	5.7	6.3	6.9	6.2	5.6	5.9	5.9	6.7	5.2	4.6	5.2	5.8	4.8	4.3	4.3	3.9
Employment	1.2	0.2	0.8	0.9	0.4	0.7	0.1	0.5	0.8	0.6	-0.2	0.6	0.5	0.7	0.4	0.7	1.4	2.2	0.3	-0.5
German Democratic Republic																				
Investment	13.0	3.6	7.6	10.1	-1.0	1.3	8.3	6.5	5.5	3.2	4.0	2.7	-1.4	3.6	-7.4	2.4	5.5	12.8	8.3	1.2
Gross fixed assets	..	5.8	5.6	5.9	6.2	8.0	5.1	4.8	5.1	4.7	5.6	4.6	5.4	4.8	4.3	5.2	4.9	4.1	4.4	4.4
Employment	0.1	0.4	0.7	0.8	0.1	-	0.9	0.7	0.7	0.6	0.1	0.5	0.3	0.3	0.4	0.2	-0.5	-0.3	0.1	-1.4
Hungary																				
Investment	9.0	11.3	0.7	-0.3	9.3	10.7	8.0	23.3	3.3	-1.8	-11.5	-8.1	0.3	-2.4	-2.2	-0.2	-6.3	5.4	-7.0	9.6
Gross fixed assets	..	8.4	8.1	7.4	7.2	9.9	6.6	7.3	9.1	8.1	6.4	4.3	4.9	5.7	4.7	3.3	5.7	4.0	3.6	..
Employment	0.1	-0.4	0.6	1.1	0.4	-0.8	-1.3	-1.0	-0.9	-1.6	-2.3	-2.3	-2.1	-2.2	-1.2	-0.3	-0.4	-1.3	-2.0	..
Poland																				
Investment	1.0	10.4	34.6	26.7	22.2	17.0	2.3	-2.4	-4.7	-15.4	-13.9	-27.2	-12.9	6.2	13.7	9.9	6.8	4.8	4.5	9.0
Gross fixed assets	..	6.3	8.9	9.4	13.8	11.1	10.6	12.3	9.6	6.2	4.6	3.4	2.4	2.8	3.0	3.4	2.3	4.1	2.6	3.3
Employment	1.9	3.0	3.9	2.9	2.4	2.6	0.2	1.0	-0.2	-0.1	0.1	-0.2	-4.7	-0.1	0.7	0.3	-2.0	0.2	-0.3	..
Romania																				
Investment	4.0	12.9	15.0	13.8	9.4	10.7	4.9	16.3	20.4	7.4	2.6	-5.8	-9.6	5.5	11.1	-2.8	4.7	-6.9	-1.3	-10.5
Gross fixed assets	..	13.0	10.6	12.0	14.3	15.6	11.9	10.6	10.0	9.5	9.8	9.2	9.7	9.1	9.6	7.6	8.7	7.2	7.1	6.1
Employment	4.3	6.6	5.6	6.9	7.1	5.3	3.8	4.1	2.6	3.9	3.2	2.0	2.1	1.7	-0.2	1.7	1.5	1.4	0.3	2.7
Eastern Europe																				
Employment	1.4	2.1	2.5	2.4	2.1	1.8	0.8	1.1	0.7	0.8	0.5	0.5	-0.9	0.4	0.3	0.6	-0.1	0.6	-0.2	..
Soviet Union																				
Investment [b]	13.0	5.2	7.1	5.5	7.1	9.3	4.7	4	4.9	0.2	4.3	4.0	2.8	5.5	3.7	4.4	8.4	5.7	5.9	7.8
Gross fixed assets	..	9.4	7.5	8.7	8.3	9.1	8.1	7.0	7.9	7.1	7.8	7.0	6.9	6.8	6.6	6.0	5.5	4.3	4.9	4.3
Employment	1.4	1.4	1.3	1.3	1.7	1.9	2.2	1.7	1.7	1.3	1.1	0.9	1.0	0.6	0.3	0.4	0.3	-0.2	-2.0	-2.6
Eastern Europe and the Soviet Union																				
Employment	1.4	1.6	1.7	1.7	1.8	1.8	1.8	1.5	1.3	1.2	0.9	0.8	0.4	0.5	0.3	0.4	0.2	0.1	-1.4	..

Sources: ECE secretariat Common Data Base, derived from national or CMEA statistics; *Statisticheskii ezhegodnik stran-chlenov SEV 1972* (CMEA statistical yearbook 1972), p.143; and plan fulfilment reports.

[a] At current prices in 1984-1988.
[b] Calculated from absolute volume figures at 1984 prices.

APPENDIX TABLE B.13

Gross agricultural output
(Annual percentage change)

	1970	1971	1972	1973	1974	1975	1976	1977	1978	1979	1980	1981	1982	1983	1984	1985	1986	1987	1988	1989	1990
Bulgaria [a]																					
Total	3.9	1.9	5.6	1.3	-1.5	7.5	4.1	-4.7	4.3	6.1	-4.6	6.4	5.3	-6.6	7.2	-11.9	11.7	-3.5	0.9	1.2	-8.6
Crop	2.3	-0.3	8.5	0.2	-7.5	7.8	5.6	-9.5	4.5	5.6	-8.7	10.2	7.9	-17.4	14.4	-22.5	22.7	-8.8	-0.3	5.3	-14.0
Animal	6.9	6.1	1.4	3.1	7.4	7.3	2.0	2.0	4.0	6.5	0.3	2.2	2.6	3.0	1.1	-2.9	3.7	-1.9	0.4	-2.7	-3.7
Czechoslovakia																					
Total	1.3	2.0	4.3	3.8	2.2	-1.0	-3.2	9.4	2.1	-3.3	4.8	-2.5	4.4	4.2	4.4	-1.6	0.6	0.9	2.9	1.8	-3.5
Crop	-4.5	0.4	4.5	4.0	1.5	-2.6	-8.2	16.8	1.7	-7.2	6.2	-5.3	13.9	2.8	6.1	-4.1	-2.5	1.8	4.0	1.7	-3.6
Animal	6.3	3.3	4.1	3.6	2.7	0.2	0.5	4.3	2.4	-0.3	3.9	-0.5	-2.0	5.4	3.1	0.4	2.9	0.3	2.1	2.0	-3.5
German Dem. Rep.																					
Total	3.8	-0.3	9.3	0.3	7.0	-2.0	-4.5	6.2	1.1	3.0	1.3	1.5	-4.1	3.9	6.6	3.9	-	-0.3	-2.1	1.6	-30.0
Crop	10.8	-5.9	18.3	-7.8	8.8	-9.6	-12.5	20.9	-	5.3	-3.2	2.3	1.5	0.9	11.5	5.3	-3.7	-0.3	-6.6	1.4	..
Animal	-	4.0	4.4	5.3	6.1	2.2	-0.6	-0.1	1.7	1.8	3.8	1.1	-7.0	5.5	4.1	3.1	2.2	-0.3	0.3	1.7	..
Hungary																					
Total	-5.7	7.6	2.6	6.3	3.2	3.7	-2.7	10.9	1.1	-1.5	4.6	2.0	7.3	-2.7	2.9	-5.5	2.4	-2.0	4.3	-1.3	-3.8
Crop	-16.4	9.5	5.8	7.8	0.5	4.7	-7.1	12.3	-1.5	-3.2	7.6	1.6	9.4	-7.5	4.9	-5.4	3.7	-5.5	7.5	0.1	-7.8
Animal	10.4	5.5	-1.0	4.5	6.4	2.5	2.7	9.6	3.7	0.1	1.9	2.4	5.3	2.2	1.0	-5.6	1.1	1.5	1.5	-2.7	0.2
Poland																					
Total	2.2	3.6	8.4	7.3	1.6	-2.1	-1.1	1.4	4.1	-1.5	-10.7	3.8	-2.8	3.3	5.7	0.7	5.0	-2.3	1.2	1.5	-2.2
Crop	4.3	1.1	7.8	6.5	-0.7	-3.0	5.0	-7.2	5.4	-3.7	-15.2	18.9	-2.5	5.9	7.4	-2.0	6.3	-2.0	-0.3	2.7	0.1
Animal	-1.1	6.6	9.0	8.2	4.2	-1.0	-8.7	13.7	2.6	1.3	-5.6	-8.9	-3.2	0.4	3.7	4.0	3.2	-2.7	3.2	-0.1	-5.2
Romania																					
Total	6.8	18.9	9.7	1.0	1.0	2.9	17.3	-0.8	-1.2	5.7	-5.0	-0.4	6.9	-	13.3	0.7	-5.5	-8.9	5.8	-5.0	-2.9
Crop	..	26.3	7.6	-3.2	0.6	0.6	21.5	-5.0	-4.3	6.5	-6.1	-1.0	15.2	-3.5	19.1	1.1	-8.5	-14.0	8.5	-1.8	-7.2
Animal	..	8.9	12.3	7.7	1.5	6.7	11.5	5.6	2.7	3.7	-3.1	0.6	-3.7	5.0	6.2	0.5	-1.4	-2.5	3.0	-8.9	2.1
Eastern Europe																					
Total	2.1	5.1	7.3	4.1	2.3	0.2	1.2	3.2	2.1	0.8	-3.7	1.9	1.5	1.2	6.8	-0.9	1.8	-2.8	2.0	0.1	-7.8
Crop	..	3.9	8.7	2.0	0.7	-1.8	1.8	1.4	1.5	-0.4	-5.9	6.5	5.3	-0.7	10.0	-2.5	1.4	-4.2	1.5	1.5	..
Animal	..	5.9	6.4	6.3	4.4	1.9	-0.8	7.4	2.7	1.9	-1.3	-2.3	-2.2	3.1	3.6	0.9	1.9	-1.3	2.1	-1.8	..
Soviet Union																					
Total	10.3	1.1	-4.1	16.1	-2.7	-5.3	6.5	4.0	2.7	-3.1	-1.9	-1.0	5.7	6.3	-0.2	0.1	5.3	-0.5	1.7	1.3	-2.8
Crop	11.8	-1.3	-7.7	27.1	-10.0	-10.5	18.4	-1.8	5.0	-5.9	-2.3	-2.6	9.6	6.3	-2.0	-1.0	6.1	-2.7	-1.4	1.0	-4.9
Animal	8.7	3.5	-0.6	6.1	5.2	-2.5	-2.4	9.4	0.8	-0.7	-1.6	0.1	2.6	6.4	1.4	1.0	4.7	1.2	4.1	1.6	-1.3
Eastern Europe and the Soviet Union																					
Total	7.6	2.4	-0.4	12.0	-1.1	-3.5	4.6	3.7	2.5	-1.8	-2.5	-0.1	4.3	4.6	2.1	-0.2	4.1	-1.3	1.8	0.9	-4.4
Crop	..	0.3	-2.5	18.3	-6.7	-7.6	12.7	-0.8	3.9	-4.2	-3.5	0.3	8.2	4.0	1.8	-1.5	4.5	-3.2	-0.4	1.1	..
Animal	..	4.3	1.7	6.2	4.9	-0.9	-1.8	8.7	1.5	0.3	-1.5	-0.8	0.9	5.2	2.1	1.0	3.7	0.4	3.4	0.5	..

Sources: ECE secretariat Common Data Base, derived from national or CMEA statistics.

Note: National data are aggregated by means of 1965 weights for total agricultural output based on CMEA investigations.

[a] Based on index numbers (1939 = 100).

Appendix B. Eastern Europe and the Soviet Union

APPENDIX TABLE B.14
Agriculture: Gross investments, gross fixed assets and employment
(Annual percentage change)

	1970	1971	1972	1973	1974	1975	1976	1977	1978	1979	1980	1981	1982	1983	1984	1985	1986	1987	1988	1989
Bulgaria																				
Investment [a]	6.0	3.7	11.5	3.8	17.1	5.1	1.4	10.9	-9.8	-1.7	6.9	10.7	-18.6	1.6	2.6	8.0	-12.1	13.0	25.8	0.1
Gross fixed assets	..	6.6	6.3	6.4	-0.4	14.5	7.3	6.6	4.7	4.5	5.3	5.3	5.0	5.1	2.6	3.5	4.4	3.8	-	9.6
Employment	-4.1	-4.2	-2.0	-4.1	-3.5	-6.3	-4.9	-4.0	-2.6	-0.1	-1.8	-1.5	-2.8	-3.1	-3.2	-2.3	-2.2	-3.5	-2.9	-5.4
Czechoslovakia																				
Investment	-5.0	5.8	9.0	18.5	10.0	13.1	-0.5	6.3	8.0	-6.6	-3.2	5.0	4.6	12.7	1.6	7.8	3.0	-1.5	0.4	-3.9
Gross fixed assets	..	5.4	5.4	5.5	6.3	6.8	7.2	6.4	6.8	6.3	6.0	6.1	5.3	5.6	5.8	6.4	5.4	5.2	4.9	4.8
Employment	-0.9	-1.5	-6.2	-3.0	-0.8	-2.2	-2.1	-2.3	-1.9	-0.7	-0.2	-0.3	-1.2	-2.0	0.1	-0.2	-0.5	-0.9	-1.6	-3.3
German Democratic Republic																				
Investment	-1.0	2.3	-2.6	4.8	9.1	0.8	2.8	3.5	-3.2	-3.9	-1.1	2.6	-7.5	-9.4	-10.8	-5.7	5.8	8.6	9.1	6.1
Gross fixed assets	..	5.6	4.8	5.6	4.3	4.2	4.8	5.1	5.0	5.4	4.9	4.9	4.3	4.0	3.6	3.2	2.9	3.0	3.4	3.3
Employment	-3.3	-2.4	-3.7	-1.9	-1.4	-0.8	-1.4	-0.5	0.5	-0.2	0.3	0.4	0.6	1.5	2.3	0.7	0.5	0.1	0.1	-1.0
Hungary																				
Investment	26.0	-4.9	-12.7	3.4	8.3	10.7	-5.8	8.8	9.6	-2.0	-11.2	8.4	-0.8	-15.9	-7.3	-7.0	6.9	21.4	-22.5	-7.3
Gross fixed assets	..	9.3	8.6	8.6	6.9	7.0	5.8	5.9	5.8	5.6	4.3	4.3	4.3	3.4	0.5	2.1	1.7	2.2	1.7	..
Employment	-1.7	-2.3	-2.5	-3.4	-3.7	-2.6	-1.9	-1.5	-0.5	0.6	0.2	-0.5	-	-0.3	-2.2	-4.1	-4.6	-3.9	-3.0	..
Poland																				
Investment	3.0	4.7	14.9	17.1	18.0	16.1	2.0	12.9	5.9	-3.6	-17.2	-12.5	-15.3	5.6	4.6	-1.9	0.4	3.6	3.5	-9.5
Gross fixed assets	..	2.9	4.2	5.2	6.1	6.4	7.0	7.2	7.0	6.5	5.7	4.0	1.9	2.0	2.6	2.4	1.6	2.1	2.1	1.5
Employment	-0.3	-0.3	-1.4	-1.8	-1.6	1.4	-0.4	1.4	-0.2	1.7	0.2	1.1	-0.5	-2.2	-1.9	-0.1	-1.2	-0.7	-2.6	..
Romania																				
Investment [a]	25.0	10.9	2.4	0.4	8.9	13.9	12.2	12.1	11.4	-1.7	4.4	10.0	-1.8	8.6	9.2	10.7	-3.4	-3.6	-5.0	3.2
Gross fixed assets	..	10.0	9.1	9.2	9.2	10.5	7.6	10.6	6.9	7.0	5.6	8.8	10.1	9.9	9.2	8.6	7.5	7.1	5.1	3.1
Employment	-3.6	-4.4	-4.9	-4.4	-4.3	-4.5	-4.7	-4.1	-4.1	-5.2	-4.6	-2.7	-1.0	0.3	0.8	-	-0.2	-0.1	0.1	-0.1
Eastern Europe																				
Employment	-2.1	-2.4	-3.2	-3.1	-2.7	-1.9	-2.4	-1.3	-1.6	-0.8	-1.7	-0.4	-0.7	-1.2	-0.9	-0.6	-1.1	-1.0	-1.7	..
Soviet Union																				
Investment [b]	12.0	14.4	9.2	10.1	8.5	9.1	4.2	2.6	4.6	1.6	1.6	2.6	1.6	3.5	-2.8	1.3	6.4	2.3	6.3	5.8
Gross fixed assets	..	7.5	10.5	8.7	11.7	9.2	7.8	7.8	7.7	6.7	6.7	6.7	7.1	5.9	5.2	4.3	4.4	4.2	2.9	2.5
Employment	-1.5	-0.7	-0.6	0.5	0.1	-1.3	0.4	-0.7	-0.2	-1.1	-0.5	-0.5	0.4	0.2	0.2	-0.7	-1.0	-1.5	-4.2	-2.6
Eastern Europe and the Soviet Union																				
Employment	-1.7	-1.3	-1.5	-0.8	-0.9	-1.5	-0.6	-0.9	-0.6	-1.0	-0.9	-0.5	-	-0.3	-0.2	-0.6	-1.0	-1.3	-3.4	..

Sources: ECE secretariat Common Data Base, derived from national or CMEA statistics; *Statisticheskii ezhegodnik stran-chlenov SEV 1972* (CMEA statistical yearbook 1972), p.143.

[a] At current prices in 1984-1988.
[b] Calculated from absolute volume figures at 1984 prices.

APPENDIX TABLE B.15
Export and import volumes
(Annual percentage change)

	1970	1971	1972	1973	1974	1975	1976	1977	1978	1979	1980	1981	1982	1983	1984	1985	1986	1987	1988	1989	1990
Bulgaria																					
Exports	8.7	8.0	11.6	9.6	8.3	12.4	13.4	14.3	10.7	13.7	12.2	8.3	11.4	4.5	4.7	7.4	-3.7	1.8	2.4	-2.3	-24.2
Imports	4.7	13.3	13.3	10.7	21.9	12.6	-2.3	5.3	7.1	2.1	4.1	9.3	3.1	5.2	2.2	10.5	3.9	-1.4	5.3	-4.6	-24.2
Czechoslovakia																					
Exports	20.7	8.4	7.7	3.5	5.0	6.8	7.5	8.9	7.5	2.9	4.9	0.3	6.1	5.7	9.5	2.6	1.2	3.4	3.2	-2.0	-4.2
Imports	15.9	5.9	4.1	9.8	10.9	1.9	3.4	7.1	3.6	2.2	-1.6	-6.9	2.9	2.1	0.3	4.6	2.7	4.3	2.9	2.7	9.7
German Dem. Rep.																					
Exports	8.8	10.1	11.6	7.3	8.2	7.0	6.1	4.3	7.7	9.3	3.7	9.8	6.2	12.0	2.3	2.3	-4.5	-0.1	-0.2	0.5	–
Imports	15.9	2.0	7.5	12.9	8.6	4.9	11.0	4.5	-0.2	6.5	5.0	-1.7	-6.2	7.2	4.8	4.1	2.9	9.0	4.7	2.4	15.0
Hungary																					
Exports	7.6	7.6	19.3	12.5	3.5	4.8	8.2	12.6	1.5	12.5	1.0	2.6	7.3	9.4	5.8	-0.3	-2.2	3.9	5.0	0.3	-4.3
Imports	27.1	17.3	-5.1	2.9	17.5	5.7	3.9	8.5	12.5	-3.3	-1.1	0.1	-0.1	3.9	0.1	1.1	2.1	3.2	-1.9	1.1	-3.4
Poland																					
Exports	10.1	6.5	15.2	11.0	12.8	8.3	5.3	7.0	5.7	6.8	-4.2	-19.0	8.7	10.3	9.5	1.3	4.9	4.8	9.1	0.2	13.7
Imports	10.4	13.8	22.1	22.7	14.1	5.0	10.2	0.2	1.6	-1.2	-1.9	-16.9	-13.7	5.2	8.6	7.9	4.9	4.5	9.4	1.5	-17.9
Romania [a]																					
Exports	3.9	9.8	4.7	18.8	2.2	3.5	11.1	7.3	5.2	5.7	1.2	11.3	-8.3	3.2	15.9	0.3	0.2	-4.3	7.4	-10.8	-46.0
Imports	8.2	3.1	10.5	10.7	13.4	-3.7	11.5	8.4	17.2	6.8	2.0	-7.2	-22.4	-3.8	10.5	8.5	18.3	-6.3	-5.8	3.7	4.0
Eastern Europe																					
Exports	10.7	8.6	11.0	9.3	7.0	7.0	7.9	8.0	6.7	7.9	3.1	2.7	5.3	8.0	7.0	2.5	-1.2	1.4	3.6	-1.9	-7.9
Imports	14.0	7.5	8.2	12.1	13.0	4.3	6.7	5.2	5.0	2.7	1.3	-4.3	-5.3	4.0	3.9	5.8	4.8	3.4	3.3	1.2	-8.6
Soviet Union																					
Exports	6.1	3.2	2.7	14.4	2.6	2.5	8.6	10.6	3.4	0.6	1.6	1.9	4.5	3.3	2.5	-4.3	10.0	3.3	4.8	–	-13.1
Imports	7.8	5.9	17.2	14.6	1.0	14.8	7.0	0.9	13.3	1.1	7.5	6.4	9.7	4.0	4.4	4.7	-6.0	-1.6	4.0	9.3	-1.4
Eastern Europe and the Soviet Union																					
Exports	7.8	5.3	6.1	12.3	4.4	4.4	8.3	9.5	4.8	3.8	2.3	2.3	4.9	5.5	4.6	-1.0	4.4	2.4	4.3	-0.9	-10.7
Imports	11.4	6.8	11.8	13.2	7.9	8.5	6.8	3.4	8.4	2.0	3.9	0.4	1.7	4.0	4.1	5.3	-0.6	1.0	3.6	5.0	-5.1

Sources: ECE secretariat Common Data Base, derived from national or CMEA statistics.

Note: National data are aggregated by means of weights calculated from 1985 US dollar trade shares.

[a] ECE secretariat estimates.

APPENDIX TABLE B.16
Energy production: Electricity, coal and crude oil
(Billion kWh, million tons)

	1970	1971	1972	1973	1974	1975	1976	1977	1978	1979	1980	1981	1982	1983	1984	1985	1986	1987	1988	1989	1990
Bulgaria																					
Electricity	19.5	21.0	22.3	22.0	22.8	25.2	27.7	29.7	31.5	32.5	34.8	37.0	40.5	42.6	44.7	41.6	41.8	43.5	45.0	44.3	44.0
Coal	29.3	27.0	27.3	26.8	24.3	27.8	25.5	25.2	25.8	28.2	30.2	29.2	32.4	32.4	32.4	30.9	35.2	36.8	34.1	34.3	31.5
Oil	0.3	0.3	0.2	0.2	0.1	0.1	0.1									0.1	0.1	0.1			
Czechoslovakia																					
Electricity	45.2	47.2	51.4	53.5	56.0	59.3	62.7	66.5	69.1	68.1	72.7	73.5	74.7	76.3	78.4	80.6	84.8	85.8	87.4	89.3	86.8
Coal	109.5	113.0	112.9	109.0	110.1	114.4	117.7	121.2	123.2	124.7	123.1	122.8	124.6	127.4	129.3	126.6	126.4	126.1	123.5	117.4	105.0
Oil	0.2	0.2	0.2	0.2	0.1	0.1	0.1	0.1	0.1	0.1	0.1	0.1	0.1	0.1	0.1	0.1	0.1	0.1	0.1	0.1	0.1
German Dem. Rep.																					
Electricity	67.6	69.4	72.8	76.9	80.3	84.5	89.1	92.0	96.0	96.8	98.8	100.7	102.9	104.9	110.1	113.8	115.3	114.2	118.3	119.0	119.0
Coal	261.6	263.7	249.2	247.0	244.1	247.2	247.4	254.1	253.3	256.1	258.1	266.7	276.0	278.0	296.3	312.2	311.3	309.0	310.3	301.0	301.0
Oil	0.1	0.1	0.1	0.1	0.1	0.1	0.1	0.1	0.1	0.1	0.1										
Hungary																					
Electricity	14.5	15.0	16.3	17.6	19.0	20.5	22.0	23.4	25.6	24.5	23.9	24.3	24.7	25.7	26.2	26.7	28.0	29.7	29.2	29.7	29.6
Coal	27.8	27.4	25.8	26.8	25.8	24.9	25.3	25.5	25.7	25.7	25.7	25.9	26.1	25.2	25.0	24.0	23.1	22.8	20.9	20.0	20.1
Oil a	1.9	2.0	2.0	2.0	2.0	2.0	2.1	2.2	2.2	2.0	2.0	2.0	2.0	2.0	2.0	2.0	2.0	1.9	1.9	2.0	1.9
Poland																					
Electricity	64.5	69.9	76.5	84.3	91.6	97.2	104.1	109.4	115.6	117.5	121.9	115.0	117.6	125.8	134.8	137.7	140.3	145.8	144.3	145.5	136.0
Coal	172.9	180.0	188.9	195.8	201.8	211.5	218.6	226.9	233.6	239.0	230.0	198.6	227.0	233.6	242.0	249.4	259.3	266.2	266.5	249.4	215.6
Oil	0.4	0.4	0.3	0.4	0.5	0.6	0.5	0.4	0.4	0.3	0.3	0.3	0.2	0.2	0.2	0.2	0.2	0.1	0.2	0.2	0.1
Romania																					
Electricity	35.1	39.5	43.4	46.8	49.1	53.7	58.3	59.9	64.3	64.8	67.5	70.1	68.9	70.3	71.6	71.8	75.5	74.1	75.3	75.9	64.2
Coal	20.5	20.6	23.2	24.9	26.9	27.1	25.8	26.8	29.3	32.8	35.2	36.9	37.9	44.5	44.3	46.6	47.5	51.5	58.8	61.3	38.2
Oil	13.4	13.8	14.1	14.3	14.5	14.6	14.7	14.6	13.7	12.3	11.5	11.6	11.7	11.6	11.5	10.7	10.1	9.5	9.4	9.2	8.0
Eastern Europe																					
Electricity	246.5	262.0	282.7	301.1	318.8	340.4	364.1	380.8	401.8	404.3	419.6	420.6	429.3	445.7	465.8	472.4	485.7	493.1	499.6	503.6	479.6
Coal	621.6	631.7	627.3	630.3	633.0	652.9	660.3	679.5	690.9	706.4	702.3	680.3	723.7	741.1	769.3	789.7	802.9	812.5	814.1	783.5	711.4
Oil	16.4	16.7	17.0	17.1	17.4	17.5	17.6	17.4	16.5	14.9	14.4	14.1	14.1	13.9	13.7	13.2	12.6	11.8	11.7	11.5	10.3
Soviet Union																					
Electricity	740.9	800.4	857.4	914.6	975.8	1038.6	1111.4	1150.1	1202.0	1238.2	1293.9	1326.0	1367.1	1418.1	1492.6	1544.0	1599.0	1665.0	1705.1	1721.7	1728.0
Coal	577.6	591.5	603.6	614.7	630.6	644.9	654.4	663.3	664.4	657.3	652.9	637.8	647.3	641.6	634.6	647.8	672.7	680.3	691.5	662.7	628.5
Oil	353.0	371.8	393.8	421.4	450.6	490.8	519.7	545.8	571.5	585.6	603.2	608.8	612.6	616.3	612.7	595.3	614.8	624.2	624.3	607.3	570.0
Eastern Europe and the Soviet Union																					
Electricity	987.4	1062.4	1140.2	1215.7	1294.5	1379.0	1475.5	1530.9	1603.9	1642.5	1713.5	1746.6	1796.4	1863.8	1958.4	2016.4	2084.7	2158.1	2204.7	2225.3	2207.6
Coal	1199.1	1223.2	1230.9	1245.0	1263.5	1297.8	1314.7	1342.8	1355.3	1355.1	1355.1	1318.1	1371.1	1382.7	1403.9	1437.4	1475.6	1492.8	1505.6	1446.2	1339.9
Oil	369.4	388.5	410.8	438.5	468.0	508.3	537.3	563.2	588.0	600.4	617.6	622.9	626.7	630.2	626.5	608.5	627.3	636.0	636.0	618.7	580.3

Source: Statisticheskii ezhegodnik stran-chlenov SEV (CMEA statistical yearbook), various issues, and ECE secretariat estimates.

a Excluding gas condensate.

APPENDIX TABLE B.17

Steel production
(Million tons)

	1970	1971	1972	1973	1974	1975	1976	1977	1978	1979	1980	1981	1982	1983	1984	1985	1986	1987	1988	1989	1990
Bulgaria	1.8	1.9	2.1	2.2	2.2	2.3	2.5	2.6	2.5	2.5	2.6	2.5	2.6	2.8	2.9	2.9	3.0	3.0	2.9	2.9	2.2
Czechoslovakia	11.5	12.1	12.7	13.2	13.6	14.3	14.7	15.1	15.3	14.8	15.2	15.3	15.0	15.0	14.8	15.0	15.1	15.4	15.4	15.5	14.9
German Dem. Rep.	5.1	5.4	5.7	5.9	6.2	6.5	6.7	6.8	7.0	7.0	7.3	7.5	7.2	7.2	7.6	7.9	8.0	8.2	8.1	7.8	5.6
Hungary	3.1	3.1	3.3	3.3	3.5	3.7	3.7	3.7	3.9	3.9	3.8	3.6	3.7	3.6	3.8	3.6	3.7	3.6	3.6	3.4	3.0
Poland	11.8	12.7	13.4	14.1	14.6	15.0	15.6	17.8	19.3	19.2	19.5	15.7	14.7	16.2	16.5	16.1	17.1	17.1	16.9	15.1	13.6
Romania	6.5	6.8	7.4	8.2	8.8	9.5	10.7	11.5	11.8	12.9	13.2	13.0	13.1	12.6	14.4	13.8	14.3	13.9	14.3	14.4	9.8
Eastern Europe	39.7	42.0	44.6	46.8	48.9	51.3	53.9	57.5	59.7	60.4	61.5	57.6	56.2	57.5	60.0	59.4	61.2	61.3	61.2	59.1	49.0
Soviet Union	115.9	120.7	125.6	131.5	136.2	141.3	144.8	146.7	151.5	149.1	147.9	148.4	147.2	152.5	154.2	154.7	160.5	161.9	163.0	160.1	154.4
Eastern Europe and the Soviet Union	155.6	162.6	170.2	178.3	185.1	192.6	198.7	204.2	211.1	209.5	209.5	206.0	203.4	210.0	214.2	214.1	221.7	223.2	224.2	219.1	203.4

Source: National statistics.

APPENDIX TABLE B.18
Grain production [a]
(Million tons)

	1970	1971	1972	1973	1974	1975	1976	1977	1978	1979	1980	1981	1982	1983	1984	1985	1986	1987	1988	1989	1990
Bulgaria																					
Total	6.9	7.2	8.2	7.4	6.7	7.8	8.6	7.7	7.6	8.4	7.7	8.5	10.1	8.0	9.3	5.5	8.6	7.4	7.9	9.6	8.0
Wheat	3.0	3.1	3.6	3.3	2.9	2.8	3.5	3.4	3.5	3.4	3.8	4.4	4.9	3.6	4.8	3.1	4.3	4.1	4.7	5.4	5.1
Maize	2.4	2.5	3.0	2.6	1.6	2.8	3.0	2.5	2.2	3.2	2.3	2.4	3.4	3.1	3.0	1.3	2.8	1.9	1.6	2.3	1.2
Czechoslovakia																					
Total	7.3	8.9	8.7	9.7	10.5	9.4	9.2	10.5	11.1	9.3	10.9	9.5	10.4	11.2	12.2	12.0	11.0	12.0	12.2	12.3	12.3
Wheat	3.2	3.9	4.0	4.6	5.1	4.2	4.8	5.2	5.6	3.7	5.4	4.3	4.6	5.8	6.2	6.0	5.3	6.2	6.5	6.4	6.7
Maize	0.5	0.5	0.6	0.6	0.6	0.8	0.5	0.8	0.6	0.9	0.7	0.7	0.9	0.7	0.9	1.0	1.0	1.2	1.0	1.0	0.5
German Democratic Republic																					
Total	6.5	7.8	8.6	8.6	9.8	9.0	8.2	8.8	9.9	9.0	9.7	8.9	10.1	10.2	11.4	11.7	11.8	11.3	9.9	10.9	..
Wheat	2.1	2.5	2.7	2.9	3.2	2.7	2.7	2.9	3.1	3.1	3.1	2.9	2.7	3.5	3.9	3.9	4.2	4.0	3.7	3.5	..
Maize	-	-	-	-	-	-	-	-	-	-	-	-	-	-	-	-	-	-	-	-	..
Hungary																					
Total	7.8	10.0	10.9	11.8	12.6	12.4	11.5	12.4	13.5	12.2	14.2	13.0	15.1	13.9	15.9	15.0	14.5	14.4	15.4	15.9	12.5
Wheat	2.7	3.9	4.1	4.5	5.0	4.0	5.1	5.3	5.7	3.7	6.1	4.6	5.8	6.0	7.4	6.6	5.8	5.7	7.0	6.5	6.2
Maize	4.1	4.7	5.6	6.0	6.2	7.2	5.1	6.0	6.7	7.4	6.7	7.0	8.0	6.4	6.7	6.8	7.3	7.2	6.3	7.0	4.5
Poland																					
Total	16.6	20.2	20.7	22.2	23.3	19.8	21.1	19.6	21.8	17.6	18.5	19.9	21.4	22.4	24.8	24.2	25.5	26.6	25.1	27.6	28.7
Wheat	4.6	5.5	5.1	5.8	6.4	5.2	5.7	5.3	6.0	4.2	4.2	4.2	4.5	5.2	6.0	6.5	7.5	7.9	7.6	8.5	9.0
Maize	-	-	-	-	-	0.1	0.2	0.2	0.1	0.2	0.1	0.1	0.1	0.1	0.1	0.1	0.1	0.1	0.2	0.2	0.3
Romania																					
Total	10.9	14.8	17.1	14.0	13.7	15.4	19.9	18.7	18.3	18.9	19.5	16.5	20.0	17.6	20.2	19.8	20.0	17.1	19.5	18.6	17.2
Wheat	3.4	5.6	6.0	5.5	5.0	4.9	6.8	6.5	6.2	4.6	6.3	5.3	6.2	5.0	7.5	5.6	6.4	6.7	8.6	7.9	7.4
Maize	6.5	7.8	9.8	7.4	7.4	9.2	11.6	10.1	9.7	11.8	10.6	8.3	10.5	10.3	9.9	11.9	10.9	7.5	7.2	6.8	6.8
Eastern Europe																					
Total	56.0	68.8	74.3	73.6	76.5	73.8	78.5	77.6	82.2	75.3	80.4	76.5	87.1	83.4	94.0	88.2	91.4	88.8	90.0	94.9	78.7
Wheat	19.0	24.4	25.6	26.6	27.6	23.8	28.7	28.7	30.1	22.7	28.9	25.9	28.7	29.1	35.8	31.7	33.5	34.7	38.2	38.2	34.4
Maize	13.5	15.6	19.0	16.6	15.9	20.2	20.5	19.7	19.3	23.5	20.3	18.5	22.9	20.6	20.6	21.2	22.1	17.9	16.2	17.3	13.3
Soviet Union																					
Total	186.8	181.2	168.2	222.5	195.7	140.1	223.8	195.7	237.4	179.3	189.1	158.2	186.8	192.2	172.6	191.7	210.1	211.4	195.1	211.1	233.9
Wheat	99.7	98.8	86.0	109.8	83.9	66.2	96.9	92.2	120.9	90.3	98.2	81.1	84.3	77.5	68.8	78.1	92.3	83.3	84.4	92.3	107.8
Maize	9.4	8.6	9.8	13.2	12.1	7.3	10.1	11.0	8.9	8.4	9.5	9.4	14.7	13.3	13.6	14.4	12.5	14.8	16.0	15.3	9.9
Eastern Europe the Soviet Union																					
Total	242.8	250.0	242.5	296.1	272.2	213.9	302.3	273.4	319.6	254.6	269.5	234.7	273.8	275.6	266.6	279.8	301.5	300.2	285.0	305.9	312.6
Wheat	118.8	123.2	111.6	136.4	111.5	90.1	125.6	120.8	151.0	113.0	127.1	107.0	113.0	106.6	104.4	109.7	125.8	118.1	122.7	130.5	142.2
Maize	23.0	28.9	28.9	29.8	28.0	27.5	30.6	30.6	28.2	31.9	29.8	27.9	37.7	33.9	34.1	35.6	34.6	32.8	32.2	32.6	23.2

Sources: ECE secretariat Common Data Base, derived from national and CMEA statistics.

[a] Including pulses.

APPENDIX TABLE B.19

Saving deposits of the population
(Billions of national currency units)

	1970	1971	1972	1973	1974	1975	1976	1977	1978	1979	1980	1981	1982	1983	1984	1985	1986	1987	1988	1989	1990
Bulgaria	4	5	5	6	7	8	8	9	9	10	10	11	12	13	14	16	16	17	18	19	20
Czechoslovakia	64	74	85	98	107	116	126	137	143	148	156	165	178	191	204	219	235	252	266	278	268
German Dem. Rep.	52	56	60	65	70	75	80	86	92	97	100	103	108	113	119	125	132	142	152	160	..
Hungary [a]	42	48	54	62	71	81	93	107	124	135	144	159	174	194	215	239	268	263	280	262	260
Poland [b]	115	134	167	210	261	303	334	371	409	457	500	665	867	1058	1237	1667	2091	2482	3695	7719	28112
Romania	..	..	..	36	41	47	55	64	80	90	98	115	118	128	139	153	167	177	186	202	249
Soviet Union	47	53	61	69	79	91	103	117	131	146	157	166	174	187	202	221	243	267	297	338	381

Sources: National statistics (CSSR, GDR, Hungary, Poland); IMF, *International Financial Statistics* (Romania); *Statisticheskii ezhegodnik stran-chlenov SEV* (CMEA statistical yearbook), various years (Bulgaria, USSR).

[a] Forint saving deposits only. Since 1987 current accounts of private entrepreneurs are excluded.
[b] For 1980, and 1985-date increased coverage.

Appendix C. International trade and payments

Data for this section were compiled from international[745] and national statistical sources, as indicated in the notes to individual tables. Regional aggregates for tables C.2-C.3 were obtained by means of weights representing 1985 shares in the US dollar value of trade.

---

[745] United Nations COMTRADE data base, IMF, IBRD, OECD, BIS.

APPENDIX TABLE C.1
World trade: Value, by region
(Billion US dollars)

	1970	1971	1972	1973	1974	1975	1976	1977	1978	1979	1980	1981	1982	1983	1984	1985	1986	1987	1988	1989	1990
Exports																					
Developed market economies	215.1	240.8	286.6	390.1	525.1	560.1	623.2	707.6	849.1	1042.2	1228.7	1210.1	1145.9	1132.9	1208.9	1251.1	1463.2	1710.9	1953.9	2089.9	2414.6
North America	59.4	61.9	70.4	97.3	133.9	142.9	157.4	166.7	194.3	244.7	293.3	311.4	287.7	282.4	314.2	309.8	317.5	352.3	439.0	484.1	520.2
Western Europe [a]	131.9	149.4	180.3	246.0	322.7	348.0	383.4	443.1	535.4	667.4	771.5	713.7	685.1	669.1	684.3	721.8	887.4	1067.1	1181.6	1255.5	1513.7
Southern Europe [b]	4.6	5.4	6.9	9.8	12.9	13.3	15.1	16.7	21.2	27.8	33.4	33.4	34.7	34.5	40.7	42.4	47.6	60.2	68.4	76.5	93.1
Japan	19.3	24.1	29.1	37.0	55.5	55.8	67.3	81.1	98.2	102.3	130.4	151.5	138.4	147.0	169.7	177.2	210.8	231.3	264.9	273.9	287.6
Developing market economies	55.3	64.2	75.6	113.3	238.3	221.9	265.8	300.0	317.5	457.4	583.3	438.4	471.6	448.4	403.4	509.6	586.1	652.9	717.6	737.5	803.1
Oil-exporting countries [c]	17.4	22.6	26.3	40.2	131.3	120.8	146.5	159.3	155.6	236.4	300.8	178.8	173.1	154.8	100.9	121.2	120.6	148.5	177.6	158.6	178.1
Non-oil developing countries	38.0	41.6	49.3	73.1	106.9	101.1	119.3	140.7	161.9	221.0	282.5	259.6	298.5	293.6	302.5	388.4	465.5	504.4	540.0	578.9	625.0
Eastern Europe and the Soviet Union	32.6	35.5	42.2	55.6	71.5	87.0	71.2	82.5	92.3	111.9	128.0	132.3	135.9	134.1	134.4	131.5	137.5	143.8	144.0	142.8	138.2
Eastern Europe [d]	19.8	21.7	26.8	34.3	43.0	51.8	42.0	46.9	52.4	62.0	70.0	71.9	71.7	70.5	72.0	74.2	77.4	80.4	82.0	80.5	79.1
Soviet Union	12.8	13.8	15.4	21.4	28.5	35.2	29.2	35.5	39.8	49.9	57.9	60.4	64.2	63.6	62.4	57.3	60.0	63.4	62.0	62.3	59.1
Total above	303.1	340.5	404.4	559.1	834.9	869.0	960.2	1090.1	1258.9	1611.5	1939.9	1780.8	1753.3	1715.5	1746.6	1892.3	2186.8	2507.5	2815.4	2970.2	3355.9
Memorandum item																					
ECE region	228.4	252.2	299.7	408.8	541.1	591.3	627.1	709.0	843.2	1051.8	1226.2	1190.9	1143.4	1120.1	1173.5	1205.5	1389.9	1623.4	1833.0	1958.8	2265.2
Imports																					
Developed market economies	224.6	249.5	299.0	410.1	585.6	589.0	679.7	770.1	888.6	1140.4	1368.9	1296.0	1215.4	1199.3	1310.4	1344.7	1523.3	1805.5	2037.9	2199.5	2540.3
North America	56.6	64.8	78.9	97.9	145.1	142.0	172.7	202.5	232.3	278.9	319.5	343.4	313.0	334.7	424.2	433.1	467.8	517.0	572.3	612.7	639.0
Western Europe [a]	139.8	154.8	183.3	255.5	350.4	359.0	409.2	461.0	540.0	705.0	846.3	750.1	711.0	682.1	693.2	722.0	860.9	1047.0	1173.2	1254.6	1510.9
Southern Europe [b]	9.2	10.1	12.9	18.2	28.1	30.2	32.9	35.2	36.4	46.7	61.8	59.6	59.9	56.1	56.9	59.0	67.1	90.4	105.1	122.5	155.1
Japan	18.9	19.8	23.9	38.4	61.9	57.9	64.9	71.3	79.9	109.8	141.3	142.9	131.5	126.4	136.2	130.5	127.6	151.0	187.4	209.7	235.4
Developing market economies	55.6	63.0	68.3	95.5	156.6	181.0	194.1	233.0	280.5	343.9	456.1	515.2	475.9	447.8	450.2	423.0	413.8	457.1	553.4	601.6	674.5
Oil-exporting countries [c]	8.9	10.5	13.2	19.1	30.9	50.9	63.1	83.9	94.7	98.0	131.5	158.1	160.4	142.3	126.0	105.1	91.8	91.1	104.1	99.0	113.5
Non-oil developing countries	46.7	52.6	55.2	76.4	125.8	130.1	130.9	149.1	185.8	245.8	324.6	357.1	315.5	305.5	324.2	317.9	322.0	365.9	449.3	502.5	561.0
Eastern Europe and the Soviet Union	33.1	36.0	43.6	58.0	77.4	100.2	81.3	89.3	101.5	117.8	133.4	134.8	127.1	122.0	120.7	125.2	132.7	132.8	135.9	143.1	148.9
Eastern Europe [d]	21.3	23.5	27.5	37.0	51.4	61.4	50.6	57.1	63.0	73.4	81.2	77.9	70.0	66.7	66.7	70.5	77.7	79.0	77.8	78.1	84.0
Soviet Union	11.7	12.5	16.1	21.0	25.9	38.8	30.8	32.2	38.5	44.4	52.2	56.9	57.1	55.4	53.9	54.8	55.0	53.8	58.0	65.0	65.0
Total above	313.2	348.5	410.9	563.6	819.6	870.3	955.1	1092.4	1270.6	1602.0	1958.5	1945.9	1818.4	1769.2	1881.3	1892.9	2069.8	2395.4	2727.2	2944.1	3363.8
Memorandum item																					
ECE region	238.8	265.7	318.8	429.7	601.0	631.4	696.1	788.1	910.2	1148.3	1361.0	1287.9	1211.0	1194.9	1294.9	1339.4	1528.4	1787.3	1986.4	2132.8	2453.9

Sources: IMF, *International Financial Statistics*, February 1992 and ECE secretariat calculations, based on national publications for the countries of eastern Europe and the Soviet Union, using consistent rouble/dollar crossrates for recalculation of trade flows denominated in transferable roubles, as explained in the note to Appendix table C.4.

[a] Austria, Belgium-Luxembourg, Denmark, Finland, France, the Federal Republic of Germany, Ireland, Italy, the Netherlands, Norway, Sweden, Switzerland and the United Kingdom.
[b] Greece, Portugal, Spain and Turkey.
[c] IMF definition covering Algeria, Indonesia, the Islamic Republic of Iran, Iraq, Kuwait, Libyan Arab Jamahiriya, Nigeria Qatar, Saudi Arabia, the United Arab Emirates and Venezuela.
[d] Including Yugoslavia.

APPENDIX TABLE C.2

World trade: Volume change, by region
(Annual percentage change)

	1970	1971	1972	1973	1974	1975	1976	1977	1978	1979	1980	1981	1982	1983	1984	1985	1986	1987	1988	1989	1990
Exports																					
Developed market economies	10.3	5.5	8.6	13.6	8.4	-4.4	11.3	4.5	6.7	6.2	4.6	2.4	-2.1	2.3	9.6	3.9	1.2	5.4	7.9	7.3	5.4
North America	8.9	0.4	9.1	20.5	5.7	-3.2	5.3	1.8	11.3	7.3	7.5	-2.0	-9.3	-2.5	9.8	0.4	1.0	10.2	15.3	8.3	7.9
Western Europe	10.1	6.0	8.5	11.2	8.1	-5.9	12.6	5.0	5.5	6.8	0.8	2.8	1.1	2.9	7.6	5.1	2.0	4.1	5.6	7.4	3.9
Southern Europe [a]	17.5	12.6	15.9	14.7	3.9	-1.9	14.2	6.7	12.0	8.4	7.8	7.5	12.9	7.1	17.6	6.6	-3.3	12.4	1.7	12.2	8.3
Japan	15.8	18.3	6.4	6.8	20.5	-0.2	21.1	8.6	0.7	0.2	17.1	10.7	-2.3	8.7	15.8	4.9	-0.6	0.4	4.4	5.0	5.6
Developing market economies [b]	9.6	7.0	12.1	8.3	1.5	-8.7	13.9	2.6	0.6	5.1	-9.0	-5.5	-6.9	1.7	6.9	0.5	8.3	11.9	11.4	6.9	3.7
Oil-exporting countries [c]	18.1	10.2	4.6	8.9	2.1	-14.0	13.4	0.4	-4.2	2.8	-15.8	-13.9	-14.1	-4.7		-3.8	11.9	3.2	13.7	8.1	4.1
Non-oil developing countries	5.0	4.9	17.0	8.0	0.3	–	14.6	5.1	6.3	9.3	2.1	4.7	0.2	6.7	11.6	3.2	7.2	15.2	10.7	6.5	3.5
Eastern Europe and the Soviet Union	7.8	5.3	6.1	12.3	4.4	4.4	8.3	9.5	4.8	3.8	2.3	2.3	4.9	5.5	4.6	-1.0	4.4	2.4	4.3	-0.9	-11.6
Eastern Europe [d]	10.7	8.6	11.0	9.3	7.0	7.0	7.9	8.0	6.7	7.9	3.1	2.7	5.3	8.0	7.0	2.5	-1.2	1.4	3.6	-1.9	-7.9
Soviet Union	6.1	3.2	2.7	14.4	2.6	2.5	8.6	10.6	3.4	0.6	1.6	1.9	4.5	3.3	2.5	-4.3	10.0	3.3	4.8	–	-13.1
Total above	10.0	5.9	9.4	12.1	6.2	-5.0	11.8	4.3	4.9	5.8	0.7	0.2	-3.0	2.3	8.5	2.7	3.4	7.0	8.6	6.7	3.8
Memorandum item																					
ECE region	9.8	4.7	8.7	13.9	7.0	-4.0	10.3	4.7	7.2	6.7	2.9	1.7	-0.8	1.9	8.2	3.3	1.8	5.8	7.9	6.7	3.5
Imports																					
Developed market economies	9.9	5.5	10.7	11.9	0.8	-7.7	14.8	4.0	6.2	7.3	-1.7	-1.9	-0.8	4.7	11.8	5.9	7.3	7.2	7.7	7.3	5.1
North America	2.0	9.0	14.1	6.9	1.0	-10.5	18.5	8.5	8.8	2.2	-6.8	2.6	-7.5	10.5	23.2	9.0	10.1	3.3	5.7	5.6	2.9
Western Europe	12.2	4.7	8.3	11.1	1.0	-5.8	14.4	1.7	5.1	9.5	1.0	-4.6	1.9	2.7	6.4	5.1	5.6	6.8	7.0	7.2	5.6
Southern Europe [a]	17.4	11.1	12.4	12.6	2.8	0.7	11.1	8.9	-0.1	5.7	6.9	6.1	7.9	3.4	10.6	6.4	–	38.5	9.5	16.1	11.0
Japan	18.7	-0.4	13.9	30.6	-0.7	-12.2	8.9	2.5	6.6	11.4	-5.1	-2.2	-0.6	1.2	10.5	–	10.5	9.0	16.6	8.3	5.8
Developing market economies [b]	8.8	8.8	3.9	14.0	18.4	6.5	5.7	10.9	6.3	2.0	9.3	8.0	-4.3	-3.3	2.4	-0.3	-2.6	6.8	11.6	8.0	3.0
Oil-exporting countries [c]	6.6	11.5	13.4	18.5	26.8	45.2	23.6	22.4	0.3	-10.2	17.2	22.7	-1.8	-12.6	-7.9	-9.9	-20.3	-5.5	8.3	5.0	2.7
Non-oil developing countries	9.2	8.4	2.3	13.0	16.8	-1.6	0.7	6.9	8.8	6.4	6.8	2.2	-5.0	1.5	6.9	3.3	4.1	10.3	12.4	8.7	3.1
Eastern Europe and the Soviet Union	11.4	6.8	11.8	13.2	7.9	8.5	6.8	3.4	8.4	2.0	3.9	0.4	1.7	4.0	4.1	5.3	-0.6	1.0	3.6	5.0	-5.1
Eastern Europe [d]	14.0	7.5	8.2	12.1	13.0	4.3	6.7	5.2	5.0	2.7	1.3	-4.3	-5.3	4.0	3.9	5.8	4.8	3.4	3.3	1.2	-8.6
Soviet Union	7.8	5.9	17.2	14.6	1.0	14.8	7.0	0.9	13.3	1.1	7.5	6.4	9.7	4.0	4.4	4.7	-6.0	-1.6	4.0	9.3	-1.4
Total above	9.7	6.4	9.2	12.5	5.3	-3.5	12.2	5.5	6.3	5.8	1.1	0.5	-1.5	2.8	9.2	4.4	4.5	6.7	8.3	7.3	4.0
Memorandum item																					
ECE region	9.0	6.6	10.7	10.0	1.6	-5.9	14.9	4.4	6.3	6.3	-1.1	-1.3	-0.9	5.4	11.9	6.5	6.3	6.6	6.4	6.9	4.0

Sources: IMF, *International Financial Statistics*, February 1992 for the developed market economies; IMF, *IFS Supplement on Trade Statistics* (Supplement Series No. 15.) and *World Economic Outlook*, May 1991 for developing countries; ECE secretariat calculations, based on national sources for southern Europe and the east European economies.

Note: For market economies and eastern Europe, weights for aggregations are US dollar trade shares in 1985, as reflected in Appendix table C.1.

[a] Includes ECE, OECD or World Bank estimates for certain sub-periods for Portugal, Turkey and Yugoslavia.
[b] IMF definitions for developing countries.
[c] See the definition applied in Appendix table C.1.
[d] Excludes Yugoslavia.

APPENDIX TABLE C.3

Western Europe and North America: Trade volume change
(Annual percentage change) [a]

	1970	1971	1972	1973	1974	1975	1976	1977	1978	1979	1980	1981	1982	1983	1984	1985	1986	1987	1988	1989	1990
Exports																					
France	15.9	8.4	14.1	10.2	9.6	-4.2	9.1	6.5	6.1	10.0	2.1	2.9	-2.9	3.4	5.4	2.7	0.5	3.7	8.7	7.8	5.0
Germany	14.7	4.1	6.4	13.9	11.0	-11.2	18.6	3.9	3.2	4.9	1.7	6.6	3.3	-0.3	9.1	5.9	1.3	2.9	6.7	8.1	1.5
Italy	8.0	7.9	12.5	1.1	7.7	3.7	11.7	7.6	10.8	7.8	-7.9	4.2	0.5	3.6	6.5	7.5	1.8	2.0	6.0	8.6	3.3
United Kingdom	2.3	7.1	1.2	12.9	5.3	-2.5	9.0	8.8	2.7	3.4	1.2	-1.3	3.3	2.2	8.4	5.8	4.0	5.6	2.5	4.3	6.6
Total 4 countries	10.7	6.3	7.8	10.7	8.9	-5.4	13.0	6.2	5.0	6.2	-0.0	3.6	1.4	1.7	7.7	5.4	1.8	3.5	6.1	7.3	3.7
Austria	7.7	3.2	11.8	8.7	11.6	-7.0	15.7	3.2	10.1	12.9	2.9	5.1	1.1	4.4	9.3	10.1	0.8	2.5	12.1	13.6	6.1
Belgium	8.5	7.8	12.7	12.9	2.9	-8.3	13.6	2.7	3.9	7.5	2.3	-	2.3	3.3	4.3	3.1	5.0	6.7	6.3	7.6	3.1
Denmark	6.7	4.2	8.0	7.4	5.2	-3.3	3.4	4.9	6.3	10.3	8.0	2.5	2.4	4.7	6.7	5.3	-	4.0	4.8	7.3	1.7
Finland	8.0	-3.7	13.5	8.5	-	-17.2	17.0	9.7	7.4	9.6	8.7	3.4	-2.2	3.4	9.9	-	1.0	3.0	-1.0	1.9	3.8
Ireland	8.4	7.1	5.0	5.7	11.9	7.3	3.8	17.7	12.0	8.1	5.4	2.3	6.2	12.3	17.9	3.1	4.0	14.2	7.0	11.3	8.6
Netherlands	11.9	8.5	12.5	10.3	14.3	-5.6	13.2	-1.3	3.9	8.9	-	1.2	-6.1	4.7	7.8	3.1	3.0	5.8	8.3	4.2	4.9
Norway	4.5	4.9	11.7	10.3	-0.8	4.0	15.3	-3.4	23.3	5.5	5.8	-2.0	1.3	7.4	9.1	3.2	-4.1	8.6	-2.0	15.0	7.0
Sweden	13.3	3.9	7.5	17.5	6.0	-9.9	4.7	1.5	7.4	8.2	-2.5	1.3	2.6	7.4	7.8	3.1	3.0	3.9	2.8	1.8	0.9
Switzerland	6.1	3.8	5.6	12.3	3.1	-9.1	13.3	11.8	3.9	2.5	2.5	3.6	-3.5	-	7.2	12.4	2.0	1.0	-2.9	5.4	4.4
Total 9 countries	9.2	5.7	9.9	12.1	6.8	-6.7	11.8	2.8	6.5	7.9	2.2	1.4	0.5	5.1	7.6	4.5	2.3	5.3	4.8	6.6	4.2
Total western Europe	10.1	6.1	8.5	11.2	8.1	-5.9	12.6	5.0	5.5	6.8	0.8	2.8	1.1	2.9	7.6	5.1	2.0	4.1	5.6	7.0	3.9
United States	8.5	-1.2	9.1	23.9	8.6	-2.1	3.5	-0.2	11.8	8.9	10.0	-3.2	-11.7	-5.5	6.8	-2.0	-0.5	13.1	18.0	10.9	9.0
Canada	10.0	5.3	9.3	10.7	-3.7	-7.3	11.9	9.0	9.9	1.8	-1.4	2.8	-1.5	7.5	18.4	6.5	4.5	3.6	9.3	1.1	4.8
Total above	9.7	4.2	8.7	14.3	7.3	-5.0	10.1	3.9	7.4	6.9	3.1	1.1	-2.5	1.2	8.3	3.6	1.7	6.0	8.7	7.4	5.2
Imports																					
France	6.6	7.5	14.0	13.7	4.3	-7.1	20.8	0.8	5.2	11.7	6.2	-3.3	3.6	-1.9	2.3	4.1	3.3	7.1	6.5	8.7	5.1
Germany	18.4	8.3	6.4	5.5	-3.9	-0.3	17.8	2.3	6.8	7.5	-	-5.0	1.4	3.9	5.3	4.2	6.1	5.4	6.4	7.3	11.9
Italy	15.6	0.3	11.0	11.2	-5.5	-10.7	15.6	-0.4	7.5	13.1	2.8	-6.6	-	-	9.0	8.8	4.5	9.5	6.9	8.3	4.5
United Kingdom	4.9	3.8	10.1	13.6	-0.1	-8.5	7.1	1.8	6.5	8.2	-4.7	-3.9	5.9	8.6	10.7	3.6	7.2	7.1	13.7	7.9	1.3
Total 4 countries	11.9	5.4	9.7	10.3	-1.5	-5.9	15.5	1.3	6.5	9.7	1.0	-4.7	2.6	2.7	6.5	4.9	5.4	6.9	8.2	8.0	6.3
Austria	18.1	8.6	14.6	10.5	2.7	-6.8	23.0	9.9	-1.6	10.5	5.0	-4.1	-2.1	7.1	8.7	4.8	5.2	5.2	8.2	14.0	8.1
Belgium	10.2	9.3	8.5	17.2	5.3	-6.3	13.5	2.4	3.5	7.9	1.0	-3.1	3.7	-	4.3	2.0	8.0	7.4	6.0	6.5	4.6
Denmark	9.7	-2.9	3.0	20.6	-6.1	-6.5	19.4	-2.3	4.8	5.7	-8.6	-5.9	-	4.8	6.9	7.5	-1.0	6.1	-1.0	1.9	0.9
Finland	21.1	-1.4	4.4	12.7	7.5	-	-3.5	-8.4	-5.3	19.4	11.6	-6.3	3.7	3.3	-	6.4	6.0	13.2	-0.8	15.1	-2.9
Ireland	3.6	5.1	8.4	13.7	1.0	-10.1	15.3	12.6	17.0	13.8	-4.9	1.2	-4.0	3.4	9.5	3.3	3.0	6.2	4.7	12.9	7.0
Netherlands	10.2	3.3	3.2	10.9	8.5	-5.2	12.3	1.2	6.0	6.8	-2.1	-7.6	1.2	2.3	6.8	6.4	4.0	6.7	7.2	2.5	5.7
Norway	12.7	1.9	-	12.8	8.2	-	11.4	7.9	-11.3	5.3	10.8	-4.0	4.2	4.0	13.5	12.0	14.8	-1.8	-9.9	-4.9	9.9
Sweden	11.5	-3.4	5.4	8.5	15.6	2.7	5.3	-3.8	-5.2	15.1	2.4	-7.0	6.3	3.5	4.5	8.7	4.0	7.7	5.4	6.8	0.8
Switzerland	14.3	5.4	6.8	6.3	-1.5	-18.2	16.7	9.5	8.7	9.3	3.7	2.4	-4.6	6.0	8.0	5.3	9.0	6.4	-7.8	5.6	2.3
Total 9 countries	12.6	3.5	5.8	12.5	5.4	-5.7	12.4	2.3	2.6	9.1	1.0	-4.4	0.6	2.6	6.4	5.7	5.9	6.5	4.8	5.8	4.2
Total western Europe	12.2	4.7	8.3	11.1	1.0	-5.8	14.4	1.7	5.1	9.5	1.0	-4.6	1.9	2.7	6.4	5.1	5.6	6.8	7.0	7.2	5.6
United States	3.2	8.8	13.4	4.7	-1.4	-12.0	21.8	10.7	10.3	0.1	-7.1	2.6	-5.1	10.4	24.0	8.7	10.5	2.6	3.8	5.8	3.7
Canada	-3.1	9.9	16.9	16.1	10.2	-5.4	7.8	0.5	3.1	11.1	-5.6	2.8	-16.4	11.0	19.7	10.4	8.1	6.2	13.7	4.8	-0.4
Total above	8.7	6.1	10.2	9.6	1.0	-7.4	15.7	4.0	6.4	6.9	-1.7	-2.3	-1.3	5.2	12.0	6.6	7.3	5.4	6.5	6.6	4.6

Source: IMF, *International Financial Statistics*, February 1992.

Note: National data are aggregated by means of weights derived from 1985 US dollar trade shares.

[a] Calculated from rounded index numbers (1985 = 100) for Belgium, Denmark, Finland, Netherlands, Norway, Sweden and Switzerland. Comparisons with the previous year are limited due to changes in methodology in France (1973, 1975, 1986), Italy (1970, 1981), UK (1970, 1973), Austria (1979,1988), Belgium (1974), Denmark (1971, 1974, 1985), Finland (1970, 1977), Greece (1977), Ireland (1975, 1985), Norway (1970, 1980), Sweden (1975, 1983), Netherlands (1985), US (1989), Switzerland (1979 imports only, 1988) and Canada (1981).

Appendix C. International trade and payments

APPENDIX TABLE C.4
Eastern Europe and the Soviet Union: Exports by main directions, 1970-1990
(Value, billion US dollars)

	1970	1971	1972	1973	1974	1975	1976	1977	1978	1979	1980	1981	1982	1983	1984	1985	1986	1987	1988	1989	1990
Bulgaria																					
World	2.00	2.18	2.63	3.32	4.02	5.17	3.76	4.43	5.11	6.22	7.16	7.41	7.51	7.09	7.23	7.39	7.60	7.84	7.55	6.65	5.16
ECE-East	1.51	1.64	2.01	2.54	2.91	3.95	2.56	3.00	3.32	3.70	3.87	3.85	4.02	4.05	3.91	4.15	5.00	4.90	4.60	4.14	2.79
ECE-West	0.32	0.34	0.39	0.49	0.56	0.56	0.67	0.72	0.83	1.49	1.84	1.63	1.46	1.43	1.43	1.32	1.03	1.11	1.15	1.36	1.22
Other	0.17	0.20	0.22	0.30	0.56	0.67	0.53	0.72	0.96	1.03	1.44	1.92	2.02	1.61	1.90	1.92	1.57	1.82	1.80	1.16	1.15
Czechoslovakia																					
World	3.79	4.18	4.92	5.99	7.24	8.70	6.40	7.29	8.24	9.36	10.48	10.40	10.34	10.09	10.00	10.55	12.16	12.36	12.38	11.99	10.73
ECE-East	2.43	2.66	3.26	3.88	4.46	5.78	3.76	4.20	4.72	5.19	5.41	5.52	5.63	5.36	5.32	5.60	6.67	6.69	6.26	5.59	3.97
ECE-West	0.92	1.00	1.12	1.51	1.99	1.99	1.85	2.16	2.41	2.96	3.58	3.27	3.22	3.16	3.18	3.34	3.74	4.05	4.46	4.91	5.44
Other	0.43	0.52	0.54	0.60	0.79	0.93	0.79	0.93	1.11	1.21	1.48	1.61	1.49	1.57	1.49	1.61	1.75	1.62	1.66	1.49	1.33
ex-GDR																					
World	4.58	5.08	6.19	7.58	9.13	11.05	8.35	8.76	9.85	11.42	12.52	14.03	15.17	15.59	15.52	17.64	16.86	16.47	15.81	16.00	16.54
ECE-East	3.13	3.50	4.39	5.26	5.95	7.74	4.68	5.28	6.02	6.91	6.65	6.79	6.79	6.60	6.37	6.73	7.48	7.28	6.53	6.03	5.84
ECE-West	1.10	1.20	1.43	1.87	2.61	2.53	2.93	2.68	2.83	3.36	4.42	5.69	6.52	7.31	7.63	9.06	7.68	7.52	7.90	8.63	9.49
Other	0.36	0.37	0.37	0.45	0.57	0.78	0.73	0.80	1.00	1.15	1.45	1.55	1.87	1.68	1.52	1.84	1.70	1.67	1.38	1.34	1.21
Hungary																					
World	2.32	2.50	3.29	4.37	5.13	6.06	4.93	5.82	6.35	7.93	8.61	8.73	8.86	8.77	8.62	8.47	9.17	9.58	10.00	9.67	9.55
ECE-East	1.44	1.62	2.15	2.80	3.22	4.10	2.73	3.25	3.45	4.14	4.33	4.65	4.62	4.32	4.17	4.43	4.95	4.79	4.46	3.96	2.98
ECE-West	0.69	0.68	0.89	1.26	1.49	1.45	1.68	1.97	2.22	2.91	3.27	2.90	2.93	3.19	3.28	2.90	3.19	3.74	4.31	4.64	5.48
Other	0.19	0.20	0.24	0.31	0.42	0.52	0.52	0.60	0.68	0.88	1.01	1.18	1.31	1.25	1.17	1.13	1.04	1.05	1.23	1.07	1.09
Poland																					
World	3.55	3.87	4.93	6.45	8.63	11.11	8.59	9.60	10.75	12.53	13.07	10.08	10.53	10.44	10.90	11.10	13.13	14.09	14.57	14.67	18.29
ECE-East	2.13	2.29	2.97	3.77	4.67	6.60	3.93	4.46	5.07	5.80	5.21	4.37	4.88	4.80	4.90	5.18	6.47	6.63	6.27	5.99	7.13
ECE-West	1.09	1.24	1.60	2.29	3.18	3.52	3.69	4.03	4.55	5.31	6.09	4.13	3.96	4.12	4.49	4.48	4.61	5.63	6.52	6.94	9.55
Other	0.33	0.34	0.35	-0.40	0.77	0.99	0.96	1.10	1.14	1.42	1.77	1.58	1.69	1.53	1.51	1.44	2.05	1.84	1.78	1.74	2.64
Romania																					
World	1.85	2.10	2.60	3.73	5.01	5.66	5.09	5.79	6.47	8.01	9.22	10.29	8.97	8.60	9.47	8.38	8.16	8.58	8.97	8.08	4.57
ECE-East	0.92	1.00	1.23	1.70	1.86	2.31	1.47	1.86	1.98	2.10	2.43	2.62	2.30	2.09	2.07	2.27	2.68	2.44	2.28	1.99	1.09
ECE-West	0.66	0.79	0.97	1.42	2.23	2.05	2.34	2.31	2.86	3.86	4.32	4.13	3.45	3.72	4.16	3.79	3.38	4.09	4.30	4.24	2.60
Other	0.27	0.31	0.40	0.61	0.92	1.30	1.29	1.63	1.62	2.05	2.47	3.54	3.22	2.79	3.24	2.32	2.10	2.04	2.39	1.85	0.89
Eastern Europe																					
World	18.10	19.92	24.56	31.44	39.16	47.77	37.12	41.69	46.77	55.46	61.06	60.94	61.38	60.59	61.74	63.53	67.07	68.93	69.29	67.06	64.84
ECE-East	11.57	12.71	16.02	19.94	23.08	30.48	19.13	22.04	24.56	27.85	27.90	27.81	28.24	27.22	26.74	28.35	33.24	32.73	30.41	27.70	23.79
ECE-West	4.78	5.25	6.41	8.84	12.06	12.10	13.15	13.87	15.70	19.88	23.54	21.75	21.54	22.95	24.17	24.90	23.63	26.15	28.64	30.72	33.85
Other	1.75	1.95	2.13	2.66	4.03	5.19	4.83	5.78	6.51	7.74	9.63	11.38	11.60	10.43	10.83	10.27	10.20	10.05	10.24	8.64	8.22
Soviet Union																					
World	12.80	13.81	15.40	21.36	28.54	35.20	29.20	35.53	39.81	49.92	57.94	60.42	64.20	63.60	62.36	57.32	60.04	63.41	62.02	62.29	59.06
ECE-East	6.76	7.24	8.12	10.01	12.41	17.99	11.04	13.03	14.87	16.68	17.81	19.01	18.66	17.76	17.53	18.09	21.93	19.90	17.07	15.17	11.10
ECE-West	2.78	3.16	3.44	5.62	9.31	9.74	11.23	13.00	13.81	20.85	26.70	26.14	27.90	28.23	27.96	23.81	19.83	23.79	25.34	27.44	31.05
Other	3.26	3.41	3.85	6.73	6.82	7.47	6.93	9.50	11.14	12.40	13.43	15.28	17.64	17.60	16.87	15.42	18.29	19.71	19.61	19.67	16.91
Eastern Europe and the Soviet Union																					
World	30.90	33.72	39.96	52.80	67.70	82.97	66.32	77.22	86.58	105.39	119.00	121.36	125.58	124.19	124.10	120.84	127.12	132.34	131.31	129.34	123.90
ECE-East	18.33	19.96	24.13	29.95	35.49	48.47	30.17	35.07	39.42	44.53	45.71	46.81	46.91	44.98	44.27	46.44	55.17	52.64	47.48	42.88	34.89
ECE-West	7.56	8.41	9.84	14.46	21.37	21.83	24.39	26.87	29.51	40.72	50.24	47.89	49.43	51.18	52.13	48.71	43.46	49.94	53.97	58.16	64.90
Other	5.01	5.36	5.98	8.39	10.85	12.66	11.76	15.28	17.65	20.13	23.05	26.66	29.24	28.03	27.69	25.68	28.49	29.76	29.85	28.30	25.13

Source: Secretariat of the United Nations Economic Commission for Europe, based on national foreign trade statistics.

Notes: Dollar values of intra-eastern and total trade were adjusted to avoid the distortions stemming from mutually inconsistent national rouble/dollar crossrates, as explained in the following paragraph. Partner country groupings: ECE-East – Soviet Union and east European former member countries of the CMEA; ECE-West – ECE market economies and Japan; Other – all remaining countries.

As an approximation to a consistent dollar valuation of rouble-denominated intra-group trade flows, the national-currency data on trade with the market economies were revalued, in national currency terms, at a common rouble-dollar crossrate and reaggregated with the data on trade with the "socialist" countries to obtain new trade totals (see United Nations Economic Commission for Europe, *Economic Bulletin for Europe*, vol.43, New York, 1991, pp.52-53 and 58-62). To generate the longest re-valued series obtainable, Hungarian crossrates (available from 1976) where used. There is thus a substantial discontinuity in the time series at 1975/76. While data for prior years may overvalue rouble-denominated trade flows, they are at least internally consistent as all countries used similar crossrates during the early period. The procedure must be considered an approximation to the desired standard of consistent valuation because intra-group trade flows contained convertible-currency components (which in 1990 were significant).

315

APPENDIX TABLE C.5
Eastern Europe and the Soviet Union: Imports by main directions, 1970-1990
(Value, billion US dollars)

	1970	1971	1972	1973	1974	1975	1976	1977	1978	1979	1980	1981	1982	1983	1984	1985	1986	1987	1988	1989	1990
Bulgaria																					
World	1.83	2.12	2.57	3.29	4.52	5.91	4.00	4.46	5.15	5.74	6.32	7.17	7.26	6.96	6.83	7.57	8.68	8.22	8.13	7.33	5.48
ECE-East	1.33	1.57	1.97	2.48	3.02	4.20	2.59	3.05	3.59	3.95	4.09	4.31	4.44	4.29	4.09	4.24	5.00	4.82	4.07	3.37	2.55
ECE-West	0.38	0.39	0.43	0.57	1.07	1.36	1.10	1.06	1.18	1.38	1.74	2.24	1.99	1.79	1.83	2.11	2.42	2.52	2.61	2.65	1.94
Other	0.13	0.16	0.17	0.24	0.43	0.36	0.32	0.35	0.39	0.42	0.49	0.63	0.82	0.87	0.91	1.22	1.26	0.89	1.44	1.31	0.99
Czechoslovakia																					
World	3.70	4.01	4.66	6.07	7.72	9.45	7.04	8.07	8.90	10.18	10.62	10.13	10.05	9.62	9.53	10.22	12.28	12.50	12.18	11.77	11.81
ECE-East	2.33	2.54	3.04	3.81	4.60	5.47	3.83	4.42	5.01	5.62	5.62	5.63	5.85	5.71	5.76	5.97	7.12	6.82	6.04	5.63	4.52
ECE-West	1.01	1.12	1.22	1.69	2.35	2.54	2.57	2.76	3.09	3.67	4.00	3.54	3.27	3.03	2.82	3.18	3.87	4.49	4.81	4.73	6.01
Other	0.35	0.34	0.41	0.57	0.76	0.72	0.65	0.89	0.80	0.90	1.01	0.96	0.90	0.88	0.95	1.07	1.28	1.20	1.33	1.41	1.28
ex-GDR																					
World	4.85	4.98	5.91	7.91	10.01	12.27	10.08	10.76	11.05	12.77	14.25	14.18	13.64	13.83	14.11	15.16	16.67	16.79	16.62	16.52	19.66
ECE-East	3.19	3.23	3.71	4.86	5.74	8.02	5.00	5.90	6.23	6.58	6.79	7.01	6.82	6.18	6.01	7.05	8.08	7.26	6.34	5.66	3.92
ECE-West	1.35	1.45	1.93	2.67	3.46	3.52	4.34	3.95	3.91	5.23	6.10	6.19	5.75	6.42	6.82	6.62	7.11	8.27	9.16	9.69	14.69
Other	0.30	0.30	0.27	0.38	0.81	0.73	0.73	0.90	0.91	0.96	1.37	0.98	1.07	1.23	1.28	1.49	1.48	1.25	1.12	1.16	1.05
Hungary																					
World	2.51	2.99	3.15	3.88	5.58	7.15	5.53	6.52	7.94	8.68	9.19	9.16	8.87	8.55	8.13	8.18	9.59	9.86	9.37	8.86	8.62
ECE-East	1.56	1.88	1.98	2.33	3.00	4.48	2.81	3.23	3.86	4.33	4.31	4.30	4.33	4.12	3.91	4.04	4.87	4.66	4.10	3.47	2.91
ECE-West	0.72	0.89	0.93	1.21	2.05	2.03	2.09	2.52	3.20	3.46	3.88	3.93	3.48	3.23	3.12	3.41	3.87	4.26	4.34	4.69	4.73
Other	0.22	0.22	0.25	0.34	0.53	0.64	0.64	0.77	0.88	0.89	1.01	0.93	1.06	1.21	1.10	0.73	0.85	0.94	0.93	0.69	0.98
Poland																					
World	3.61	4.04	5.33	7.87	10.80	13.31	11.47	11.88	12.65	14.00	14.71	11.39	9.50	9.38	9.72	10.43	12.31	12.69	12.99	12.94	12.62
ECE-East	2.36	2.58	3.08	3.91	4.69	6.18	3.90	4.63	5.17	5.64	5.90	5.66	5.29	5.13	3.36	5.51	7.08	6.50	5.59	4.92	5.46
ECE-West	0.98	1.18	1.89	3.49	5.42	6.34	6.85	6.36	6.44	6.76	6.82	4.60	3.32	3.24	3.36	3.80	4.15	4.75	5.96	6.57	6.19
Other	0.27	0.28	0.35	0.46	0.68	0.80	0.72	0.90	1.05	1.60	1.99	1.13	0.89	1.01	1.09	1.12	1.08	1.44	1.44	1.44	2.16
Romania																					
World	1.96	2.10	2.62	3.49	5.27	5.65	5.07	5.81	7.34	9.15	11.06	10.09	7.27	6.16	6.43	6.70	6.41	6.36	5.36	5.83	6.89
ECE-East	0.94	0.97	1.17	1.41	1.74	2.22	1.52	1.86	1.97	2.23	2.32	2.69	2.19	2.00	1.94	2.18	2.94	2.55	2.23	2.18	1.92
ECE-West	0.81	0.89	1.14	1.58	2.65	2.40	2.28	2.62	3.50	4.01	4.26	3.61	2.01	1.43	1.58	1.55	1.55	1.12	1.02	1.03	2.24
Other	0.21	0.25	0.31	0.50	0.88	1.02	1.27	1.33	1.87	2.92	4.48	3.79	3.07	2.72	2.91	2.97	1.92	2.68	2.11	2.62	2.73
Eastern Europe																					
World	18.45	20.24	24.25	32.50	43.90	53.75	43.19	47.49	53.03	60.53	66.14	62.13	56.55	54.50	54.75	58.26	65.95	66.41	64.65	63.25	65.08
ECE-East	11.72	12.77	14.95	18.80	22.79	31.30	19.64	23.08	25.82	28.35	29.01	29.59	28.92	27.44	26.98	28.98	35.10	32.61	28.38	25.24	21.28
ECE-West	5.25	5.92	7.53	11.20	17.01	18.18	19.22	19.26	21.32	24.51	26.79	24.10	19.82	19.14	19.54	20.67	22.96	25.41	27.90	29.37	35.81
Other	1.48	1.55	1.76	2.50	4.10	4.27	4.32	5.15	5.89	7.68	10.34	8.43	7.81	7.92	8.24	8.61	7.89	8.39	8.37	8.64	9.18
Soviet Union																					
World	11.73	12.48	16.09	21.01	25.95	38.77	30.79	32.21	38.48	44.37	52.22	56.91	57.12	55.39	53.95	54.76	55.02	53.79	58.04	64.98	64.96
ECE-East	6.63	7.26	9.27	10.97	12.26	17.15	10.29	11.82	14.72	15.73	16.26	16.54	17.26	16.77	16.51	17.59	20.34	19.87	18.15	17.12	15.04
ECE-West	3.02	3.11	4.45	6.37	8.67	14.20	14.55	13.78	16.70	20.55	24.47	26.55	27.11	25.94	25.00	24.28	23.43	22.63	27.53	33.34	35.38
Other	2.08	2.12	2.36	3.67	5.02	7.42	5.95	6.60	7.06	8.09	11.49	13.81	12.74	12.67	12.44	12.90	11.24	11.30	12.36	14.52	14.54
Eastern Europe and the Soviet Union																					
World	30.18	32.72	40.33	53.51	69.85	92.52	73.98	79.70	91.51	104.90	118.36	119.03	113.67	109.89	108.70	113.02	120.97	120.21	122.69	128.24	130.04
ECE-East	18.35	20.03	24.22	29.77	35.05	48.45	29.94	34.90	40.53	44.07	45.27	46.13	46.19	44.22	43.49	46.57	55.43	52.48	46.53	42.37	36.33
ECE-West	8.27	9.03	11.99	17.57	25.68	32.38	33.77	33.05	38.02	45.06	51.26	50.65	46.93	45.08	44.54	44.94	46.40	48.04	55.43	62.71	71.19
Other	3.56	3.66	4.12	6.17	9.12	11.69	10.27	11.75	12.95	15.77	21.83	22.25	20.55	20.59	20.67	21.51	19.13	19.69	20.73	23.16	23.72

Source: Secretariat of the United Nations Economic Commission for Europe, based on national foreign trade statistics.

Notes: Dollar values of intra-eastern and total trade were adjusted to avoid the distortions stemming from mutually inconsistent national rouble/dollar crossrates, as explained in the following paragraph. Partner country groupings: ECE-East – Soviet Union and east European former member countries of the CMEA; ECE-West – ECE market economies and Japan; Other – all remaining countries.

As an approximation to a consistent dollar valuation of rouble-denominated intra-group trade flows, the national-currency data on trade with the market economies were revalued, in national currency terms, at a common rouble-dollar crossrate and reaggregated with the data on trade with the "socialist" countries to obtain new trade totals (see United Nations Economic Commission for Europe, *Economic Bulletin for Europe*, vol.43, New York, 1991, pp.52-53 and 58-62). To generate the longest re-valued series obtainable, Hungarian crossrates (available from 1976) where used. There is thus a substantial discontinuity in the time series at 1975/76. While data for prior years may overvalue rouble-denominated trade flows, they are at least internally consistent as all countries used similar crossrates during the early period. The procedure must be considered an approximation to the desired standard of consistent valuation because intra-group trade flows contained convertible-currency components (which in 1990 were significant).

Appendix C. International trade and payments

APPENDIX TABLE C.6
East-west trade: Value of western exports, by country of origin
(Billion US dollars)

	1970	1971	1972	1973	1974	1975	1976	1977	1978	1979	1980	1981	1982	1983	1984	1985	1986	1987	1988	1989	1990
Austria	0.48	0.49	0.54	0.76	1.36	1.51	1.50	1.68	1.98	2.45	2.46	2.08	2.00	1.92	1.95	2.08	2.43	2.52	3.01	3.20	4.36
Belgium-Luxembourg	0.21	0.23	0.30	0.52	0.87	0.89	0.83	0.82	0.94	1.12	1.35	1.17	0.98	1.11	0.98	1.13	1.08	1.10	1.06	1.33	1.31
Denmark	0.11	0.13	0.13	0.19	0.28	0.31	0.27	0.29	0.34	0.36	0.34	0.29	0.22	0.22	0.27	0.30	0.41	0.33	0.43	0.58	0.84
Finland	0.35	0.32	0.43	0.51	0.88	1.28	1.45	1.65	1.71	1.74	2.76	3.63	3.71	3.41	2.72	3.11	3.51	3.36	3.43	3.62	3.67
France	0.71	0.78	0.98	1.45	1.79	2.78	2.86	3.14	3.31	4.42	5.04	4.01	2.99	3.49	3.18	3.12	2.93	3.28	3.62	3.62	3.94
Germany	1.93	2.26	2.97	4.89	7.33	8.29	7.83	8.78	10.25	11.88	12.31	9.86	9.57	9.75	9.06	9.47	12.03	13.16	14.69	16.93	19.61
Greece	0.14	0.10	0.13	0.21	0.31	0.31	0.31	0.39	0.42	0.40	0.59	0.40	0.45	0.37	0.33	0.37	0.32	0.31	0.25	0.45	0.52
Iceland	0.01	0.02	0.02	0.02	0.04	0.04	0.04	0.06	0.06	0.07	0.09	0.08	0.06	0.06	0.07	0.07	0.06	0.06	0.08	0.07	0.05
Ireland	0.01	0.01	0.01	0.01	0.03	0.04	0.02	0.03	0.04	0.08	0.11	0.08	0.07	0.09	0.05	0.08	0.11	0.11	0.09	0.15	0.25
Italy	1.08	1.17	1.19	1.48	2.43	2.86	2.43	2.94	3.18	3.75	3.83	3.41	3.34	3.65	3.33	3.74	4.07	4.83	4.95	5.97	7.78
Netherlands	0.23	0.26	0.33	0.46	0.74	0.81	0.79	0.93	1.02	1.22	1.49	1.44	1.10	1.15	0.95	1.04	1.20	1.35	1.29	1.64	1.87
Norway	0.06	0.06	0.09	0.13	0.16	0.24	0.25	0.25	0.33	0.25	0.30	0.37	0.24	0.25	0.17	0.17	0.18	0.22	0.31	0.32	0.43
Portugal	0.01	0.01	0.01	0.01	0.02	0.04	0.08	0.08	0.07	0.09	0.09	0.08	0.09	0.08	0.09	0.09	0.08	0.09	0.10	0.15	0.10
Spain	0.09	0.07	0.11	0.14	0.25	0.27	0.31	0.29	0.37	0.57	0.62	0.65	0.41	0.52	0.57	0.68	0.45	0.55	0.49	0.65	0.68
Sweden	0.30	0.30	0.32	0.50	0.77	1.07	0.98	0.96	1.02	1.27	1.33	1.12	0.89	0.77	0.77	0.85	0.91	0.96	1.10	1.24	1.33
Switzerland	0.25	0.26	0.35	0.51	0.74	0.91	0.91	1.05	1.27	1.28	1.26	1.03	0.92	0.91	0.89	0.98	1.29	1.54	1.67	1.77	2.04
Turkey	0.08	0.08	0.09	0.12	0.16	0.12	0.17	0.18	0.33	0.30	0.49	0.35	0.31	0.24	0.28	0.33	0.30	0.32	0.58	1.01	0.97
United Kingdom	0.66	0.70	0.72	0.87	1.10	1.43	1.33	1.67	2.09	2.30	2.86	2.26	1.68	1.57	1.85	1.68	1.87	2.04	2.29	2.41	2.65
Western Europe	6.71	7.24	8.72	12.77	19.26	23.21	22.36	25.19	28.72	33.55	37.31	32.31	29.00	29.53	27.52	29.29	33.23	36.16	39.43	45.11	52.39
United States	0.49	0.53	0.97	2.00	1.72	3.09	3.73	2.85	3.97	6.05	4.12	4.61	3.87	3.30	4.47	3.74	2.42	2.59	4.06	5.68	4.72
Canada	0.16	0.19	0.37	0.42	0.19	0.64	0.76	0.57	0.76	1.01	1.82	1.96	2.08	1.56	1.78	1.32	1.08	0.72	1.08	0.72	1.11
North America	0.65	0.72	1.34	2.42	1.91	3.73	4.49	3.42	4.73	7.06	5.95	6.57	5.95	4.85	6.25	5.06	3.49	3.31	5.14	6.39	5.83
Japan	0.47	0.54	0.73	0.82	1.74	2.26	2.85	2.77	3.25	3.12	3.57	3.95	4.34	3.29	2.90	3.25	3.78	3.16	3.87	3.77	3.45
Developed market economies	7.83	8.50	10.79	16.02	22.91	29.19	29.70	31.38	36.70	43.72	46.82	42.83	39.29	37.68	36.67	37.59	40.51	42.63	48.45	55.28	61.67

Sources: United Nations commodity trade data (COMTRADE); OECD, *Monthly Statistics of Foreign Trade*, Series A, Paris, September 1991.

Note: Data cover reported balances (f.o.b.-f.o.b) with seven east European countries (Albania, Bulgaria, Czechoslovakia, Hungary, Poland, Romania, Yugoslavia) and the Soviet Union.

APPENDIX TABLE C.7

East-west trade: Value of western imports, by country of destination

(Billion US dollars)

	1970	1971	1972	1973	1974	1975	1976	1977	1978	1979	1980	1981	1982	1983	1984	1985	1986	1987	1988	1989	1990
Austria	0.34	0.39	0.44	0.60	0.87	0.93	1.08	1.24	1.37	1.75	2.33	2.40	2.10	1.98	2.27	2.22	2.24	2.27	2.43	2.52	3.27
Belgium-Luxembourg	0.15	0.20	0.24	0.36	0.52	0.55	0.52	0.66	0.75	0.95	1.49	1.32	1.72	1.42	2.10	1.55	1.41	1.70	1.74	1.71	2.16
Denmark	0.12	0.12	0.14	0.25	0.36	0.45	0.51	0.42	0.49	0.67	0.67	0.45	0.51	0.44	0.54	0.52	0.50	0.51	0.51	0.54	0.70
Finland	0.39	0.45	0.46	0.60	1.39	1.43	1.48	1.64	1.64	2.42	3.57	3.53	3.48	3.44	3.06	2.93	2.59	3.06	2.80	3.18	3.03
France	0.43	0.54	0.68	0.99	1.27	1.58	1.87	2.15	2.40	3.17	5.09	4.85	3.99	3.90	3.73	3.66	4.25	4.41	4.73	4.69	5.90
Germany	1.28	1.50	1.86	2.77	3.46	3.71	4.64	5.13	6.34	8.91	9.52	8.43	8.66	8.69	9.46	9.39	10.30	11.19	11.74	13.08	17.43
Greece	0.11	0.12	0.16	0.19	0.19	0.24	0.39	0.42	0.62	0.61	0.62	0.51	0.51	0.46	0.74	0.73	0.57	0.73	0.65	0.78	0.94
Iceland	0.01	0.02	0.02	0.03	0.06	0.05	0.06	0.07	0.06	0.09	0.10	0.08	0.09	0.08	0.08	0.07	0.06	0.08	0.08	0.08	0.10
Ireland	0.03	0.03	0.04	0.05	0.08	0.08	0.08	0.11	0.12	0.17	0.13	0.10	0.12	0.13	0.14	0.14	0.17	0.17	0.16	0.19	0.22
Italy	0.94	1.01	1.31	1.77	2.13	2.03	2.65	2.83	3.16	4.07	5.58	4.94	5.49	5.73	6.62	5.53	5.54	6.30	7.05	8.03	8.89
Netherlands	0.18	0.22	0.28	0.40	0.59	0.74	0.90	1.01	1.17	1.86	2.17	2.41	3.04	3.06	2.76	2.88	1.76	2.19	1.98	2.29	2.72
Norway	0.08	0.15	0.13	0.18	0.19	0.23	0.31	0.37	0.25	0.36	0.32	0.33	0.40	0.27	0.33	0.32	0.26	0.38	0.42	0.46	0.67
Portugal	0.01	0.02	0.02	0.04	0.05	0.08	0.15	0.14	0.12	0.18	0.21	0.24	0.11	0.10	0.08	0.07	0.08	0.08	0.09	0.10	0.09
Spain	0.06	0.06	0.14	0.19	0.30	0.41	0.39	0.32	0.35	0.51	0.70	0.73	0.76	0.77	0.81	0.64	0.57	1.23	1.52	1.71	1.81
Sweden	0.28	0.28	0.34	0.46	0.77	0.90	0.96	0.99	0.93	1.54	1.37	1.03	1.16	1.36	1.21	1.16	1.02	1.44	1.47	1.53	1.61
Switzerland	0.14	0.15	0.17	0.26	0.37	0.35	0.51	0.61	0.86	1.16	1.43	1.23	1.15	1.03	0.94	0.88	0.83	0.74	0.68	0.73	0.81
Turkey	0.10	0.12	0.15	0.16	0.24	0.22	0.28	0.32	0.35	0.57	0.77	0.79	0.39	0.70	0.88	0.60	0.81	0.87	1.03	1.42	2.09
United Kingdom	0.56	0.56	0.62	0.81	1.02	1.36	1.71	1.97	2.05	2.66	2.68	1.47	1.72	1.74	2.14	1.84	2.08	2.68	2.80	2.82	3.09
Western Europe	5.24	5.94	7.18	10.09	13.87	15.35	18.50	20.40	23.03	31.66	38.77	34.84	35.40	35.30	37.87	35.13	35.02	40.04	41.90	45.85	55.53
United States	0.29	0.28	0.42	0.63	1.05	0.90	1.14	1.14	1.48	1.57	1.66	1.82	1.30	1.60	2.37	2.28	2.36	2.51	2.79	2.63	2.83
Canada	0.07	0.08	0.11	0.14	0.19	0.17	0.20	0.19	0.20	0.27	0.25	0.24	0.17	0.18	0.21	0.20	0.22	0.26	0.46	0.45	0.49
North America	0.35	0.37	0.53	0.77	1.24	1.07	1.33	1.32	1.68	1.84	1.90	2.06	1.46	1.77	2.57	2.48	2.58	2.78	3.25	3.07	3.32
Japan	0.46	0.48	0.59	1.07	1.51	1.21	1.22	1.47	1.48	1.99	1.90	1.58	1.39	1.53	1.63	1.47	1.74	2.31	2.93	3.21	3.47
Developed market economies	6.05	6.79	8.29	11.93	16.62	17.62	21.05	23.20	26.20	35.48	42.58	38.48	38.25	38.60	42.07	39.08	39.35	45.13	48.08	52.14	62.32

Sources: As for Appendix table C.6.

Note: Data cover reported balances (f.o.b.-f.o.b) with seven east European countries (Albania, Bulgaria, Czechoslovakia, Hungary, Poland, Romania, Yugoslavia) and the Soviet Union.

a Including trade between the Federal Republic of Germany and the German Democratic Republic.

APPENDIX TABLE C.8

East-west trade: Western trade balances by western country
(Billion US dollars)

	1970	1971	1972	1973	1974	1975	1976	1977	1978	1979	1980	1981	1982	1983	1984	1985	1986	1987	1988	1989	1990
Austria	0.13	0.10	0.10	0.16	0.49	0.58	0.42	0.44	0.61	0.69	0.12	-0.32	-0.10	-0.06	-0.32	-0.14	0.19	0.25	0.58	0.68	1.09
Belgium-Luxembourg	0.06	0.03	0.06	0.16	0.35	0.34	0.31	0.16	0.19	0.17	-0.15	-0.14	-0.74	-0.31	-1.13	-0.41	-0.33	-0.60	-0.68	-0.37	-0.86
Denmark	-0.02	0.02	-0.01	-0.06	-0.08	-0.14	-0.24	-0.13	-0.16	-0.31	-0.34	-0.17	-0.29	-0.23	-0.27	-0.22	-0.09	-0.18	-0.08	0.04	0.13
Finland	-0.04	-0.14	-0.02	-0.09	-0.51	-0.15	-0.03	0.01	0.07	-0.68	-0.82	0.11	0.23	-0.03	-0.34	0.18	0.92	0.30	0.63	0.44	0.64
France	0.28	0.24	0.31	0.46	0.52	1.20	0.99	0.99	0.91	1.25	-0.05	-0.83	-1.00	-0.41	-0.55	-0.54	-1.32	-1.14	-1.11	-1.08	-1.96
Germany	0.65	0.76	1.11	2.12	3.87	4.58	3.19	3.65	3.91	2.97	2.79	1.42	0.90	1.06	-0.40	0.08	1.73	1.97	2.95	3.85	2.18
Greece	0.02	-0.02	-0.02	0.02	0.12	0.08	-0.08	-0.03	-0.20	-0.21	-0.02	-0.11	-0.07	-0.09	-0.41	-0.36	-0.25	-0.42	-0.40	-0.33	-0.42
Iceland	-	-	-	-	-0.02	-0.01	-0.02	-	-	-0.02	-0.01	-0.01	-0.03	-0.02	-0.01	-0.01	-	-0.02	-	-0.01	-0.05
Ireland	-0.02	-0.02	-0.03	-0.04	-0.05	-0.05	-0.06	-0.07	-0.08	-0.09	-0.02	-0.02	-0.05	-0.04	-0.08	-0.06	-0.05	-0.06	-0.07	-0.04	0.04
Italy	0.14	0.15	-0.12	-0.29	0.31	0.83	-0.22	0.11	0.02	-0.32	-1.76	-1.53	-2.15	-2.08	-3.29	-1.78	-1.47	-1.46	-2.11	-2.06	-1.11
Netherlands	0.05	0.04	0.05	0.06	0.15	0.07	-0.11	-0.08	-0.15	-0.64	-0.68	-0.97	-1.95	-1.91	-1.81	-1.84	-0.55	-0.83	-0.69	-0.65	-0.86
Norway	-0.02	-0.09	-0.04	-0.05	-0.03	0.01	-0.06	-0.13	0.08	-0.11	-0.03	0.04	-0.16	-0.02	-0.16	-0.15	-0.08	-0.16	-0.12	-0.14	-0.24
Portugal	-	-0.02	-0.01	-0.03	-0.03	-0.03	-0.07	-0.06	-0.05	-0.09	-0.12	-0.16	-0.02	-0.02	0.02	0.02	-	0.01	0.01	0.05	0.01
Spain	0.03	0.01	-0.03	-0.05	-0.05	-0.14	-0.08	-0.03	0.02	0.07	-0.08	-0.08	-0.35	-0.25	-0.24	0.03	-0.11	-0.67	-1.03	-1.07	-1.13
Sweden	0.02	0.01	-0.02	0.04	-0.01	0.16	0.01	-0.03	0.08	-0.27	-0.04	0.09	-0.28	-0.59	-0.45	-0.32	-0.11	-0.48	-0.38	-0.28	-0.28
Switzerland	0.11	0.11	0.18	0.25	0.37	0.57	0.40	0.43	0.41	0.12	-0.17	-0.20	-0.23	-0.12	-0.05	0.10	0.46	0.80	0.99	1.04	1.23
Turkey	-0.01	-0.03	-0.06	-0.05	-0.08	-0.10	-0.12	-0.15	-0.02	-0.27	-0.28	-0.45	-0.08	-0.46	-0.60	-0.27	-0.51	-0.54	-0.45	-0.41	-1.11
United Kingdom	0.10	0.14	0.10	0.06	0.08	0.07	-0.38	-0.30	0.04	-0.36	0.18	0.79	-0.04	-0.17	-0.29	-0.16	-0.21	-0.64	-0.51	-0.41	-0.44
Western Europe	1.48	1.30	1.54	2.68	5.40	7.86	3.86	4.79	5.68	1.89	-1.46	-2.53	-6.40	-5.77	-10.35	-5.84	-1.79	-3.88	-2.46	-0.74	-3.14
United States	0.20	0.25	0.55	1.38	0.67	2.19	2.59	1.72	2.49	4.48	2.47	2.79	2.57	1.70	2.10	1.46	0.06	0.08	1.27	3.05	1.89
Canada	0.09	0.11	0.26	0.28	-	0.47	0.56	0.38	0.56	0.74	1.58	1.72	1.91	1.38	1.57	1.11	0.86	0.46	0.62	0.27	0.62
North America	0.29	0.35	0.81	1.66	0.66	2.66	3.16	2.10	3.05	5.22	4.04	4.51	4.48	3.08	3.67	2.58	0.91	0.54	1.90	3.32	2.51
Japan	0.01	0.06	0.14	-0.25	0.24	1.05	1.63	1.29	1.77	1.13	1.67	2.37	2.95	1.76	1.27	1.78	2.04	0.85	0.94	0.56	-0.01
Developed market economies	1.78	1.72	2.50	4.09	6.30	11.57	8.65	8.18	10.50	8.24	4.25	4.35	1.04	-0.93	-5.41	-1.49	1.16	-2.50	0.38	3.14	-0.65

Sources: As for Appendix table C.6.

Note: Data cover reported balances (f.o.b.-f.o.b) with seven east European countries (Albania, Bulgaria, Czechoslovakia, Hungary, Poland, Romania, Yugoslavia) and the Soviet Union.

a Including trade between the Federal Republic of Germany and the German Democratic Republic.

APPENDIX TABLE C.9
East-west trade: Western exports, imports and balances by eastern country
(Billion US dollars)

	1970	1971	1972	1973	1974	1975	1976	1977	1978	1979	1980	1981	1982	1983	1984	1985	1986	1987	1988	1989	1990
Western exports to:																					
Albania	0.02	0.02	0.02	0.04	0.05	0.06	0.04	0.06	0.07	0.09	0.12	0.13	0.15	0.11	0.11	0.10	0.08	0.08	0.11	0.16	0.19
Bulgaria	0.33	0.32	0.35	0.49	0.85	1.10	0.94	0.90	1.10	1.23	1.61	1.85	1.55	1.56	1.44	1.83	2.19	2.34	2.37	2.39	1.56
Czechoslovakia	0.78	0.91	0.99	1.33	1.71	1.86	2.06	2.06	2.32	2.74	2.94	2.30	2.12	1.91	1.87	2.12	2.70	3.28	3.49	3.54	4.75
Hungary	0.62	0.74	0.83	1.11	1.78	1.83	1.81	2.31	2.99	2.96	3.25	3.19	2.85	2.57	2.50	2.80	3.45	3.87	3.95	4.60	5.37
Poland	0.87	1.03	1.65	3.10	4.52	5.41	5.43	4.94	5.51	5.92	6.41	4.19	3.15	2.81	2.84	3.02	3.26	3.84	4.73	6.00	7.55
Romania	0.70	0.75	0.98	1.35	2.04	1.99	1.99	2.29	2.97	3.75	3.87	3.00	1.65	1.26	1.34	1.38	1.59	1.22	1.17	1.13	2.29
Yugoslavia	1.95	2.15	2.17	3.08	4.70	4.79	4.13	5.54	6.45	8.39	8.16	6.88	5.72	5.51	5.28	6.01	7.43	7.91	8.68	9.81	13.57
Eastern Europe	5.26	5.93	6.99	10.49	15.64	17.03	16.42	18.11	21.42	25.08	26.36	21.53	17.20	15.73	15.38	17.26	20.68	22.54	24.49	27.63	35.28
Soviet Union	2.57	2.58	3.80	5.52	7.27	12.16	13.28	13.27	15.28	18.64	20.46	21.30	22.09	21.95	21.29	20.34	19.83	20.08	23.96	27.65	26.39
Eastern Europe and the Soviet Union	7.83	8.50	10.79	16.02	22.91	29.19	29.70	31.38	36.70	43.72	46.82	42.83	39.29	37.68	36.67	37.59	40.51	42.63	48.45	55.28	61.67
Total	1.09	1.21	1.55	1.87	2.41	2.72	2.99	3.08	3.77	4.96	5.39	4.90	4.32	4.66	4.02	4.19	5.36	6.67	7.00	7.39	15.21
Western imports (f.o.b.) from:																					
Albania	0.01	0.01	0.01	0.02	0.04	0.05	0.04	0.06	0.05	0.11	0.11	0.12	0.13	0.11	0.11	0.08	0.10	0.09	0.12	0.14	0.13
Bulgaria	0.22	0.23	0.25	0.34	0.39	0.37	0.45	0.48	0.55	0.85	0.94	0.81	0.76	0.69	0.70	0.67	0.71	0.72	0.71	0.75	0.94
Czechoslovakia	0.67	0.77	0.88	1.19	1.43	1.53	1.60	1.77	2.05	2.59	3.05	2.58	2.53	2.48	2.58	2.51	2.96	3.34	3.63	3.93	4.63
Hungary	0.50	0.53	0.75	1.04	1.26	1.18	1.36	1.59	1.80	2.41	2.69	2.38	2.16	2.22	2.43	2.49	2.88	3.55	3.92	4.31	5.44
Poland	0.98	1.12	1.40	1.98	2.68	2.98	3.40	3.63	4.04	4.75	5.18	3.41	3.13	3.10	3.70	3.69	3.99	4.67	5.42	5.81	8.45
Romania	0.51	0.58	0.74	1.03	1.47	1.56	1.85	1.79	2.19	3.05	3.30	3.35	2.44	2.59	3.51	3.28	3.44	3.88	3.82	3.68	2.59
Yugoslavia	0.86	0.96	1.36	1.84	1.99	1.72	2.24	2.46	2.82	3.55	3.87	3.20	3.33	3.85	4.27	4.62	5.90	7.44	8.66	9.45	11.44
Eastern Europe	3.74	4.19	5.40	7.44	9.26	9.38	10.95	11.78	13.50	17.31	19.13	15.85	14.47	15.03	17.30	17.33	19.97	23.69	26.28	28.07	33.62
Soviet Union	2.32	2.59	2.90	4.49	7.36	8.24	10.10	11.42	12.69	18.17	23.45	22.63	23.79	23.57	24.78	21.75	19.37	21.43	21.80	24.07	28.69
Eastern Europe and the Soviet Union	6.05	6.79	8.29	11.93	16.62	17.62	21.05	23.20	26.20	35.48	42.58	38.48	38.25	38.60	42.07	39.08	39.35	45.13	48.08	52.14	62.32
Total	0.92	1.06	1.22	1.61	2.14	2.33	2.55	2.78	3.27	4.04	5.06	4.76	5.00	5.00	4.94	4.83	5.52	6.20	6.47	6.58	7.20
Western trade balances with:																					
Albania	0.01	0.01	0.01	0.02	0.02	0.02	0.01	0.01	0.03	-0.02	0.01	–	0.02	-0.00	-0.00	0.02	-0.03	-0.01	-0.01	0.02	0.06
Bulgaria	0.11	0.10	0.10	0.15	0.46	0.73	0.48	0.42	0.56	0.38	0.67	1.04	0.79	0.87	0.74	1.16	1.48	1.61	1.67	1.64	0.62
Czechoslovakia	0.11	0.14	0.11	0.14	0.28	0.33	0.47	0.29	0.27	0.14	-0.11	-0.27	-0.41	-0.56	-0.71	-0.39	-0.26	-0.06	-0.14	-0.38	0.12
Hungary	0.13	0.21	0.08	0.07	0.52	0.65	0.45	0.72	1.19	0.55	0.57	0.81	0.70	0.35	0.06	0.30	0.57	0.33	0.03	0.30	-0.07
Poland	-0.11	-0.09	0.24	1.12	1.83	2.43	2.03	1.31	1.47	1.18	1.23	0.78	0.02	-0.29	-0.86	-0.67	-0.73	-0.82	-0.69	0.19	-0.91
Romania	0.19	0.17	0.25	0.32	0.57	0.43	0.14	0.50	0.78	0.70	0.57	-0.35	-0.78	-1.33	-2.17	-1.89	-1.85	-2.66	-2.65	-2.55	-0.30
Yugoslavia	1.09	1.19	0.80	1.24	2.71	3.06	1.89	3.08	3.63	4.84	4.30	3.68	2.39	1.66	1.01	1.39	1.53	0.47	0.02	0.36	2.13
Eastern Europe	1.53	1.74	1.59	3.05	6.38	7.65	5.47	6.33	7.91	7.77	7.24	5.68	2.73	0.70	-1.92	-0.08	0.71	-1.15	-1.79	-0.44	1.65
Soviet Union	0.25	-0.02	0.91	1.03	-0.09	3.92	3.18	1.85	2.58	0.47	-2.99	-1.33	-1.69	-1.62	-3.49	-1.41	0.46	-1.35	2.16	3.58	-2.30
Eastern Europe and the Soviet Union	1.78	1.72	2.50	4.09	6.30	11.57	8.65	8.18	10.50	8.24	4.25	4.35	1.04	-0.93	-5.41	-1.49	1.16	-2.50	0.38	3.14	-0.65
Total	0.17	0.15	0.33	0.26	0.26	-0.39	0.44	0.30	0.49	0.92	0.33	0.14	-0.68	-0.34	-0.92	-0.64	-0.16	0.46	0.53	0.81	8.01

Sources: As for Appendix tables C.6-C.8.

Appendix C. International trade and payments

APPENDIX TABLE C.10
Eastern Europe and the Soviet Union: Balance of payments in convertible currencies
(Billion US dollars)

	1970	1971	1972	1973	1974	1975	1976	1977	1978	1979	1980	1981	1982	1983	1984	1985	1986	1987	1988	1989	1990
Bulgaria																					
Merchandise export	0.5	0.5	0.5	0.7	0.9	1.0	1.1	1.2	1.5	2.4	3.3	3.4	3.1	2.7	3.3	3.3	2.7	3.3	3.5	3.1	2.5
Merchandise import	0.5	0.5	0.6	0.8	1.1	1.8	1.5	1.5	1.5	1.8	2.5	3.1	2.6	2.7	3.0	3.7	3.5	4.2	4.5	4.3	3.3
Balance	-	-	-	-0.1	-0.2	-0.8	-0.4	-0.3	0.1	0.5	0.8	0.3	0.5	0.1	0.3	-0.4	-0.8	-1.0	-1.0	-1.2	-0.8
Invisibles	-	-	-	-	-	-0.1	-	-0.3	0.1	0.1	0.1	0.3	0.3	0.2	0.4	0.3	0.1	0.2	0.1	-0.1	-0.4
Current account	-	-0.1	-	-0.1	-0.2	-0.9	-0.4	-0.3	0.1	0.6	0.9	0.6	0.8	0.3	0.7	-0.1	-0.7	-0.8	-0.8	-1.3	-1.2
Czechoslovakia																					
Merchandise export	0.8	1.0	1.2	1.6	2.2	2.1	2.1	2.5	2.9	3.5	4.4	4.2	4.1	4.0	4.0	3.9	4.3	4.5	5.0	5.4	6.0
Merchandise import	0.9	1.0	1.2	1.7	2.4	2.5	2.8	3.1	3.3	4.1	4.4	3.9	3.4	3.2	3.1	3.2	4.1	4.7	5.1	5.0	6.8
Balance	-0.1	-0.1	-	-0.2	-0.2	-0.4	-0.7	-0.6	-0.4	-0.5	-	0.3	0.7	0.8	0.9	0.7	0.2	-0.1	-0.1	0.4	-0.8
Invisibles	0.1	0.1	0.1	0.2	0.1	0.1	0.2	-	-	-	-0.3	-0.3	-0.1	0.1	0.2	0.1	0.2	0.2	0.3	-0.1	-0.3
Current account	-	-	0.1	-	-	-0.3	-0.6	-0.6	-0.4	-0.5	-0.3	0.1	0.6	0.9	1.1	0.8	0.5	0.1	0.1	0.3	-1.1
Hungary																					
Merchandise export	0.6	0.6	0.9	1.5	2.1	2.2	2.3	2.7	3.2	4.1	4.9	4.4	4.8	4.8	4.9	4.2	4.2	5.0	5.5	6.4	6.3
Merchandise import	0.7	0.8	0.9	1.4	2.5	2.5	2.5	3.0	4.0	4.2	4.6	4.4	4.2	4.1	4.0	4.1	4.7	5.0	5.0	5.9	6.0
Balance	-0.1	-0.2	-0.1	0.1	-0.4	-0.3	-0.2	-0.4	-0.8	-0.2	0.3	-	0.7	0.8	0.9	0.1	-0.5	-	0.5	0.5	0.3
Invisibles	-	-	-	-0.1	-0.1	-0.2	-0.2	-0.4	-0.5	-0.7	-0.6	-1.2	-1.0	-0.7	-0.8	-1.0	-1.0	-0.9	-1.3	-2.0	-0.2
Current account	-0.1	-0.3	-0.1	-	-0.5	-0.5	-0.4	-0.8	-1.2	-0.8	-0.4	-0.7	-0.3	0.1	0.1	-0.8	-1.5	-0.9	-0.8	-1.4	0.1
Poland																					
Merchandise export	1.1	1.3	1.6	2.3	3.5	4.1	4.3	4.7	5.3	6.1	7.4	5.0	4.5	4.8	5.3	5.1	5.3	6.2	7.2	7.6	10.9
Merchandise import	1.0	1.1	1.8	3.6	5.6	6.9	7.0	6.6	7.4	8.2	8.2	5.8	4.3	3.9	3.9	4.0	4.3	5.1	6.3	7.3	8.6
Balance	0.1	0.2	-0.2	-1.3	-2.1	-2.8	-2.7	-1.9	-2.1	-2.1	-0.8	-0.8	0.3	0.9	1.4	1.1	1.0	1.0	0.9	0.2	2.2
Invisibles	0.1	0.1	0.2	0.2	-	-0.2	-0.1	-0.3	-0.4	-1.2	-1.8	-2.4	-2.5	-2.3	-2.2	-1.7	-1.7	-1.4	-1.5	-2.1	-1.5
Current account	0.1	0.3	-	-1.1	-2.1	-3.0	-2.8	-2.1	-2.4	-3.4	-2.6	-3.2	-2.3	-1.4	-0.8	-0.6	-0.7	-0.4	-0.6	-1.8	0.7
Romania																					
Merchandise export	0.7	0.8	1.1	1.7	2.6	2.8	3.4	3.7	4.0	5.4	6.5	7.2	6.2	6.3	6.9	6.3	5.1	5.9	6.5	6.0	3.4
Merchandise import	0.8	0.9	1.1	1.7	2.9	2.9	3.3	3.8	4.6	6.5	8.0	7.0	4.7	4.6	4.7	4.8	3.2	3.4	2.9	3.4	5.1
Balance	-0.1	-0.1	-0.1	-0.1	-0.3	0.1	0.1	-0.1	-0.6	-1.2	-1.5	0.2	1.5	1.7	2.2	1.4	1.9	2.4	3.6	2.6	-1.7
Invisibles	-0.1	-0.1	-	-0.1	-0.2	-0.1	-0.1	-0.2	-0.2	-0.5	-0.9	-1.0	-0.9	-0.8	-0.6	-0.5	-0.5	-0.2	-1.5	0.3	0.1
Current account	-0.1	-0.1	-	-0.2	-0.5	-0.3	-0.1	-0.3	-0.4	-1.7	-2.4	-0.8	0.7	0.9	1.5	0.9	1.4	2.2	3.6	2.9	-1.7
Yugoslavia																					
Merchandise export							4.9	5.2	5.8	6.8	9.1	10.4	10.5	6.3	6.6	6.5	7.2	8.6	9.6	10.5	11.8
Merchandise import							6.8	9.0	9.6	12.9	14.0	13.5	12.5	8.1	7.8	8.3	9.7	9.6	10.2	12.0	16.5
Balance							-1.9	-3.8	-3.8	-6.1	-4.9	-3.2	-2.0	-1.8	-1.2	-1.8	-2.5	-1.0	-0.6	-1.5	-4.7
Invisibles							1.7	2.5	2.5	2.4	2.6	2.0	1.5	2.1	2.0	2.1	2.7	2.1	2.8	3.5	1.8
Current account							0.2	-1.3	-1.3	-3.7	-2.3	-1.0	-0.5	0.3	0.9	0.3	0.2	1.1	2.2	2.0	-2.9
Eastern Europe																					
Merchandise export	3.7	4.1	5.3	7.7	11.3	12.3	13.2	14.8	16.9	21.4	26.4	24.6	22.8	28.9	31.0	29.2	28.8	33.5	37.4	39.1	40.9
Merchandise import	3.9	4.4	5.7	9.2	14.4	16.7	17.1	18.0	20.8	24.9	27.7	24.2	19.2	26.4	26.6	28.1	29.5	32.1	34.1	38.0	46.3
Balance	-0.2	-0.2	-0.3	-1.5	-3.2	-4.4	-3.9	-3.2	-3.8	-3.5	-1.3	0.5	3.6	2.5	4.5	1.2	-0.7	1.4	3.4	1.1	-5.4
Invisibles	-0.1	-	0.2	0.2	-0.2	-0.5	-0.3	-0.8	-1.0	-2.3	-3.4	-4.6	-4.1	-1.3	-1.0	-0.7	-0.1	-0.1	0.4	-0.5	-0.6
Current account	-0.2	-0.2	-0.1	-1.3	-3.4	-4.9	-4.2	-4.0	-4.8	-5.8	-4.7	-4.1	-0.5	1.1	3.5	0.5	-0.8	-1.3	3.7	0.6	-6.0
Soviet Union																					
Merchandise export	4.8	5.1	5.7	9.5	13.6	14.2	16.6	20.7	22.8	30.9	38.2	39.1	43.4	44.2	43.3	36.9	34.6	40.8	42.7	45.1	48.8
Merchandise import	4.3	4.6	6.2	9.0	12.0	18.7	19.3	18.8	21.8	26.7	34.8	39.9	39.1	38.0	36.6	36.2	33.3	32.7	39.2	47.4	50.2
Balance	0.4	0.5	-0.5	0.5	1.6	-4.5	-2.7	1.9	0.9	4.1	3.4	-0.7	4.3	6.2	6.7	0.7	1.4	8.1	3.5	-2.3	-1.4
Invisibles	0.5	0.3	0.3	0.6	0.7	0.3	0.1	-	-	0.1	-0.4	-0.9	-0.7	-0.4	-	-0.7	-0.9	-1.0	-1.2	-1.7	-3.1
Current account	0.9	0.8	-0.2	1.1	2.4	-4.2	-2.6	1.9	1.0	4.3	3.0	-1.6	3.6	5.8	6.7	0.1	0.4	7.1	2.3	-4.0	-4.3
Eastern Europe and the Soviet Union																					
Merchandise export	8.5	9.3	11.1	17.1	24.9	26.5	29.8	35.5	39.7	52.3	64.7	63.8	66.2	73.1	74.4	66.2	63.5	74.3	80.1	84.2	89.6
Merchandise import	8.2	8.9	11.8	18.1	26.4	35.3	36.4	36.9	42.6	51.6	62.5	64.0	58.3	64.4	63.2	64.3	62.7	64.8	73.3	85.4	96.5
Balance	0.2	0.3	-0.8	-1.0	-1.5	-8.9	-6.6	-1.3	-2.9	0.8	2.1	-0.3	7.9	8.7	11.2	1.9	0.7	9.5	6.8	-1.2	-6.9
Invisibles	0.4	0.3	-0.5	-0.2	0.5	-0.1	-0.2	-0.8	-0.9	-2.3	-3.9	-5.5	-4.8	-1.7	-1.0	-1.3	-1.1	-1.1	-0.8	-2.1	-3.7
Current account	0.7	0.7	-0.3	-0.2	-1.0	-9.1	-6.8	-2.1	-3.8	-1.5	-1.7	-5.8	3.0	7.0	10.2	0.6	-0.3	8.4	6.0	-3.3	-10.6

Sources: ECE secretariat Common Data Base. National statistics for Bulgaria, Czechoslovakia, Hungary (revised data for 1982-1990; IMF, *Balance of Payment Statistics* for 1971-1981), Poland, Romania and Yugoslavia (IMF data for 1976-1982). ECE estimates for the Soviet Union. For these two countries trade balances reflect trade with all developed and developing market economies (non-socialist countries *plus* Yugoslavia) based upon national foreign trade statistics.

Note: Substantial discontinuities in the series are indicated by ‖.

APPENDIX TABLE C.11
Eastern Europe and the Soviet Union: Gross debt, foreign currency reserves and net debt in convertible currencies
(Billion US dollars)

	1970	1971	1972	1973	1974	1975	1976	1977	1978	1979	1980	1981	1982	1983	1984	1985	1986	1987	1988	1989	1990
Gross debt																						
Bulgaria	0.7	0.8	1.0	1.1	1.8	2.7	3.3	3.8	4.4	4.6	4.9	4.1	3.5	3.1	2.9	4.1	5.5	7.4	9.1	10.7	11.1
Czechoslovakia	0.3	0.4	0.6	0.7	1.0	1.0	1.7	2.4	3.0	3.8	6.8	6.3	5.8	5.2	4.7	4.6	5.6	6.7	7.3	7.9	8.1
Hungary	1.0	1.5	1.9	2.3	3.1	3.9	4.5	5.2	7.6	8.3	9.1	8.7 ‖	10.2	10.7	11.0	14.0	16.9	19.6	19.6	20.4	21.3
Poland	1.2	1.1	1.2	2.6	5.2	8.4	12.1	14.9	18.6	23.7	24.1	25.9	26.3	26.4	26.9	29.3	33.5	39.2	39.2	40.8	48.5
Romania	1.0	1.2	1.2	1.6	2.6	2.9	2.8	3.6	5.1	7.2	9.6	10.2	9.8	8.9	7.2	6.6	6.4	5.7	1.9	0.7	1.2
Yugoslavia	2.1	2.8	3.5	4.3	5.1	6.0	7.5	10.1	12.5	16.0	18.5	20.6	19.9 ‖	19.0	18.8	18.4	19.2	20.5	18.9	17.3	16.5
Eastern Europe	6.0	7.8	9.5	12.6	18.8	24.9	32.1	40.1	51.1	63.5	73.0	75.8	75.5	73.2	71.6	77.0	87.1	99.0	96.0	97.8	106.7
Soviet Union	1.6	2.6	4.2	6.0	8.1	15.4	20.9	22.7	24.4	26.1 ‖	25.2	29.0	28.4	26.9	25.6	31.4	37.4	40.2 ‖	49.4	58.5	62.5
Eastern Europe and the Soviet Union	7.6	10.4	13.7	18.6	26.9	40.3	52.9	62.8	75.5	89.7	98.1	104.8	103.9	100.1	97.2	108.4	124.5	139.2	145.4	156.3	169.2
Addendum: GDR	1.1	1.4	1.5	2.2	3.2	5.2	6.0	7.5	9.3	11.1 ‖	13.6	14.4	12.6	12.1	11.6	13.6	16.1	19.1	20.2	33.0	..
Foreign currency reserves [a]																						
Bulgaria	..	..	0.1	..	0.3	0.4	0.4	0.5	0.6	0.7	0.8	0.8	1.0	1.2	1.4	2.1	1.4	1.1	1.8	1.2	0.6
Czechoslovakia	0.3	0.3	0.5	0.5	0.4	0.3	0.4	0.5	0.6	1.0	1.8	1.0	0.8	0.8	1.0	0.9	1.1	1.4	1.6	2.2	1.1
Hungary	0.2	0.2	0.3	0.3	0.6	0.9	1.2	1.1	0.9	1.2	1.4	0.9	0.7	1.2	1.6	2.2	2.3	1.6	1.5	1.2	1.1
Poland	0.3	0.4	0.4	0.6	0.5	0.6	0.8	0.4	0.8	0.6	0.1	0.3	0.6	0.8	1.1	0.9	0.7	1.5	2.1	2.3	4.5
Romania	..	..	..	0.2	0.2	0.5	0.6	0.3	0.4	0.5	0.3	0.4	0.4	0.5	0.7	0.2	0.6	1.4	0.8	1.9	0.5
Yugoslavia	0.1	0.2	0.7	1.3	1.1	0.8	2.0	2.0	2.4	1.3	1.4	1.6	0.8	1.0	1.2	1.1	1.5	0.7	2.3	4.1	5.5
Eastern Europe	0.9	1.1	1.9	2.9	3.1	3.6	5.4	4.8	5.7	5.3	5.8	4.9	4.3	5.5	6.9	7.3	7.5	7.7	10.0	12.9	13.2
Soviet Union	1.0	1.2	1.9	2.6	3.5	3.1	4.7	4.4	6.1	8.8	8.6	8.5	10.0	10.9	11.3	13.1	14.8	14.1	15.3	14.7	8.6
Eastern Europe and the Soviet Union	1.9	2.3	3.8	5.5	6.6	6.7	10.1	9.2	11.8	14.1	14.4	13.4	14.4	16.4	18.3	20.3	22.4	21.8	25.3	27.6	21.8
Addundum: GDR	0.2	0.2	0.3	0.3	0.5	1.6	0.8	0.9	1.3	2.0 ‖	2.0	2.2	1.9	3.4	4.5	6.2	7.5	9.0	9.5	9.5	..
Total assets [b]																						
Hungary	0.6	0.8	1.0	1.5	1.7	2.0	2.3	2.4	3.1	3.3	3.7	3.2 ‖	2.9	3.8	4.4	5.9	6.2	5.9	5.6	5.5	5.2
Romania	..	..	..	..	..	..	..	..	..	2.0	1.7	1.9	2.3	2.9	3.6	3.0	3.1	3.2	3.3	3.1	3.2
Net debt (reflecting foreign currency reserves)																						
Bulgaria	0.7	0.8	0.9	1.1	1.5	2.3	2.9	3.3	3.8	3.9	4.1	3.3	2.5	1.9	1.5	2.0	4.1	6.3	7.3	9.5	10.5
Czechoslovakia	..	0.1	0.1	0.2	0.6	0.7	1.3	1.9	2.3	2.8	5.0	5.4	5.0	4.4	3.8	3.8	4.5	5.3	5.7	5.8	7.0
Hungary	0.8	1.3	1.6	2.0	2.5	3.0	3.3	4.1	6.7	7.1	7.7	7.8 ‖	9.5	9.5	9.4	11.8	14.6	18.0	18.2	19.1	20.2
Poland	0.9	0.7	0.8	2.0	4.7	7.8	11.3	14.5	17.8	23.2	24.0	25.6	25.7	25.6	25.8	28.4	32.8	37.7	37.1	38.5	44.0
Romania	1.0	1.2	1.2	1.4	2.4	2.3	2.2	3.3	4.7	6.6	9.2	9.8	9.3	8.4	6.5	6.4	5.8	4.3	1.1	-1.2	0.7
Yugoslavia	2.0	2.6	2.9	3.0	4.0	5.2	5.6	8.1	10.1	14.7	17.1	19.0	19.1	18.0	17.7	17.3	17.7	19.8	16.6	13.2	11.1
Eastern Europe	5.2	6.7	7.5	9.7	15.7	21.4	26.7	35.3	45.4	58.3	67.1	70.9	71.1	67.8	64.6	69.8	79.5	91.3	86.1	84.9	93.5
Soviet Union	0.6	1.4	2.3	3.4	4.6	12.3	16.2	18.3	18.3	17.3	16.6	20.5	18.4	16.0	14.2	18.3	22.5	26.1	34.1	43.8	53.9
Eastern Europe and the Soviet Union	5.8	8.1	9.8	13.1	20.3	33.7	42.9	53.6	63.7	75.6	83.7	91.4	89.5	83.7	78.9	88.1	102.1	117.4	120.1	128.7	147.4
Addendum: GDR	0.9	1.2	1.2	1.9	2.7	3.6	5.2	6.6	8.1	9.1 ‖	11.6	12.3	10.7	8.7	7.1	7.3	8.6	10.1	10.7	23.5	..
Net debt (reflecting total assets)																						
Hungary	0.4	0.7	0.9	0.8	1.4	1.9	2.3	2.9	4.5	5.0	5.4	5.5 ‖	7.3	7.0	6.5	8.0	10.7	13.7	14.0	14.9	16.1
Romania	..	..	..	..	..	..	..	..	..	5.2	7.8	8.2	7.5	6.0	3.6	3.6	3.3	2.5	-1.4	-2.4	-2.0

Sources: ECE secretariat Common Data Base. National statistics for Bulgaria (1980-1990), GDR (1989), Hungary (revised data 1982-1990), Poland, Romania (1970-1990), Yugoslavia (1983-1990) and Soviet Union (1988, 1990). Bulgaria, GDR and the Soviet Union (including CMEA banks) prior to discontinuity: BIS/OECD *Statistics on External Indebtedness: Bank and Trade Related Non-Bank External Claims on Individual Borrowing Countries and Territories*, Paris and Basle (various years). BIS/OECD figures are adjusted here to to include gross claims of the Federal Republic of Germany vis-à-vis the GDR arising from clearing exchanges). For these three countries data reflect convertible currency debt vis-à-vis reporting institutions only and thus exclude any claims of developing countries. IMF, *International Financial Statistics*, October 1991; BIS, *International Banking and Financial Market Developments* (various issues); Yugoslavia: World Bank, *World tables 1989-1990*, prior to discontinuity.

Note: Substantial discontinuities in the series are indicated by ‖.

[a] For Bulgaria, GDR and Soviet Union, assets with BIS reporting banks; also for other countries prior to discontinuity in series.
[b] International reserves *plus* other assets (mainly trade credits). Hungarian gold reserves at national valuation: $275/oz (1982-1985); $320/oz (1986-1990). Romania's gold reserves valued at SDR 35/oz.

In addition to its regular review of recent economic developments in Europe and North America, the Division for Economic Analysis and Projections of the United Nations Economic Commission for Europe, in Geneva, also publishes research studies with a longer time perspective.

Recent publications include:

"Eastern imports of machinery and equipment, 1960-1985", *Economic Bulletin for Europe*, vol.38, No.4, Published by Pergamon Press for the United Nations, December 1986

"Aspects of capital formation in manufacturing industry", *Economic Survey of Europe in 1986-1987*, New York, 1987, Sales No. E.87.II.E.1

"Demographic change and public expenditure", ibid.

"Agricultural inputs and efficiency 1970-1985" (in the centrally planned economies), ibid.

"Energy production, consumption and trade" (in the centrally planned economies), ibid.

"Five-year plans 1986-1990 in eastern Europe and the Soviet Union", ibid., chapter 4

"World imports of engineering goods, 1961-1985", *Economic Bulletin for Europe*, vol.39, No.4, Published by Pergamon Press for the United Nations, December 1987

"Aspects of intra-west European trade in manufactures, 1962-1985", *Economic Survey of Europe in 1987-1988*, New York, 1988, Sales No. E.88.II.E.1

"Wage rigidity in western Europe and North America" ibid.

"Agricultural country profiles for eastern Europe and the Soviet Union, 1981-1985", ibid.

"Structural changes in industry of eastern Europe and the Soviet Union, 1971-1990", ibid.

"Eastern consumer goods imports from market economies, 1962-1986", ibid.

"Review of current and prospective economic reforms", ibid.

"East-west agricultural and food trade: development and prospects", *Economic Bulletin for Europe*, vol.40, No.3, Published by Pergamon Press for the United Nations, 1988, chapter 3

"Long-term prospects in ECE countries: National and international aspects", *Economic Bulletin for Europe*, vol.40, No.4, Published by Pergamon Press for the United Nations, 1988

"The effects of west European integration on imports of manufactures from eastern and southern Europe" *Economic Survey of Europe in 1988-1989*, New York, 1989, Sales No. E.89.II.E.1

"Retail trade in eastern Europe and the Soviet Union", ibid.

"A note on recent developments in east-west trade in services", *Economic Bulletin for Europe*, vol.41, (1989), Sales No. E.89.II.E.26

"East-west trade in investment goods, 1970-1987", ibid.

"Economic reform in the east: a framework for western support", *Economic Survey of Europe in 1989-1990*, New York, 1989, Sales No. E.90.II.E.1

"The broader policy framework for 1990 and beyond", ibid.

"Developments in the service sector", ibid.

"International initiative in support of eastern reforms", ibid.

"Some implications of a German monetary union", ibid.

"Economic integration and the export performance of west European countries outside the EC", ibid.

"Europe's trade in engineering goods: Specialization and technology", ibid.

"The broader policy framework for 1990 and beyond", ibid.

"The unification of Germany", *Economic Bulletin for Europe*, vol.42, 1990, Sales No. E.90.II.E.37

"The Free Trade Agreement between Canada and the United States", ibid.

"Explaining unemployment in the market economies: theories and evidence", *Economic Survey of Europe in 1990-1991*, New York, 1989, Sales No. E.91.II.E.1

"The hard road to the market economy: problems and policies", ibid.

"Developments in the service sector", ibid.

"External economic relations of the Baltic States", *Economic Bulletin for Europe*, vol.43, 1991, Sales No. E.91.II.E.39

"Economic growth in the market economies, 1950-2000", *Economic Commission for Europe, Discussion Papers, Volume 1 (1991), No.1*

"Five years of *Perestroika*: Results, problems, prospects", *Economic Commission for Europe, Discussion Papers, Volume 1 (1991), No.2*

Back issues of the *Economic Survey of Europe* (from 1948) and the *Economic Bulletin for Europe* (from 1949) are available in microfiche form (which can be supplied as printed pages).

Your source of information: *United Nations publications*